American Cultural Leaders

American Cultural Leaders

From Colonial Times to the Present

Justin Harmon, Mary E. Metcalf, Tony Pipolo, Donna Singer,
John C. Tibbetts, Ann Waldron

Editors
Amy Lewis
Paula McGuire

Consulting Editors
Robert J. Clark
Richard M. Ludwig
Peter Westergaard
Princeton University

ABC-CLIO
Santa Barbara, California
Denver, Colorado
Oxford, England

Library of Congress Cataloging-in-Publication Data

American cultural leaders : from colonial times to the present /
    Justin Harmon . . . [et al.] ; editors, Amy Lewis, Paula McGuire ;
    consulting editors, Robert J. Clark . . . [et al.].
        p.   cm. — (Biographies of American leaders)
        Includes bibliographical references.
        1. Arts, American.   2. Arts, Modern—United States.   3. Artists—
    United States—Biography—Dictionaries.   I. Harmon, Justin.
    II. Lewis, Amy.   III. McGuire, Paula.   IV. Series.
    NX503.A49   1993
    700'.92'273—dc20
    [B]   93-36284

ISBN 0-87436-673-9
00 99 98 97 96 95 94 93   10 9 8 7 6 5 4 3 2 1   (cloth)

BIOGRAPHIES OF AMERICAN LEADERS
Developed by Visual Education Corp., Princeton, New Jersey

ABC-CLIO, Inc.
130 Cremona Drive, P.O. Box 1911
Santa Barbara, California, 93116-1911

This book is printed on acid-free paper ⊗.
Manufactured in the United States of America

Contents

List of American Cultural Leaders

Preface

A merican Cultural Leaders is a biographical reference work containing 360 profiles of men and women who have made major contributions to American cultural, or artistic, life. Each of these profiles is an attempt to combine a brief account of an individual's life with an overview and assessment of the work produced and, in turn, its effect on other artists and the growth of a recognizably *American* expression of culture since the Colonial period.

As in the previous two volumes in this series, *American Political Leaders* and *American Social Leaders,* the task of the consulting editors has been to identify the cultural leaders included in this book and to review for accuracy and balance each profile submitted by the six writers.

Before beginning to choose which leaders were to be included, we had to decide what our understanding of culture in America is. One of *Webster's* definitions of culture is "an acquaintance with and taste in fine arts, humanities, and broad aspects of science as distinguished from vocational and technical skills." Leaving science aside as beyond the scope of the present undertaking, we found ourselves still faced with an enormous range of cultural activities. After long discussion, we chose six fields: art, dance, film, literature, music, and theater. Because of space limitations we have omitted television, radio, and certain other forms of entertainment, as well as journalism and criticism. Space limitations also dictated making certain choices among leaders, since we wanted to cover the historical phases of each field as well as the many kinds of performers and creators. So in music, for example, we had space for only two female jazz singers, and we chose Bessie Smith and Billie Holiday. The fact that we did not include Ma Rainey or Ella Fitzgerald in no way suggests that the latter are not leading artists in our opinion; the omission reflects only the necessity to make a difficult choice among several possible subjects, in this field as well as in many others.

We believe that the leaders finally selected present not only outstanding representatives in their fields, but also a broad-based overview of American culture as a whole. The rich field of American art is represented by painters, sculptors, designers, architects, and photographers. Examples of these are Colonial painters John Singleton Copley and Benjamin West, nineteenth-century landscape artists Albert Bierstadt and George Inness, and twentieth-century Abstract Impressionist Jackson Pollock and Pop artist Andy Warhol. Augustus Saint-Gaudens and Daniel Chester French appear among the profiles of sculptors, and Ansel Adams, Dorothea Lange, and Edward Weston among those of photographers.

Much attention has been paid to the field of architecture, starting with the first European-trained professional, Benjamin Latrobe. Henry Hobson Richardson, Louis Sullivan, and the firm of McKim, Mead & White represent the period between the Civil War and World War I. Regional considerations have been viewed in the work of Bernard Maybeck and the firm of Greene and Greene, as well as Frank Lloyd Wright, who not only created a new domestic architecture for the Midwest, but was also of considerable influence internationally. Space is devoted to twentieth-century immigrant architects Walter Gropius and Ludwig Mies van der Rohe, as well as to such Post-Modernists as Michael Graves and Richard Meier.

Finally, central to the history of developments in the crafts and industrial design are Duncan Phyfe, cabinetmaker of the Federal period; Louis Comfort Tiffany, artist in glass and metals of a century ago; and more recently, Claire McCardell, innovative designer of fashions for women, and Raymond Loewy, who tried his hand at almost everything in the American environment.

Each of the three major strands that make up the complex tradition of American dance is represented: the modern dance movement by such pioneers as Isadora Duncan and Martha Graham; the dance found in such popular entertainment forms as vaudeville, musical comedy, and film by Fred Astaire and Bojangles Robinson; and the European classical ballet tradition by the master choreographer who redefined it for the United States, George Balanchine. But also included are such figures as Alvin Ailey, Agnes de Mille, Jerome Robbins, and Paul Taylor, who by combining these three strands created a distinctly American approach to dance.

Much of the film tradition in the world has been defined by Hollywood, though it was influenced by the talent of many Europeans who came to America to work—both directors and actors—including Ernst Lubitsch, Carl Laemmle, Charlie Chaplin, and Greta Garbo. Their profiles stand alongside those of pioneers D. W. Griffith, Mack Sennett, and Irving Thalberg, as well as Marlon Brando, Henry Fonda, Katharine Hepburn, and Orson Welles, among others, with glimpses of the workings of famous studios and the star system they founded.

In literature, the profiles start in the eighteenth century with Philip Freneau and move on to such nineteenth-century writers as Louisa May Alcott, James Fenimore Cooper, Nathaniel Hawthorne, and Mark Twain, and the rich twentieth century of F. Scott Fitzgerald, Ernest Hemingway, Flannery O'Connor, John Updike, and Richard Wright, among many others. At least a dozen writers might have been included here had they not appeared earlier in *American Social Leaders;* examples include Horatio Alger, H. L. Mencken, Upton Sinclair, and Harriet Beecher Stowe. Three nineteenth-century writers were of such importance and varied talent that they are included in both volumes: Ralph Waldo Emerson, Henry David Thoreau, and William Dean Howells. W. H. Auden and T. S. Eliot, two twentieth-century writers who spent much of their lives in England, were so influenced by their American years that they have been included in this volume.

American music comes in many flavors, from indigenous popular forms like ragtime, jazz, blues, folk, rock, country, and Tin Pan Alley, to the "classical music" designed for the concert hall or opera stage. All are represented here, chiefly by their most innovative creators—composers and those performers who in their improvisations create new musical ideas and new ways of making music. On nearby pages you will find such unlikely companions as Louis Armstrong and Milton Babbitt, John Coltrane and Aaron Copland, or Jimi Hendrix and Victor Herbert. A few other performers are also included, preeminent figures such as Marian Anderson, Jascha Heifetz, Frank Sinatra, and Arturo Toscanini. Three musical profiles portray people who are neither composers or performers: the Steinways, who developed the modern grand piano; John and Alan Lomax, who preserved so much of American folk music for posterity; and John Hammond, the record producer, who shaped the popular music of the middle decades of this century almost as much as the musicians he brought together.

The field of the American theater includes playwrights, directors, producers, actors, and actresses. A few of these profiles reflect the nineteenth century—David Belasco, Edwin Booth, Augustin Daly, and Edwin Forrest, but the greater number of profiles come from the twentieth century. This distinguished group includes George Abbott, Katharine Cornell, Lillian Hellman, Elia Kazan, Eugene O'Neill, and Tennessee Williams, from whose creativity and enterprise has developed a theater singularly formed by the American spirit and way of life.

American culture, as we see it, then, is defined through the creative activities of the many men and women included in this book. What the curious reader will also discover, we hope, are the cultural debts these subjects often owe to those who have come before them, both American and European, and the many connections between the fields included. Movements such as Abstract Expressionism, Imagism, Modernism, Realism, and Naturalism are not always confined to just one field of culture or the arts—they have an overriding definition that can apply to both art and literature, both theater and the dance, for example. Likewise, the work of artists in one field is borrowed by innovators in another or may have a clear impact in the development of a new tradition. As often as possible, we have tried to point out these connections, either through specific definitions or descriptions, or through a simple system of cross-references. We think that readers, including high school students, college students, and many adults, will find much valuable information in these pages and will be able to view the incredible variety in American culture in a new light.

Robert J. Clark
Richard M. Ludwig
Peter Westergaard

Editors' Note

The profiles included in this volume aim to provide the student or general reader with biographical and general background information to help place the subjects within their field of culture and in relationship to other fields. Significant events in cultural history are described, important terms are defined, and cross-references are supplied. Each profile contains a brief bibliography for further reference, and the reader is urged to consult a library for additional materials. Black-and-white portraits illustrate many of the subjects.

A User's Guide follows, illustrating the special features of each profile.

Editorial development of the book was provided by Visual Education Corporation of Princeton, New Jersey. The editors wish to acknowledge P. Adams Sitney, Professor of the Council of the Humanities and the Visual Arts at Princeton University, for editorial advice; Meagan Freer, Joan Louise Horn, and Douglas Kincade, for fact-checking; Laura Daly, for copyediting; Cindy Feldner for keying and proofreading; and Susan Hormuth, for picture research.

Amy Lewis
Paula McGuire

User's Guide to Entry Format

Below is a description of the entry format used in this book; a sample entry appears on the facing page.

Headnote: The headnote contains the following parts:

Entry Name: Profiles are arranged alphabetically by the last name of the subject profiled. The subject's full name is used in the heading, including any middle name(s). If the subject was commonly known by initials (T. S. Eliot), a nickname (Leadbelly), or a shortened version of his or her given name (Woody Guthrie), this form is included in the text of the profile. Some profiles are presented as a "multiple entry" that lists two or more subjects in the order of the appearance within the entry.

Date of Birth/Death: If the exact date of birth or death is unknown, it is preceded by the abbreviation "ca."

Occupation(s): The most significant occupations of the subject's life are listed in alphabetical order.

Summary of Subject's Significance: Provides a general description of the subject's importance in his or her field of endeavor.

Cross-References: To aid the reader's use of the volume, a simple cross-reference system has been devised. Within the profiles, the printing of names in SMALL CAPITALS indicates a cross-reference, of which there are two kinds. The first is a name printed in small capitals, which indicates that the subject mentioned has a profile that will be found in its alphabetical position. The second kind of cross-reference features a name in small capitals preceded by the word "see." This indicates that the reader may turn to that profile for an explanation of a term or an event just mentioned.

Bibliography: Each profile contains a brief bibliography listing sources for further reference. The author, title, and date or dates of publication are included for each source. Sources are in alphabetical order by the last name of the author. Works by the same author are organized chronologically by year of publication. The reader is encouraged to consult a library for additional materials.

Headnote

Neutra, Richard Joseph

(April 8, 1892–April 16, 1970)
Architect

Summary of Subject's Significance

A seminal figure in twentieth-century American architecture, Richard Neutra was the major American pioneer of the International style and spurred the development of a new direction in the regional architecture of southern California. He also exerted substantial influence through his books and lectures.

Neutra was born in Vienna, Austria, and studied there at the Institute of Technology, then at the University of Zurich in Switzerland. After service as an Austrian artillery officer during World War I, he worked for Swiss landscape architect Gustav Ammann and developed the concept that architecture must harmonize with nature. He was also influenced significantly by Viennese architecture, especially the subway stations designed by Otto Wagner, and the design philosophy of Adolf Loos, who espoused unadorned or stripped architecture and the use of industrial prefabrication. He worked for the Berlin architect Erich Mendelsohn from 1921 to 1923 before immigrating to the United States in 1923, where he felt the future of architecture rested. He became a naturalized citizen in 1929.

Cross-Reference

After design positions in New York City, Chicago, and with FRANK LLOYD WRIGHT in Wisconsin, Neutra formed the Architectural Group for Industry and Commerce with Rudolph Schindler in Los Angeles (1925–early 1930s). His first building, the Jardin Apartments in Los Angeles (1927), was made of reinforced concrete with cantilevered balconies and bands of metal-framed windows. It was one of the first International style struc-

Cross-Reference

tures in the country (see LUDWIG MIES VAN DER ROHE). This style, which originated in Europe in the early 1920s, embraced the machine aesthetic and championed unadorned, often boxlike structures of concrete, steel, and glass.

Neutra humanized the style by emphasizing the relationship between a structure and its site, and by approaching design as a means to serve the organic nature of man, a concept he labeled Bio-realism. His international reputation came with the 1929 Lovell House, a 3-story structure noted for its steel frame sheathed with concrete and glass, masterfully integrated with the natural landscape of the Hollywood Hills.

A hallmark of Neutra's work is the interrelationship between interior and exterior space, as exemplified by his use of sliding glass doors to extend the classrooms outward at Corona

Avenue School in Los Angeles (1934). This became a prototype for the city's school designs. This fusion of the modernist idiom with the regional considerations initiated a new phase of southern California architecture.

In the 1930s Neutra designed several modular experimental houses composed of steel and plywood, such as Hollywood director JOSEF VON STERNBERG'S house in Northridge (1935). The architect was particularly adept at designing multiple-housing units, such as the Indian pueblo–inspired Strathmore Apartments in Los Angeles (1938) and five housing projects in California and Texas for the Federal Housing Authority (1939–1941). After World War II, Neutra expanded his practice, designing such varied projects as the Lincoln Memorial Museum at Gettysburg, Pennsylvania (1959), the U.S. Embassy in Karachi, Pakistan (1960), a theater in Düsseldorf, Germany (1959), and the Dayton Museum of Natural History (1959) in Ohio.

Cross-Reference

Neutra was in partnership with Robert Alexander, a planner, in the 1950s, and later with his son, Dion.

Neutra lectured worldwide and wrote extensively about architecture. Among his most influential books are *How America Builds* (1927) and *Survival Through Design* (1954). He won many awards and design competitions and became the first architect honored on the cover of *Time* magazine (1949). One of his fascinating, though never realized, projects was a plan (1926–1930) for an ideal future city, called Rush City Reformed, which idealized, on a human scale, transportation, living, and working in the twentieth century.

BIBLIOGRAPHY

Boesiger, Willy (ed.), *Richard Neutra, Buildings and Projects, 1923–1966*, 3 vols., 1966; Hines, Thomas S., *Richard Neutra and the Search for Modern Architecture: A Biography and History*, 1981; McCoy, Esther, *Richard Neutra*, 1960; Neutra, Richard J., *Life and Shape*, 1962.

Bibliography

Acknowledgments

John Ashbery	"The One Thing That Can Save America," copyright © 1975 by John Ashbery, from *Self-portrait in a Convex Mirror* by John Ashbery. Used by permission of Viking Penguin, a division of Penguin Books USA Inc.
W. H. Auden	From W. H. *Auden: Collected Poems* by W. H. Auden, edited by Edward Mendelson. Copyright 1937, 1940, 1951 and renewed 1965, 1968, 1969 by W. H. Auden. Reprinted by permission of Random House, Inc.
Stephen Crane	Used by permission of the University Press of Virginia
Emily Dickinson	From *The Complete Poems of Emily Dickinson* edited by Thomas H. Johnson. Copyright 1929 by Martha Dickinson Bianchi; Copyright © renewed 1957 by Mary L. Hampson. By permission of Little, Brown and Company
Emily Dickinson	Reprinted by permission of the publishers and the Trustees of Amherst College from *The Poems of Emily Dickinson*, Thomas H. Johnson, ed., Cambridge, Mass.: The Belknap Press of Harvard University Press, Copyright © 1951, 1955, 1979, 1983 by the President and Fellows of Harvard College.
Robert Frost	From *The Poetry of Robert Frost* edited by Edward Connery Lathem. Copyright © 1969 by Henry Holt and Company, Inc., copyright © 1970 by Lesley Frost Ballantine, copyright 1942, 1944 by Robert Frost. Reprinted by permission of Henry Holt and Company, Inc.
Allen Ginsberg	"Sunflower Sutra" from *Collected Poems* 1947–1980 by Allen Ginsberg. Copyright 1955 by Allen Ginsberg. Reprinted by permission of HarperCollins, Publishers, Inc.
Randall Jarrell	Excerpt from "The Death of the Ball Turret Gunner" from *The Complete Poems* by Randall Jarrell. Copyright © 1945, 1969 by Mrs. Randall Jarrell. Reprinted by permission of Farrar, Straus Giroux, Inc.
Randall Jarrell	Excerpt from "The Woman at the Washington Zoo" reprinted by permission of Rhoda A. Weyr as agent.
Archibald MacLeish	Excerpt from "Ars Poetica" from *New and Collected Poems, 1917–1982* by Archibald MacLeish. Copyright © 1985 by the Estate of Archibald MacLeish. Reprinted by permission of Houghton Mifflin Company.
Edna St. Vincent Millay	Excerpt from "Renascence" copyright 1917, 1945 by Edna St. Vincent Millay.
Sylvia Plath	6 lines from "Elm" from *Ariel* by Sylvia Plath. Copyright © 1963 by Ted Hughes. Reprinted by permission of HarperCollins Publishers Inc.
Gertrude Stein	"A Carafe, That Is a Blind Glass" and excerpt from "Sacred Emily" from *Selected Writings of Gertrude Stein* by Gertrude Stein, edited by Carl van Vechten. Copyright 1946 by Random House, Inc. Reprinted by permission of Random House, Inc.
Wallace Stevens	Excerpts from "Sunday Morning" and "The Idea of Order at Key West" from *The Palm at the End of the Mind; Selected Poems and a Play by Wallace Stevens*, edited by Holly Stevens. Copyright © 1971 by Holly Stevens. Reprinted by permission of Alfred A. Knopf, Inc.

American Cultural Leaders

Abbott, George Francis

(June 25, 1887–)
Director, Playwright, Producer

George Abbott has had the longest track record of commercial hits in the history of the American stage. He has lived to be over 100 years old and has remained the quintessential Broadway showman.

Abbott grew up in the small upstate New York village of Salamanca. When he was eleven years of age, after his father declared bankruptcy, the family moved to Cheyenne, Wyoming, where the boy spent several idyllic years living among the cowboys and colorful characters of the region (some of whom were incorporated into his later plays). After disciplinary problems at school led to his transferral to the Kearney Military Academy in Nebraska, Abbott restlessly drifted through a variety of jobs. At the University of Rochester he began writing plays. Realizing that he had at last found his calling, he enrolled at Harvard University in 1912 and took drama courses under the legendary professor George Pierce Baker. Soon afterward Abbott moved to New York, where he worked as an actor and writer at many theaters and for dozens of productions. His first appearance as an actor on Broadway was in 1913 in *A Misleading Lady.*

His first big success as a playwright, *The Fall Guy* (1925), written in collaboration with James Gleason, encouraged him to devote his full time to writing, producing, and directing. Between 1925 and 1939 he was involved in

Copyright *Washington Post;* Reprinted by permission of the D.C. Public Library

more than thirty shows, including some of his greatest successes. Among the plays he wrote or collaborated on were *Broadway* (1926) and *Three Men on a Horse* (1935), two of his greatest personal successes; among those he produced were *Twentieth Century* (1932), *Boy Meets Girl* (1935), *On Your Toes* (1936), *Room Service* (1937), and *The Boys from Syracuse* (1938). Like many other successful playwrights in the late 1920s, he cashed in on the talking picture boom and adapted some of his plays for the screen, notably *Coquette* (which was MARY PICKFORD's first sound film), as well as other projects, like Erich Maria Remarque's *All Quiet on the Western Front* (1929).

He boasted in his autobiography that, from 1935 to 1963, he always had at least one play running on Broadway. Indeed, among the later productions were such standouts as *Pal Joey* (1940), *On the Town* (1944), *A Tree Grows in Brooklyn* (1951), *The Pajama Game* (1954), *Damn Yankees* (1955), and *A Funny Thing Happened on the Way to the Forum* (1962). Among his last shows were the failed musical *Music* (1976) and a revival of *On Your Toes* in 1983, when he was ninety-five years old. He worked best not as a solitary creator but as an enthusiastic collaborator and play doctor. About his first production of *On the Town,* for example, he wrote: "We all worked together on this show in the way that I love to work: each

---

putting forth his opinion, yet remaining objective, and subordinating everything to the main end."

BIBLIOGRAPHY

Abbott, George, *Mister Abbott*, 1963.

Adams, Ansel Easton

(February 20, 1902–April 22, 1984)
Photographer

Ansel Adams was the most famous photographer in America and was celebrated for his images of the landscapes of the western United States.

Adams was born in San Francisco in 1902 to Carlie and Olive Adams. The family home was located in a remote area near the western edge of the city, and the child spent idyllic years in natural settings. However, the family business, a lumber company, failed in 1907 and soon his father was deeply in debt. Because Ansel was unable to adapt to a succession of schools, he received private tutoring. At home he learned to play the piano and for a time considered a career in music. He changed his mind, however, when he first encountered the medium of photography. At thirteen he visited the Panama-Pacific International Exposition and was fascinated by the photography exhibits. He took his first camera, a Kodak Box Brownie, along on a family vacation to Yosemite and took his first pictures.

Beginning in 1919 Adams worked during his summers at Yosemite as the custodian of the Sierra Club's headquarters. He began to take trips into the high country of the Sierra Nevada and encountered unfenced country that never seemed to have been touched by humans. "From that day . . . my life has been colored and modulated by the great earth-gesture of the Sierra."

He began publishing his photographs of the area in the *Sierra Club Bulletin*. At that time "art" photographs were popularly assumed to look smudgy in a vaguely impressionistic way, the results of soft focus and bromoil prints.

Adams rejected these pictorial techniques and worked toward a more direct approach that preserved the clarity of the mountains. He found the special qualities he desired in light in the early morning hours or in inclement weather. Yosemite and the Sierra were his first subjects, but he soon traveled through the Southwest, California, and north to Alaska.

Through a friend, Cedric Wright, Adams met Albert Bender, a supporter of the arts in the Bay Area who became his patron. While putting together his first portfolio early in 1927, Adams decided to photograph the famous mountain, Half Dome, in the Yosemite valley. Here he made an important discovery: by using a red filter he created an emulsion density that printed the blue sky in black tones. *Monolith, the Face of Half Dome* (1927) was a breakthrough. Through "visualization," as Adams termed it, he could plan in advance of the exposure how best to achieve a desired effect.

In 1928 he had his first one-man exhibition at the Sierra Club in San Francisco; more than 500 more exhibitions would follow in his lifetime. Adams and his wife, Virginia, settled into a house adjoining his family home. A year later a meeting with Paul Strand in Taos, New Mexico, inspired Adams finally to commit his life to photography. He began taking on commercial assignments and writing articles about photography, including a regular column for the magazine *The Fortnightly*. In 1933 he opened the Ansel Adams Gallery at 166 Geary Street in San Francisco. A meeting with ALFRED STIEGLITZ that year led to an exhibition at Stieglitz's gallery in 1936—the first exhibition given a photographer since a showing of Paul Strand in 1917. In 1937 Adams moved his family to Yosemite. There he had increased access to the landscape for his photographs while he maintained his studio and business contacts in San Francisco, five hours away.

By exercising as much care in the reproduction of his images as he did in their execution, Adams began producing at this time book collections that were distinguished by their exquisite concept and craftsmanship. Three of the early ones were especially notable—*Taos Pueblo* (1930) contained images that were printed directly onto the book paper; *Making a Photograph* (1935), a technical volume, had its images hand-tipped onto the page; and *Sierra Nevada: The John Muir Trail* (1938) appeared in an oversized format. More than thirty other titles followed, all of them exceptional works of printing.

The 1940s were the most productive years of his career. He developed the zone system of simplified applied sensitometry that divided the tonal scale into eleven zones, from black (zone 0) to white (zone 10). Using this system, the photographer could assess the general contrast range of his subject and determine what specific area related to the tonal zones of the desired print. Some of the images from these years were expansive and heroic. *Moonrise* (1941)—arguably the best-known image in the art of photography, *The Tetons and Snake River* (1942), *Clearing Winter Storm* (1944), and *Winter Sunrise* (1944) were all epic vistas—in James Alinder's words, "visual equivalents to American values." Other images, by contrast, were more intimate. *Sand Bar, Rio Grande* and *Sand Dunes, Sunrise* achieved an almost abstract quality, as if the act of seeing, not the subject, were most important. Some of his commercial assignments included the documenting of the Japanese American internees in the Manzanar relocation camp—published in 1944, *Born Free and Equal* was his statement about the unfortunate results of blind prejudice. The late 1940s also saw the beginning of a series of technical books. *Camera and Lens and Portfolio I*

would be followed by six more books over the next three decades.

By the time Adams moved to a new house and studio in the Carmel highlands in the early 1960s, he was producing fewer images. His stature as one of America's most important photographers, however, was assured. His home was the meeting place of prominent artists, environmentalists, and musicians. He continued his efforts on behalf of conservation, a priority he had first established decades earlier, in 1935, when he successfully had lobbied Congress for the establishment of the Kings Canyon region of the Sierra Nevada as a national park. President Jimmy Carter honored him with the Presidential Medal of Freedom in 1980.

Adams was involved in the most important photography organizations of the day. He helped found Group f/64 with EDWARD WESTON in 1932, was on the board of directors of the Sierra Club from 1934 to 1971, established the photography department at the California School of Fine Arts in San Francisco in 1946, founded the photography magazine *Aperture* in 1952, and was the founder and chairman of the board of the Friends of Photography from 1967 to 1980. In 1975 he established his archive at the Center for Creative Photography at the University of Arizona.

Adams sought in his images of the West to capture the idea of a pure, unspoiled America. His credo was expressed as early as 1932 when his f/64 group presented its manifesto: "Pure photography is defined as possessing no qualities of technique, composition or idea, derivative of any other art form." His greatest images were made with a view camera and 8-by-10-inch negatives, lenses that gave extreme optical sharpness, and contact prints possessing a full tonal range on glossy paper. Despite his amazing technical facility, he insisted the artist's eye and mind came first. There was nothing worse, he taught, than a sharp picture of a fuzzy concept.

Active to the end, he died in 1984 of a heart ailment. Later that year Congress passed the California Wilderness Bill, setting aside more than 100,000 acres as the Ansel Adams Wilderness Area between Yosemite National Park and the John Muir Wilderness Area. A mountain peak in Yosemite that he had first climbed in 1921 was officially named Mount Ansel Adams.

BIBLIOGRAPHY

Alinder, James, and John Szarkowski, *Ansel Adams: Classic Images*, 1985; Newhall, Nancy, *Ansel Adams, the Eloquent Light*, 1963.

Adams, Henry Brooks

(February 16, 1838–March 27, 1918)
Biographer, Historian, Novelist

Henry Adams wrote historical meditations and novels that described an erosion of social unity in the late nineteenth century caused by the substitution of scientific inquiry for religious faith. His work reflected a sense of personal alienation that became typical of poets in the modern era.

Adams was born in Boston of a wealthy family with a long tradition of civic service. His great-grandfather, John Adams, served as the second president of the United States; his grandfather, John Quincy Adams, as its sixth president. His own father, Charles Francis Adams, was a statesman and historian who served as minister to England during the Civil War.

After graduating from Harvard in 1858, Adams worked first as a correspondent from Washington for the Boston *Daily Advertiser.* He later served as secretary to his father in England, where he also wrote for the Boston *Courier* and the *New York Times.* In 1870 he became editor of the *North American Review,* to which he had contributed, and an assistant professor of history at Harvard for the next seven years.

After completing two biographies, *The Life of Albert Gallatin* (four vols., 1879) and *John Randolph* (1882), Adams studied the papers of Thomas Jefferson and James Madison, preparing his nine-volume *History of the United States of America During the Administrations of Thomas Jefferson and James Madison* (1889–1891). This series depicted the nation at a moment of transition from European influence to dominance on the international scene.

Adams married Marian Hooper of Boston in 1872, though little is known of their years together. She committed suicide in 1885, and for reasons unknown he omitted any mention of their marriage in his autobiographical prose.

Adams's first novel, *Democracy,* was published anonymously in 1880. The book satirizes social and political life in Washington and explores the roots of corruption in government. His second novel, *Esther,* published under the pseudonym Frances Snow Compton in 1884, is thought to offer some insight into Adams's own marriage. The book's heroine falls in love with a minister, but their relationship founders because of their differing religious views. The novel certainly reflects Adams's own loss of religious faith, a fact he attributed to inroads made by scientific inquiry.

After his wife's death, Adams traveled to the Far East and to Europe with his two closest friends, the geologist Clarence King and the painter John La Farge. He found in two French cathedrals the symbols he needed to describe his own philosophy regarding humanity's inner need for unity. His two books, *Mont-Saint-Michel and Chartres* (printed privately in 1904, published in 1913) and *The Education of Henry Adams* (printed privately in 1907, published in 1918), explore the loss of stable social values with the advent of scientific discovery and the substitution of reasoning for faith.

Adams died in March 1918 after a long illness. In 1919 he was awarded a posthumous Pulitzer Prize for his *Education.* During the next twenty years, four volumes of Adams's letters, carefully edited, revealed the richness of his interests and imagination.

BIBLIOGRAPHY

Harbert, Earl, *The Force So Much Closer Home: Henry Adams and the Adams Family,* 1977; Stevenson, Elizabeth, *Henry Adams: A Biography,* 1955.

Ailey, Alvin

(January 5, 1931–December 1, 1989)
Choreographer, Dancer

Known for his portraits of the black experience in America, Ailey drew crowds with accessible, often theatrical dances and critical barbs for alleged commercialism. He had a special affection for DUKE ELLINGTON's music, and his company, pioneering modern repertory groups, danced popular Ailey works and those of other choreographers.

Born in Rogers, Texas, Ailey was raised by his mother. As a child he attended the Baptist church; its rituals and gospel meetings helped shape his work. In 1942 he moved with his mother to Los Angeles, California, where she found employment at the Lockheed aircraft factory.

Ailey attended Thomas Jefferson High School in Los Angeles and went on to UCLA to study romance languages. He took classes with dancer/choreographer Lester Horton, a West Coast pioneer of American dance. According to Ailey, Horton was a primary influence: "He was not only a master choreographer, but a painter, designer, [and] sculptor, and [was] very much

Alvin Ailey City Dance Theater; Washington Performing Arts Society; Copyright *Washington Post;* Reprinted by permission of the D.C. Public Library

involved with ethnic groups." Ailey chose dance over college and joined the Horton company in 1953. Horton died of a heart attack a few months later.

Ailey began to choreograph and to design costumes and sets for the Horton company. In the summer of 1954 the company participated in Ted Shawn's Jacob's Pillow Dance Festival in Massachusetts (see RUTH ST. DENIS and TED SHAWN). That fall Ailey found a job in New York City dancing in TRUMAN CAPOTE's *House of Flowers.* Living in New York allowed him to study with teachers MARTHA GRAHAM, Doris Humphrey, Hanya Holm, and Karel Shook, later ballet master of the Dance Theatre of Harlem.

By 1958 Ailey and a small group of black dancers presented a program showcasing black culture at the 92nd Street Young Men's Hebrew Association in New York. *Dance Magazine* reported, "As a dancer, Mr. Ailey is exceptional. He reminds one of a caged lion full of lashing power that he can contain or release at will." The success led to tours and other New

York performances. In 1960 Ailey produced *Revelations*, a dance suite based on gospel songs and spirituals with a striking interplay of movement and music that many consider his masterpiece. During the sixties Ailey and his company toured extensively and was better received in Europe than at home. By 1972 the Ailey group took up residence at City Center as the Alvin Ailey American Dance Center.

Despite financial straits, strains of touring, and many appearances on Broadway, Ailey continued to choreograph, creating works for his company and others. After he stopped dancing in 1965, he produced *Sea Change* for the American Ballet Theater (1972), as well as dances for the Paris Opera Ballet and the Ballet of La Scala, Milan, and provided choreography for SAMUEL BARBER's opera *Antony and Cleopatra.*

Ailey had worked with Ellington in 1970 when they collaborated on *The River.* In 1975 Ailey choreographed *The Mooche* danced to an Ellington score. The work celebrated four black female performers. In May 1976 he presented *Black, Brown and Beige,* again to Ellington's music, in which, according to critic Joseph Mazo, he employed favorite elements of his dance vocabulary: "arabesques, diagonal lines and semicircles, short steps combined with large movements of the arms, backward arches of the torso, long yearning reaches."

Ailey, according to the *New York Times,* "suffered a breakdown in 1980, and was hospitalized after a number of public outbursts." In the late eighties he received awards from the Kennedy Center and New York City. Dance honors included the 1987 Samuel H. Scripps American Dance Festival Award, the 1979 Capezio Award, and the 1975 *Dance Magazine* Award. He died in New York in 1989.

BIBLIOGRAPHY

Hodgson, M., *Quintet: Five American Dance Companies,* 1976; Long, R. A., *The Black Tradition in American Dance,* 1989.

Albee, Edward Franklin

(March 12, 1928–)
Playwright

E dward Albee, an important playwright throughout the decade of the 1960s, is best known for *Who's Afraid of Virginia Woolf?* and the Pulitzer Prize–winning *A Delicate Balance.* His work has often been called the Theater of the Absurd.

Albee was born in Virginia and adopted by Reed and Frances Albee in 1928. He was raised in Larchmont, New York. His adoptive father was heir to part of the Keith-Albee Theatre Circuit, and young Edward at an early age had an insider's view of show business. He went to a succession of boarding schools, where he was in constant trouble because of his lack of discipline and truancy. Although he did poorly in his studies, he excelled in writing poetry. His formal education ended after a year and a half at Trinity College in Hartford, Connecticut. Early in the 1950s he settled in Greenwich Village and for the next decade drifted through a variety of odd jobs—"any job so long as it had no future," he recalled. His experience in the theater world seems to have been no less desultory, although during his frequent forays to the theater districts he discovered the work of playwrights who would prove to be influential to his own development: TENNESSEE WILLIAMS, EUGENE O'NEILL, and Samuel Beckett.

On his thirtieth birthday in 1958 he wrote *The Zoo Story,* a one-act play, which won the Vernon Rice Memorial Award. It took a circuitous route to Off-Broadway, first being premiered in Berlin, Germany, in 1959 before playing in 1960 at the Provincetown Playhouse on a double bill with Beckett's *Krapp's Last Tape* in 1960. *The Zoo Story* contains many of the styles and themes that would surface in Albee's later plays. Its construction, which is economical and uncluttered, leads from a quiet opening to a violent climax and a quick curtain. One character, Peter, is a modest, middle-aged loner who is goaded into a fight by Jerry, a young derelict clearly on the edge. Ironically, Jerry's death results in an awareness of life for Peter. Connections are examined between love and aggression, fantasy and experience, reality and art.

Among the short plays that followed were two fifteen-minute works, *Fam and Yam* (1959) and *The Sandbox* (1959). More fully realized works were *The American Dream* (1961) and *The Death of Bessie Smith* (1961). The former was a ruthless dissection of a well-to-do American middle-class family, childless, loveless, rotten at its core; the latter was a grim indictment of the racist, mean-spirited employees of a Memphis hospital. Both were chosen as the best plays of the 1960–1961 season by the Foreign Press Association.

Who's Afraid of Virginia Woolf? (1962) was Albee's first full-length play and, arguably, his finest work. Certainly its run of 644 performances on Broadway and its New York Drama Critics' Circle Award firmly established his reputation. Albee had long had the idea of a play whose central idea would be the exorcism of a nineteen-year-old fantasy child created by a middle-aged couple. Again, the themes of marital and family dysfunction came to the fore. Tragedy and comedy, fantasy and realism, the cruelty of the "fun and games" (like Hump the Hostess and Get the Guests) are all deftly interwoven as George and Martha and their two guests career about in a difficult embrace of conciliation and destruction. The play later became a movie, starring Elizabeth Taylor and Richard Burton.

None of Albee's subsequent plays have had a Broadway run longer than four or five months. Several plays have been derived from other works. *The Ballad of the Sad Café* (1963) was an adaptation of CARSON McCULLERS's novel, and it utilized a narrator in order to preserve some of the original prose. *Everything in the Garden* (1967) was drawn from a play by the English dramatist Giles Cooper. Two plays have garnered him Pulitzer Prizes—*A Delicate Balance* (1966), another domestic drama, which was derivative of *The Cocktail Party* by T. S. ELIOT; and *Seascape* (1975), which had the startling novelty of two characters who dressed as huge sea lizards.

Albee's plays have become notorious for the absurdist devices and situations that have baffled and antagonized audiences. *Tiny Alice* (1964) takes place inside a huge castle belonging to "Miss Alice." It depicts the struggles of a lay brother, Julian, who has been sent by the Cardinal to collect a large donation from her. Instead, Julian is seduced by Miss Alice and confronts the limits of his faith and sanity. *Box* (1968) consists of a bare stage occupied only by a giant cube. A woman's voice is heard commenting on various topics and themes. *Quotations from Chairman Mao Tse-Tung* (1968) juxtaposes bromides from the Chinese ruler with doggerel verse recited by an old lady. *Listening* (1977), originally conceived as a radio play, is full of word games about death and suicide played out against an expressionistic fountain. Although complex and confusing to many viewers, Albee insists that these plays are understandable when the viewer opens his mind, "to receive impressions without immediately categorizing them, to sense rather than know, to gather rather than immediately understand."

BIBLIOGRAPHY

Amacher, Richard E., *Edward Albee*, 1982; Kolin, Philip C. (ed.), *Conversations with Edward Albee*, 1988; McCarthy, Gerry, *Edward Albee*, 1986; Rutenberg, Michael E., *Edward Albee: Playwright in Protest*, 1969.

Alcott, Louisa May

(November 29, 1832–March 6, 1888)
Novelist, Short-Story Writer

Best known for her domestic novels, especially *Little Women,* Louisa May Alcott created in the popular imagination an ideal of American family life, rooted in the realities of daily existence but graced by a principled faith in the humane potential embodied in the young.

Born in Germantown, Pennsylvania, Alcott moved with her family to Boston in 1834. There her father, Bronson Alcott, founded the Temple School to practice his theories of education, which involved tapping into children's intuitive knowledge through free expression. The school failed after six years, and the family moved to Concord, Massachusetts, where they became neighbors and friends of RALPH WALDO EMERSON, HENRY DAVID THOREAU, and NATHANIEL HAWTHORNE. Louisa, educated at home by her father, also received instruction from Emerson and Thoreau.

Bronson Alcott tried unsuccessfully to found a utopian vegetarian community, Fruitlands (near Harvard, Massachusetts), in 1843. Louisa worked as a teacher, seamstress, and domestic servant to contribute to the family income. By 1848 she had begun to write for publication; her writing eventually became the family's support.

Her first book, *Flower Fables,* a collection of fairy tales, was published in 1854. She wrote numerous short thrillers, many of them serialized in magazines, under the pseudonym A. M. Barnard. Her own name became known when she published *Hospital Sketches* (1863), which recounted her experiences as a volunteer nurse at a military hospital in Washington, D.C., during the Civil War.

Alcott's first adult novel, *Moods* (1864), a study of an unsuccessful marriage, received negative reviews. The publication of *Little Women* (1868–1869), however, earned her an international reputation, and the novel and its sequels, the so-called *Little Women Series,* became phenomenal best-sellers.

Little Women draws on Alcott's own family life. The March sisters, Meg, Jo, Beth, and Amy, lived an idealized version of the life Alcott and her own sisters, Anna, Elizabeth, and May, had known. The Alcott's poverty is romanticized, but readers are given a realistic view of the dramas at the core of family life. The Marches appealed both to juveniles and adults. Into the many details of their lives are bound Alcott's acute perceptions about human nature and relations.

Alcott wrote a second series of books featuring the Marches, including *Little Men* (1871), in which Jo successfully runs a school for boys on the principles identified by Bronson Alcott, as well as *Jo's Boys and How They Turned Out* (1886), about the lives and careers of Jo's children. The success of the *Little Women* series also made it easier for Alcott to sell other books for adolescents, including *An Old-Fashioned Girl* (1870), *Eight Cousins* (1875), and *Jack and Jill* (1880).

Alcott continued to write more than just domestic novels. Her thriller *A Modern Mephistopheles* (1877) recounts the story of a failed poet who, like Goethe's Faust, makes a pact with the devil. *Work: A Story of Experience* (1873) is a novel about the efforts of a poor girl to support herself as a seamstress, a domestic servant, and a companion. "Transcendental Wild Oats" (1874) is a brief memoir of her father's effort to found Fruitlands.

Alcott suffered recurring ill health after her Civil War nursing experience, during which she had contracted typhoid fever. She died in March 1888, at the age of fifty-five, on the day of her father's funeral.

BIBLIOGRAPHY

Meigs, Cornelia, *Louisa May Alcott and the American Family Story,* 1970; Saxton, Martha, *Louisa May: A Modern Biography of Alcott,* 1977.

Allen, Woody

(December 1, 1935–)
Actor, Film Director, Writer

Woody Allen began as a gag writer and stand-up comic to become one of America's foremost independent filmmakers. While his wit and point of view reflect a New York sensibility, his films—humorously expressing the anxieties of modern-day life—have achieved international recognition.

Allen (originally Allen Stewart Konigsberg) was born in the Bronx but raised in Brooklyn. His parents, Martin and Nettie, were of European Jewish descent, his father an engraver of jewelry, his mother a bookkeeper. An average student at Midwood High School, he spent his time listening to jazz and going to the movies. He was inspired by CHARLIE CHAPLIN and the MARX BROTHERS, among others, to send original gags to newspapers—under his pen name Woody—in the hope of being discovered. Allen's passion for old movies is lovingly evoked in *The Purple Rose of Cairo* (1985).

Following high school, he briefly attended New York University and City College. During the 1950s he wrote for television, including Sid Caesar's *Your Show of Shows,* but his personal material was more effectively realized through his own delivery in night clubs.

His persona was that of the anxious Jewish *schlemiel* in an indifferent world. Unlike Mort Sahl, a mentor, and Lenny Bruce, a contemporary, Allen did not satirize the establishment or politics so much as himself. He turned his nervousness into his strength, creating a quirky, unique style combining the cleverness of Groucho Marx, the lightness of Bob Hope, and the helplessness of Stan Laurel.

In 1965 he began publishing short stories and essays in *The New Yorker,* later collected in three volumes. His story "The Kugelmass Episode" won the O. Henry Award, and several plays were produced on and off Broadway, including *Don't Drink the Water* (1966) and *Play It Again, Sam* (1969), both of which were made into films.

Allen's first involvement with film was as screenwriter for and supporting actor in *What's New, Pussycat?* (1965), a British farce with Peter Sellers, and *What's Up, Tiger Lily?* (1966), a cleverly dubbed Japanese film for which he wrote extra sequences.

His directing debut was *Take the Money and Run* (1969), which took the form of a string of gags unconcerned with narrative structure. This style characterized his early films, permitting free range over many aspects of contemporary culture, from dictatorships and revolutions in *Bananas* (1971), to sex in *Everything You Always Wanted to Know about Sex (But Were Afraid to Ask)* (1972), health fads and consumer products in *Sleeper* (1973), and romantic love and Russian literature in *Love and Death* (1975).

Allen's interest in narrative and character grew with *Annie Hall* (1977), which won Academy Awards for Best Picture, Director, Screenplay, and Actress (Diane Keaton). Some films, however, were strained imitations of favorite directors Ingmar Bergman—*Interiors* (1978)—and Federico Fellini—*Stardust Memories* (1980).

Allen's status as a director was clinched with *Manhattan* (1979), which critic Andrew Sarris called "the only great movie of the Seventies." The film epitomized Allen's love affair with New York; its glossy black-and-white photography and music by GEORGE GERSHWIN functioned both as a nostalgic re-creation and as a state of mind for his characters.

New York figures prominently in his work: *Broadway Danny Rose* (1984) is a tribute to a generation of New York–style performers; *Radio Days* (1987), a semiautobiographical look at Allen's youth in Brooklyn; and "Oedipus Wrecks," a hilarious sketch in the anthology film *New York Stories* (1989), about the character's attempt to find true love and avoid his mother's disapproval. Films set outside the city—*A Midsummer Night's Sex Comedy* (1982) and *September* (1987)—seem to lack a cohesive identity.

Allen's films are increasingly preoccupied with the meaning of love and being and the inevitability of death. However humorous their situations, his characters are obsessed with questions of how to live in a modern world bereft of traditional values. These themes are prevalent in *Hannah and Her Sisters* (1986), a seriocomic study, in a Chekhovian vein, of the interactions of three sisters, their love lives, and their ambitions, and in which the Allen character faces the prospect of death. Morality is scrutinized in *Crimes and Misdemeanors* (1989), a complex interweaving of two stories, one suggesting that life may have no meaning, the other that crime sometimes does pay. *Husbands and Wives* (1992) explores the crisis of modern marriage and the need for stimulating relationships between men and women.

Allen's screen persona experiences these conditions with a degree of personal angst quite unique. Scholar Graham McCann says that his "*schlemiel* is something of a first for American comedy: a man who is extremely vulnerable, inadequate, insecure, and often helpless." The quest for identity often accom-

panying such feelings is brilliantly parodied in *Zelig* (1983), in which a man's chameleonlike abilities enable him to assume any persona, point of view, or physical condition in order to fit into society.

The continuity between Allen's early comic material, his writing, and the characters he plays has tended to blur the line between fiction and reality in his work, sometimes with unfortunate consequences. For example, when in 1992 his personal life with longtime companion Mia Farrow—star of many of his films—and her children came under scrutiny, the media cited lines and behavior from Allen's movies as if these were indistinguishable from his private life.

Allen has occasionally acted in films of other directors, notably *The Front* (1976), Martin Ritt's critique of the Hollywood blacklist during the McCarthy era, and in Paul Mazursky's *Scenes from a Mall* (1991).

BIBLIOGRAPHY

Lax, Eric, *Woody Allen: A Biography,* 1991; McCann, Graham, *Woody Allen: New Yorker,* 1990.

Anderson, James Maxwell

(December 15, 1888–February 28, 1959)
Playwright

Maxwell Anderson wrote thirty-three plays in the thirty-five years from 1923 until 1958, including satires, fantasies, historical plays, and strong modern tragedies. He was the only major twentieth-century American playwright to succeed in creating blank verse drama.

Anderson was born in Atlantic, Pennsylvania, the son of a Baptist minister who served

churches in Pennsylvania, Ohio, Iowa, and North Dakota. He graduated from the University of North Dakota in 1911 and taught high school English for two years until he went to Stanford University as a teaching fellow. In 1914, after he earned his master's degree, he taught in a San Francisco high school and in 1917 joined the faculty of Whittier College in California. Even though Whittier was a Quaker college, the authorities fired Anderson because of his pacifist views during World War I. Turning to journalism, he worked for a newspaper in Grand Forks, North Dakota, then for the San Francisco *Chronicle* and *Bulletin,* and finally for *The New Republic.*

Anderson wrote his first play, *White Desert,* in 1923, a verse tragedy set in North Dakota about the consequences of marital jealousy. The next year he collaborated with Laurence Stallings, who had served in World War I, on a realistic antiwar play, *What Price Glory?* which presented war as horrible, not romantic, in brutally frank language. Since the play was immensely successful, Anderson resigned from *The New Republic* to write for the stage full time. Stallings and Anderson collaborated in 1925 on two other plays, both unsuccessful: *First Flight,* about an episode in the life of Andrew Jackson, and *The Buccaneer,* about the pirate Henry Morgan. *Gods of the Lightning,* produced in 1928, was the first of two plays Anderson would write about the Sacco-Vanzetti case. (This controversial case involved two Italian anarchists who were tried and convicted of murder in Massachusetts in 1921. Many liberals thought they had been tried for their radical views rather than for a proven crime, and protest demonstrations were held in the United States and abroad. Sacco and Vanzetti were executed in 1927.)

Elizabeth the Queen (1930), a romantic tragedy about historical characters written in blank verse, was the first modern American verse play to be commercially successful. Audiences loved it, and Anderson went on to write more historical plays: *Night over Taos* (1932), about Spanish resistance to American advances in early–nineteenth-century New Mexico; *Mary of Scotland* (1933), which starred HELEN HAYES as Mary Queen of Scots; *Valley Forge* (1934), about George Washington; and *Wingless Victory* (1936), a story of a doomed interracial marriage in seventeenth-century New England.

He also wrote contemporary plays, including the Pulitzer Prize–winning *Both Your*

Houses (1933), a political satire on dishonest congressmen. One of his greatest successes was *Winterset* (1935), a verse tragedy and Anderson's second play based on the Sacco-Vanzetti case. It starred Burgess Meredith and won the first New York Drama Critics' Circle Award. Reviewers compared the theme of *Winterset* with *Hamlet. High Tor* (1937), was an ambitious satirical fantasy, and *The Star Wagon,* produced the same year, was a science-fiction play.

Resenting drama critics and feeling that together with producers they had too much power over playwrights, Anderson in 1938 helped found the Playwrights' Producing Company, along with ROBERT SHERWOOD, Elmer Rice, Sidney Howard, and S. N. Behrman. The Playwrights' Company, as it came to be known, was very successful.

In 1939, *Key Largo,* a verse play dealing with an idealistic American volunteer in the Spanish Civil War, won him great respect for "its probing of the bases of man's ethical faith." As the United States became involved in World War II, he wrote three antiwar plays: *Candle in the Wind* (1941), set in occupied Paris; *The Eve of St. Mark* (1942), about an American farm boy killed in World War II; and *Storm Operation* (1944), about U.S. soldiers in North Africa. They were followed by several ambitious historical plays, including *Joan of Lorraine* in 1946, starring INGRID BERGMAN; *Anne of the Thousand Days,* about Anne Boleyn, an unqualified success in 1948; and a play about the trial and death of Socrates called *Barefoot in Athens* in 1951.

Anderson's energy led him to still other challenges. He first collaborated with KURT WEILL in 1938 on the musical *Knickerbocker Holiday,* which satirized Franklin D. Roosevelt's New Deal program. He also wrote the book and lyrics for another Weill musical, *Lost in the Stars* (1949), which was based on South African writer Alan Paton's novel *Cry, the Beloved Country.* He adapted William March's novel *The Bad Seed,* an intense portrait of a vicious child, in 1954. It was his last play.

Anderson had very definite theories about writing, which he set forth in *The Essence of Tragedy* (1939). He believed, among other things, that a play must deal with the inner life and contain a conflict between good and evil. The protagonist must represent the forces of good and must win; he or she should be a better person at the end of the play than at the beginning; and excellence on the stage is always moral excellence. Anderson spent a lifetime living up to these high standards.

BIBLIOGRAPHY

Shivers, Alfred S., *The Life of Maxwell Anderson*, 1983.

Anderson, Marian

(February 17, 1902–April 8, 1993)
Singer

Marian Anderson, the first black star at the Metropolitan Opera, was applauded in Europe long before U.S. audiences came to admire and accept her gifts. Fine musicianship guided this magnificent contralto voice of remarkable range in a repertoire that included difficult art songs along with deeply felt Negro spirituals.

Born in Philadelphia, Pennsylvania, Anderson grew up singing in the Union Baptist Church. She began vocal training when she was in her third year of high school. After graduating from South Philadelphia High School, she began to study with Giuseppe Boghetti in Philadelphia.

National Archives

On August 26, 1925, the winner of a competition, she appeared with the New York Philharmonic Orchestra at Lewisohn Stadium in New York. The *New York Times* reported, "Miss Anderson made an excellent impression. She is endowed by nature with a voice of unusual compass, color and dramatic capacity." Ten years later the newspaper declared, "There can be no question that Miss Anderson, alike by virtue of her great, gorgeous voice, her art of song, the emotional, indeed the spiritual and mystical elements of her nature that repeatedly lend her work the character of a consecration . . . ranks today among the few imposing vocal confrontations of the age."

Anderson's early success in New York led to a contract with the powerful concert manager Arthur Judson. More concertizing and higher fees followed. On Judson's recommendation she began study with Frank La Forge, a well-known vocal coach. Subsequently she went abroad, making her debut in London at Wigmore Hall in 1930. She went on to successful tours of Germany and Scandinavia and even met Finnish composer Jan Sibelius.

Conductor ARTURO TOSCANINI heard Anderson sing in Salzburg, Austria, and remarked that a voice like hers is heard "once in a hundred years." Anderson returned to America a more mature artist and received critical kudos for her Town Hall recital in 1935. In his *New York Times* review Howard Taubman stated, "Let it be said at the outset: Marian Anderson has returned to her native land one of the great singers of our time."

In 1939 Miss Anderson was slated to perform at Constitution Hall in Washington, D.C. When the Daughters of the American Revolution, proprietors of the hall, refused Anderson permission to sing there, the issue gained national attention. The president's wife, Eleanor Roosevelt, resigned from the DAR and helped reschedule the concert at the Lincoln Memorial. There, on Easter Sunday, April 9, 1939, Anderson, with her habitual dignity, sang to an audience of some 75,000. Her program included "America," Franz Schubert's "Ave Maria," and three spirituals.

Anderson continued to concertize. Finally, disgracefully late in her career, she was invited to sing at the Metropolitan Opera in New York by Rudolph Bing, the general manager. There,

on January 7, 1955, she made her debut as Ulrica in Verdi's *Un ballo in maschera* (The Masked Ball). In her fifties, no longer in her vocal prime, she was nonetheless the first black singer to appear at the Metropolitan. Though she left the opera house in 1956, she had led the way for other singers of color.

Anderson's farewell tour concluded with a recital at Carnegie Hall on April 19, 1965; a tribute there in 1977 celebrated her seventy-fifth birthday and the artistry that marked her career. Among her awards are the Presidential Medal of Freedom (1963), a Congressional Gold Medal (1978), and the first Eleanor Roosevelt Human Rights Award of the City of New York (1984).

BIBLIOGRAPHY

Anderson, Marian, *My Lord What a Morning: An Autobiography,* 1956; Vehanen, Kosti, *Marian Anderson, a Portrait,* 1941, rep., 1970.

Anderson, Sherwood Berton

(September 13, 1876–March 8, 1941)
Novelist, Short-Story Writer

Sherwood Anderson, best known for his story cycle, *Winesburg, Ohio* (1919), wrote about small-town life in the Midwest and about the effects of industrialization on the lives of people. He developed a simple prose style close to the rhythms of speech, which influenced many writers who followed.

Born in Camden, Ohio, and raised in Clyde, the town that would become the model for Winesburg, Anderson was one of seven children. His father, a house painter, barely supported the family, and Anderson left high school after only a year to help out. He finally earned his diploma at the age of twenty-three after enlisting in the army but failing to see

action in Cuba during the Spanish-American War.

Anderson went to Chicago, finding work first in advertising and then in the mail-order business. In 1904 he married and in 1907 established his own business manufacturing a roofing compound in Elyria, Ohio.

Anderson began trying to write and gradually became disillusioned with his material life. Suddenly, in 1912, he experienced a personal crisis; he left his office one day in a "fugue state" and woke up in a hospital four days later. He then left his wife and children, moved to Chicago, and tried to establish himself as a writer.

In his first novel, *Windy McPherson's Son* (1916), Anderson explored his own youth in a small midwestern town, particularly his relationship with his father. The protagonist, Sam McPherson, has grown up in squalor. His life has been dominated by his alcoholic father. The novel traces his efforts to attain material success and the consequences of those efforts on his relationships with women.

Anderson's two subsequent books, *Marching Men* (1917) and *Mid-American Chants* (1918), are exhortations. In the former, a novel set in Pennsylvania, the protagonist leads workers in protest against the excessive demands of industry; the latter offers "chants" in a style reminiscent of the work of the poet WALT WHITMAN.

Anderson was living in Chicago in 1915 when he began writing the twenty-three sketches that became *Winesburg, Ohio*, his best-known work. Each sketch featured a "grotesque," a character who had become irrevocably fixated on a single idea or truth. Each character's limited view cuts him or her off from real human companionship; each is linked by the interest of a young reporter, George Willard, to whom some of them tell their stories. George has set out to try to understand human character; he works at the behest of his mother, a desperately lonely woman who prays that before she dies George will be able to "express something" for them both. In the end, George leaves Winesburg, and we assume he has become the author of the sketches, though the book casts doubt on whether the "truth" known by any of the characters can be fully communicated.

In *Poor White* (1920), considered one of Anderson's more successful novels, the author again portrayed America's industrialization, linking men's drive for material success and their failures with women. Anderson then published two volumes of short stories, *The Triumph of the Egg* (1921) and *Horses and Men* (1923). In his novel *Dark Laughter* (1925), he depicts the corruption of white men, suggesting that only African Americans have escaped the corrupting influences of our civilization.

Feeling that his powers as a fiction writer were failing, Anderson built a house near Marion, Virginia, in 1926, and with the profits from *Dark Laughter* he bought two newspapers, one Republican and the other Democratic, which he subsequently edited.

Anderson wrote a series of autobiographical works: *A Story Teller's Story* (1924), *Tar: A Midwest Childhood* (1926), and the posthumously published *Sherwood Anderson's Memoirs* (1942). Each fictionalizes the facts of his life and offers insight into the writer's imagination.

During the Great Depression of the 1930s Anderson traveled to mills and factories throughout the South. These explorations produced two novels, *Beyond Desire* (1932) and *Kit Brandon: A Portrait* (1936), and two nonfiction works, *Perhaps Women* (1931) and *Puzzled America* (1935). In these books, Anderson celebrated the persistence and determination of the workers he had met.

Anderson died suddenly in March 1941, while en route to South America.

BIBLIOGRAPHY

Howe, Irving, *Sherwood Anderson,* 1951; Townsend, Kim, *Sherwood Anderson: A Biography,* 1987.

Arbus, Diane

(March 14, 1923–July 26, 1971)
Photographer

Diane Arbus, who began as a fashion photographer, later became known for her images of freaks, outcasts, and idiosyncratic characters.

She was born Diane Nemerov in 1923 in New York City into a well-to-do Jewish family prominent in the fur and clothing business. With her brother, Howard (later a Pulitzer Prize–winning poet), and sister, Renee, she grew up pampered and rather spoiled in several lavish Park Avenue and Central Park West apartments. She was able to pursue interests in painting at the Ethical Culture School on Central Park, the Fieldston School in the Riverdale section of the Bronx, and the Cummington School of the Arts in Northampton, Massachusetts. The work of painter George Grosz—especially the images of a harsh and debauched lifestyle—fascinated her. "I had visions of being a great sad artist and I turned all my energies toward it," she later recalled.

In 1941, at the age of eighteen, she married Allan Arbus, whom she had met while he was employed in her father's department store. She took advantage of his tenure with the photography division of the Signal Corps to learn the elements of the medium; she later advanced her studies by working with photographer Berenice Abbott. After the war they went into the fashion photography business together. Influenced by the elegant studio work of EDWARD STEICHEN and Louise Dahl-Wolfe, they photographed clothing, accessories, and models for *Vogue, Glamour,* and *Harper's Bazaar.* However, Diane, who was studying in the late 1950s with Lisette Model, a photographer known for her images of grotesques and outcasts, seemed more interested in prowling the night streets and visiting circuses and sideshows with her Rolleiflex camera, photographing "the losers of the world," as she put it (Susan Sontag has termed them the "Halloween Crowd")—the bums, bag ladies, and freaks. She went to the Bellevue Morgue, Welfare Island, mental asylums, nudist camps, and slaughterhouses. Some of these images appeared in *Esquire* magazine in 1960. "Diane was fascinated by weirdos," recalled an associate. "Not just by their weirdness, but by their *commitment* to weirdness."

Arbus's last decade was marked by her total commitment to this more personal and independent expression. *Harper's Bazaar* published her "Portraits of Eccentrics" in 1961. She received two Guggenheim Fellowships, in 1963 and 1966, free-lanced for *Esquire, Show,* and the *New York Times Magazine,* and taught photography courses at the Parsons School of Design, Rhode Island School of Design, and the Cooper Union. Regarding her images of freaks, she remarked, "There's a quality of legend about freaks. Like a person in a fairy tale who stops you and demands that you answer a riddle. Most people go through life dreading they'll have a traumatic experience. Freaks were born with their trauma. They've already passed their test in life. They're aristocrats." The camera was her "license" for her insatiable curiosity, her uncontrollable urge to nose around among the more unlikely characters and situations of life. At the same time, as she said, the camera helped her "scrutinize reality" so intensely that "it becomes fantastic." In her best work she was not interested in the chance accidents of life. Rather, as Hilton Kramer writes, "The subjects face the camera with interest and patience. They are fully aware of the picture-making process. They collaborate. It is this element of participation . . . that gives these pictures their great dignity." During her lifetime, her work appeared in three major museum exhibitions, all of them group shows. After her death, retrospective exhibitions appeared in museums in the United States, Europe, Japan, New Zealand, and Australia.

"My work doesn't do it for me anymore," she said in 1971. The intense bouts of depression she had suffered all her life were catching up with her. She was found dead, her wrists slit, lying in her bathtub. A note was found in her journal dated that day. It read, simply, "The last supper."

BIBLIOGRAPHY

Arbus, Diane, *Diane Arbus,* 1972; Bosworth, Patricia, *Diane Arbus: A Biography,* 1984.

Arlen, Harold

(February 15, 1905–April 23, 1986)
Songwriter

An extraordinary number of Arlen's hits are now classics, from "Over the Rainbow" and "Stormy Weather" to "One for My Baby" and "That Old Black Magic." Many reveal the songwriter's affection for blues and jazz and demonstrate his contributions to the popularization of black music; some helped singers to stardom.

Born in Buffalo, New York, Hyman Arluck, later known as Harold Arlen, was the son of a cantor and grew up singing in the choir at his father's synagogue. Early classical piano studies gave way to jazz when Arlen was twelve, and by the time he was sixteen he was playing piano in movie houses and on Lake Erie excursion boats.

The youngster also formed his own band, the Snappy Trio, which was later expanded into the Yankee Six. Eventually Arlen joined a local dance orchestra, the Buffalodians, as vocalist, pianist, and arranger and went with the group to New York City in 1927. Once there, Arlen moved over to Arnold Johnson's band and sang with the Johnson ensemble in *George White's Scandals of 1928.*

Arlen began to write arrangements, including some pieces for FLETCHER HENDERSON's band, worked as a solo piano/vocal act in vaudeville, and recorded as a singer with BENNY GOODMAN, Red Nichols, and Joe Venuti.

In 1929 Arlen met lyricist Ted Koehler (1894–1973) and with him wrote a hit, "Get Happy." According to *The New Yorker,* GEORGE GERSHWIN thought the song had "the most ex-

citing finale [he'd] ever heard." The success convinced Arlen to turn from performer to songwriter. Between 1930 and 1934 Arlen and Koehler wrote songs for revues at the Cotton Club in Harlem, among them "Stormy Weather," "Between the Devil and the Deep Blue Sea," and "I've Got the World on a String," works that suggest the blues while conforming to most Tin Pan Alley conventions.

In 1934, with E. Y. ("Yip") Harburg (1898–1981) and IRA GERSHWIN (1896–1983), Arlen completed the music for *Life Begins at 8:40,* his last revue, and began to write for Hollywood, moving there in 1935. Over the next twenty years he collaborated with Harburg, creating songs like "It's Only a Paper Moon" (1932), and "Happiness Is a Thing Called Joe" (1943), and with Ira Gershwin, "The Man That Got Away" (1954).

Arlen and Harburg's greatest triumph came with *The Wizard of Oz* in 1939. One of the earliest films to use song and dance to build plot and character, it included "Over the Rainbow," an Academy Award–winning song. Later the team collaborated on two Broadway musicals, *Bloomer Girl* (1944) and *Jamaica* (1957).

From 1940 to 1945 Arlen worked with lyricist Johnny Mercer (1909–1976) to fashion songs for motion pictures, including "Blues in the Night," "That Old Black Magic," "One for My Baby," and "Ac-cen-tchu-ate the Positive." In addition the team collaborated on Broadway shows: *St. Louis Woman* (1946), revised in

1959 as *Free and Easy,* and *Saratoga* (1959). *Free and Easy* added a song with lyrics by Ted Koehler, "Come Rain or Come Shine."

Many consider *House of Flowers* (1954), a Broadway show created with novelist TRUMAN CAPOTE, Arlen's finest work. Composer Alec Wilder, writing in *American Popular Song,* called it "Arlen's most ambitious and beautiful score."

Harold Arlen moved back to New York in 1955 and was described in *The New Yorker* that year as "a worried-looking, friendly man, with thick black hair and sparkling eyes." In New York Arlen continued to write for Hollywood as well as for Broadway. He wrote his last song with his old associate E. Y. Harburg in 1976, "Looks Like the End of a Beautiful Friendship."

Always partial to blues and jazz, Arlen often wrote for black casts and frequently explored black themes. According to Alec Wilder, Arlen's "love for . . . jazz players and their marvelous inventiveness . . . had a profound effect on [his] songs." For example, melodies might rise or fall an octave, as in "Stormy Weather" and "Over the Rainbow," and were often driven by complex rhythms and extended phrases adapted from blues and jazz idioms.

Harold Arlen died in New York City at eighty-one, leaving an impressive list of evergreens, songs that live beyond their original film or show.

BIBLIOGRAPHY

Furia, P., *Poets of Tin Pan Alley: A History of America's Great Lyricists,* 1990; Jablonski, E., *Harold Arlen: Happy with the Blues,* 1961; Wilder, A., *American Popular Song: The Great Innovators, 1900–1950,* 1972.

Armstrong, Louis

(ca. 1898–July 6, 1971)
Jazz Musician

Louis Armstrong is one of the towering figures in the history of jazz. A virtuoso performer, he was a master of the melodic improvisations, daring experiments in tone and pitch, and rhythmic ideas that have inspired generations of musicians.

Armstrong gave his birth date as July 4, 1900, but an earlier date, 1898, month and day unknown, seems likely. Born in New Orleans to Willie Armstrong, a laborer, and Mayann, a domestic and sometime prostitute, Louis grew up poor in Storyville, New Orleans's red-light district, a few blocks filled with dance halls and brothels and the constant swirl of music—the blues and a ragtime on the verge of becoming jazz. Willie abandoned Mayann at the time of Armstrong's birth.

Armstrong developed his extraordinary ear singing in a barbershop quartet, but it was the Colored Waifs' Home for Boys (he was sentenced there for delinquency) that he was exposed to the cornet. Released from the Home when he was in his early teens, he returned to Storyville, borrowed instruments, sat in at local establishments, and learned his way around the cornet and the rags, marches, and songs of the day.

Joe "King" Oliver, a jazz cornetist in the city, an important musical figure, and Armstrong's hero, befriended the youngster, gave him opportunities to play, and, in time, presented him with an instrument. Storyville was closed down in 1917, and, after Oliver went to Chicago the next year, Louis replaced him in what was considered the leading jazz band of New Orleans, a group led by trombonist Kid Ory. Working in dance halls and in Fate Marable's riverboat bands, the new professional honed his musical skills, learning how to read and play whatever was set before him.

In 1922 Oliver invited Armstrong to Chicago to play in his popular Creole Jazz Band at Lincoln Gardens, a black dance hall. A recording in Oliver's 1923–1924 series reveals the strength and musicianship of Armstrong's improvised second cornet parts to Oliver's lead, notably in "Dippermouth Blues." Musicians began to recognize Armstrong as a leader in "hot" music.

Armstrong's developing rhythmic concepts were realized as jazz emerged, a relaxed style less stiff than ragtime. Jazz depended on extensive use of syncopated rhythms and surprising patterns of off-beat, staggered accents fitted within a constant tempo. It also depended on a musician's ability to "swing," that is, to accent the notes a certain way while at the same time propel the music forward. And it was Armstrong, more than any other player, who defined swing. Through it he demonstrated his brilliance as an architect of spontaneous but disciplined improvisations, as an instrumental virtuoso, and as a soloist who transcended the traditional group, or ensemble, improvisation of New Orleans.

In 1924 he married Lillian Hardin, the band's pianist. The second of Louis's four wives, she encouraged Armstrong to go to New York City that year to join the FLETCHER HENDERSON Orchestra, a big band. Though he chafed under the strict Henderson rhythms, he found an outlet and an opportunity in the solos, such as on "Copenhagen," where his free-flowing improvisations enchanted listeners and strengthened his musical reputation. He began to play with other groups and, in 1925, made a remarkable recording with BESSIE SMITH, "St. Louis Blues." Some of his New Orleans–style recordings of this time include SIDNEY BECHET, the noted clarinetist and soprano saxophonist.

Back in Chicago in November 1925, Armstrong began a series of some sixty re-

cordings under his own name. Including the famous "Big Butter and Egg Man," "Potato Head Blues," and "Struttin' with Some Barbecue," they are known collectively as the Hot Five and the Hot Seven, which, according to Armstrong biographer James L. Collier, "because of their profound effect on later music, are one of the most important bodies of recordings in 20th century music." He goes on to say that the recordings "provide an astonishing record of Armstrong's musical growth—his quick electric climb to artistic maturity."

It was during these years in Chicago that Armstrong switched from cornet to trumpet, a more brilliant instrument, and here, too, that he made his first scat recording. Scat, a manner of singing using nonsense syllables, presents the voice as a solo instrument. Singing was to become an integral part of his performance.

The earliest of the series reflected New Orleans ensembles. In successive recordings, Armstrong's solos became more important, and he sang more frequently after the success of his scat singing on "Heebie Jeebies." By 1928 Armstrong's more modern small band included Earl Hines, a leading jazz pianist.

In 1929 Armstrong made recordings of then popular songs, such as "I Can't Give You Anything But Love," "Some of These Days," "When You're Smiling," and dozens of others. His example often made these songs the standards of the future among younger jazz players and fans. That same year he appeared in the Broadway revue *Hot Chocolates* with music by Fats Waller, and he helped popularize such featured numbers as "Ain't Misbehavin'" and "Black and Blue." And he adopted the form he was to use until 1947—a big band as background for his vocal and instrumental solos.

By the mid-1930s, the music known as "Swing" (the Swing Era would last from approximately 1935 to 1945), music Armstrong's work had largely founded, had become the popular idiom—there were Swing bands in dance halls, large movie houses, and on radio. Ideas from Armstrong's classics, such as "Mahogany Hall Stomp" or "Gut Bucket Blues" echoed through other bands, but Armstrong himself did not often make guest appearances or find himself played on disc jockey shows. His career depended as much on his humorous vocals such as "Brother Bill" or "(I'll Be Glad When You're Dead) You Rascal You," as on his more ambitious instrumental efforts such as "Swing That Music" or "Jubilee." And he began to appear in films, notably *Pennies from Heaven* with Bing Crosby in 1936 and an ill-starred effort called *New Orleans* in 1947.

The era of the big band was drawing to a close, and in 1947 Armstrong appeared in a specially arranged concert at New York's Town Hall with a small ensemble, including trombonist Jack Teagarden, drummer Sidney Catlett, clarinetist Barney Bigard, Earl Hines, and others. The artistic success of the evening was evident, and Armstrong soon cut back permanently to a small group he called his "All Stars." Using a repertory that went back to his early years but also including a selection of vocal-instrumental successes, Armstrong was now the "grand old man of jazz" pursuing a grueling schedule of appearances. His appearances included songs like "Blueberry Hill" and "Cold, Cold Heart" that soon passed on to younger performers, and songs he made standards such as "Mack the Knife" from *Threepenny Opera* and the title song from the Broadway show, *Hello Dolly,* probably the most successful single of his career.

The All Stars toured the world—the United States, Australia, the Far East, Europe, South America, Africa. Armstrong's international travels, some under the auspices of the U.S. State Department, earned him a new nickname, Ambassador Satch, in addition to the many others: Dippermouth, Pops, Satchelmouth, Satchmo. A heart attack in 1959 and other health problems led to fewer performances and finally to his death in 1971.

BIBLIOGRAPHY

Armstrong, Louis, *Swing That Music,* 1939, *Satchmo,* 1954, and *A Self-portrait,* 1971; Collier, J. L., *Louis Armstrong: An American Genius,* 1983; Jones, M., and J. Chilton, *Louis: The Louis Armstrong Story 1900–1971,* 1971; Schuller, G., *Early Jazz: Its Roots and Development,* 1968.

Ashbery, John Lawrence

(July 28, 1927–   )
Poet

The poetry of John Ashbery echoes but denies traditional poetic forms. Avoiding even self-consistency, it defies the reader's effort to find patterns that might convey its sense. This constant variety reflects the Post-Modern conviction that the poet can no longer ground his work in a set of metaphysical beliefs.

Ashbery was born in Rochester, New York, and grew up in nearby Sodus. He attended Deerfield Academy and earned his bachelor's degree at Harvard University in 1949 and his master's degree in English literature at Columbia University in 1951.

Ashbery worked for three years writing copy for Oxford University Press and then McGraw-Hill Book Company. He won a Fulbright Fellowship and traveled to Paris, where he lived from 1955 until 1966 and worked as an art critic for the European edition of the New York *Herald Tribune* and for *Art International.* Returning to New York, he edited *Art News* before becoming a professor of English at Brooklyn College in 1974.

Ashbery's poetry was influenced by his association with Abstract Expressionist painters (notably JACKSON POLLOCK and ROBERT MOTHERWELL) and with a group of avant-garde poets based in New York. Like others in the New York school, he developed a poetic style marked by richness of detail and long, contemplative argument. His own hallmark became the use of unconnected lyric phrases, strung together without transition in a manner resembling a collage, defying the reader to make sense of the whole.

Some Trees (1956), Ashbery's first book of poems, was chosen by the poet W. H. AUDEN to be published in the Yale Series of Younger Poets. The poet takes traditional forms—sonnet, eclogue, canzone—and subverts them, refusing to meet traditional expectations for coherence. In his second book, *The Tennis Court Oath* (1962), Ashbery explores more open forms, creating lyric pastiches and avoiding consistent structure from poem to poem. The poet once described his penchant for constant self-revision as "doing the recalcitrant thing."

Regarding the difficulty he presented to readers, Ashbery once wrote:

I know that I braid too much my own
Snapped-off perceptions of things as they come to me.
They are private and always will be.

One of his critics, Richard Howard, emphasizes Ashbery's revolutionary notion that "the world not only contains but *is* his poem, and that he cannot, in order to write, draw the world into himself as has traditionally been attempted, but must rather extrude himself into the world, must flee the center in order to be on the verge at all points."

In *Rivers and Mountains* (1966), Ashbery developed his long, meditative style. "The Skaters," which runs half the length of the book, characteristically draws together scattered pieces of experience in a discursive manner. Ashbery continued in this more synthetic mode in *The Double Dream of Spring* (1970), which cleverly reflects on an absence of philosophical or religious frames to give sense to modern life. The prose poems in *Three Poems* (1972) are set up like a dialectical argument, though within each poem the speaker loses himself among the complexities of life and language.

Self-Portrait in a Convex Mirror (1975) won the three major literary prizes of 1976: the National Book Award, the National Book Critics Circle Award, and the Pulitzer Prize. The book continues Ashbery's metaphysical explorations in a manner the poet described as "essayistic."

Among Ashbery's recent works are *Houseboat Days* (1977), *As We Know* (1979), *Shadow Train* (1981), *A Wave* (1984), which earned him the 1984 Bollingen Prize, and *April Galleons* (1987). His formal experiments have included a volume of fifty poems of four quatrains each, as well as a series of one-line poems. His poems often seem to follow the flow of thought without purpose and without conclusion.

Ashbery also has written a novel with James Schuyler, *A Nest of Ninnies* (1969); *Three Plays* (1978); and a book of art criticism, *Reported Sightings* (1989).

He continues to live and write in New York City.

BIBLIOGRAPHY

Bloom, Harold (ed.), *John Ashbery,* 1985; Lehman, David (ed.), *Beyond Amazement: New Essays on Ashbery,* 1980; Shapiro, David, *John Ashbery: An Introduction to the Poetry,* 1979.

Astaire, Fred

(May 10, 1899–June 22, 1987)
Choreographer, Popular Dancer, Singer

One of America's favorite entertainers, Fred Astaire danced with a winning, effortless style that drew life from ingenious combinations of tap, ballroom, and ballet dancing. The debonair, elegant dancer moved top hat and tails, his signature, from Broadway to Hollywood, where he became a star.

He was born Frederick Austerlitz in Omaha, Nebraska, the son of brewer Frederick E. Austerlitz and younger brother of Adele. Astaire's father had emigrated from Vienna, Austria, and found his way to the Midwest. Adele showed early promise and their mother, Ann, an enthusiastic supporter, brought the two children to New York in 1904, adopted the stage name Astaire, found dance instruction for the youngsters, and tried to spot a break in the entertainment world for a brother-sister song and dance act.

The duo made their debut in vaudeville in 1906 and continued their stage apprenticeship for over a decade. By 1917 Adele and Fred Astaire were appearing in stage musicals and by the time Fred's sister left the stage to marry in 1932,

Library of Congress

the popular team had ten musicals to their credit. Adele Astaire was the favorite. "The perfect dancing team since they were children," notes writer Arthur Jackson, "the Astaires came, were seen, and conquered with their personal dancing style and strangely enough, Adele's winsome personality rather than Fred's retiring demeanor."

The Astaires' last show together was *The Band Wagon,* in 1931, but they had sparkled and dazzled earlier in two GEORGE GERSHWIN musicals, *Lady, Be Good!* (1924) and *Funny Face* (1927), and Vincent Youmans's *Smiles* (1930).

Fred Astaire was paired with Claire Luce in COLE PORTER's *Gay Divorce* in 1932. The show ran only thirty-two weeks, but it contained Astaire's choreography for the romantically seductive "Night and Day." Jackson points out that *Gay Divorce* "made Fred Astaire a star . . . in his first solo performance." The show was made into the film *The Gay Divorcée,* starring Astaire and Ginger Rogers, in 1934.

In assessing the show *New York Times* reviewer

Brooks Atkinson wrote, "As a solo dancer Mr. Astaire stamps out his accent with that lean nervous agility that distinguishes his craftsmanship, and he has invented turns that abound in graphic portraiture. But some of us cannot help feeling that the joyousness of the Astaire team is missing now that the team has parted." Others were less kind, and one critic suggested, "Two Astaires are better than one."

Fearing that he would not fare well without his sister, Astaire rethought his position. Hollywood beckoned and films seemed the answer. In 1933 Astaire headed for California. That year he appeared in *Flying Down to Rio* with Ginger Rogers. He went on to dance with Rogers in nine more films, including *Top Hat* (1935), *Swing Time* (1936), and *Shall We Dance* (1937), movies considered by many to be among the best musicals ever made.

For Astaire, dancing was not enough. A perfectionist, he involved himself with film staff and choreographers, especially Hermes Pan, his long-time associate. Astaire expressed both story and character through dance sequences, and dances were filmed with long, sweeping shots that avoided closeups. The result was a heightened sense of the close interplay between dancers.

In the forties and fifties Astaire continued to develop new dance routines, always carefully rehearsed, with stars like Eleanor Powell, Rita Hayworth, Judy Garland, and Bing Crosby. In 1949 Astaire received a special Academy Award for his contributions to films. His studiedly casual singing inspired songs by IRVING BERLIN, Gershwin, Youmans, and Cole Porter, and he made his mark in dramatic roles, on television, and with his own songs.

But it is Astaire's dancing that sticks in the mind. Dance critic Arlene Croce writes that "Astaire was the first dancer to establish himself on the screen, and the greatest. He raised technical standards in every department— camerawork, cutting, synchronization, scoring. He inspired the best efforts of the best song writers, and his personal style set a criterion for masculine elegance that has persisted through two generations." She adds this about his partnership with Ginger Rogers: "With Astaire and Rogers, it's a matter of total professional dedication; they do not give us emotions, they give us dances, and the more beautifully they dance, the more powerful the spell that seems to bind them together."

Astaire died in Los Angeles in 1987 of pneumonia.

BIBLIOGRAPHY

Adler, B., *Fred Astaire: A Wonderful Life*, 1987; Croce, A., *The Fred Astaire and Ginger Rogers Book*, 1972, rep., 1977; Thomas, B., *Astaire: The Man, the Dancer*, 1984.

Auden, Wystan Hugh

(February 21, 1907–September 29, 1973)
Playwright, Poet

An Englishman who emigrated to America in midcareer, W. H. Auden turned from an early mastery of the complex techniques of his contemporaries—especially William Butler Yeats and T. S. ELIOT—to a poetry that was simpler, more traditional, and more directly reflective of the moral imperative he felt it needed to make art meaningful.

Wystan Hugh Auden was born on February 21, 1907, in York, England, the son of a doctor and a nurse who shared broad intellectual interests and a commitment to public service. At

Oxford, Auden was at the center of a circle of young writers—including Stephen Spender, Cecil Day Lewis, and Louis MacNeice, as well as Christopher Isherwood, then a medical student at Cambridge—known for their left-liberal politics and their consuming interest in the poetics of such current writers as Eliot and A. E. Housman.

Auden's friendship with Isherwood, which had begun in acquaintance at their prep school, St. Edmund's, blossomed in Berlin, where they often spent time together between 1929 and 1933. They discussed politics, especially the Nazi menace and Auden's growing interest in communism, and caroused together, sharing in the nightlife of the city's homosexual community.

After 1929 Auden taught preparatory school for five years. His first two volumes, *Poems* (1930) and *The Orators* (1932), established his poetic reputation. "Paid on Both Sides," a short play in prose and verse published in *Criterion* by Eliot in 1930 and republished in *Poems*, was influenced by Eliot's early work in its tight weaving of diverse images and allusions. Other poems in the volume reflect Auden's facility with a wide range of verse techniques and his deepening preoccupation with morality and politics. *The Orators* earned him the highest accolade from a *Criterion* reviewer who called the volume "the most valuable contribution to English poetry since [Eliot's] *The Waste Land.*"

With Isherwood, Auden wrote three plays: *The Dog Beneath the Skin, or, Where Is Francis?* (1935), *The Ascent of F6* (1936), and *On the Frontier* (1938). Typically, Auden wrote the verse portions and Isherwood the prose. One unhappy critic accused them of "putting Marxist pap into bourgeois bottles."

Look, Stranger! (1936; published in the United States as *On This Island* in 1937) is dedicated to Erika Mann, the German writer Thomas Mann's daughter, whom Auden had married in 1935 as a kindness, in order to provide her with a passport out of Nazi Germany. They never lived together. In the dedication to the volume, Auden described a need for dis-

ciplined thought and expression to answer the moral chaos of the time. In their directness and simplicity, the lyric poems in the volume suggest the course Auden would follow. Like MARIANNE MOORE, whose verse he admired, he worked to approximate the patterns of speech in order to express more plainly what he hoped was a clear-eyed view of the world.

Auden traveled to Spain for two months in 1937 to observe the civil war. His poem "Spain," written upon his return, reflects both his sympathy with the Loyalist, antifascist cause and his horror at the brutality of some of its adherents.

The outbreak of war between China and Japan led Auden and Isherwood to travel to China in 1938. Together they wrote *Journey to a War* (1939). Auden's sequence of twenty-seven sonnets, "In Time of War," attempts to create an intellectual framework explaining the outbreak of world war. The poet expresses a faith in the power of human reason and love—a stance that marked his liberalism and alienated many, more radical thinkers.

Auden and Isherwood emigrated to the United States in 1939. Auden wrote that he sought "to live deliberately without roots." The move was criticized by those who regarded it as an abandonment of the liberal causes Auden had championed, but Auden had come to feel overwhelmed by unending debate. He effectively gained distance on English literary and political life by adopting for himself the status of a detached, objective observer.

Auden divided his time between New York City, where he taught at the New School for Social Research and at Barnard College, and other teaching jobs at the University of Michigan, Swarthmore, Bryn Mawr, and Bennington. He was naturalized in 1946.

Shortly after arriving in New York, Auden had met Chester Kallman, who became his lifelong companion, even though he was eighteen years of age and Auden was thirty-two. Together, in 1947 and 1948, they wrote the libretto for IGOR STRAVINSKY's opera *The Rake's Progress*, which premiered in Venice in 1951.

Another Time (1940) gathers the last of the poems Auden had written in Europe with early poems he wrote in the United States. The volume includes some of Auden's best-known works, such as "Musèe des Beaux Arts," "The Unknown Citizen," and "September 1, 1939." Auden later sought to retract this last poem, named for the date Germany invaded Poland at the start of World War II, for what he regarded as its inauthenticity, in spite of its containing his most famous single line: "We must love one another or die." Many readers criticized the poems in *Another Time* for their more traditional forms and meters and for their plain reflectiveness. Auden was discarding the structural complexity and the reliance on imagery typical of the popular modernists.

Auden had begun revising some of his earlier poems, imprinting them with his discontent with liberal politics and his growing commitment to Christianity. *The Double Man* (1941) included some of these revisions. Auden had become an avid reader of the works of the Christian philosopher Søren Kierkegaard, who believed that faith came as a result of personal crisis. "For the Time Being," the title poem in a volume published in 1944, is dedicated to Auden's mother, a devout Anglo-Catholic, who died in 1941. The poem depicts a manger scene and puts updated language in the mouths of Mary, Joseph, and the shepherds.

The Age of Anxiety (1947) won the Pulitzer Prize in 1948 and inspired LEONARD BERNSTEIN'S Second Symphony. The book is a psychological exploration of a woman and three men in a bar on Third Avenue in Manhattan. Auden sought to demonstrate how ordinary individuals, with all their faults and idiosyncracies, can yet aspire to the heroic.

In 1951 Auden published *Nones* and in 1955, *The Shield of Achilles*, which won the National Book Award. *Nones* contains Auden's own favorite poem, "In Praise of Limestone":

> If it forms the one landscape that we, the
>   inconstant ones,
> Are consistently homesick for, this is chiefly
> Because it dissolves in water.

Both volumes typify Auden's mature style: themes vary widely, but, in their careful simplicity, the poems engage the reader without apparent effort.

Auden received the Bollingen Prize in Poetry in 1954. In 1956 he was elected to a five-year term as professor of poetry at Oxford. His volumes *Homage to Clio* (1960), *About the House* (1965), and *City without Walls* (1969) featured poems on personal themes.

BIBLIOGRAPHY

Carpenter, Humphrey, *W. H. Auden: A Biography*, 1981; Miller, Charles H., *Auden: An American Friendship*, 1983; Osborne, Charles, *W. H. Auden: The Life of a Poet*, 1979.

Babbitt, Milton Byron

(May 10, 1916–)
Composer

Milton Babbitt is one of the most influential American composers, theorists, and teachers since World War II. His discovery of the systematic properties of pitch relationships inherent in ARNOLD SCHOENBERG's twelve-tone method led him to new ways of organizing not only pitch, but rhythm, dynamics, and tone color as well.

Born in Philadelphia, Pennsylvania, Milton Byron Babbitt was raised in Jackson, Mississippi. At four he was playing the violin and a few years later studied clarinet and saxophone. By the time Babbitt graduated from high school in 1931 at the age of fifteen, he was already playing in jazz groups and composing popular songs.

Babbitt's father, an actuary, had stimulated the youngster's interest in mathematics and when Babbitt entered the University of Pennsylvania in the fall of 1931, he planned on becoming a mathematician. But music continued to tempt him and before long he transferred to New York University, switched his major, and studied with composers Marion Bauer and Philip James. He graduated with a B.Mus. in 1935.

Early on Babbitt was interested in the compositions of EDGARD VARÈSE and IGOR STRAVINSKY, and later fascinated by the tonal explorations of Arnold Schoenberg and others. At the time twelve-tone music was known to few Americans, and those who encountered it tended to dislike it.

After graduating from New York University, Babbitt continued his studies privately with composer ROGER SESSIONS, who had just joined the faculty at Princeton University. Babbitt enrolled in graduate study at Princeton, joined the music faculty there in 1938, and in 1942 earned the M.F.A. in music, one of the first such degrees granted by the university. His twelve-tone work *Composition for String Orchestra* (1940) was composed during this period.

Babbitt's interest in mathematics remained. During World War II he conducted research in Washington, D.C., and was a member of the mathematics faculty at Princeton (1943–1945). At the time he was not composing. Rather, he concentrated on developing a study of the abstract properties of the twelve-tone system used by Schoenberg. The result, *The Function of Set Structure in the Twelve-tone System* (1946), submitted as a Ph.D. dissertation in music, was not accepted because of its difficulty and was never published. Princeton University finally awarded Babbitt the Ph.D. in 1992. He began to work again as a composer and between 1946 and 1948 he produced music for films and the score for an unproduced Broadway musical, *Fabulous Voyage.*

Babbitt returned to Princeton in 1948 as a member of the music faculty and in 1960 succeeded Roger Sessions as the Conant Professor of Music. In 1959 he became director of the Columbia-Princeton Electronic Music Center. He has been a member of the composition faculty at the Juilliard School (appointed in 1973), and has taught at the Salzburg Seminar in American Studies, the Berkshire Music Center, and the New England Conservatory of Music. He lectures widely, has received many honors, including a Pulitzer Prize Special Citation for "his life's work as a distinguished and seminal American composer," and has long been active in contemporary music organizations. Babbitt has been a MacArthur fellow since 1986.

Babbitt worked intensively to extend and formalize aspects of the twelve-tone serialism initiated and developed by Schoenberg. Schoenberg, as scholar Eric Salzman notes, "established a carefully coordinated set of relationships, not only between the parts but between the various aspects or dimensions of the musical discourse."

But, Salzman adds, "the first works in which linear succession, harmonic simultaneity, duration (including rhythm and tempo), dynamics, articulation, register, and timbre are all strictly derived from a single, all-inclusive premise were written . . . by Milton Babbitt." Salzman goes on to note Babbitt's *Three Compositions for Piano* and his compositions for four instruments and twelve instruments in 1948. What had been a method for Schoenberg became a system as a result of Milton Babbitt's work.

The composer set down his theories and system in the early sixties in such essays as "Some Aspects of Twelve-tone Composition," "Set Structure as a Compositional Determinant," and "Twelve-tone Rhythmic Structure and the Electronic Medium." He thought that "the twelve-tone set must absolutely determine *every* aspect of the piece," and he once said, "I believe in cerebral music, and I never choose a note unless I know why I want it there." Babbitt's ideal was "a really autonomous music that does not depend upon analogies with tonal music."

Long intrigued with electronic developments, in the late fifties Babbitt began working with RCA's new electronic sound synthesizer, the MARK II, at the newly reorganized Columbia-Princeton Electronic Music Center. The synthesizer allowed precise definition and readjustment of pitched and nonpitched sound. Salzman suggests that the composer's "interest in electronic techniques has been not so much in matters of new sounds as in the possibilities of control." Because of the synthesizer's ability to refine musical elements, it offered new possibilities. One Babbitt innovation is known as the time-point set idea in which duration is considered by the composer to be "a measure of distance between pitch points." With interval interpreted as duration, a set of intervals could be programmed with precision. Electronic works like *Composition for Synthesizer* (1961) and *Ensembles for Synthesizer* (1962–1964) "have been primarily concerned with new ways of organizing time and form perception," says Salzman.

A natural outgrowth of Babbitt's interest in electronic music has been his combination of live performance with tape, as in two works for soprano and synthesizer: *Vision and Prayer* (1961, text by Dylan Thomas) and *Philomel* (1964, text by John Hollander). The latter uses live voice, recorded vocal material, and electronic sound. In this melding of music and po-etry, says Salzman, "language becomes a kind of musical expression, while the music becomes articulate and precise, almost like language."

Babbitt continued to explore and refine sound relationships, always within a strict formal context, as in the chamber work *Arie da capo* (1973–1974), *A Solo Requiem* (1979) for soprano and two pianos (a setting of several poetic texts), and *The Head of the Bed* (1982) for soprano, flute, clarinet, violin, and cello, the text drawn from John Hollander.

Milton Babbitt's music provokes mixed reactions. Some believe his experiments have produced only inaccessible music. Others admire his experiments with sound and his comprehensive, systematic approach to the twelve-tone system. An important theorist, his teaching and his work has been a major influence on succeeding generations of composers and theorists. He has been a lifelong advocate for a rational discourse about music, thus changing the American musical intellectual scene single-handedly and irrevocably.

BIBLIOGRAPHY

Ewen, D., "Milton Babbitt," *Composers of Tomorrow's Music,* 1972; Machlis, J., *Introduction to Contemporary Music,* 1961; Salzman, E., *Twentieth Century Music: An Introduction,* 1967.

Balanchine, George

(January 22, 1904–April 30, 1983)
Choreographer

Balanchine created an exciting, exacting dance idiom rooted in classical ballet but reflecting twentieth-century upheaval through carefully articulated movement. He choreographed over 200 works and helped develop an American audience for ballet during his years leading the New York City Ballet, which he cofounded with Lincoln Kirstein.

Born in St. Petersburg, Russia, Georgi Melitonovitch Balanchivadze was the middle child of three. His parents planned to enter him in a military academy, but, at nine, when he was too young for soldiering, his mother had him audition with his sister, Tamara, for the Imperial School of Ballet in St. Petersburg. He was accepted, his sister was not.

At first a reluctant dancer, Balanchivadze changed his mind when he performed as a cupid in *The Sleeping Beauty.* Overwhelmed by the dancers, the scenery, the enchanting Maryinsky Theatre, he decided that dance was a worthy endeavor.

When Balanchivadze graduated from the ballet school in 1921 (after 1918 the school became the Soviet Academy for Opera and Ballet), he was hired by the Maryinsky corps de ballet. Almost immediately he enrolled at the nearby Petrograd State Conservatory of Music and there studied music theory and piano for three years while he continued dancing.

In 1924 he toured Europe, one of the seven Soviet State Dancers. With four others he refused to return home when ordered, and subsequently was invited to join Sergei Diaghilev's Ballets Russes. Diaghilev, short of choreographers, named Balanchivadze principal choreographer in 1925. It was Diaghilev who suggested the name change to Balanchine. When Balanchine injured his knee in 1926, his performing career ended, but he stayed on with the Ballets Russes as choreographer until Diaghilev's death in August 1929.

Balanchine created ten works for the Ballets Russes. The most important was *Apollon Musagète* (1928) with music by IGOR STRAVINSKY. The title was later changed to *Apollo.* Now considered a masterwork of the twentieth-century repertory, *Apollo* is based on a style of unique, choreographic movement that emphasizes the shapes of dancers' bodies rather than their individual personalities.

Balanchine's biographer, Bernard Taper, writes, "At the height of the jazz age, [Balanchine] evolved a new classicism, which serenely embodied the classical virtues of clarity and grandeur and yet in spirit and in style of movement was more up to date and adventurous than the run of ultra-modern ballets. With *Apollo* . . . Balanchine started out on

what was to be the central, though not the only, line of development in his career."

It was Stravinsky's music that set Balanchine on an important course. The score of *Apollo* taught Balanchine that he could clarify dance by simplifying. He realized, Taper says, "that like tones in music and shades in painting, gestures have certain family relations, which as groups impose their own laws." All of his subsequent choreography, said Balanchine, "was affected by this realization." Balanchine, almost alone among choreographers, had a deep understanding of musical structure, from the music of Tchaikovsky to Stravinsky, Anton von Webern, PAUL HINDEMITH, and KURT WEILL.

After Diaghilev's death, the Ballets Russes dissolved, and Balanchine took a number of jobs in Europe. He established Les Ballets 1933, which performed for one season. One of Balanchine's ballets created for the group, *The Seven Deadly Sins*, was reworked for the New York City Ballet years later.

Lincoln Kirstein, an American arts patron, watched a performance of Les Ballets 1933 and invited Balanchine to form a company in the United States. Kirstein dreamed of indigenous ballet in America: American dancers performing in American companies. The pair formed the School of American Ballet in 1933 and its company, the American Ballet, in 1935. Critic Edwin Denby observed that there were no stars, and went on to say, "By concentrating on form and the whole ensemble, Balanchine was able to bypass the uncertainties of the individual dancer." The starless system promoted high quality and eventually produced many lead dancers. Balanchine's first American ballet, the abstract *Serenade* (1934), was performed by the company, and later became the signature work of the New York City Ballet.

By 1936 Balanchine was also staging musicals on Broadway. In *On Your Toes*, a RICHARD RODGERS and Lorenz Hart production, he changed the relationship of the dance and the musical when he dropped the chorus line as backdrop for lead performers and designed functional dance routines central to the action.

"Slaughter on Tenth Avenue" is a notable example.

Balanchine became a U.S. citizen in 1939 and had a two-year stint with the Ballet Russe de Monte Carlo. In 1946 Balanchine and Kirstein established a new subscription ballet company called the Ballet Society.

The first work Balanchine created for the Ballet Society was *The Four Temperaments*, with music by Paul Hindemith. It is considered one of his greatest works, one that connects its four parts with a common vocabulary of movement. *New Yorker* critic Arlene Croce wrote of it, "The world of *The Four Temperaments* is wild and swarming with possibilities, yet if we could pass the choreography through a computer . . . there would probably not be more than six [gestures]—maybe eight."

In 1947 the City Center in New York became the sponsor of the company. In 1948 the Ballet Society was renamed the New York City Ballet. Balanchine was its artistic director; he remained so for thirty-five years, creating two to five new ballets a year. Some of the greatest dancers of the century performed with the company, and the NYCB gained international acclaim for its excellence.

Balanchine expanded the American audience for classical dance as he opened up ballet technique, raised standards, and built a telling language from abstract gesture. Absorbing the culture of his adopted land, he set GEORGE GERSHWIN songs to dance in *Who Cares* and turned Vivaldi and Corelli into *Square Dance*. He had a particular affinity for Stravinsky, creating thirty-nine works from the composer's scores, including the stark, intense *Agon* (1957).

Balanchine suffered a heart attack in 1979, was hospitalized for a neurological disorder late in 1982, and died of pneumonia in 1983 in New York.

BIBLIOGRAPHY

Taper, B., *Balanchine: A Biography*, 1984; Tracy, R., *Balanchine's Ballerinas: Conversations with the Muses*, 1983.

Baldwin, James Arthur

(August 2, 1924–December 1, 1987)
Essayist, Novelist

James Baldwin, author of the novel *Go Tell It on the Mountain* (1953), wrote about the effects of race, religion, and sexuality on personal identity. In numerous essays, he articulated a deep moral concern about the effects of racism, not only on African Americans, but on whites, their society and culture.

Baldwin was born in Harlem and raised by his mother, Berdis, and stepfather, David, a storefront preacher. At the age of fourteen, even as he began to write with the encouragement of several of his teachers, he preached in various Harlem churches, gaining the reputation of a prodigy. In 1942 Baldwin left home and the church for Greenwich Village, where he held a succession of odd jobs while he wrote essays and reviews, a few of which were published in New York journals. In 1948 he moved to Paris, where he settled for a decade.

Go Tell It on the Mountain, Baldwin's first novel, is the story of fourteen-year-old John Grimes and his salvation in a pentecostal church. John is confused by his emerging sexuality, by his ambivalent feelings toward his father, and by his anger toward whites. While he experiences a rebirth in his father's church, he still must choose whether and how to face the impoverished world outside its walls.

In 1955 Baldwin published *Notes of a Native Son*, a collection of essays that had appeared in such magazines as *Commentary* and *Partisan Review*. Its subjects ranged from the protest novel to interracial encounters in Europe, and Baldwin emerged as a prominent African American spokesperson. "I'm only black if you think you're white," he wrote. In his novel *Giovanni's Room* (1956), Baldwin explored the complexities of love and sex between men and women, and men and other men.

In 1957 Baldwin returned from Paris, feeling that he should use his growing fame to further the cause of the American civil rights movement. A trip to the South that year provided the material for the title essay in *Nobody Knows My Name* (1961), a collection of writings on "the question of color" and the artist's role in a racist society.

The best-selling novel *Another Country* (1962) depicts racial and sexual tensions among a circle of friends coping with life amid the poverty and violence of New York City. *The Fire Next Time* (1963) includes two essays, both in the form of letters. Baldwin recollects his own experience as a preacher in Harlem and examines the movement created by the Black Muslims, warning of the pent-up rage of African Americans. He wrote, "God gave Noah the rainbow sign, no more water, the fire next time." The book confirmed Baldwin's place as a leading advocate for civil rights, and for two years he traveled, preaching his new gospel.

In 1964 Baldwin's *Blues for Mr. Charlie* opened on Broadway. The drama addressed the contrasting approaches to the civil rights struggle taken by the nonviolent activist

National Archives

Martin Luther King, Jr., and the black militant Malcolm X.

Going to Meet the Man (1965) contains eight short stories. The title story studies the moral and sociological roots of racism by examining the violent behavior of a white sheriff's deputy. *Tell Me How Long the Train's Been Gone* (1968) follows the career of a famous black actor and observes his searches for meaningful love and for an activism that can be effective in fostering social change.

Among Baldwin's subsequent works were dialogues on race with the anthropologist Margaret Mead and the African American poet Nikki Giovanni; an autobiographical essay, *No Name in the Street* (1972); the novel *If Beale Street Could Talk* (1974), about a young Harlem couple's struggle against racism; and a children's book about growing up black, *Little Man, Little Man* (1976). His last novel, *Just Above My Head* (1979), describes the efforts of an African American musician to cope with his homosexuality and the demands of his art in a racist environment.

Suffering from ill health, Baldwin nevertheless managed to lecture at several colleges in the 1980s and to write *Evidence of Things Not Seen* (1985), about a series of child murders in Atlanta, as well as to collect a book each of his poetry and essays. He died of cancer in France in 1987.

BIBLIOGRAPHY
Campbell, James, *Talking at the Gates: A Life of James Baldwin*, 1991; Weatherby, William J., *James Baldwin: Artist on Fire*, 1989.

Baraka, Imamu Amiri

(October 7, 1934–   )
Essayist, Playwright, Poet

Over three decades and through writings in various genres, Amiri Baraka has chronicled changes in black consciousness and culture. His own political evolution as an individual committed to social justice for African Americans is mirrored in essays, poems, and plays that seek to describe a revolution to come.

Baraka was born Everett LeRoy Jones to middle-class parents in Newark, New Jersey. After graduating from high school in 1951 he spent a year on a science scholarship at the Newark campus of Rutgers University, then transferred to Howard University to study English literature. (It was at this time that he changed the spelling of his name to LeRoi.) After two years he left without a degree, joined the U.S. Air Force, and spent three years on duty in Puerto Rico. In a 1954 interview he was quoted as saying, "The Howard thing let me understand the Negro sickness. . . . But the Air Force made me understand the white sickness. It shocked me into realizing what was happening to me and others."

In 1957, after a discharge from the service, Jones moved to Greenwich Village and became a disciple of the Beat poet ALLEN GINSBERG, whose work reflects his disaffiliation from society and anarchic individualism. Jones founded and coedited two influential avant-garde journals, *Yugen* (1958–1962) and *The Floating Bear* (1961–1963). His first volume of poetry, *Preface to a Twenty Volume Suicide Note*, was published in 1961.

Jones visited Cuba in 1960 and met a number of Third World intellectuals who urged him to reexamine his art. By the time of *The Dead Lecturer* (1964), he was seeking urgently to find a medium for black activism.

Jones's play *Dutchman* (1964) won an Obie Award and established his reputation. The protagonist, Clay, is a black intellectual and would-be poet, who is picked up by a beautiful white woman, Lula, on a New York subway. When Clay's revolutionary potential becomes evident, he is executed by white society. In *The Slave* (1964), the protagonist, Walker Vessels, has progressed to militancy. He abandons his ineffectual poetry for action.

The System of Dante's Hell (1965) is Jones's only novel. Based on his adolescent years in Newark, it equates the slums he knew firsthand with the nine circles of Dante's Inferno, but with this difference: Jones's hell is "in the head, the torture of being the unseen object, and, the constantly observed subject."

With the assassination of Malcolm X in 1965, Jones became a Black Cultural Nationalist committed to finding African American values through art. In 1967 he returned to Newark to found a community center, Spirit House, and, joining the Kawaida sect of the Black Muslims, adopted the African name Imamu ("spiritual leader") Amiri Baraka ("blessed prince"). (He later dropped Imamu.)

Tales (1967), a short-story collection, documents the time he spent in Harlem and his desire to recreate the language of his tribe. The poems in *Black Magic* (1969) reject liberalism in favor of revolutionary violence. Baraka produced a number of plays—including *Jello* (1965), *A Black Mass* (1966), and *Madheart* (1967)—that openly proclaimed the superiority of black over white and man over woman. *Raise Race Rays Raze* (1971), written in a black idiom, is a collection of essays that made it clear that Baraka thought black art and Black Power were synonymous. "No movement shaped or contained by Western culture," he argued, "will ever benefit Black people. Black power must be the actual force and beauty and wisdom of Blackness . . . reordering the world."

By 1973 Baraka had rejected Black Cultural Nationalism as racist and become a Marxist. He was committed to the idea that art should be used as a weapon of revolution, and his plays continued to address political themes. For example, *The Motion of History,* produced in 1977, dramatizes instances over four centuries of the ruling class pitting poor blacks and whites against each other so as to obscure their common interest in revolution.

In 1979 Baraka joined the African studies department at the State University of New York at Stony Brook. He was promoted to professor in 1984, and he continues to teach and write. He won the 1984 American Book Award from the Before Columbus Foundation for his work *Confirmation: An Anthology of African-American Women.*

BIBLIOGRAPHY

Baraka, Amiri, *The Autobiography of LeRoi Jones,* 1984; Bentson, Kimberly W., *Amiri Baraka: The Renegade and the Mask,* 1976.

Barber, Samuel

(March 9, 1910–January 23, 1981)
Composer

Barber's conservative approach, lyricism, and fine workmanship won over conductors and audiences alike: his music was playable and understandable. Most avant-garde musicians, however, scorned him, resenting his embrace of tonality, his lack of rebellion against the old style, and the popularity of his work.

Born in West Chester, Pennsylvania, near Philadelphia, Samuel Barber started piano lessons at age six, studied cello briefly, and even composed a short opera to be performed by himself and his sister, Sara. His interest in vocal music began early, in part because the great American contralto Louise Homer encouraged him. Homer was his mother's sister and Sidney Homer, the singer's husband, was a composer of songs.

Barber graduated from West Chester High School in 1926, but two years earlier, at fourteen, he had entered the Curtis Institute in Philadelphia for formal musical training, a member of its first class. (Curtis had been founded by the wealthy Philadelphian Mary Louise Curtis Bok; later she was to become Barber's generous supporter.)

At Curtis, Barber studied composition, conducting, piano, and voice. For a time singing seemed a possible career. He performed in recitals at Curtis, later studied voice in Vienna, and in 1935 sang in recitals broadcast by NBC. But Barber developed, too, as a composer at Curtis. Many of the works he wrote during his eight years there illustrate his emerging style—the long lyric line, use of instrumental color, and fine setting of words—and remain part of the repertory: the *Serenade* for string quartet, *Dover Beach* (which he recorded as vocalist in 1935), and the Cello Sonata, among others.

Barber's career was encouraged and punctuated by awards, from the Bearns Prize of Columbia University in 1928 for his Violin Sonata, and for the overture to *The School for Scandal* in 1933, to the Pulitzer Prize for the 1957 opera *Vanessa,* and for the 1962 Piano Concerto. Premieres of various works were led by conductors like Artur Rodzinski (Cleveland

Orchestra, 1937), ARTURO TOSCANINI (NBC Symphony Orchestra, 1938), and commissions from individuals like John Nicholas Brown and soprano Eleanor Steber or foundations supported many of Barber's works. It was Toscanini who first presented *Adagio for Strings*, an orchestral arrangement of the second movement of Barber's String Quartet, in 1938. It was to become Barber's most popular composition.

In 1939 Barber returned to Curtis and taught composition there until 1942. In 1943 he purchased a house in Mount Kisco, New York, with GIAN CARLO MENOTTI, whom he had met during his student days at Curtis. Barber did most of his composing at Capricorn, the Mount Kisco house, until it was sold in 1973. The *Capricorn Concerto* (1944), for flute, oboe, trumpet, and strings, with its dissonance, angular lines, and wide leaps, "is a witty concerto grosso," according to scholar Joseph Machlis, "the composer's bow to Stravinskyan neoclassicism."

Barber was drafted in 1943 and assigned to the U.S. Army Air Force. After his discharge at the end of World War II, he returned to Europe on a Guggenheim Fellowship. In 1948 he became a consultant to the American Academy in Rome. Thanks to important commissions in the 1940s and 1950s, he composed the Cello Concerto, dance scores (*Medea*, revised as *The Cave of the Heart*, for MARTHA GRAHAM, and *Souvenirs*, for the Ballet Society of New York), vocal works like *Knoxville: Summer of 1915*

(from James Agee's novel *A Death in the Family*), and a piano sonata.

Vanessa, an ambitious four-act opera, libretto by Menotti, was completed in 1957 and performed by the Metropolitan Opera and at the Salzburg Festival in Austria. *Vanessa* was awarded the 1958 Pulitzer Prize in music.

Barber won a second Pulitzer Prize for his 1962 Piano Concerto, commissioned by his music publisher, G. Schirmer, to mark the firm's centenary. Another important commission was for the opera *Antony and Cleopatra* (the libretto by Franco Zeffirelli, after Shakespeare), planned to celebrate the opening of the new Metropolitan Opera House at Lincoln Center in New York City. The huge production was designed and directed by Zeffirelli. In the opera the battle of Actium was to be staged with full-scale ships. Unfortunately, the turntable jammed. Many thought the opera's failure was due to Zeffirelli's elaborate production. In 1975 a new version with the libretto reshaped by Menotti was staged by the Opera Theater of the Juilliard School in New York. It proved more successful.

Barber died in New York in 1981.

BIBLIOGRAPHY

Broder, N., *Samuel Barber,* 1954; Machlis, J., *Introduction to Contemporary Music,* 1961.

Barnum, Phineas Taylor

(July 5, 1810–April 7, 1891)
Circus Impresario, Showman

Phineas T. Barnum, who claimed a sucker was born every minute, promoted all kinds of entertainment—circuses, freak shows, and concerts of such European artists as Jenny Lind.

He was born in Bethel, Connecticut, the son of Philo F. Barnum and Irena Taylor. Until he was twenty-five years old he did various kinds of work, including storekeeping, bartending, running an abolitionist newspaper, and selling tickets for a theater.

He was running a sideshow of freaks and curiosities in 1835 when he discovered Joice Heth, a black woman who said she was 161 years old and had been George Washington's nurse. After Barnum took charge of her and put her in his show, his career took off. When Heth died a year later, an autopsy showed she was only half the age that Barnum claimed for her. Barnum buried her in his family plot and protested that he had acted in good faith and had been the victim of a hoax.

After Heth's death, Barnum continued to tour his show for a while, but after a few years at loose ends, in 1842 without gold but, as he said, with "much brass," he managed to buy both the American Museum and its rival, Peale's Museum, in New York. He opened his own successful American Museum, which became a great attraction for tourists and New Yorkers.

In his museum Barnum put on exhibition such hoaxes as the Feejee Mermaid and the bearded lady, who was probably not a lady at all, as well as worthwhile exhibits of fossils and natural history specimens. Short melodramas and farces were performed on the museum's stage. The most popular exhibit was General Tom Thumb, a dwarf named Charles Sherwood Stratton, who, under Barnum's sponsorship, became a great celebrity.

Barnum took Tom Thumb to Europe in 1844, showing him in Paris and in London to Queen Victoria. In London he lectured at St. James Hall on "The Science of Money Making, and the Philosophy of Humbug" to large crowds. In England he was also quite struck with the Royal Pavilion in Brighton, a house that George IV built in a lavish Indian and Oriental style. Barnum copied it for his own home in Bridgeport, Connecticut, called it Iranistan, and opened it to the public, for a fee. It was a success until it was completely destroyed by fire in 1857. At his home Barnum also had an elephant that went into action pulling a plow whenever a train passed by.

In 1850 Barnum persuaded singer Jenny Lind, called the "Swedish Nightingale," who was at the height of her fame in Europe, to come to America for a long tour. Her visit began a long tradition of European artists coming to America.

Barnum turned to politics in the 1860s, running successfully for the Connecticut legislature and unsuccessfully for the U.S. Congress.

His last great enterprise was the circus, which he billed as "The Greatest Show on Earth." His circus, with three rings under a big tent, the "Main Top," opened in Brooklyn on April 10, 1871. After that the circus's annual opening, usually in Madison Square Garden, marked the official arrival of spring in New York. Fire destroyed the circus and the American Museum in 1872.

Barnum presided over the circus's metamorphosis from a wagon show to a railroad show and from gasoline flares to electricity. As younger men began to compete with him, he combined forces with his biggest competitor, James A. Bailey, and formed the Barnum & Bailey circus, which opened in 1881. In 1882 Barnum bought Jumbo, whom he advertised as the world's largest elephant, for $10,000 from England's Royal Zoological Gardens. In the United States Barnum billed Jumbo as "The Only Mastodon on Earth." Newspapers ran drawings of Jumbo feeding from third-story windows when he was in a parade. After a locomotive hit and killed Jumbo in 1885, Barnum bought Alice and advertised her as Jumbo's widow.

In 1889 Barnum took his circus to London. When he circled the arena in an open carriage, he received as much applause as any of the other acts. He wrote several books, including his autobiography, *Life of P. T. Barnum Written by Himself* (1854), *The Humbugs of the World* (1865), and *Struggles and Triumphs* (1869).

BIBLIOGRAPHY

Saxon, A. H., *Phineas T. Barnum: The Legend and the Man*, 1989.

Barrymore, Lionel

(April 28, 1878–November 15, 1954)

Barrymore, Ethel

(August 15, 1879–June 18, 1959)

Barrymore, John

(February 15, 1882–May 29, 1942)
Actors

Lionel, Ethel, and John Barrymore, who themselves were descended from actors, were called the Royal Family of the American Theater. Distinguished by handsome faces, strong talent, and memorable roles, the three became legendary figures of both the stage and screen.

All three of the Barrymores were born in the Philadelphia home of their maternal grandmother, Louisa Lane Drew, who raised them since their own parents, themselves actors, were often away from home. Mrs. Drew managed the Arch Street Theater, where she allowed the children to watch from a box on Saturday afternoons when their father performed there. Otherwise, in spite of their theatrical lineage for four generations, they had little contact with the theater. "We became actors," Ethel Barrymore said, "not because we wanted to go on the stage, but because it was the thing we could do best."

Lionel Barrymore, the oldest, was educated in Philadelphia, London, and Seton Hall Academy in East Orange, New Jersey. When he was fifteen he played a coachman in *The Rivals* in a production in which his grandmother Louisa Drew played Mrs. Malaprop. Lionel really wanted to be a painter and did a poor job of his walk-on part. When he was eighteen, he enrolled at the Art Students League in New York. After he had been there three years, family fortunes demanded that he earn a living, and he went on the stage, playing Max in Hermann Sudermann's *Magda*. He made his Broadway debut on September 27, 1900, in James A. Herne's *Sag Harbor*. In 1902 his sister, Ethel, helped him get the role of an Italian organ-grinder in *The Mummy and the Humming Bird*, which starred his uncle John Drew. Lionel worked hard at this role, rehearsing with two experienced actors for hours and studying the way Italians in New York talked and moved. He stole the show from his uncle and decided to concentrate on character parts.

Lionel still longed to be an artist and moved to Paris to study art. After three years, again forced to earn money, he came back to the United States and the stage.

D. W. GRIFFITH hired him to act in motion pictures in New Jersey. He played many roles for Griffith between 1909 and 1912, and moved to Hollywood when it became headquarters for the new industry. Later he divided his time between Hollywood and the Broadway stage.

On stage in 1917, he was the wicked Colonel Ibbetson opposite his brother, John, as the hero in *Peter Ibbetson*, adapted from the George du Maurier novel by John Raphael. He badly wanted and got the part of Milt Shanks in Augustus Thomas's *The Copperhead*. He appeared again with his brother as the evil Neri in *The Jest*, a play that Edward Sheldon adapted from the Italian *La Cena delle Beffe* especially for the Barrymore brothers. Lionel also played Macbeth, but he was a failure.

He accepted a proposal from producer Jesse Lasky of Paramount to appear in movies for $10,000 a picture and never went back on the stage. Among his most memorable films are *Rasputin and the Empress* in which he starred with John and Ethel; *Arsene Lupin* with John; *Mata Hari* with GRETA GARBO; and *Grand Hotel* with John and Garbo, all from 1932. In 1931 he won an Academy Award for his role in *A Free Soul*.

In the 1930s Barrymore injured his hip and spent the rest of his life in a wheelchair. The role of Dr. Gillespie in the "Dr. Kildare" series was written for him so that he could continue to act. Every year he read Dickens's *Christmas Carol* over the radio.

Ethel Barrymore went to the Academy of Notre Dame in Philadelphia. Like Lionel, she made her stage debut when she was fifteen, with her grandmother in *The Rivals*. At sixteen she replaced Elsie De Wolfe in the road company of *The Bauble Shop* with her uncle John Drew, who helped her get a number of other small roles in New York. She went to London in 1897 with a production of *Secret Service*, writ-

ten by and starring William Gillette. Back in this country, she began working for the producer Charles Frohman. In 1901 Frohman gave her the star's part, Madame Trentoni, in *Captain Jinks of the Horse Marines* by CLYDE FITCH, then the country's most successful playwright. As Madame Trentoni, Ethel had to be a comedian, act with pathos, and sing and dance, and she succeeded radiantly in everything. "Dear Miss Barrymore," wrote one critic, "New York is at your feet."

She played the straight dramatic title role in Somerset Maugham's *Lady Frederick* in 1908 and later had a great success in Maugham's *The Constant Wife* in 1926. Arthur Wing Pinero wrote *Mid-Channel* in 1910 especially for her, and she later appeared in his *Trelawny of the Wells*. Night after night in 1919 standing-room-only crowds came to see her as a slightly tarnished Lady Helen in Zoë Akins's *Déclassée*. In 1923 she played Lady Teazle with her uncle John Drew in a Players Club production of *The School for Scandal* that celebrated Drew's fifty years in the theater.

At the urging of her brothers, she went to Hollywood in 1932 to star with them in the film *Rasputin and the Empress*. Lionel played the monk Rasputin, Ethel the czarina, and John Prince Youssoupoff. It was at this point that the three Barrymores came to be called the Royal Family. Publicity for the film pictured the siblings as rivals competing for attention, with someone suggesting that the movie be called "Disputin' and the Empress." The Barrymores impishly went along with the publicity, although Ethel disliked the experience and left Hollywood as soon as she could.

Ethel's last great stage success was as Miss Moffatt, the dedicated teacher in Emlyn Williams's autobiographical play *The Corn Is Green* in 1940. Critics termed her performance "magnificent," commenting that she played the role forcefully, but with compassion.

The range of her talents was enormous. She appeared in vaudeville, on radio, and in many movies, winning an Academy Award in 1944 for her work as Ma Mott in *None But the Lonely Heart*. She died in her sleep in 1959.

John Barrymore, who had classic good looks, was known as the Great Profile. After being expelled from Georgetown Academy, he was sent to Seton Hall, where Lionel had gone. When he was fifteen he went to England to King's College, Wimbledon. Like Lionel, he wanted to become an artist, and he studied at the Slade School of Art in London. Back in New York, he enrolled at the Art Students League but did not go to classes, studying instead with the painter George Bridgman.

He made his first professional theatrical appearance in Chicago on October 31, 1903, playing Max in *Magda*, a role Lionel had done several years before. He made his New York debut in Clyde Fitch's *Glad of It* a few months later. Traveling for several years with a touring company that went to Australia and San Francisco gave him a great deal of experience.

In 1909 he appeared in the title role in *The Fortune Hunter,* and over the next five years the handsome young actor became the idol of women theater goers. At a friend's urging in 1916 John began to try dramatic roles and played the bank clerk in John Galsworthy's *Justice.* He was a resounding success in the title role in *Peter Ibbetson,* with Lionel as the villain, in 1917. As he often did, though, John became bored with the role and gave it up.

He became a seasoned Shakespearean actor, beginning with *Richard III* in 1920. He worked with a voice coach to learn how best to handle Elizabethan verse. For the first time, he said, he felt like the character he was playing. Critics called him a genius and the public loved him. Exhausted from the effort of learning his lines and playing the difficult role (he did an acrobatic fall in heavy armor), he collapsed in complete exhaustion after twenty-seven performances.

When he opened in *Hamlet* in 1922, one critic wrote, "There never has been such a great actor at any time, there never has been such shattering beauty in art." After taking *Hamlet* to England in 1925, he gave up the theater for fourteen years while he made movies. He became ill while making a film in 1933 and was troubled with lapses of memory caused by excessive use of alcohol. In March 1939 he returned to the stage in a comedy, *My Dear Children,* for a long run, although he had trouble remembering his lines. Back in Hollywood, he collapsed at a movie rehearsal and died ten days later in Hollywood Hospital.

BIBLIOGRAPHY

Alpert, Hollis, *The Barrymores,* 1964; Kotsilibas-Davis, James, *The Barrymores: The Royal Family in Hollywood,* 1981.

Barth, John Simmons

(May 27, 1930–   )
Novelist

Intending to revive what he considers the dying tradition of the novel, John Barth, author of *Giles Goat-Boy,* writes fiction that relies on elaborate framing devices, parody, and wit to explore the claims of art and the problems of self-consciousness.

Barth was born and raised on the eastern shore of Maryland, in the town of Cambridge. He enrolled on an academic scholarship at the Johns Hopkins University in 1947. There he completed his bachelor's and then a master's degree in creative writing, and began study on a doctorate in the aesthetics of literature, which he never completed, due to the financial pressures of an early marriage and family.

As an undergraduate, Barth worked at the classics library at Hopkins and, while filing books in the Oriental section, discovered and read numerous tale-cycles, including *The Ocean of Story*, the *Arabian Nights*, and the *Decameron*. These cycles of stories, in which a tale was structured to set up another, which in turn framed yet another, profoundly influenced his own approach to fiction.

Teturo Maruyama; Little, Brown and Company

In 1953 Barth began teaching English at Pennsylvania State University and started writing his own *Decameron*, a cycle of tales arising from the history of the Eastern Shore. While he wrote only half of the 100 stories he had projected before abandoning his "Dorchester Tales," Barth adapted characters from the cycle for later novels and even transplanted one tale almost verbatim as a chapter in the long novel *The Sot-Weed Factor* (1960).

Barth intended his first published novel, *The Floating Opera* (1956), to be a "nihilistic comedy." It would be the first in a series of three such novels, unrelated except by theme, each of which would "concern some sort of bachelor, more or less irresponsible, who either rejects absolute values or encounters their rejection."

The protagonist of *The Floating Opera*, Todd Andrews, is writing in 1954 about the day in 1937 when he decided to commit suicide because there was "no final reason for living." In the end Todd finds there is no final reason to die, either, so he spares himself. The narrative rambles chattily through a scene in a foxhole during World War I, a love affair, and a protracted and comical legal dispute.

If Todd accepts relative values, Jacob Horner, the irresponsible bachelor in *The End of the Road* (1958), is an unredeemable nihilist, rejecting completely the possibility of making moral distinctions about the choices he faces. Jake meets Joe Morgan, a relativist, and starts an affair with Joe's wife, Rennie. Their competition to win Rennie becomes a philosophical debate of sorts, which neither wins, since the novel ends with Rennie's death.

Barth decided to change fictional styles for the final novel in his nihilistic trilogy. *The Sot-Weed Factor* was to be a historical novel, deliberately inflated in length and with a convoluted plot that parodied the eighteenth-century tradition of the questing hero. *The Sot-Weed Factor* is based on a 1708 poem by Ebenezer Cooke of Maryland. Cooke himself is the novel's irresponsible bachelor, a virgin who decides to test himself against the prostitutes and highwaymen of the New World. His tutor in the ways of the world is Henry Burlingame, who assumes the identities of nine different historical characters, embodying the notion that no single, unyielding stance is tenable in life.

In *Giles Goat-Boy* (1966) Barth creates yet a more elaborate frame, comprising the memoirs of George Giles as fed into, edited by, and printed out from a campus computer, then re-edited by George's son, emended by a struggling academician, and edited yet again by its publishers. Barth furthers the point he made in *The Sot-Weed Factor* about art as a distortion of reality, but here he carries it into actual fantasy. In *Giles Goat-Boy*, the world is a giant university, where east and west campuses behave as the United States and Russia, campus unrest substitutes for world war, and the president and trustees act as Jesus and his disciples. *Giles Goat-Boy* brought Barth's first financial success: it appeared briefly on the best-seller list.

Lost in the Funhouse (1968) is a cycle of tales united by a common theme: the plight of the storyteller and the story in modern society, where the possibilities for fiction have been exhausted. The fictions, among them "Title," "Autobiography," and "Life-Story," are primarily about their own processes.

Chimera (1972) includes three novellas, the stories of Dunyazade, supposedly Scheherazade's sister, and two middle-aged mythic heroes, Bellerophon and Perseus. The theme is again the modern plight of narrative

art. *Chimera* won Barth the National Book Award.

Letters (1979) updates the epistolary novel and reorchestrates characters from Barth's first six books. Barth's subsequent fiction, including *Sabbatical: A Romance* (1982), *The Tidewater Tales: A Novel* (1987), and *The Last Voyage of Somebody the Sailor* (1991), carries forward his exploration of the relation between narration and reality.

Barth lives in Chestertown, Maryland, and teaches at the Johns Hopkins University.

BIBLIOGRAPHY

Harris, Charles B., *Passionate Virtuosity: The Fiction of John Barth*, 1983; Schulz, Max F., *The Muses of John Barth*, 1990.

Beach, Amy Marcy Cheney

(September 5, 1867–December 27, 1944)
Composer, Pianist

Amy Beach was the first American woman to gain recognition as a composer. In a time when women, if they composed at all, might be expected to produce sentimental parlor music, Beach was composing ambitious orchestral, choral, and chamber music that was widely performed at home and abroad.

Amy Marcy Cheney Beach was the only child of Charles Abbott Cheney, a businessman, and Clara Imogene (Marcy) Cheney, a pianist and singer. Beach, born in Henniker, New Hampshire, was a precocious child. She taught herself to read by age three and by four she was composing piano pieces and playing four-part hymns by ear.

The family moved to Chelsea, Massachusetts, in the early 1870s. When Beach was six, her mother began formally to teach her piano. A year later she was playing Handel,

Beethoven, Chopin, and her own works in public recitals.

The Cheneys, of distinguished New England lineage, rubbed shoulders with Boston's intellectual elite. As a result, their daughter's progress was followed closely by a group that included OLIVER WENDELL HOLMES, HENRY WADSWORTH LONGFELLOW, and Henry Harris Beach, a physician who lectured at Harvard. She and Beach were to marry in 1885.

She made her debut in 1883 and first performed with the Boston Symphony Orchestra in 1885. After marriage she concertized less, donated her fees to charity, and, encouraged by her husband, spent more time composing. In 1892 Beach's first large work, a Mass for chorus, soloists, orchestra, and organ, was presented by the Boston Handel and Haydn Society.

Later that year her work for contralto and orchestra, entitled *Eilende Wolken,* a scene and aria from German poet Friedrich von Schiller's *Mary Stuart,* was introduced by the Symphony Society of New York under Walter Damrosch. It was the first work by a woman composer heard at these concerts. She composed *Festival Jubilate* for the dedication of the Women's Building of the World's Columbian Exposition in 1893.

After her husband died in 1910, Beach sailed for Europe to establish herself there as a soloist and composer. Germany was especially receptive. One critic, Ferdinand Pfohl, described her as a "virtuoso pianist . . . [with] a musical nature tinged with genius." She performed her new piano concerto in Germany and a piano quintet composed in 1907. A critic praised the quintet's "scrumptiously Straussian melody."

Beach returned home in 1914 after the outbreak of World War I and moved to New York in 1915. Winters she toured, summers she practiced and composed in her cottage on Cape Cod, Massachusetts, or, from 1921 on as a fellow at the MacDowell Colony in Peterborough, New Hampshire. Surviving her husband by over three decades, she died of a heart ailment in New York.

Amy Beach's music was rooted in romanticism and influenced sometimes by Brahms, occasionally by French composers like Debussy, even perhaps by EDWARD MACDOWELL. Her Symphony of 1896 was the first ever produced by an American woman and the first to be performed by an American orchestra. She has been called sentimental and criticized for her dependence on chromaticism, but she nonetheless possessed considerable technical mastery. Her lyricism was especially pronounced in pieces where flowing melodies lie well for the voice; these songs were popular among recitalists.

BIBLIOGRAPHY

Ammer, C., *Unsung: A History of Women in American Music,* 1980.

Bechet, Sidney Joseph

(May 14, 1897–May 14, 1959)
Jazz Musician

Bechet, along with LOUIS ARMSTRONG, was an outstanding early jazz soloist. He helped gain the saxophone its place in jazz and his passionate, eloquent, yet restrained improvisations bent notes and time to suggest an elegant, earthy blues feeling. His innovations influenced saxophonists Johnny Hodges and JOHN COLTRANE.

Grandson of a slave, Bechet was born to a Creole family in New Orleans and was surrounded by music from the beginning. Self-taught, he picked up the clarinet very early, some say by the age of six. Though he never could read music, in his youth he received pointers from older clarinetists, among them Lorenzo Tio, Jr., "Big Eye" Nelson, and George Baquet. Around 1910, still in his early teens, he was already playing with New Orleans bands.

In 1914 he left New Orleans and played throughout the South in touring shows and carnivals and began what became his habitual restless wandering. He played in bands, among them one led by King Oliver, the idol of the young Louis Armstrong. In 1919 Bechet was engaged for a European tour by Will Marion Cook, who led a large concert band, the Southern Syncopated Orchestra. He was to be featured in jazz specialties.

Ernest Ansermet, a young Swiss conductor, heard Bechet in London and wrote, "There is an extraordinary clarinet virtuoso who . . . composed perfectly formed blues on the clarinet. I wish to set down the name of this artist of genius. . . ."

In a London junk shop, Bechet discovered a soprano saxophone, the instrument he was to make his own. The sax, with its appealing strength and command, was especially suited to Bechet's decorative treatment of melodic line and allowed a penetrating mellowness of tone in higher registers not possible on the clarinet. It became Bechet's primary instrument, though he continued to perform on the clarinet.

In 1919 the temperamental Bechet left the Southern Syncopated Orchestra to tour with a small ragtime band led by Benny Peyton, a drummer. In the 1920s Bechet toured Europe, the United States, and Russia, and by mid-decade was working, though briefly, in New York with the DUKE ELLINGTON Orchestra. Bechet's ability to swing, surpassed only by Louis Armstrong's, pushed the Ellington group toward jazz. Bechet's influence lived on in Johnny Hodges's work. Hodges was an Ellington musician from 1928 on who played earlier with bands in Harlem at Bechet's own place, Club Basha.

Bechet recorded with Louis Armstrong in Chicago in 1924 and 1925. These discs, important documents of New Orleans jazz, reveal the musical climate and achievements of the 1920s. As the popularity of hot dance music waned in the 1930s, Bechet dropped out of sight for a time and comanaged a tailor shop, but his lot improved late in the decade with the revival of New Orleans music. Recast as a great jazz pioneer, in 1949 he returned to Europe and became a major star. He settled permanently in France and lived there until his death in 1959.

BIBLIOGRAPHY

Bechet, Sidney, *Treat It Gentle*, 1960; Schuller, Gunther, *Early Jazz: Its Roots and Development*, 1968; Williams, Martin, *Jazz Masters of New Orleans*, 1967.

Belasco, David

(July 25, 1853–May 14, 1931)
Playwright, Producer, Theater Owner

David Belasco, whose innovations in the stagecraft of realism and spectacle melodrama at the turn of the century spearheaded a new era in modern American drama, was one of the most influential producers in the history of the American theater.

He was born in 1853 in San Francisco to Portuguese Jews recently immigrated from England. As a young actor, he toured with such important playwrights of the day as Dion Boucicault and James A. Herne (with whom he collaborated on several plays, including *Hearts of Oak*, 1880). From 1876 to 1880 he adapted novels and plays from the East Coast and brought them to several California theaters, including the Egyptian Hall in San Francisco, for which he developed his interest in exotic and spectacular lighting and stage effects. After his arrival in New York City in 1882 as stage manager for the Madison Square Theater, the Great Wizard, as Alexander Woollcott dubbed him, began writing and producing many of the plays for which he is best known.

In the category of intimate realism were his collaborations with Henry C. DeMille. *The Wife* (1887), *The Charity Ball* (1889), and

Men and Women (1890) satirized the social pretentions of society and business. Belasco spared no expense to appoint his sets in the most realistic manner possible. One of the more notorious examples was his production of the gritty social problem play, Eugene Walter's *The Easiest Way* in 1909, when he purchased a lodging house room and transferred its cheap furniture and broken fixtures intact to the theater stage.

In the category of melodramas—Belasco's real forte—were plays full of action and spectacular scenic effects. "I believe," he

Library of Congress

wrote, "in a play that deals with life in its moments of importance, in a crisis of emotion." In *The Heart of Maryland* (1895), which established him as an independent producer for the rest of his career, the heroine, Maryland Calvert, silences an order to execute her lover by making a spectacular leap from a belfry onto the tolling bell. *Madame Butterfly* (1900), written in collaboration with John Luther Long, was famous for its complicated lighting effects, especially the extraordinary twelve-minute "dusk-to-dawn" vigil maintained by the heroine Cho-Cho-San. *The Girl of the Golden West* (1905) re-created on stage the scenery of a California dawn in 1849 in the prologue to the first act, the fury of a blizzard in the second act, and the suggestive horror of a thriller in the last act (the dripping blood that interrupts the famous card game and reveals the hiding place of the highwayman, Dick Johnson). The latter two plays were adapted for the opera stage by Giacomo Puccini, *Madame Butterfly* in 1904 and *The Girl of the Golden West* in 1910.

Dubbed the Bishop of Broadway because of his clerical mode of dress, Belasco was, by the turn of the century, the owner of several the-

ater houses in New York City and, in general, one of the most powerful and influential figures of the American theater. He even took on the powerful New York booking and theater house monopoly (see LEVI SHUBERT) when he attacked in court its unscrupulous and unethical business operations. Ironically, although the syndicate was eventually indicted by a grand jury for criminal conspiracy in restraint of trade, Belasco himself was to join forces with it in 1909.

In 1913, sensing new and wider potential audiences for his works, he turned to the developing medium of the motion picture. For the Protective Amusement Company, an amalgamation of the forces of Klaw/Erlanger and the Biograph Motion Picture Company, he released in 1913 and 1914 the film rights to several of his collaborations with Henry C. DeMille. At the same time, for his more scenically spectacular melodramas, he worked with the Jesse L. Lasky Feature Play Company (whose chief director was the young CECIL B. DeMILLE, son of Henry C.), and saw his plays filmed in the natural locations that could only be poorly approximated at best on stage. Belasco was enthusiastic about these new scenic opportunities, declaring in an open letter to the film trade in 1914: "On the stage we must give you a bit of painted canvas for Niagara Falls or the Nile; you show us the real thing. The world is your stage." Among the filmed plays for the Lasky company were *The Girl of the Golden West* and *The Warrens of Virginia* (both produced in 1915).

Belasco was more of an organizer and collaborator than a creative individual. He spoke of himself as a playwright, not a dramatist, that is, as a worker who fashions scripts from available materials with the help of diverse hands, then transforms them into theatrical events with every resource of stagecraft at his disposal. He was a master of effect, not so much of the literary art. "Lights are to drama what music is to the lyrics of a song," he wrote in his autobiography, *The Theatre through Its Stage Door* (1919). "The greatest part of my success in the theatre I attribute to my feeling for colors, translated into effects of light."

The decline that marked Belasco's later years was due in part to his resistance to the growing "little theater" movement and to the emergence of a younger generation of playwrights, like Eugene O'Neill, who passed him by. But his later years were replete with many honors, including election to the Moscow Art Theatre and the reception of the Order of Chevalier of the French Legion of Honor. Active to the last, he developed pneumonia while rehearsing a play in the winter of 1930. He died from a heart attack a year later.

BIBLIOGRAPHY

Marker, Lise-Lone, *David Belasco: Naturalism in the American Theatre*, 1975; Tibbetts, John C., *The American Theatrical Film*, 1985; Timberlake, Craig, *The Bishop of Broadway*, 1954.

Bellow, Saul

(June 10, 1915–)
Novelist, Short-Story Writer

Saul Bellow, the Nobel Prize–winning author of *Herzog* and *Humboldt's Gift*, writes fiction that confronts the modern dilemma of individuals trying to find meaning in their lives, despite social chaos. Broadly concerned with defining human values, Bellow's work is deeply rooted in a sense of Jewish tradition and culture.

Born in Lachine, Quebec, in 1915 of Russian Jews who had emigrated two years earlier, Bellow was raised in Montreal and Chicago. He studied at the University of Chicago and Northwestern University, from which he earned a bachelor's degree in sociology and anthropology in 1937. He then pursued a year's graduate work in anthropology at the University of Wisconsin at Madison. He supported himself at the start of his writing career through a succession of editorial and teaching jobs, including a post at the University of Minnesota. After winning a Guggenheim Fellowship in 1948, Bellow took up brief residence in Paris. He then spent a decade in New York, including two years on the faculty of New York University, before return-ing to Chicago in 1962, where he continues to live and work as a member of the faculty of the University of Chicago.

Joseph, the protagonist of Bellow's first novel, *Dangling Man* (1944), asks a question at the heart of all Bellow's fiction: "How should a good man live; what might he do?" Bellow sees humanity in the modern age as deeply torn by the loss of traditional values. His main characters, most of them intellectuals, search for meaning and purpose in their lives, seeking to ground their behavior in some larger system of beliefs.

Awaiting induction into the service during World War II, Joseph quits his job and stays home to read books. Alone in his room for days at a time, he ponders the value of friendship and family and comes to question the moral basis of life itself. Finally, to save himself from the futility of his own musings, he actively enlists in the army.

In *The Victim* (1947), Asa Leventhal lives quietly, lest he risk roiling the waters of his personal and professional lives. But his domestic peace is soon broken by the illness of his nephew, Mickey, and the frantic pleadings of his sister-in-law, Elena. Moreover, an old colleague, Kirby Allbee, returns to accuse Asa in the most scathing and anti-Semitic terms of deliberately plotting his professional ruin. As he faces these sudden pressures, Asa must come to terms with his uneasiness over the uncertainties in his life without cutting himself off from human feeling.

Like his predecessors in Bellow's fiction, the protagonist of *The Adventures of Augie March* (1953) ponders the human condition as he seeks to understand his own circumstances. Bellow adapted the picaresque novel (depicting the travels of a rogue-hero) to allow Augie March to offer his impressions of "the length and breadth of America." Beginning in his native Chicago, which he renders as a modern Babylon, Augie is driven by restlessness outward toward Mexico and finally Europe. An innocent, Augie meets a number of "reality instructors" who seek to indoctrinate him into their own ways of thinking and acting; Augie witnesses and resists political manipulation and sexual perversion. At the end of the novel, married and living in Europe, Augie remains at heart "a traveling man," struggling to achieve a sense of himself in the world. The novel won Bellow his first National Book Award, in 1954.

Like Asa Leventhal, Wilhelm Adler, the protagonist of *Seize the Day* (1956), has ceased trying to find significance in his life; rather, he wishes to find simplicity. At forty-four, he has faced divorce and professional failure, and he makes a final, desperate attempt to succeed financially by investing his last $700 in the commodities market. The man to whom he entrusts his savings, however, absconds. Wilhelm's illusions are lost, and he finds release at the funeral of a complete stranger, where he weeps alone beside the corpse.

Henderson the Rain King (1959) is a comic fantasy of a trip to Africa. Eugene Henderson, a Connecticut millionaire facing a midlife crisis, seeks an escape from the chaos of his life. In Africa, Henderson encounters two primitive tribes and a series of mishaps that

force him to confront his dual fears of living and dying. Henderson returns home, a man reborn.

In *Herzog* (1964), the protagonist has discovered the infidelity of an ex-wife with his one-time friend. Devastated, Moses Herzog spends most of his time lying down, writing letters he never mails to friends and enemies and even to public figures. At last he decides to murder his ex-wife, Madeleine, and her lover, Gersbach. However, when he finds himself looking into the bathroom window of Madeleine's house, he sees Gersbach bathing Herzog's own daughter. Herzog sees his own traits surviving in the little girl and knows he cannot carry out his revenge. *Herzog* earned Bellow a second National Book Award, in 1965.

Bellow also wrote short fiction, collected in *Mosby's Memoirs* (1969) and later in *Him with His Foot in His Mouth* (1984). He also tried his hand at play writing; *The Last Analysis* was produced on Broadway in 1964.

In *Mr. Sammler's Planet* (1970), Bellow offers a view of a man poised on the boundary between this world and the next. Arthur Sammler, an octogenarian and a survivor of two world wars who lost his wife in the Holocaust, has grown weary of life's demands. Appalled by the moral chaos he sees as he roams the streets of New York City, Sammler hopes to disengage himself. En route to the hospital to visit his dying nephew, Sammler encounters a pickpocket who physically threatens him and involves him in a succession of events that implicate Sammler in the degradation around him. In the end Sammler sees that only the humane values of his nephew provide a framework that makes life livable. Bellow received yet a third National Book Award, for *Mr. Sammler's Planet*, in 1971.

In *Humboldt's Gift* (1975), Bellow concerns himself with the plight of the artist in the modern Babylon. A successful writer, Charlie Citrine feels he must carry on for his deceased friend and mentor, the poet Von Humboldt Fleischer, whom Citrine believes was destroyed by the pressures of materialistic society. (Humboldt is based on Bellow's own friend, the poet and fiction writer DELMORE SCHWARTZ.) As Citrine mentally reconstructs Humboldt's life, he attempts to strip his own of these pressures. He receives two posthumous gifts from Humboldt: an absurd play that will probably make a successful film, and a model for his own life.

Humboldt's Gift won Bellow a Pulitzer Prize in 1976; he received the Nobel Prize for Literature the same year.

The need felt by a central character to get past appearances to some saving reality is a theme in all of Bellow's fiction, including his more recent novels, *The Dean's December* (1982) and *More Die of Heartbreak* (1987).

However, in two subsequent novellas, *A Theft* and *The Bellarosa Connection*, both published in 1989, Bellow seems to push his usual ponderings into the background, concentrating instead on the warmth and wit of his central characters.

BIBLIOGRAPHY

Bradbury, Malcolm, *Saul Bellow*, 1982; Dutton, Robert R., *Saul Bellow*, 1982; Harris, Mark, *Saul Bellow, Drumlin Woodchuck*, 1980; Miller, Ruth, *Saul Bellow: A Biography of the Imagination*, 1991.

Benton, Thomas Hart

(April 15, 1889–January 19, 1975)
Painter

Thomas Hart Benton, known as a Regionalist painter, is noted for his vigorous, realistic narrative easel murals and paintings that portrayed everyday life in the United States.

Benton, named after his great-uncle, Missouri's first senator, was born in Neosho, Missouri. His father was a lawyer and later a U.S. congressman. The young Benton said he painted his first mural when he was six years old; he drew a long train in charcoal on the new cream-colored wallpaper on the stairway wall of his parents' home. The disapproval that met this effort did not discourage him.

He continued a passionate interest in drawing and at seventeen, despite his father's desire for him to become a lawyer, got a job drawing cartoons for the Joplin *American* for $14 a week. In 1907 he went to Chicago to study at the Art Institute, where he sneaked into the life classes instead of drawing plaster casts as beginners were supposed to do. At nineteen his

mother helped him go to Paris, where he studied for three years at the Académie Julian. He flirted briefly with the new movements, Cubism and Synchronism (styles of painting that were rocking the Paris art world with natural forms reduced to geometrical ones), but he returned home most influenced by traditional artists like El Greco and the painters of the Italian Renaissance. "I wallowed in every cockeyed 'ism' that came along, and it took me ten years to get all that modernist dirt out of my system," he said.

Benton took part in the Forum Exhibition of Modern American Painters in 1916 in New York. He was a gallery director in New York and a teacher at the Art Students League in New York City, where his most important student was JACKSON POLLOCK, who later became famous for his "action" paintings. After service as a draftsman in the U.S. Navy during World War I, Benton worked for ten years on a series of paintings of groups of people to illustrate themes from American history, folklore, and daily life. He and other Regionalist painters believed that the heartland of America was the source of the country's strength. He developed his own style, using contrasting colors and rhythmic lines to depict human figures, often somewhat distorted, in action. His subjects ranged from Southern revivalist preachers to midwestern farmers scything hay, from railroad workers to soldiers and sailors in city honky-tonks.

In the 1930s Benton began painting murals. Sites included the New School for Social Research in New York (1930–1931), the Whitney Museum of American Art (1932), the Indiana pavilion at the Chicago World's Fair (1933), Indiana University at Bloomington (1933), and the Missouri State Capitol in Jefferson City (1936). This last mural showed Frankie and Johnny and Kansas City's Boss Pendergast.

Benton was always controversial. Political conservatives considered him a radical, and to modernist painters he was a traitor to his generation because of his realism.

In 1936 Benton went back to Missouri to teach at the Kansas City Art Institute. His work changed further as he turned to easel paintings of nudes, still lifes, and landscapes. In *Susan-nah and the Elders* (1938), an outstanding example of his later work, Benton gave the Old Testament story a midwestern setting; the elders are grim-faced farmers hiding behind a tree while in the foreground the angular, naked Susannah prepares to bathe. In the background a prim white church stands, symbolizing the religiosity in rural American life. He also set in the Midwest the classical myth in which Hercules wrestles with Achelous, who changed himself into a bull. *Achelous and Hercules* (1947) shows a barebacked farm youth wrestling a long-horned bull, while applauding girls sit on a horn of plenty that spills vegetables and fruit into the foreground.

He was painting in his Kansas City studio when he collapsed; he died of heart disease soon afterward.

BIBLIOGRAPHY

Adams, Henry, *Thomas Hart Benton: An American Original*, 1989; Benton, Thomas Hart, *Thomas Hart Benton and the Indiana Mural: The Making of a Masterpiece*, 1990; Burroughs, Polly, *Thomas Hart Benton: A Portrait*, 1981.

Bergman, Ingrid

(August 29, 1915–August 29, 1982)
Actress

E xemplifying classical beauty and nobility, Swedish-born Ingrid Bergman was one of the most beloved actresses of the 1940s until personal scandal destroyed her Hollywood career. Following work in Europe, she reclaimed her reputation and won her second of three Oscars for her performance in *Anastasia*.

Born in Stockholm, Bergman was an only child. Her German-born mother died when she was three and her father, who owned a camera shop and photographed her constantly, died when she was thirteen. She lived briefly with relatives until age seventeen, when she auditioned successfully for the government-sponsored Royal Dramatic School. By age twenty-four she was one of the leading actresses in Sweden.

Following several offers from Hollywood, she played in *Intermezzo: A Love Story* (1939), a remake of her 1936 Swedish film of the same title. The film's producer, David O. Selznick, convinced he had found another Garbo, signed her to a Hollywood contract. Bergman moved to California with her husband, Dr. Peter Lindstrom, and their young daughter, Pia.

Except for two minor films in 1941, Bergman was cast opposite Hollywood's biggest male stars and achieved instantaneous success. In 1941 she was the hapless prostitute terrorized by Spencer Tracy in *Dr. Jekyll and Mr. Hyde*, and won praise for her stage performance in EUGENE O'NEILL's *Anna Christie*, which opened in San Francisco and toured across the country. In 1942 she was loaned to Warners to star with Humphrey Bogart in *Casablanca*, her most popular movie. In 1943 she appeared with GARY COOPER in an adaptation of ERNEST HEMINGWAY's *For Whom the Bell Tolls*, for which she was nominated for an Oscar; and in 1944 she won her first Oscar for her performance as the besieged wife of Charles Boyer in the suspense melodrama *Gaslight*.

A box-office draw throughout the 1940s, she appeared in ALFRED HITCHCOCK's *Spellbound* (1945) with Gregory Peck and *Notorious* (1946) with CARY GRANT. In *The Bells of St. Mary's* (1945) she played a nun, and she was *Joan of Arc* in 1948. Partly owing to the image she projected in the latter two, audiences idealized her as a woman of morally impeccable character, an image that was shattered in 1949 when she left her husband and career to work and live with the director Roberto Rossellini in Italy.

Still married to Lindstrom, Bergman's affair with Rossellini was much publicized and shortly after their first film together, *Stromboli* (1950), she gave birth to the first of her three children with Rossellini. Granted a divorce from Lindstrom, she married Rossellini but was denounced in the press and in the U.S. Senate, where it was suggested she be banned from the country for "moral turpitude." Not until 1972 did the Senate enter an official apology in the Congressional Record.

Between 1950 and 1955 she and Rossellini made six more films, several of which are highly regarded by film scholars, particularly *The Greatest Love* (1951), in which Bergman plays a frivolous upper-middle-class woman whose life is transformed after the death of her son, and *Journey in Italy* (1954), in which she and George Sanders play an estranged couple whose meanderings end in their sudden reconciliation.

Her professional and personal relationship with Rossellini ended shortly after; the marriage itself was annulled in 1957. Bergman made a "comeback" in *Anastasia* (1956), playing the daughter of the last Russian czar. She won the Oscar for Best Actress and regained her popularity and respect with American audiences. In 1958 she married Lars Schmidt, a Swedish theatrical producer.

The success of *Anastasia* led to other projects, most notably the romantic comedy *Indiscreet* (1958), costarring Cary Grant; the missionary drama *The Inn of the Sixth Happiness* (1958); and a television production of HENRY JAMES's *The Turn of the Screw* (1959), for which she won an Emmy, television's equivalent of the Oscar.

Still active on the stage, she appeared in Robert Anderson's *Tea and Sympathy* and Ibsen's *Hedda Gabler* in Paris, Turgenev's *A Month in the Country* in London, and O'Neill's *More Stately Mansions* in New York. Her films in the 1960s and 1970s, however, were undistinguished. For a small part in *Murder on the Orient Express* (1974) she won her third Oscar, for Best Supporting Actress. She appeared in Vincente Minnelli's last and flawed film, *A Matter of Time* (1976), as well as in Swedish director Ingmar Bergman's *Autumn Sonata* (1978). She received a posthumous Emmy for her portrayal of Golda Meir, prime minister of Israel from 1969 to 1974, in the television movie *A Woman Called Golda* (1982).

Bergman and Schmidt were divorced in 1974, but remained friends until her death in

1982. Her daughter Pia Lindstrom is a television journalist in New York, and another daughter, Isabella Rossellini, who bears a striking resemblance to her mother, is an actress and a model.

BIBLIOGRAPHY

Bergman, Ingrid, *My Story*, 1980; Leamer, Laurence, *As Time Goes By*, 1986; Quirk, Laurence J., *The Complete Films of Ingrid Bergman*, 1989; Taylor, John Russell, *Ingrid Bergman*, 1983.

Berlin, Irving

(May 11, 1888–September 22, 1989)
Songwriter

Perhaps the most prolific songwriter ever, Irving Berlin published some 1,500 songs—from "Alexander's Ragtime Band" to "White Christmas." Beloved from Broadway to Hollywood, he responded to changing times and tastes with Main Street language and downhome images as he set Americans singing with his always irresistible melodies.

Berlin, the youngest of eight children, was named Israel by his parents, Moses and Lena Baline, and was born in Mohilev, Russia. Driven from Russia by persecutions of Jews, the Balines reached New York in 1892 and settled on the Lower East Side. Moses Baline, a cantor, died three years later.

The young Israel had two years of schooling before hard times forced him to work selling newspapers and singing on the streets. After he landed a job as a singing waiter at Pelham's Café in Chinatown, he wrote "Marie from Sunny Italy" with the restaurant's pianist, M. Nicholson. Baline's name appears on the sheet music as I. Berlin. The song, published in 1907, earned him 37½ cents in royalties. By 1909 he

Library of Congress

was working as a lyricist and song plugger, and, a year later, he was performing his own songs in *Up and Down Broadway*, a revue.

In 1911 Israel Baline changed his name legally to Irving Berlin. That same year he had a major success, his first, with the jaunty "Alexander's Ragtime Band." It was played again and again for dance-crazy Americans. Though not strictly ragtime, "Alexander's Ragtime Band" became one of Tin Pan Alley's greatest ragtime hits. Tin Pan Alley, New York's West 28th Street music publishing district, referred to the area's constant musical din.

The next year, a ballad, "When I Lost You," reflected Berlin's mood after his bride's death of typhoid six months after the wedding. Burying himself in work, he wrote his first complete score and lyrics in 1914: *Watch Your Step*, a show designed for dancers Vernon and Irene Castle. Berlin, constantly creating, usually at night, contributed to New York revues and operettas—from *Ziegfeld Follies* in 1911 to *The Century Girl* in 1916, and even performed in London as the "King of Ragtime" in 1917.

Drafted into the U.S. Army, he cajoled his World War I superiors into mounting an all-soldier revue, *Yip, Yip, Yaphank* in 1918. It included the song "Oh, How I Hate to Get Up in the Morning," but "God Bless America" was discarded as unsuitable. After discharge Berlin formed his own music publishing firm, Irving Berlin Music, Inc., in 1919, and two years later, with producer Sam H. Harris, built the Music Box Theatre.

The Music Box, still on West 45th Street, opened in September 1921 and was to stage Berlin's revues and showcase his popular songs. Berlin, a good businessman, maintained control of his works. Along with staging his own productions, the hard-working Berlin was writing music for the Ziegfeld Follies, including in 1919, the hit "A Pretty Girl Is Like a Melody," and for Broadway musicals like *The Cocoanuts* (1925), which starred the MARX BROTHERS.

In 1926 Berlin married socialite Ellin Mackay, the daughter of a Catholic millionaire. Furious, Clarence Mackay disinherited the bride. Berlin's wedding gift, the rights to the song "Always," more than compensated for her financial loss. In 1946, twenty years later, Mrs. Berlin received $60,000 in royalties from the song. Ironically, her father's fortune was wiped out by the Great Depression.

Berlin began to pull out of a long dry period with the 1932 success of *Face the Music* ("Let's Have Another Cup o' Coffee") and of *As Thousands Cheer*, in 1933, both written with Moss Hart (see under GEORGE SIMON KAUFMAN). The latter, a clever revue, was based on pages from a daily newspaper. It included a revised "Easter Parade" (from the failed *Smile and Show Your Dimple*), representing the rotogravure section, "Heat Wave" (weather), and the moving "Supper Time" (news), with Ethel Waters singing about the lynching of a black man.

Berlin, taken up by Hollywood, produced successful songs for successful movies, among them, "Cheek to Cheek" and "Top Hat, White Tie, and Tails," for *Top Hat* (1935), with FRED ASTAIRE and Ginger Rogers; "Let's Face the Music and Dance," for *Follow the Fleet* (1936);

and "I've Got My Love to Keep Me Warm," for *On the Avenue* (1937).

But it was *Holiday Inn* (1942), starring Bing Crosby and Fred Astaire, that launched "White Christmas." Berlin had doubts about the song and recalled, "I didn't think it would be a hit. But Crosby saw something there. . . . When he read the song he just took his pipe out of his mouth and said to me, 'You don't have to worry about this one, Irving.'" Crosby was right.

World War II brought Berlin back to familiar territory with another all-soldier revue, *This Is the Army* (1942, film 1943). "This Is the Army, Mr. Jones" and "I Left My Heart at the Stage Door Canteen" became hits. Berlin toured with the show for three and a half years, earning $10 million for army relief, and once again portrayed the sleepy soldier singing "Oh, How I Hate to Get Up in the Morning." But "God Bless America," originally intended for the World War I revue, turned out to be the showstopper.

The postwar *Annie Get Your Gun* (film version 1950) opened in 1946 and became Berlin's longest-running musical. Starring ETHEL MERMAN, the show included the hit song "There's No Business Like Show Business." *Call Me Madam* followed in 1950 (film 1953). Twelve years later, in 1962, the final Berlin show, *Mr. President*, opened. It ran for eight months, received lukewarm reviews, and was to be Berlin's Broadway farewell. He died in Manhattan, years later, at 101.

Alec Wilder writes of Berlin as "the best all-around, overall songwriter America has ever had." Wilder's admiration stems from Berlin's "uncanny ability to adjust to the demands or needs of the moment, the singer, or the shift in popular mood," and he notes that Berlin "represented, in song, every phase of musical fashion for forty-five years or more."

BIBLIOGRAPHY

Bergreen, Laurence, *As Thousands Cheer: The Life of Irving Berlin*, 1990; Wilder, Alec, *American Popular Song*, 1972.

Bernstein, Leonard

(August 25, 1918–October 14, 1990)
Composer, Conductor, Pianist, Teacher

Leonard Bernstein's indefatigable enthusiasm and prodigious talents expressed themselves over a broad range of musical endeavors. He was at home in the television studio and on the podiums of the world's great orchestras. His compositions include everything from symphonies to Broadway musicals.

He was born in Lawrence, Massachusetts. Samuel Bernstein, his father, the son of a scholar-rabbi, had immigrated from the Ukraine; Jennie, his mother, went to work as a child in the Lawrence textile mills. When the family acquired an upright piano in 1928, young Bernstein, the oldest of three children, began lessons, first with a neighbor, later with a faculty member of the New England Conservatory.

From the prestigious Boston Latin School, Bernstein went on to Harvard University to study music and, following graduation in 1939, continued his training at the Curtis Institute in Philadelphia. At Tanglewood, the Massachusetts summer home of the Boston Symphony Orchestra, Bernstein met conductor SERGE KOUSSEVITZKY and in 1942 became Koussevitzky's Berkshire Music Festival assistant.

That fall, despite his father's objections to music as a career, Bernstein went to work for the music publishers Harms-Remick. His duties included arrangements and notating improvisations by jazz players like tenor saxophonist COLEMAN HAWKINS and pianist Earl Hines. The following summer he became assistant conductor of the New York Philharmonic Orchestra. His big moment came November 14, 1943, when guest conductor Bruno Walter fell ill. Bernstein was recruited to conduct, the broadcast performance proceeded, and a front-page review in the *New York Times* followed.

In demand as a guest conductor, Bernstein appeared with important orchestras the following season and was signed to replace LEOPOLD STOKOWSKI as music director of the New

York City Symphony Orchestra, a post he held until 1948. He conducted the American premiere performance of Benjamin Britten's opera *Peter Grimes* at the Berkshire Music Festival in 1946, and went on to lead orchestras in Europe and Israel.

Bernstein also composed works like the Clarinet Sonata (1941–1942); Symphony no. 1 ("Jeremiah"), the winner of a New York Music Critics' Circle Award; and *Fancy Free,* choreographed by JEROME ROBBINS. The ballet was expanded into the engaging musical *On the Town* in 1944. Five years later, Bernstein appeared as piano soloist in a performance of his Symphony no. 2 ("The Age of Anxiety"), conducted by Koussevitzky.

The next dozen years were just as full and productive. Bernstein married and became head of the orchestra and conducting departments at the Berkshire Music Center and professor of music at Brandeis University. He continued to compose for the stage, producing *Trouble in Tahiti* in 1952, *Candide* in 1956, and the hit musical *West Side Story* in 1957. He also composed music for the film *On the Waterfront,* released in 1954.

Conductor Bernstein directed soprano MARIA CALLAS at La Scala in 1953 (the first American on the podium at that distinguished Milan opera house), served as codirector with Dmitri Mitropoulos of the New York Philharmonic Orchestra in 1957, and in 1958 was appointed music director of the Philharmonic, the first American-born conductor to hold the post. Now a world figure, he toured with the Philharmonic, conducted at the Metropolitan Opera, published a book, appeared on groundbreaking television series, and built an impressive list of recordings.

At his height as a conductor, on December 15, 1971, Bernstein led his 1,000th concert with the New York Philharmonic. The whole world watched and listened when, in 1989, at the fall of the Berlin Wall Leonard Bernstein led the moving performances of Beethoven's Ninth Symphony, substituting *Freiheit* (freedom) for *Freude* (joy) in the magnificent choral finale.

Bernstein believed in the universal language of music and in musical excellence, whether found in jazz and popular song or in the symphony. He was not willing, he said, "to spend my life as ARTURO TOSCANINI did, studying and restudying the same fifty pieces of music. . . . I want to compose. I want to play the piano. I want to write for Hollywood. I want to write symphonic music."

Bernstein did those things and more, buoyed by an enthusiasm for life that was expressed in hectic schedules, political activism, personal dynamism, and a broad range of contributions to stage, screen, and concert hall. He died of cancer in 1990.

BIBLIOGRAPHY

Gradenwitz, Peter, *Leonard Bernstein*, 1987; Peyser, Joan, *Bernstein: A Biography*, 1987.

Berry, Charles Edward Anderson

(ca. January 15, 1926–   )
Rock and Roll Musician

If you tried to give Rock 'n' Roll another name, you might call it 'Chuck Berry,'" said John Lennon. As Lennon suggests, it would be hard to overestimate Berry's influence. His lyrics captured the pulse of American teenage life, and his music became the blueprint for a generation of young guitarists.

Though Berry says he was born October 18, 1926, in St. Louis, Missouri, others give the date as January 15, 1926, and the place as San Jose, California. Critic John Rockwell notes that "Berry deliberately obscured his early years; sources differ as to his date of birth, and the year was long given as 1931." Chuck Berry grew up in a working-class family. The Berry family life revolved around church, and every week young Chuck attended Sunday school followed by church services without fail. By the time he reached Sumner High School in St. Louis, he began to pursue singing and guitar playing of popular love songs at backyard parties. Berry's guitar instruction came from chord books and casual help from friends, such as Ira Harris. Berry would take his guitar along, and while he waited for a haircut, Harris would show him a few passages. He was a de-

termined student who ultimately would add aspects of Charlie Christian's swing, T-Bone Walker's showmanship, and Louis Jordan's rhythm and blues to a foundation of Chicago style blues as played by the likes of MUDDY WATERS and Elmore James.

On New Year's Eve 1953, Berry was asked to join Sir John's Trio for an engagement at the newly opened Cosmopolitan Club in East St. Louis, Illinois, which was a considerable step up from other clubs he played. As Berry recalls, "[The Cosmopolitan] was four times as big, . . . six times as plush and ten times as popular." Berry, on guitar and vocals, joined Johnnie Johnson, leader and pianist, and Ebby Harding on drums. Joe Lewis was hired to play bass on holidays. The band continued to grow in popularity, owing greatly to Berry's showmanship and style, and soon was renamed the Chuck Berry Trio.

Country-western, usually called hillbilly music around St. Louis, also played a significant role in Berry's brew of influences. Berry would try out his versions of current country hits on his predominantly black audiences. "After they laughed at me a few times, they began requesting the hillbilly stuff and enjoyed trying to dance to it," remembers Berry.

In 1954, on the advice of Muddy Waters, Berry sought an audition with Leonard Chess of Chess Records in Chicago. Chess liked a song named "Ida Red" but suggested Berry change the name to "Maybellene." "Maybellene" and its flip "Wee Wee Hours" were recorded in 1955. It was the first of what would become a string of hits Berry recorded for Chess. "Maybellene" climbed the charts and made the playlist of New York disc jockey Alan Freed. Freed is often credited with inventing the term "rock and roll," and his radio show was tremendously influential with teenagers. Berry was on a roll now and hit the charts with one great song after another. Among them are "You Can't Catch Me" and "Roll Over Beethoven" (1956), "School Days" and "Rock and Roll Music" (1957), "Johnny B. Goode" and "Sweet Little Sixteen" (1958), "Back in the USA" (1959), and "Bye Bye Johnny" (1960). As much as his music was a hit, so were his live performances. Berry knew the value of showmanship and kept the crowds worked to a frenzy with his flashy angular poses and staggered steps. One particular strut he performed came to be known as the duck walk and was as much imitated as his guitar style.

At the peak of his popularity in 1959, Berry was arrested for violating the Mann Act, and in 1961 was sentenced to three years in the Terre Haute, Indiana, Federal Prison. By the time he reached prison in 1961, rock and roll had changed. Buddy Holly and Ritchie Valens had been killed in a plane crash, and Elvis Presley

was in the army. Now Berry's career was on hold. Despite this setback, after his release in 1963 Berry took up his career again. "Nadine," "Promised Land," and "No Particular Place to Go" were released the next year and Berry was back on the charts. He recorded through the sixties and one song, "My Ding-a-ling," climbed to number one on the pop charts in 1972.

The year 1979 brought a performance at the White House followed two months later by a conviction for tax evasion. He had failed to report $110,000 from 1973 concerts and served 120 days in the federal prison at Lompoc, California. In 1986 Berry was inducted into the Rock 'n' Roll Hall of Fame, and work began on a video tribute to him culminating in a live filmed performance a year later on his sixtieth birthday, featuring Keith Richards of the Rolling Stones. The film, entitled *Hail, Hail Rock 'n' Roll*, was released to much acclaim.

Every guitarist who plays rock and roll owes a debt to Chuck Berry, and his lyrics are considered the poetry of American popular culture. Probably the most praised of early rock stars, *The Rolling Stone Record Guide* suggests, "Chuck Berry is to rock what Louis Armstrong was to jazz."

BIBLIOGRAPHY

Berry, Chuck, *Chuck Berry: The Autobiography*, 1987; De Witt, H., *Chuck Berry: Rock 'n' Roll Music*, 1981; Reese, K., *Chuck Berry: Mr. Rock and Roll*, 1982.

Berryman, John

(October 25, 1914–January 7, 1972)
Poet

John Berryman, best known for *The Dream Songs*, wrote poems that reflected on the artist's struggle to produce despite the indifference of society and the limitations of his own talent and character. His carefully measured verse took liberties with syntax and style, yielding sometimes surprising insights into the narrative persona.

Born John Allyn Smith in McAlester, Oklahoma, Berryman lived on a farm before moving with his family to Florida in 1926. His father committed suicide that year, an event that would haunt the boy throughout his life. When his mother remarried, her new husband, John Angus Berryman, adopted him and moved the family to New York City.

Berryman attended Columbia University, graduating in 1936, then spent two years as a Kellett fellow at Cambridge University. He taught at Wayne State University, Harvard University, Princeton University, and the University of Iowa before joining the faculty of the University of Minnesota in 1955. He remained at Minnesota until his death.

Berryman's early work appeared in *Five Young American Poets* in 1940, along with that of RANDALL JARRELL, and then in his own book, *Poems* (1942). His first full-length volume, *The Dispossessed* (1948), and his sonnets, written while he taught at Princeton from 1946 to 1951 but published as *Berryman's Sonnets* in 1967, demonstrated his skill at revitalizing traditional poetic forms.

With *Homage to Mistress Bradstreet* (1956), Berryman found his own poetic style, one marked by inversions of syntax, indirect narration, and vivid imagery. In the title poem, which comprises fifty-seven eight-line stanzas, the poet allows the narrator's modern voice to mingle with and contradict his colonial subject's. The poem relates the personal hardships faced by the seventeenth-century American poet Anne Bradstreet.

Berryman began what would become his greatest work, *The Dream Songs*, in 1955. This series of poems explores the inner turmoil of a middle-aged poet as he struggles to satisfy his artistic ambitions despite alcoholism and a mediocre talent. This work, sometimes described as a verse novel, traces the narrator's deepening alienation from a society that seems to reject his gift, as well as his growing sense of despair. The poems, 385 in all, each comprising three six-line stanzas, were first published as *77 Dream Songs* (1964) and *His Toy, His Dream, His Rest* (1968). They were republished together as *The Dream Songs* in 1969.

Berryman's subsequent works treat his own life quite directly. *Love and Fame* (1970) offers autobiographical glimpses of his education and his career. *Delusions, Etc.* (1972), published just after his death, concerns his religious inclinations. Three final volumes came out posthumously: *Recovery* (1973), a novel based on Berryman's battle with alcoholism; *The Freedom of the Poet* (1976), a book of essays and stories; and *Henry's Fate* (1977), previously unpublished poems.

Berryman was honored with the Pulitzer Prize in 1965, and the National Book Award and the Bollingen Prize in 1969. His death by his own hand on January 7, 1972, was an act he had sometimes contemplated in his poetry.

BIBLIOGRAPHY

Haffenden, John, *The Life of John Berryman,* 1982; Mariani, Paul, *Dream Song: The Life of John Berryman,* 1990; Simpson, Eileen, *Poets in Their Youth,* 1982.

Bierstadt, Albert

(January 7, 1830–February 18, 1902)
Painter

Albert Bierstadt's huge, panoramic landscapes of the American West were wildly popular with the public and with wealthy collectors in the years after the Civil War.

Bierstadt was born in Solingen, Germany, near Düsseldorf on the Rhine. He came to the United States with his parents when he was an infant, and went to school in New Bedford, Massachusetts. Deciding to become a painter, in 1853 Bierstadt returned to Germany, this time to study art in Düsseldorf, where he learned to observe carefully and to draw painstakingly. From there he went to Rome, where artists from all over Europe went to study.

Returning to the United States in 1857, he went out west the next year with a surveying expedition that mapped an overland wagon route from St. Louis to the Pacific. He left the expedition to record with pencil and paint the country around the Wind River where the Shoshone Indians lived. The sketches he made would be the foundation of his landscape painting for many years thereafter. In 1859 he went back east and settled in New York City, painting vast, monumental landscapes based on his western sketches. These landscapes awed the viewers who flocked to see them. The tremendous scale, the unearthly light, and the generous detail in the pictures impressed them. Although influenced by early photographers, he had the painter's advantage—he could change and improve the landscape to get the effect of unspoiled grandeur that he wanted. Bierstadt's vision of the unspoiled

Library of Congress

West helped to shape the nation's ideas about the region. His national reputation grew and collectors clamored for his work. Banners advertising *The Rocky Mountains* (1863) were hung across Broadway when it was shown in New York. Vincent Scully has written of this painting that Bierstadt leads the viewer deep into a picture and has him focus across a glassy pool in the middle of the canvas, while at the same time the viewer's eye is picking up a whole 180-degree arc of vision as the mountains open up around him.

During the Civil War, he traveled in the South, painting large pictures such as *Attack on a Union Picket Post* and *The Bombardment of Fort Sumter*, both painted in 1862.

Bierstadt returned to the West in 1863 with a journalist named Fitzhugh Ludlow, who wrote a book about the journey, *The Heart of the Continent* (1870). The artist's continued success was spectacular; he was a rich man and the darling of the critics. His paintings, so large that they could not hang in ordinary homes, brought the highest prices ever paid to an American painter at that time.

Museums began to buy his paintings, and the U.S. government purchased *The Discovery of the Hudson* (1875) for the Capitol in Washington, D.C.

Bierstadt was a handsome man with an air of dignity and confidence. In 1867, when he was thirty-seven, he built a luxurious thirty-five room house at Irvington-on-Hudson, New York, which later burned. He lived at various times in the White Mountains, in Boston, in New York

City, and in San Francisco, and traveled in Europe, Canada, and the Bahamas, searching for exotic scenes. He painted a few big canvases of European landscapes, like *Storm on the Matterhorn*. In 1885 he began painting wildlife, as John James Audubon had done.

His success began to dim as the century faded. Collectors were interested in French painters and now found his work lacking in charm and warmth. It was said that his colors were not "natural," but chosen according to a formula by which his vegetation was a lush green, his lakes and rivers ice blue, and his skies unreal shades of pink and blue. In 1889 his painting *The Last of the Buffalo* was refused by a jury of New York artists who were selecting American paintings for the Universal Exposition in Paris. By the time he died, he was completely out of fashion.

In recent years Bierstadt's work has won new appreciation. His large works are admired for their grandeur and his small oil sketches, painted directly from nature, for their freshness and spontaneity.

BIBLIOGRAPHY

Anderson, Nancy, *Albert Bierstadt, Art and Enterprise*, 1990; Britsch, Ralph A., *Bierstadt and Ludlow: A Painter and Writer in the West*, 1980.

Bingham, George Caleb

(March 20, 1811–July 7, 1879)
Painter, Politician

George Caleb Bingham, who pursued a career in art and another in politics, painted scenes of everyday life along the Missouri River, which in his time was on the Western frontier.

Born on a plantation near Charlottesville, Virginia, Bingham moved when he was eight to Franklin, Missouri. A severe attack of measles when he was nineteen caused him to lose all his hair, and he wore a wig from then on. He was still a young man when the artist Chester Harding, who had gone to Missouri to do a portrait of Daniel Boone, encouraged him to become a portrait painter. Bingham earned a living through his portraits for several years.

Bingham married Elizabeth Hutchison, the first of his three wives, in 1836. In 1837 he studied briefly at the Pennsylvania Academy of the Fine Arts in Philadelphia. From 1840 to 1844 he lived in Washington, D.C., and painted portraits of politicians.

Politics drew Bingham back to Missouri, where he painted scenes of life along the Missouri and Mississippi rivers. His most famous picture is *Fur Traders Descending the Missouri* (1845), which he first called *French Trader and His Half-Breed Son*. The boy and his father float serenely down the river in a canoe, with a small black bear cub chained to the bow. The two figures face the viewer directly, on their silent journey down the pristine river that will take them to civilization. Spare and lean, they are outlined sharply against the misty background of the trees on the opposite bank.

Another river scene is *Raftsmen Playing Cards* (1847), which shows two boatmen playing cards while three others watch attentively. Again, the figures in the foreground are sharp and vivid, while the banks of the river are muted. That same year, the American Art-Union bought Bingham's *The Jolly Flatboatmen* for reproduction as its annual colored aquatint engraving and distributed it to its 10,000 members. Overnight Bingham became a celebrity, the master of Western genre.

In 1846 he was elected as a Whig to the Missouri legislature, but his opponent contested the election and was upheld by the Democratic legislature. In 1848 Bingham ran again against the same opponent and won.

Bingham saw himself as a painter of "our political characteristics" in Missouri, and he would paint politicians and elections almost as often as rivermen. In *The Verdict of the People* (1854) a portly man in a suit and tie standing on the steps of a building reads out the election results to a large crowd around him. A drunken boatman sprawls in the foreground, and one man rejoices with uplifted hands. Little boys cavort. The figures are arranged in the street setting, as one critic has said, with the expertise of a Venetian master. Bingham noted that everyone who saw it said it was his best work.

Bingham was good at drawing figures and was a careful draftsman and painter. He kept a file of sketches of Missouri people to use as he needed them for his accurate, compelling pictures of everyday life on his home ground.

In 1856 he went to Paris, then to Germany, where he studied for two years at the Düsseldorf Academy. The Düsseldorf school was extremely rigid, and most critics feel that Bingham did far better work before he went abroad to study. His fresh point of view is lacking in his later paintings, which are more theatrical and pretentious.

Bingham successfully continued his political life, serving admirably as state treasurer from 1862 to 1865 and adjutant general of Missouri in 1875.

BIBLIOGRAPHY

Bloch, E. Maurice, *The Paintings of George Caleb Bingham*, 1986; Rash, Nancy, *The Painting and Politics of George Caleb Bingham*, 1991.

Bishop, Elizabeth

(February 8, 1911–October 6, 1979)
Poet

Elizabeth Bishop, who traveled widely and lived many years abroad, reflected in her verses both the landscapes of her Nova Scotia childhood and the tropics she grew to love. Considered by many a "poet's poet," she experimented with many forms and styles.

Bishop was born in 1911 in Worcester, Massachusetts. Her father died eight months later, and her mother suffered a nervous breakdown from which she never recovered. Bishop lived with her mother's family in Great Village, Nova Scotia, for her first six years, then with her father's parents in Worcester.

As a child she withdrew from these traumas into a world of poetry and fairy tales. In her early teens, she discovered the works of WALT WHITMAN, EMILY DICKINSON, and HENRY JAMES. At Vassar College, she and MARY MCCARTHY were among four students who founded the literary magazine *Con Spirito*. Also at Vassar, she met the poet MARIANNE MOORE, who became her mentor and friend.

In 1935 Bishop began the travels that became so important in her life and work. She went to Brittany and Paris, North Africa and Spain. In 1937 she first visited Key West, Florida. After another sojourn in Europe, she settled in Key West for several years. Her poems, many of them inspired by the places she had visited, began to appear in small literary magazines.

Bishop's first book of poetry, *North & South*, published in 1946, is striking for the contrast between the earlier poems, written in the North, and the later poems, written in the

South. The earlier poems are witty and intro-spective; the later works celebrate the lush-ness of life in the tropics. Her poetic syntax is that of the best prose. She developed a rhyth-mic style for her free verse that set a fixed number of stressed syllables per line, effec-tively controlling their flow.

North & South earned her a Guggenheim Fellowship and a consultancy in poetry at the Library of Congress. Some critics felt that Bish-op's persona was too much repressed in her work; others saw a strong current of emotion beneath the placid surface of her poetry. Bishop herself experimented widely with forms and styles, from the traditional to the surreal, and struggled with finding the right distance from her subject matter. Her goal was stylistic subtlety above all else.

Bishop's second book, *A Cold Spring*, was collected with *North & South* and published under the title *Poems* in 1955. One poem, "Over 2,000 Illustrations and a Complete Con-cordance," trades on the challenge of seeing afresh what many others already have wit-nessed. "At the Fishhouses" reflects on the balance between sea and shore. *Poems* won her the Pulitzer Prize in 1956.

In 1951 Bishop began a fateful voyage around South America. Becoming ill, she re-cuperated with friends in Brazil. She fell in love with the country and stayed twenty years. She turned much of her energy to translation, including most notably poetry by Carlos Drummond de Andrade, and she wrote a pictorial history, *Brazil*, with the editors of *Life* magazine.

Questions of Travel (1965) explores the altered awareness of one who arrives in a strange country as a tourist but comes to know the country as an insider. A second section reflects back on the Nova Scotia the poet knew as a child and, particularly in the poem "In the Village," conveys poignantly and with careful control her sense of loss. *Questions of Travel* led to a series of academic appointments—first at the University of Washington in Seattle, later at Harvard—that brought her to the United States for part of each year. She moved to Boston in 1974.

Complete Poems was published in 1969, earning a National Book Award and affirming Bishop's reputation. *Geography III* (1976), which used the physical world as a metaphor for the self, won the National Book Critics Cir-cle Award. Such poems as "In the Waiting Room" and "Crusoe in England" explored ar-tistic intuition and the effects of solitude on the imagination.

Bishop died suddenly of a stroke in Boston on October 6, 1979.

BIBLIOGRAPHY

Kalstone, David, *Five Temperaments*, 1977; Stevenson, Anne, *Elizabeth Bishop*, 1966.

Booth, Edwin Thomas

(November 13, 1833–June 7, 1893)
Actor

Edwin Booth, whose father and two brothers were also on the stage, became one of America's great tragic actors and the first to win a European reputation.

Booth was born near Bel Air, Maryland, the son of Junius Brutus Booth, a great English actor who had played Richard III at Covent Garden in London at age twenty, Shylock at twenty-two, and King Lear at twenty-four. He came to America in 1821 and acted steadily for thirty years. Edwin was one of ten children born to the Booths in America. When he was very young he started going on theatrical trips to look out for his father, whose heavy drinking exacerbated his mental instability.

Young Booth's first appearance on the stage was in Boston in 1849. It was a minor part in a production of Shakespeare's *Richard III* with his father in the title role. In New York he took minor roles several times in plays opposite his father until the night in 1851 when he had to take his father's place, with no warning, as Richard III. After this Booth was hired by a Baltimore theater at $6 a week, but he did a very poor job, giving no hints of his future greatness.

In 1852 he and his father went to San Francisco, where Edwin's brother, Junius Brutus Booth, Jr., managed the Jenny Lind Theater. Edwin Booth played a variety of roles and sometimes acted as a handy man. Booth and another actor named D. C. Anderson lived in a shack on a small plot they called the Ranch. The two of them went on an acting tour to Australia with actress Laura Keene, a trip that ended in financial disaster. On the way home, Anderson and Booth stopped off in Honolulu and Booth played Richard III before King Kamehameha IV. Booth stayed on in California, acting in San Francisco and Sacramento, and then with a company that toured mining towns.

When he returned to the East, he was a polished performer with a style that drew a great deal from his father's, who in turn had been influenced by the English actor Edmund Kean. Edwin had learned to compensate for his shortness of height (he was only five feet, six inches tall). By and large, he kept to tragic roles, realizing that his strength did not lie in comedy or romantic parts that demanded a youthful, vibrant leading man. He was intellectual, even solemn, by nature but endowed with a mellifluous voice.

Booth played in Baltimore; toured the South; went to New York, where he played Hamlet, Richelieu, King Lear, and Romeo; and was greeted as "the Hope of the living Drama." He went on to Boston, which was still considered the most important audience in America,

and there, in April 1857, he played Sir Giles Overreach in Philip Massinger's *A New Way to Pay Old Debts*. His appearance was a triumph. He was at the top of his profession.

On July 7, 1860, he married Mary Devlin, a young actress who retired from the stage. The following year they traveled to London, where he played Shylock, Sir Giles, and Richelieu, his most popular role, and his wife gave birth to a daughter, Edwina. Back in the United States, he was playing at the Winter Garden in New York when his young wife died. Booth retired temporarily but came back to manage the Winter Garden, where he mounted many well-received Shakespearean plays, among them a *Julius Caesar* in which he played Brutus, Junius Brutus Booth, Jr., played Cassius, and his younger brother, John Wilkes Booth, played Marc Antony. The next night, November 26, 1864, he began his famous 100-performance run as Hamlet, the longest run the play had ever had. Hamlet, melancholy and intellectual, was the role that suited Booth best. Less than a month after the play closed, Booth again retired temporarily when he heard that John Wilkes Booth had assassinated President Lincoln at Ford's Theater on April 14, 1865.

Returning to the theater in 1866, he staged lavish productions. In 1867 the Winter Garden burned, destroying scenery, costumes, a library, and his collection of portraits of theatrical personages. He built his own theater, called Booth's, which he opened on February 3, 1869, starring in *Romeo and Juliet*. He married his Juliet, Mary McVicker, who then retired from the stage. She later became insane and died in 1881.

Booth was responsible for some of the most artistic productions ever seen in this country. A poor businessman, however, he went bankrupt and lost his theater in 1873 during a time of economic distress. He continued to act, but in other people's theaters. From 1880 to 1882 he was in Germany and England; in London he was invited to act in Henry Irving's Lyceum, where he and Irving alternated as Iago and Othello.

Back in the United States he acted constantly, distinguishing himself in Chicago during a performance of *Henry II,* when a lunatic in the audience fired a gun at him. He never for a moment stepped out of his role. He gave his home on Gramercy Park in New York City to the Players Club, which he had helped found, retaining an apartment there until his death.

His last appearance was as Hamlet at the Brooklyn Academy of Music in 1891.

BIBLIOGRAPHY

Kimmel, Stanley, *The Mad Booths of Maryland,* 1940; Ruggles, Eleanor, *Prince of Players,* 1953.

Brando, Marlon

(April 3, 1924–)
Actor

Marlon Brando, arguably the first Method actor, exploded on the New York stage in 1947 when he originated the role of Stanley Kowalski in *A Streetcar Named Desire.* By 1954, having made six movies, Brando had established a screen persona as a sullen and sensitive tough guy and had become the most influential—and imitated—actor of his generation.

Brando was born (as Marlon Brando, Jr.) in Omaha, Nebraska, in 1924. His father was a manufacturer of chemical products and insecticides, and his mother was a quasi-professional actress. Expelled both from high school and a military academy, he had a series of odd jobs before drifting to New York in 1943 and enrolling in a Dramatic Workshop at the New School for Social Research. His teacher was Stella Adler, famous disciple of the even more famous Russian theater director Konstantin Stanislavsky. Brando's debut on stage was as Jesus Christ in a 1944 Workshop production of Gerhart Hauptmann's *Hannele's Way to Heaven.* Subsequently, he had small parts in plays of Molière and Shakespeare, then secured the role of the oldest son of immigrant Norwegians in the long-running play *I Remember Mama* (1944) by John Van Druten. He next appeared in Maxwell Anderson's *Truckline Cafe* and George Bernard Shaw's *Candida,* and with actor Paul Muni in *A Flag is Born,* all in 1946.

It was the torn T-shirt performance in ELIA KAZAN's production of TENNESSEE WILLIAMS's *A Streetcar Named Desire,* however, that placed him in the front rank of the profession. His combination of animal magnetism and soulful vulnerability made him the prototype of the Method approach to acting promulgated by the newly established group known as the Actors' Studio. He quickly drew the attention of Hollywood, where he was to make his biggest impact. Even in his first minor film, *The Men* (1950), in which he played a paraplegic war veteran confined to a wheelchair, the raw power underlying his controlled gestures and brooding glances came through. While his performance reflected the Method's call for the actor to creatively discover the psychological truth of a role within himself or herself, it is equally true that Brando's performing instincts shaped the impression of what Method acting was both for actors and for the general public.

In the next few years he solidified his persona in the screen version of *Streetcar* (1951), as a Mexican revolutionary in *Viva Zapata!* (1952), as a motorcycle rebel in *The Wild One* (1954), and as a sensitive dockworker in *On the Waterfront* (1954), for which he won his first Academy Award. Kazan, who directed him in all but the third, called him "the only genius I ever met in the field of acting."

Following this initial period, however, Brando never again found a series of roles that so aptly utilized his unique mixture of charisma and volatility. During the rest of the 1950s, his range was wide—from Marc Antony in *Julius Caesar* (1953) and Napoleon in *Desirée* (1954) to the gambler Sky Masterson in the Damon Runyon musical *Guys and Dolls* (1955) and the Okinawan Sakini in *Teahouse of the August Moon* (1956)—but perhaps only as the sensitive Nazi officer in *The Young Lions* (1958) were his original strengths visible.

He began the 1960s as the Southern drifter opposite the sexually deprived Anna Magnani in Tennessee Williams's *The Fugitive Kind* (1959), but his acting was considered a parody of the behaviorisms that made him famous. Partly owing to disappointing roles, he directed himself in *One-Eyed Jacks* (1961), a psychological western, and developed a reputation for being uncooperative and unreliable, dragging out expensive productions like *Mutiny on the Bounty* (1962). He showed some talent for comedy in *Bedtime Story* (1964) and CHARLIE CHAPLIN's last directorial effort, *A Countess from Hong Kong* (1967), in which he played opposite Sophia Loren. His most

challenging role in the 1960s, however, was as the homosexual army officer in John Huston's *Reflections in a Golden Eye* (1967).

Just when critics were writing him off as no longer serious, Brando gave two memorable and very different performances in 1972, as *The Godfather* and as a middle-aged man coming to terms with the death of his wife in *Last Tango in Paris*. Although he was awarded his second Oscar for the former, he refused it, denouncing all awards as meaningless. At the Oscar ceremony in 1973, an American Indian woman spoke in his stead about government mistreatment of the Indians, a subject of deep concern for Brando. His few screen appearances since then—notably but briefly in *Superman* (1978) and *Apocalypse Now* (1979) and the charming if parodic replay of his *Godfather* performance in *The Freshman* (1990)—were, according to him, only to make money to support the many social causes to which he has been devoted.

BIBLIOGRAPHY

Garfield, David, *The Actors Studio*, 1984; Grobel, Lawrence, *Conversations with Brando*, 1991; Schickel, Richard, *Marlon Brando*, 1991.

Buck, Pearl Sydenstricker

(June 26, 1892–March 6, 1973)
Novelist

Pearl S. Buck is best known for her novels about China, particularly *The Good Earth*. She wrote prolifically about the lives and struggles of common people, demonstrating a consistent and deep-running faith in their ability, not just to improve their own circumstances, but to change their society.

Pearl Sydenstricker was born in Hillsboro, West Virginia, to Presbyterian missionary parents who took her to Chinkiang, China, as an infant. She was educated at a boarding school in Shanghai. She later attended Randolph-Macon Woman's College in Virginia, graduating in 1914. Returning to China, she married John Lossing Buck, a missionary, and taught

English at the University of Nanking from 1921 to 1931. She published her first book, *East Wind, West Wind* in 1930.

Her second book, *The Good Earth* (1931), made her immediately famous. The novel tells the story of a Chinese peasant farmer and his struggle to attain prosperity through the land. Told on an epic scale, the story traces the lives of Wang Lung, his three wives, and his family. Its sympathetic rendering of China's common people won the book a wide audience, and Buck was honored with the Pulitzer Prize in 1932. She wrote two sequels, *Sons* (1932) and *A House Divided* (1935). The three novels were published together as a trilogy, *The House of Earth*, in 1935.

Eventually, Buck began to question the role of Western missionaries in China. In 1933 she resigned any association with the Presbyterian missions after publishing an article critical of missionary personnel. The next year she returned to the United States. She divorced her first husband (with whom she had one daughter) in 1935 and married Richard J. Walsh, her publisher.

Buck set about writing biographies of her parents. *Fighting Angel*, her father's story, and *The Exile*, her mother's, were published in 1936. The two books were well-received and may have helped Buck win the Nobel Prize for Literature in 1938.

The author became coeditor of *Asia* magazine in 1941. Active in promoting intercultural exchange through the East and West Association, she served as the group's director from 1941 to 1951.

Copyright *Washington Post*; Reprinted by permission of the D.C. Public Library

Buck also took an interest in international adoption, founding Welcome House, an adoption agency, in 1949. She and her husband themselves adopted eight children. Her humanitarian interests found further expression through the Pearl S. Buck Foundation, which she established in 1964.

Buck was an optimist, and many of her novels address the personal qualities requisite to finding happiness and success. *Dragon Seed* (1942), for example, reflects on the need of the young to acquire wisdom through experience. The sage Ling Tan has learned the value of the land and the importance of apportioning it equitably. His children, however, must learn this lesson for themselves and come to recognize their father's wisdom only later.

It is often the case in Buck's fiction that women characters are wiser than the men in their lives. Wang of *The Good Earth* is well intentioned but awkward in his dealings with others. Buck's novels *Pavilion of Women* (1946), *Peony* (1948), and *Letter from Peking* (1957) also reflect this perspective. Buck's other fiction for adults includes *Come, My Beloved* (1953), *Stories of China* (1964), *The Good Deed and Other Stories of Asia, Past and Present* (1969), *East and West* (1975), and *The Lovers and Other Stories* (1977).

Buck translated *All Men Are Brothers* (two volumes, 1933) from the Chinese of Shui Hu

Chan. She wrote two volumes of autobiography, *My Several Worlds: A Personal Record* (1954) and *A Bridge for Passing* (1962). She also produced numerous plays and books for children

Pearl Buck died in Danby, Vermont, on March 6, 1973.

BIBLIOGRAPHY

Doyle, Paul A., *Pearl S. Buck*, 1980; Harris, Theodore F., *Pearl S. Buck: A Biography*, 2 vols., 1969–1971; Stirling, Nora, *Pearl S. Buck: A Woman in Conflict*, 1983.

Burnham, Daniel Hudson

(September 4, 1846–June 1, 1912)
Architect, City Planner

Daniel Burnham was a brilliant organizer who pioneered modern civic design in America and was the founder of the City Beautiful movement. With his first partner, John Wellborn Root, he produced some of Chicago's most famous skyscrapers and was in the forefront of the modern movement in architecture as an adherent of the Chicago school.

Born in Henderson, New York, Burnham moved to Chicago in 1855. He was a poor student and failed the entrance exams for Harvard University and Yale University. After pursuing assorted jobs, such as store clerk, miner, and Illinois state senate candidate, Burnham gained his first architectural training and experience working in the offices of Loring and Jenney (1867–1868). He served a brief apprenticeship in the Chicago architectural firm of Carter, Drake & Wight (1872), where he met John Wellborn Root. Root was a multitalented man from an affluent southern family, who had studied architecture and music in England and received an engineering degree from New York University. In 1873 the two men formed the Chicago-based architectural firm of Burnham and Root.

A propitious partnership, they complemented each other perfectly. Burnham, who was aggressive, persuasive, and people-oriented, had a command of the technical, utilitarian, and financial aspects of architecture and became the firm's planner and administrator. Root, a shy dreamer with the formal training and experience, became the designer. They produced many new buildings and residences in the wake of the 1871 Chicago fire. Their earliest commissions were residences for some of Chicago's elite, such as the home for stockyard magnate James B. Sherman (1874), whose daughter Burnham married.

However, Burnham wanted to produce "big buildings" for "big businessmen." During the 1880s, Burnham and Root began doing just that, creating three famous Chicago skyscrapers for developers Peter & Shepherd Brooks: the Montauk building (1881–1882), the Rookery building (1885–1887), and the Monadnock building (1889–1891). The Rookery, influenced by the style of HENRY HOBSON RICHARDSON, was noted for Root's exquisite ornamentation and Burnham's interior plan of a light court surrounded by four connecting wings, which became a model for skyscraper layouts. The sharply outlined, dark, unembellished Monadnock building became an emblem of modernist design.

In 1890 the firm built the first all-steel skeleton-framed structure, Chicago's Rand McNally building. Their 20-story, steel-skeletoned Masonic Temple (Chicago, 1892) was the world's tallest building at the time. The firm reorganized as D. H. Burnham & Company in 1891 as a result of Root's untimely death that year, and established branch offices in New York City and San Francisco. Thereafter, Burnham worked with several design partners and moved toward the Beaux-Arts style and neoclassicism. Chicago's Reliance building (1895; begun with Root, finished with Charles B. Atwood) heralded the steel-framed, glass-skinned skyscrapers of the twentieth century. Burnham's skyscrapers aligned him with the Chicago school, an architectural group prominent in establishing the modern movement. Capitalizing on the technological advances of central heating and elevators, the group spearheaded the development of the modern steel and glass skyscraper, espousing a stripped down, proportionally balanced, functional design.

One of Burnham's major achievements was as organizer/chief of construction/chief consulting architect for the Chicago World's Columbian Exposition in 1893, for which he gathered an impressive group of artists and architects. The Expo's "White City," with its formal, ordered, axially oriented plan and neoclassical architecture became the catalyst for Burnham's City Beautiful movement. He promoted city planning on a grand scale that would give American cities a certain cultural parity with the great European cities. The City Beautiful movement became the major motivating force in urban design from the 1890s to the 1920s, and Burnham became famous as a master city planner for such cities as Cleveland, Ohio (1903), San Francisco (1905), and Manila, the Philippines. He served as chairman of the commission for completing plans for Washington, D.C. Perhaps his greatest achievement was the 1909 "Plan of Chicago," in collaboration with Edward Bennett, with realization of many of its aspects. A careful integration of pragmatic, aesthetic, and ideological concerns, the plan detailed the development of a 60-mile ra-

dius around the city center. It provided for a radial and concentric system of boulevards to connect city center to the suburbs and link suburbs to each other, and a network of parks throughout the city and for 20 miles along Lake Michigan, among other features. In 1904 Burnham collaborated with landscape architect Jens Jensen to construct Grant Park and begin the park system.

Among Burnham's other architectural successes were Chicago's Railway Exchange building (1903), Philadelphia's Wanamaker's department store (1910), London's Selfridge's store, and New York's striking triangular-shaped Fuller, or Flatiron, building (1903). The aegis of his neoclassical style, commonly called Burnham Baroque, was Union Station in Washington, D.C. (1903–1907), which formed an integral part of his city plan. It is noted for its arched entrance porch and barrel-vaulted waiting-room ceiling, which was expressed as the building's dominant exterior feature.

Burnham was also one of the shapers and benefactors of the American Academy in Rome (founded in 1894). He was appointed by President William Howard Taft as the first chairman of the National Commission of Fine Arts (1910). After his death, the firm continued with two of his sons in partnership with Ernest Robert Graham, and later reorganized as Graham, Anderson, Probst & White. As both architect and planner, Burnham followed his own dictim: "Let your watchword be order and your beacon beauty."

BIBLIOGRAPHY

Burnham, Daniel H., and Edward Bennett, *Plan of Chicago*, rep., 1970; Hines, Thomas S., *Burnham of Chicago, Architect and Planner*, 1979; Moore, Charles, *Daniel H. Burnham: Architect, Planner of Cities*, rep., 1968.

Burroughs, Edgar Rice

(September 1, 1875–March 19, 1950)
Novelist

Edgar Rice Burroughs, best known as the creator of Tarzan, wrote more than seventy books, most of them jungle adventures or science-fiction romances, during the first half of the twentieth century.

Born in Chicago, Burroughs was educated at Phillips Academy in Andover, Massachusetts, and at the Michigan Military Academy, graduating in 1895. He served briefly in the U.S. Seventh Cavalry and then held a succession of disappointing jobs as a manager in businesses ranging from stationery stores to family mining and manufacturing concerns. He began writing fantasy stories at the age of thirty-six.

Burroughs's first published story was serialized in *All-Story Magazine* in 1912 and later published in hardcover as *A Princess of Mars* (1917). The first of a series of eleven interplanetary romances, *A Princess of Mars* concerns an earthling, John Carter, who becomes a citizen of Mars (known as Barsoom). Over the course of the series, Carter travels about Barsoom and one of its moons, comes to know many of the nomadic peoples who inhabit the planet, and even becomes its most powerful warlord. He marries a princess, Dejah Thoris, a beautiful red-skinned woman who is human—except that she lays eggs.

Burroughs's first full-length book was *Tarzan of the Apes* (1914). Tarzan, the abandoned son of a British nobleman, Lord Greystoke, is raised in the jungles of Africa by a tribe of apes. Benefiting both by his noble heritage and freedom from constraining social norms, Tarzan grows to be a man of tremendous strength and prowess. He learns the languages of the animal species and embarks on a string of fabulous adventures.

The "Tarzan" series stretched to twenty-one novels, which, by the 1940s, had sold 25 million copies and had been translated into fifty-six languages. A 1918 film based on *Tarzan of the Apes* was a smash success; a long series of "Tarzan" films followed. The Tarzan character also served as the basis for comic strips and radio and television shows.

A second string of science-fiction novels began with *At the Earth's Core* (1923). The "Pellucidar" series was based on the premise that a second world existed beneath the earth's hollow mantle. This world featured primitive humans and creatures that had survived the dinosaur age. Among the six "Pellucidar" novels is one in which Tarzan visits the earth's core.

In 1924 Burroughs published *The Land That Time Forgot,* in which a submarine crew discovers an island inhabited by primitive life forms. Like those in the "Pellucidar" series, the book includes speculation on evolutionary processes that may have been informed by Burroughs's studies at Michigan Military Academy. In *The Moon Maid* (1926), the moon has a hollow mantle and an interior world accessible through its visible craters. After a spaceship from the earth visits the moon, the lunar inhabitants invade and conquer the earth using its own technologies. A third science-fiction series concerns Carson Napier's adventures on Venus, beginning with *Pirates of Venus* (1934).

Burroughs's works fit fictional genres already pioneered by others. He did not invent the novel about the feral man, nor the interplanetary romance, nor the hollow-earth novel. However, he had a knack for suspenseful storytelling and an ability to render vividly the many wonders encountered by his heroes in the jungle or in the other worlds they explored. These qualities have allowed his work to endure where similar tales have not.

After 1919 Burroughs lived in California, serving as mayor of Malibu Beach in 1933. He died in Los Angeles in 1950.

BIBLIOGRAPHY

Lupoff, Richard A., *Edgar Rice Burroughs, Master of Adventure*, 1965; Porges, Irwin, *Edgar Rice Burroughs: The Man Who Created Tarzan*, 1975.

Cage, John Milton, Jr.

(September 5, 1912–August 12, 1992)
Composer

John Cage's revolutionary concepts questioned centuries of disciplined musical development and established new freedoms for the avant-garde. His inventive, sometimes witty tinkering with convention led to new ideas about instruments, performers, audiences, and composition.

The son of an inventor, John Milton Cage, Jr., was born in Los Angeles, California. At twelve he had his own weekly radio show, which featured his piano performances and those of others in his Boy Scout troop. In 1928 he graduated from Los Angeles High School, the class valedictorian, and continued his education at Pomona College.

In 1930 Cage left Pomona for Europe, traveling to cities like Paris, Berlin, and Madrid. He immersed himself in music and architecture, studied contemporary piano works, wrote poetry, and painted. While in Majorca, he composed his first piano pieces. When he returned home, he studied piano with Richard Buhlig because Buhlig had performed piano works of ARNOLD SCHOENBERG.

In 1933 Cage went to New York to study theory and composition and attended composer Henry Cowell's classes in nontraditional music at the New School for Social Research. When he returned to California in the fall of 1934, he studied counterpoint, analysis, and harmony with Arnold Schoenberg, a recent arrival in the United States. At the University of California, Los Angeles, he took courses in theory and became involved in a dance group as

composer and accompanist. Four years later he was in Seattle, Washington, as composer-accompanist for Bonnie Baird's dance classes at the Cornish School of the Arts, met MERCE CUNNINGHAM, and began a long association with the dancer.

In 1938 Cage joined the faculty at Mills College in California. He was intrigued by the possibilities offered by percussion ensembles. In *First Construction in Metal* (1939), he used sleigh bells, thunder sheets, and brake drums to explore intricate rhythms. After he moved to New York in 1942, he organized percussion concerts that included his works and attracted media attention. He was also writing music for Cunningham and touring with the dance company as accompanist, eventually becoming its music director.

Cage developed the idea of the prepared piano and wrote compositions for it. The piano, with objects like nails, wood, or rubber bands placed between its strings, produced odd percussive sounds. He also began to tinker with electrically produced sounds for composing. In *Imaginary Landscape no. 3* (1942), he used variable-speed turntables, an electric buzzer, an amplified marimba, and an amplified coil of wire. Tone color rather than pitch had become the primary means of differentiating sounds in these compositions. Rhythmic interest led to explorations of Eastern music and studies in Eastern philosophy. Cage continued to teach, travel, and tour with Merce Cunningham. By 1950 he was studying the *I Ching,* the Chinese book of changes, its message for each person based on chance.

Cage extended the concept of chance to his compositions, including the performer as a compositional element. *Music for Piano I* (1952), for instance, is written in whole notes, but it is the instrumentalist who determines the duration of each. *Imaginary Landscape no. 4* (1951), for twelve radios (two people at each), involves performers changing stations and volume according to precise instructions; the way the piece sounds in any one performance will depend on what is on the air at that time. "Now structure is not put into a work, but comes up in the person who perceives it himself," he said. His "4'33'''" (1952), most often performed with piano, is at once the most extreme and clearest expression of such principles. In it the pianist is expected to enter, sit at the piano, and do absolutely nothing for exactly four minutes and thirty-three seconds. All the listeners have to hear are audience noise and whatever sounds may penetrate from out-

side. If they can listen intently enough, they may indeed be able to make a piece for themselves.

Audiences often suspected or ridiculed Cage's innovations. He turned to artists like JASPER JOHNS and ROBERT RAUSCHENBERG or dancers like Merce Cunningham for understanding, and he became a strong influence on composers like PHILIP GLASS. Cage's writings, especially the collection *Silence* (1939–1961), is, according to *New York Times* critic John Rockwell, "the most influential conduit of Oriental thought and religious ideas into the artistic vanguard—not just in music but in dance, art and poetry as well." Cage died in Manhattan on August 12, 1992, of a stroke.

BIBLIOGRAPHY

Brindle, R. S., *The New Music*, 1975; Nyman, M., *Experimental Music, Cage and Beyond*, 1974.

Calder, Alexander Stirling

(July 22, 1898–November 11, 1976)
Sculptor

With his invention of the mobile, Alexander Calder incorporated motion into sculpture and created a new twentieth-century art form. His mobiles and, later, his stationary sculptures, called stabiles, won him international fame.

Calder was born in Lawnton, Pennsylvania, now part of Philadelphia. His mother, Nanette Lederer, was a painter and his father, Alexander Stirling Calder, a sculptor. His grandfather, Alexander Milne Calder, also a sculptor, created the 37-foot statue of William Penn that stands on top of Philadelphia's City Hall. Sandy Calder, as the grandson was called, played in his father's studio as a toddler and, at four, posed for the elder Calder's *Man Cub*. The

young Calder demonstrated his mechanical aptitude by remaking his toys when he was very young. He was particularly fascinated with an eighteenth-century toy that demonstrated the operation of the solar system.

After growing up in New York and California, Calder resolved to become an engineer and graduated from the Stevens Institute of Technology in Hoboken, New Jersey, in mechanical engineering. He worked as an engineer, lumberjack, and seaman before he went to New York to study at the Art Students League. While he was an art student, he worked as a freelance illustrator for the *National Police Gazette*, which assigned him to cover prizefights and circuses. He attended the circus for two weeks in 1925 and, impressed by the balance in motion of the animal and human performers, made lively linear drawings that would be the source for many of his subsequent works.

In 1926 he went to Paris, where he attended classes at the Académie de la Grande Chaumière. He began making toylike figures of animals out of wire, and went on to create an entire circus in miniature, with animals, clowns, and acrobats of wire, wood, string, cloth, and cork. The circus and other moving sculptures, like *Fishbowl with Crank*, in which fish seemed to swim at the turn of a crank, enchanted thousands, including the distinguished French painter and writer Jean Cocteau and the Spanish Surrealist painter Joan Miró. For years, Calder continued to refine and add to *Circus*, which is often on exhibition at the Whitney Museum of American Art in New York, where children of all ages study it in rapt fascination.

After a visit to the Paris studio of the Dutch abstract artist Piet Mondrian in 1930, Calder turned from representational art to abstract paintings and sculptures. He made movable sculptures that were abstract designs of metal globes or disks in bold, basic colors balanced on wires. When he began using welding to join the parts of his mobiles, he brought a new industrial technique to art. Motion constantly changed the composition of the sculpture as the elements moved, forming new relationships. At first Calder used pulleys and small motors to move the parts of his mobiles, but by 1932 he had begun leaving it to air currents or the touch of a hand for movement.

MARCEL DUCHAMP coined the word "mobile" for Calder's moving sculptures and organized

Library of Congress

the first exhibition of them in Paris in 1932. They were shown for the first time in the United States that same year. Calder won international attention for his kinetic mercury fountain in the Spanish pavilion at the 1937 Paris World's Fair.

Calder created all kinds of mobiles, large and small, including some in stage sets he designed for the dancer MARTHA GRAHAM. He built one large mobile for the New York World's Fair of 1939–1940. During World War II, when metal was scarce, he made stabiles, known as constellations, mainly out of wood. His *Teodelapio* (1962), a 59-foot stabile in Spoleto, Italy, is so big that trucks can drive between its "legs." One of his largest stabiles is the 70-foot-high stainless steel *Man*, which he made for the 1967 Montreal World's Fair. His monumental abstract stabiles stand crablike in open spaces in cities and college campuses throughout the world.

He also made stabile-mobiles that combined motion and repose. One of the most admired of these is *Spirale* (1958) for the Paris headquarters of the United Nations Educational, Scientific, and Cultural Organization.

In the 1950s he created a series of wall-mounted wire constructions called "towers," and experimented with mobiles and sound. Many museums have staged exhibitions of his work, including the enormous retrospective (361 objects) in 1964 at the Guggenheim Museum in New York that attracted more visitors than any other show at the museum up to that time.

Calder was prolific throughout his long, successful career. His work is noted for its wit and good-humored mischief, as well as its abstract form. He made models for his sculptures with hand tools and supervised their actual construction at the foundry. His mastery of balance and leverage reflects his years of engineering-school training, although he said he often experimented by trial and error. Calder and his wife, the former Louisa James, a painter and weaver, divided their time between a house in Roxbury, Connecticut, and one in Saché, a village near Tours in France.

In addition to his abstract sculptures, Calder produced jewelry, drawings, bronze figures, tapestries, and paintings in oil and gouache. He wrote several books, including *Animal Sketching* (1926) and *An Autobiography with Pic-* *tures* (1966). He also illustrated books. The *New York Times* named him one of the ten best children's book illustrators of the half century from 1900 to 1950 for such works as *Fables of Aesop* (1931).

BIBLIOGRAPHY

Arnason, H. H., *Calder*, 1961; Arnason, H. H., and Ugo Mulas, *Calder*, 1971; Calder, Alexander, *An Autobiography with Pictures*, 1966, and *Calder at the Zoo*, 1974; Sweeney, James Johnson, *Calder*, 1971.

Caldwell, Erskine Preston

(December 17, 1903–April 11, 1987)
Novelist

Erskine Caldwell wrote vivid fictional chronicles of the lives of the poor in the rural South during and after the Great Depression. His *Tobacco Road* shocked sensibilities in the 1930s with its unflinching portrayal of a family brought low by grinding poverty.

Caldwell was born in Moreland, Georgia, in 1903. His college years were divided among three schools: Erskine College, the University of Virginia, and the University of Pennsylvania. He worked briefly as a reporter for the *Atlanta Journal*, spent several years in Hollywood as a screenwriter, and later worked as a correspondent in Mexico, Spain, Czechoslovakia, Russia, and China.

In 1932 Caldwell achieved recognition with *Tobacco Road.* Jeeter Lester, a Georgia sharecropper too poor to plant a crop, lives in a shack with his mother, his ailing wife, and two of their children. Caldwell uses humor to play against his characters' gravity and their tragic circumstances. *Tobacco Road* was made into a play in 1933 that ran on Broadway for seven years.

An equally successful but more humorous novel, *God's Little Acre* (1933), depicts shiftless Georgia mountaineers. The protagonist, Ty Ty Walden, has dedicated the income from an acre of his property to supporting the church, but he constantly changes the location of the acre according to his needs of the moment.

As in other Naturalistic fiction, Caldwell's characters are oppressed by circumstances beyond their control, whether of heredity or environment. Flight seems pointless to them. Some are mentally deficient or perverse. Caldwell's treatment of grotesque characters and Southern social themes has been compared to WILLIAM FAULKNER's. Consistent with his portrayal of the seaminess of his characters' lives, Caldwell's frank rendering of sex marked a major departure in literature in the 1930s, though it became commonplace afterward.

Though Caldwell published over forty books of fiction, none measured up to his early successes. His critical reputation never reached the level of other Southern writers—WILLIAM FAULKNER, EUDORA WELTY, CARSON MCCULLERS, and FLANNERY O'CONNOR. But by the year 1962 sales of his books had reached 25 million copies and continued to grow, especially in Europe. Among his better novels are *Trouble in July* (1940), depicting racism in the South; *All Night Long* (1942), about guerrilla warfare in Russia; *Tragic Ground* (1944), on wartime prosperity among Georgia farmers; *A Place Called Estherville* (1949), again concerning Southern race relations; *Love and Money* (1954); *Jenny by Nature* (1961); and *The Weather Shelter* (1969).

Some of Caldwell's best work is found in his collections of short stories, including *Kneel to the Rising Sun* (1935), *Georgia Boy* (1943), and *When You Think of Me* (1959). "Candy-Man Beechum" is his most anthologized story. "Saturday Afternoon" is an unforgettable account of a lynching.

Caldwell also collaborated on four books with his second wife, the photographer Margaret Bourke-White: *You Have Seen Their Faces* (1937), *North of the Danube* (1939), *Say! Is This the U.S.A.?* (1941), and *Russia at War* (1942).

Caldwell died in 1987.

BIBLIOGRAPHY

Corwin, James, *Erskine Caldwell*, 1984.

Callas, Maria

(December 4, 1923–September 16, 1977)
Opera Singer

Maria Callas's distinctive voice, technical mastery, and galvanizing dramatic presence signaled her as a strong force in the revival of the operas of Rossini, Donizetti, and Bellini.

Born in New York City, Maria Callas (Cecilia Sophia Anna Maria Kalogeropoulou) returned to her parents' Greek homeland in 1937 to study music. She was three when the family name was changed to Callas.

Callas graduated from the eighth grade at New York's Public School 189 and promptly sailed for Greece with her mother Evangelia. Evangelia Callas was determined to prepare her gifted daughter for a vocal career and had no qualms about leaving an unhappy marriage.

In Greece, Callas studied with soprano Elvira de Hidalgo at the Athens Conservatory and became totally immersed in music. Her intensive studies were productive: she sang her first leading role, Tosca, at the Athens Opera on July 4, 1941. She was not yet eighteen.

During the next three years she went on to sing other leading roles in Greece.

She returned to New York in 1945, where her singing impressed Giovanni Zenatello. He hired her to perform the title role in Ponchielli's *La Gioconda* in Verona, Italy. Her Verona appearance, August 2, 1947, was so successful that she was asked to sing demanding roles in Verdi and Wagner operas throughout Italy.

Conductor Tullio Serafin helped Callas broaden her opera repertory, and under his guidance she began to master Italian opera roles like Bellini's Norma. She reached her greatest heights playing Norma, Tosca, Anna Bolena, and other dramatic roles, and she sang them in opera houses around the world, including La Scala in Milan, Italy, and the Metropolitan Opera in New York.

The Callas legend rested not only on her vocal career but on a stormy personal life that was the subject of endless media attention. Her forays into high society and her reputed temperaments were fascinating to press and public alike. A perfectionist, some of her difficulties stemmed from intense self-criticism and the vocal difficulties that plagued her.

Many believe Callas was like no other artist. She always projected excitement and drama and possessed a kind of personal electricity that engaged audiences immediately. Her voice was distinctive—highly centered, even edgy, often free of vibrato, and always in tune. Her technique and musicianship were superb. Strikingly self-possessed, she used her instinct, intelligence, training, and sense of the dramatic to draw audiences into the music. She was criticized for vocal imperfections, though her performances provoked comparisons with the greatest singers known.

Maria Callas made her last operatic appearance as Tosca at Covent Garden on July 5, 1965, and became a Greek citizen in 1966. In 1973 she toured Europe, the Far East, and the United States with tenor Giuseppe di Stefano, though her voice was losing strength. She died quite suddenly in Paris, France, at age fifty-three.

BIBLIOGRAPHY

Ardoin, J., *The Callas Legacy,* 1977, rev., 1982; Stassinopoulos, A., *Maria Callas: The Woman behind the Legend,* 1981.

Capote, Truman

(September 30, 1924–August 25, 1984)
Journalist, Novelist, Playwright, Short-Story Writer

Truman Capote wrote fiction, as well as prose works that depended on fictional techniques to engage and entertain the reader. His book *In Cold Blood,* the account of a multiple murder on a Kansas farm, started a vogue for what he called the nonfiction novel.

Born Truman Streckfus Persons in New Orleans, he lived with a succession of relatives after age four when his parents divorced. His mother later remarried a businessman named Capote, and he adopted his stepfather's surname. As a child, he often made up stories as a way to stave off loneliness; by age ten he had decided he would be a writer.

Capote attended the Trinity School and St. John's Academy in New York City, then public schools in Greenwich, Connecticut. At age seventeen, he decided he had finished his formal education, and, finding a job as an errand boy at the *New Yorker,* he devoted his free time to writing his own stories. The publication of his short story "Miriam" in *Mademoiselle* in June 1945 attracted attention and won him his first O. Henry Memorial Award for the Short Story and his book contract. The story is typical of much that came after: evoking isolation and dread, it seemed intended largely to produce a shudder in the reader.

Capote's first novel, *Other Voices, Other Rooms* (1948), made him a best-selling author at age twenty-three. While the book demonstrated Capote's talent, the sensation surrounding its publication may be attributed to its then-shocking subject matter: homosexuality. The protagonist, Joel Knox, searches for his father. Failing to find him and afraid to face life alone, Joel attaches himself to a transvestite named Randolph, who encourages him to reject the "normal" world. Many critics were horrified that Capote would leave Joel with Randolph at the end of the novel. John W. Aldridge suggested, in fact, that the characterizations had no basis in reality: Joel and Randolph "belong eternally to the special illusion Capote has created; outside it, they do nothing and are nothing," he wrote. In fact, Joel was unique among Capote's early protagonists in that he remained functional at the end of the story.

The pieces in *A Tree of Night and Other Stories* (1949) continue to evoke psychological terror. Without exception, the central characters come to realize that their lives are empty and meaningless. The story "Shut a Final Door" won first prize in the 1948 O. Henry Memorial Award.

After publishing his second book, Capote sailed for Europe, where he lived for many years. In addition to his fiction, he wrote travel pieces and profiles of such artists as André Gide and Isak Dinesen, collected in *Local Color* (1950).

The Grass Harp (1951), written in Sicily, draws on Capote's boyhood experiences. The novel centers on a bunch of young rebels who join together in an idyllic, though temporary, withdrawal from society. Capote mixed comedy and pathos, and, though he used a first-person narrator, critics noted he seemed to have moved away from the subjectivity of his early fiction.

Capote began to work in theater and films. His dramatization of *The Grass Harp* opened on Broadway in 1952; a musical adaptation of one story, "The House of Flowers," was staged in 1954, with the book by Capote and music by HAROLD ARLEN. Neither was financially successful. Capote collaborated with the movie director John Huston on *Beat the Devil* in 1954; while not commercially successful, the film has become a classic among critics.

Capote became interested in nonfiction writing and soon convinced himself that the genre had enormous artistic potential. As part of his exploration of the genre, he followed the touring company of *Porgy and Bess* on a Russian tour and reported in a pair of long *New Yorker* articles, which were later published as a book, *The Muses Are Heard* (1956). While seeming to remain objective, Capote manipulated details of his story to create an effect similar to fiction.

Capote returned to the United States and wrote *Breakfast at Tiffany's* (1958). The novel is a witty depiction of life in New York City and of the fortunes of Holly Golightly, an innocent young woman who makes her way by accepting money from the men she "dates." It is one of Capote's lighter works; though Holly faces an uncertain future, she remains capable of influencing the world around her.

Intrigued by the possibility of a nonfiction novel, Capote began searching for a subject. In November 1959, he read a story in the *New York Times* about the murders of a farmer and three family members. He left soon after for Holcomb, Kansas, where he began the six years of research and writing that yielded *In Cold Blood* (1966), which told the story of the Clutter family and the two psychopaths who were eventually executed for their murders. The book ignited an immediate controversy: Capote claimed he had invented a new literary form; some critics questioned whether it was right for a writer to make money from so enormous a tragedy. The book earned Capote millions.

Among the book's unquestioned accomplishments were a detailed rendering of the lives and manners of the people of western Kansas, an intimate portrait of the mind of one of the murderers, Perry Smith, and a telling account of the limitations of the criminal justice system in dealing with psychopathic personalities. A film version of *In Cold Blood* was released in 1967.

Capote's subsequent works included *The Dogs Bark: Public People and Private Places* (1973) and *Music for Chameleons* (1980), both collections of his nonfiction. Capote worked for years on a project he called *Answered Prayers*, which was to be a long and complex intermingling of fact and fiction. Several excerpts were printed in magazines in the mid-1970s, but the work was never completed. It was published in its final, unfinished form in 1987.

In the last years of his life, Capote's health and his work suffered badly, at least in part as a result of chronic alcoholism and repeated drug abuse. Because of his celebrity—he enjoyed making gossipy appearances on television talk shows and delivering vituperative lectures at college campuses—his breakdown became a public spectacle. He died on August 25, 1984.

BIBLIOGRAPHY

Brinnin, John Malcolm, *Dear Heart, Old Buddy,* 1986; Clarke, Gerald, *Truman Capote: A Biography,* 1988; Reed, Kenneth T., *Truman Capote,* 1981.

Capra, Frank

(May 18, 1897–September 3, 1991)
Film Director

Frank Capra, director of such classics as *It Happened One Night* and *It's a Wonderful Life,* was one of Hollywood's greatest populist filmmakers. Celebrating the triumphs of the ordinary man over the system, his work, one critic said, "brought the meaning of the American Dream alive for generations of moviegoers."

Born in Palermo, Italy, Francesco was the sixth surviving child of Rosaria and Salvatore Capra, a farmer with unpromising prospects. In 1903 the family emigrated to Los Angeles, joining older son Ben. Frank peddled papers while attending elementary school and learning English. At Manual Arts High School, his best friend was James Doolittle (later to be a World War II general and hero), the real-life prototype of the idealistic characters played by GARY COOPER and JAMES STEWART in Capra's films.

While an excellent student, Capra's education distanced him from his family. He was determined to succeed in America, where, he said, "a six-year old newsboy [could] grow and

The Museum of Modern Art/Film Stills Archive

dream, and . . . make his dreams materialize into realities"—sentiments echoed in many of his films. Capra studied engineering at Throop College of Technology, where an English teacher inspired him to write. He earned a few dollars selling gags for MACK SENNETT comedies. Graduating from Throop in 1918, he served in the army during World War I and became an American citizen in 1920.

Capra's entry into movies was in 1919 at the Christie Film Company, producer of slapstick comedies. As an apprentice, he was set builder, prop boy, and assistant director. In 1921 he directed his first one-reeler, *Fulta Fisher's Boarding House,* inspired by a Rudyard Kipling poem about lowlifes. A New York reviewer called it a "masterpiece of realism."

In 1924 he worked, uncredited, for Hal Roach on five "Our Gang" comedies, and was hired by Sennett to cowrite scenarios for two-reelers. He directed his first two features—*The Strong Man* (1926) and *Long Pants* (1927)—for comic Harry Langdon.

In 1928 Capra began his association with Columbia Pictures and production head Harry Cohn, directing six silent features in his first year. In the early sound period he directed four films with Barbara Stanwyck, including *The Bitter Tea of General Yen* (1933); *Platinum Blonde* (1931), a Jean Harlow vehicle; *American Madness* (1932), an account of the Great Depression; and *Lady for a Day* (1933), a Damon Runyon fable of an apple vendor transformed into a perfect lady, which Capra remade in 1961 as *Pocketful of Miracles*—his final film—with BETTE DAVIS.

Capra brought Columbia into the big time in 1934 with *It Happened One Night*, a romantic comedy about a spoiled heiress and a down-to-earth newspaper man, with special reverberations for the depression era. The sleeper of the year, it was the first film to win Academy Awards in all major categories: Picture, Director, Actor (Clark Gable), Actress (Claudette Colbert), and Screenplay (Robert Riskin). Capra's *You Can't Take It with You*, based on the GEORGE S. KAUFMAN/MOSS HART play, also won Oscars for Best Picture and Director in 1938.

More memorable, however, are Capra's genuine slices of Americana: *Mr. Deeds Goes to Town* (1936), which gave him his second Oscar for directing, and in which Gary Cooper plays naive everyman Longfellow Deeds, who inherits $20 million and wants to give it to the poor; and *Mr. Smith Goes to Washington* (1939), in which James Stewart plays young idealist Jefferson Smith, fighting corruption in the U.S. Senate. In both films, Jean Arthur excels as a smart-talking gal from the "real" world, drawn to the small-town innocence and idealism of the title characters.

While some critics found such films sentimental, dismissing them as "Capra-corn," others perceived the darker implications of Capra's vision of America. Critic Andrew Sarris noted that Capra espoused "the tyranny of the majority" and "the innate conformism of the common man." *Meet John Doe* (1941), Capra's first film after leaving Columbia, is a gloomy fable in which the title character (Cooper again) almost commits suicide upon discovering he's been used by a corrupt politician to mislead the multitude.

From 1942 to 1945 Capra worked for the U.S. Army, producing and supervising propagandistic documentaries on the Second World War, including the celebrated "Why We Fight" series, seven films explaining and justifying America's involvement in the war. The first, *Prelude to War*, won an Oscar for Best Documentary in 1942.

Capra's first film after the war was *It's a Wonderful Life* (1946), in which James Stewart plays a man who tries to end his life on Christmas Eve because he thinks it's been a failure and is saved by his guardian angel. It has become a perennial television favorite during the Christmas season.

State of the Union (1948), another story of American politics, pitting corruption against idealism, stars Spencer Tracy and KATHARINE HEPBURN. During the 1950s Capra directed two lesser comedies with Bing Crosby, *Riding High* (1950) and *Here Comes the Groom* (1951); several educational films for television; and *A Hole in the Head* (1959), in which FRANK SINATRA sings the Oscar-winning song "High Hopes."

Capra's autobiography, *The Name above the Title*, often rings with the idealized tone of his films. Biographer Joseph McBride challenges Capra's claims, creating a more complex picture of a man of ambition and determination, not without flaws. Yet, in vindication of Capra's belief in the "American Dream," three children from his second marriage (a fourth died young) inherited their father's drive for success: Frank, Jr., is a film producer; Tom, a television producer; and daughter Lulu, a professor of literature and philosophy.

BIBLIOGRAPHY

Capra, Frank, *The Name above the Title*, 1971; Carney, Raymond, *American Vision: The Films of Frank Capra*, 1986; McBride, Joseph, *Frank Capra: The Catastrophe of Success*, 1992.

Carter, Elliott Cook, Jr.

(December 11, 1908–)
Composer

Admired by musicians, recipient of many honors, the intellectual Elliott Carter created his own idiom. His complex, highly disciplined language is made meaningful by the intersection and interaction of its individual parts. Pitch, rhythm, and dynamics, for example, generate an intricate structure of changing tempos that impels the music forward.

Born in New York, Elliott Cook Carter, Jr., graduated from Horace Mann High School in 1926 and went on to Harvard University. There he studied harmony and counterpoint with Walter Piston and Gustav Holst, and earned a B.A. in English (1930) and an M.A. in music (1932). After completing his Harvard studies, he went to Paris to study at the Ecole Normale de Musique and privately with Nadia Boulanger, the renowned teacher and conductor.

Carter returned to the United States in 1935 and the following year began to contribute to *Modern Music* (until 1946). From 1937 to 1940 he was music director of Lincoln Kirstein's Ballet Caravan, and a suite based on his 1939 ballet score, *Pocahontas,* won the Juilliard Publication Award in 1940.

In 1940 Carter left the Ballet Caravan for St. John's College, Annapolis, Maryland, where he taught music, Greek philosophy, and mathematics and developed, with philosopher Scott Buchanan, a new teaching approach that brought music back into the academic mainstream. Carter composed Symphony no. 1 in 1942, and in 1943, when he was serving as music consultant to the Office of War Information in Washington, D.C., he composed settings for the poetry of ROBERT FROST and WALT WHITMAN. A 1944 orchestral work, *Holiday Overture,* won first prize in 1945 at the Independent Music Publishers' contest.

Though Carter spent most of his time composing (he was awarded Guggenheim Fellowships in 1945 and in 1950), he served as a faculty member of several institutions after he left St. John's: Peabody Conservatory, 1946–1948; Columbia University, 1948–1950; Queens College, 1955–1956; Yale University, 1960–1962; and Cornell University as Andrew D. White Professor-at-Large, 1967–1968.

Carter's exposure to the work of contemporary composers (CHARLES IVES, EDGARD VARÈSE, ROGER SESSIONS, PAUL HINDEMITH, AARON COPLAND, and Alexander Scriabin) and to the ferment of the modern movement (as in the work of Joyce, Proust, and the German Expressionist painters) helped develop his viewpoints and technique. He leaned toward moderation and toward a style that was accessible, as in *The Harmony of Morning* (1944) for women's voices and small orchestra, though in the joyous *Holiday Overture* of the same year, Carter began to use blocks of contrasting tempos and textures for the first time.

In the Piano Sonata (1945–1946) Carter began to forsake the neoclassical formalities and shift his emphasis to considerations of tone color and instrumental playing technique. Scholar Eric Salzman points out that "at the end of the 1940's and early in the 1950's Carter began to expand his vocabulary in the direction of a non–twelve-tone instrumental chromaticism." The *Variations for Orchestra* (1954–1955) reveal Carter's serial approach to intervals and dynamics, and by the String Quartet no. 2 (1959), "one hears the tone-row behind his melodic method," notes critic Peter Yates.

There is new intensity of feeling in the Sonata for Cello and Piano (1948), which, according to scholar Joseph Machlis, "sets forth the principle of 'metric modulation' as well as Carter's subtle insight into the problem of sonority and balance." In a metric modulation what had been some fraction of the beat in the previous tempo becomes the beat in the new tempo. Thus, in a metric modulation from

$\flat$ = 60 to $\flat$ = 80, the tempo in the first section is one beat every second and in the second section one beat every three quarters of a second. What had been written as a dotted eighth is now written as a quarter note, and steady sixteenth notes continue on as triplet eighths. A rhythmic pattern that was aligned with the beat in one way becomes aligned in a totally different way. This allows the interpenetration of many separate and distinct rhythmic layers.

"The effect I am interested in producing," said Carter, "is one of perceived large scale rhythmic tension, sometimes involving the anticipation of the impending final coincidence of all the disparate rhythm layers at some key moment."

Carter's String Quartet no. 2 brought him a Pulitzer Prize in 1960. Characteristically demanding of players, the work individualizes each instrument, gives it an inherent character, embodied, as Carter says, "in a special set of melodic and harmonic intervals and of rhythms that result in four different patterns of slow and fast tempi with associated types of expression."

The composer's interest in poetry and its incorporation into a musical fabric surfaced again with such works as *A Mirror on Which to Dwell* (1975) on poems of ELIZABETH BISHOP,

Syringa (1978) on poems by JOHN ASHBERY and various ancient Greek poets translated by the composer, and *In Sleep, in Thunder* (1981) on poems by ROBERT LOWELL. The 1980s saw a long succession of complex instrumental masterpieces, many of which reveal Carter's long and fruitful association with some of the most distinguished performers in the United States. They include two more string quartets, *Changes,* a work for solo guitar, and *Night Fantasies,* his most ambitious work for solo piano.

Elliott Carter, according to Peter Yates, is a cautious radical who became concerned with expression and imagination, with technique as a means, not an end. Though Carter's writings deplore the contemporary composer's predicament, Carter himself received his share of honors, including degrees from institutions like Swarthmore College, Princeton University, and Oberlin College, as well as numerous commissions and prizes.

BIBLIOGRAPHY

Schiff, D., *The Music of Elliott Carter,* 1983; Stone, E., and K. Stone (eds.), *The Writings of Elliott Carter,* 1977.

Cassatt, Mary Stevenson

(May 22, 1844–June 14, 1926)
Painter

Mary Cassatt, the only American invited to exhibit with the Impressionists in France, became famous for her paintings of women and children. She was also a printmaker.

Cassatt was born in Allegheny City, Pennsylvania, a suburb of Pittsburgh, and moved to Philadelphia with her parents in 1849. In 1851, when she was six, her family moved to Europe. They lived there four years, spending time in Paris, Heidelberg, and Darmstadt.

Back home, Cassatt became interested in art, and in 1861 she began instruction at the Pennsylvania Academy of the Fine Arts in Philadelphia. For four years she drew from casts of classical sculpture, studied life drawing, and copied pictures in the academy's collection. It was exactly the same kind of classical art training that Claude Monet, Edgar Degas, and other artists were undertaking in France.

In 1866 Cassatt returned to Paris and settled with family friends so that she could continue her art training. She studied with Jean-Léon Gérôme and Thomas Couture and also worked on her own, copying paintings at the Louvre. In this period she was producing sentimental oil paintings and pastels of children and small landscapes, some with young women sitting on the grass, sketching.

In 1870 the Franco-Prussian War drove her home to Philadelphia, but she was back in Europe in 1872. Maintaining her base in Paris, she traveled to Parma, Italy, to learn engraving and to study the technique of the Renaissance painter Correggio, especially the way he handled chiaroscuro, the play of light and shadow in a painting. She went to Spain, Belgium, and the Netherlands to study and copy works by Velázquez, Goya, Rubens, and Hals.

The judges for the Salon, the big annual art exhibition in Paris, accepted one of her paintings in 1872 and others in each of the next four years. This was a rare honor for an American artist. Edgar Degas, who was painting candid scenes of Parisian life, saw her painting, *Ida*, in the Salon of 1874 and said, "It's true. This is someone who feels as I do."

The admiration was mutual, but Cassatt did not meet Degas until 1877, when someone brought him to her studio. Her true masters, she said, were Courbet, Manet, and Degas. She was one of the few American artists of her day in Paris who admired the Impressionists, who were then considered radical and outrageous. (In their zeal to capture light with short, swift strokes of color, the Impressionists produced pictures that the public considered "unfinished.") Degas invited Cassatt to exhibit with him and his friends—including Monet, Pissarro, Renoir, Manet, Cézanne, Sisley, and Gauguin—in the Fourth Exhibition of Impressionists in 1879. "I accepted with joy," she said. "I hated conventional art. I began to live." She showed eleven paintings. Degas considered her a protégée and actually helped paint the background of her *Little Girl in a Blue Armchair* (1878).

Cassatt's style changed as her friendship with the Impressionists ripened. She used brighter colors, and her pictures began to re-flect a new realism, an effort to capture people in natural poses. She adopted Impressionist techniques, but not their obsession with landscape and outdoor light.

By this time Cassatt's parents and sister were living with her in Paris. In 1880 a visit from her brother Alexander and his wife and four children probably inspired her paintings, which attracted attention and acclaim at the next Impressionist exhibition. "Ravishing!" said one critic. "Only a woman can paint infancy." She continued to paint mothers and children over the years, switching from middle-class mothers and their offspring to peasant women and children until her work took on the tenderness that viewers find particularly moving.

In 1890 an exhibition of Japanese woodblock prints in Paris excited Cassatt and Degas, who saw it together. Cassatt began to work again at printmaking—aquatints and drypoints—which she saw as a technical challenge. She worked in her studio, painting in oils or pastels, all day and at night sat down with her family and worked on graphics, in which she experimented more freely with line and color. It is generally agreed that Cassatt did her best, most powerful work in the 1890s, including *The Bath* (1892) and *The Boating Party* (1894), with their strong patterns and lines.

Cassatt settled in the country at the Château de Beaufresne, near Le Mesnil-Théribers, surrounded by 45 acres of land on which she grew roses and vegetables. Her eyes began to fail around 1910, and she did little work after that. In her old age, she came to dislike the late work of Monet, Cézanne, Matisse, and the sculptor Rodin. She quarreled with Degas and with other old friends. She had had a circle of admirers in the United States, but it was only after her death in 1926 that she gained greater appreciation in her own country.

BIBLIOGRAPHY

Hale, Nancy, *Mary Cassatt*, 1975; Mathews, Nancy Mowll, *Mary Cassatt*, 1987.

Cather, Willa Sibert

(December 7, 1873–April 24, 1947)
Novelist, Short-Story Writer

Set variously in Nebraska, the American Southwest, and her native Virginia, the novels and stories of Willa Cather reflect a keen sense of place and the values of the American pioneers. Her best-known books are *My Ántonia* and *Death Comes for the Archbishop*.

Cather was born in Back Creek Valley, near Winchester, Virginia. At the age of ten, she moved with her family to a farm near Red Cloud, Nebraska, where she grew up with a keen awareness of the pioneer tradition. In 1891 she began her studies at the University of Nebraska at Lincoln, supporting herself by working as a journalist and drama critic for the *Nebraska State Journal*.

In 1896 Cather moved to Pittsburgh, Pennsylvania, where she became editor of the magazine *Home Monthly*. A year later, she resigned her position to teach Latin and English at a public high school. She published her first book, a collection of poetry called *April Twilights*, in 1903 and her first collection of fiction, *The Troll Garden*, in 1905.

The stories in *The Troll Garden* address the intersection of the vulgar and the beautiful. In "The Sculptor's Funeral," the body of the artist Harvey Merrick is returned to his home village for burial, but few of the citizens show any appreciation for Merrick or his accomplishments. "A Wagner Matinee" depicts the transformation wrought in a simple plainswoman by the music at a concert.

Library of Congress

In 1906 Cather became an editor at *McClure's Magazine*. Two years later she was promoted to managing editor. In 1912 she quit her job to devote full time to writing; she published her first novel that same year. Cather later disparaged *Alexander's Bridge*, saying she preferred to think of *O Pioneers!* (1913) as her novelistic debut. In the latter book, she returned to the Nebraska farm families she had known as a child. *O Pioneers!* tells the success story of Alexandra Bergson, a young Swedish immigrant who inherits her father's farm. Alexandra survives a set of challenges, first from her two mean-spirited, jealous brothers, Lou and Oscar, then from the death of her beloved younger brother, Emil, who is murdered by a Czech farmer with whose wife he had fallen in love.

Four subsequent novels continue Cather's exploration of her Nebraska heritage. *The Song of the Lark* (1915) tells the story of the life of a celebrated singer; the singer's childhood is based on Cather's own life at Red Cloud, and her career follows that of Cather's good friend, the opera singer Olive Fremstad. *My Ántonia* (1918), one of Cather's most celebrated works, depicts the journey of Ántonia Shimerda, the daughter of Bohemian immigrants, who leaves the Nebraska farm to seek a life of greater sensitivity but returns to marry an old friend, Anton Cuzak, after she is deserted by a railway conductor who leaves her pregnant. *One of Ours* (1922), inspired by the death of Cather's cousin during World War I, tells the story of an idealistic Nebraska farm boy who enlists in the army to escape a failed marriage and dies thinking he has saved the world for democracy. The novel was awarded a Pulitzer Prize. *A Lost Lady* (1923), again drawn from the life of a Midwestern acquaintance of Cather's, depicts Marian Forrester, the young wife of an aristocratic railroad builder, who survives his death and the sudden loss of her home and fortune by making a new life for herself with an English husband in South America.

Youth and the Bright Medusa (1920) was Cather's second collection of short fiction. Four stories were reprinted from *The Troll Garden;* most of the rest concern the lives of artists and singers.

In *The Professor's House* (1925), Cather relates the story of a professor of history, who, despite having won a prestigious literary prize for his history of the Spanish in North America, has grown disillusioned with his life and work and depressed over his family's apparent materialism. When his wife insists they buy a fancy new house, he also insists they retain the homely old one. After he nearly dies there from asphyxiation during a gas leak, he realizes he must make peace with his family and with himself.

Death Comes for the Archbishop (1927), the first of three historical novels, is regarded by many critics as Cather's finest. It tells the story of the fictional bishop Jean Marie Latour and his vicar Joseph Vaillant, who bring order to the diocese of New Mexico and build a cathedral in the wilderness, despite enormous hardship. Told in retrospect from the archbish-op's deathbed, the story is episodic. The novel is based on the true story of two French missionaries who organized the Catholic diocese of New Mexico when the United States acquired the territory from Mexico.

Soon after the publication of *Death Comes for the Archbishop,* Cather's father died and her mother suffered a severe stroke. Cather immersed herself in the writing of *Shadows on the Rock* (1931). Set in seventeenth-century Quebec, the novel recounts a year in the life of Cécile Auclair, the young daughter of an apothecary. The historical personages Count Frontenac and Bishop Laval also figure in the story.

Cather returned for a last visit to Red Cloud after her mother died in 1931; she preferred thereafter to call New York City her home. She returned fictionally, however, with *Obscure Destinies* (1932), a collection of three Midwestern stories. Included was "Old Mrs. Harris," regarded by some as her finest story.

Sapphira and the Slave Girl (1940), Cather's third historical novel, is set in her native Virginia. It recounts a true story, in which her grandmother rescues a slave belonging to her own parents and helps her escape to Canada via the Underground Railroad.

Cather wrote a few more stories and began another novel, but her health deteriorated, making work difficult. She died on April 24, 1947, of a cerebral hemorrhage.

BIBLIOGRAPHY

O'Brien, Sharon, *Willa Cather: The Emerging Voice,* 1987; Woodress, James, *Willa Cather: A Literary Life,* 1987.

Chaplin, Charles Spencer

(April 16, 1889–December 25, 1977)
Film Actor/Director/Producer

Charles Chaplin is the most important comic genius in the history of motion pictures. As Charlie or the Tramp, a mustachioed figure in baggy trousers, derby hat, frayed cutaway jacket, and cane, he is the most instantly recognized movie icon in the world.

Born in London, Chaplin's parents, Charles and Hannah, were vaudeville artists, though Chaplin never remembered living with his father. His mother took odd jobs to support Charles and older brother Sydney, but the family ended in a workhouse. At age seven Chaplin was in an orphanage for destitute children where, in addition

The Museum of Modern Art/Film Stills Archive

to suffering flogging and indignities, he learned to read and write. His mother was institutionalized several times, and his father died of alcoholism at age thirty-seven. This Dickensian childhood of poverty and starvation is reflected in the theme of Chaplin's art: the plight of the underdog.

Charles and Sydney developed slapstick routines for Fred Karno's Fun Factory, playing music halls in England and the continent. By age nineteen Chaplin was a principal clown, with Stan Laurel as his understudy. In 1910 he came to the United States with the troupe, making his first appearance before an American audience at the Colonial Theater in New York City.

He went back to England in 1912, but returned to the United States that year and was offered a film contract by MACK SENNETT, the creator of Keystone Comedies, who had seen Chaplin perform.

At Keystone he devised the costume that made him famous. Assembling used clothes—from Fatty Arbuckle's baggy pants to an overtight jacket and undersized bowler hat—he created what biographer Roger Manvell called a "study in contrasts." The mustache used by actor Mack Swain was cut down so that "no nuance of expression would be lost." With the cane as symbol of the man-about-town, the character was "at once tramp and city man, hobo and genteel man of the world," an ageless, mythic clown in the tradition of Harlequin and Pierrot.

Chaplin felt that Keystone's comedies—the shot-by-shot lead up to the final chase—were not conducive to his conviction that "nothing transcended personality." He learned how to edit improvisational action, but insisted on directing himself. Sennett, however, directed him in the feature-length *Tillie's Punctured Romance* (1914) starring comedienne Marie Dressler.

Aware of his box-office appeal, Chaplin left Keystone for Essanay where, between February 1915 and May 1916, he directed and starred in fourteen two-reelers, including *The Tramp* (1915), in which his most memorable screen persona crystallized. The character was inspired by a real hobo whose gestures and expressions Chaplin studied and who he said possessed an "irresponsible joy of life."

Chaplin developed an acting style in which personality dominated the comic action, perfecting a range of facial expressions for every situation—"comic dumbfoundedness, tongue-in-cheek triumph at getting away with murder, affected innocence twisting into a fatuous grin, a coy smirk at a nude statue, sudden laughter in moments of success, scowls of outrage when faced with evil opponents, or deadpan nonchalance when playing the drunk doing outrageous things," as described by Manvell.

At Essanay he discovered Edna Purviance, his leading lady in thirty-four films. Her last appearance was in Chaplin's dramatic feature *A Woman of Paris* (1923), which he directed but in which he did not star.

In 1916 Chaplin moved to Lone Star Mutual where he produced and directed some of his finest shorts, including *The Pawnshop* and *The Rink* (both 1916), and *Easy Street, The Immigrant*, and *The Adventurer* (all 1917). At First National he produced and directed a dozen films, including *Shoulder Arms* (1918), *The Pilgrim* (1923), and his first full-length feature, *The Kid* (1921).

By 1918, the most popular film star in the world, Chaplin was praised for his work's comic and human values. Ever the misfit and social outsider, his screen persona had special appeal to immigrants whose struggles to adapt to American society were mirrored in Chaplin's poignant but resilient characterizations. His expert pantomime enhanced and universalized his impact.

Chaplin's personal life at the time was beset with scandal, as it would be throughout his career. His penchant for young women led to two disastrous marriages ending in divorce: in 1918 to Mildred Harris, in 1924 to Lita Grey; both were sixteen.

In 1919 Chaplin, with actors MARY PICKFORD and Douglas Fairbanks and director D. W. GRIFFITH, formed United Artists, which released his next seven features. Following *A Woman of Paris* was *The Gold Rush* (1925), an epic-style comedy in which Charlie strikes it rich in the Klondike and becomes a million-aire. A critical and box-office hit, it is the film he wished to be remembered by.

Litigation over his second marriage interfered with the production and release of *The Circus* (1928), which Chaplin fails to even mention in his autobiography. His three subsequent films were all judged great achievements.

City Lights (1931) brought Chaplin's inspired mixture of pathos and humor to a new level, and he added musical composition to his talents. *Modern Times* (1936) was a brilliant satire of the age of the machine and unemployment, although many thought that, as a nontalking film made years after the arrival of sound, it indicated that Chaplin's art could not survive into the sound era.

They were proved wrong with *The Great Dictator* (1940), a serious and hysterical spoof of Hitler and Mussolini, in which Charlie played both Hitler and a look-alike Jewish barber who accidentally trades places with the dictator and gives a speech espousing peace. Chaplin's real-life resemblance to Hitler was much commented on throughout the 1930s, and his films were banned in Nazi Germany.

Chaplin's costar in *Modern Times* and *The Great Dictator* was Paulette Goddard, who became his third wife in 1936; they were divorced in 1940. Both films drew criticism from many quarters. Chaplin was accused of sympathizing with leftist causes and of being a communist, which he denied. It did not help that he never became an American citizen.

Chaplin was married for the fourth and last time in 1943 to Oona O'Neill, daughter of the famous playwright EUGENE O'NEILL. She was seventeen and he fifty-four. They had seven children and the marriage lasted until his death.

Chaplin's troubles with the U.S. government throughout the decade were compounded by further personal scandals. His bitterness is reflected in *Monsieur Verdoux* (1947), a critique of the hypocrisies of bourgeois society that was generally misunderstood. In 1952 he made *Limelight*, a nostalgic drama about an aging clown who saves the life of a young ballerina. In it he appears on stage with fellow comic great BUSTER KEATON.

Following its release, Chaplin left for Europe with his family. His reentry permit was rescinded, and he was warned that upon return he would face charges of a "political nature and of moral turpitude." He did not return to the United States until 1972, when he was feted and praised for his life's work by the Film Society at Lincoln Center, New York.

In the interim, he lived in Switzerland and directed two final films: *A King in New York*

(1956) and *The Countess from Hong Kong* (1966), a failed comedy starring MARLON BRANDO and Sophia Loren.

BIBLIOGRAPHY

Chaplin, Charles, *My Autobiography*, 1964; Manvell, Roger, *Chaplin*, 1974; Robinson, David, *Chaplin, His Life and Art*, 1985; Sobel, Raoul, and David Francis, *Chaplin: Genesis of a Clown*, 1977.

Chopin, Katherine O'Flaherty

(February 8, 1851–August 22, 1904)
Novelist, Short-Story Writer

In her fiction, Kate Chopin sought to explore the inner lives of women. Though her novel *The Awakening* so shocked the critics that it effectively ended her brief career, it has been recognized since for its realistic rendering of women's social plight at the turn of the century.

Born Kate O'Flaherty to a prominent St. Louis family, she was educated at the Academy of the Sacred Heart. She graduated in 1868 and two years later married Oscar Chopin, a Creole and a prosperous businessman.

When her husband died of swamp fever in 1882, Chopin spent two years running the family cotton plantation in Louisiana, then returned to St. Louis with her six children. She began to write fiction, publishing her first short stories in 1889. Over the next fifteen years, she published two novels and wrote over 100 short stories, printed in *Harper's, Atlantic,* and *Vogue,* as well as newspapers in St. Louis and New Orleans.

Chopin's first novel, *At Fault* (1890), was privately published. It concerns a woman in the Cane River section of Louisiana who has compelled a man to remarry his ex-wife, a drunk-

ard, in order to rescue her, a course she comes to regret having advocated. Chopin herself had learned to observe people without judging them, and the story reflects her dislike of moralists.

Bayou Folk, her first collection of stories, appeared in 1894 and earned Chopin a reputation as a writer of local color, especially Creole and Cajun. The twenty-three stories it contains typify Chopin's work in several ways. They show her interest in depicting the inner life of women and her naturalistic concern with the ways in which social and biological forces affect behavior. They demonstrate her propensity for using scenic detail to reflect her characters' emotions. They also prove she could take local characters and create for them situations that suggested universal themes.

"Madame Célestin's Divorce," first published in *Bayou Folk,* concerns a woman who, in the absence of her drunkard husband, begins a flirtation with a lawyer. She aggressively pursues a divorce until her husband returns home and reawakens her deep emotional and sexual bond with him. "Désirée's Baby" offers a commentary not only on racial bias, but on marriage as an institution that enslaves women.

Chopin's second collection of stories, *A Night in Acadie,* was published in 1897. Its twenty stories made use of the same Louisiana settings as the earlier stories and even reintroduced some of the same characters. Included were "A Respectable Woman," which daringly left its protagonist, a happily married woman, on the brink of adultery; "Regret," the story of an independent woman who has spurned the attention of men but who realizes at age fifty that she wants children; and "Athénaïse," which deals with the sexual awakening of a young woman and the flowering of her marriage at the moment her husband acknowledges her right to make her own choices about their relationship.

In 1897 Chopin's publisher returned the manuscript for her third collection of stories and suggested she try writing a novel. Chopin continued her efforts to have the collection published but also began *The Awakening.* She never succeeded in getting the short-story volume printed, though many of the pieces had appeared individually in periodicals. Two volumes of Chopin's *Complete Works* were published in 1969 and include these stories, some of them now considered among her best.

The Awakening (1899) tells the story of Edna Pontellier, who marries a Creole from New Orleans and finds she must struggle to adapt to his culture. Confused by her emerging sexuality but determined to know her own mind and heart, she begins an affair and later leaves her husband and their two children to start an independent life. Once liberated she knows she cannot go back to her marriage, but she fears for the effect her ruined reputation will have on her children. Finally, she commits suicide by swimming into the ocean, an act that describes her final assertion of will despite the lack of real freedom.

While critics recognized the technical mastery represented in *The Awakening,* they could not accept the author's refusal to condemn its protagonist. The book was banned by some libraries, and Chopin was shunned by the St. Louis literary establishment. Discouraged, she published only five more stories before her death in 1904.

BIBLIOGRAPHY

Elwell, Barbara C., *Kate Chopin,* 1986; Seyersted, Per, *Kate Chopin: A Critical Biography,* 1969.

Church, Frederick Edwin

(May 4, 1826–April 7, 1900)
Landscape Painter

Frederick E. Church became famous in the middle of the nineteenth century for his flamboyant landscape paintings of natural marvels: Niagara Falls, erupting volcanoes, and enormous icebergs.

Church was born to a wealthy family in Hartford, Connecticut. He took art lessons from two teachers before 1844, when he went to Catskill, New York, to study with THOMAS COLE, a founder of the Hudson River school of painting and at that time the nation's most famous landscapist. Church made rapid progress, and a year later he showed his first picture at the National Academy of Design. In 1848 he set up his studio in New York City and began taking pupils himself.

Church's paintings were more realistic than his teacher's, and he was not interested in allegory, as Cole was. When Church showed *West Rock, New Haven* (1849) with its meticulously detailed hay wagon and farm workers in the foreground, someone said that his works were as accurate as prints from the new daguerreotype photography. Unlike most artists who were his contemporaries, Church did not feel the need to go to Europe to study. He traveled widely in America, painting scenes in Vermont, New Hampshire, Maine, Virginia, Kentucky, and the region of the Upper Mississippi.

His *Niagara*, painted in 1857 from the Canadian shore, was enormously popular because of its realism. People marveled at how wet the water and spray looked and admired the rainbow effect in the falls. John Ruskin, the English art critic, said that it was the finest painting of water in the world. Lithographs of *Niagara* had enormous sales.

The work of the German explorer and naturalist Baron Alexander von Humboldt, who wrote several travel books and a scientific work, *Cosmos* (1845–1862), influenced Church enormously. Humboldt believed that landscape painting was one of the three ways for humans to express their love of nature. (The other two were poetic description and the cultivation of exotic plants.) Humboldt urged artists to discover the ruins and wildlife of South America. Church, convinced that the artist should combine scientific accuracy with the depiction of beauty, went there in 1853. In Ecuador he stayed in the house where Humboldt had lived and traveled by mule, by boat, and on foot through Ecuador and Colombia, sketching volcanoes, waterfalls, and wilderness. Back in New York, he painted pictures based on these sketches.

Church was also a showman where art was concerned. He put on display in his studio in New York one of the largest of these, *Heart of the Andes* (1859), 10 feet wide and more than 5 feet tall. The painting was filled with precise details of Andean plants and trees, a waterfall and stream in the foreground, and a background of soaring purple mountains beneath a cloud-scattered blue sky. The room where the picture hung had no windows. Church put black curtains on the walls, used gas jets to light the painting, and placed palm trees and other tropical plants in the room to give it the right atmosphere. The response to the picture was overwhelming. Crowds paid admission to see the picture, and Church distributed tubes of paper to use as spyglasses so that the viewers could feel themselves closer to the picture. Newspapers carried poems written in its honor. Preachers commended the picture's morally uplifting content. "Glorious," "magnificent," "finest picture ever painted in this country," were some of the descriptions used to describe it.

On a second trip to South America, Church made the sketches for his three paintings of smoke gushing from the volcano of Cotopaxi, the smoke turning red in the light of the setting sun. Church also traveled in Europe and the Middle East, always searching for exotic terrain to paint. In 1859 he went to Labrador, where he made sketches for a large canvas called *The Icebergs* (1861).

At the peak of his career Church developed rheumatoid arthritis. He was forced to cut back on his work, although he continued to produce oil sketches. He and his wife, the former Isabel Carnes, whom he had married in 1860, lived in a large mansion, Olana, that Church had begun building on the Hudson River, near the town of Hudson, in 1870. Strongly influenced by Moorish architecture, Olana has turrets, minarets, patterned ceilings, as well as elaborately landscaped grounds with spectacular views of the Hudson. Church lived there until he died in 1900. Now the property of New York State, Olana, with its original furnishings collected by Church from all over the world, is open to the public.

BIBLIOGRAPHY

Kelly, Franklin, *Frederick E. Church*, 1989.

Cole, Thomas

(February 1, 1801–February 11, 1848)
Painter

Thomas Cole was the first important landscape painter in America and a founder of the Hudson River school of nineteenth-century American landscapists.

Cole was born in 1801 in Bolton-le-Moors, England, and was apprenticed at fourteen to a designer of calico prints in Nottinghamshire and later to a wood engraver in Liverpool. In his spare time he played the flute and roamed the English countryside. He read a book about the beauty of North America and his enthusiasm persuaded his father, an unsuccessful woolen manufacturer, to emigrate. The family arrived in Philadelphia in 1819.

Cole did wood engraving in Philadelphia and then in Steubenville, Ohio, where he wandered through the unspoiled wilderness along the Ohio River. Deciding to become a painter, he decorated chairs for a chair maker in return for art supplies. He wanted to paint landscapes, but he started out with portraits for which he could earn money. By the time he was twenty-one, he was a not-too-successful itinerant portrait painter.

Beginning in 1823, Cole spent two years in Philadelphia, studying from time to time at the Pennsylvania Academy of the Fine Arts. In 1825 he moved to New York, where he was an immediate success as a landscape painter. Three well-known painters, John Trumbull, Asher B. Durand, and William Dunlap, saw his work in a shop window and sought him out. They bought some of the pictures he had painted along the Hudson River at Palisades and Weehawken, New Jersey, and found other buyers for his landscapes. The poet William Cullen Bryant was one of Cole's patrons and became a close friend. Another author, JAMES FENIMORE COOPER, also admired his work extravagantly. Cole's landscape paintings became well known at the same time that writers were reassessing the current attitudes toward nature. RALPH WALDO EMERSON inspired writers

and artists alike with his 1836 essay *Nature,* which revealed his love for the natural scenes of this country and expressed the main principles of Transcendentalism (an American philosophical movement that had lasting effects on religion, literature, art, and social reform movements in the nineteenth century and later).

Cole's painting from nature in the Catskill Mountains along the Hudson gave rise to the Hudson River school, a group of landscape painters who flourished in the mid-nineteenth century. The Hudson River painters admired nature and emphasized the grandeur and nobility of the country in their dramatic, colorful paintings. Cole believed that the scene was all-important and that techniques, including use of color and chiaroscuro (light and shade), should always be subservient to the subject and not ends in themselves. While he did many sketches in pencil and in oils, he always completed the landscape in his studio.

In 1828 he began painting imaginary landscapes like *The Garden of Eden* and *Expulsion from Paradise,* but these were based on real scenes. A grant from a Baltimore art collector, Robert Gilmor Powell, made it possible for him to visit England and Italy from 1829 to 1832. He found his native England depressing, but he thought Florence "a painter's paradise." In Florence his studio was in the building with Horatio Greenough, an American sculptor, and in Rome he occupied a studio on the Pincian Hill that had once been used by Claude Lorraine, a French landscape painter. While he was in Italy he had the idea for a series of paintings that would tell the story of a civilization from its beginning to its end.

After Cole returned from Europe, Luman Reed, a New York art collector, commissioned him to paint a series, *The Course of Empire* (1836). The five paintings have the same natural setting, each in a different stage of development or decay. *The Savage State* shows an unspoiled natural scene. In *The Arcadian or Pastoral State* shepherds are tending sheep and farmers tilling the soil. *The Consummation of Empire* shows a handsome city at the height of its power. *Destruction* depicts the downfall of the city. In *Desolation* nature takes over the ruins of the city. Despite the fact that important people admired the series, Cole was afraid that the public would not receive these allegorical paintings as well as they had his landscapes. He was right. Because of their moral content, the public professed to like them, but when it came to pictures for their own homes, Americans wanted "American scenes," or landscapes. They wanted the *truth*.

America's landscape still awed Cole. All nature in America was art, he said, "primeval forests, virgin lakes and waterfalls," with none of Europe's famous sites like Tivoli or Terni in Italy that were "hackneyed and worn by the daily pencils of hundreds" of sketchers. Along with art lovers, he was convinced that landscape painting had a "happy and civilizing influence" on the country, that it provided intellectual stimulation and fostered a love of nature and beauty. One of his most famous landscapes is *The Oxbow (the Connecticut River near Northampton)*, painted in 1836. In it an artist on a rocky hilltop paints the magnificent horseshoe bend of the river in the tranquil, sunlit valley below. Waterfalls were a favorite subject of Cole's. For example, he painted *View of the Falls of Munda near Portage on the Genesee Falls, New York (Mountain Landscape with Waterfall)* in 1847.

Cole lectured, wrote essays and poetry, even tried architecture, entering the competition for the Ohio State Capitol in 1838. In 1844 he accepted the only pupil he ever had on a formal basis, FREDERICK E. CHURCH, who also became famous as a landscape painter.

Another collector commissioned *The Voyage of Life*, a series of four paintings that Cole began in 1839 and included *Childhood, Youth, Manhood,* and *Old Age*. Cole joined the Anglican Church and began a religious series to be called *The Cross and the World*. It was never completed; Cole died in 1848 while working on one picture for that series, *The Pilgrim of the Cross at the End of His Journey*. William Cullen Bryant eulogized the artist at his funeral held at the National Academy of Design, which Cole had helped found.

BIBLIOGRAPHY

Bargell, Matthew, *Thomas Cole*, 1991; Powell, Earl A., *Thomas Cole*, 1990.

Coleman, Ornette

(March 9, 1930–   )
Jazz Musician

When Ornette Coleman shattered established musical patterns with startling instrumental innovations in tone, color, and texture in his free-form improvisations, he opened up dramatic new horizons for jazz. His individualistic approach set off new energies in improvisation and challenged the limits of earlier styles.

Coleman was born in Fort Worth, Texas. At fourteen he acquired an alto saxophone and taught himself to play it using a piano instruction book. After a year's hiatus as a result of an athletic injury, he returned to music and took up the tenor sax because it provided opportunities for jobs with rhythm and blues groups.

He did not apply for college after high school graduation. Rather, he spent the rest of 1949 touring the South with rhythm and blues bands. Long-haired, bearded, he was already a rebel capable of arousing strong feelings. Once, patrons in Baton Rouge, Louisiana, beat him and ruined his instrument.

Back home in Forth Worth, Coleman bought a used alto sax and in 1950 traveled to Los Angeles with Pee Wee Crayton's band. There he worked, studied theory from textbooks, and jammed at night. Inspired by compositions of THELONIOUS MONK and CHARLIE PARKER, Coleman's avant-garde approach was unpopular. It was not until the late 1950s that he made his first recordings: *Something Else* and *Tomorrow Is the Question.* The latter demonstrates an established style, one that defied conventional rhythm, melody, and harmony.

Championed by critic Nat Hentoff and encouraged by pianist John Lewis and jazz scholar Gunther Schuller, Coleman, sponsored by Atlantic Records, went to Massachusetts in 1959 to attend the Lenox School of Jazz. The debut of the Coleman quartet at the Five Spot in Manhattan later that year set off public awareness of free jazz. A remarkable record made in 1960 called *Free Jazz,* a thirty-seven-minute improvisation for double jazz quartet, was to shape the decade's music.

Response to Ornette and his white plastic sax was mixed. Supporters like Hentoff, Schuller, and LEONARD BERNSTEIN were delighted with Coleman's jolting style. Detractors, many of them practicing jazz musicians, criticized his violations of conventions and his lack of formal training.

In 1962 Ornette Coleman retired to teach himself trumpet and violin. When he returned, his performances were just as controversial. Trumpeter MILES DAVIS and bassist Charles Mingus deplored the free-form group sounds produced by Coleman's quartet. By the early 1970s Coleman, revitalized by a visit to Morocco, began to experiment with the sounds of rock, funk, and fusion (see MILES DAVIS).

In 1981 Coleman founded Prime Time, an electric band, and has since been honored with a weeklong festival in Hartford, Connecticut, where his chamber works were performed. A 1991 Carnegie Hall concert review by Jon Pareles chides Coleman for the sound and its sometimes incongruous effect. The piano, once banished from the ensemble to free the group from chords, had been not so successfully reintroduced.

Coleman, who was awarded Guggenheim Fellowships for composition in 1967 and 1974, once told Nat Hentoff, "What I'm trying to do is make my playing as free as I can . . . if you put a conventional note under my note, you limit the number of choices I have for my next note. If you do not, my melody may move freely in a far greater choice of directions."

BIBLIOGRAPHY

Harrison, M., *A Jazz Retrospect,* 1976; Williams, M., *Jazz Masters in Transition, 1957–1969,* 1970.

Coltrane, John William

(September 23, 1926–July 17, 1967)
Jazz Musician

John Coltrane's astonishing technical mastery, spiritual tone, and lengthy improvisations left a mark on music and on admiring musicians. Inspired by multicultural sources from Indian sitar to African drums, Coltrane stretched the boundaries of jazz and enriched its vocabulary. He also reestablished the soprano saxophone as a major jazz instrument.

Born in Hamlet, North Carolina, John William Coltrane, an only child, grew up in a religious household; both grandfathers were ministers. Early on he moved with his parents to High Point, 100 miles away,

Shaw Artists Corporation; Courtesy of the New York World and Telegram and Sun Collection at the Library of Congress

to live with his maternal grandparents. Coltrane's mother sang and played piano. His father, J. R., ran a dry-cleaning and tailoring shop and played the violin and ukelele. He died when Coltrane was twelve. In 1940 his family moved to Atlantic City, New Jersey, moving three years later to Philadelphia, Pennsylvania.

Coltrane played clarinet and alto sax in a community band led by the Reverend Warren Steele and graduated from William Penn High School in Philadelphia in 1943. He entered the Ornstein School of Music in Philadelphia to study performance and composition. While there he learned alto sax technique from Mike Guerra and the theories of bitonality and scale-based improvisation from Dennis Sandole.

After a year as clarinetist in a navy band, Coltrane returned to Philadelphia from Hawaii in 1946. He continued his studies with Guerra, played alto sax with Joe Webb and King Kolax

bands, and listened well to cornetist DIZZY GILLESPIE and alto sax virtuoso CHARLIE PARKER.

In 1947 Coltrane took up the tenor saxophone to join Eddie ("Cleanhead") Vinson, an alto saxophonist, and played whichever instrument the occasion demanded. He performed rhythm and blues with Jimmy Heath, Howard McGhee, Earl Bostic, and Dizzy Gillespie and made his first recording with Gillespie in 1949. The next years show Coltrane alternating between homebase Philadelphia and touring.

During 1953 and 1954 Coltrane played with a septet led by alto sax player Johnny Hodges. By now committed to the tenor sax, Coltrane was developing his own individual style. In 1955 he was invited to play with the MILES DAVIS quintet. Though critics disliked his "harsh tone" and fragmented phrasing, Coltrane nonetheless played with restless energy as he explored rhythmic and harmonic possibilities. In late 1956 he interrupted his career to break his destructive habits of heroin and alcohol. He mastered his addictions by the spring of 1957 and that year was hired by THELONIOUS MONK. A year of rededication to music was intensified by a spiritual awakening that sprang from his battle with drugs. The album *A Love Supreme* documents the experience.

Coltrane's tenure with the Monk quartet was short and fraught with contractual difficulties. He returned to play with Miles Davis and with other small groups that included

Cannonball Adderley, Bill Evans, and Philly Joe Jones. In 1960 he purchased a soprano saxophone. His hard-earned technique displayed a growing knowledge of harmony and an expanding style of improvisation. Critic Ira Gitler suggests that Coltrane's solos were "sheets of sound," the results of efforts to produce "continuous music" while creating harmonic improvisations. This new direction was inspired in part by music for harp.

By his mid-thirties Coltrane was the leading tenor saxophonist. In 1960 Coltrane established his own avant-garde quartet with pianist McCoy Tyner, drummer Elvin Jones, and bass Jimmy Garrison. Financial and artistic success and tours of Europe did not keep Coltrane from continuing his search for new sounds. The quartet's first record, *My Favorite Things*, with Coltrane on soprano sax, reveals his per-

sistent explorations of chromatic lines set against modal backdrops (see MILES DAVIS).

Coltrane's experiments with sound attracted large audiences, though they did not always please his sidemen. Some moved on. New additions to the group included his second wife, Alice (piano), and a number of drummers who adapted complex African rhythms. Coltrane died in New York in 1967 leaving a legacy of avant-garde jazz, a reputation as a virtuoso instrumentalist, and disciples who had benefited from his generous spirit.

BIBLIOGRAPHY

Simpkins, C. O., *Coltrane*, 1975; Thomas, J. C., *Chasing the Trane: The Music and Mystique of John Coltrane*, 1975.

Cooper, Gary

(May 7, 1901–May 13, 1961)
Actor

Gary Cooper embodied the mythic qualities of the American folk hero. Combining shyness and inner strength, he defined a quiet masculinity in a variety of roles. "Coop," as he was known, expressed more with a "yup" or a "nope" than many actors could with lines of dialogue.

A leading actor for thirty years, Cooper was born Frank James Cooper and raised on a ranch in Montana, where he became the expert horseman evidenced in his westerns. His parents being English, he attended grammar school for three years in Bedfordshire, England. Returning to America in the early 1920s, he attended Grinnell College but never graduated. An aspiring cartoonist, he sought work in Chicago, but without success.

In Hollywood he worked as a stuntman and an extra in B westerns until producer SAMUEL GOLDWYN cast him in *The Winning of Barbara*

Worth in 1926. An actress suggested he change his name to Gary. Under contract to Paramount Pictures, he appeared in twenty films over the next four years, including *It* (1927) with infamous "flapper" Clara Bow, and the classic western *The Virginian* (1929), which drew greater attention to him.

He played a foreign legionnaire in *Morocco* (1930) opposite MARLENE DIETRICH, a sophisticated gent in *Design for Living* (1933), and an adventurous hero in *The Lives of a Bengal Lancer* (1935), but these were less memorable than the films he made with directors FRANK CAPRA and HOWARD HAWKS. Capra's *Mr. Deeds Goes to Town* (1936) and *Meet John Doe* (1941) were perfect vehicles for Cooper's natural persona. In both he played a homespun American everyman exploited by politicians and opportunists. Capra remarked that "every line in his face spell[ed] honesty." In

Hawks's *Sergeant York* (1941) as the pacifist Tennessee farm boy who became a hero in World War I, Cooper won both the New York Film Critics' Circle Award and his first Oscar for Best Actor.

His unforced acting style prompted ERNEST HEMINGWAY, his hunting partner for twenty years, to say, "If you made up a character like Coop's, nobody would believe it. He's just too good to be true." His performance as ballplayer Lou Gehrig in *Pride of the Yankees* (1942) reinforced the impression.

In *The Fountainhead* (1949) he played an idealistic architect modeled on FRANK LLOYD WRIGHT. During production Cooper had a much publicized affair with costar Patricia Neal, which almost broke up his marriage to Veronica Balfe, whom he had married in 1933.

His career was sliding in the early 1950s when he played the town sheriff besieged by outlaws in the low-budget western *High Noon* (1952), costarring newcomer Grace Kelly. His performance won him his second Oscar and etched his pained and rugged face into the minds of filmgoers. *Springfield Rifle* (1952) and *Man of the West* (1958) brought his commanding presence as a western hero full circle.

Shortly before his death, he was made an officer in the Order of Arts and Letters by the French government, one of many international tributes he received.

BIBLIOGRAPHY

Dickens, Homer, *The Complete Films of Gary Cooper*, 1991; Kaminsky, Stuart, *Coop: The Life and Legend of Gary Cooper*, 1980; Swindell, Larry, *The Last Hero*, 1980.

Cooper, James Fenimore

(September 15, 1789–September 14, 1851)
Novelist, Social Critic

James Fenimore Cooper, author of the Leatherstocking tales of the early frontier, was the first writer to capture the popular imagination with myths rooted in America's own history. He wrote romances whose heroes embodied the ideals—courage, integrity, love of the wilderness—of a nation destined to expand and prosper.

Cooper was born in Burlington, New Jersey. When he was a year old, his father, Judge William Cooper, founded the frontier settlement at Cooperstown, New York, and there Cooper grew up on a manorial estate on Otsego Lake. Judge Cooper was a successful entrepreneur and prominent Federalist politician who served two terms in the U.S. House of Representatives. His son seemed doubtful about how to rival his father's achievements. After a dangerous prank got him expelled from Yale University in 1805, he prepared for a naval career, first as a merchant seaman and then as a midshipman in the navy in 1808.

His father's death and a promise to his fiancée, Susan De Lancey, prompted Cooper to leave the navy in 1811. His expectation that he could support his new wife comfortably on his inheritance, however, was dashed by a host of legal claims against his father's estate, and Cooper found himself financially dependent on the De Lanceys, a condition he felt was intolerable. His decision to attempt a novel—apparently after Susan challenged him to make good on a boast he could write a better book than one he had been reading—changed his circumstances, making him financially independent and bringing him fame.

Cooper's first book, *Precaution* (1820), a courtship novel, was published anonymously.

Though it won favorable reviews in the United States and abroad, it was not nearly so successful as Cooper's second novel, *The Spy: A Tale of the Neutral Ground* (1821). In *The Spy,* Cooper adopted what was to become his characteristic voice: strongly masculine and emphatically American. Set in the days of the revolutionary war, it was a romance after the fashion of the British writer Sir Walter Scott, featuring larger-than-life characters and events drawn together in such a way as to typify a period in history. *The Spy* answered a demand for historical romance rooted in America's own past; its fantastic success launched Cooper's career as a writer.

Cooper moved from rural Scarsdale, New York, to New York City and quickly achieved a series of literary successes. Between 1823 and 1827, he published three of the five books in his famous Leatherstocking series of frontier novels—*The Pioneers* (1823), *The Last of the Mohicans* (1826), and *The Prairie* (1827)—as well as the two novels that established the genre of the modern sea novel, *The Pilot* (1823) and *The Red Rover* (1827).

Although they were not written chronologically, the Leatherstocking tales related the life story of the wilderness scout and trapper Natty Bumppo—also known as Leatherstocking, Hawkeye, Pathfinder, and Deerslayer—an illiterate but a man of extraordinary courage, integrity, and skill. The books constitute an American epic, relating the story of the exploration of the frontier in terms of human heroism, a majestic landscape, and a sense of national destiny. They also depict the environmental degradation that is the consequence of the expansion of white civilization. Like the American Indians he helps supplant, Bumppo finds his God in the wilderness; while Bumppo sees the progress of white civilization as inevitable, the novel suggests that the future will be best served by a democracy whose leaders respect the land and its resources.

The grandeur of the high seas figured prominently in Cooper's maritime fiction, and, like Natty Bumppo, successful sailors found their God in nature. *The Pilot* and *The Red Rover* are romances; later sea novels, such as *The Wing-and-Wing* (1842) and *The Oak Openings* (1848), ranged to explorations of serious moral dilemmas and affirmations of deep religious faith.

In 1826 Cooper traveled with his family to Europe intending to learn more about its culture and society. The Coopers ended by staying seven years, based in Paris, at the behest of Cooper's friend, the Marquis de Lafayette, the French statesman who had helped fight the American Revolution. At Lafayette's urging, Cooper wrote a laudatory description of the American democratic experiment, *Notions of the Americans* (1828). He also began a series of novels rooted in European history, such as *The Bravo* (1831), which explored the failings of aristocratic forms of government.

Cooper returned to the United States in 1833 and to Cooperstown a year later. His popularity had waned with critics who felt he had become a European aristocrat and wished he would return to writing American adventure stories. Instead, Cooper devoted himself to five volumes based on his European travels, published between 1836 and 1838, and a *History of the Navy of the United States of America* (1839).

Dedicated as he was to the ideals of a democracy, Cooper had been born into an American ruling class. He came to suspect that democrats advocating a classless society were themselves motivated by economic incentives that belied their rhetoric. In a succession of treatises and novels, he began to point out what he regarded as the excesses of American democracy and to defend the rights of individuals and the right to property. Two noteworthy books were *The American Democrat* (1838), a tract on American institutions and political ideals, and *Home as Found* (1838), a satiric novel.

Cooper completed his Leatherstocking series with *The Pathfinder* (1840) and *The Deerslayer* (1841). He then began three novels—*Satanstoe* (1845), *The Chainbearer* (1845), and *The Redskins* (1846)—chronicling the rise of the Littlepage family and their struggles to protect their property against Indians and squatters.

Cooper's final novel, *The Ways of the Hour* (1850), concerned a murder trial. He died in Cooperstown, one day short of his sixty-second birthday.

BIBLIOGRAPHY

Dekker, George, *James Fenimore Cooper the Novelist*, 1967; Railton, Stephen, *James Fenimore Cooper: A Study of His Life and Imagination*, 1978.

Copland, Aaron

(November 14, 1900–December 2, 1990)
Composer

In replacing old conventions with a startling new musical language, composer Aaron Copland changed the course of twentieth-century American music. His complex rhythms and surprising, often dissonant harmonies created a new style that everybody could recognize as American.

The fifth child of Polish and Lithuanian parents, Copland was born in Brooklyn, New York. His early musical interest led to progressively more advanced work, and, after graduation from Boys' High School in 1918, he studied harmony, counterpoint, and sonata form with the conservative Rubin Goldmark.

National Archives

In 1920 he went to Paris. "It was where the action seemed to be," he recalled in 1985. "[IGOR] STRAVINSKY was living there, and the whole new 'group of six' with Milhaud and Poulenc." In Paris, Copland met Nadia Boulanger, organist, conductor, teacher of composition, and a founder of a school of music for Americans at Fontainebleau. Boulanger trained and inspired generations of American musicians. Aaron Copland, the first to enroll at the new institution, studied with her until 1924.

Boulanger led students away from traditional nineteenth-century forms and encouraged experiments in harmony, rhythm, structure, and diction. Copland later described those years as the most important musical experience of his life. Among the distinguished Americans that followed him to Fontainebleau were Virgil Thomson, ROGER SESSIONS, Roy Harris, Walter Piston, and PHILIP GLASS.

Copland returned to New York with an important commission from Nadia Boulanger to write a concerto for organ for her American appearances. The Symphony for Organ and Orchestra was performed in 1925 by the New York Symphony under Walter Damrosch.

Copland was eager to write an "American" work. "I had experimented a little with the rhythms of popular music in several earlier compositions, but now I wanted frankly to adopt the jazz idiom and see what I could do with it in a symphonic way." The results were

Music for Theatre (1925) and Concerto for Piano and Orchestra, which he performed with the Boston Symphony Orchestra under SERGE KOUSSEVITSKY in 1927, a performance that annoyed conservative critics and enraged some members of the audience.

A 1929 work, the *Symphonic Ode* embodied the characteristics of Copland's early compositions: stylized rhythms, dissonance, and a certain grandness. He turned next to a more austere, complex style in the *Piano Variations* (1930) and the *Short Symphony* (1933). "During the mid-30's," Copland noted, "I began to feel an increasing dissatisfaction with the relations of the music-loving public and the living composer. . . . It seemed to me that we composers were in danger of working in a vacuum. . . . I felt that it was worth the effort to see if I couldn't say what I had to say in the simplest possible terms."

In the thirties and forties, then, Copland turned to folk music for ideas, to cowboy songs, and New England and Quaker hymns. What emerged were ballet scores that employed striking, spontaneous rhythms and transparent and deliberately simple orchestral textures to evoke a nostalgia for rural America: *Billy the Kid* (1938); *Rodeo* (1942) for AGNES DE MILLE; and *Appalachian Spring* (1944) for MARTHA GRAHAM, which won a Pulitzer Prize. Patriotic works of the World War II years, *Lincoln Portrait* and *Letter from Home,* gained public acceptance but were never as popular as the ballets. In the 1940s scores for such films as *Our Town* (based on the play by THORNTON WILDER), *The Red Pony* (based on the short story by JOHN STEINBECK), and *The Heiress* (based on the novel *Washington Square* by HENRY JAMES) brought Copland's music to an even wider public. The score for *The Heiress* earned an Academy Award. Other compositions included Concerto for Clarinet and String Orchestra (1948), commissioned by BENNY GOODMAN, and the Third Symphony (1946), an expansive, personal, and very American work.

In the fifties and sixties Copland offended his audiences again by experimenting with ARNOLD SCHOENBERG's now out-of-fashion twelve-tone techniques. Late works like *Connotations* (1962) and *Inscape* (1967) were more complex, less accessible, and slow to win public acceptance.

For Copland, synthesis was at the heart of his always finely crafted work. He gave early expression to this concern in the 1930s when he said, "I occasionally had the strange sensation of being divided in half—the austere, intellectual modernist on the one side, the accessible popular composer on the other."

There is no question about Copland's importance as an enthusiastic supporter of new American music. From the twenties onward he worked to promote American composers and their work. With Roger Sessions he founded the Copland-Sessions Concerts in New York (1928–1931). President of the American Composers Alliance from 1937 to 1945, he also served as a member of the executive board of directors of the League of Composers. From 1940 until he retired in 1965, he was a leading faculty member of the Berkshire Music Center in Tanglewood and helped make it a center for contemporary music. In 1932 he directed the first festival of contemporary music at Yaddo, the artists' colony in Saratoga Springs, New York.

In his tireless efforts to promote new music, Copland wrote articles and books and lectured throughout the world. He taught at Harvard in 1935 and 1944, and returned in 1951, the first American composer to deliver the Norton Lectures there. Prior to his death in 1990, he received many honors in addition to the Pulitzer Prize and the Academy Award, among them, the New York Music Critics' Circle Award, the Gold Medal of the National Institute of Arts and Letters, the Presidential Medal of Freedom, the Howland Prize of Yale University, and honorary degrees from Princeton, Oberlin, Harvard, and other institutions.

BIBLIOGRAPHY

Smith, J. F., *Aaron Copland, His Work and Contribution to American Music,* 1955.

Copley, John Singleton

(ca. July 26, 1738–September 9, 1815)
Painter

John Singleton Copley, the greatest of America's colonial artists, had a successful career in this country as a portrait painter and, later, in England as both a history painter and a portraitist.

He was born in Boston, Massachusetts, where his stepfather, Peter Pelham, a portrait painter and engraver as well as dancing teacher, taught him the basics of art. A precocious pupil, Copley had mastered engraving by the time he was fifteen and was soon making careful, accurate anatomical drawings.

Before he was twenty, Copley was a successful portrait painter with plenty of commissions. He painted realistic, brilliantly colored pictures that revealed the character of each sitter. His clients included prominent businessmen and their wives and Bostonians who would become leaders of the American Revolution. He painted Paul Revere, a silversmith, with one of his silver teapots in his hand, as well as Samuel Adams and John Hancock, both delegates to the Continental Congress and signers of the American Declaration of Independence.

Copley married a rich woman, Sussannah Farnum Clarke, and built a house on Beacon Hill. His wife and her family were loyal to the Crown, while Copley sympathized with the people who were working for American independence.

In 1766 he sent a painting, *The Boy with the Squirrel,* which showed his half-brother Henry Pelham at a table playing with a baby squirrel, to BENJAMIN WEST, an American painter living in England. Although he had some constructive criticism, West admired the picture and got it into the exhibition of the Society of Artists of Great Britain. The painting made Copley famous in England and won him election as a Fellow of the Society of Artists. Over the years, West wrote to Copley, advising him to visit Europe to study for three or four years.

Copley would have liked nothing better. He complained to West that in America there were no examples of art from which he could learn, except for a few indifferently executed prints. But since the death of his stepfather, his mother and younger stepbrother depended on him for support and he hated to give up the excellent income he was making from his painting, unless he could be assured of making money in England.

In 1771 Copley spent a few months in New York, where he set up a studio in a house on Broadway and painted thirty-seven portraits. Life in Boston was becoming perilous for Loyalists. The tea that spurred the Boston Tea Party had been consigned to Copley's father-in-law. It was a good time to leave. Copley sailed from Boston for England in June 1774, leaving his wife and children in the care of Henry Pelham.

In England, Copley met Sir Joshua Reynolds, the most important painter in England at that time, and visited the Royal Academy, which was founded to provide classes in art and to stage annual exhibitions of painting and sculpture. Copley was interested to note that "the Students had a naked model from which they were Drawing." By September, Copley was in Paris, looking at pictures and sculptures. He traveled throughout Italy to study art and antiquities and returned to London by way of Germany, the Netherlands, and Belgium. He had been anxious for his wife and children to leave Boston because they would be considered enemies of the country, and he was relieved to greet them in London on his return.

The Copleys settled in a house on Hanover Square and lived there the rest of their lives. His reputation had preceded him to England and he had no trouble making a living as an artist. He continued to paint portraits, which were more elaborate and artificial than his

American work. Copley wanted badly to be known as a painter of historical events as well as a portraitist. In 1778 he painted *Watson and the Shark*, which illustrates a story told him by Brook Watson, a London businessman who commissioned the picture. In his youth Watson had lost a leg to a shark while he was swimming in Havana harbor, and Copley showed him being pulled from the water by a group of men in a rowboat. There are at least two versions of this dramatic picture. Engravings of it were immensely popular and, in fact, still are.

Copley painted other history pictures, including *The Death of the Earl of Chatham in the House of Lords* (1779–1781), which showed the fifty-five lords who had been present when the earl, who had been William Pitt, died; *The Death of Major Peirson* (1782–1784); and *The Siege of Gibraltar* (1785–1791). His history paintings sold well, partly because Copley did careful research to make every detail accurate. However, critics do not consider them as powerful as his portraits or his *Watson and the Shark*.

Copley worked very hard, usually from early morning until twilight. He tired of life as an exile but could not go back to America because of the press of work. He remained loyal to the revolutionaries in America, and when King George III acknowledged that the colonies were independent, Copley painted a U.S. flag in the background of his portrait of Elkanah Watson, an American privateer. He painted portraits of John Adams and John Quincy Adams when they visited England.

In the last years of his life, Copley was depressed and often unable to paint. He quarreled with many of his friends and died deeply in debt. His son, a brilliant lawyer and later Lord Chancellor of England, was made Lord Lyndhurst.

BIBLIOGRAPHY

Flexner, James Thomas, *America's Old Masters*, rev., 1980; Morgan, John Hill, *John Singleton Copley*, 1939.

Cornell, Katharine

(February 16, 1893–June 9, 1974)
Actress

Katharine Cornell, one of the greatest actresses of the American stage, typified the romantic school of acting. She starred in a wide range of roles, including Elizabeth Barrett Browning, Candida, Juliet, and Joan of Arc.

Cornell was born in Berlin, Germany, in 1893 while her father was studying to be a physician. After the family returned to a prosperous home in Buffalo, New York, she grew up absorbed in her two great passions, sports (she was a champion amateur swimmer and tennis player) and acting (her father abandoned med-

icine when she was eight to manage a local theater). It was not until her mid-teens, however, when she saw Maud Adams in *Peter Pan* at her father's theater, that she decided the stage would be her life. Cornell, who had always thought herself odd looking and ill-proportioned—the distinctive, widely set eyes, the large, irregular mouth, and the strong shoulders—began her apprenticeship with the Jessie Bonstelle stock company, where she voraciously absorbed everything she could.

Kit, as her friends called her, made her Broadway debut in 1921 in Rachel Crothers's

Nice People, which costarred Tallulah Bankhead. Soon after her marriage to director Guthrie McClintic, Cornell launched on a series of memorable roles that made her reputation—as Sydney Fairfield, the daughter of a mentally disturbed father in *A Bill of Divorcement* (1921); Laura Pennington, a homely woman in *The Enchanted Cottage* (1923); Candida, the wise married woman faced with a romantic entanglement in the George Bernard Shaw play of that name (1924); Iris March, the notorious free-lover in *The Green Hat* (1925); and Elizabeth Barrett Browning, the invalid poet in *The Barretts of Wimpole Street* (1931).

Although Cornell initially disliked the role of Elizabeth Barrett, it had autobiographical significance in that its depiction of the stifling relationship between the poet and her overly possessive father paralleled Cornell's own insecure childhood. It also became her greatest success, running to capacity audiences at the Empire Theatre for a record 372 performances, and continuing after 1932 for several cross-country tours.

Hollywood beckoned, but she refused many lucrative offers; indeed, she never made a motion picture. Instead, the movie roles of Sydney Fairfield and Elizabeth Barrett, went to, respectively, KATHARINE HEPBURN and Norma Shearer.

Cornell spent the World War II years touring for the soldiers, reviving (against the advice of government officials who believed her legitimate roles would be above the audiences' taste) her roles of Candida and Elizabeth Barrett. Winning over the tough GIs elicited Cornell's memorable remark, "We must never forget this, never; we've seen an audience born."

When Cornell appeared with a young MARLON BRANDO in a revival of *Candida* in 1946, the event marked the confluence of two acting styles, her romantic gesture as opposed to his "psychological realism." She continued an active career, including *The Dark Is Light Enough* (1955) and, in her last appearances, Mrs. Patrick Campbell in *Dear Liar* (1960). She died of pneumonia in 1974. To the end, said Christopher Plummer, who costarred with her in *The Dark Is Light Enough*, Cornell "gave the theater the romantic quality it should have—the dream of it was alive in her hands—the religion of it."

BIBLIOGRAPHY

Cornell, Katharine, *I Wanted to Be an Actress*, 1939;
Mosel, Tad, *Leading Lady*, 1978.

Cram, Ralph Adams

(December 16, 1863–September 22, 1942)
Architect

Architect Ralph Adams Cram is best known for his Gothic Revival buildings at the U.S. Military Academy and Princeton University and for the Cathedral of St. John the Divine in New York City.

Cram was born in Hampton Falls, New Hampshire. For his fifteenth birthday, his parents gave him a book on house building by the British architect Charles J. Richardson. Inspired by this book, the young Cram built models of houses and cities. When there was no money for his college education after he graduated from high school, he began as an apprentice to the architects Arthur Rotch and

George T. Tilden in Boston in 1881. In 1886 he won $500 in a competition for the design of the Suffolk County Court House, Massachusetts, and used the money for a trip to Europe in 1886, visiting Germany, France, Italy, and England.

Back in Boston, he tried various kinds of work, including a short time as art critic for the *Transcript,* a Boston newspaper. Cram returned to architecture and won $1,300 for second prize in a competition for an addition to the Massachusetts State House. He and Charles Francis Wentworth formed an architectural partnership in 1890 and soon began to specialize in the design of churches.

A Christmas Eve midnight mass in the church of San Luigi dei Francesi in Rome had a profound effect on Cram, and he had been looking for a spiritual home for himself. His father had been a Unitarian minister, but Cram detested the Reformation and the Renaissance and most of what had happened to the Roman Catholic church since the Council of Trent in the sixteenth century. He found what he wanted in the Anglo-Catholic wing of the Episcopal church, and was baptized and confirmed in Boston. He regarded pre-Reformation England as an ideal society as far as architecture, religion, and social life were concerned, and he believed that Gothic architecture had been the "perfect expression of Northern and Western Christianity for five centuries." Although the Gothic had been rudely cut off by the Renaissance and the Reformation, he believed it could be developed further in modern times.

Cram took on twenty-one-year-old BERTRAM GOODHUE as head draftsman in 1890, and in 1895 the firm became Cram, Wentworth & Goodhue. Goodhue worked with Cram on Gothic Revival designs for All Saints' Church, Ashmont (1892–1913), in the Boston suburb of Dorchester; on the Euclid Avenue Presbyterian Church (now Church of the Covenant) (1907–1941) in Cleveland; Calvary Church (1905–1928) in Pittsburgh, and on several other Episcopal churches.

Cram claimed later that he could visualize any architectural project in three dimensions and could draft plans at quarter-scale, but that he depended on Goodhue to work out the decorative details, which were sometimes very inventive and abstract.

The firm, which had become Cram, Goodhue & Ferguson in 1898, won the competition for revamping the U.S. Military Academy at West Point, New York, in 1903. Goodhue took responsibility for designing the chapel and two of the cadet barracks, while Cram did the post headquarters, riding hall, and power plant. They worked together on the other buildings, all in the Collegiate Gothic made by the Late Gothic Revival.

Goodhue and Cram drifted apart—St. Thomas Church (1906–1914) on Fifth Avenue in New York was the last project on which they collaborated. Cram was appointed supervising architect of Princeton University in 1907, and his firm designed the Graduate College (1911–1913), the chapel (1925–1928), and one other dormitory, Campbell Hall (1907–1909).

While Cram is best known for his work in the Gothic style, he said that he "tried in every case to fit each building to its tradition, purpose, and geographic place." When Rice Institute (now Rice University) in 1910 commissioned Cram to design its new campus in Houston, Texas, he turned from Gothic to a Mediterranean style that included Italian and Byzantine features with rich colors of brick, marble, and tiles. He designed neo-Georgian buildings for Wheaton, Williams, and Sweet Briar colleges and for Phillips Exeter Academy.

He also designed the chapel at St. George's School (1920–1928) in Newport, Rhode Island. But his largest ecclesiastical project was the Cathedral of St. John the Divine in New York City. He received the commission in 1912, when the cathedral authorities decided they wanted a Gothic structure instead of the Romanesque building begun twenty years earlier and far from finished. Although the nave was completed in Cram's lifetime, the huge building is still under construction.

By the 1930s, Cram was considered the dean of American traditional architects. He taught architecture at the Massachusetts Institute of Technology and wrote several books that offered Gothic and Christian solutions to the world's problems. He died in Boston of pneumonia at the age of seventy-eight.

BIBLIOGRAPHY

Cram, Ralph Adams, *My Life in Architecture*, 1936; Daniel, Ann Miner, *The Early Architecture of Ralph Adams Cram*, 1978; Doumato, Lania, *Ralph Adams Cram*, 1978; Muccigrosso, Robert, *American Gothic: The Mind of Ralph Adams Cram*, 1980; Tucci, Douglass Shand, *Ralph Adams Cram: American Medievalist*, 1975.

Crane, Harold Hart

(July 21, 1899–April 27, 1932)
Poet

During a career that spanned less than a decade, Hart Crane wrote poetry that celebrated America's urban, industrial culture. His best-known poem, *The Bridge* (1930), casts the Brooklyn Bridge as a symbol of human achievement, unifying beauty and functionality.

Born in Garrettsville, Ohio, Crane began writing poetry at the age of thirteen. The son of a wealthy but dictatorial candy manufacturer and of a doting, neurotic mother, he had a troubled adolescence. In 1916 his parents separated, and he dropped out of Cleveland's East High School. He traveled to New York City to write and to prepare himself for college, though he never attended. An avid reader, Crane educated himself through the works of such writers as Christopher Marlowe, EDGAR ALLAN POE, WALT WHITMAN, Fyodor Dostoyevski, T. S. ELIOT, and CARL SANDBURG.

To support himself, Crane held a succession of jobs in Cleveland, Akron, and New York, as a worker in a munitions plant, a reporter for the Cleveland *Plain Dealer,* advertising manager at the *Little Review,* and an advertising copywriter and salesman. Meanwhile, his poems began to appear in the *Little Review, Poetry,* and *The Dial.*

Crane's first collection of poems, *White Buildings,* appeared in 1926. Many of the poems address the theme of the artist's isolation from the society he loves. "The Wine Menagerie," one of his most ambitious, is set in an urban bar, and its subject is the visionary dream world of the poet. The six-poem series called "Voyages" reflects Crane's profound love of the sea. He imagines himself united with a lover, a merchant seaman, crossing a seascape. Inevitably, the sea and the lover merge in the poet's mind.

In the three-poem suite called "For the Marriage of Faustus and Helen," Crane invokes Marlowe. The poems strive to unify American technology and traditional notions of beauty. Helen is evoked variously in images of a cityscape, in the playing of a jazz band in a skyscraper, and through the eyes of a pilot. Crane described "For the Marriage of Faustus and Helen" as an answer to the cultural pessimism of T. S. Eliot. Faustus is bidden to enjoy Helen's beauty; the poet's perceptions should be fired by emotion rather than intellect.

After his father refused him financial assistance, Crane applied for and received the generous support of Otto Kahn, financier and patron of the arts, in order to devote himself to writing *The Bridge* (1930). First conceived in 1923 as "a mystical synthesis of America," it took almost seven years to complete. *The Bridge* takes its shape from Eliot's *Waste*

Land, which Crane judged as "good, of course, but so damn dead." Crane intended his 1,200-line poem to answer his predecessor's pessimistic view of the modern city. The protagonist awakes, strolls across the Brooklyn Bridge into Manhattan, roams the streets of the city, and returns home at night via the subway. Such historical and literary figures as Christopher Columbus, Pocahontas, Walt Whitman, Edgar Allan Poe, and EMILY DICKINSON, all regarded as "bridges," appear as Crane attempts to weave together "the Myth of America." He took on a formidable task, and so does the reader, but like Eliot, EZRA POUND, and James Joyce, he believed in the mythic or symbolic qualities in literary subjects and the poet's skill in fusing disparate images into a historical unity.

In 1931 Crane traveled to Mexico on a Guggenheim Fellowship, intending to write a long poem on Montezuma and the Spanish conquest. His efforts were fruitless, though he did compose some shorter poems, including a brilliant lyric entitled "The Broken Tower." He became friends there with the American writer KATHERINE ANNE PORTER and the Mexican painter David Siqueiros and grew increasingly despondent and totally unable to control his addiction to alcohol. During the return voyage to the United States in April 1932, Crane committed suicide by leaping from the stern of the ship into the sea.

In 1933, less than a year after Crane's death, Waldo Frank edited *The Collected Poems of Hart Crane,* in which half of the poems appeared for the first time. Arguments over the quality of these verses and the causes of the poet's suicide have been and will be endless.

BIBLIOGRAPHY

Clark, David R., *Critical Essays on Crane,* 1982; Quinn, Vincent, *Hart Crane,* 1963; Spears, Monroe K., *Hart Crane,* 1965; Unterecker, John, *Voyager: A Life of Hart Crane,* 1969.

Crane, Stephen Townley

(November 1, 1871–June 5, 1900)
Novelist, Poet, Short-Story Writer, War Correspondent

During his brief career, Stephen Crane, author of *The Red Badge of Courage,* wrote novels and stories that explored the minds of men struggling against destructive forces in themselves or in other men. His work particularly influenced the development of the war novel in American literature.

Born in Newark, New Jersey, Crane was descended from clergy on both sides. His father, the Reverend Jonathan Townley Crane, served as presiding elder of Methodist churches around Newark. His mother, Mary Peck Crane, was a public speaker on religious and reform issues. The family tradition of civic activism dated to the American Revolution. An ances- tor, Stephen Crane, had served as president of the Colonial Assemblies.

Crane was the youngest of fourteen children, five of whom died in early childhood. After Crane's father died in 1880, the family lived, under difficult financial circumstances, in Port Jervis, New York, and Asbury Park, New Jersey. At age sixteen, Crane began to contribute to a column written by his brother Townley in the *New York Tribune.* He attended two boarding schools before enrolling first at Lafayette College and then at Syracuse University, but he seemed more interested in playing baseball than in studying and never earned a degree.

During his single semester at Syracuse in 1891, Crane began drafting *Maggie: A Girl of the Streets*. Published in 1893, at his own expense and under the pseudonym Johnston Smith while Crane was working as a journalist in New York City, the novel became known for its naturalistic rendering of life in the Bowery. Maggie Johnson is a child of the tenements. Victimized by everyone around her, from the drunken mother who abuses her, to her lover, Pete, who abandons her, to the minister who shrinks from her pleas for help, Maggie is foredoomed to failure. In desperation she turns prostitute and finally drowns herself in the East River.

Crane was only twenty-one when he began writing *The Red Badge of Courage* (1895), regarded by many as the finest Civil War novel ever written. The story, written before Crane had ever witnessed armed conflict, relates the experience of Henry Fleming, a young Union soldier who overcomes the panic he experiences when he first sees battle by leading his regiment in a charge on the second day. Crane called the book "a study of fear"; it considers the basis in instinct of both courage and cowardice. War became Crane's metaphor for existence, and he would return to the subject both as a war correspondent and as a novelist.

At twenty-three, Crane wrote the verses that appeared in *The Black Riders* (1895). Its spare lyrics prefigured the work of the Imagists, who favored the use of clear, concise images and free verse. A second volume of poetry, *War Is Kind* (1899), included a typical Crane parable poem:

Library of Congress

A man said to the universe:
"Sir, I exist!"
"However," replied the universe,
"The fact has not created in me
A sense of obligation."

With the instant success of *The Red Badge of Courage* upon its publication in 1895, Crane talked the Bacheller and Johnson newspaper syndicate into sponsoring a trip to the American West and Mexico. The trip furnished the material for such tales as "Horses—One Dash," "The Bride Comes to Yellow Sky," and "The Blue Hotel," all written later and published between 1896 and 1898.

In 1896 Crane republished *Maggie* under his own name and issued a collection of short stories, *The Little Regiment and Other Episodes of the American Civil War*. The six stories consistently contrast veterans with those uninitiated in the realities of war. Crane wrote admiringly of veterans for their cool nerve and dependability in the heat of battle, as well as for their cynicism.

His newspaper syndicate sent Crane to Jacksonville, Florida, to cover a private military expedition to Cuba. He was shipwrecked aboard the *Commodore* on New Year's Day 1897. Crane imaginatively recreated the experience in his story "The Open Boat," regarded as one of his finest. The story became the title piece for *The Open Boat and Other Tales of Adventure* (1898).

While in Jacksonville, Crane fell in love with Cora Taylor, who ran a brothel, the Hotel de Dream. Cora accompanied him to Greece, where he worked as a war correspondent for the New York *Journal*. She became the first woman war correspondent, writing under the name Imogene Carter.

When the war between Greece and Turkey ended, the pair went to London and then, in July 1897, rented a house in Surrey. In April 1898 Crane left for Cuba to report on the Spanish-American War, writing first for the New York *World* and later for the New York *Journal*. When the war ended in August, Crane stayed on to write the first draft of *Active Service*, a novel about the Greek war, which he revised and published upon his return to England early in 1899.

He and Cora settled in a Sussex manor house called Brede Place and began entertaining a string of guests in grand fashion. Near bankruptcy, Crane tried to write his way out of debt, but he succeeded only in ruining his health. He died of tuberculosis during a trip to Germany in June 1900, at the age of twenty-eight.

Published posthumously were *Whilomville Stories* (1900), a collection of tales of childhood; *Wounds in the Rain* (1900), journalistic sketches and short stories; and *Last Words* (1902), a miscellany. Crane left an unfinished novel, *The O'Ruddy*, which was completed by Robert Barr and published in 1903.

BIBLIOGRAPHY

Berryman, John, *Stephen Crane*, 1950; Colvert, James B., *Stephen Crane*, 1984; Stallman, R. W., *Stephen Crane: A Biography*, 1968.

Crumb, George Henry

(October 24, 1929–   )
Composer

George Crumb's exotic sound world is unlike any other composer's. It builds its textures from unusual sounds or from unusual combinations of familiar sonorities. There is a ritual, almost dreamlike, quality to his compositions that can be broken suddenly as if some intense but unknown drama had taken place.

Born in Charleston, West Virginia, George Crumb gained his early musical training from his musician parents. He attended Mason College of Music and Fine Arts in Charleston, where his father was a member of the faculty, and earned his B.Mus. in 1950. In 1953 he received an M.Mus. at the University of Illinois and a D.M.A. at the University of Michigan in 1959, where he studied with Ross Lee Finney.

Following graduate school, Crumb went on to teach at the University of Colorado (1959–1964) and at the State University of New York at Buffalo (1964–1965). In 1965 he was appointed professor and composer-in-residence at the University of Pennsylvania.

From the beginning, Crumb was interested in the structural roles that timbre and rhythm might be made to play. His orchestral work, *Echoes of Time and the River* (1967), won a Pulitzer Prize in 1968. He had already been awarded generous grants by foundations (Rockefeller, 1964; Guggenheim, 1967; and National Institute of Arts and Letters, 1967).

Echoes of Time and the River, performed by the Chicago Symphony Orchestra, established Crumb's reputation. The score calls for groups of musicians to walk around the stage, per the subtitle, *Four Processionals for Orchestra*. In this audiovisual performance the players whisper, shout, whistle, and tap out the composer's name in Morse code. A gong changes pitch as it is immersed in a bucket of water.

By 1970 Crumb was exploring sonority even further and was especially concerned with the ways tone qualities can be combined. Two 1970 works, *Black Angels: Thirteen Images from the Dark Land*, for electric string quartet, and *Ancient Voices of Children*, for soprano, boy soprano, oboe, mandolin, harp, electric piano, toy piano, and percussion, illustrate this interest.

The composer acknowledges that soprano Jan DeGaetani affected the composition of *Ancient Voices*. Her virtuosity and "also the timbral flexibility . . . the very dark timbre of her voice . . . that . . . fits Lorca very well. It's that quality I see in his poetry. I hear a dark timbre in his Spanish words." The composer has set much of poet Federico Garcia Lorca's work to music, including collections for soprano: *Madrigals*, volumes I and II in 1965 and volumes III and IV in 1969.

Crumb extended the possibilities of instruments themselves by trying new playing methods, such as bottleneck banjo techniques, and he sometimes introduced instruments like the musical saw or musical glasses along with experimental sound sources. His treatment of the piano is especially noteworthy, both as a solo instrument and in ensemble, as he probed its possibilities for coloration and he has been particularly inventive for the voice.

In Crumb's scores, which are usually of very large size, a kind of time-space outline is created within which action and movement are notated along with sound. Symbols, gestures, entrances, and exits are all meaningful. Crumb notes in *Night of the Four Moons* (1969) that the work "might be enhanced by a discreet use of stage lighting effect," and, "if the work is performed in a quasi-theatrical manner, the singer might be dressed in Spanish cabaret costume."

Crumb notes in *Black Angels* that "the amplification of the stringed instruments is intended to produce a highly surrealistic effect. The performers also play maracas, tam-tams, and water-tuned crystal glasses, the latter played with the bow for the 'glass-harmonica' effect in GOD-MUSIC."

Makrokosmos I: 12 Fantasy Pieces after the Zodiac (1972), for amplified piano, developed dramatic ties among the subjects, which depend on the acoustical and psychological elements of individual performances as well as on metric relationships and contrasts.

Crumb's work reflects conversational Baroque instrumental relationships of the seventeenth and eighteenth centuries rather than the expressionist and serial concepts explored by Crumb's predecessors. To Crumb the performer provided a special kind of dramatic energy that, combined with risks of performance, eclipsed the attractions of micro precisions offered by the synthesizer or computer. Crumb was not after bel canto (beautiful singing) in his use of the human voice; rather, he rejected conventional vocal effects. The score might call for shouting, whispering, humming, hissing, and sometimes singing, though singing was never included for vocal display.

Medieval ideas intrigue Crumb. He flirts with numerology and mirror images. Both *Makrokosmos I* and *Black Angels* reflect his interest in medieval astronomical, arithmetical, geometric, and musical concepts. Symbols, invisible to listeners, appear in the score and on occasion fragments of medieval music are quoted. Sometimes performers wear masks, recite numbers, or march, though since 1980 Crumb has depended more on the score and has concentrated on enriching his music rather than engaging listeners with stage business.

Surrealism is present in Crumb's work, though writer Gilbert Chase notes: "While it would be misleading to tag Crumb as a musical surrealist—his achievement is too varied and original for that limitation—there is nevertheless an underlying affinity, and no composer has explored and exemplified more deeply and imaginatively the hidden sources of surrealistic expression than this mystic superrealist from West Virginia." Crumb himself said that "music might be defined as a system of proportions in the service of a spiritual impulse."

Crumb's many awards include an International Rostrum of Composers Award (1971), a KOUSSEVITZKY recording award (1971), Guggenheim and Fromm Foundation awards (1973), and a Ford Foundation Award (1976). He was elected to membership in the National Institute of Arts and Letters in 1975.

BIBLIOGRAPHY

Gagne, C., and T. Caras (eds.), *Soundpieces: Interviews with American Composers,* 1982; Rockwell, J., *All American Music: Composition in the Late Twentieth Century,* 1983.

Cummings, Edward Estlin

(October 14, 1894–September 3, 1962)
Poet

In his idiosyncratic verse, the modern poet E. E. Cummings (who styled his name "e. e. cummings" until the 1930s) sought to capture the aliveness of each moment. He used typography, punctuation, and syntax to create surprises to free his readers of linguistic habit.

Born and raised in Cambridge, Massachusetts, Edward Estlin Cummings was the son of a Harvard professor and ordained minister. From the age of eight he wrote almost a poem a day, playing with such established forms as the ballad and the sonnet.

Horace Liveright Inc., N.Y.; Courtesy of the New York World Telegram and Sun Collection at the Library of Congress

At Harvard, Cummings joined the staff of the *Harvard Monthly,* where he befriended JOHN DOS PASSOS, a young fiction writer. He received his B.A. in 1915, an M.A. in 1916, and helped organize the Harvard Poetry Society. Eight of Cummings's poems were published in *Eight Harvard Poets* in 1917.

Cummings's work during this period reflects his notion that poems were visual objects. He staggered words on a page to draw attention to their densities. In one poem, he ran the type back and forth across the page, forcing the reader to read lines alternately from left to right and right to left.

Cummings joined the Norton-Harjes Ambulance Corps on April 7, 1917, the day after the United States entered World War I. While serving in the French countryside, he and a friend aroused the suspicions of the French censors by writing letters home that were critical of the war. They were detained for three months on suspicion of espionage, an experience that provided the material for an autobiographical novel, *The Enormous Room* (1922).

Returning to New York, Cummings devoted most of his time to painting. He was inspired by the work of the Cubists, who reduced natural forms to geometric shapes. In July 1918, Cummings was drafted by the army and was sent for six months to Fort Devens in Massachusetts for training. During this time, he wrote many of the poems that filled his next three published volumes.

Also during this time, Cummings began an affair with Elaine Orr Thayer, the wife of a college friend, Schofield Thayer. She became pregnant with Cummings's child shortly after he was discharged by the army in 1919. Cummings's daughter, Nancy, was given Thayer's surname.

Cummings and Dos Passos toured Europe together in 1921, arriving in Paris in March. During the next two years there Cummings began what became a lifelong friendship with the American poet EZRA POUND.

Cummings's first book of poems, *Tulips and Chimneys*, came out in 1923. The tulips are free-verse lyric poems; the chimneys are sonnets. Typically, the poems celebrate the individual while condemning humankind.

Cummings married Elaine Orr Thayer in March 1924 and adopted Nancy in April. Three months later, Orr had fallen in love with another man and asked for a divorce. Cummings lost a custody battle for Nancy, and she was raised without knowing he was her father.

Over the next twenty years, Cummings became a popular and controversial poet. His work, considered outrageously modern by some, contained themes of rebellion, love, faith in the true individual, and fear and loathing for what he called "unworld," the unfeeling masses. They featured condensed syntax, odd typographical arrangements, wild puns, and playful titles, such as *is 5* (1926), which, Cummings wrote his mother, is "short for Twice Two Is Five."

Cummings's play *Him* (1927) mixes dramatic vignettes with circus sideshows, vaudeville routines, and burlesque. The protagonist, Him, represents Cummings's Everyman—the lowercase *i* of his poetry.

Nine nonsense stories were published as a book with no title in 1930 and were followed by a volume of poetry, *ViVa*, in 1931. Cummings's sole published collection of artwork also came out in 1931. Its title, *CIOPW*, is an acronym for "charcoal, ink, oil, pencil, watercolor."

A travel diary kept during a trip to the Soviet Union in 1931 formed the basis for *Eimi* (1933). Its title, "I am" in Greek, reflects Cummings's rejection of the collective stressed in the Soviet Union. His antipathy toward the Soviet Union grew into a broad dislike of leftist ideology.

Cummings had married Anne Barton in 1929 and divorced her in 1932. He then met Marion Morehouse, who became his companion and common-law wife for the rest of his days. Like her predecessors in Cummings's affection, Morehouse was a great beauty.

The depression economy hindered publication of Cummings's next book, *No Thanks*, which finally appeared in 1935 in a printing subsidized by his mother. The volume was dedicated to the fourteen publishers who had turned it down, their names arranged on the page in the shape of a funeral urn.

Though Cummings never renounced the stylistic idiosyncracies that make his work so recognizable (and which some criticized as formulaic), he did address sober themes. The collection *50 Poems* (1940) contains "my father moved through dooms of love," an elegy in tone. The poems in *1 × 1* (1944) reflect seriously on love as the means by which oneness is reached. *Santa Claus* (1946), a play in verse about a girl looking for her lost father, reflects Cummings's lost relationship with his own daughter. *Xaipe* (1950), or "Rejoice" in Greek, contains elegies as well as satires.

In 1952 Cummings was invited to be Charles Eliot Norton Professor at Harvard. His autobiographical talks there were collected as *i: Six Nonlectures* in 1953. Throughout the decade, Cummings read his own poetry to capacity crowds all over the country.

Cummings received the National Book Award for *Poems 1923–1954* (1955). He was awarded the Bollingen Prize in poetry in 1958.

The collection *95 Poems* (1958) was the last to be published during his lifetime. He died at his family farm in Madison, New Hampshire.

BIBLIOGRAPHY

Dumas, Bethany K., *E. E. Cummings: A Remembrance*, 1974; Kennedy, Richard S., *Dreams in the Mirror: A Biography of E. E. Cummings*, 1980.

Cunningham, Merce

(April 16, 1919–   )
Choreographer, Dancer

Cunningham's provocative, unpredictable choreography comments on life and challenges audiences. Though he broke down barriers dividing modern dance and ballet, he always maintained the highest technical standards. In using the random to create carefully structured works, he built new and independent relationships for dance with music and the visual arts.

Born in Centralia, Washington, Merce (Mercier) Cunningham entered the Cornish School in Seattle at eighteen, intending a career in the theater. "After he began to study modern dance there," says David

Stephen Mark Needham and the Cunningham Dance Foundation Inc.

Vaughan, archivist at the Merce Cunningham Dance Foundation, "he realized the theater for him meant dance, and switched his courses accordingly." Cunningham studied dance with Bonnie Bird, a former member of MARTHA GRAHAM's company. His studies in music and composition with JOHN CAGE began a lifelong association with the composer.

Cunningham met Martha Graham at Mills College, Oakland, California, in 1939 and was invited to join the Graham company as male soloist. Based in New York he stayed with Graham until the mid-1940s; danced in many Graham works, among them *El Penitente* (1940) and *Appalachian Spring* (1944); and studied, too, at GEORGE BALANCHINE's School of American Ballet, where he later taught modern dance.

Cunningham's first solo concert (1944), in collaboration with John Cage, presented music

and dance structured independently of one another. The solo dance and percussionist music were of the "greatest aesthetic elegance," wrote critic Edwin Denby.

The Cunningham company was formed in 1953 (PAUL TAYLOR was a member of the first performance group), the school six years later, in 1959. Cunningham had participated in summer workshops at Bennington College in Vermont and Black Mountain College in North Carolina, which were sources for the new company's dancers. By 1964 Cunningham was touring the world presenting his many works choreographed for the company.

Cunningham became acquainted with the New York school of painters (see BARNETT NEWMAN). Artists were intrigued because he gave them a free hand, as he did composers, often not seeing or hearing final work until it and his choreography were complete. ROBERT RAUSCHENBERG and JASPER JOHNS became important collaborators.

Cunningham's dance technique, according to David Vaughan, "combined the leg action and pelvic turn-out of ballet with the flexibility of the torso of the modern dance." Breaking with representational, expressionistic modern dance, Cunningham moved from formal structure to chance combinations, using ballet techniques performed barefoot. His method of composition discarded collaborative conventions, putting together scenic design, music, and dance only after each element was separately completed. One of the first choreographers to use electronic music, live and taped, Cunningham is considered a great innovator, one who stretched rules as he experimented with time, space, and motion.

BIBLIOGRAPHY

Hodgson, M., *Quintet: Five American Dance Companies*, 1976; Klosty, J., *Merce Cunningham*, 1975; Sontag, S., et al., *Cage, Cunningham, Johns: Dancers on a Plane*, 1990.

Daly, John Augustin

(July 20, 1838–June 7, 1899)
Playwright, Producer, Theatrical Manager

Augustin Daly brought the best plays and actors of his time to American audiences and took American acting companies to Europe, gaining new status for this country's theater.

Daly was born in Plymouth, North Carolina, the son of a sailor. When his father died, his mother took him and his brother to New York City, where Augustin grew up in love with the theater. He was able to see the great romantic actors of the time and, inspired, organized amateur theatricals for the children in his neighborhood.

By 1856, still in his teens, he was writing plays and had rented a hall in Brooklyn where he produced a variety of plays. He was also a drama critic and wrote regularly for the weekly *Sunday Courier* and other New York newspapers.

His first play was *Leah the Forsaken* (1862), an adaptation of a German novel that dealt with the persecution of the Jews in eighteenth-century Austria. He adapted other plays from German, French, and English novels and finally produced on his own his first original play, *Under the Gaslight*, in New York in 1867. Daly became famous for theatrical spectacles; in *The Red Scarf* (1869), the hero, tied to a log about to be sawed in half, is rescued by the heroine. Another of his melodramas featured a burning Hudson River steamboat.

In 1869 Daly began to establish his own company of actors at the Fifth Avenue Theatre, which he leased. There he produced English comedies but also began to support American playwrights. He directed his actors to perform in a more natural, "normal" way, instead of in the declamatory style with exaggerated gestures then in fashion. In 1871 he produced one of his own plays, *Horizon*, and adapted *Divorce* from the novel *He Knew He Was Right* by Anthony Trollope, changing the setting to America and using colloquial American speech for the dialogue. The play ran for 200 performances, a staggering achievement at the time.

Daly said he wanted to bring together the finest actors he could find and to offer the best new plays along with the classics. He believed in a true repertory company, where all the actors could play both comic and serious parts, heroes and villains. He was strict and demanding with his actors, whom he chose carefully and used according to their talents as he saw them. It was a disappointment to him that American critics did not always like the new American plays.

After the Fifth Avenue Theatre burned in 1873, he leased the New York Theatre and renamed it Daly's Fifth Avenue Theatre. For a while he operated two more theaters, but after 1873 he confined himself to the New Fifth Avenue Theatre at 28th Street. One of his own most successful plays, *Pique*, appeared there in 1875. After the last of his original plays, *The Dark City*, failed in 1877, the financial loss forced him to give up his theater.

He visited England, met English actors and managers, and returned in 1879 to open the Old Broadway Theatre as Daly's Theatre with an astonishing company that included John Drew, Ada Rehan, and Otis Skinner. He offered fare that was made up mostly of his own adaptations of European novels. In 1884 and 1886 Daly toured with his company in England; on the second trip he took the first English-speaking company of any importance in 300 years to Germany and then went on to Paris. On a third trip he took *The Taming of the Shrew*, possibly the first time a Shakespearean comedy had been produced in Europe by an American company. Parisians were not impressed, but they did like his productions of *As You Like It* and *The School for Scandal*, which he took over on a later trip. In 1893 Daly opened his own theater in London, where he produced a hit version of *Twelfth Night*, and continued to produce Shakespeare in America.

Over the years, Daly built up what one theatrical historian has called the "finest and most complete interpretative instrument for the drama that America has seen." His reputation is unique in the annals of nineteenth-century drama.

BIBLIOGRAPHY

Daly, Joseph F., *The Life of Augustin Daly*, 1917; Felheim, Marvin, *The Theater of Augustin Daly*, 1956.

Davis, Alexander Jackson

(July 24, 1803–January 14, 1892)
Architect, Draftsman

Downing, Andrew Jackson

(October 30, 1815–July 28, 1852)
Author, Horticulturist, Landscape Gardener

Alexander Jackson Davis, a preeminent architect of the pre–Civil War era and a leader in the revival of many styles, is noted for his romantic eclecticism and especially for Gothic Revival houses. Through professional association, he and Andrew Jackson Downing, one of America's first architectural critics and an influential proponent of the picturesque in landscaping, became the leading domestic tastemakers of the mid-nineteenth century.

Davis was born in New York City, grew up in Newark, New Jersey, and Utica and Auburn, New York, and worked briefly as a printer's assistant in Alexandria, Virginia, before becoming an architectural illustrator for a New York bookseller (1823). Apprenticed to architect J. R. Brady, he traveled through New England (1827–1828) and learned about architecture by observing and executing meticulously detailed drawings. He then worked as a draftsman for architect Ithiel Town, an innovator in the Greek Revival style (symmetrical, templelike buildings, usually with columned porticoes), who made him a partner in 1829. Town & Davis (New York, 1829–1835) became the first fully organized architectural firm in the country and gained recognition for such Greek Revival structures as the state capitols in Raleigh, North Carolina (1833–1842), and Indianapolis, Indiana (1831–1835), and the domed Customs House in Boston (1833–1842). From the late

1830s, Davis concentrated on the design of romantic suburban and country houses. He established his own practice in 1843.

Davis called himself an architectural composer who put the beauty of pictorial composition ahead of function and structure. He influenced American designers and builders through a series of portfolios, *Rural Residences* (first one in 1838), containing Gothic Revival designs with full views, floor plans, and elevations for all types of houses from villas to farmhouses. These houses were characterized by asymmetry, variety, and picturesqueness, and featured pointed arches, bay windows, deep verandas, complicated brackets, steeply pitched roofs, and ornamental chimneys. These images reflected the romantic tenor of the times and complemented the irregular aspects of nature emerging in picturesque landscaping design. Davis's "Rustic Cottage style" became the prototype for countless structures across the country. These four-bedroom houses incorporated board-and-batten siding (vertical planks with their joints covered by thin wooden strips). Larger houses were of stone.

Davis's association with Andrew Jackson Downing (1840s–1852) reinforced his predilection for the Gothic Revival style. Downing, born in Newburgh, New York, began his career by working in the family nursery business, conducting horticultural investigations, and publishing the results in various magazines. His 1841 book, *A Treatise on the Theory and Practice of Landscape Gardening*, brought international recognition, and he was hailed as the apostle of landscape design. His other books, *Cottage Residences* (1842) and *The Architecture of Country Houses* (1850), for which Davis did the drawings, popularized picturesque landscape design as inherently American and promoted the improvement of rural architecture. Davis's drawings illustrating the houses in appropriate landscape settings and Downing's philosophical and practical explanatory text helped revolutionize architectural book publishing.

As editor of *The Horticulturist* (1846–1852), a "journal of rural art and rural taste," Downing said, "A tasteful house [is] a barrier against vice, immorality, and bad habits," and convinced Americans that even the simplest cottage could be tasteful. He believed that "architectural beauty must be considered conjointly with the beauty of the landscape or situation." By the mid-1840s, people were remarking that nobody "builds a house or lays out a garden without consulting Downing's works." His promotion of picturesque parks for city dwellers influenced the great landscape architect FREDERICK LAW OLMSTED.

Downing encouraged the cultural milieu for Davis's works to flourish, and Davis gave concrete shape to Downing's ideas. The Knoll (now called Lyndhurst) overlooks the Hudson River in Tarrytown, New York, and is considered Davis's masterpiece in the Gothic style (1838–1842, enlarged 1865–1867). The house, as later extended by the same architects, harmonizes with nature through asymmetrical massing (including a square tower) and its sweeping veranda. Inside it has vaulted ceilings and even Gothic-style furniture.

An example of Davis's "Suburban Gothic villa" style is the Waddell house in New York City (1844–1845), with its asymmetrical plan highlighted by large and small octagonal towers flanking a central gabled projection. Fascinated by light, Davis often used large expanses of windows, and installed dark glass here to create a mysterious effect. He was also noted for imaginative smaller structures, such as gate lodges, chapels, and observatory towers, to embellish larger estates.

Davis produced about thirty houses in the versatile Italianate villa style, a variation of the Gothic characterized by flatter roofs, rounded openings, and more restrained detail. For Belmont, Llewellyn S. Haskell's Italianate villa near Belleville, New Jersey (1850–1852), Davis juxtaposed two towers of divergent shape and height.

With Haskell and Downing, Davis planned the first architecturally integrated community in the country—Llewellyn Park in the hilly area of West Orange, New Jersey. Begun in the early 1850s, this picturesque village has roads that curve through a terrain of craggy slopes, tree clusters, ravines, and streams, with many Gothic-style homes designed by Davis (only a few survive).

By the 1850s, Davis was serving a widespread clientele, often working through the mail for clients he never met, designing houses he never saw. Several elements of his designs, such as board-and-batten siding, became part of American vernacular architecture. Although he was never able fully to recover his practice after interruption by the Civil War, Davis left his mark on the evolution of the American house. As for his philosophical soul-mate, Downing, his immense influ-

ence continued, even after his tragic death in a steamboat disaster on the Hudson River.

BIBLIOGRAPHY

Davies, Jane B., "Alexander Jackson Davis: Architect of Lyndhurst," *Historic Preservation,* 1965; Lynes, R., *The Tastemakers,* 1954; Newton, Roger Hale, *Town & Davis, Architects: Pioneers in American Revivalist Architecture, 1812–1870,* 1942; Peck, Amelia (ed.), *Alexander Jackson Davis, American Architect, 1803–1892,* 1992; Tatum, George B., *Alexander Jackson Downing: Arbiter of American Taste,* 1950 (unpublished dissertation, Princeton University).

Davis, Bette

(April 5, 1908–October 6, 1989)
Actress

For most of her career, Bette Davis reigned as Hollywood's toughest and most resilient actress. Her impersonations of spirited, strong-willed women echoed her own struggles against studio politics to win better scripts and directors. Wide-eyed, perennially waving a cigarette in the air, Davis brought life even to the most mediocre material.

Born in Lowell, Massachusetts, Ruth Elizabeth Davis came from a strong Yankee background. Her parents divorced when she was seven. Her mother placed her and her sister in boarding school and moved to New

Copyright *Washington Post;* Reprinted by permission of the D.C. Public Library

York, where the children joined her in 1917. She called herself Bette after the character in Balzac's novel *Cousin Bette,* and was determined to be an actress.

Davis read for EVA LE GALLIENNE's Repertory Group but was not admitted to the school. Her first professional acting job was in Rochester, New York, under director George Cukor; she made her New York City debut in 1929 at the Provincetown Playhouse in *The Earth Between.* At a time when experienced stage actresses were needed in "talking pictures," she took a screen test and won a $300 a week contract at Universal Pictures; she moved to Hollywood with her mother in 1930.

Her first film was *Bad Sister* (1931). Playing opposite George Arliss in *The Man Who Played God* (1932) led to a contract with Warner Brothers, the studio with which she fought over the next decade. While cast in over a dozen films in the next few years, it was her performance as the slatternly waitress Mildred in *Of Human Bondage* (produced by RKO in 1934) that drew attention to her acting ability and won her the first of ten Oscar nominations. She won the Best Actress Award twice within the next three years, the first for *Dangerous* (1935), the second for *Jezebel* (1938), and is reputed to have given the name Oscar to the Academy Award when she remarked that the backside of the statuette resembled that of her then-husband Ham Oscar Nelson. The nickname stuck.

Despite her feud with Warners, her most successful and profitable period was there between 1938 and 1949. She appeared in twenty-five films, only one of which, *The Little Foxes* (1941)—the adaptation of the celebrated LILLIAN HELLMAN play—was made outside the studio. Most notable were *Dark Victory* (1939), in which she played a spoiled socialite facing death; *Juarez* (1939), in which she was the mad Empress Carlotta; *The Private Lives of Elizabeth and Essex* (1939), the first of two impersonations of Queen Elizabeth I; *The Letter* (1940), based on a Somerset Maugham play; *Now, Voyager* (1942), in which she and costar Paul Henreid commemorate their love in perhaps the most famous cigarette scene in movie history; and *Mr. Skeffington* (1944), in which she ages fifty years with her favorite costar, Claude Rains.

Her last film at Warners was *Beyond the Forest* (1949), a flop, but containing the line, "What a dump!" which became a standard part of every female impersonator's Davis routine. After leaving Warners, she made *All About Eve,* one of her most famous films, which won five Oscars, including Best Picture of 1950. She played the fading stage actress Margo Channing, "the role of a lifetime," which ironically marked the turning point in her career.

Of her acting, one critic called her a "vulgar, bullying actress, who . . . made mannerism a virtue," while another observed that Davis "needed her bad scripts as sorely as they needed her."

Although her reign as a major star had passed, she played a number of striking characters throughout the 1950s and 1960s, including Elizabeth I again in *The Virgin Queen* (1955), a Bronx housewife in *The Catered Affair* (1956), Catherine the Great in *John Paul Jones* (1959), and Apple Annie in *A Pocketful of Miracles* (1961). At one point, not getting any film offers, she placed an ad in a Los Angeles newspaper as an experienced actress looking for work.

Her most memorable roles of the 1960s were in two horror films that became cult classics: in *What Ever Happened to Baby Jane?* (1962) she is an emotionally disturbed woman who was once a famous child star, and in *Hush . . . Hush, Sweet Charlotte* (1965) she is the slightly deranged heiress of a southern plantation harassed by cousin Olivia de Havilland.

Unlike many of her colleagues, who believed television an inferior medium, Davis appeared on many programs during the 1950s and 1960s—including *General Electric Theater, Alfred Hitchcock Presents, Perry Mason, Gunsmoke,* and *Wagon Train*—and made more than a dozen television movies in the 1970s and 1980s. Her last theatrical features were *The Whales of August* (1987), costarring legendary silent screen star Lillian Gish, and *Wicked Stepmother* (1989), a botched production that she abandoned midway.

Davis was married four times, first to high school sweetheart Ham Nelson in 1932; second in 1940 to aircraft engineer Arthur Farnsworth, who died in 1943; third to William Grant Sherry in 1945; and immediately after divorcing him in 1950, to Gary Merrill. A daughter, Barbara, was born to Davis and Sherry; and she and

Merrill adopted two children, Michael and Margot, but were divorced in 1960. Davis published an autobiography in 1962, and in *This 'n That*, she rebuts her daughter's book, *My Mother's Keeper*, which drew an unflattering picture of the star. She died of breast cancer in France at age eighty-one.

In addition to her Oscars, Davis was the first woman to receive the Life Achievement Award from the American Film Institute.

BIBLIOGRAPHY

Davis, Bette, *The Lonely Life*, 1962; Davis, Bette, with Michael Herskowitz, *This 'n That*, 1987; Hyman, B. D., *My Mother's Keeper*, 1985; Leaming, Barbara, *Bette Davis*, 1992; Ringgold, Gene, *The Complete Films of Bette Davis*, 1966, rev., 1990; Stine, Whitney, *I'd Love to Kiss You: Conversations with Bette Davis*, 1990; Stine, Whitney, with Bette Davis, *Mother Goddam*, 1974.

Davis, Miles Dewey, III

(May 25, 1926–September 28, 1991)
Jazz Musician

Miles Davis was always at the cutting edge of modern jazz as he helped set new styles from cool to modal to fusion. His extraordinary trumpet improvisations and fine ensemble work pushed boundaries of rhythm, harmony, and melody and continuously posed musical challenges that suggested future paths for jazz.

Davis, the son of a dental surgeon, Miles Dewey Davis, and Cleota Henry Davis, was born in Alton, Illinois, twenty-five miles north of East St. Louis. At thirteen he began to study trumpet with Elwood Buchanan and two years later joined the musicians' union to play professionally in the area. In September 1944 he went to New York to study at the Juilliard School of Music and to search out jazz saxophonist CHARLIE PARKER, whom he admired.

Miles left his classical studies at Juilliard in the fall of 1945 and immersed himself in the jazz of Harlem and 52nd Street. Charlie Parker and DIZZY GILLESPIE were his mentors. Under their influence the young Davis absorbed the language and techniques of jazz and started to develop his own style. Davis began to record in 1945, played in 52nd Street clubs, and eventually joined Charlie Parker's quintet, with whom he recorded an early bebop session. In 1947 he made his first recording as a leader and began to experiment with a new, more densely textured style that became the cool jazz so popular on the West Coast. With John Lewis and Gerry Mulligan, Davis played in a nine-piece band at New York's Royal Roost; their recordings, under Davis's name, were later reissued as *Birth of the Cool*.

From mid-1949 to 1953 Davis was addicted to heroin. As a result, his performance and creativity became unreliable. He was able to overcome his addiction in 1954 and made some recordings with small groups. That year the tune "Walkin'" rejected cool jazz and introduced hard bop. Miles's revitalized improvisations, heard at the Newport Jazz Festival in 1955, were greeted with enthusiasm. He had brought together some remarkable musicians: JOHN COLTRANE, tenor sax; Red Garland, piano; Paul Chambers, bass; and Philly Joe Jones, drums. The quintet's mix of energy and understatement achieved an extraordinary balance. The group recorded six albums in 1955–1956.

From 1954 to 1958 Davis mastered his ballad style and strengthened his improvisational skills. With arranger Gil Evans's orchestrations Davis demonstrated the richness of orchestral jazz, especially as a backdrop for his relaxed and subtle improvisations. In 1959 he was experimenting with modality, his more linear reaction against music thick with chords. (Modal jazz is based on modes, or scales other than the major or minor ones, and may use repeating bass figures instead of chord patterns.) He recorded *Kind of Blue,* an album of modal jazz that profoundly influenced jazz of the sixties, with pianist BILL EVANS and others. Sidemen John Coltrane and Julian ("Cannonball!") Adderley continued everafter to explore the melodic implications of the session, and the ground-breaking recording helped shape the outlook of younger jazz musicians.

Davis continued his exploration of the possibilities of modal concepts through the 1960s, and by 1968 he was using electronic instruments and rock rhythms in recordings like the best-selling *Bitches Brew.* The mix of jazz and rock so characteristic of Davis's work between 1968 and 1971 became known as fusion. Some scorned the style as commercial. Others thought it coherent, evocative, and exciting.

During the 1970s bad health plagued Davis, and his music reflected diminished energy. He broke both legs in a 1972 automobile accident but emerged from retirement in 1981 to make an album, *The Man with the Horn,* and to perform at the Kool Jazz Festival that year.

A moving, haunting tone, inner tension, and constantly changing style established Miles Davis as an important innovator, and he was an influence for decades. He died in Santa Monica, California, in 1991.

BIBLIOGRAPHY

Baker, D., *The Jazz Style of Miles Davis,* 1980; Carr, I., *Miles Davis,* 1982; Davis, M., and Q. Troupe, *Miles: The Autobiography,* 1989; Feather, L., *From Satchmo to Miles,* 1972.

Davis, Stuart

(December 7, 1894–June 24, 1964)
Painter

Stuart Davis, at first a traditional painter of realistic works, became a central figure in the development of American abstract painting in the 1920s.

Davis was born in Philadelphia to artist-parents, both of whom had studied at the Pennsylvania Academy of the Fine Arts. When Davis was seven, his family moved to East Orange, New Jersey, and ten years later, in 1911, he began to commute to New York to study at the art school run by ROBERT HENRI.

Davis followed Henri's unorthodox advice to get out of the classroom and paint the everyday life of the city. He painted in the style of the Ashcan school (see ROBERT HENRI), a group of eight New York artists who chose to paint slum dwellers, ethnic groups, and outcasts. He exhibited five "ashcan" paintings in the 1913 Armory Show in New York City, which was organized by American artists in revolt against the reactionary National Academy of Design. It not only displayed new developments in American art, but brought modern European paintings by Impressionists, Symbolists, Post-Impressionists and Neo-Impressionists, Fauves, and Cubists to this country as well.

Like other young artists, Davis changed his style after he saw these paintings. He wrote in his autobiography that he was "enormously excited by the [Armory] show" and that he "responded particularly to Gauguin, Van Gogh, and Matisse." He wanted to find a way to paint the frenzy of American life, and these painters, with their broken brush strokes and brilliant colors, fascinated him. Davis decided that he "would quite definitely have to become a *modern* artist."

Davis began to paint in more abstract ways. He painted landscapes from several different perspectives. He experimented with collages and painted imitations of collages, making copies of package labels, for instance. "I soon learned to think of color more or less objectively, so that I could paint a green tree red without batting an eye. Purple or green faces didn't bother me at all," he said.

For years, however, his trees had the shape of trees, and his faces looked like faces, in spite of the arbitrary colors. In 1927 he dropped his concern with representation and began trying to synchronize objects or landscapes, seen at different times, into a "single focus." He nailed an eggbeater, an electric fan, and a glove to a table and methodically drew and painted them over and over, thus producing his famous *Eggbeater* series. He said he concentrated on the "logical elements" and eliminated "optical truths." The result was his own kind of abstraction, based on a science of organizing and simplifying what he felt. His pictures of the eggbeater, he said later, were the basis of everything he painted afterward.

Davis insisted that his abstract paintings had subject matter. To maintain they did not, he argued, was the same thing as saying that life had no subject matter. "Some of the things that have made me want to paint . . . are the brilliant colors on gasoline stations, chain-store fronts, and taxicabs . . . fast travel by plane, auto, and airplane; electric signs; the landscape and boats of Gloucester, Massachusetts; five-and-ten-cent store kitchen utensils; music and radio; Earl Hines's piano. . . ."

After a successful one-man show in 1927, Davis spent a year in Paris painting street scenes, including *Place Pasdeloup, Place de Vosges,* and *Rue Vercingétorix.* Streets and buildings became flat planes of color and lines indicated doors, windows, shutters, paving stones, and street lamps. Having experimented with Cubism and other styles, Davis found his own way of painting.

During the 1930s Davis painted several murals, some on commission and two for the Federal Art Project, one of several government programs that helped artists and provided art for public spaces during the depression. One mural, *Men Without Women,* was originally at Radio City Music Hall (it is now at the Museum of Modern Art); *Swing Landscape* is at Indiana University. Davis, who had worked for the leftist magazine *The Masses* in his teens, joined the Artists' Union in 1934 and helped organize the American Artists' Congress in 1936. Other leftists wanted him to make his work less abstract and more political, but Davis refused.

"In the last fifteen years of his life, Stuart Davis made some of the greatest paintings any American has made in this century," critic Roberta Smith said in the *New York Times.* Smith called these works, which include *The Paris Bit* and *Colonial Cubism,* "rigorous yet casually assured concoctions of color, shape and language."

Troubled by cataracts and ill health, Davis continued to paint his brilliant abstracts until his death.

BIBLIOGRAPHY
Wilkin, Karen, *Stuart Davis,* 1987.

de Kooning, Willem

(April 24, 1904–   )
Painter

Willem de Kooning, a member of the New York school, was a major figure in the development of Abstract Expressionism in the 1940s. His most celebrated paintings are his *Woman* series of the early 1950s.

De Kooning was born in Rotterdam in 1904 and grew up in the uncertain circumstances of a divided home, alternately in the care of his mother and father. At the age of twelve he was apprenticed to a firm of commercial artists and decorators, Jan and Jaap Gidding. His precocious talent for drawing encouraged him to enroll in evening classes at the Rotterdam Academy of Fine Arts and Techniques. His training was thorough, ranging from perspective and proportion studies to classes in art theory and history, and he became a skilled professional—equally adept at carpentry, furniture design, and portraiture.

In 1926 he embarked for America in an unorthodox fashion: he hid himself aboard a ship bound for Newport News, slipped off and worked on a coal ship headed for Boston, and eventually arrived in Hoboken, New Jersey. He has admitted that one of the lures of this country was his romanticized notion of the American eagle: "[T]he shield, the medieval shield they have with the stars on top and the stripes on the bottom, was almost like the heraldic period of the Crusaders, with the eagle; as a child I used to be absolutely fascinated by this image." Despite his inability to speak English, he was able to make a living as a house painter. Gradually, he found other work in commercial art and sign painting.

During his tenure with the Federal Art Project in 1935, de Kooning first showed publicly one of his paintings, a study for a never-completed mural project provisionally entitled *Abstraction* (subsequently destroyed). Despite the hardships of the depression, he decided to commit himself to a full-time career in painting. One of his first important subjects was a series of images of his wife-to-be, Elaine Fried, whom he met in 1937. These *Women* paintings were early examples of a subject that would preoccupy him for the rest of his life. He was also painting at this time a series of male figure studies in a vaguely Cubist manner, most of them conveying a sense of sadness and loss. By contrast to these series, there was also a number of abstract works based on still-life motifs. In 1942 his work was officially presented to the public for the time, along with that of two other first-timers, JACKSON POLLOCK and Lee Krasner, in a group show sponsored by the decorating firm of McMillen, Inc.

De Kooning was acquiring a reputation as an artist who was never satisfied with individual works. Frequently he would destroy his paintings, wipe them out, or abandon them in various stages of incompleteness. These acts, according to historian Thomas B. Hess, were not admissions of failures, but a defiance of the concept of "finish" that was still so much a part of the Parisian artistic tradition. If de Kooning abandoned an unfinished painting, it was to leave it as a record of processes and obstacles; if he destroyed a work outright, it was a "destruction that opens the way to a fresh beginning."

De Kooning's first one-man show in April 1948 marked his official public endorsement. Soon he was a popular teacher at Yale University and in New York with FRANZ KLINE, the organizer of "the Club," which brought together for Friday night debates painters Jackson Pollock, BARNETT NEWMAN, and ROBERT MOTHERWELL. Meanwhile, his paintings, particularly his figure studies, were acquiring increasingly vivid colors and vigorous pictorial tensions. His numerous *Woman* paintings from 1950 to 1955 displayed fragmented anatomical shapes and oscillating figure-ground relationships. ("The landscape is in the Woman," he said in 1955, "and there is Woman in the land-scapes.") In a style that in the early 1950s Harold Rosenberg would dub action painting, his brush swept across the canvas, leaving drips and blobs and, in general, achieving a sense of simultaneous creation and destruction. The *Woman* series—what Hess calls "lacerated goddesses"—became at once de Kooning's most famous and most notorious work. Critics pronounced them "monstrous" and "repellent." De Kooning himself claimed: "I always started out with the idea of a young person, a beautiful woman. I noticed them change. Somebody would step out—a middle-aged woman. I didn't mean to make them such monsters." This energy abated somewhat in his later work, after the mid-1960s, when a more gentle and lyrical expression predominated. De Kooning's legacy to a later generation of Pop artists (see Roy Lichtenstein) was profound. Paintings like *Gotham News* (1955–1956) displayed randomly placed images as well as typescript that was offset from newspapers. Banal cigarette ads were the basis for *T-Zone* (1949). And the "pinup girl" icons, like Marilyn Monroe, were assimilated into his *Woman* series in 1954.

De Kooning returned to a completely abstract style in his late work, so in the final analysis, his forms possess both abstract and representational qualities. "Even abstract shapes must have a likeness," he once declared. Fame, fortune, and artistic independence eventually came to de Kooning in the 1960s. He was elected to the National Institute of Arts and Letters in 1960, and in 1964 he was awarded the Presidential Medal of Freedom.

BIBLIOGRAPHY

de Kooning, Willem, "What Abstract Art Means to Me," *Museum of Modern Art Bulletin*, Spring 1952; Hess, Thomas B., *Willem de Kooning*, 1968; Janis, Harriet, and Rudi Blesh, *De Kooning*, 1960.

de Mille, Agnes George

(September 18, 1909–)
Choreographer, Dancer

Agnes de Mille's dance narratives draw on American themes to express the national spirit and style in ballets and in musical theater alike. Her lively landmark choreography for *Oklahoma* pioneered the use of dance to further the plot and forever changed the relationship of dancing and the Broadway musical.

Born in New York, Agnes de Mille, the granddaughter of political economist Henry George and the niece of movie mogul Cecil B. DeMille, grew up in Hollywood, California. Dazzled early on by a performance of the great ballerina Anna Pavlova, dance became the child's obsession. "My life was wholly altered by her," de Mille said later. At fourteen she was allowed to study ballet, though dance was deemed unsuitable as a career.

After graduating from UCLA, de Mille, supported by her now divorced parents, tried to hone her skills, find work, and make her way. She made her concert debut in 1927, dancing solos in the ballet *Stagefright* and performing other character sketches.

From 1929 to 1940 de Mille toured at home and abroad, studied with Marie Rambert, and in England danced with the Rambert and Anthony Tudor companies before settling in New York where in 1940 she joined the Ballet Theater (later the American Ballet Theater) and successfully choreographed Broadway shows: *Hooray for What?* and *Swingin' the Dream*.

Her career took off in 1942 with a ballet, *Rodeo*, created for the Ballet Russe de Monte Carlo. De Mille starred in the dance-mime performance, a girl-gets-boy story set in the American West. Aaron Copland's music and de Mille's choreography were a hit and de Mille, called by critic Edwin Denby "a great actress-dancer . . . raised," he said, "the standards—in dance construction, in humor of character and situation, and, best of all, in American savor." It was, Denby wrote, the "first great success [of] American local-color ballet."

Broadway's 1943 *Oklahoma* changed the use of dance on Broadway. In the Richard Rodgers and Oscar Hammerstein II musical, dances spring naturally from the action, heighten sentiment, make a point, and were performed superbly. Denby noted in 1943 that de Mille "seems to come closer to the secret of our common movement than other native dancers have."

De Mille continued to choreograph for Broadway musicals until 1963, including *One Touch of Venus* (1943), *Paint Your Wagon* (1951), and *110 in the Shade* (1963). At the same time she was creating works for the Ballet Theater like *Fall River Legend* (1948), *The Harvest According* (1952), and *The Wind in the Mountains* (1965), the latter based on an early American folk song.

In 1992 at age eighty-six Agnes de Mille choreographed *The Other*, a new ballet to the music of Schubert. *The Other*, writes Jean Battey Lewis in the *New York Times*, "draws on her skill at pacing and creating dramatic tension, but it also has a quiet simplicity, a purity sometimes seen late in an artist's life."

De Mille, a candid and gifted writer, has published autobiographical works and books about dance. Her most recent, a biography of Martha Graham (*Martha: The Life and Work of Martha Graham*), was published in 1991.

BIBLIOGRAPHY

de Mille, Agnes, *Dance to the Piper*, 1952, and *America Dances*, 1980.

DeMille, Cecil Blount

(August 12, 1881–January 21, 1959)
Film Director/Producer

For many people, Cecil B. DeMille's name is synonymous with Hollywood. One of the first filmmakers to settle there, his sense of spectacle and showmanship symbolized Hollywood as the producer of colossal entertainment. He also endeared himself to millions in the late 1930s as the host of a popular radio program, *The Lux Radio Theatre*.

DeMille was raised in Washington, North Carolina, although he was born while his parents were vacationing in Ashfield, Massachusetts. His father, Henry Churchill DeMille (changed from the original "de"), an English teacher, also preached sermons and wrote plays, some in collaboration with playwright David Belasco. His wavering between the ministry and play writing augured Cecil's signatory filmmaking style: telling well-constructed stories with moralistic messages. His English mother, Mathilda, also a teacher, ran a school for girls after her husband's death and later opened a theatrical agency.

Young Cecil ran away from Pennsylvania Military College to enlist for the Spanish-American War, but was rejected as under age. Interested in theatrics, he enrolled in the American Academy of Dramatic Arts in 1898 and made his acting debut in New York City in 1900. While on a performance tour, he met and married actress Constance Adams in 1902.

Without success he wrote plays, collaborating with his brother William, as well as Belasco. As manager of his mother's agency, he met vaudeville musician Jesse L. Lasky, with whom he remained friends for fifty years. In 1913 Lasky ventured into film production with his brother-in-law SAMUEL GOLDWYN. They formed the Jesse L. Lasky Feature Play Company and made the inexperienced DeMille director general.

Their first film was *The Squaw Man* (1914) starring Dustin Farnum, who had performed it on stage. DeMille went to Los Angeles where other filmmakers were working and rented a barn in a quiet farming village west of the town, called Hollywood. The real estate soon became invaluable, and the site developed into the film capital of the world.

DeMille produced and directed his first twenty-three films with Lasky. In 1916 the company merged with ADOLPH ZUKOR's Famous Players, becoming Famous Players–Lasky, the production arm for Paramount Pictures, for which DeMille continued to make most of his next twenty-five films. He left Paramount in 1925, releasing films through other outlets, then made his first three sound films for Metro-Goldwyn-Mayer. Returning to Paramount, he produced and directed his remaining fifteen films there between 1932 and 1956.

DeMille is primarily associated with biblical and historical spectacles, expensively produced and showcasing all-star casts. His silent version of *The Ten Commandments* was the most expensive film up to 1923, and his 1956 version, his final film, was—at $13.5 million—the most expensive production of its time.

Others included *The King of Kings* (1927), *The Sign of the Cross* (1932), *The Crusades*

The Museum of Modern Art/Film Stills Archive

(1935), *The Plainsman* (1937), *Union Pacific* (1939), *Reap the Wild Wind* (1942), *Unconquered* (1947), *Samson and Delilah* (1949), and his only movie to win the Academy Award for Best Picture, *The Greatest Show on Earth* (1952), an epic about circus life made with the cooperation of Ringling Brothers–Barnum and Bailey Circus.

DeMille was more versatile in the silent period; in addition to western, adventure, and war films, he made a number of domestic and social dramas, such as *Old Wives for New* (1917), *Don't Change Your Husband, For Better or Worse,* and *Male and Female* (all 1919), and *Why Change Your Wife?* (1920). As their titles suggest, these films were equally bent on combining melodrama with moralizing.

Joan the Woman (1917) revealed DeMille's eye and taste for spectacle. His longest film to date, it starred opera diva Geraldine Farrar and typified DeMille's propagandistic approach to historical subjects. The film celebrated America's entry into World War I, and further encouraged the British to help France in order to expiate historic guilt for their part in the execution of the French martyr Joan of Arc.

Explicitly relating historical and biblical subjects to contemporary life was DeMille's trademark, consistent with his aim to sermonize. *The Ten Commandments* (1923) tells parallel stories—ancient and modern—to underline its message. In this respect, DeMille reflected a messianic tendency of several silent filmmakers who believed that film was a universal language that could change the world.

DeMille is credited with certain technical innovations, including "Rembrandt lighting," the method of lighting a part of a face or object rather than an entire scene. *The Cheat* (1915) is a dramatic example. He also extended the settings for scenes to the bedroom and the bathroom. Elaborate baths were designed for stars like Gloria Swanson (for *Don't Change Your Husband*) and Claudette Colbert (*Cleopatra*, 1934). This guaranteed a modest amount of nudity and sexual innuendo, which spiced up his morality tales.

DeMille's name became a household word when, between 1936 and 1944, he hosted *The Lux Radio Theatre*, an hour-long program dramatizing films with live actors. Its audience rivaled those for President Franklin D. Roosevelt's "fireside chats." While DeMille was paid handsomely, he left in 1945 over a dispute of principle with the radio artists union.

Always the conservative, DeMille headed a faction of the Directors Guild during the McCarthy era in the 1950s, which tried to mandate that every member sign a loyalty oath. The idea was squelched when JOHN FORD confronted DeMille at a meeting to vote on the question.

DeMille remained married to Adams all his life. They had two children and adopted two others.

BIBLIOGRAPHY

DeMille, Cecil B., and Donald Hayne (ed.), *Autobiography*, 1959; Higham, Charles, *Cecil B. DeMille*, 1973; Ringgold, Gene, and De Witt Bodeen, *The Complete Films of Cecil B. DeMille*, 1969.

Dickinson, Emily Elizabeth

(December 10, 1830–May 15, 1886)
Poet

Writing in seclusion in Amherst, Massachusetts, in the mid-nineteenth century, Emily Dickinson created subtle lyric poems of rare range and power. She is unquestionably one of America's finest poets, but her complete work was not published until long after her death.

Dickinson was born in Amherst to a family prominent in the history of Amherst College. Her grandfather, Samuel Fowler Dickinson, helped found the college, and her father, Edward Dickinson, a lawyer, served as its treasurer for thirty-seven years. Her father's business dealings made him one of the wealthiest men in Amherst; he served for many years in the Massachusetts legislature and for a single term in the U.S. House of Representatives.

Dickinson was schooled at Amherst Academy and then for a year at Mount Holyoke Female Seminary in South Hadley, Massachusetts. She studied languages and literature, as well as mathematics and science. Though it was unusual for a woman of her day to receive so much formal education, Dickinson was not expected to begin a career. Quite the opposite; her family expected her to return home and to help keep the household until such time as she would marry, when she would begin to serve the same function for her husband.

On this point, her father may have been more vehement than most. As a young man, he wrote a series of articles for a local newspaper decrying women who had any ambition besides seeing to the comfort of men in the home. He adamantly opposed women's suffrage. It seems unlikely he took much interest in his daughter's talent, if indeed he recognized it at all. His expectations for his son were quite different: Austin was meant to follow his father in business.

Dickinson lived a private life, so private in fact that little is known about it. She left Amherst only a handful of times, in order to travel to Washington, D.C., Philadelphia, or

Boston. She never married. Only seven of her poems were published during her lifetime. It is uncertain even when she began to write; the best estimates range between ages nineteen and twenty-four. We do know that the bulk of her verse was written between 1859 and 1865. There also has been a good deal of speculation about why she wrote—whether a single trauma or sadness in her life, such as a lost love, caused her need to create poetry. To these questions, there are no answers, only conjectures.

Dickinson's poems—1,775 of them—were found among her papers after her death by her sister, Lavinia. All were undated, few were titled. In some cases, more than a single version of a poem or even a line had been kept, and it was impossible to know which had been Dickinson's preference. Only a rough chronology could be ascertained by observing subtle changes in the author's handwriting.

Dickinson's family and friends chose to publish the poems. There were too many to print all at once, so they were issued in a series of volumes. Unfortunately, the editors—Thomas Wentworth Higginson and Mabel Loomis Todd—often chose to "smooth out" irregularities of rhythm, rhyme, and punctuation. A definitive edition of Dickinson's poetry, with most of the variants in their original form, did not exist until 1955, when the three-volume *Poems of Emily Dickinson*, edited by Thomas H. Johnson, was published.

Dickinson's poetry often concerns religious themes. She grew up among Puritans but rejected the notion of a vengeful God. Though she took quite seriously the question of faith, she sometimes directed her humor at the existential dilemma: "Of course—I prayed— / And did God Care? / He cared as much as on the Air / A Bird—had stamped her foot—."

The form of Dickinson's short lyric poems seems to be derived in part from the hymns she heard in childhood, though she introduces subtle variations in rhythm and in some cases substitutes assonance for rhyme. If they served no other purpose, these variations prevent her often short verse lines from approaching singsong.

The poet often wrote about the related questions of eternity and mortality ("Because I could not stop for Death— / He kindly stopped for me—"). She also wrote about passion ("Wild Nights—Wild Nights! / Were I with thee / Wild Nights should be / Our luxury!") and about domestic happiness. She eulogized the humble and satirized the pretentious ("How dreary—to be—Somebody! / How public—like a Frog— / To tell one's name—the livelong June— / To an admiring Bog!").

Dickinson's poems always feature a directness of observation that is almost childlike. The poet herself described the characteristic quality of her poetry as "awe." The intensity of her vision comes through with the simplest of images: "How still the Bells in Steeples stand / Till swollen with the Sky, / They leap upon their silver Feet / In frantic Melody!"

In her only meeting with Thomas Wentworth Higginson, Dickinson offered her own description of the quality that makes poetry: "If I read a book [and] it makes my whole body so cold no fire can ever warm me I know *that* is poetry. If I feel physically as if the top of my head were taken off, I know *that* is poetry. These are the only way I know it. Is there any other way."

Dickinson has been called the greatest American woman poet as well as the greatest American poet. Whatever the final reckoning, she wrote poems whose range and intensity have seldom been equaled by writers in English.

BIBLIOGRAPHY

Donoghue, Denis, *Emily Dickinson*, 1969; Sewall, Richard B., *Emily Dickinson*, 1974; Wolff, Cynthia Griffin, *Emily Dickinson*, 1986.

Diebenkorn, Richard Clifford, Jr.

(April 22, 1922–March 30, 1993)
Painter

R ichard Diebenkorn belonged to a generation of painters in the 1940s who were a part of the Abstract Expressionist movement; however, in his subsequent shifts between abstract and figurative painting, he remained essentially independent of any specific style.

Diebenkorn was born in Portland, Oregon, in 1922. He studied painting in a number of institutions in California and New Mexico. Although he began his career as a painter of still lifes and interiors, he shifted between the abstract and the figurative—from geometric severity to a more sensual expressiveness. As a result of an association in the 1940s with MARK ROTHKO at the California School of Fine Arts, he pursued Abstract Expressionism and Color Field work (see BARNETT NEWMAN). Later in 1955, however, stimulated by the example of a number of Bay Area artists, particularly David Park, he began an important figurative period. "It was almost as though I could do too much too easily," he recalled, explaining the reasons for this shift. "There was nothing hard to come up against. And suddenly the figure painting furnished a lot of this." People, landscapes, and interiors, such as *Woman on Porch* (1958) and *Prisoners' Harbor, Santa Cruz Island* (1958) fused Abstract Expressionist gestures and brush strokes with figurative imagery. In this turning from abstraction to more figurative paintings, it was Diebenkorn more than anyone who preserved the abstractionist's sense of the construction of a painting. The colors, cool and searingly hot, celebrated the sun-drenched Bay Area locales. *Interior with Book* (1959) is typical of this period in that it combined all three priorities: even though no figure is included in the room, there is a felt presence in the disposition of the chair and the book, and a landscape is visible through large windows.

In 1967 he began a long series of abstract images entitled Ocean Park (the name of a coastal area west of Los Angeles), a series that he worked on into the 1980s. Generally, he tended here to use areas of color rather than line, arranging pictorial space asymmetrically into large open areas activated by smaller formal elements. Critic Hilton Kramer has written that here the primacy of Matisse's influence on Diebenkorn is revealed, inasmuch as they display that ideal "of *luxe* and *calme* that was so much a part of Matisse's vision." Kramer regarded these works as "among the finest pictures anyone anywhere has produced in the last ten years."

Diebenkorn was an acknowledged master of abstraction and had few rivals as a sensitive colorist. He worked on sheets of cut and pasted paper, building up layers of acrylic, gouache, crayon, and charcoal. His style remains instantly recognizable: horizontal lines ruled in pencil dividing the picture space into rectangular plots, subtly harmonized planes of color, and a dry, textured paint thin enough to allow underpainting to show through. According to art critic Richard B. Woodward, he never concealed the influences on his work by Cézanne, early Matisse, Mondrian, the Cubists, and Rothko. "He gladly carries the burden of modernist painting and represents the best kind of academic: rigorous, methodical, staunch in his convictions. . . . In today's climate he may look stuffy and mirthless, but he stands taller for never having been a prankster." Hilton Kramer, lamenting in 1974 the relative lack of public acclaim accorded Diebenkorn, predicted that his retrospective at the Whitney Museum that year would change all that: "Henceforth it will be impossible to write seriously about the arts of our time—and not only in America—without taking Diebenkorn's achievement into account."

Diebenkorn died at his home in Berkeley in 1993.

BIBLIOGRAPHY

Kramer, Hilton, "Richard Diebenkorn," *The Revenge of the Philistines*, 1985; Tarshis, Jerome, "Bay Area Figurative Movement," *Vogue*, December 1989; Woodward, Richard B., "Richard Diebenkorn at the Museum of Modern Art," *Art News*, March 1989.

Dietrich, Marlene

(December 27, 1901–May 6, 1992)
Film Actress, Singer

Perhaps more than any other film star, Marlene Dietrich epitomized the concept of glamour during Hollywood's Golden Age. Her fame is forever linked with director JOSEF VON STERNBERG, who discovered her and directed her best films.

Born Maria Magdalena von Losch (of which Marlene is a contraction) of middle-class parents in Berlin, the exact date of her birth is the first of many unsettled biographical mysteries. Her father was killed during World War I, and as a teenager raised by her mother, grandmother, and aunts, she lived in what she called a woman's world. She graduated from Augusta Victoria School for Girls in 1918 and entered Weimar Konservatorium to study violin. Against her mother's wishes, she began acting, and in 1921 she auditioned for the Max Reinhardt School of Drama.

Dietrich played minor roles in plays and films throughout the 1920s. Then, in 1929, she was seen by American director Josef von Sternberg in the play *Two Bow Ties*. Against the producer's—and everybody else's—wishes, Sternberg cast her in the role of the seductive cabaret singer Lola-Lola in *The Blue Angel* (1930), Germany's first sound film, which he had been invited from Hollywood to direct. Dietrich made instant history by upstaging Emil Jannings, the "official" star of the film.

Encouraged by Sternberg, she left Berlin—and her husband and young daughter—and went to Hollywood to sign a contract with Paramount Pictures, where, between 1930 and 1935, she made six more films with Sternberg. These were unquestionably her most successful and memorable movies, following which most of her films were mediocre. In her autobiography she asserts that she owed Sternberg everything: "I was nothing but pliable material on the infinitely rich palette of his ideas and imaginative faculties." She never got over the extraordinary way in which he photographed what she considered her "unphotogenic" face.

Through the artful combination of lighting, camera angle, composition, and set design, Sternberg created a complex visual texture in which Dietrich's face, sculpted with shadows and illumination, evoked more mystery and allure than any actress before or after her with the exception of GRETA GARBO. In *Morocco* (1930), *Dishonored* (1931), *Shanghai Express* (1932), *Blonde Venus* (1932), *The Scarlet Empress* (1934), and *The Devil Is a Woman* (1935), the camera often lingers silently and lovingly in close-up on her face, beyond the story's needs and without especially revealing any nuances of the characters. The look was frequently inscrutable, readable in a dozen different ways. The Dietrich mystique that thus emerged was less a result of acting than a product of the art of Hollywood illusion, a supreme example of the power of cinema, in its most glamorous era, to create a "star" defined by her celluloid incarnation.

Of her other films, noteworthy ones include *Desire* (1936), ERNST LUBITSCH's *Angel* (1937), *Destry Rides Again* (1939), *Manpower* (1941), BILLY WILDER's *A Foreign Affair* (1948) and *Witness for the Prosecution* (1958), ALFRED HITCHCOCK's *Stage Fright* (1950), and ORSON WELLES's *Touch of Evil* (1958). In several of these she also sang in her inimitable sultry style. Her last film appearance was in a worthless effort called *Just a Gigolo* (1978).

Dietrich was an avid anti-Nazi and renounced her German citizenship in the early years of the Second World War. She brought her daughter, Maria, to America and remained married all of her life to Rudolf Sieber (they married in 1924), although they were often on different continents. She actively worked to support the American war effort both domestically and on a USO tour of the European front from 1943 to 1946.

In 1953 she embarked on a wholly new career as a singer and performer, first in night clubs and eventually in concert halls all over the world, and in 1972 did a television special called *I Wish You Love*. Frequently, her costume was top hat, white tie, and tails, a look that she introduced in the film *Morocco* and continued to cultivate, keeping alive what observers often called her androgynous mystique. Said critic Kenneth Tynan: "She had sex but no particular gender. . . . Marlene lives in a sexual no man's land—and no woman's either. She dedicates herself to looking rather than to being sexy." Her one-woman show became internationally famous over the next two decades, especially after she met songwriter Burt Bacharach, to whom she attributed her later musical success.

Dietrich enjoyed deep friendships with some of the century's most famous men and women, including American writer ERNEST HEMINGWAY, French singer Edith Piaf, and English playwright Noel Coward. The actor Maximilian Schell made a documentary about her in 1984, for which she refused to be photographed, but is heard on a tape recorder mocking his questions and repudiating virtually every legend and story about her. She died in Paris at age ninety.

BIBLIOGRAPHY

Dietrich, Marlene, *Marlene Dietrich's ABC*, 1961, and *Marlene*, 1987; Frewin, Leslie, *Dietrich*, 1967; Higham, Charles, *Marlene*, 1977; Spoto, Donald, *Falling in Love Again, Marlene Dietrich*, 1985; von Sternberg, Josef, *Fun in a Chinese Laundry*, 1965; Walker, Alexander, *Dietrich*, 1984.

Disney, Walter Elias

(December 5, 1901–December 15, 1966)
Film and Television Animator, Producer

Creator of Mickey Mouse, Walt Disney achieved preeminence in movies and television and revolutionized the leisure industry with his theme park, Disneyland. Founder of the largest studio in the world devoted to animated films, he produced such classics as *Snow White and the Seven Dwarfs* and *Fantasia*, and was equally successful with live-action productions such as *Mary Poppins*.

Born Walter Elias Disney in Chicago, he was the fourth son of Elias and Flora Disney. As a result of several family moves, Disney attended grammar school in Kansas City and high school in Chicago, as well as art classes at the Kansas City Art Institute and the Chicago Institute of Art. In his leisure time he was always drawing. In late 1918 he went to France as an ambulance driver in the final days of World War I.

Employed at an advertising company in 1920, he met Ub Iwerks, who later helped develop the Disney style. At the Kansas City Film Ad Company, Disney learned enough about stop motion photography to set up a studio, where he made animated spoofs and fairy tales known as Laugh-O-Grams, but went bankrupt in 1923.

The Museum of Modern Art/Film Stills Archive

Moving to Hollywood, Disney, with his brother, Roy, and Iwerks, produced a fifty-six-film series inspired by *Alice's Adventures in Wonderland*, involving interaction between a six-year-old girl and cartoon characters. In 1927 he conceived the "Oswald the Lucky Rabbit" series for Universal Studios, but lost rights to the character. He vowed never to work for someone else again.

With Mickey Mouse, Disney created a character whose optimism appealed enormously to depression-era audiences. Mickey was introduced to the public in *Steamboat Willie* (1928), the first cartoon to use synchronized sound, Disney himself providing vocalizations for Mickey, Minnie Mouse, and the ship's parrot. Other characters followed, including Pluto, Goofy, and Donald Duck, the studio's most successful star, first seen in *The Wise Little Hen* (1934).

Competition impelled Disney to develop another kind of cartoon, in which music was used to tell a story. With *The Skeleton Dance* (1929), a series of over seventy "Silly Symphonies" was initiated, representing the Disney Studio's most creative work: *Flowers and Trees* (1932) was the first cartoon in color and the first to win an Academy Award in the new "Cartoon Short Subject" category; Oscars also went to *Three Little Pigs* (1933), *The Old Mill* (1937), and *The Ugly Duckling* (1939), the last "Silly Symphony."

Knowing the future belonged to features, in 1934 Disney began his most ambitious project, requiring 750 artists and quadrupling the original budget. Certain that it would bankrupt the studio, the industry labeled it Disney's Folly. When it premiered on December 21, 1937, *Snow White and the Seven Dwarfs*, based on the Grimm's fairy tale, made instant film history. Disney received a Special Academy Award for "a significant screen innovation," and the film, universally acknowledged as a movie milestone, earned $8 million on its initial release, four times its cost.

Entering its golden age, the Disney Studio achieved a level of success that continued unabated for five decades, producing a stream of animated classics, live-action films, and documentaries, garnering numerous awards.

Among the studio's best animated features are *Pinocchio* (1940); *Fantasia* (1940), a collaboration with conductor LEOPOLD STOKOWSKI, featuring the music of Bach, Beethoven, Tchaikovsky, Moussorgsky, and others; *Dumbo* (1941); *Bambi* (1942); *Cinderella* (1950); *Alice in Wonderland* (1951); and *Peter Pan* (1953). *Sleeping Beauty* (1959), Disney's most ambitious and expensive animated film, was a financial disaster, but had dazzling animation effects set to the score of Tchaikovsky's ballet of the same name.

The studio also produced dozens of public service films for the U.S. government, the armed forces, and various institutions. During

World War II it provided brilliant animation for the "Why We Fight" series supervised by Frank Capra. Even its cartoons served the war effort, notably the Oscar-winning *Der Fuehrer's Face* (1942), in which Donald Duck has a nightmare that he is in Nazi Germany.

Treasure Island (1950) was the first all live-action feature and the first in a series of swashbuckling adventures produced at Disney's British studio, which also included *The Story of Robin Hood* (1952) and *Kidnapped* (1960)—all with British casts. Among the most successful ventures in live-action were *20,000 Leagues under the Sea* (1954), *Old Yeller* (1957), and *The Parent Trap* (1961).

One of Disney Studio's biggest commercial and critical hits was *Mary Poppins* (1964), a lavishly produced musical integrating a live-action story of a British nanny (Julie Andrews) with ingenious animated sequences. The film was nominated for thirteen Academy Awards and won five awards (including Best Actress for Andrews).

Disneyland, the studio's first television venture, premiered on ABC in October 1954. Its programming, representing the diversity of the Disney product, included many of its cartoons, live-action and nature subjects, but new material premiered as well, like the "Davy Crockett" series. Other Disney television programs included *The Mickey Mouse Club*, an instant success at its premiere in 1955; *Zorro*, a weekly adventure series; and *The Wonderful World of Color*, which premiered on NBC in 1961.

The view of America—and life in general—projected through the varied products of the Disney Studio was remarkably consistent. Whether embodied in the contests between good and evil in *Snow White* or *Sleeping Beauty*, or in the celebration of traditional family and patriotic values through heroes like Johnny Tremain and Davy Crockett, Disney's

was the personality and vision that marked every work. This was both his genius and the reason, over the years, that so many artists and directors—including loyal collaborators like Ub Iwerks—found him tyrannical and left the Disney Studio.

Perhaps the ultimate symbols of Disney's empire are the two amusement parks he created. The first, Disneyland, opened in Anaheim, California, in 1955, and the second, Walt Disney World, in Orlando, Florida, in 1971. Today, versions of Disneyland exist around the world. The Disney company was and is one of the most successful merchandising businesses of the century, producing numerous commodities linked to its films, including books, comics, records, toys, clothes, games, and watches. The income from such sources reached $130 million annually by 1986.

After Disney's death in 1966, the studio's fortunes varied but have markedly improved since the late 1970s. Under the banner of Touchstone Pictures it has produced many live-action successes, including *Splash* (1984), *The Color of Money* (1987), and *Who Framed Roger Rabbit* (1988), coproduced by Steven Spielberg, an extraordinary integration of live action and animation. An ebullient tribute to the achievements of Disney and his contemporaries, the film's animation won a Special Academy Award. The Studio's pure animation impulse was revitalized with *The Little Mermaid* (1989), *Beauty and the Beast* (1991), and *Aladdin* (1992).

BIBLIOGRAPHY

Finch, Christopher, *The Art of Walt Disney*, 1973; Holliss, Richard, and Brian Sibley, *The Disney Studio Story*, 1988; Maltin, Leonard, *The Disney Films*, 1973; Mosley, Leonard, *Disney's World*, 1985.

Dixon, Willie James

(July 1, 1915–January 29, 1992)
Bass Player, Singer, Songwriter

Dixon, a mover in the Chicago blues, wrote for fellow Mississippians MUDDY WATERS and HOWLIN' WOLF. His songs transposed the gentler Delta blues into keyed-up city music that touched black migrants' roots while it addressed urban realities.

Willie Dixon was one of fourteen children and grew up on a farm near Vicksburg, Mississippi. In the late twenties he visited Chicago but went home to Mississippi shortly. By the early thirties he was writing and selling songs to local musicians and had joined a gospel group, the Jubilee Singers. He returned to Chicago in 1936 to become a fighter and won the Illinois State Golden Gloves heavyweight championship in 1937. Subsequently he quarreled with his manager and gave up boxing.

Dixon met Leonard ("Baby Doo") Caston, a Mississippi-born guitarist/pianist, at the gym, learned to play bass, and turned to music. Working with Caston and blues groups, he sang and played bass with the Five Breezes, recorded by Bluebird in 1940. In 1941 he refused the draft. "I didn't feel I had to go because of the conditions that existed among my people," he said later. After a brief time in jail, he established the Four Jumps of Jive, who were recorded by Mercury.

With Baby Doo Caston he founded a vocal group, the Big Three Trio, in 1945. A year later "Wee Wee Baby, You Sure Look Good to Me" was a hit. By 1948 Dixon was working studio sessions for Chess Records and went full-time with Chess after the Big Three Trio disbanded in 1952.

Dixon recorded on bass and as a singer for Chess. Though valued for his solid performances, he found his niche in songwriting. He'd been listening to Muddy Waters. "There was quite a few people around singing the blues," he said, "but most of 'em was singin' all *sad* blues. Muddy was givin' his blues a little pep ... I began tryin' to think of things in a peppier form."

In 1954 "Hoochie Coochie Man" appeared. The song, says critic Robert Palmer, "featured stop-time riffs, the whole band phrasing them in unison—dah *dah* dah dat!" Through the fifties, Dixon continued to write songs for performers like Little Walter, Buddy Guy, and Magic Sam. His creations for Howlin' Wolf became classics: "Back Door Man," "Wang Dang Doodle," "Little Red Rooster," and "You Can't Judge a Book by Its Cover."

Dixon played bass at Chess sessions for rock stars CHUCK BERRY and Bo Diddley and took the Chicago blues to Europe as bandleader for the American Folk Blues Festival from 1962 to 1964. His songs inspired groups like the Yardbirds and the Rolling Stones. He recorded for Columbia, Capitol, and others, wrote a song for MARTIN SCORSESE's film *The Color of Money* (1986), and produced a Bo Diddley revamp of "Who Do You Love" for the movie *La Bamba* (1987). Dixon died in Burbank, California.

BIBLIOGRAPHY

Keil, C., *Urban Blues,* 1966; Palmer, R., *Deep Blues,* 1981.

Dos Passos, John Roderigo

(January 14, 1896–September 28, 1970)
Essayist, Novelist

John Dos Passos wrote fiction and history that lionized the rights and the promise of the individual against the corruptions of capitalism and war. The radical structure of his three-part *U.S.A.* earned it praise as one of the most ambitious American novels of this century.

Born John Madison on January 14, 1896, in a Chicago hotel room, he was the son of a successful lawyer and grandson of a Portuguese immigrant. His parents were not free to marry until 1910, after his father's first wife had died. Until that time, the boy and his mother lived quietly, traveling in Europe much of the time and receiving his father's visits surreptitiously. The youth took his father's name in 1912.

This period of domestic normalcy was short-lived. Dos Passos's mother died in 1915, his father in 1917. It took years to establish claim to some part of his father's estate, though eventually Dos Passos took title to his father's Virginia farm.

Dos Passos and his college friend E. E. CUMMINGS both had poems published in *Eight Harvard Poets* in 1917, shortly after graduating from Harvard University. Eager to see the war in Europe, Dos Passos went to study in Spain, eventually joined the Norton-Harjes Ambulance Corps and served in France (as did E. E. Cummings), and later enlisted with a U.S. Army medical unit.

Three Soldiers (1921) established his career as a writer. A polemical novel, it follows the wartime fortunes of three young men from different ethnic backgrounds and classes. War is depicted as the tool of a capitalistic society bent on stifling individual freedom. Widely read, the book became a model for many subsequent novels in which war itself becomes a character.

During the 1920s Dos Passos traveled throughout the United States and journeyed to Europe, Africa, the Middle East, and Russia. He wrote prolifically, publishing four novels, two travel books, two plays, and a volume of poetry.

Manhattan Transfer (1925) offers a cross section of life in New York City. All of the characters are affected by the city, which is depicted as a wasteland. Motivated by greed and a lust for power, they form a microcosm of the larger industrial society.

In 1927 Dos Passos published *Facing the Chair,* a defense of Nicola Sacco and Bartolomeo Vanzetti, two avowed anarchists who many believed to have been falsely convicted of two murders amid public backlash against radicals.

The plays *The Garbage Man* (1926; first produced as *The Moon Is a Gong* in 1925), *Airways, Inc.* (1928), and *Fortune Heights* (1933) drew on real-world events and offered pastiches of popular culture. They depict the search for happiness and belief in a society crushed by its own material ambitions.

Dos Passos was deeply concerned with social history. In 1928 he traveled to Russia, though he returned only modestly impressed by the Communist experiment.

His masterpiece, *U.S.A.* (1938), was published as three separate novels—*The 42nd Parallel* (1930), *1919* (1932), and *The Big Money* (1936)—and then collected as a massive trilogy. In this work Dos Passos mingled fact and fiction to create a new type of narrative. The reader eventually realizes that the social background of twentieth-century America is, in fact, the main character. Woven together with fictional passages are excerpts from newspaper stories and popular songs, impressionistic sketches from the author's memory, and biographies of real Americans. As in *Manhattan Transfer,* the fictional characters represent all walks of life. The scheme of the books was modernist in its self-consciousness and complexity; the volumes created a stir among writers and other intellectuals.

Dos Passos visited Spain during its civil war (1936–1939). While he supported the Left against the Fascist rebels, he turned irrevocably against the Communist party after a friend died in a bloody purge. Dos Passos returned from Europe convinced that, whatever its faults, America represented humanity's only hope. He began a lengthy study of American history, especially the era of Thomas Jefferson.

In a tragic automobile accident in 1947, Dos Passos's wife, Katharine F. Smith, was killed and he himself lost an eye. He was devastated but continued to write. In 1949 he married Elizabeth Holdridge, and the next year they had a child, Lucy.

During the last years of his career, Dos Passos devoted most of his energies to American history. He wrote studies of political and social leaders—such as *The Head and Heart of Thomas Jefferson* (1954) and *The Men Who Made the Nation* (1957)—as well as more general studies, including *Mr. Wilson's War* (1962) and *The Shackles of Power: Three Jeffersonian Decades* (1966).

Dos Passos returned to the techniques that had made *U.S.A.* successful in his novel *Midcentury: A Contemporary Chronicle* (1961), which recorded the decline of the labor movement and celebrated free enterprise. His final novel, *Century's Ebb: The Thirteenth Chronicle* published posthumously in 1975, also showed some of the power of his earlier technique.

BIBLIOGRAPHY

Landsberg, Melvin, *Dos Passos' Path to U.S.A.: A Political Biography 1912–1936*, 1972; Ludington, Townsend, *John Dos Passos: A Twentieth-Century Odyssey*, 1980.

Dreiser, Theodore Herman Albert

(August 27, 1871–December 28, 1945)
Novelist

In his novels, Theodore Dreiser depicted individuals caught hopelessly between natural drives and ambitions and a society that imposed moralistic limitations and impossible expectations for material success. He shocked readers in the early twentieth century with highly documented fictionalizations of real-life tragedies whose circumstances belied conventional mores.

Dreiser was born in 1871 into a large family living on the edge of poverty in Terre Haute, Indiana. His father, who had been crippled in an accident, was employed only occasionally. Dreiser himself worked as a janitor before a former teacher insisted on paying his expenses for a year at Indiana University.

Dreiser broke into journalism, working for newspapers in Chicago, St. Louis, Pittsburgh, and New York. He was encouraged to write fiction by his eldest brother, Paul, who had earned fame as a songwriter under the name Paul Dresser.

Dreiser came to be deeply affected by the evolutionary theories of the English philosopher Herbert Spencer. Like other novelists of the group called Naturalists, he became convinced that the universe was ruled by natural laws humanity had no hope of contravening. Dreiser emulated the fiction of Émile Zola; a novel, he wrote, should be "perhaps an absolutely accurate biography—not a lot of elusive imaginings and romanticism, but a literal transcript of life as it is." Though his style has been called elephantine, Dreiser argued he needed a mass of details to make the case that American society was flawed, its morals narrow and repressive, its goals monetary.

Dreiser finished his first novel, *Sister Carrie,* in 1900. The book was based in part on the experiences of a sister of his who had eloped with the cashier of a Chicago bar after he had stolen a large sum of money from his employer's safe. The novel's heroine, Carrie Meeber, is a small-town girl bent on making her future in the big city. She soon learns that her only route to riches is through men, and she takes and then abandons a series of lovers in order to succeed as an actress and to climb socially.

The book was accepted with enthusiasm by FRANK NORRIS for publication by Doubleday, Page & Company, but when the publisher Frank Doubleday returned from Europe he objected to the book on grounds of immorality. Doubleday sought to have Dreiser withdraw the manuscript. When Dreiser refused, the company fulfilled the letter of the contract but neither advertised nor distributed the book. Norris sent out review copies, but the critics were as appalled as Doubleday: a sinful woman remains unpunished.

The furor over the novel exhausted Dreiser. He spent two years recovering from depression. Unable to write, he first edited dime novels, then two magazines. His brother Paul found him a job at Butterick Publications, a publisher of women's magazines, and by 1907 he was promoted to managing editor at a handsome salary. But Dreiser lost this job in 1910, when he was exposed as the seducer of an employee's young daughter. The affair also ended his ten-year marriage to Sara White.

He returned to his writing and published *Jennie Gerhardt* in 1911. The heroine embodies a virtue not found in Carrie Meeber: she remains loyal to the two lovers who abandon her, to her disapproving father, to the natural daughter she loses to typhoid, and to the orphans she later adopts.

In 1912 Dreiser published *The Financier,* the first novel of his so-called Trilogy of Desire,

which traced the fortunes of a fictional captain of industry, Frank Cowperwood. Based on the real-life exploits of a Chicago-based transportation magnate, the novels were meticulously documented and portrayed a ruthless self-promoter bent on achieving wealth, power, and sexual gratification. By the time the second novel, *The Titan,* was ready for publication in 1914, the first had become so controversial that a new publisher had to be found. The third novel, *The Stoic,* was published posthumously in 1947.

The "Genius" (1915), the most autobiographical of Dreiser's works, depicts conflicting drives toward sex and success at the heart of a young artist. The novel was withdrawn by its publisher after being labeled obscene by the New York Society for the Suppression of Vice. Dreiser's subsequent battle against the censors was credited with easing the way for a new generation of writers.

In *An American Tragedy* (1925), a massive novel, Dreiser again explores the effect of the law of the jungle on a man ill-equipped to advance or even to defend himself. Based on a celebrated murder case, the novel examines the plight of Clyde Griffiths, convicted in the drowning death of his pregnant fiancée. Griffiths had hoped to free himself to marry a wealthy woman, but the novel leaves vague whether he is truly culpable in his fiancée's death. Many readers felt assured Dreiser was blaming an immoral society rather than a weak hero. *An American Tragedy,* craftily titled, became a best-seller, and Dreiser lived well on the proceeds until the stock market crash of 1929.

Dreiser traveled to the Soviet Union in 1927 as a guest of the government. With JOHN DOS PASSOS and others, he formed a committee in 1931 to investigate working conditions among coal miners in Bell and Harlan counties, Kentucky. He later joined the Communist party.

Between 1925 and 1945, Dreiser wrote several books of memoirs, essays, and history, including *Chains* (1927), *Dreiser Looks at Russia* (1928), *The Carnegie Works at Pittsburgh* (1929), *My City* (1929), *Tragic Amer-*

ica (1931), and *America Is Worth Saving* (1941).

In 1944 Dreiser married Helen Richardson, who had been his mistress for many years. He died in Hollywood, California.

BIBLIOGRAPHY

Lundquist, James, *Theodore Dreiser*, 1974; Swanberg, W. A., *Dreiser*, 1965.

Duchamp, Henri-Robert-Marcel

(July 28, 1887–October 2, 1968)
Painter, Sculptor

Library of Congress

Marcel Duchamp was this century's foremost modernist. He absorbed the important art movements of his youth, like Cubism and Futurism and prefigured the modern development of Dadaism, Surrealism, Pop, and Conceptual art. Duchamp spent only part of his life in the United States, but he affected significantly American concepts about the boundaries of art.

Duchamp was born in the Rouen region of Normandy, France, in 1887, the third of six children. Like his two older brothers, Gaston and Raymond, he showed a precocious ability for drawing and sketching. It seemed only natural that, like them, he would aspire to be an artist.

Duchamp quickly absorbed the art movements that were burgeoning around him. At age fifteen, he executed a *Landscape at Blainville* (1902) in the Impressionist manner. Two years later, after joining his brothers at the Académie Julian, his paintings showed the influence of Cézanne. Soon he was using the bold, discordant palette of the Fauves and their leader, Matisse, and experimenting with Cubism, an art movement in which natural forms are reduced to geometrical ones. In his brothers' studio he met the Cubists Fernand Léger, Roger de la Fresnaye, Robert Delaunay, and Francis Picabia. The works of these artists, as well as the chronophotographs of Étienne-Jules Marey, were absorbed in *The Sonata* and *Portrait (Dulcinea)* (both 1911), which suggested not only the fracturing of the image but its movement through space. *Sad Young Man in a Train* and *Coffee Mill* (both 1911) displayed a Futuristic concern with the dynamism of machinery with sexual overtones. Stop-motion imagery would appear in subsequent works for the rest of his painting career.

Shortly afterward, Duchamp executed the first version of the painting that brought him great notoriety—*Nude Descending a Staircase* (1911; the second and final version was completed a year later). Based on a text by the Symbolist poet Jules Laforgue, it transformed a nude woman into a mechanized abstraction in downward motion. He sent it to the Salon des Indépendants. Its rejection alienated Duchamp forever after from affiliation with any art groups. When it was shown in New York City at the legendary 1913 International Exhibition of Modern Art (the epic Armory Show; see STUART DAVIS), it incurred the lion's share of critical outrage.

Meanwhile, Duchamp abjured painting in 1913, taking a job as a library clerk in the Bibliothèque Sainte-Geneviève. He cast about for an entirely different means of image making and conceptualizing. "It's very difficult to escape from the prison of tradition," he said. "Education is so strong; it holds you like a chain." He experimented with the element of chance, composing music by drawing the notes out of a hat. He brought a wine bottle rack and the front wheel of a bicycle into his studio. When he signed his name on the rack, he undermined at a stroke the whole tradition of Western art. These were the first of his famous "readymades"—defined once and for all in 1934 by Surrealist leader André Breton as "manufactured objects promoted to the dignity of objects of art through the choice of the artist."

After the outbreak of World War I, Duchamp came to America. He was an instant celebrity, and he was able to keep a studio in New York City on the proceeds of French lessons that he gave to well-to-do admirers. In 1917 he selected and signed some of his most famous readymades, a snow shovel (*In Advance of the Broken Arm*) and a urinal (*Fountain*). When the Society of Independent Artists, which Duchamp had helped found, refused to exhibit it as a piece of sculpture, he scornfully replied: "It is a fixture you see every day in plumbers' show windows. The only works of art America has given [us] are her plumbing and her bridges." Almost as controversial was his "assisted" readymade entitled *L.H.O.O.Q.*, a reproduction of the *Mona Lisa* on which he drew a goatee and mustache (1919).

In his work Duchamp was pursuing a parallel course with the Dada movement in Europe, the most aggressively radical trend in art history. To Duchamp, who carefully kept some distance from the movement, Dada was "a sort of nihilism . . . a way to get out of a state of mind—to avoid being influenced by one's immediate environment or by the past, to get away from clichés—to get free."

Throughout the 1920s Duchamp experimented in a variety of media. He appeared in René Clair's Dadaist short film *Entr'acte* (1924), in which he was seen playing chess (a favorite activity); served as a kind of agent for the sculptor Brancusi; and manufactured several motion machines, notably *Revolving Glass*—five rectangular glass plates attached to a metal rod that was turned by a motor. (In 1932 he would coin the term "mobile" to describe ALEXANDER CALDER's moving metal sculptures.) He startled everyone with a temporary "identity alteration" when he took on the female alter ego of "Rrose Sélavy." He even brought to a "definitive stage of incompletion" a work that had preoccupied him for ten years, *The Bride Stripped Bare by Her Bachelors, Even (the Large Glass)*—called by historian Calvin Tomkins "the most enigmatic and by all odds the most complex work of art produced in our time." The work is actually two works—*Large Glass*, a 9-foot-high object that stands today in the Philadelphia Museum of Art, and a collection of ninety-three written notations regarding *Large Glass* that Duchamp collected between 1911–1920 and published in facsimile in 1934 as *Boite Verte (Green Box)*. Together, the two pieces—what Duchamp described as "a wedding of mental and visual relations"—constituted a witty use of mechanistic forms to express a sardonic vision of the frustrations of physical love. (A second version was made in 1961 by Duchamp and Ulf Linde and is presently in the Moderna Museet, Stockholm.)

In the 1930s the Surrealists, led by André Breton, courted the elusive Duchamp, in so many ways one of the founders of the movement in which imagery is based on fantasy or the subconscious. Breton's monograph on him in 1935, *Lighthouse of the Bride*, laid the basis for his future reputation. Although Duchamp avoided a close entanglement with the movement, he did assist Breton in installing the 1938 International Exhibition of Surrealism in Paris. He also worked on a series of color experiments and optical illusions (*Rotoreliefs* in 1935 and *Coeurs volants* [Fluttering Hearts] in 1936) based on retinal scintillation anticipating by thirty years the Op art of the 1960s. Otherwise, he lived reclusively in his little studio on the Rue Larrey. This abode has become famous in art history because of its Duchamp-designed door, a paradox on hinges, as it were, which served alternately to close either the bathroom or the main entrance (and could thus be open and shut at the same time).

After several trips back and forth to Paris, Duchamp returned to New York for good in 1942 and established spartan quarters in a small studio over a commercial building at 210 West 14th Street. For the next two and a half decades he seemed content to be a kind of elder statesman among a younger generation of artists. It was an ironic position, writes Calvin Tomkins: "[C]onsidered the anti-artist of all time, the complete iconoclast who had once proposed, as a readymade, the use of a Rembrandt painting as an ironing board, he nevertheless worked quietly and generously to promote the careers of younger artists and to further the development of modern art." He became an American citizen in the 1950s, married for a second time, and soon saw a revival of interest in his work. When Walter

Arensberg died in 1954, his vast collection of Duchamp's works was bequeathed to the Philadelphia Museum of Art. In 1963 the Pasadena Art Museum mounted a large Duchamp exhibition, the first major retrospective show of his work ever presented anywhere. Moreover, Duchamp assisted in the publishing of several books devoted to his work. A younger generation of painters from the Abstract Expressionist (see BARNETT NEWMAN), Pop art (see ROY LICHTENSTEIN), and Op art movements, paid him tribute. Ironically, the master of "antiart" was now effectively canonized as a patron saint of modern art.

Duchamp took his twilight fame in stride. "Society takes what it wants," he said. "The artist himself doesn't count.... The work of art is always based on the two poles of the onlooker and the maker, and the spark that comes from that bipolar action gives birth to something—like electricity. But the onlooker has the last word, and it is always posterity that makes the masterpiece."

BIBLIOGRAPHY

View, Marcel Duchamp Number, Series V, No. 1, 1945; Hamilton, Richard, *The Bride Stripped Bare by Her Bachelors, Even,* 1960; Tomkins, Calvin, *The World of Marcel Duchamp,* 1966.

Duncan, Isadora

(May 26, 1878–September 14, 1927)
Dancer

S parking the modern dance movement and challenging the status quo, the dynamic beauty Isadora Duncan tripped barefoot to Wagner and Brahms, dressed uncorseted in Greek tunics, and liberated movement from tradition. She is still influential for the expressionism of her performance and the high guiding principles of her schools.

Born in San Francisco, California, during the Bay Area rage for Greek Revival, Isadora Duncan was trained in ballet as a child. The precise nature of this early discipline is not documented, but it is clear that early on she rejected classic techniques for her own style based on natural movement.

A concert dancer, Duncan worked for theatrical manager AUGUSTIN DALY in Chicago and New York before traveling to Europe in 1900. There her career blossomed. She toured with the American Loïe Fuller, who capitalized on the magic of billowing fabric and movement. Fuller understood the technological potential of stage lighting and in her theatrical presentations interpreted music through light and color, not through choreography.

In Europe, Duncan gave recitals and lecture-demonstrations and traveled to Budapest and Berlin (1903), St. Petersburg (1904), and London and New York (1908). Her affinity for classic art was becoming clear though Duncan's espousal of beauty was intuitive and emotional, never academic. Dance writer Don McDonagh observed that she "tried to create serious truth through the beauty of expressive movement . . . and appropriated concert-level music for the dance steps." In 1905, for example, she performed her *Iphigenia in Aulis* to Gluck's 1774 score. One of her dancers, Marie-Therese, said of her performance, "gliding, swaying she achieves an almost unearthly lightness."

Duncan's private life was unconventional and unsettled. She bore three children out of wedlock: a son to the wealthy Paris Singer, a daughter to the gifted actor-producer Edward Gordon Craig (both children drowned in the Seine River in 1913), and a third child who died in infancy. Following the tragedy in 1913,

Duncan retired from the stage and concentrated on teaching, but returned to the theater during World War I. According to British dance critics Mary Clarke and Clement Crisp, "her art then acquired the dark and massive qualities to which it was best suited," as in the 1917 *Marche Slav*, performed to the music of Tchaikovsky.

By 1921 she was in Russia again, where she established a school and married the poet Sergei Esenin. Esenin accompanied Duncan on an American tour marked by criticism like that from evangelist Billy Sunday: "The Bolshevik hussy doesn't wear enough clothes to pad a crutch." Duncan's marriage ended in 1924 and she returned to Europe. Dogged by financial problems, failed schools, and despair, she retreated to Nice and her studio, performing occasionally, always attempting to raise money. She gave her last concert in Paris in 1927 and that year died motoring in Nice, strangled by her long scarf caught in the car's spoked wheel.

Clarke and Crisp write that "no dancer has ever inspired so many fine artists . . . in their representations is seen the life of Duncan's art, its grandeur and its freedom, and its power to excite. It is this that has inspired the impulse behind the entire modern dance movement."

BIBLIOGRAPHY

Duncan, I., *My Life*, 1927, rep., 1955; Steegmuller, F., *Your Isadora*, 1974.

Dylan, Bob

(May 24, 1941–   )
Singer/Songwriter

A central figure in the urban folk movement of the 1960s and 1970s, Bob Dylan, first known for protest songs, would move far beyond the narrow tradition of folk music and ultimately influence the content of rock as well.

Born Robert Allen Zimmerman in Duluth, Minnesota, Dylan moved with his family to the small iron-mining town of Hibbing in the mid-forties. He had a keen interest in music and, self-taught, he played the guitar, harmonica, and piano. In high school Dylan was part of the Golden Chords, a rock and roll band. Emulating his movie hero James Dean, Dylan acted the defiant outsider, riding his motorcycle and dreaming of leaving small-town life for the big city. In 1959 he arrived in Minneapolis, where he spent three semesters at the University of Minnesota, evidently more interested in pursuing a career as a folksinger than in his classes. Accounts differ, but it was apparently at this time that he first used the stage name of Bob Dylan.

He went east in 1961 in search of WOODY GUTHRIE, the folksinger, who was then ill in a New Jersey hospital. He visited Guthrie regularly and began to perform in Greenwich Village at Gerdes' Folk City. After JOHN HAMMOND signed him for Columbia Records, his first album, *Bob Dylan*, issued in 1962, included two Dylan songs, "Talkin' New York" and "Song to Woody." The recording reveals his admiration for Guthrie, bluesmen HUDDIE LEDBETTER and Big Joe Williams, and country singers HANK WILLIAMS and Jimmie Rodgers.

In 1963 Dylan began to hit his stride on the album *The Freewheelin' Bob Dylan* with the songs "Blowin' in the Wind," "A Hard Rain's a-Gonna Fall," and "Masters of War." With the 1964 album *The Times They Are a-Changin'*, he had the public's attention for his songs of social protest. Other performers, like Peter, Paul and Mary and Joan Baez, were to record Dylan songs successfully. *Another Side of Bob Dylan*, issued later that year, however, turned away from social causes and revealed a more personal tone.

Dylan was impressed by the success of the Beatles and the Rolling Stones, who had revitalized the spirit of rock and roll. One side of Dylan's *Bringing It All Back Home* (1965) introduces electric blues. This album, along with *Highway 61 Revisited*, uses blues and folk to fashion a kind of rock that critic Jon Pareles considers "one of the artistic peaks of rock music" because of the quality of the lyrics and singing and the intensity of performance. That year Dylan's song "Mr. Tambourine Man," performed by The Byrds, was folk-rock's first hit single. "Like a Rolling Stone," his first commercial hit, climbed the charts, as did "Rainy Day Women Nos. 12 & 35" in 1966.

A motorcycle accident in July 1966 was nearly fatal. Recuperating in Woodstock, New York, Dylan wrote songs and recorded, the results released much later as *The Basement Tapes* (1975). His musical backup, The Band, began to perform on its own. In 1968 Dylan appeared at a concert honoring Woody Guthrie, recorded "John Wesley Harding," and explored country music on *Nashville Skyline* (1969), an early country-rock recording.

During the seventies Dylan performed to wildly mixed reviews from the critics. He had a successful tour with The Band in 1974, recorded, and with Joan Baez and others formed a touring group, the Rolling Thunder Revue. Scenes from one performance, broadcast by NBC-TV, were included in *Renaldo and Clara* (1978), a film directed by Dylan. In 1979 Dylan announced that he had become a fundamentalist Christian, which was reflected in *Slow Train Coming* and *Saved*.

Dylan continues into the 1990s exploring a wide range of sounds and styles, working with musicians both legendary and obscure, forever defying pressures to pander to anything other than the direction of his heart. Although millions have looked to his songs for direction, he claims he never intended to be a voice of a generation. In his own words, "I told them not to follow leaders, to watch parking meters. I wasn't going to fall for that, for being any kind of leader."

BIBLIOGRAPHY

Cott, J., *Dylan,* 1984; Mellers, W., *A Darker Shade of Pale,* 1985; Scaduto, Anthony, *Bob Dylan,* 1973; Shelton, R., *No Direction Home: The Life and Music of Bob Dylan,* 1986.

Eakins, Thomas

(July 25, 1844–June 25, 1916)
Painter

Thomas Eakins, who considered himself a "scientific realist," was primarily interested in the human figure and is most famous for his portraits and his pictures of athletes, including swimmers, boxers, and rowers.

Eakins was born in Philadelphia, went to high school there, and studied at the Pennsylvania Academy of the Fine Arts, the oldest art school in America, where he learned the basics of his art. In 1866 he went to Paris to study with Léon Bonnat, Jean Léon Gérôme, and the sculptor A. A. Dumont. On a long trip to Spain, he was impressed by the work of the Spanish realists Velázquez and Goya.

When the Franco-Prussian War broke out in 1870, he went back to Philadelphia and stayed there the rest of his life. He studied anatomy at the Jefferson Medical College, acquiring a basis for his mastery of drawing the human figure. A by-product of his anatomical studies was his fascination with surgical operations and autopsies. The operating theater was the subject of the large canvas that is generally considered his masterpiece, *The Gross Clinic* (1875), which dramatizes the pedagogical moment as well as the calm confidence of the surgeon. Dr. Samuel Gross, in the center of the picture, explains the operation to intent students, while the anesthetician and nurses concentrate on their work. The picture shocked most people.

Blood was considered indelicate, and the patient's naked thigh, bared for the operation, was thought to be obscene. Eakins painted this picture for the Centennial Exposition of 1876 in Philadelphia, but it was rejected by the art exhibition and hung in the medical section of the exposition. Fourteen years later Eakins painted another operation, *The Agnew Clinic* (1889), which is less focused and less dramatic.

Eakins was as interested in athletic events as he was in anatomical dissection. His paintings of boat races and boxing matches again reveal his full command in drawing the human figure. *Max Schmitt in a Single Scull* (1871) shows one of his friends in a rowing shell. Eakins, who often went rowing with Schmitt on the Schuylkill River, painted himself at the oars of another shell in the background. Eakins took infinite care with his pictures, and for this painting he did scale drawings of the boats, oars, and bridges. He had invented a system that used trigonometry to place the figures and landscape in the correct perspective and proportion. To study the effects of sunlight, he made rag models of the figures and built a model scull from a cigar box. Using thick pigment in the foreground and transparent glazes for the distant shadows, he achieved the illusion of total reality.

In *William Rush Carving His Allegorical Figure of the Schuylkill River* (1877), Eakins recreated an event that had taken place in 1809 involving the Philadelphia sculptor and carver of figureheads for ships, who used nude models when that practice was extremely rare in the United States. Rush had caused a small scandal by using a society girl as his nude model for his wooden carving *Water Nymph and Bittern*. In Eakins's painting, Rush works in the shadowy background. His model, a graceful young woman, a dictionary on her shoulder instead of the bittern of Rush's sculpture, is in the foreground, her clothes scattered on the chair beside her. A chaperon sits in the shadows on the right, knitting. Eakins produced several versions of this picture, which can be read as an allegory of artistic creation and the problems of the artist in a conventional society.

Eakins painted many portraits, all of them honest, and sitters often complained about these uncompromising likenesses. One of his best portraits shows his father, who had taught penmanship to well-to-do Philadelphia children, in a painting called *The Writing Master* (1882). His father's hands are old, full of wrinkles and age spots, and his head, with its spare gray hair, is painted faithfully without flattery. People criticized his portrait of WALT WHITMAN (1887), but Whitman defended it, saying that only an unusual person would appreciate it. "I only knew of but one artist," Whitman said, "and that's Tom Eakins, who could resist the temptation to see what they ought to be rather than what is."

He did not beautify Susan Hannah Macdowell, one of his art students, whom he married in 1881. In *The Pathetic Song* (1881), Miss Macdowell stands to sing, sheet music in her hand. Her gray taffeta dress, with its bustle, train, and pleated ruffles, is meticulously painted; so is her face, which although not flattered by the painter's brush, is warm and filled with the emotion of the song she sings.

The Swimming Hole (1883), with its group of male swimmers (his students) diving, swim-ming, and lounging on a rock wall, demonstrates Eakins's concern with the nude. He loved watching boxing matches, and his *Between Rounds* (1899) depicts a trainer fanning the boxer, seated on a stool in the corner of the ring.

When Eakins, who taught at the Pennsylvania Academy for many years, gained authority there, he drastically revised the curriculum and cut out classes in illustration, art history, and composition, emphasizing perspective and the study of the live model instead of classical casts. He let students begin oil painting immediately instead of making them draw for years. The students still studied anatomy and took part in dissections, which Eakins believed was as essential to art as to medicine. He made students study the actions of the body, and once to show how the pelvis worked, removed the loincloth from a male model. Some of his female students complained, and Eakins's insistence on nude models led the academy's trustees to dismiss him in 1886. Most of his students approved of his teaching methods, and many of them withdrew and started the Art Students League of Philadelphia, where Eakins taught without pay for seven years.

Eakins's work was rarely appreciated in his lifetime, and he made very little money from his painting. When the Pennsylvania Academy gave him a gold medal late in his life, he showed up to receive it wearing bicycling clothes. He said at the ceremony that the academy, which had failed to support his teaching, had its nerve giving him a medal. He rode his bicycle over to the mint and sold the gold medal for $75 in cash. He died in 1916 at the age of seventy-one.

BIBLIOGRAPHY

Goodrich, Lloyd, *Thomas Eakins*, 1982; Johns, Elizabeth, *Thomas Eakins, the Heroism of Modern Life*, 1983.

Eames, Charles

(June 7, 1907–August 21, 1978)
Architect, Furniture Designer

Charles Eames was one of the most important designers in the post–World War II period. His innovations in furniture design helped to bring America out from the shadow of European designers.

Eames was born in St. Louis in 1907. He attended the Washington University School of Architecture from 1924 to 1926. He opened his own office in St. Louis in 1930. Six years later he accepted a fellowship at the Cranbrook Academy near Detroit, where he studied under ELIEL SAARINEN. Later he directed its department of experimental design. At Cranbrook he and EERO SAARINEN, Eliel's son, began experimenting with molded plywood chair designs. Working along the lines of the International style of the 1930s (see LUDWIG MIES VAN DER ROHE), the two men stressed the functional character of their chairs. In 1940 these designs won them first prize in the Museum of Modern Art's "Organic Design Chair Competition."

One of Eames's trademarks was to differentiate clearly between the upper and lower structural elements of his chairs. He introduced complex, multidirectional curves in the molding, manipulating a single sheet of wood to form the seat, the back, and the arms in a sculptural manner. By contrast, this molded seat unit was mounted on slender legs of steel rods. The resulting compound curves were emphatically three-dimensional, relating the chairs to sculpture that must be seen not in profile but in the round. This anticipated subsequent work in molded plastics.

After marrying a Cranbrook colleague, painter and designer Ray Kaiser (with whom he would collaborate on many of his designs), Eames moved to Venice, California. During World War II the U.S. Navy commissioned him to produce molded plywood stretchers and splints. This experience, in turn, inspired his famous postwar "Eames chair." It consisted of two molded wooden elements, seat and back, attached to a light metal frame by shock-absorbing rubber pads. The Herman Miller Furniture Company began manufacturing the chair in 1946 (and continues to do so today). That same year the Museum of Modern Art gave him a one-man show. Meanwhile, he was working on "metal stamping," by which he hoped to design the metal furniture of the future. These designs were incorporated into a new molded plastic technique developed by the Herman Miller Furniture Company in 1950. Other Eames designs of the period included the 1948 bucket-shaped, one-piece plastic chair, the DAR molded fiberglass shell chair in 1949, the DKR dining or desk chair (the "Bikini") in 1953, and the famous 1956 lounge chair and ottoman (the twentieth century's answer to the old wing or club chair). He also designed sofas, tables, radio cabinets, and other household objects.

In 1949 Charles and Ray Eames designed their house in Pacific Palisades, California, the Case Study House, that was among the most important domestic buildings of its time. Mass-produced materials that could be ordered from catalogs were utilized, including stock window and door elements, normally used in the construction of factories. In effect, it was a collection of ready-mades, anticipating the boom in prefabricated structures. It owed something of its clarity to the emerging influence of Mies van der Rohe's steel-and-glass buildings in Chicago.

Eames appeared at a time when American designers were still working in primarily European idioms. Imported furniture dominated the contract market. "I think of myself officially as an architect," he said; "I can't help but look at the problems around us as problems of structure—and structure is architecture." His impact was international. He influenced Scandinavian designers like Finn Juhl and Arne Jacobsen, as well as British designers. It is no exaggeration to say that much of progressive furniture design since World War II is indebted to his innovations in form and materials.

BIBLIOGRAPHY
Bates, Elizabeth Bidwell, and Jonathan L. Fairbanks, *American Furniture, 1620 to the Present*, 1981; Clark, Robert J., et al., *Design in America: The Cranbrook Vision, 1925–1950*, 1983; Eames, Charles, *Furniture for the Design Collection of the Museum of Modern Art*, 1973.

Eliot, Thomas Stearns

(September 26, 1888–January 4, 1965)
Critic, Playwright, Poet

In 1948 T. S. Eliot won the Nobel Prize for Literature and was cited as "a leader and champion of a new period in the long history of the world's poetry." Among his greatest poems are "The Love Song of J. Alfred Prufrock," *The Waste Land*, and the *Four Quartets*.

Eliot was born in St. Louis, Missouri, in 1888 to a family of prominent clergy and educators. His grandfather, William Greenleaf Eliot, had transplanted the family from Boston to St. Louis, where he founded Smith Academy and Washington University.

Eliot's skill as a poet became evident at Harvard University, where he was editor of the literary magazine *Harvard Advocate*. While an undergraduate, Eliot discovered the French Symbolists, admiring especially the ironic detachment of Jules Laforgue. Eliot developed a distaste for romanticism and an attachment to literary tradition. He earned his B.A. in 1909 and then spent a year in Paris at the Sorbonne.

Four great early poems, written in the period 1910 to 1911, revolve thematically around problems of isolation. "Portrait of a Lady" depicts a woman talking and a man who cannot

The Nobel Foundation

answer, captive in his own thoughts. In "The Love Song of J. Alfred Prufrock," a middle-aged intellectual in a sterile society futilely tries to find meaning in his life. In "Preludes" and "Rhapsody on a Windy Night," a woman exists only as an image in the soul of a man. Eliot used allusion, irony, and a quality of open-endedness to reach past the thematic isolation of the poems and involve the reader.

From 1911 to 1914 Eliot pursued graduate study in philosophy at Harvard. He spent the following academic year at Oxford, then stayed in London an additional year working on his dissertation. Convinced that the work of contemporary philosophers was inadequate to the spiritual challenges of the time, he abandoned thought of an academic career and settled permanently in England to write.

In 1915 Eliot married Vivien Haigh-Wood, an English woman whose subsequent descent into madness drained him financially and contributed to a desperate sense of isolation and guilt. In this same year his friendship with the expatriate American poet EZRA POUND led to the publication of "The Love Song of J. Alfred Prufrock" in *Poetry* magazine in Chicago. In

1917, Pound persuaded Harriet Shaw Weaver to publish in London the first collection of Eliot's remarkably original poems, *Prufrock and Other Observations*.

Eliot worked briefly as a teacher and for nine years as a banker. He supplemented his income by working at night on reviews and essays. In 1920 he published *The Sacred Wood*, a collection of essays addressing the poet's artistic isolation. In "Tradition and the Individual Talent," Eliot advocates a poetry born of a dialogue between the contemporary poet and the Western literary masters.

Struggling against what he felt was modern poetry's formlessness, Eliot began a series of poems in quatrains. "The Hippopotamus," "Sweeney Erect," "Sweeney Among the Nightingales," and "Whispers of Immortality" are densely written satiric poems, layered with allusions.

In "Gerontion," Eliot began to explore possibilities for transcending isolation. Civilization is presented as a sea of cultural and spiritual debris floating in the mind of an old man. Yet the poet suggests linkages among these fragments by imaging the houses—mental and physical—that contain them.

Eliot's long poem, *The Waste Land*, explores the breakdown of civilization, but also of the poet's personal life. In 1921, on the verge of a nervous breakdown, Eliot spent two months in a Swiss sanitorium. There he completed *The Waste Land*. The poem appeared in October 1922 in the first issue of *Criterion*, the journal Eliot edited for the next seventeen years.

In *The Waste Land*, Eliot experimented with what he called the "mythical method." The poem is intended to be true to history by depicting what Eliot saw as the chaos of modern life; at the same time, it is faithful to art by referring to a mythology, an ordering mechanism.

The Waste Land refers to myths and religions from many places and times and includes fragments from the work of other poets. These are organized around themes relating to death, sex, and finally regeneration. While the poem ends in pessimism about the possibility of re-

vitalizing civilization, it does suggest that the individual can give his own life meaning.

In 1925 Eliot joined the publishing house of Faber and Gwyer (later Faber and Faber), a move that helped him financially. In 1927 he was confirmed in the Church of England and naturalized as a British subject. In 1933 he and Vivien separated permanently.

"The Hollow Men," published in *Poems, 1909–1925* (1925), alludes to Dante's *The Divine Comedy*, Shakespeare's *Julius Caesar*, and Joseph Conrad's *Heart of Darkness*. Deeply pessimistic, the poem seems to count Eliot among the spiritually dead.

Ash Wednesday (1930) marks a departure in the tone of Eliot's poetry. It describes the waste land, but it allows for the possibility that death may be followed by rebirth. The poem signals Eliot's turning to Christianity for a structure to make possible both his life and art.

In the 1930s, Eliot published his *Selected Essays* (1932) and three collections of lectures: *The Use of Poetry and the Use of Criticism* (1933), *After Strange Gods: A Primer of Modern Heresy* (1934), and *The Idea of a Christian Society* (1939).

In 1935, in Canterbury, England, Eliot saw the first successful production of his first play, *Murder in the Cathedral*. The drama about Thomas à Becket and King Henry II alternates passages in lyric and prose form. In 1939 he completed a second play, *The Family Reunion*, but the London opening was a grave disappointment. In the same year, Eliot composed *Old Possum's Book of Practical Cats* as light verse for his godchildren.

In the 1930s and early 1940s, Eliot wrote four poems—"Burnt Norton," "East Coker," "The Dry Salvages," and "Little Gidding"—gathered in 1943 as *Four Quartets*. Eliot regarded them as his finest work. In the poems, he acknowledges that life is experienced in fragments, but he refers especially to those moments of understanding in which one glimpses the pattern of one's life. These moments form the theme and structure of the four poems.

In 1948 Eliot received England's Order of Merit, as well as the Nobel Prize for Literature.

In 1950 he was inducted into the French Legion of Honor and won the New York Drama Critics' Circle Award for *The Cocktail Party,* a play published that year. He won the U.S. Presidential Medal of Freedom in 1964.

In 1957 he married Valerie Fletcher, his former secretary at Faber and Faber. At the end of his life, he seems to have found the wholeness he had long sought in his life and work. He died in London on January 4, 1965.

BIBLIOGRAPHY

Ackroyd, Peter, *T. S. Eliot: A Life,* 1984; Chiari, Joseph, *T. S. Eliot: A Memoir,* 1982; Matthews, T. S., *Great Tom: Notes Toward the Definition of T. S. Eliot,* 1974.

Ellington, Edward Kennedy

(April 29, 1899–May 24, 1974)
Composer, Jazz Musician

One of America's great composers, Duke Ellington created such standards as "Mood Indigo" and "Sophisticated Lady" in addition to jazz and sacred works. He used vocal and instrumental timbres ingeniously to produce striking new textures, many of which became regular components of the immediately recognizable "Ellington sound."

Born in Washington, D.C., Ellington grew up in a stable, affectionate family. His father, a butler, provided a comfortable home life and steered his son toward a career as an artist. At seven Ellington began to study piano. He continued with musical studies at school and with a private teacher, Henry Grant.

At Armstrong High School, a Washington manual training school for blacks, he won a National Association for the Advancement of Colored People poster contest. Subsequently offered a scholarship to the Pratt Institute of Fine Arts in Brooklyn, New York, Ellington declined, already drawn by ragtime and opportunities to play at dances and parties. By 1918 he was making a good living painting commercial signs and performing in public.

Ellington went to New York in 1922 to try his musical wings. He failed miserably. He and his Washington sidemen, Otto ("Toby") Hardwicke, bass and sax, and Sonny Greer, drums, had joined Wilbur Sweatman's band, but after a few months, discouraged, returned to Washington, D.C.

Early in 1923 pianist Fats Waller convinced Ellington that Manhattan was the place to be. Ellington and his Washingtonians, among them Elmer Snowden, banjo, and Arthur Whetsol, trumpet, headed there to work for Ada Smith, later known as "Bricktop" in continental café society, and, under Snowden's direction, to work at Barron Wilkins' Club in Harlem.

When the band was hired downtown by the Hollywood, later to become the Kentucky Club, Ellington took over as leader and Fred Guy replaced Snowden on banjo. The small group played at the Kentucky Club between 1923 and 1927 and began to increase in size. Additions included two trumpets, one of them Bubber Miley, trombone Joe ("Tricky Sam") Nanton, baritone sax Harry Carney, clarinet and tenor sax Rudy Jackson, and bass Wellman Braud. Ellington, Guy, Greer, and Braud, the rhythm section, stayed together for a decade.

In 1927 the band moved to Harlem's noted Cotton Club. Ellington's star was rising. The orchestra expanded again, adding clarinetist Barney Bigard, saxophonist Johnny Hodges, and trumpeters Freddie Jenkins and Cootie Williams. Continuing at the club until 1932, the band was often broadcast, appeared in *Check and Double Check* (1930), a film with Amos 'n' Andy, and performed around the country. These years established Ellington's lead in the jazz world and consolidated his reputation for high standards in improvisation and in orchestral jazz.

Recordings of this period included many "jungle style" numbers. The sound, original to Ellington and Miley, depends on special effects (plunger mutes, mutes on all the brasses, tomtoms, and unusual combinations of instruments). "Mood Indigo," a hit in the popular market, made Duke famous around the world. Ellington's growing success depended in part on his individual players, each with unique tone color and timbre. The special qualities each brought to the ensemble were blended by Ellington into a distinctive sound that defied replication.

Ellington's successes were accompanied by heightened creativity. In 1931 he experimented with longer compositions. *Creole Rhapsody* was followed by *Reminiscin' in Tempo* and *Diminuendo and Crescendo in Blue.* Popular hits of the period include "Sophisticated Lady," recorded in 1933; "Solitude," in 1934; and "In a Sentimental Mood," in 1935. In other works his orchestrations matched melody in importance, as in *Daybreak Express* and *Blue Harlem.*

Between 1932 and 1942, Ellington's most productive decade, the band toured the United States and Europe (in 1933 and 1939). The group contained six brasses, four reeds, and four rhythm instruments. In 1939 there were three major additions: Billy Strayhorn, arranger, composer, and second pianist; Jimmy Blanton, bass; and Ben Webster, tenor sax. Strayhorn's "Take the A Train" became the band's theme. From 1939 to August 1, 1942, the date a recording ban began (see CHARLIE PARKER), Ellington's work was, according to many, his most superb. During these years he composed "Concerto for Cootie," "Ko-Ko," and "Cotton Tail."

New instrumentalists came on board during the 1940s. By 1946 there were eighteen in the band, including Ray Nance, who played trumpet and violin. Unfortunately, as musicians came and went the musical stability of the preceding years evaporated. Ellington's com-

positions and performance reflected the uncertainty.

A series of ambitious annual Carnegie Hall Concerts began in January 1943 and showcased Ellington works, such as *Black, Brown and Beige,* his first long composition. Though not recorded because of the ban, the piece was important because it created a major concert work from jazz elements. Other longer Ellington compositions were introduced in subsequent years, among them *Liberian Suite* and *Night Creature.* At the premiere of *Night Creature,* in March 1955, the Ellington band joined forces with the Symphony of the Air.

Despite a changing roster of musicians, Ellington continued to compose and to tour during the 1950s. He created the film score for Otto Preminger's *Anatomy of a Murder* (1959) and recorded with JOHN COLTRANE, Charles Mingus, and others. In his final years Duke turned to composing sacred music. He was honored with degrees from Howard University, 1963; Yale University, 1967; and was awarded the Presidential Medal of Freedom in 1969. He continued to direct the band until his death in New York in 1974. His son, Mercer, took over the band.

Ellington was a perpetual innovator. Today many of his ideas are taken for granted: casting the voice as a jazz instrument, breaking and expanding the three-minute record time, using the concerto form to display jazz soloists. Most know Ellington through his songs, but critics and musicians admire the way he wrote for and led his orchestra. Billy Strayhorn commented, "Duke plays the piano, but his real instrument is his band."

BIBLIOGRAPHY

Dance, S., *The World of Duke Ellington,* 1970; Rattenbury, K., *Duke Ellington: Jazz Composer,* 1990; Schuller, G., *Early Jazz: Its Roots and Musical Development,* 1968, and *The Swing Era: The Development of Jazz, 1930–1945,* 1989; Ulanov, B., *Duke Ellington,* 1946, rep., 1975.

Ellison, Ralph Waldo

(March 1, 1914–   )
Essayist, Novelist

Ralph Ellison, whose novel *Invisible Man* has become a classic of modern American fiction, has written compellingly of the experience of African Americans in a society that has tended to ignore their problems.

Ralph Waldo Ellison was born and educated in Oklahoma City. Among the role models available to him in his youth, he was deeply impressed by the jazz musicians, and when he entered Tuskegee Institute in Alabama in 1933, he expected to study classical music.

In 1936, while still an undergraduate, Ellison headed for New York City, intending to work there for a summer. He never returned to Tuskegee. The following year, he met RICHARD WRIGHT, who asked him to write a review for a magazine called *New Challenge*. Wright influenced Ellison's ideas about social justice and provided a literary role model.

Among Ellison's early stories published in *New Masses*, a left-wing magazine, are a number that present characters and situations that foreshadow Ellison's novel *Invisible Man.* "Slick Gonna Learn" is an example of a story that also shows Wright's influence.

During the years surrounding World War II, Ellison wrote and abandoned a book-length manuscript and composed a series of stories— such as "Flying Home"—that explored the concept of the antihero, or protagonist notable for the lack of heroic qualities. In 1945 he began to concentrate his efforts on *Invisible Man,* though the novel had been on his mind for some time. He worked seven years on the manuscript; the book was published in 1952.

Invisible Man concerns the travels of an unnamed African American man from the South to the North and from ignorance to understanding. The narrative is framed by a prologue and an epilogue in the protagonist's voice, set in an underground room in which he has taken refuge from the hurt and hardship of life outside.

The action of the story begins in the South during the Great Depression as the protagonist graduates from high school and prepares to enter an all-black college. He arrives at college with naive dreams of success, but he grows disillusioned by the corruption he sees in the hollow philanthropy of a white trustee and the naked ambition of the black college president. After a painful encounter in which he tries to show a founder of the school how most southern blacks live, the protagonist is expelled. He heads to New York City in search of a job. When he fails to find white-collar employment, he signs on at a paint factory, again with bad results. After he rouses a crowd witnessing an eviction, he catches the attention of the Brotherhood, a radical group similar to the Communist party. He hopes to work within the Brotherhood for social change, but he finds himself hampered there by tokenism. After a Harlem race riot in which his physical safety is threatened, the protagonist realizes he must deal explicitly with the issue of race and the invisibility of the black man in white America, and he goes underground.

Invisible Man was published as the American civil rights movement was beginning to emerge. The book quickly became known, not just for its literary quality, but for its articulation of many of the values of the movement. The novel earned the National Book Award in 1953, as well as honors from the National Newspaper Publishers Association and the National Academy of Arts and Letters.

In 1964 Ellison published a collection of essays, *Shadow and Act,* which contained his reflections on literature—particularly his own literary career—music, and race.

Excerpts have been printed from a long second novel on religion and politics, but the book remains unpublished after three decades. A second collection of essays, *Going to the Territory,* was published in 1986.

Ellison has held a number of visiting professorships at such institutions as the University of Chicago, the University of California at Los Angeles, and Yale University. He retired in 1979 after nine years as Albert Schweitzer Professor in the Humanities at New York University. He is a recipient of both the Presidential Medal of Freedom, awarded to him in 1969 by President Lyndon B. Johnson, and the National Medal of Arts.

Ellison continues to live and write in New York City.

BIBLIOGRAPHY

Benston, Kimberly W. (ed.), *Speaking for You: The Vision of Ralph Ellison*, 1987; Bloom, Harold, *Ralph Ellison*, 1986; Busby, Mark, *Ralph Ellison*, 1991.

Emerson, Ralph Waldo

(May 25, 1803–April 27, 1882)
Essayist, Lecturer, Poet

Ralph Waldo Emerson, a leader of the movement known as Transcendentalism, was one of the foremost writers and thinkers of the nineteenth century. His essay "Self-Reliance" articulated a particularly American notion of the independence of the individual within society.

Emerson was born in Boston, the son of a prominent minister. William Emerson, who represented the sixth generation of Emerson ministers, preached a brand of Christian tolerance that came to be known as Unitarianism. He and his wife, Ruth Haskins Emerson, had eight children, of whom three died in infancy; Ralph was the fourth born. When William died in 1811, he left his family in difficult financial circumstances, and his spinster sister, Mary Moody Emerson, joined the family to help raise the children.

The young Emerson attended Boston Public Latin School and then entered Harvard University at the age of fourteen. Though he was not an outstanding student, while at Harvard he began the first volume of a journal that he continued throughout his life and from which he drew much of the material for his later writings.

After four years as a teacher at a girls' school, Emerson returned to Harvard as a di-

vinity student in 1825. He earned his master's degree the following year and began to serve a number of New England churches as a guest minister. In 1829 he accepted the pastorate of the Second Church of Boston.

In 1828 in Concord, New Hampshire, Emerson had met Ellen Tucker, a seventeen-year-old poet. They married the following year, despite Ellen's ill health. Ellen died in 1831 of tuberculosis. Emerson grieved for years, and began to question his beliefs as well as his devotion to the ministry. In time he began to find his pastoral duties increasingly difficult. While he enjoyed writing and preaching, he disliked many of the ceremonial aspects of his work. When his request to be relieved of the responsibility of performing the sacrament of the Lord's Supper was denied by the elders of his church, he resigned his position.

Emerson departed for Europe on Christmas Day 1832. In England he met the poets Samuel Taylor Coleridge and William Wordsworth, and the essayist and historian Thomas Carlyle, with whom he became lifelong friends. Three years after their first encounter, Emerson edited Carlyle's masterpiece, *Sartor Resartus*, for its first American publication.

Upon his return to the United States in 1833, Emerson launched a new career as a philosopher. He offered lectures on natural history, biography, and the philosophy of history.

The following year he moved to Concord, Massachusetts, where he met and married Lydia Jackson of Plymouth. The couple bought a house and there entertained a circle of intellectuals from Boston and Concord who came to be known as founders of the Transcendentalist movement. Among this group were Bronson Alcott, an educator and the father of LOUISA MAY ALCOTT; Margaret Fuller, a feminist and journalist; and HENRY DAVID THOREAU, the writer and philosopher who became Emerson's disciple.

In 1836, the day after the group known as the Transcendental Club began meeting at his home, Emerson published his first book, *Nature*. The book encapsulates many of the ideas Emerson developed throughout his life as a philosopher. Emerson rejected the notion that the route to truth was through an understanding of culture through history; rather, he argued that individuals had access to truth through their own intuition. Nature, he wrote, engages the intuition and makes individuals aware of what he called the Oversoul: the supernatural essence or spirit that resides within each person and that is universal, eternal, and moral.

Nature was the first important statement of the Transcendentalists, who took their name from the idea that certain universal truths transcended the philosophical categories established by Aristotle. Though the book sold poorly, it ignited controversy.

In 1837 Emerson returned to Harvard to address the Phi Beta Kappa society. His lecture, published that year as "The American Scholar," argued that Americans should declare their cultural independence from Europe and exhorted his listeners to intellectual self-confidence. OLIVER WENDELL HOLMES called the published essay "our intellectual Declaration of Independence."

The following year, Emerson ignited the biggest controversy of his career by declaring during an address at the Harvard Divinity School that historical Christianity blasphemed by focusing so intently on the details of Christ's biography. Christ should not be worshiped as the Son of God, he argued, as much as revered as an example of the divinity each individual might achieve. The talk raised such a stir that Emerson was not invited back to his alma mater for thirty years.

In 1840 the Transcendentalists decided to publish a journal, *The Dial.* Emerson and Fuller edited the journal together for two years, then Emerson edited the journal alone for another two, after which time it folded.

In the early 1840s, Emerson published two volumes of essays that began to apply his universal principles to more particular personal and political themes. In 1841 his first series of *Essays* addressed such matters as "History," "Love," and "Friendship." The volume also included Emerson's most famous essay, "Self-Reliance," in which he revisited the question of the moral primacy of the individual and argued that social cooperation could undermine the individual's integrity. This emphasis on the individual was integral in the evolution of the literary movement called romanticism.

Essays: Second Series (1844) treated such subjects as "Politics," "Gifts," and "Character." Its most significant essay, "Experience," marked a turning point in Emerson's career. He reconsidered the value of subjective perception, questioning whether it could render sufficiently the truths that lay beyond the self. The individual could be trapped by limiting factors such as his own temperament, which distorted reality and rendered it impossible to know anything absolutely. Emerson came to feel that his work on epistemology, or the theory of knowledge, had led him nowhere.

Emerson began to lecture more widely. He published his first volume of *Poems* in 1847 and continued collecting his lectures for publication. The poems influenced such writers as WALT WHITMAN and EMILY DICKINSON with their simple language and concrete imagery; some, such as "Brahma," "Threnody," and "Each and All," expressed elements of his philosophy in memorable lines. Emerson's subsequent book, *Representative Men* (1850), constituted a series of biographical sketches of such great men as William Shakespeare, Johann Wolfgang von Goethe, and Michel de Montaigne. *English Traits* (1856) offered Emerson's impressions after a visit abroad in 1847.

Emerson began to involve himself more in political debate. He spoke publicly in opposition to the Fugitive Slave Act (1850), which required Northerners to cooperate with slavery by returning escaped slaves to their Southern masters. He also spoke in favor of women's equality.

In *The Conduct of Life* (1860) and particularly in the book's introductory essay, "Fate," Emerson turned to the practical question of how one should live. He lacked a practical answer. Without an absolute reality in which to ground a standard of conduct, individuals simply had to do the best they could.

In his later years, Emerson enjoyed a rapprochement with Harvard, where he lectured in 1867 and 1870 and even was elected to the Board of Overseers. He traveled widely, as far as California in 1871, then to Europe and Egypt in 1872.

He died in 1882.

BIBLIOGRAPHY

Allen, Gay Wilson, *Waldo Emerson,* 1981; Barish, Evelyn, *Emerson: The Roots of Prophecy,* 1989; Rusk, Ralph L., *The Life of Ralph Waldo Emerson,* 1957.

Evans, William John

(August 16, 1929–September 15, 1980)
Jazz Musician

Bill Evans's delicate tone, dense harmonies, and refined pianistic improvisations helped develop a postbop language and influenced pianists like Chick Corea, Herbie Hancock, and Keith Jarrett. His compositions, except for a few such as "Waltz for Debby," were tied to his style of improvising and have not become standards.

Born in Plainfield, New Jersey, Evans began to study piano at six, violin at seven, and flute at thirteen. As a teenager he played in an amateur jazz band and won a music scholarship to Southeastern Louisiana University. After graduating in 1950, he toured with Herbie Fields's band until he was drafted in 1951.

Stationed at Fort Sheridan, Evans played flute in the U.S. Army band and met and studied with composer George Russell. Russell's modal ideas (see MILES DAVIS) helped shape Evans's style. Evans recorded *All About Rosie,* Russell's work for the piano, in 1957.

After discharge from the army in 1954, Evans headed for New York and the Mannes College of Music for graduate study. Almost immediately he found work playing and recording, including an album date with Charles Mingus for *East Coasting* (1957). Evans's own first album included "Peace Piece" (1959).

In 1958 Miles Davis invited Evans to join his sextet, which included JOHN COLTRANE. A 1959 session produced *Kind of Blue.* The album is considered historic by many critics. Davis presented his musicians with bare outlines of modes on which to construct improvisations. According to Evans's liner notes, musicians were handed the outlines as recording was to begin. The resulting improvisations were beautiful and coherent. Evans's own performance, especially his harmonic approach, writes Brian Priestley, "was significant in softening the edges of conventional sequences and pointing the way for pianists to cope with modal jazz."

Over the next twenty years Evans worked with trios and recorded as soloist, in duos, and in ensembles. *Jazz Abstractions*, with pianist John Lewis and saxophonists ORNETTE COLEMAN and Eric Dolphy, blended jazz with contemporary concert music. On *Conversations with Myself*, thanks to multitrack technology, Evans played three piano parts simultaneously.

Evans's trio, with bassist Scott LaFaro and drummer Paul Motian, was "capable of uncanny interplay," say Lyons and Perlo, and "set new standards for the trio form." The three rhythm instruments used as equal voices transformed elements of rhythm, harmony, and melody into ever-shifting designs. LaFaro's death in 1961 ended the collaboration.

Evans's jazz world was torn by "crow-jim," reverse discrimination, which, Grover Sales says, described "all whites as copyists at best and rip-off exploiters at worst." Miles Davis's response was, "I don't care if he's purple, blue, green, or polka dotted Bill has the piano sound I want in my group." Evans performed until shortly before his death in New York City at age fifty-one.

BIBLIOGRAPHY

Lyons, L., *The Great Jazz Pianists*, 1983; Taylor, B., *Jazz Piano*, 1982.

Faulkner, William Cuthbert

(September 25, 1897–July 6, 1962)
Novelist, Short-Story Writer

William Faulkner crafted a set of intricately woven stories and novels depicting the tragic lives of a people inhabiting a fictional county in rural Mississippi. His extraordinary imaginative power and the depth of his insight into the human condition have led to his reputation as one of America's greatest novelists.

Born William Falkner in New Albany, Mississippi, Faulkner moved to Oxford, Mississippi, at the age of five. His father, Murry Falkner, owned a livery stable and then a hardware store, finally becoming business manager of the

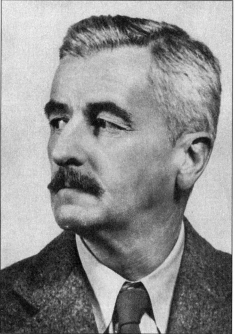
The Nobel Foundation

University of Mississippi in Oxford.

Faulkner dropped out of school in the eleventh grade. Anxious to serve in the military during World War I but unable to join the U.S. Army because he was too short, Faulkner signed on with the Canadian Division of the Royal Air Force. The war ended before he could see combat, but he received his commission as a second lieutenant in 1918. It was during this period that Faulkner changed the spelling of his name, adding the *u* from an earlier family spelling.

After the war, Faulkner was admitted to the

University of Mississippi as a special student, but he dropped out early in his sophomore year. He did begin to write stories and poems for student publications, however. He held a number of odd jobs—house painter, dishwasher, store clerk—as he tried to establish himself as a writer. In 1922 he became postmaster for the University of Mississippi, a job at which he was inept and which he resigned in 1924.

A fellow townsman, Phil Stone, helped Faulkner by suggesting authors to read and keeping him in touch with literary movements of the day. Faulkner had gone with Stone to New Haven, and later moved to New York in order to try to become acquainted with the literati. Stone also helped finance the publication of Faulkner's first book, a collection of poems called *The Marble Faun* (1924).

In 1925 Faulkner moved to New Orleans, where he became acquainted with SHERWOOD ANDERSON. Anderson encouraged him to write his first novel, *Soldier's Pay* (1926), and gave it to his own publisher. An experimental novel about World War I, the book did not sell.

Late in 1925, Faulkner took a walking tour through Italy, Switzerland, and France; the trip provided material for later stories. Faulkner then returned to Mississippi, where he wrote *Mosquitoes* (1927), a satiric novel about the New Orleans artistic community.

With his third novel, *Sartoris* (1929), Faulkner began to mine the territory in northern Mississippi in which he had grown up. He invented Yoknapatawpha County and its county seat of Jefferson, a composite of several Mississippi towns. He drew upon the characters he had known in childhood and upon his own family history. Faulkner's great-grandfather, William Clark Falkner, provided the model for Colonel John Sartoris, while his grandfather, John Wesley Thompson Falkner, seems the likely source for "Old Bayard" Sartoris. The novel focuses on "Young Bayard" and his bitter return from World War I to his small-town home, where his violent anger puts him at odds with the more genteel ways of his kinsfolk and the townspeople.

Faulkner's imaginative return to his roots unleashed a torrent of creative energy, and he wrote a series of major novels in quick succession. In 1929 he published *The Sound and the Fury*, his first radical experiment in narrative form and, by some estimates, his finest work. The novel tells the tale of the Compson family from four different perspectives in succession: through the eyes of the idiot son Benjy; his hypersensitive, intellectual brother Quentin; their greedy, petty-minded brother Jason, and finally Dilsey, the black servant who really holds the family together. The Compson family had been southern aristocracy, but have fallen: the mother to whining and imagined illness, the father to drink, and a daughter, Caddy, to sexual debauchery.

In *As I Lay Dying* (1930), Faulkner again used multiple streams of consciousness—this time creating fifty-nine separate interior monologues and time shifts—to tell the tale of a disintegrating southern family, the Bundrens. Written in only six weeks, the novel describes the death of a poor woman who lives in the hills and her family's obstacle-laden journey to Jefferson to bury her.

Faulkner claimed to have written *Sanctuary* (1931) in only three weeks, but when it came back from the publisher in galley form, he decided it was so bad he had to tear it down and rewrite it, bearing personally the expense of resetting the galleys. The novel describes lawyer Horace Benbow's efforts to exonerate Lee Goodwin of rape and murder charges. Benbow's work is thwarted, however, when the rape victim, Temple Drake, lies to protect the real villain, and Goodwin is killed by townspeople. Perhaps owing to the shocking nature of the story, *Sanctuary* became Faulkner's first popular success.

In *Light in August* (1932), Faulkner fashioned a plot of enormous complexity, featuring a large cast of characters whose psychologies he probed using multiple flashbacks and shifts in chronology. The story centers on Joe Christmas, who does not know whether he is black or white and who is taunted mercilessly by the children in the orphanage where he has been placed by his white grandfather. In later years, he begins an affair with a wealthy white woman who wishes to exploit him and pushes him to assume a black identity. When Joe murders her, he is hunted down and brutally killed.

Absalom, Absalom! (1936), considered by some to be Faulkner's masterpiece, reintroduces the character of Quentin Compson and follows his detective work as he tries to uncover the story of Thomas Sutpen, a local plantation owner murdered many years before. Sutpen's dreams of social prominence had been dashed when, returning from meritorious service in the Civil War, he found his son gone and his plantation in ruins. His attempt to produce a new heir with a poor white girl led to his death at the hands of her grandfather.

Faulkner turned his attention to shorter fiction, occasionally lengthening a short story into a thin novel; *The Unvanquished* (1938), *The Hamlet* (1940), and *Go Down, Moses* (1942) are examples.

The author frequently reintroduced characters from earlier stories. Lucas Beauchamp, the black hero of Faulkner's story "The Fire and the Hearth," is saved from a lynching in his novel *Intruder in the Dust* (1948). Temple Drake, the rape victim of *Sanctuary*, comes to atonement in *Requiem for a Nun* (1951). Not all of Faulkner's fiction, however, arose from Yoknapatawpha County. *A Fable* (1954) retells the story of Christ's passion through the experience of a French corporal on the Western Front during World War I.

The Town (1957) and *The Mansion* (1959) complete the story of the rise of the poor white Snopes family, begun in *The Hamlet. The Reivers* (1962), Faulkner's final book, is a nostalgic and amusing account of a boy's initiation into manhood.

Faulkner became internationally known after he was awarded the Nobel Prize for Literature in 1949. Whereas previously he had spent most of his time in Oxford, traveling to Hollywood from time to time to work on movie screenplays, afterward he traveled widely for the U.S. Department of State. Meanwhile, the honors continued. He won the National Book Award for *The Collected Stories of William Faulkner* in 1951 and for *A Fable* in 1955, the Pulitzer Prize for *A Fable* in 1955 and for *The Reivers* in 1963, and the Gold Medal for Fiction of the National Institute of Arts and Letters in 1962.

Faulkner died of a heart attack on July 6, 1962.

BIBLIOGRAPHY

Blotner, Joseph, *Faulkner: A Biography,* 1974, rev., 1984; Karl, Frederick R., *William Faulkner: American Writer,* 1989; Minter, David, *William Faulkner: His Life and Work,* 1981; Oates, Stephen B., *Faulkner: The Man and the Artist,* 1987.

Fitch, William Clyde

(May 2, 1865–September 4, 1909)
Playwright

C lyde Fitch, a prolific playwright in a twenty-year career at the turn of the century, wrote sixty popular historical dramas and plays that combined social satire with melodrama and comedy.

Fitch was born in Elmira, New York, the son of a Union army officer. As a child, he directed neighborhood children in melodramas that he wrote himself. His favorite was *Bluebeard.* He created the costumes, built the scenery, and acted in his productions.

He attended high school for a year in Hartford, then went to a high school for boys in Holderness, New Hampshire. He enrolled at

Amherst in 1882, where he contributed to nearly every issue of the *Student* and was also its editor.

When his fraternity was planning an entertainment to which they had invited the faculty, they discovered that their one-act operetta, called *Il Jacobi*, was not long enough. In less than two hours, Fitch wrote a second act that was better than the first.

He did everything in the dramatic society—designed costumes and scenery, painted a curtain, and produced William Wycherley's *The Country Wife*. He usually played female roles, including Peggie Thrift in *The Country Wife*, Constance in Oliver Goldsmith's *She Stoops to Conquer*, and Lydia Languish in Richard Brinsley Sheridan's *The Rivals*.

Against the wishes of his father, Fitch went to New York determined to be a writer. He had a letter of introduction to Edward A. Dithmar, the drama critic of the *New York Times*, who began taking him to first nights at the theater. Meanwhile, Fitch wrote stories and short plays and was able to sell children's stories and verses.

When the actor Richard Mansfield asked Dithmar, in 1890, who could write a play for him about Beau Brummell, the famous eighteenth-century dandy, Dithmar recommended Fitch. Fitch conferred with Mansfield and wrote the play. Mansfield had terrible misgivings about the young playwright's ability and at the last minute almost canceled the opening. It was an instant hit, and Fitch's career was launched.

During the 1898 season he had sellouts simultaneously in Chicago (*Nathan Hale*) and Philadelphia (*The Moth and the Flame*). In 1901 he had four successful plays running at one time in New York: *The Climbers; Captain Jinks of the Horse Marines*, with ETHEL BARRYMORE; *Lover's Lane;* and a revival of *Barbara Frietchie*. Fitch's most outstanding plays were combinations of social satire and melodrama. *The Climbers*, his first serious play, satirized people who were ambitious for money and social status. *The Truth*, regarded as Fitch's best play, looked at the problems of truth and lies in marriage. In *The Girl with the Green Eyes*, the heroine is pathologically jealous.

Theater owners and managers let Fitch have his way with his plays, and he cast and directed them himself, paying attention to the most minute details of the production. Actors liked his direction. Today's critics fault him for his invariably happy endings, but he wrote to please the audiences of his day. He needed to earn money to maintain his lavish lifestyle.

His last play was *The City*, which shows how the stresses of urban life magnify weaknesses and strengths that would be undetected in the country. It was produced after Fitch's death in Europe at the age of forty-four. One critic has said, "If we took Fitch's words and correctly illustrated them, they would give to future generations a better idea of American life from 1890 to 1910 than newspapers or historical records."

BIBLIOGRAPHY

Moses, Montrose J., and Virginia Gerson, *Clyde Fitch and His Letters*, 1924.

Fitzgerald, Francis Scott Key

(September 24, 1896–December 21, 1940)
Novelist, Short-Story Writer

F Scott Fitzgerald is best known as the voice of the 1920s. While his artistic reputation rests most securely on *The Great Gatsby,* Fitzgerald produced works, such as *This Side of Paradise* and *Tender Is the Night,* that have become equally a part of the myth of America's Jazz Age.

Fitzgerald was born in St. Paul, Minnesota, and named for a distant relative of his father's and the author of "The Star-Spangled Banner." Fitzgerald was sent to private schools, St. Paul Academy in Minnesota and Newman Academy in Boston. He enrolled at Princeton University in 1913 but left before the end of his junior year because of physical illness and an unsatisfactory academic record. In 1917 he enlisted in the army as a second lieutenant.

Fitzgerald spent his time before shipping overseas at work on a novel drawn from his college days. A draft of "The Romantic Egotist" was rejected by Charles Scribner's Sons. After the armistice that ended World War I, Fitzgerald hastily revised the novel, hoping its publication would induce Zelda Sayre, a society belle he had met at a country club dance, to marry him. Charles Scribner's Sons accepted the revised draft, now called *This Side of Paradise,* and the couple were married eight days after its publication in 1920.

The novel tells the story of Amory Blaine, a wealthy Princeton student who engages in a series of flirtations until he finally falls in love. Blaine is devastated when the object of his desire rejects him in favor of another, wealthier man, but he finds and learns to appreciate a vein of self-sacrifice.

This Side of Paradise was considered a daring and emotionally honest account of the lives and values of many young people in an era of optimism and excess, glamour and decadence. The novel became an immediate success, and Fitzgerald was instantly famous. The Fitzgeralds celebrated with an extended honeymoon—a string of all-night parties and drunken adventures they later called "the greatest, gaudiest spree in history."

The success of the novel opened the door to the lucrative magazine market, and Fitzgerald sold story after story to feed his extravagant lifestyle. *Flappers and Philosophers* (1920) and *Tales of the Jazz Age* (1922) collected stories he had written earlier in order to capitalize on his popularity. *The Beautiful and Damned* (1922), a tragic novel about the dissipated lives of a wealthy young artist and his wife, was another attempt to draw a story out of his own experience.

The Fitzgeralds had a daughter, Frances Scott (nicknamed Scottie) in 1921. Subsequently, they divided their time between the United States and Europe, where they lived in Paris and on the French Riviera.

In 1925 Fitzgerald published the book that became his acknowledged masterpiece, *The Great Gatsby.* Jay Gatsby is a man of fabulous wealth who gives lavish parties at his mansion in a posh Long Island town. He is the reincarnation of James Gatz, a man of humble origins who made a fortune bootlegging alcohol during Prohibition. Gatsby can buy anything but love; his pursuit of Tom Buchanan's wife, Daisy, is frustrated and ultimately leads to his own murder. The novel exposes the hollow values of the Jazz Age, with its economic and social corruptions. It also turns on its ear the particularly American myth of the self-made man who achieves success through his integrity and plain hard work.

All the Sad Young Men (1926), a collection of stories published on the heels of *The Great Gatsby,* includes two of Fitzgerald's best-known stories, "The Rich Boy" and "Winter Dreams."

The stock market crash of 1929 ended the Jazz Age, and the Fitzgeralds' lives changed irrevocably. Frustrated in her own work as a writer and a dancer, Zelda showed increasing signs of instability during the years after the publication of *The Great Gatsby*. Finally, in 1930, she had a complete breakdown, the first of several. Diagnosed as schizophrenic, she spent the last eighteen years of her life in a series of private sanatoriums. The cost of her medical care almost ruined her husband, who wrote story after story for magazines in order to maximize his income. Even magazine fees were at depressed levels, however, and he was forced to work so quickly that he himself later characterized much of his work during this period as "trash."

Distraught over Zelda's mental state, guilt-ridden over his inability to provide a stable home for Scottie, and disappointed with his work, Fitzgerald wrote three essays in 1935 for *Esquire* magazine that recorded his personal crisis. The essays—"The Crack-Up," "Pasting It Together," and "Handle with Care"—captured some of the mood of the 1930s and are now considered among his best work.

Fitzgerald's fourth novel, *Tender Is the Night* (1934), tells the story of the brilliant young psychiatrist Dick Diver, whose life is ruined by his marriage to the beautiful Nicole Warren, a schizophrenic he hopes to cure. Nicole is based transparently on Zelda;

Fitzgerald went so far as to use Zelda's letters and medical records in the novel. Though the book was released to favorable reviews, neither it nor a companion volume of short stories, *Taps at Reveille* (1935), sold well in the depression-era market.

Still desperate for money, Fitzgerald turned to Hollywood, where he earned a handsome salary as a screenwriter on such projects as *A Yank at Oxford*, *Three Comrades*, and, briefly, *Gone with the Wind*. His life in Hollywood provided material for Fitzgerald's unfinished novel, *The Last Tycoon*, a tragic story about a motion picture producer, published posthumously in 1941.

Toward the end of his life, Fitzgerald apparently found a measure of happiness in an affair with Sheilah Graham, a motion picture columnist. Nevertheless, a life of excess and of emotional hardship had taken its toll. He died of a heart attack in 1940.

BIBLIOGRAPHY

Bruccoli, Matthew J., *Some Sort of Epic Grandeur: The Life of F. Scott Fitzgerald*, 1981; Mellow, James R., *Invented Lives: F. Scott and Zelda Fitzgerald*, 1984.

Fonda, Henry Jaynes

(May 16, 1905–August 12, 1982)
Actor

Henry Fonda, prominent actor of stage and screen for half a decade, was one of the great natural resources of the American cinema. Like GARY COOPER and JAMES STEWART, he exemplified the homespun American of integrity and softspoken grit.

He was born Henry Jaynes Fonda in Grand Island, Nebraska, to a family of Christian Sci-

entists. His father ran a small printing company in Omaha. Graduating from Omaha Central High School in 1923, he studied journalism at the University of Minnesota for two years but dropped out.

At twenty Fonda worked for the Omaha Community Playhouse and became hooked on acting. He worked with community theaters on

Cape Cod, in Washington, D.C., and Easthampton, Long Island. While in Massachusetts with the University Players Guild, he met actress Margaret Sullavan, with whom he had a turbulent, short-lived marriage.

In 1932 Fonda played small parts on Broadway. His first big lead in *The Farmer Takes a Wife* won praise—for what the playwright Marc Connelly described as his "gee-gosh, foot-dragging quality," a performance he recreated in the film version of 1935, his first movie.

Fonda excelled in sophisticated comedies (*The Lady Eve,* 1941), serious social realism (*Twelve Angry Men,* 1957), biographical dramas (*Young Mr. Lincoln,* 1939), westerns (*My Darling Clementine,* 1946), war epics (*The Longest Day,* 1962), and political dramas (*Advise and Consent,* 1962, and *The Best Man,* 1964).

While a natural in these film genres, he never abandoned the stage, appearing on Broadway and nationally in such plays as *Mister Roberts* (1948), *The Caine Mutiny Court-Martial* (1954), *Two for the Seesaw* (1958), and *Clarence Darrow* (1974), his enormously successful one-man show.

His film embodiments of men of conscience confronting injustice are best epitomized in his young Lincoln; in Tom Joad, a poor migrant worker in *The Grapes of Wrath;* in the one jury member who makes a difference in *Twelve Angry Men;* and in the honorable navy officer Mister Roberts, who wars against the corrupt captain of his ship. In all, Fonda's persona radiates with moral conviction, his face an infallible register of his sincerity.

A true democrat, Fonda identified with the politics and sympathies of American lawyer

The Museum of Modern Art/Film Stills Archive

Clarence Darrow. David Rintels, revising his text of the Darrow show, said, "If a line doesn't sound right coming out of Fonda's mouth, it means the line isn't true. He had an unerring sense of what is right."

Fonda's patriotism impelled him to volunteer in the navy during World War II but to oppose American involvement in Vietnam—a position more aggressively taken by his daughter, Jane, also an actress.

One of Fonda's few villains was a cold-blooded killer in the epic *Once Upon a Time in the West* (1969), a huge success in Europe but not with American audiences who could not accept him in such a role.

Besieged by several illnesses in the last years of his life, his final film was *On Golden Pond* (1980), costarring Jane Fonda and KATHARINE HEPBURN, about an elderly couple spending probably their last summer in New England. Fonda and Hepburn won Oscars for their performances; the year before he was awarded the Academy's Special Achievement Award for his "enduring contribution to the art of motion pictures."

Fonda also received a special Tony Award in 1979 for his outstanding contribution to the American theater, and in 1978 the American Film Institute's Life Achievement Award. In 1979 he was one of five Americans honored at the Kennedy Center by President Jimmy Carter for their contributions to American culture. The others were AARON COPLAND, Ella Fitzgerald, MARTHA GRAHAM, and TENNESSEE WILLIAMS.

Fonda's private life had its share of tragedy. In addition to the ill-fated marriage with Margaret Sullavan, his second wife—heiress

Frances Brokaw and mother of Jane and Peter, also an actor—committed suicide in 1950; two subsequent marriages ended in divorce. His fifth wife, Shirlee Adams, was with him at his death.

BIBLIOGRAPHY

Collier, Peter, *The Fondas*, 1991; Fonda, Henry, with Howard Teichmann, *My Life*, 1981; Thomas, Tony, *The Complete Films of Henry Fonda*, 1983.

Ford, John

(February 1, 1895–August 31, 1973)
Film Director

John Ford, the only Hollywood director to win five Academy Awards, was America's most honored filmmaker. No other director so fully explored the American past, from revolutionary days through Vietnam. Ford's canvas was often epic, but his characters were always human.

As recorded in the official registry of Cape Elizabeth, Maine, Ford was born John Martin Feeney into an Irish Catholic family. Raised in Portland by immigrant parents, he—a seaman like his father—worked on freighters during his vacations from high school.

Failing to be appointed to Annapolis in 1914, he went to Hollywood where his brother, Francis Ford, was directing western serials. As Jack Ford he was property man, stunt rider, assistant cameraman, and played bit parts. Learning so much about filmmaking, he later mastered "cutting in the camera," the technique of getting the desired shot in a single take, leaving no excess footage to be edited.

His directing debut was *The Tornado* (1917), a two-reel western that he also wrote and played in. He directed nearly sixty films by 1924—short and feature-length, many of them westerns featuring actor Harry Carey—when he made *The Iron Horse*, an epic about the building of the transcontinental railroad.

He experimented early with outdoor sound in *Napoleon's Barber* (1928) and directed three to four films a year throughout the 1930s, notably *Arrowsmith* (1931), from SINCLAIR Lewis's novel; *The Lost Patrol* (1934); *The Informer* (1935), for which he won his first Oscar and Victor McLaglen won for Best Actor, and which was the first movie to win the Best Picture Award from the New York Film Critics; *Stagecoach* (1939), which made John Wayne a star and was the first of nine westerns Ford filmed in Monument Valley, Arizona, a setting now inextricably associated with his films; and *Young Mr. Lincoln* (1939), with a memorable performance by HENRY FONDA.

Ford began the 1940s with an adaptation of JOHN STEINBECK's *The Grapes of Wrath* (1940), for which he won his second Oscar and with another brilliant performance by Fonda; and *How Green Was My Valley* (1941), which won the Oscar for Best Picture of the Year and gave Ford his third Oscar.

During World War II, as lieutenant commander in charge of the U.S. Navy's film unit, he produced and directed training films and documentaries. While making *The Battle of Midway* (1942), a twenty-minute record of the Japanese attack on the American naval base, he was wounded and later decorated with the Legion of Merit, the Air Medal, and the Purple Heart. The film won an Oscar as Best Documentary of 1942.

Between the late 1940s and mid-1950s Ford made a number of westerns that have become classics: *My Darling Clementine* (1946), with Fonda as Wyatt Earp; *Wagon Master* (1950); his trilogy on the U.S. Cavalry—*Fort Apache*

(1948), *She Wore a Yellow Ribbon* (1949), and *Rio Grande* (1950); and *The Searchers* (1956).

The last four starred John Wayne, whose most complex and moving performance was in *The Searchers,* regarded by many international scholars as the finest western ever made and one of America's greatest films. Wayne was also splendid in *The Quiet Man* (1952), a charming comedy filmed in Ireland costarring Maureen O'Hara, which won Ford his fourth Oscar, and in *The Wings of Eagles* (1957), a biography about navy man Frank Wead who became a screenwriter after becoming paralyzed.

In his last active decade Ford did some television work, made five more westerns—including *The Horse Soldiers* (1959), *Two Rode Together* (1961), and *The Man Who Shot Liberty Valance* (1962)—as well as *The Last Hurrah* (1958), about Boston politics; the comedy *Donovan's Reef* (1963); and his last feature, *Seven Women* (1965), an offbeat, underrated drama about missionaries in China.

Ford paid tribute to the Irish by filming plays of Sean O'Casey—*The Plough and the Stars* (1936)—and Eugene O'Neill—*The Long Voyage Home* (1940), and short stories of several Irish writers in *The Rising of the Moon* (1957), filmed in Dublin. Many films are leavened with colorful characters of Irish ancestry played by Victor McLaglen, Barry Fitzgerald, Ward Bond, Mildred Natwick, and Donald Crisp, who, along with Wayne, Fonda, O'Hara, Jane Darwell, and others used repeatedly, virtually constituted Ford's stock company.

In addition to his Oscars, Ford was named Best Director four times by the New York Film Critics. Ironically, none of these awards acknowledged the westerns now judged to be his best work. His direction has been universally praised by such giants of the film world as Orson Welles and the Swedish director Ingmar Bergman.

In 1973 Ford was the first recipient of the American Film Institute's Life Achievement Award at a ceremony attended by then president Richard Nixon, who also awarded him the Presidential Medal of Freedom, the nation's highest civilian honor.

BIBLIOGRAPHY

Anderson, Lindsay, *About John Ford,* 1981; Bogdanovich, Peter, *John Ford,* 1978; Ford, Dan, *Pappy,* 1979; Gallagher, Tag, *John Ford: The Man and His Films,* 1986; Sarris, Andrew, *The John Ford Movie Mystery,* 1975; Sinclair, Andrew, *John Ford,* 1979.

Forrest, Edwin

(March 9, 1806–December 12, 1872)
Actor

E dwin Forrest, the first great American actor, was blessed with immense charm and power and a commanding voice. He acted in the exaggerated, declamatory style then in fashion, taking on both Shakespearean roles and new American plays, which he commissioned to promote native drama.

Forrest was born in Philadelphia. The manager of the South Street Theater noticed how handsome he was when he was only eleven and asked him to fill in for an actress who was sick. Forrest was thrilled to play the small role of Rosina in *Rudolph, or, The Robber of Calabria* by John D. Turnbull. He made his real debut at fourteen in *Douglas, or, The Noble Shepherd* by the Reverend James Home at the Walnut Street Theater and resolved to make acting his career. He toured with a company that played mostly frontier towns, joined a circus as a tumbler, and finally found an acting job in New Orleans, where he enjoyed the rough and ready life.

In 1825 Forrest was working in Albany, New York, supporting the great English actor Edmund Kean. Kean liked Forrest and gave him invaluable advice on acting. Forrest was an apt pupil, good-looking, muscular, and tempestuous. When he made his New York debut at the Park Theatre in *Othello* in 1826, the Bowery Theatre immediately lured him away for $800 a year. Forrest was immensely popular with Bowery audiences for several seasons. He was very much a man of the people, and upper-class audiences (more inclined to go to the Park than the Bowery) were not always comfortable with his sometimes crude vigor and his display of muscular arms and legs. In his second year at the Bowery, however, he was earning $200 a night, and from then on he was one of the best-paid actors in America.

Three years later he was back at the Park Theatre, offering prizes for new American plays. The first American actor to encourage native playwrights, he paid more than $20,000 over the years for nine works. The first prize in 1829 went to John Augustus Stone for *Metamora,* a play about Indians in which Forrest acted for years.

In 1834 Forrest, now a wealthy man, decided to move to Europe. In London he was a spectacular success as Spartacus at Drury Lane, the first American actor to appear in a leading role in London. He also met Catherine Norton Sinclair, and they were married in 1837.

In 1845 Forrest again visited London. Unemployment was rampant in the theater that season. One of those out of work was the famous William Macready, who had been extremely popular with American audiences on a tour a few years before. English actors supposedly resented the American interloper, and when Forrest appeared as Macbeth, a group in the audience hissed him. Without any actual proof, Forrest thought Macready was behind the insult.

Forrest was in Edinburgh when Macready played Hamlet. He went to the performance,

sat in a box, and hissed loudly when Macready was pretending to be mad. Many English people were angry with Forrest, and he made things worse by writing a letter to the London *Times* defending his actions.

Macready came back to America for another tour in 1848–1849. He wound up his tour in New York and was to make his farewell appearance at the Astor Place Opera House on May 8, 1849. A mob of Forrest supporters packed the theater and shouted so loudly that Macready could not play Macbeth. Forrest was acting at the Broadway Theatre and was not directly involved, but he was accused of encouraging the rowdies. Macready's friends persuaded him to try again, and on May 10 they packed the house themselves. Outside, an angry mob gathered, throwing rocks at the opera house, breaking windows, and attempting, literally, to tear it down. The Seventh Regiment was called out and smuggled Macready out of the theater unharmed. The mob started fighting the militia, and someone gave the order to fire. Twenty-two persons were killed and thirty-six wounded.

Forrest's life was disintegrating in other ways. He and his wife had a noisy, expensive divorce and, with suits and counter-suits, the proceedings dragged on for years. He spent more and more time alone in a vast, gloomy house he built in Philadelphia but occasionally made personal appearances, with enormous success, in New York, Chicago, and San Francisco. Finally, unable to act on stage because of gout and rheumatism, he read plays, standing behind a lectern. In his last appearance, he read *Othello* in Boston in 1872. That same year he died, leaving his estate to a home for retired actors, which became the Forrest Home in Philadelphia.

BIBLIOGRAPHY

Moody, Richard, *Edwin Forrest: First Star of the American Stage,* 1960.

Foster, Stephen Collins

(July 4, 1826–January 13, 1864)
Composer

Scores of Stephen Foster down-home songs speak of nineteenth-century dreams and nostalgia. Foster lives on through nonsense ditties like "Oh! Susanna" and through sentimental yearnings for plantation life like "My Old Kentucky Home." These familiar tunes, once popularized by blackface minstrel show performers, are now prized Americana.

Stephen Collins Foster was the second youngest of ten children. Born in Lawrenceville (now part of Pittsburgh), Pennsylvania, on the fiftieth anniversary of the Declaration of Independence, he was the son of William Barclay Foster and Eliza Clayland Tomlinson Foster.

Library of Congress

Foster seems to have been self-taught. He played the flute and the violin and could pick out tunes on the piano, though the family did not encourage his passion for music. His brother Morrison remembered the first piano composition, "The Tioga Waltz," written in 1841. Foster's first printed song, "Open Thy Lattice, Love," was issued in 1844.

Having arranged for a suitable job in business for the young man, the family hoped for the best as Foster headed down the Ohio River to work as a bookkeeper for his brother Dunning. He was struck by the singing of slave deckhands on the steamer during the trip, and the influence of black music was strong in the songs he continued to write. Some of his tunes, such as "Old Uncle Ned" and "Oh! Susanna," were published and gained some popularity. As a result, Foster decided to make songwriting his career, went back to his parents' home in Allegheny, Pennsylvania, and married Jane McDowell in 1850.

At this time, minstrel shows were a popular form of stage entertainment. White performers in blackface mimicked a variety of African Americans ranging from city dandies to plantation workers. They sang in dialect, spoke a kind of nonsense language, played fiddle, banjo, bones, and tambourine, and danced with exaggerated movements. They were enormously influential in conveying an idea of black culture to the American public, though the music they performed had few traits that were strictly African American, and had an important influence on American songwriting and jazz.

Foster made a publishing agreement with Firth, Pond & Co., who advised him to contact minstrel bands to introduce his songs to the public. He composed about thirty songs for minstrels and gave one such group, the famous Christy's Minstrels, exclusive first-performance rights to all new songs he wrote, including "Camptown Races," "Massa's in de Cold, Cold Ground," and "My Old Kentucky Home." He even allowed Christy to claim credit as author and composer for one of his most successful, "Old Folks at Home," written in 1851. He was to regret the gesture and never received credit for the song during his lifetime.

Foster wrote some of his finest songs between 1850 and 1856, among them "Jeanie with the Light Brown Hair" in 1854 and "Gentle

Annie" in 1856. Unfortunately, the family always lived a little beyond its means. Account books reveal debts and borrowings. In 1857 Foster sold future rights to already published songs to settle overdrawn royalty accounts. By 1860 he was overdrawn at his publishers again, and he sold all future rights for $1,600. With the overdraft deducted, his balance was $203.36. He settled debts in Allegheny and moved his family to New York.

With him he brought "Old Black Joe," a song written at home. It was the last success before he began the tragic downward spiral caused by poor financial management, domestic crisis (his wife and daughter returned to Allegheny), and alcoholism. Foster ground out songs, often with inferior lyrics by others, and spent whatever cash he earned for subsistence and alcohol. As the Civil War raged, death came to Foster at Bellevue Hospital in New York.

Foster wrote about 200 songs and a few instrumental works. Many were in the sentimental vein so popular at the time—love songs or nostalgic evocations like "Old Dog Tray." In some there are hints of European traditions—the Irish in "Jeanie with the Light Brown Hair," genteel British American stage music in "Stay, Summer Breath," even the Donizetti or Bellini of Italian opera in "Beautiful Dreamer," published posthumously. A handful are Civil War songs supporting the Union, among them, "We Are Coming, Father Abraham."

The first American nominated to the Hall of Fame for Great Americans, Foster is remembered, too, by a memorial collection of his papers housed at the University of Pittsburgh.

BIBLIOGRAPHY

Hamm, C., *Yesterdays: Popular Song in America,* 1979; Howard, J. T., *Stephen Foster: America's Troubadour,* 1934, rev., 1962.

Frankenthaler, Helen

(December 12, 1928–   )
Painter

Helen Frankenthaler, who has produced immensely large canvases, moved from the figurative painting of her teens to Abstract Expressionism. When she was still only twenty-four, she invented "color stain" painting, which had a profound influence on a number of painters.

Frankenthaler was born in New York, the daughter of a judge on the New York State Supreme Court who used to walk the streets of the city with his daughter, pointing out architectural and historic monuments. She went to private schools in Manhattan, including one year at the Dalton School, where the Mexican painter Rufino Tamayo was in charge of studio classes. Tamayo instilled in her the beginning of a professional attitude toward art, and

Frankenthaler decided when she was in her mid-teens to become an artist. She went to Bennington College, where the painter Paul Feeley taught. During nonresident semesters she worked at various jobs in the art world or took studio courses at the Art Students League.

Very soon, before she was twenty-three, her work appeared in a group show in a New York gallery, and she had a one-person show. She became involved immediately in Abstract Expressionism (see BARNETT NEWMAN), a new school of painting whose artists believed in free brushwork to "express" emotions without using representational images. Abstract Expressionism, the first art movement to develop independently in the United States (though with the influence of European immigrants), was becoming an international phenomenon. In 1952, after a summer of sketching landscapes in Nova Scotia, Frankenthaler, influenced by ARSHILE GORKY's use of line, JOHN MARIN's watercolors, and JACKSON POLLOCK's technique of dripping paint on the canvas, took off on her own course. She nailed a 7-by-10-foot piece of unprimed cotton duck to the floor of her studio. She thinned oil paints with turpentine until they were almost like watercolors, then applied them to the canvas. The result was *Mountains and Sea*, an abstraction in her own "color-stain" or "soak-stain" technique. Frankenthaler continued to apply thin washes of paint in small areas, often with a turpentine "halo," on a relatively empty raw canvas. Her pictures have a somewhat ethereal, yet immediate and direct effect. Other painters, including Kenneth Noland and MORRIS LOUIS, picked up the "soak-stain" method for their own work.

Frankenthaler experimented with various methods of painting; she used thick layers of paint in 1954 and 1955 and huge colored "line" drawings like *Nude* in 1958. In the sixties she began to roll or drip thicker acrylic paints on the canvas. This gave her areas of color hard edges instead of halos of oil. The opaque hues and firmer edges made her shapes more definite, more designed, but made possible islands of color that could be abstractions of natural forms. The color shapes sometimes were moved to the edges of the canvas, leaving a defined void at the center.

Frankenthaler still followed her instincts as she painted, instead of making preliminary sketches. She has said of her work that accidents are lucky if the artist knows how to use them: "People who hope for a tool of accident without having had real limits or a 'self-censor'—a discipline—often wind up with a mess." Ruthless cropping and discarding maintained her standard, with one painting often the result of ten discarded efforts.

In 1958 she met and married ROBERT MOTHERWELL, an older Abstract Expressionist, and they lived in New York and in the summer in Provincetown on Cape Cod in Massachusetts. In 1971 Frankenthaler and Motherwell were divorced.

In 1967 her *Guiding Red* was exhibited prominently in the U.S. Pavilion at the world's fair in Montreal. "I was guiding the red and the red was guiding me," she said of the painting. It was at that time her largest work, 30 feet high and 16 feet wide. In 1976 and 1977 Frankenthaler painted in the West, and critics have written of the "golden or calcified light" suffusing her pictures. In the 6-by-9-foot *M* (1977), the light seems to come from an unearthly source behind the picture. Although abstract, these pictures suggest landscapes, and Frankenthaler speaks of "having the landscape in my arms."

Frankenthaler, who works in New York, has experimented with sculpture and printmaking, trying both lithographs and woodcuts.

BIBLIOGRAPHY

Carmean, E. A., Jr., *Helen Frankenthaler: A Painting Retrospective*, 1989; Elderfield, John, *Helen Frankenthaler*, 1989.

French, Daniel Chester

(April 20, 1850–October 7, 1931)
Sculptor

D
aniel Chester French, who sculpted heroic themes in a naturalistic but elegant style, produced some of the most famous sculptures in America, including *The Minute Man* in Concord, Massachusetts, and the seated figure of Abraham Lincoln in the Lincoln Memorial in Washington, D.C.

He was born in Exeter, New Hampshire, the son of a prominent and well-to-do lawyer. When Daniel was six, his father decided to practice in Boston and moved the family to Concord, Massachusetts, then the center of New England literary and intellectual life. French modeled with clay as a child and one time carved some comic figures from turnips, which led his stepmother to suggest that he become a sculptor.

Boston had no school for sculpture at that time, but French picked up a rudimentary knowledge of armatures, the frameworks used to support figures being modeled. He studied anatomy with William Rimmer at the Lowell Institute and drawing with WILLIAM MORRIS HUNT, a Boston painter.

In 1873 the people of Concord and Lexington decided to put a monument on the battlefield to mark the 100th anniversary of the first battle of the revolutionary war. French was asked to create a sculpture, and worked ten hours a day in his Boston studio to make a model 27 inches high of a Minute Man. He modeled a "handsome young man, bareheaded, in long waistcoat, shirt sleeves rolled up, throat bare, with his musket in his right hand, his left resting on a plow behind him," ready to leave for battle. For models, French used a cast of the Hellenistic Greek *Apollo Belvedere* and his own reflection in a mirror. French got the job, and on April 19, 1875, the statue was unveiled before a crowd of 10,000 people that included President Ulysses S. Grant. An engraving of *The Minute Man* was placed on war bonds and postage stamps during World War II.

By the time his statue was unveiled, French was in Italy, studying under an American sculptor named Thomas Ball, who recognized that French had "more than talent." When he came back to the United States, his father was assistant secretary in the Treasury Department and young French settled in a studio in Washington. He soon had three commissions for sculptural groups for public buildings—the St. Louis Customs House (1876–1878), the Philadelphia Court House (1883), and the Boston Post Office (1885). He also had commissions to do busts of RALPH WALDO EMERSON and Bronson Alcott, intellectuals from his old neighborhood. "This is the face I shave," Emerson said when he saw French's work.

In the early 1880s he did the bronze seated figure of John Harvard, now in front of University Hall at Harvard University; a statue of former governor and senator Lewis Cass, which the State of Michigan placed in Statuary Hall of the Capitol in Washington, D.C.; and *Dr. Gallaudet Teaching a Deaf Mute* for the Columbia Institute for the Deaf in Washington (now Gallaudet College). French took models of these three sculptures to show to the famous American sculptor AUGUSTUS SAINT-GAUDENS when he went to Paris to study at the Ecole des Beaux-Arts for two years.

Later, Saint-Gaudens, director of sculpture for the World's Columbia Exposition in Chicago in 1893, asked French to design the 75-foot allegorical statue *The Republic* in the lagoon of the Court of Honor, the central space in the architectural composition of the fair. With Edward Potter, who designed the horses in French's work, he did the *Triumph of Columbia* over the peristyle, the entrance from Lake Michigan.

Again in collaboration with Potter, he did three equestrian statues—*Ulysses S. Grant* in Philadelphia's Fairmount Park (1899); *George Washington*, presented to France by the

Washington Memorial Association (1900); and *Joseph Hooker* (1903) outside the State House in Boston. At this time he also did *Alma Mater* for Columbia University.

French was a member of the commission that recommended placing a memorial to Abraham Lincoln at the opposite end of the axis from the Capitol, and sculpted the heroic, pensive figure of Lincoln for the memorial (1911–1922). He also did a standing figure of Lincoln for Lincoln, Nebraska.

French's work is full of stylized verve. People respond to it immediately. Although not as deep in conception nor as rich in results as

Saint-Gaudens, no other American sculptor has received such appreciation from the public.

He continued to work until he died in his sleep at his country home, Chesterwood, in Stockbridge, Massachusetts, when he was eighty-one. Chesterwood is now a museum of French's life and work.

BIBLIOGRAPHY

Adams, Adeline Valentine, *Daniel Chester French: Sculptor,* 1932; Richman, Michael, *Daniel Chester French, an American Sculptor,* 1976.

Freneau, Philip Morin

(January 2, 1752–December 18, 1832)
Editor, Essayist, Poet

Philip Freneau is often called the poet of the American Revolution because he published reams of patriotic verse rousing the rebels to battle. He was also an accomplished lyric poet who helped break the formal bonds of traditional verse, making way for the higher-soaring romantics of the nineteenth century.

Freneau was born of Huguenot ancestry in New York City and raised in New Jersey, on a farm in what is now Matawan. He was educated at home and in private schools before attending Princeton University, then known as the College of New Jersey. There, with classmates James Madison and Hugh Henry Brackenridge, he composed a collection of verse called *Satires Against the Tories.* With Brackenridge, he also wrote a commencement poem, "The Rising Glory of America" (1771), and a novel, *Father Bombo's Pilgrimage to Mecca,* published for the first time in its entirety in 1975.

After graduation in 1771, Freneau taught at schools in New York and Maryland. He continued to write, publishing his first volume of poetry, *The American Village,* in 1772. When the

American Revolution began in 1775, Freneau was living in New York City, composing satiric poems, published as *General Gage's Soliloquy* and *General Gage's Confession.*

In 1776 Freneau left to spend two years on the island of Santa Cruz in the West Indies, where he worked as a planter's secretary and wrote an idyllic poem about the splendor of island life, "The Beauties of Santa Cruz" (1776). He also produced "The House of Night" (1776), in which he sought to rationalize his absence from the mainland during the early battle for independence.

Freneau left for home in 1778 but was captured en route by the British. He was released shortly after the Battle of Monmouth, which laid waste to his home fields. These experiences galvanized in him a patriotic fervor. He joined a militia and helped run supplies through the British naval blockade. He also wrote patriotic verse published in Brackenridge's *United States Magazine* in 1779.

Captured again by the British during a privateering expedition to the West Indies in 1780, Freneau was held aboard British prison ships in New York Harbor. He was so appalled by the cruel treatment he and his fellow prisoners received there that he wrote his vitriolic poem, *The British Prison-Ship* (1781), upon his release. Freneau then went to Philadelphia, where he worked for a while as a postal clerk and for three years as an editor of the *Freeman's Journal.* He contributed many of his own poems inveighing against the British.

At the end of the war, Freneau went to sea, captaining vessels along the Atlantic coast from 1785 until 1791. During these years, he published his verse in newspapers in the ports he visited. His name became known as the verses were reprinted in newspapers up and down the coast.

Two of Freneau's most lyrical poems, "The Wild Honey Suckle" (1786) and "The Indian Burying Ground" (1788), were published during this period. They marked the American beginning of the literary transition to romanticism. "The Wild Honey Suckle," for example, embodies the notion of the ephemeral quality of beauty:

> From morning suns and evening dews
> At first thy little being came
> If nothing once, you nothing lose,
> For when you die you are the same;
> The space between, is but an hour,
> The frail duration of a flower.

After his marriage to Eleanor Forman in 1790, Freneau decided to return to land-based employment. In 1791 he accepted an appointment by President THOMAS JEFFERSON as translator in the State Department and established the *National Gazette* in Philadelphia. For two years, he used the *Gazette* to attack policies of Federalist party politicians, particularly Alexander Hamilton, and to advocate the principles of the more liberal Republicans.

Freneau returned to New Jersey, establishing the *Jersey Chronicle* in 1795. When that paper failed, he went to New York as editor of the *Time-Piece; and Literary Companion;* this appointment lasted only about a year, however, as the Alien and Sedition Acts of 1798 effectively muzzled Freneau's freewheeling attacks on the opposition party in power.

In 1798 he again retired to Mount Pleasant, his New Jersey farm, contributing a series of essays in the name of Robert Slender to the *Aurora* newspaper in Philadelphia. Slender is an everyday man who views government in the plainest terms:

> Had I . . . the disposal of but half the income of the United States, I could at least so order matters, that a man might walk to his next neighbour's without splashing his stockings, or being in danger of breaking his legs in ruts, holes, gutts, and gullies.

Freneau grew weary of public life. When Jefferson was elected president in 1800, Freneau felt he could retire to life as a private citizen. Between 1803 and 1807, poverty drove him to again become a sea captain, but from 1807 until his death in 1832 he remained in New Jersey.

In 1809 Freneau published a two-volume edition of his collected poems, and in 1815 he added some new poems prompted by the outbreak of the War of 1812. More urbane than his revolutionary verses, they looked wittily at both sides in the conflict.

Freneau's last years were spent quietly, at work on a volume of poems he never published. He died of exposure at the age of eighty while trying to pick his way home across the fields during a blizzard.

BIBLIOGRAPHY

Axelrod, Jacob, *Philip Freneau: Champion of Democracy,* 1967; Leary, Lewis, *That Rascal Freneau,* 1941.

Frost, Robert

(March 26, 1874–January 29, 1963)
Poet

Robert Frost made his debut as a poet when he was almost forty, yet he quickly demonstrated the skills of a major craftsman. He is remembered for the New England countryside he evokes in such poems as "Mending Wall" and "Birches," as well as for his deceptively simple style.

Born in San Francisco, Frost was taken to Lawrence, Massachusetts, after his father's death in 1885 and was raised among his mother's family. After graduating from Lawrence High School in 1892, a covaledictorian with his future wife, Elinor White, he briefly attended Dartmouth College. He worked in a textile mill and as a teacher before enrolling at Harvard University as a special student in 1897. After two years he left Harvard to become a farmer, settling on property in Derry, New Hampshire, purchased for him by his grandfather.

During his family's twelve years in Derry, Frost learned he had no real knack for farming, but he taught after 1905 at Pinkerton Academy and dedicated spare hours to writing poetry.

In 1912, at the age of thirty-eight, Frost sold the farm and took his family to England, hoping to establish himself as a poet. During his three years in London, he met with such poets as EZRA POUND and William Butler Yeats, and he published *A Boy's Will* (1913) and *North of Boston* (1914), the latter including some of his best-known poems, such as "Mending Wall" and "Home Burial." The two books secured his reputation. He returned home amid the tumult of World War I.

Settling his family briefly on a farm in Franconia, then in Plymouth, New Hampshire, Frost continued his career as a teaching poet and sometime farmer. He taught for four years at Amherst College. He also helped found the Bread Loaf School of English at Middlebury College in 1920.

Frost published *Mountain Interval* in 1916 and *New Hampshire* in 1923. The former volume included "The Road Not Taken" and "Birches," the latter "The Axe-Helve" and "Stopping by Woods on a Snowy Evening." *New Hampshire* won him his first Pulitzer Prize.

Frost felt that a poem "begins in delight and ends in wisdom." It must be about something that matters, and it must move the reader to a new understanding. Frost believed that a simple, concrete metaphor was the best vehicle to carry the sense of a poem. He sought to capture the vitality of the spoken word, using plain language and playing against regular meters:

> I shall be telling this with a sigh
> Somewhere ages and ages hence:
> Two roads diverged in a wood, and I—
> I took the road less traveled by,
> And that has made all the difference.

In an era when modern poets such as Ezra Pound and T. S. ELIOT were experimenting with new poetic forms and ideas, Frost's accessibility and morality soon made him seem outdated. Some critics now insist that Frost's sensibility was in fact Post-Modern, that he understood only too well the source of the modernists' doubt in God and alienation from society, but that he chose to communicate this indirectly and in seemingly traditional forms.

Frost's published volumes after 1922 included *West-Running Brook* (1928), which contained "Once by the Pacific" and "Tree at My Window"; *A Further Range* (1936), with "Two Tramps at Mud Time" and "Design"; *A Witness Tree* (1942), with "The Silken Tent" and "The Gift Outright"; *Steeple Bush* (1947), with "Directive"; and *In the Clearing* (1962).

"Design" reflects Frost's sense that God is inscrutable, if not dangerous. It acknowledges that appalling sights exist in nature and questions the notion of a grand design. "Two Tramps at Mud Time" meditates on the value of work to the equilibrium of the individual, especially when work is motivated by need.

"The Silken Tent" offers the example of a young woman who maintains a striking individuality at the same time she is bound willingly by "countless ties of love and thought / To everything on earth."

In his own life, Frost knew deep sadness. The deaths of three of his children, as well as the death of his wife in 1938, had a profound effect on him. However, Frost's public persona as a genial country poet made him a popular reader and lecturer. He held appointments variously at Wesleyan University, the University of Michigan, Dartmouth College, Yale University, and Harvard University. He was honored four times with the Pulitzer Prize and read "The Gift Outright" at the inauguration of President John F. Kennedy in 1961. He received the Bollingen Prize posthumously.

BIBLIOGRAPHY

Barry, Elaine, *Robert Frost*, 1973; Pritchard, William H., *Frost: A Literary Life Reconsidered*, 1984; Sergeant, Elizabeth S., *Robert Frost: The Trial by Existence*, 1960; Thompson, Lawrance, *Robert Frost*, 3 vols., 1966–1977.

Garbo, Greta

(September 18, 1905–April 15, 1990)
Film Actress

The most famous Hollywood actress of all time, Greta Garbo embodied romance and mystery in the silent era and the 1930s, playing tragic heroines such as Anna Karenina and Camille. Retired from films in 1941 to live a reclusive existence, she remained a fascinating enigma for the next fifty years.

Born Greta Lovisa in Stockholm to Karl and Anna Gustafsson, she had an older brother and sister and lived in poor circumstances. She left school at thirteen to care for her ill father. At age fourteen, when he died, she worked in a department store where she drew attention and was cast in a publicity short. In 1922 she

The Museum of Modern Art/Film Stills Archive

appeared as a bathing beauty in the slapstick feature *Peter the Tramp*.

Interested in theater, she won a two-year scholarship to Stockholm's Royal Dramatic Theater Academy, where Swedish film director Mauritz Stiller noticed her and took her under his wing. He made her lose twenty pounds, taught her how to move and dress, and took her out in public to develop her social graces. He changed her name to Garbo and cast her in *The Saga of Gosta Berling* (1924), based on a celebrated novel by Selma Lagerlöf.

Impressing film reviewers in Berlin, Garbo was invited by German director G. W. Pabst to play in *The Joyless Street* (1925). Simultaneously, Stiller signed a contract with LOUIS B. MAYER, head of Metro-Goldwyn-Mayer studios, on the condition that Garbo go to Hollywood with him. In one of the most nearsighted judgments of film history, Mayer was at first reluctant to take Garbo because "in America men don't like fat women."

Unpredictably, Garbo became MGM's biggest star, making twenty-four movies there between 1926 and 1941. Even before her first film, *The Torrent*, was released in early 1926, the studio realized that she was a screen sensation. Stiller was assigned to direct her second film, *The Temptress* (1926), but problems with studio executives resulted in his dismissal, and direction was completed by Fred Niblo. Stiller returned to Sweden in 1928 and died a year later, leaving Garbo to grieve over her mentor for many years.

In her third film, *Flesh and the Devil* (1927), assigned to Clarence Brown, her favorite director, Garbo was cast opposite John Gilbert, Metro's biggest male star at the time. The film's sizzling love scenes, reflecting Garbo and Gilbert's passionate off-screen affair, made it a huge box-office success. One critic remarked, "Never in our screen career have we seen seduction so perfectly done."

Garbo demanded a salary increase commensurate with her drawing power, and MGM, in order to profit from the gossip, acceded, raising her weekly salary from $600 to $5,000. She immediately was cast again with Gilbert in *Love* (1927), a modern-dress version of Tolstoy's *Anna Karenina*. Although their affair continued, they never married.

In the remaining two years of the decade, she made six more films, including *The Divine Woman* (1928). Based on the life of the actress Sarah Bernhardt, it was the first time Garbo received top billing above the male lead. *A Woman of Affairs* (1929) was her third film with Gilbert. In reviewing *The Kiss* (1929), her last silent film, critic/playwright ROBERT SHERWOOD judged it mediocre, but called Garbo "the best actress in the world,"

warranting comparison with Eleanora Duse, Helen of Troy, and Venus.

Garbo shunned Hollywood society, avoiding interviews and appearances at premieres, preferring privacy and simple living. Though a plain, unglamorous dresser by nature, her screen image exerted a huge influence on women's fashions, hairstyles, and makeup. Her genius was that she knew intuitively exactly how she projected on the screen. The studio complied with her requests for closed sets because Garbo claimed it was the only way she could make her face express things it would not ordinarily.

Afraid that sound would destroy her image and career, as it had done to many others—including Gilbert—MGM delayed casting her in a talking film until 1930 with *Anna Christie*. With her deep throaty voice, so well suited to the character in this adaptation of EUGENE O'NEILL's play, directed by Brown, Garbo's mystique was, if anything, intensified. "I can't decide whether it's baritone or bass," said one critic, but "there isn't another like it. Disturbing, incongruous, its individuality is so pronounced that it would belong to no one less strongly individual than Garbo herself."

Garbo became an even bigger star, by the early 1930s earning a record $270,000 per movie. She played opposite Clark Gable in *Susan Lenox: Her Fall and Rise* (1931) and was the German spy *Mata Hari* (1932), costarring Ramon Novarro.

In 1932 she was one of an all-star cast in the Academy Award–winning *Grand Hotel*, in which she played a fading, world-weary dancer, briefly regenerated by an affair with shady aristocrat JOHN BARRYMORE. This role epitomized the air of romantic disillusionment that pervaded nearly all of Garbo's performances and spilled over into the public's impression of her private life.

In 1933 she played opposite Gilbert for the last time in *Queen Christina*, again about a doomed love affair and one of her most memorable films. The last shot of the movie is a dazzling long close-up take of Garbo's face, holding every secret longing and unfulfilled wish in a mask of the eternal feminine. She remade *Anna Karenina* in 1935 with Fredric March, and in 1937 George Cukor directed her in *Camille,* which, along with *Ninotchka* (1939), was one of her two best films.

In the latter, a brilliant satire directed by ERNST LUBITSCH, Garbo revealed a talent for comedy as the sober Soviet envoy seduced by Melvyn Douglas and Parisian society. Advertised with the quip "Garbo Laughs!" the film was a critical and box-office success, leading MGM to conclude, erroneously, that her image should change into that of a "fun-loving American glamour girl," according to biographer John Bainbridge. The result was *Two-Faced Woman* (1941), again costarring Douglas. The critic of *Time* magazine said of her character's loose behavior, "It is almost as shocking as seeing your mother drunk." Garbo is reputed to have said about Metro's decision, "They've dug my grave." It was her last film.

Leaving Hollywood at age thirty-six, Garbo was approached repeatedly to make a comeback but was never able to agree on scripts. She became an American citizen in 1951 and lived in total privacy in a Manhattan apartment. Pursued by fans, photographers, and the press whenever she went out, she was forced to wear nondescript clothes and sunglasses in public. It was not uncommon to hear strangers, store owners, or celebrities remark that they "spotted Garbo" on the street or in an East Side store.

She was twice voted Best Actress by the New York Film Critics for her performances in *Anna Karenina* and *Camille,* and received an honorary Oscar in 1954, which she naturally was not present to accept. Though she had publicized relationships with several noted men, including director Rouben Mamoulian, conductor LEOPOLD STOKOWSKI, and nutrition theorist Gayelord Hauser, she remained unmarried.

BIBLIOGRAPHY

Bainbridge, John, *Garbo,* 1971; Bruman, Sven, *Conversations with Greta Garbo,* 1991; Gronowicz, Antoni, *Garbo: Her Story,* 1990; Zierold, Norman, *Garbo,* 1969.

Garden, Mary

(February 20, 1874–January 3, 1967)
Singer

G arden's superb acting abilities and versatile voice brought special qualities to her interpretations of operatic roles like Debussy's Mélisande, Charpentier's Louise, or Richard Strauss's Salome. The great Scottish-born soprano used publicity masterfully to further her career and to compete with the other high-powered singers of the day.

Born in Aberdeen, Scotland, Mary Garden came to the United States as a child. She studied singing in Chicago and later in Paris with Antonio Trabadelo and Lucine Fugère. While in Paris, Garden met Albert Carré, director of the Opéra-Comique, and on April 10, 1900, she made her very successful debut there in Gustave Charpentier's *Louise,* eventually her most famous role.

In 1902 composer Claude Debussy and Carré chose Garden to play the female lead in *Pelléas et Mélisande* over objections by Maurice Maeterlink, whose play had inspired the opera. The production was initially problem-ridden, but by the end of the season, thanks to the efforts of Garden, Carré, and conductor André

Messager, it was a triumph. Garden's success as Manon in Paris and in London convinced Massenet to compose the opera *Chérubin* for her.

On November 25, 1907, Garden made her American debut at Hammerstein's Manhattan Opera House as Thaïs in the American premiere of Massenet's opera. She was praised as an outstanding singing actress. The production of *Pelléas et Mélisande*, which premiered in the United States on February 9, 1908, supported by an imported Parisian cast, was another popular success.

In 1910 Garden made her debut at the Chicago Grand Opera as Mélisande, and for twenty years thereafter she was the company's leading soprano. In the 1921–1922 season she directed the company. Among her presentations was the American premiere of Prokofiev's *Love for Three Oranges*. Though her artistic abilities were unquestioned, it was a season fraught with difficulties, financial and other.

Garden was basically a lyric soprano, but she displayed remarkable versatility in taking on coloratura roles like Violetta and Juliet and heavier roles like Carmen and Salome. In 1927 she sang in the first American performances of Arthur Honegger's *Judith* and in 1930 in Franco Alfano's *Risurrezione,* sung in French. Garden took over the tenor role of Jean in Massenet's *Le jongleur de Notre Dame* and in that part made her final Chicago appearance, January 24, 1931. Following her retirement from the operatic stage, she presented Debussy lecture-recitals in 1934 and 1935 and lectures from 1948 to 1955. She died in Inverurie, Scotland, January 3, 1967.

BIBLIOGRAPHY

Garden, M., and L. Biancolli, *Mary Garden,* 1951; Wagenknecht, E. C., *Seven Daughters of the Theatre,* 1964.

Garland, Hannibal Hamlin

(September 14, 1860–March 4, 1940)
Autobiographer, Critic, Novelist, Short-Story Writer

Hamlin Garland's fictional renderings of Midwestern farm life during the late nineteenth century contributed not only to public understanding of the hardships settlers faced working their homesteads, but also, through their unflinching detail, to the evolving literary tradition known as Realism.

Garland was born near West Salem, Wisconsin, in 1860 and lived in Iowa until 1881, when his family moved to a homestead in the Dakota Territory. He remained behind to establish in 1883 his own homestead in what is now McPherson County, South Dakota.

The 1880s were a period of economic depression for farmers. Because of the amount of land under cultivation, new farm machinery, and high crop yields, agricultural products glutted the markets and prices fell sharply. The resulting privations of farm life deeply affected Garland.

In 1884 he became first a student and then a teacher at the Boston School of Oratory. After a trip home to visit his ailing mother in 1887, he returned to Boston to write the six stories collected in *Main-Travelled Roads* (1891). The stories, about the hard life of the farmer, are minutely observed, in the emerging tradition of American realistic fiction; they also can be considered naturalistic, because the characters' lives are dominated by forces outside their control: nature, heredity, environment. Though they are carried by Garland's deep emotion, the stories are not all somber: "Mrs. Ripley's Trip" is comic, and "Among the Corn Rows" ends optimistically.

All together, Garland wrote thirty such short stories, many of them published as *Prairie Folks* (1892) and *Wayside Courtships* (1897) and later combined in *Other Main-Travelled Roads* (1910). Critics agree these stories constitute his most enduring legacy.

In 1894 Garland published his one work of literary criticism, *Crumbling Idols,* in which he advocates a fictional realism rooted in detailed observation and steadfast adherence to the truths of life in the writer's geographic region. He labeled his method "Veritism."

Library of Congress

Four Garland novels are generally considered noteworthy, though some critics have said two of them are overly influenced by politics. *Jason Edwards: An Average Man* (1892) promotes the notion—espoused by the economist Henry George—that a single tax on property owners, substituting for all other taxes, would relieve laborers of their heavy economic burden. *A Spoil of Office* (1892) attacks political corruption and crusades for a populist redistribution of wealth.

A Little Norsk (1892) describes the bleak farm life of an orphaned Norwegian girl. *Rose of Dutcher's Coolly* (1895), considered Garland's finest novel, tells the story of a Wisconsin farm girl who, rebelling against the stric-

tures of farm life, struggles to send herself to college and to become a writer in Chicago.

Garland spent the next twelve years writing popular novels about Indians and the American West, achieving his first financial success with *The Captain of the Gray-Horse Troop* (1902). His writing, however, lost the bite of social criticism.

In 1917 Garland began a series of autobiographical works with *A Son of the Middle Border* that once again achieved the literary recognition his early fiction had enjoyed. He wrote three more volumes of family history: *A Daughter of the Middle Border* (1921), for which he received a Pulitzer Prize; *Trail-Makers of the Middle Border* (1926); and *Back-Trailers from the Middle Border* (1928).

In his later years, Garland published a number of literary reminiscences, including *Roadside Meetings* (1930), *Companions on the Trail* (1931), *My Friendly Contemporaries* (1932), and *Afternoon Neighbors* (1934). He died on March 4, 1940.

BIBLIOGRAPHY

Holloway, Jean, *Hamlin Garland: A Biography,* 1960; McCullough, Joseph R., *Hamlin Garland,* 1978.

Gehry, Frank Owen

(February 28, 1929–)
Architect

Frank Gehry is a highly original, idiosyncratic designer whose works, until recently, have been closely identified with southern California. Early noted for his economical, unpretentious style and his use of unusual materials, he has since designed more monumental buildings of unusual shape and gained an international reputation.

Gehry was born Frank Owen Goldberg in Toronto, Canada, and moved to Los Angeles with his family in 1947. He changed his name to Gehry in the early 1950s and received an architectural degree from the University of Southern California, Los Angeles, in 1954. He worked as a project designer for Victor Gruen & Associates (1953–1954), then served in the U.S. Army Special Services division (1955–1956). After graduate study in city planning at Harvard University (1956–1957), Gehry worked as project designer for the Los Angeles firm of Pereira & Luckman (1957–1958), then as designer and planner for André Remondet in Paris (1961). In 1962 he established his own firm, Frank O. Gehry & Associates, Inc., in Los Angeles.

Although Gehry's designs spring from a Post-Modernist (see MICHAEL GRAVES) preference for complexity of form, he is a true maverick who works in a range of styles and types. His firm's first project, the Kay Jewelers Office Building in Los Angeles (1963), is an eclectic mix of influences from the Japanese and from FRANK LLOYD WRIGHT. The O'Neill Hay Barn in Orange County, California (1966), introduced two hallmarks of his style: the use of prefabricated stock building components and the conception of a building as a sculptural object. Composed of telephone poles and corrugated metal, the barn shows his deliberate choice to clad structures with materials traditionally relegated to other minor building types in order to create an inexpensive, unpretentious "cheapskate architecture." Gehry has said, "I approach each building as a sculptural object,

a spatial container, a space with light and air, a response to context and appropriateness of feeling and spirit." Even his inexpensive, playfully shaped, durable cardboard furniture collection (1969–1973), called Easy Edges, reflects these design concepts.

Painter Ron Davis's house in California's Malibu Hills (1972, additions in 1977), reveals Gehry's emphasis on minimal construction and functional flexibility. Strongly defined outer walls are constructed of corrugated, galvanized, unpainted metal panels and are set off by parallelogram windows and skylights. The design was influenced by the building's relationship to its trapezoidal-shaped site and Davis's paintings, creating illusory views as one approaches and the feeling of forced perspective once inside.

During the 1970s and 1980s Gehry designed shopping malls, corporate headquarters, school and museum complexes, private residences, and several art exhibitions, such as the much-praised Treasures of King Tutankhamen (1978) for the Los Angeles County Museum of Art. The Mid-Atlantic Toyota Distributorship Warehouse/Offices in Glen Burnie, Maryland (1978), reveals his use of distortion and juxtaposition of shapes and cheap materials, with metal supports and bridges creating patterns against the corrugated roof and the colorful, multisize partitions. His mini-campus for L.A.'s Loyola Marymount University Law School (1981–1984) melds a cluster of two classroom buildings, a chapel, and a moot court, all informally placed and creating an irregular courtyard, and a larger student/office center. The facades of this complex offer a mixture of materials, colors, and historical allusion. The glazed chapel's interior reveals exposed wooden structural elements, creating an unfinished or "in progress" appearance. This visibility of construction elements is a dominant aspect of Gehry's design vocabulary and reflects his desire to capture the immediacy of the act of painting in his architecture.

One of Gehry's most famous structures is his home in Santa Monica (1978–1979), which initially elicited loud protests from his neighbors because of its bizarre appearance. He took "a dumb little house with charm" and "deconstructed" it, stripped the interior walls and ceilings to reveal the construction elements, then clad it on three sides with a shell of chain-link fencing, corrugated metal, and unpainted plywood. Surrealist effects are created by the spatial ambiguity of a new door opening to the original door, and frames of the original windows left for viewing the new parts of the house.

Gehry is particularly noted for his museum structures, especially those for children, such as the Cabrillo Marine Museum in San Pedro, California (1979), designed to encourage hands-on experience. He renovated an armory for Los Angeles's California Aerospace Museum (1982–1984), creating an assemblage of individual units (his preferred design approach) of different sizes, shapes, and colors unified by a dramatic facade featuring a jet fighter cantilevered in nosedive position.

Although Gehry was originally regarded as a regional architect, he moved into the international arena in the late 1980s with the acclaimed Vitra Design Museum near Basel, Switzerland (1988–1990), a white fantasy of curves and angles. He designed the festive high-tech entertainment complex of shops, restaurants, night clubs, and rodeo for Euro Disneyland outside Paris (1988–1992). Other current projects include the American Center in Paris (scheduled to open in 1993) and the Walt Disney Concert Hall, Los Angeles (scheduled to open in 1996). He has said that his work is in the spirit of the ancient Roman builder and scholar Vitruvius: "All in pursuit of firmness, commodity, and delight."

Gehry's "free-spirited" approach has served as a catalyst for younger architects, especially through his stints as visiting critic at several universities and the wide publication of his work.

BIBLIOGRAPHY

Bletter, Rosemarie Haag, et al., *The Architecture of Frank Gehry,* 1986; Goldberger, "Studied Slapdash," *New York Times Magazine,* January 18, 1976; Nairn, Janet, "Frank Gehry: The Search for 'No Rules' Architecture," *Architectural Record,* June 1976.

Gershwin, George

(September 26, 1898–July 11, 1937)
Composer, Conductor, Pianist

Gershwin, Ira

(December 6, 1896–August 17, 1983)
Lyricist

George Gershwin, admired by Ravel and other European composers, wrote songs for Tin Pan Alley, Broadway, and Hollywood, as well as more ambitious works like *Rhapsody in Blue* and *Porgy and Bess.* Jaunty Gershwin songs, many with clever lyrics by his brother Ira, cheered the thirties and continue as favorites.

Moishe Gershovitz (Morris Gershvin) and Rose Bruskin, both Russian immigrants, married in New York in 1895. Their first child, Israel (Ira), was followed by a second son, Jacob

(George), Arthur, in 1900, and Frances, the only girl, in 1906. Morris Gershvin (the name appears as Gershvin or Gershwin) changed jobs often and the Gershwins moved frequently to be near his place of employment—twenty-two times between 1895 and 1917.

Neither parent was musical, but in 1910 the family purchased a piano, ostensibly for their eldest son. It became clear quickly that George Gershwin was the musical child. In 1912, after two years of instruction from neighborhood teachers, Gershwin was accepted by Charles Hambitzer, who took the youngster under his wing, introduced him to the concert hall, and taught him pieces by Debussy, Liszt, and Chopin.

In 1914 Gershwin dropped out of the New York High School for Commerce to go to work as a song plugger for Jerome H. Remick & Co., a music publishing firm. Day after day of playing honed Gershwin's piano technique and turned him into an experienced accompanist.

Gershwin began to compose songs and dreamed of moving from Tin Pan Alley (the district where many publishers of popular music were located) to Broadway. There people like JEROME KERN, another New York songwriter with European-Jewish roots, were writing entire scores for the most sophisticated musical stage. In 1917 Gershwin left Remick to take a position as rehearsal pianist for *Miss 1917*, a show written by Kern and VICTOR HERBERT.

One year later, Max Dreyfus, head of Harms, another music publisher, recognized Gershwin's talent and offered him $35 a week for the publishing rights to future songs. Before George Gershwin was twenty-one, he was known as a pianist, had written the score for a Broadway show, *La La Lucille* (1919), published songs, and had a publisher committed to issuing more.

Gershwin wrote sixteen full scores between 1919 and 1925. "Swanee," sung by Al Jolson in 1920, was a hit. He composed music for *George White's Scandals* (1920–1924), provided scores for several shows, contributed songs to others, and wrote twice for the London stage. In 1924 he created the score for *Lady, Be Good!*

Songs like "Fascinating Rhythm" and "Oh, Lady, Be Good!" with lyrics by Ira Gershwin, are still popular.

But it was band leader PAUL WHITEMAN who catapulted Gershwin to fame. Whiteman's concert "An Experiment in Modern Music" was held at Aeolian Hall, February 12, 1924. Whiteman had commissioned Gershwin to write and perform a serious jazz composition for the occasion; the result was *Rhapsody in Blue*.

The audience loved the jazzy, spirited work. Though reviews were mixed, George Gershwin's name was made, not just as a song writer, but as a serious composer. In *Rhapsody in Blue* Gershwin combined the materials of popular music, like syncopated rhythms and bluesy harmonies, with his Tin Pan Alley experience and classical studies to create a concert work. He had studied harmony, counterpoint, orchestration, and musical form with Edward Kilenyi for four years, and the piece reflects his efforts.

Gershwin continued to write for the musical theater, producing ten scores and one collaboration between 1926 and 1935. He also published *George Gershwin's Song-book* in 1932, wherein he pointed out that his "rhythms . . . are more or less brittle; they should be made to snap, and at times to crackle." He was concentrating, too, on concert music and study, working with Rubin Goldmark, Wallingford Riegger, and Henry Cowell in the 1920s. A 1928 trip to Europe with his brother Ira and others allowed Gershwin to complete the score for a tone poem, *An American in Paris*. The next year he conducted the New York Philharmonic in a performance of the work at Lewisohn Stadium and was the conductor and soloist for *Rhapsody in Blue*.

Gershwin wrote most of another concert work, *Second Rhapsody for Piano and Orchestra*, while he and Ira were producing the music for a Hollywood film, *Delicious* (1931). The thirties saw more successful Gershwin brothers musicals, among them *Girl Crazy* (1930) and *Of Thee I Sing* (1931). The latter won a Pulitzer Prize. Tireless, George Gershwin toured, performed, wrote songs, and studied composition with constructivist Joseph Schillinger between 1932 and 1936.

While working with Schillinger, Gershwin, collaborating with his brother, wrote a full-length opera, *Porgy and Bess* (1935). The ambitious work, based on Dubose Heyward's novel *Porgy*, brought together African American folk music and opera. The work is popular today, though when it opened, it ran only 124 performances and was a financial failure.

Early in 1937 Gershwin was plagued by bouts of dizziness and depression and fell into a coma on July 9. Operated on for a brain tumor, he died in Hollywood. Novelist JOHN O'HARA wrote, "George Gershwin died on July 11, 1937, but I don't have to believe it if I don't want to." Critic/composer Virgil Thomson commented, "George Gershwin was an exquisite maker of tunes. There is life in them and grace and a wonderful sweet tenderness.... They are music, our music, everybody's music."

Ira continued to write his slangy, sophisticated lyrics after his brother died, collaborating with KURT WEILL, Jerome Kern, and HAROLD ARLEN. He died in Beverly Hills in 1983.

BIBLIOGRAPHY

Gershwin, Ira, *Lyrics on Several Occasions,* 1959; Jablonski, Edward, *Gershwin: A Biography,* 1987, and *Gershwin Remembered,* 1992.

Gillespie, John Birks

(October 21, 1917–January 6, 1993)
Jazz Musician

A trumpet virtuoso, who with CHARLIE PARKER instigated the bop revolution, Dizzy Gillespie inspired scores of instrumentalists by walking the musical high wire. His driving improvisations displayed fertile imagination, incredible technical skill, lightning contrasts, and cascading notes as he puffed out his cheeks and blew a misshapen trumpet.

The youngest of nine children, Gillespie was born in Cheraw, South Carolina. His father, a bricklayer and weekend musician, died when Dizzy was ten. At twelve Gillespie

Photo by Charles Stuart; Courtesy of the New York World Telegram and Sun Collection at the Library of Congress

began to play trombone, a year later trumpet, and subsequently cornet. In 1932 the talented Gillespie was studying harmony and theory at Laurinburg Technical Institute in North Carolina; the school band needed a trumpet player. While at Laurinburg he practiced trumpet and piano with little instruction but great enthusiasm.

By 1935 Gillespie had dropped out of school to join his family in Philadelphia and found work with the Frankie Fairfax band. An admirer of trumpeter Roy Eldridge, Gillespie learned many Eldridge solos from another Fairfax trumpet player, Charlie Shavers. Gillespie began to sound like Eldridge, adopting his idol's phrasing, tone quality, vibrato, even his melodic ideas. It was the Fairfax group that called Gillespie "Dizzy." The nickname reflected his perpetual high jinks, and it stuck.

In 1937 Gillespie went to New York. He played with several groups and eventually signed on with Teddy Hill to replace Eldridge. After a two-month summer tour of France and England with the group, he returned to New York and free-lanced with various ensembles, among them the Savoy Sultans, Mercer Ellington, and the Alberto Socarras Afro-Cuban band. Eventually he returned to play with Hill.

It was a step up for Gillespie when he was hired by Cab Calloway in 1939. He joined Chu Berry (saxophone) and Cozy Cole (drums) as soloists with the high-paid black band. Cuban trumpeter Mario Bauza, a member of the Calloway group, stimulated Dizzy's interest in interweaving Afro-Cuban music with jazz. Gillespie began to move away from the Eldridge style and to incorporate new sounds in his playing, including more complex jazz patterns that came to be known as bop or bebop.

During a 1940 tour with Calloway, Gillespie met saxophonist Charlie Parker. Of similar progressive leanings, they continued their acquaintance in New York after-hours sessions with THELONIOUS MONK, Kenny Clarke (drums), and other young experimenters. Gradually bop emerged, its intricate rhythms and harmonies fired by virtuoso improvisations played at breakneck speed. Later Gillespie wrote in liner notes, "I learned rhythm patterns from . . . Charlie Parker, the other side of my heartbeat." The dramatic new sound is documented in a 1941 recording, "Kerouac," made at Minton's Uptown Playhouse, the famous Harlem spot where musicians jammed. That year Gillespie quarreled with Calloway and was fired.

Gillespie moved on to work with bandleaders Benny Carter and the singer Ella Fitzgerald. In 1942 he toured with Charlie Barnet and Les Hite. In 1943 he played with Calvin Jackson, Lucky Millinder, DUKE ELLINGTON, and Earl Hines (whose band included Parker), and with

small groups in jazz clubs on 52nd Street. An early 1940s recording with Millinder introduces Dizzy playing the first real bop solo with swing band backing, "Little John Special." Dizzy developed the riff (a short rhythmic phrase designed to be repeated with a constantly changing relation to the beat) for his composition "Salt Peanuts."

Billy Eckstine, a singer with the Hines band, formed his own bop band in 1944 and hired Gillespie as soloist and music director. Bop was on its way, known at the very least by musicians. Gillespie, given to startling contrasts in range and complexity, was at the forefront of the new style. That year he made some early bop recordings with small ensembles, among them a group led by COLEMAN HAWKINS, and another by Charlie Parker.

Gillespie tried leading a big band in 1945. Unsuccessful financially, he turned next to a bop quintet with Parker and later expanded the group to a sextet. When he tried a big band again, it lasted four years. The ensemble experimented with integrating Afro-American jazz and Afro-Cuban rhythms. Chano Pozo, the Cuban conga drummer, joined the rhythm section and, with Gillespie, recorded George Russell's "Cubano Be/Cubano Bop" and "Manteca," the latter written by Pozo and Gillespie.

By 1947 Gillespie's rhythm section included John Lewis on piano, Milt Jackson on vibraphone or piano, Kenny Clarke on drums, and Ray Brown on bass. The four eventually formed the Modern Jazz Quartet. Other bop musicians joined the band periodically, including trombonist J. J. Johnson and saxophonist JOHN COLTRANE.

Money problems forced Gillespie out of the big band business in 1950. After a short stint as soloist with Stan Kenton's band, Gillespie founded another sextet and in 1951 organized his own record company, Dee Gee, again a financially unrewarding venture.

In 1953 someone accidentally bent the bell on Gillespie's trumpet. Dizzy played it, liked the sound, and the odd-shaped instrument, built especially for him, became a trademark. After leading small groups for a time, Gillespie formed yet one more big band, this time to tour the Middle East, Greece, and Yugoslavia for the U.S. State Department. Two years later, he took another large group on tour to South America. Unable to sustain a big band without financial support, he resumed his work with small groups. He continued to perform and record in smaller ensembles into the 1980s.

In 1976 *New Yorker* jazz columnist Whitney Balliett pointed out Gillespie's evolution "from the Roy Eldridge imitator he was to the baroque wonder he became." But even as early as the sixties, critic Ralph Gleason was writing in liner notes of Gillespie as "one of the great musicians in jazz history, a trumpet virtuoso without peer and an experimenter and innovator . . . still searching and exploring. 'What knocks me out about him,' a fellow trumpet player once [said], is that there he is, night after night, all these years, when he *could* play it safe and he doesn't.'"

BIBLIOGRAPHY

Horricks, R., *Dizzy Gillespie and the Be-bop Revolution*, 1984; James, M., *Dizzy Gillespie*, 1959.

Ginsberg, Allen

(June 3, 1926–   )
Poet

Allen Ginsberg's poems, particularly his early works *Howl* and *Kaddish*, embody the values and aesthetic of the Beat Generation of writers in the 1950s and 1960s. They reflect anarchic individualism and a reliance on amplified sensory experience.

Ginsberg was born in Newark, New Jersey, in 1926 and graduated from Columbia University in 1948. Until 1956 he worked variously as a dishwasher, a welder at the Brooklyn Navy Yard, and a merchant sailor. His association with the novelist Jack Kerouac and others of the so-called Beat Generation in Greenwich Village led to appearances as a character in works of fiction by Kerouac and Lionel Trilling even before he had earned any literary reputation of his own.

The Beats espoused voluntary poverty and general disaffiliation from society; they sought illumination through release from social and literary conventions. In their works, they hoped to capture the process of experience, not just a verbal record.

Ginsberg achieved recognition as a poet with the publication of *Howl*, a Beat anthem, in 1956. Written in long lines derived stylistically from WALT WHITMAN, the poem is a diatribe against a society Ginsberg saw as militaristic and materialistic. Ginsberg decries the fate of "the best minds of my generation," leading lives that are self-destructive; they are made outlaws by a false social order. The poet establishes his identification with human suffering and insists that all existence, no matter how limited, is sacred. Ironically, while the poem was carefully structured and the product of a slow gestation, it seemed almost improvisational and came to represent the notion that poetry might be spontaneous.

Howl and Other Poems (1956) included three other well-known works: "America," "A Supermarket in California," and "Sunflower Sutra." The sutra (Sanskrit for thread or string of precepts) opens:

> I walked on the banks of the tincan banana dock and sat down under the huge shade of a Southern Pacific locomotive to look at the sunset over the box house hills and cry.

After 1956 Ginsberg traveled a great deal, living in the Far East during 1962 and 1963. He became a public figure, a guru of the new generation, appearing frequently at readings and social protest rallies all over the world, and was identified with his advocacy of Zen Buddhism, gay liberation, the drug culture, and pacifism (for which he invented the phrase "flower power"). His poems grew to reflect their function as performance pieces: they took on the incantatory quality of Indian mantras.

Another celebrated poem is *Kaddish* (the Hebrew word for a prayer of mourning), a long prophetic poem focused on the life and death of the poet's mother, which was collected in *Kaddish and Other Poems, 1958–1960* (1961). Sadder in tone than *Howl*, the poem is similar nonetheless, in that it comprises a long, flowing rush of data, both sensory and intellectual.

Other volumes by Ginsberg include *Airplane Dreams: Compositions from Journals* (1968), *The Gates of Wrath: Rhymed Poems 1948–1952* (1972), and *White Shroud: Poems 1980–1985* (1986). *The Fall of America: Poems of These States 1965–1971* (1973) won a National Book Award.

Ginsberg lives and writes in New York City.

BIBLIOGRAPHY

Merrill, Thomas F., *Allen Ginsberg*, 1969; Miles, Barry, *Ginsberg: A Biography*, 1989; Mottram, Eric, *Allen Ginsberg in the 60's*, 1972.

Glasgow, Ellen Anderson Gholson

(April 22, 1873–November 21, 1945)
Novelist

The novelist Ellen Glasgow is generally recognized as one of the first distinctive literary voices to emerge in the South after the tumult of the Reconstruction era. A fine regional writer, she brought dead-on realism and polished wit to works that chronicled a social revolution in the first three decades of the twentieth century.

Born in Richmond, Virginia, in 1874, Glasgow was educated at home and in private schools in Richmond. She started to lose her hearing at the age of sixteen and eventually became deaf.

Glasgow witnessed the hardships associated with the South's Reconstruction after the Civil War, and she wrote unsentimentally about the transition from its aristocratic past to a time marked by the gradual rise of a middle class to economic and political power. She wrote social history marked by the "blood and irony" she believed it merited.

Her first two novels—*The Descendant* (1897) and *Phases of an Inferior Planet* (1898)—were set in New York, though they featured Southern characters. Both typify the clear-eyed realism she pursued in her later novels.

Glasgow then wrote a series of novels, beginning with *The Voice of the People* in 1900, that comprised a social history of Virginia from the Civil War to World War I. These included *The Battle-Ground* (1902), *The Deliverance* (1904), *The Romance of a Plain Man* (1909), *The Miller of Old Church* (1911), *Virginia* (1913), and *Life and Gabriella* (1916).

Though they featured characters and events that were entirely fictional, these works are historical in the sense that they sought to depict manners and the political and economic forces of an earlier era. Glasgow treats these subjects with detachment and irony; her tone marked a departure from a literary tradition besotted with mourning over the loss of old Southern ways.

In 1925 Glasgow published *Barren Ground*, regarded by many as her greatest novel. Dorinda Oakley, a Virginia farm girl, disappointed by the man she loves, Jason Greylock, goes to New York to find work and learns to be self-sustaining. She rejects the hand of a young doctor, then returns to the family farm after her father's death. Through her own resourcefulness, she not only manages the farm, but makes it profitable. She marries a local storekeeper to make a home for his children and, after his death, takes in her dissolute former love, Jason, who soon dies from alcoholism. The story turned the conventional Southern romance on its ear. Glasgow once noted proudly that it recounts what might happen "wherever the spirit of fortitude has triumphed over the sense of futility."

In 1926 Glasgow published *The Romantic Comedians,* the first in her so-called Queenborough trilogy, set in a fictional Richmond. A novel of manners, the book describes the marriage of a young girl to an old judge; it satirizes the social customs of the surviving Southern aristocrats. *They Stooped to Folly* (1929), subtitled "A Comedy of Morals," chronicles strong-minded women from three generations of a Virginia family. In *The Sheltered Life* (1932),

Glasgow treats her historic themes by exploring the memory of a very old man, a retired general, who shares a household with female relatives trying to live by social traditions of the nineteenth century.

The two final novels published during Glasgow's lifetime are grimmer than any work that preceded them. *Vein of Iron* (1935) locates the strength in the character of a woman, Ada Fincastle, who meets a series of misfortunes—marital and familial—during her life in the mountains and towns of Virginia before and during the Great Depression. *In This Our Life* (1941), which despairs of modern life in Queenborough, finally earned Glasgow a Pulitzer Prize in 1942.

Glasgow died November 21, 1945. Her book *Beyond Defeat,* a sequel to *In This Our Life,* was published posthumously in 1966.

BIBLIOGRAPHY

Auchincloss, Louis, *Ellen Glasgow,* 1964; Rouse, Blair, *Ellen Glasgow,* 1962; Santas, Joan Foster, *Ellen Glasgow's American Dream,* 1966.

Glass, Philip

(January 31, 1937–)
Composer

Philip Glass has reacted strongly against compositional complexity. His spare, tonal music suggests ties with Minimalist painting, sculpture, and dance, and his ensemble's use of amplification and pulsing rhythm connect him to the rock movement.

Born in Baltimore, Maryland, Philip Glass studied flute at the Peabody Conservatory before continuing his musical education at the University of Chicago, where he earned his B.A. in 1956. He went on to the Juilliard School for training in composition (B.A. 1959, M.A. 1961) and to the Aspen Music Festival (summer 1960) where he studied with composer Darius Milhaud. From 1963 to 1965 he went to France on a Fulbright Scholarship and studied with Nadia Boulanger. A Ford Foundation grant (1961–1963) placed him in the Pittsburgh public schools as composer-in-residence.

While Glass was in France he worked with Ravi Shankar, the famous Indian sitarist, to notate the raga improvisations so that Western musicians could play them for the sound track of the film *Chappaqua*. As Glass came to understand the meter of the film score, he discovered the inherent possibilities of rhythmic musical structure and wrote his first stripped down Minimalist music for the avant-garde Paris theater company that was to become Mabou Mimes in the early seventies. Based in New York's SoHo district, the group was named for a Nova Scotia town where they had worked together. Glass, as resident composer for Mabou Mines, produced some dozen scores for the company over the next twenty years.

Glass traveled to India, North Africa, and Central Asia in 1965 and 1966 and returned to New York in the spring of 1966. There he met Steve Reich and Arthur Murphy, who were also composing Minimal music, and the three worked together performing their own works.

In 1968 the composer formed the Philip Glass Ensemble, which included amplified instruments and performed in concert. In 1970 Kurt Munkacsi joined the ensemble as sound designer and mixer, thus making sound engineering a component of a concert music ensemble in live performance. Munkacsi sits at the center facing the performers. "By placing Kurt in the center, facing us," Glass writes, "he can respond to our sound mix needs and mix for the house at the same time."

In the late sixties, Glass, at home with visual arts as well as with music, began to perform in art galleries and museums like the Guggenheim. By 1970 he was appearing outside New York—at the Walker Art Center in Minneapolis and on tour, often sponsored by university art galleries in the United States and abroad. In 1971, Glass, with gallery owner Klaus Kertess, founded a record company and began to record his own work.

As Glass became known abroad, he was invited to perform at festivals overseas. In 1974 he produced a large-scale concert of his work at Town Hall, New York. Two years later, November 21, 1976, his opera *Einstein at the Beach* was performed by a company put together by Glass and others at the Metropolitan Opera House on a "dark" (no regular performance) night, and he became well known in the United States. Key to *Einstein*'s succès d'estime were the striking visual images created by Glass's collaborator, the director and designer Robert Wilson.

Glass won a three-year grant from the Rockefeller Foundation in 1978. His opera *Satyagraha*, commissioned by the city of Rotterdam, was performed at the Netherlands Opera in 1980, as well as in New York. By 1982 Glass had signed a recording contract with CBS and in 1984 his third opera, *Akhnaten*, was performed in Stuttgart, Germany, in Houston, Texas, and in New York.

Glass, now popular, was developing his audience and diversifying his style. Rock bands like Talking Heads felt the impact of his work, and Glass noted in a 1982 interview that "the most important and vital new music scene today, for me, has been in the clubs."

BIBLIOGRAPHY

Cagne, C., and T. Caras (eds.), *Soundpieces: Interviews with American Composers*, 1982; Glass, P., *Music by Philip Glass*, 1987; Rockwell, J., *All American Music: Composition in the Late Twentieth Century*, 1983.

Goldwyn, Samuel

(August 27, 1882–January 31, 1974)
Producer

Pioneer Samuel Goldwyn produced many of Hollywood's popular classics. Renouncing partnership in the two biggest corporate mergers of the film industry—which eventually led to Paramount Pictures and Metro-Goldwyn-Mayer—Goldwyn preferred to produce movies independently. His brusque and colorful expressions, composed of malapropisms and mixed metaphors, became known as Goldwynisms.

Born Schmuel Gelbfisz (Samuel Goldfish) in Warsaw, Poland, the eldest of six children, his parents were poor Hasidic Jews. He received an Orthodox education and could read Hebrew. His father ran a small antique store, but he died when Samuel was only fifteen.

Dreaming of migrating to America to "make something of himself," he first went to England and worked until he accumulated enough money to sail to Canada, arriving in America in 1895. In Gloversville, New York, he was a salesperson for a glove factory, then a partner in the company.

In 1910 he married Blanche Lasky, whose brother, Jesse, a vaudeville producer, was interested in filmmaking. He and Samuel formed the Jesse L. Lasky Feature Play Company. Their first movie was *The Squaw Man* (1913), one of the earliest long (about one hour) features made in Hollywood and the directorial debut of Cecil B. DeMille.

The film's success sparked interest in the company, which merged with Adolph Zukor's Famous Players, the foundation of what became Paramount Pictures. Differing with Zukor, Goldwyn sold his shares for almost a million dollars, a huge sum in those days. In 1917 he joined Broadway producers Edgar and Archibald Selwyn to make films of notable plays, but this, too, dissolved. It was at the time of their association that the name Goldwyn was formed from the first syllable of Goldfish and the last syllable of Selwyn.

He became an independent producer in 1922, but his company went bankrupt and merged in 1924 with what became Metro-Goldwyn-Mayer. Again, he withdrew with a substantial settlement, leaving only his name as part of MGM. In 1926 he became a member of United Artists, a cooperative of independent producers—including MARY PICKFORD, D. W. GRIFFITH, and CHARLIE CHAPLIN—who distributed their own pictures. In 1941 he sold his stock to the corporation and released his films thereafter mainly through RKO.

Goldwyn believed that the prime ingredient in films was the story, and spared no expense hiring noted writers—such as Ben Hecht, Moss Hart (see GEORGE S. KAUFMAN/MOSS HART), SINCLAIR LEWIS, LILLIAN HELLMAN, and ROBERT SHERWOOD—as well as the most respected directors and actors. While his directors were not always free to do their best work, a list of Goldwyn productions includes such respectable titles as JOHN FORD's *Arrowsmith* (1931), King Vidor's *Street Scene* (1931) and *Stella Dallas* (1937), and HOWARD HAWKS's *Ball of Fire* (1941).

Perhaps his most successful and critically acclaimed films were those directed by William Wyler, including *Dodsworth* (1936), *Wuthering Heights* (1939), *The Little Foxes* (1941), and *The Best Years of Our Lives* (1946). The New York Film Critics chose *Wuthering Heights* as Best Picture of 1939 over *Gone with the Wind*. *The Best Years of Our Lives* won seven Oscars, including Best Picture, and Goldwyn himself won the IRVING G. THALBERG Award for creative producing. Despite all this, Wyler and Goldwyn did not get along.

Goldwyn's subsequent output was less critically and financially successful. His last two productions were ambitious adaptations of the American musicals *Guys and Dolls* (1955) and *Porgy and Bess* (1959). While they were not disasters, they failed to do justice to the genius of the originals.

Among the stars whose careers Goldwyn launched were the humorist Will Rogers; GARY COOPER, whose first important film was *The Winning of Barbara Worth* (1926); vaudevillian Eddie Cantor, introduced to films in Goldwyn's production of *Whoopee!* (1930); and Danny Kaye, who made several films for Goldwyn, including *The Secret Life of Walter Mitty* (1947) and the popular *Hans Christian Andersen* (1952).

He introduced Vilma Banky whose films with Ronald Colman were among Goldwyn's successes in the 1920s. On the other hand, his biggest gaffe was spending hundreds of thousands of dollars on Polish actress Anna Sten, whom he considered another Garbo. The public did not agree.

Investing his own money, Goldwyn oversaw every aspect of his films. Though a perfectionist, his taste was generally crude and his aim not above the average viewer's intelligence. Consequently, even his more "prestigious" projects—such as *Wuthering Heights*—were often accused of being simpleminded and pseudoartistic.

Nevertheless, he assumed full responsibility: "My pictures were my own.... My mistakes and my successes were my own. My one rule was to please myself; and if I did that, there was a good chance I would please others." Indeed, his primary talent, as even Wyler conceded, was his ability to market his movies.

Goldwyn and Blanche Lasky had a daughter, Ruth, but were divorced in 1915. In 1925 he married actress Frances Howard; their son, Samuel, Jr., is currently a well-known movie producer.

BIBLIOGRAPHY

Berg, A. Scott, *Goldwyn: A Biography*, 1989; Easton, Carol, *The Search for Sam Goldwyn*, 1975; Griffith, Richard, *Samuel Goldwyn: The Producer and His Films*, 1956; Marx, Arthur, *Goldwyn*, 1976.

Goodhue, Bertram Grosvenor

(April 28, 1869–April 23, 1924)
Architect

Bertram Goodhue began his career as an architect designing Gothic Revival buildings with RALPH ADAMS CRAM and ended working on his own on modern buildings, such as the Nebraska State Capitol.

Goodhue was born in Pomfret, Connecticut, of well-to-do parents. He was a precocious artist, learning from his mother, who sketched and painted. He did not have much formal education, but he was a voracious reader. He sketched with great skill and spent long days out of doors in the country around Pomfret. He put on the walls of his attic studio the motto "Art pre-exists in Nature, and Nature is reproduced in Art."

When he was fifteen, he went to New York to work as an office boy for architect James Renwick, who had designed Saint Patrick's Cathedral in New York. He was ambitious and when he was twenty-one entered an open competition for the design of a cathedral in Dallas—and won. He took the commission with him when he joined Ralph Adams Cram's Boston firm as head draughtsman, but the Dallas cathedral was never built. Cram and Goodhue designed many churches in the Gothic Revival style, including All Saints, Ashmont (1892–1913), in the Boston suburb of Dorchester. Cram said of Goodhue, "I had neither the power nor the patience to work out any sort of decorative detail. At this point Bertram entered the equation, to go on without a break to the completion of the work."

When Cram, Goodhue, and Ferguson won the commission in 1903 to design new buildings for the U.S. Military Academy at West Point, Goodhue opened the firm's New York office. At West Point, Goodhue designed the chapel (1903–1910) and two barracks and worked with Cram on other buildings. He married Lydia T. Bryant of Boston in 1902, and the couple settled in New York. After Goodhue and Cram designed St. Thomas Church (1906–1914) on Fifth Avenue in New York, with Goodhue doing the bulk of the work, the two men parted ways.

Goodhue stayed in New York and designed several more Gothic Revival churches there. His work for the Cathedral of the Incarnation (1911–1924) in Baltimore was strongly influenced by what he saw of the modern Gothic cathedral that was under construction in Liverpool, England, in 1913. For the Panama-California Exposition (1911–1915) in San Diego, he designed buildings that were strongly Spanish in character. In a design for Saint Bartholomew's Church (1914–1918) in New York, he used a Romanesque-Byzantine style.

Later Goodhue moved toward greater abstraction of forms without abandoning his devotion to ornament. The most important of his works in this mode is the Nebraska State Capitol (1920–1932), marked by horizontal lines and stepped masses, contrasting with the vertical lines of the domed tower. He also designed the National Academy of Sciences in Washington (1920–1924).

He died in his prime, at age fifty-four.

BIBLIOGRAPHY

Oliver, Richard, *Bertram Grosvenor Goodhue*, 1983; Whitaker, Charles Harris (ed.), *Bertram Grosvenor Goodhue: Architect and Master of Many Arts*, 1925.

Goodman, Benjamin David

(May 30, 1909–June 13, 1986)
Bandleader, Clarinetist

B enny Goodman, the King of Swing, ushered in the big band era and delighted a generation of fans. Known for lilting tempos and high ensemble standards, he improvised seamlessly, constantly exploring harmonic and instrumental possibilities. By hiring both black and white musicians for public performances, Goodman broke existing color barriers.

The son of Eastern European parents, Goodman, one of twelve children, was born in Chicago, Illinois, to Dora and David Goodman. David supported the family by working in the stockyards or at a tailoring shop.

It was David who arranged for Goodman and two of his brothers to receive musical training at a local synagogue. Goodman moved on to Jane Addams's Hull House, where he studied clarinet with band director James Sylvester. Franz Schoepp, a classically trained clarinetist, taught Goodman for two years. A superior teacher, Schoepp gave Goodman an excellent technical foundation and a serious attitude toward musicianship.

In 1921 Goodman's imitation of Ted Lewis, a vaudeville clarinetist, at the Central Park Theater in Chicago launched his career. The next year, a student at Harrison High School, he played with the Austin High School Gang, a group that included Jimmy McPartland, Bud Freeman, Frank Teschemacher, and Dave Tough, who had attended the same Chicago high school and were inspired by older New Orleans jazz musicians. And certainly he listened to King Oliver, LOUIS ARMSTRONG, and clarinetists like Jimmie Noone.

Goodman joined the musicians union in 1923. He met cornetist Bix Beiderbecke that year. Beiderbecke's lyricism and quiet understatement helped shape Benny's style. Hired in 1925, Goodman joined Ben Pollack's band in Los Angeles. The group returned to Chicago in 1926, and that year Benny recorded his first solo, "He's the Last Word." In 1928 the band went to Manhattan. Goodman remained with Pollack until 1929 when he decided to settle in New York. He established himself as a free-lancer, working for radio, at recording studios, and on Broadway. He played in orchestras for *Strike Up the Band* and *Girl Crazy,* two GEORGE GERSHWIN shows, and he met JOHN HAMMOND and pianist Teddy Wilson, both central to his later success. In fact, Goodman married Hammond's sister, Alice, in 1941.

With Hammond's encouragement Goodman formed his first big band in 1934. He was booked at Billy Rose's new Music Hall and later that year was featured on "Let's Dance," an NBC radio series. Drummer Gene Krupa joined the band, and, at the urging of Hammond, Goodman hired FLETCHER HENDERSON as arranger. High performance standards, unusual for the time, were evident in the broadcasts.

A 1935 jam session led Goodman to invite Teddy Wilson to record with Krupa and himself.

As the Benny Goodman Trio they recorded four sides. Goodman's solo on "After You've Gone" displays both his dazzling technique and his always disciplined presentation. In August, sponsored by Music Corporation of America, the band concluded a discouraging tour. On August 21, in what Goodman believed to be his final band performance, lightning struck. The huge crowd at the Palomar Ballroom in Los Angeles, electrified by the music, roared its approval. The performance excited the public and the critics and ushered in the swing era. Benny Goodman was toasted as the King of Swing. From 1936 until the early 1940s the popular Goodman band dominated the market.

At the time of Goodman's big band triumphs, he experimented with smaller ensembles. A trio or quartet was featured in performances and spelled the big band. These groups pioneered the public appearance of racially mixed ensembles. The quartet—Goodman, Krupa, Wilson, and Lionel Hampton (vibraphone)—made musical history.

In the late 1930s Goodman explored classical music, initially at John Hammond's instigation. Hammond, who played viola, put together a string group and with Goodman played the Mozart Clarinet Quintet. Goodman's interest grew and he began study with Reginald Kell, the reigning classical clarinetist. Goodman went on to appear with major American orchestras and to record works by LEONARD BERNSTEIN, Claude Debussy, IGOR STRAVINSKY, and others. He contributed to the repertory by commissioning pieces for clarinet from Bela Bartok (1938), AARON COPLAND (1947), and PAUL HINDEMITH (1947).

Goodman's illness in the early forties forced the band to dissolve. However, later the same year he reformed it and began to play more modern arrangements. Eventually Goodman hired bebop musicians like Fats Navarro and Charlie Christian, but he never really embraced the new style.

For thirty years Goodman toured the world, appeared in films like *A Song Is Born* (1948), recorded, and even held a repeat Carnegie Hall concert in 1978 to mark the fortieth anniversary of the ground-breaking 1938 event. A film

biography, *The Benny Goodman Story*, appeared in 1956, and Benny received a Kennedy Center Honors award in 1982. Goodman died in New York City in 1986.

BIBLIOGRAPHY

Collier, J. L., *Benny Goodman and the Swing Era*, 1989; Kappler, F., and G. Simon, *Giants of Jazz: Benny Goodman*, 1979; Schuller, G., *The Swing Era: The Development of Jazz, 1930–1945*, 1989.

Gorky, Arshile

(April 15, 1905–July 21, 1948)
Painter

A rshile Gorky took two radical French art styles—Cubism, in which natural forms are reduced to geometrical ones, and Surrealism, in which imagery is based on fantasy or the subconscious—into a new kind of American painting in the 1940s. His work helped to lay the foundation for Abstract Expressionism, America's contribution to world art.

Gorky (Vosdanik Adoian) was born in a village on Lake Van in Turkish Armenia. His father left home in 1908 to avoid the Turkish military service and eventually reached America with Gorky's older sisters. Gorky and his younger sister, Vartoosh, remained with their mother.

Gorky went to high school in Erevan in Caucasian Armenia, where the three of them had fled as refugees, and received some education in Tiflis. After his mother died of starvation, Gorky and Vartoosh managed to make their way to Providence, Rhode Island, where their father lived. Gorky went to the Rhode Island School of Design, the New School of Design in Boston, and Grand Central School of Art in New York, where he also taught until 1931. He learned more, he said, from galleries and books than from schools.

It was in 1925, soon after he had moved to Greenwich Village in New York, that Gorky adopted the name by which he is known; it means "bitter one." Two versions of a painting, *The Artist and His Mother* (1926–1936), which shows a sad, dark-eyed boy standing stiffly beside a seated woman with a shawl around her head, indicate something of Gorky's loneliness. It was based on a photograph taken in 1912.

Gorky worked through several stages in his painting as he felt the influence of various painters. In the 1920s he was drawing on the Cubists and Cézanne, who he said was "the greatest artist . . . that has lived." In the 1930s he painted like Picasso, who was now "the world's greatest artist." In 1935 the WPA Federal Art Project, a government program designed to help artists during the Great Depression, commissioned Gorky to do a mural for the Newark Airport Administration Building. In the early 1940s he was painting dreams, drawing on his unconscious as the Surrealists did. His *Garden in Sochi* (1941) demonstrates his interest in Surrealism.

In 1941 Gorky married Agnes Magruder. Finally, approaching forty, he found his own splendid abstract style, using thin bursts of brilliant color and graphic black lines. Surrealism continued to influence his work, as in *The Liver Is the Cock's Comb* (1944), a noteworthy example of this period. The shapes in his pictures were forms from nature that he had observed on visits to his wife's family's farm in Virginia. Sometimes these natural forms were microscopically small, twisted into grotesque shapes, which are interpreted as references to his own body, which was battling cancer. His work became more improvisational, as demonstrated in *Summation* (1947), *The Plough and the Song II* (1946–1947), and *Dark Green Painting* (ca. 1948).

Gorky lived in abject poverty. Julien Levy, whose gallery showed Gorky's work each year after 1945, wrote that "art was religion" for Gorky, and described the ragged, patched coat he wore in the winter.

The last years of Gorky's life were full of horror. In January 1946 a fire in his Connecticut studio destroyed 27 paintings and 300 drawings. The next month he underwent cancer surgery. His painting *Agony* (1947) reflects his wretchedness. In 1948 his neck was broken and his painting arm injured in an automobile accident. His marriage disintegrated. He hanged himself in Sherman, Connecticut, after writing on a wooden crate, "Goodbye My Loveds."

BIBLIOGRAPHY

Lader, Melvin P., *Arshile Gorky*, 1985; Rosenberg, Harold, *Arshile Gorky: The Man, the Time, the Idea*, 1962; Waldman, D., *Arshile Gorky*, 1981.

Gottschalk, Louis Moreau

(May 8, 1829–December 18, 1869)
Composer, Pianist

Pianist Louis Gottschalk was one of the first American musicians to gain world recognition. His compositions included variations on contemporary operatic and minstrel music, as well as Latin American motifs. One of his popular pieces, *Banjo,* contained musical quotations from STEPHEN FOSTER and transformed banjo techniques into showy piano style.

Gottschalk's father, Edward, a merchant born in London, emigrated to New Orleans in the 1820s, where Louis Moreau, one of eight, was born. Gottschalk's mother, Marie, fled to Louisiana from Haiti during the 1790s slave rebellion.

Young Gottschalk, called Moreau by the family, began study with François Letellier at five; two years later he was proficient enough to substitute for his teacher at the organ of St. Louis Cathedral during Mass. In response to Letellier's urging, the Gottschalks sent their precocious eldest to Paris in May 1842.

There Gottschalk studied piano and composition. On April 2, 1845, the fifteen-year-old gave a recital at the Salle Pleyel. By 1849 Gottschalk was the darling of Paris, and by 1850 the completion of a trilogy of Louisiana-inspired piano pieces assured him a reputation as a composer. The young virtuoso, so thought Europeans, had now become the musical spokesperson for America.

After touring Switzerland and Spain, Gottschalk returned home in 1853. His father's death that October put Gottschalk under pressure to support the family, and he began to compose pieces, such as *The Last Hope, Bamboula,* and *Tremolo.* These and other sentimental works depended on musical clichés and sentimental titles, but they did please audiences.

In 1856, after concertizing in the United States, Gottschalk sailed for Cuba. He toured the Caribbean and Latin America before returning to Cuba in 1860, where he conducted an opera season in Havana. The composer created his finest piano works at this time, among them *Souvenir de Porto Rico,* along with Symphony no. 1 (A Night in the Tropics), and a one-act opera.

A lucrative touring contract lured Gottschalk back to the United States in 1862. When he reached California in April 1865, he estimated he had given 1,100 American recitals and traveled some 95,000 miles. In September an alleged involvement with a female student in California prompted a scandal and Gottschalk sailed for South America. Though eventually exonerated, he never returned home. In South America Gottschalk composed, conducted, and concertized until his death in a suburb of Rio de Janeiro in 1869.

BIBLIOGRAPHY

Loggins, V., *Where the World Ends: The Life of Louis Moreau Gottschalk,* 1958.

Graham, Martha

(May 11, 1894–April 1, 1991)
Choreographer, Dancer

Martha Graham placed modern dance on a par with ballet as an art form. As the fledgling new dance form left the vaudeville stage for the concert hall, the Graham technique made it into a powerful, codified idiom that expressed raw emotion, drove choreography, and profoundly changed the dance world.

Martha Graham, daughter of George Graham, a physician who treated mental disorders, and Jane Beers, moved with her family from Allegheny, Pennsylvania, to Santa Barbara, California, in 1908. After completing high school in 1913, she entered the Cumnock School in Los Angeles, graduating from the junior college in 1916. Cumnock of-

Library of Congress

fered training in dance, drama, and self-expression along with the usual academics.

In 1911 Dr. Graham had taken his daughter to a RUTH ST. DENIS performance. Graham was mesmerized, but her father, a strict Presbyterian, ruled dance inappropriate as a profession. It was not until 1916, after Dr. Graham's death, that the young woman, with her family's blessing, entered the newly established Denishawn School, run by St. Denis and TED SHAWN, in Los Angeles. Graham was twenty-two, old for a beginning dancer, when she started her studies with Denishawn, then the only major dance company to work outside balletic tradition.

St. Denis did not see Graham's potential. Shawn, however, recognized her talent and determination. He used her for a pageant, then as a teacher during his World War I military service. On Shawn's return to Denishawn, Graham continued to teach and to dance small roles. Her break came in 1920 when Shawn created his Aztec dance, *Xochitl,* for her. It was her first major performing opportunity, and Shawn noted it "made the most of [her] exotic features and allowed her body freedom of movement that ranged from the tigerish and primitive to the passionate and regal."

Graham left Denishawn in 1923 for John Murray Anderson's *Greenwich Village Follies.* She soon knew that neither the exotica of Denishawn nor the commercial theater would satisfy her. She went to the Eastman School of Music in Rochester, New York. There she taught dance and began to create her own works. On April 18, 1926, she made her concert debut at the 48th Street Theater in New York with works that still reflected the theatrics of Denishawn, but, as critic Robert Salin noted in 1953, "the spirit was new and as bracing as a salty sea wind." In 1927 Graham founded the Dance Repertory Theater, later the Martha Graham School of Contemporary Dance, and began to recruit dancers.

With courage and determination Graham was beginning to develop her own dance idiom. "My dancing," she said, "is not an attempt to interpret life in the literary sense. It is an affirmation of life through movement." Her technique stemmed from breathing and took its form from contracting and release, exhaling and inhaling. The result was a stark, expressive, angular style with large dramatic movements rather than graceful gestures. In the 1930 solo *Lamentation,* Graham, garbed in a tube of jersey, became grief rather than merely suggesting it. Through her body's sharp, intense angles, she was anguish, "the thing itself," she said, "not just a pretty picture of it."

Graham's abstract experiments were not always well received, though in 1930, her portrayal of the chosen maiden in the revival of IGOR STRAVINSKY's *Rite of Spring* brought her

recognition. Gradually she drew high-quality students, and her choreography became ever more adventurous. In the end it was her choreography, created out of a powerful new dance idiom, rather than dancing itself that marked her achievement.

In the 1930s, *Primitive Mysteries* (1931), based on American Indian dances she had seen in the Southwest, and *American Provincial* (1934) and *Frontier* (1935), which celebrated American pioneer background, explored the American spirit. Guided by her musical director Louis Horst, Graham sought out scores by contemporaries like SAMUEL BARBER, GIAN CARLO MENOTTI, and AARON COPLAND. Copland's score for the 1944 *Appalachian Spring* won the Pulitzer Prize.

Graham, a thorough-going Modernist, rejected the literal for abstraction and searched for forms with resonant meanings. *Frontier* began her thirty-two-year collaboration with sculptor ISAMU NOGUCHI. His simple, spare set helped heighten the power of Horst's score and Graham's solo. Noguchi remarked on Graham's "drive that motivated her to strip the dance to its stark rudiment."

In the 1940s Graham turned to literary figures. *Letter to the World* (1940) explored EMILY DICKINSON, while *Deaths and Entrances* (1943) portrayed the sisters Charlotte, Emily, and Anne Brontë, English writers. She went on to probe Greek mythology in works like *Cave of the Heart* (1946), *Errand into the Maze* (1947), and *Clytemnestra* (1958).

As Graham grew older, she steered younger dancers to difficult roles but retained less exhausting parts for herself. She gave her last stage performance at seventy-five but continued to manage, direct, and tour with her troupe for another twenty years. *Maple Leaf Rag* (1990), the last of the over 180 works she created and directed, premiered six months before her death in 1991. She died of cardiac arrest in her New York apartment. Her autobiography, *Blood Memory* (1991), was published posthumously.

Graham's honors range from the Presidential Medal of Freedom to the Medal of Honor from the city of Paris. Her school and company trained dancers who were inspired by her teaching and determination and spawned generations of performers, choreographers, and teachers, including MERCE CUNNINGHAM and PAUL TAYLOR. A tiny, thin figure with arched eyebrows and a red slash of a mouth, she was, says AGNES DE MILLE, "a gigantic figure. She started

not only a whole school of dance, but a whole new form of theater."

BIBLIOGRAPHY

Graham, M., *Blood Memory*, 1991; McDonough, D., *Martha Graham: A Biography*, 1973; Stodelle, E., *Deep Song: The Dance Story of Martha Graham*, 1984.

Grant, Cary

(January 18, 1904–November 29, 1986)
Actor

A leading man in Hollywood for thirty years, Cary Grant was the epitome of romantic elegance and sophistication. While he has had many imitators, no other actor ever matched his blend of wit, worldliness, and chivalrous charm, qualities that graced performances in comedies, thrillers, and adventure films alike.

Born Archibald Alec Leach in Bristol, England, he was the only surviving child of working-class parents. His father was employed in the garment industry; his mother suffered a nervous breakdown and entered a mental institution when he was ten. He ran away at thirteen to join the Bob Pender troupe of comics and acrobats, which performed in New York in 1920. When the group broke up in 1922, he remained in the United States and worked as a carnival barker at Coney Island.

Leach continued his vaudeville performances throughout North America with former members of the Pender troupe, settling mainly in New York. He began his acting career in several shows produced by Arthur Hammerstein and J. J. SHUBERT. In 1931 he joined Shubert's St. Louis Repertory Company and had leading roles in operettas. A Hollywood screen test won him a contract at Paramount, where his name was changed to Cary Grant. He changed it legally in 1942.

Grant based his screen persona on the English playwright Noel Coward, spending end-

less time imitating his walk and voice, until finally, he said, "I became that person." His very presence in a movie elicited words like "class" and "polish." No one wore a tuxedo as definitively, yet he was equally at ease in street clothes or military garb.

He made a good impression in his first film, *This Is the Night* (1932), and in *Blonde Venus* (1932) with MARLENE DIETRICH, but it was costarring with MAE WEST in *She Done Him Wrong* (1933) and *I'm No Angel* (1933) that made him a star.

By the end of the 1930s, he had made twenty more films, including such classics as *Sylvia Scarlett* (1936), *Bringing Up Baby* (1938), and *Holiday* (1938)—all with KATHARINE HEPBURN—*Topper* and *The Awful Truth* (both 1937), and *Gunga Din* and *Only Angels Have Wings* (both 1939).

He continued this string of successes with *His Girl Friday* (1940), costarring Rosalind Russell, *The Philadelphia Story* (1940), again with Hepburn, and *Suspicion* (1941), his first of four memorable suspense thrillers directed by ALFRED HITCHCOCK. The others were *Notorious* (1946) with INGRID BERGMAN, *To Catch a Thief* (1955) with Grace Kelly, and *North by Northwest* (1959). All four explored a cruel underside to Grant's suave personality.

New York Times critic Vincent Canby remarked that Grant's different characters shared a "profound urbanity"—in serious and comedic roles, he possessed a "lightness of heart and touch . . . far more adaptable than was ever immediately apparent."

Like many of the screen's greatest personalities, Grant never received an Academy Award for a particular performance, but in 1970 was awarded a special Oscar for his lifetime contribution. Even his two Oscar nominations—for *Penny Serenade* (1941) and CLIFFORD ODETS's *None But the Lonely Heart* (1944)—were for atypical performances in which his strongest features were less apparent.

In 1942 Grant became a U.S. citizen. He had also become one of the first actors to declare independence from the studio system, working first in Britain for Grand National, then for Columbia and RKO. By the 1950s he was earning $300,000 per film.

Among his later successes were *I Was a Male War Bride* (1949), *An Affair to Remem-ber* (1957), *Operation Petticoat* (1959), and *Charade* (1963). His last screen appearance was in *Walk, Don't Run* (1966), in which, uncharacteristically but perhaps symbolically, he does not win the girl in the end.

Grant was married five times and divorced four. His first, third, and fourth wives were the actresses Virginia Cherrill, Betsy Drake, and Dyan Cannon, the last of whom bore him his only child, Jennifer, in 1966. His second wife was Woolworth heiress Barbara Hutton. At his death he was married to longtime companion Barbara Harris.

BIBLIOGRAPHY

Godfrey, Lionel, *Cary Grant*, 1981; Higham, Charles, and Roy Moseley, *Cary Grant: The Lonely Heart*, 1989; Nelson, Nancy, *Evenings with Cary Grant*, 1991; Wansell, Jeffrey, *Haunted Idol*, 1983.

Graves, Michael

(July 9, 1934–   )
Architect, Designer

A leader in the Post-Modernist movement in architecture, Michael Graves is a prolific designer of furniture, textiles, and murals, as well as of buildings. In addition, his ideas about the nature and function of architecture, and about color and decoration, have influenced the profession substantially.

Graves was born in Indianapolis, Indiana, and exhibited artistic talent early in his childhood. Encouraged by his parents to pursue an architectural career, he attended the University of Cincinnati and graduated with a B.S. degree in architecture (1958). After receiving an M.A. from Harvard University (1959), he won the Rome Prize, spending two years in residence at the American Academy in Rome, where interaction with other artists and exposure to the great works of classical and Re-naissance art were an influence in the gradual formation of his ideas on architecture in relation to humanity, nature, and history.

Upon returning to the United States, Graves began a fruitful association with Princeton University, first as a lecturer in architecture (1962), and finally as full professor (from 1972). He opened his own firm in Princeton, New Jersey, in 1964, and gained recognition for his designs in the "Forty Under Forty" Exhibition at the Architectural League in New York City (1966). His early designs, such as the Union County Nature and Science Museum (1967) in Mountainside, New Jersey, and the addition to the Paul Benacerraf house in Princeton (1969) reflect the influence of the work in the 1920s by the Swiss architect Le Corbusier with emphasis on white geometric forms and primary colors, complicated by unusual details. In the early 1970s Graves was linked with other Corbusian-influenced architects (Peter Eisenman, RICHARD MEIER, John Hejduk, Charles Gwathmey), who were then known as the New York Five. A book called *Five Architects* (1972) promoted their concept of architectural design as the "making of form."

By the mid-1970s Graves had shifted from Corbusian-influenced designs to a more heterogeneous style. He emerged in the forefront of the Post-Modernist movement, which stressed assembling forms of the past into new juxtapositions and the use of eclectic ornamentation and rich colors. He has become known for the unusual ways in which he blends elements of ancient Greek and Roman architecture with neoclassical and modern forms, and for his insistence that these historical allusions, and color, make the thematic content of his buildings more "readable." Graves views architecture as a "metaphor of nature," and as the representation "in physical form [of] the symbolic and mythic aspirations" of society. His aim has been to reestablish the "common language" of architecture.

One of Graves's most famous and controversial works is the Public Service Building in Portland, Oregon (1980–1982). Although it has been criticized as a "beribboned Christmas package," and a combination "cookie jar and jukebox," this milestone of Post-Modern architecture has also been praised for energy-efficient design and the bold, quasi-classical presence that it brings to the city center. Above a dark-green colonnaded base rises a huge block with small windows. On the front, two pilasterlike vertical bands support a gigantic keystone. Other memorable features include the stylized lateral garlands and the much-loved sculpture *Portlandia*, crouching above the entrance portal.

His San Juan Capistrano Regional Library (1982–1984) in California, which echoes somewhat the Spanish mission ruins nearby, is a nod to regionalism, while the Humana Building (1982–1986) in Louisville, Kentucky, with its red granite base and pink granite tower, is a complicated, but striking, tribute to the tradition of the tall, elegantly profiled skyscraper.

As an "architectural storyteller," Graves tries to create "metaphorical landscapes" in which the parts of a building (such as foundations, walls, doors, and columns) suggest nature (a roof is like the sky) or the human form (a base is like a human foot), with color coding to underscore the function and significance of the structural element (blue for sky or water). He is also interested in what he has termed figurative architecture (as opposed to a completely abstract architecture). "I believe people make a natural association with form, color, and the composition of elements, while decoration and detailing help communicate a building's purpose and spirit." When he designed the Swan and Dolphin hotel-convention complexes (1987–1990) at Disney World in Orlando, Florida, he focused on the relationship of the architecture to the other fantasies of the place and tried to create an "aesthetic mythology." The facades are metaphorical seascapes and banana groves, with huge swans, dolphins, and scalloped fountains as decorations, evoking the stage scenery of musicals in the 1930s or the flamboyant temporary architecture of a world's fair.

As a diversified designer, Graves has also produced furniture, rugs, textiles, posters, exhibition booths, a best-selling teakettle, a tea service, and a clock, among other items. His murals, such as the one for the School of Architecture, University of Texas at Austin (1974), have garnered much acclaim. His sketches and drawings for architectural projects have also been critically praised and sold as independent works of art.

BIBLIOGRAPHY

Frampton, Kenneth, and Colin Rowe, *Five Architects: Eisenman, Graves, Gwathmey, Hejduk, Meier*, 1972; Graves, Michael, *Buildings and Projects*, 2 vols., 1982, 1988; Jencks, Charles, *The Language of Post-Modern Architecture*, 1977.

Greene, Charles Sumner

(October 12, 1868–June 11, 1957)

Greene, Henry Mather

(January 23, 1870–October 2, 1954)
Architects

The brothers Charles and Henry Greene, who created the California bungalow style of the late nineteenth century, were cited by the American Institute of Architects in 1952 as "formulators of a new and native architecture."

The Greenes were born in Brighton, Ohio, near Cincinnati, but when they were young, their father moved the family to St. Louis. With their mother, they moved, this time temporarily, to her family's farm at Wyandotte, West Virginia, while their father was in medical school. There they became acquainted with the natural world of plants, trees, and rocks, which made a profound impression on them.

With the family back in St. Louis, the brothers went to Calvin Woodward's Manual Training School, the first manual training school in America. Calvin Woodward was a disciple of William Morris, the English artist who founded the Arts and Crafts movement (see GUSTAV STICKLEY), which called for the revival of handicrafts and the reform of architecture by using traditional building crafts. There the Greenes learned to use tools and materials properly and acquired high standards for workmanship.

When Charles Greene graduated in 1887, he waited for a year so that he and Henry could enter the Massachusetts Institute of Technology together to study architecture. They found that the curriculum contrasted sharply with the craftsmanlike atmosphere of the Woodward Manual Training School, but they became interested in classical Greek architecture and studied scale, proportion, and composition intensively. They finished the MIT program, which included two years of classroom work and two years of apprenticeship in Boston architectural firms.

While they were working as apprentices in Boston, they were exposed to the shingled houses of HENRY HOBSON RICHARDSON and his followers and spent time in the Museum of Fine Arts in Boston, where they first became acquainted with Oriental art forms.

In late 1893 they went to Pasadena, where their parents had recently moved. They admired the landscape and the way Californians lived. They also were impressed with the Mission churches that Spanish missionaries had built on the West Coast. They opened an office when a friend of their father's asked them to design a small house in Pasadena and called themselves Greene and Greene. Over the years they worked out their own style, drawing on their Arts and Crafts training and their knowledge of the Shingle Style, Chinese furniture, Japanese buildings, and California missions. One of their early designs, the Arturo Bandini house in Pasadena (1903), was one story and shaped like a U around a courtyard.

The California bungalows, as their homes came to be called, featured low-pitched roofs with wide overhangs, broad porches and terraces, and open plans. They were made of natural materials—shingles, wood, brick, and stone. Builders seized upon the Greenes' ideas, and by the 1920s whole subdivisions of American cities were covered with California bungalows in all sizes.

The Greenes performed wonders with wood. They were experts at working with it themselves, and they trained expert craftsmen. RALPH ADAMS CRAM, who was principally a neo-Gothicist, had high praise for the Greenes' work, which he said had "an honesty that is sometimes almost brazen." They combined wood with stone and used exposed joints. They also designed the terraces, furniture, carpets, and light fixtures, as well as the landscape and garden around a house.

The Freeman A. Ford House in Pasadena (1904) was of 2 stories and completely enclosed a patio. The Robert R. Blacker house in Pasadena (1907–1909) was less adventurous in plan, but was a crucial turning point in their career. It brought together their disparate interests and talents in a unified work of house, furnishings, and landscape. The Charles M. Pratt house in Ojai (1909) has an unusually rambling, free-form plan. The house for David B. Gamble in Pasadena (1908–1909) contains the original furniture and is the best-preserved example of the Greenes' work.

In 1909 Charles Greene began to withdraw from the firm. He took his family (he had married Alice Gordon White in 1901) to England for a year, where he painted in oils and watercolors and rested. Henry Greene, who had married Emeline Augusta Dart in 1899, stayed behind to oversee the work in progress. After Charles returned to the United States, the firm had fewer commissions. Taste was changing, and their work was expensive because of the high standards they maintained. In 1916 Charles and his family moved to Carmel, California, where he spent the rest of his life, writing, designing, and carving. Henry remained in southern California until his death in 1954. Charles died in 1957.

BIBLIOGRAPHY

Current, William R., and Karen Current, *Greene and Greene—Architects in the Residential Style,* 1974; Makinson, Randell L., *Greene & Greene: Architecture as a Fine Art,* 1977, and *Charles and Henry Greene and Their Work,* 1978; Strand, Janann, *A Greene and Greene Guide,* 1974.

Griffith, David Wark

(January 22, 1875–July 23, 1948)
Film Director, Producer

D W. Griffith, whose film *Birth of a Nation* revolutionized the industry, was the single most important and influential figure in the development of the American narrative film.

Born in a village near Louisville, Kentucky, Griffith's father, Jacob Wark Griffith, was a colonel for the Confederacy and an officer in the early Ku Klux Klan. Owing to family misfortune, the boy had to work as a shop assistant in Louisville, where he became fascinated with the theater and went on stage at age seventeen against his family's wishes. He experienced hunger and hard times between stock engagements in the 1890s, taking odd jobs to make a living while acting part time and writing.

He married Linda Arvidson in 1906 and sold his first play, *A Fool and a Girl,* for $700 in 1907. At the same time he began writing scenarios for the Biograph Film Company in New York, occasionally acting in the films, directed by Edwin S. Porter, then in 1908 made his debut as director with *The Adventures of Dollie.*

Between 1908 and 1913 Griffith made nearly 500 one- and two-reeler films, in which he advanced the art of narrative and dramatic filmmaking through experiments with framing, editing, lighting, camera angles, and shot sizes. While he was not the first filmmaker to use a close-up, he developed a sophisticated use of it within a story that intensified its emotional impact.

Much of his material was drawn from the Bible and such nineteenth-century writers as EDGAR ALLAN POE and Charles Dickens. While his themes stressed universal truths and Christian values, generally unquestioned in his day, he was also sensitive to social injustice and moral hypocrisy. His heroes were strong men of conscience and action, his heroines pure and virtuous, but he did not flinch from realistic depictions of the corruptions and evils of human nature.

Library of Congress

Griffith began to move to feature-length films with *Judith of Bethulia,* a four-reel biblical drama made in 1913. Following this, he left Biograph and produced his own films, beginning with *The Battle of the Sexes; The Escape; Home, Sweet Home;* and *The Avenging Conscience;* all released in 1914.

In 1915 he released a three-hour epic, *The Birth of a Nation,* his most famous film and undoubtedly one of the two or three most important—as well as controversial—silent films ever made. Hugely successful and provocative, it advanced the state of film art with its panoramic evocation of American history, its ambitious narrative structure, its attention to characterization and period detail, and its technical achievements. With cameraman Billy Bitzer, Griffith experimented with new photographic techniques, often with tinted film stock to evoke mood and special lighting effects.

Griffith balanced long-distance shots of battlefields and marching soldiers with expressive close-ups of characters. Scenes broken up through different camera setups created a more varied perspective on the action. Inspired by the novels of Charles Dickens, which in their serialized forms often ended installments with cliffhanging situations, leaving the reader in a state of suspense, Griffith developed the editing technique of parallel cutting, which allowed him to cut from one situation to another and develop separate lines of the narrative, increasing dramatic tension. The finale of the film utilizes the technique in depicting a group of whites besieged by blacks as the Ku Klux Klan rushes to the rescue.

Beyond its technical achievements, the film demonstrated indisputably the social and political impact of the motion picture medium. Based on the novel *The Clansman* (1905) by Thomas Dixon, a white supremacist, the film's portrayal of the post–Civil War conditions in the South, legitimizing the rise of the Ku Klux Klan, aroused protests nationwide, especially at a time when the Klan was newly activated in parts of the South. Though Griffith always expressed surprise at accusations of racism, the film still encounters protests when it is revived.

In 1916 he made *Intolerance,* another long, even more ambitious epic, which told four separate stories set in four different historical periods—the time of the Babylonian Empire, the story of Christ, the massacre of the Huguenots in sixteenth-century France, and a modern-day tale of social injustice. Griffith cut back and forth from one story to another, developing situations and characters, until in the final reel the shifts became more and more rapid, highlighting the common theme of intolerance through the ages. While the film was not a commercial success, its importance in the evolution of film language and structure has long since been acknowledged.

Between 1918 and 1924 Griffith produced and directed eighteen features, most notably *Hearts of the World* (1918), a sympathetic view of post–World War I Germany; *Broken Blossoms* (1919), a moving drama of interracial love; *Way Down East* (1920), a melodrama climaxing in a tense chase across icefloes and waterfalls; *Orphans of the Storm* (1921), an epic of the French Revolution; *America* (1924), the story of the American Revolution; and *Isn't Life Wonderful* (1924). All of these were released by United Artists, the company he jointly formed in 1919 with CHARLIE CHAPLIN, MARY PICKFORD, and Douglas Fairbanks.

Griffith worked with what became his own stock company, which included Lillian Gish, who appeared in many of his most important films, giving especially moving performances in *Broken Blossoms, True Heart Susie* (1919), *Way Down East,* and *Orphans of the Storm.*

Between 1925 and 1931 Griffith directed his six last films, including his only two sound works, *Abraham Lincoln* (1930), starring Walter Huston, and *The Struggle* (1931), a drama about alcoholism.

Virtually inactive for the next seventeen years, Griffith lived in hotels, writing poems and plays that he failed to complete. In 1936 he divorced Linda Arvidson and married Evelyn Baldwin, age twenty-six. He received an hon-

orary Academy Award in 1936 and was made First Honorary Life Member of the Directors Guild of America in 1938. Hal Roach hired him as consultant and general assistant on *One Million, B.C.* (1940), which was inspired by *Griffith's Man's Genesis* (1912).

While Griffith spent his remaining years in limbo, visited occasionally by old friends who had worked with him, like Gish and Mae Marsh, he continued to try writing various screenplays. In 1947, separated from his second wife, he took up residence at the Knickerbocker Hotel in Hollywood, where he was to die alone the following year. Griffith's influence on the development of film is incalculable and can be seen in the work of countless directors.

BIBLIOGRAPHY

Arvidson, Linda, *When the Movies Were Young,* 1925, rep., 1969; Gunning, Tom, *D. W. Griffith and the Origins of the American Narrative Film,* 1991; Henderson, Robert M., *D. W. Griffith: His Life and Work,* 1972; Schickel, Richard, *D. W. Griffith: An American Life,* 1984.

Gropius, Georg Walter Adolf

(May 18, 1883–July 5, 1969)
Architect

Walter Gropius, an influential teacher and administrator, was a leader in the development of the twentieth-century International style in architecture. He founded the Bauhaus, a design school in Weimar and Dessau, Germany, and later directed architectural education at Harvard University.

Gropius was born in Berlin, the son of an architect who was head of the Berlin Art School. He studied briefly at the Institute of Technology in Munich in 1903 and, later, at the

Institute of Technology in Berlin. After a tour of Spain in 1907, he began work in Neu Babelsberg/Berlin in the office of Peter Behrens, the most important design studio in Germany. Behrens, who designed factories as well as houses and furniture, influenced Gropius with his ideas for transforming industry through improved design.

In 1910 Gropius opened his own office. His first big commission, in 1911, a shoe-last factory at Alfeld an der Leine, was one of the first buildings in the world to have glass walls and unrelieved cubic blocks. From 1913 to 1914 he designed a model factory office building for the Deutscher Werkbund exhibition in Cologne. (The Werkbund, in which Gropius was interested, was a German association of avant-garde manufacturers and architects that worked to create a new industrial art based on good design and sound construction through collaboration of artists, artisans, architects, and manufacturers.)

Gropius spent four years in the German army from 1914 to 1918, and during that time married Alma Schindler Mahler, widow of the composer Gustav Mahler. They were divorced after World War I, and Gropius married Ise Frank in 1923.

After Gropius's wartime service, the grand duke of Saxe-Weimar appointed him to reorganize the Weimar school of arts and crafts and the Weimar Art Academy. Gropius combined the schools to form the Bauhaus, "house of building," a reversal of the German word, Hausbau, which means "building of a house." The name underlined Gropius's principle that the school should teach both fine art and crafts, which are allied with architecture, the basis of all art. The curriculum was designed to unite art with both industry and daily life. Artists and craftspersons learned the basics of form, color, and materials, then entered workshops in carpentry, metal working, pottery, wall painting, weaving, graphics, typography, and stagecraft. (The Bauhaus did not actually teach architecture until 1927.) A team, composed of an artist and a craftsperson, taught each workshop. Gropius assembled an outstanding faculty that included the painters Paul Klee, László Moholy-Nagy, and Wassily Kandinsky, the architect Marcel Breuer, and the designer Josef Albers.

Gropius continued his private architectural practice, designing a house for Adolf Sommerfeld in Berlin (1921) made of teak timbers salvaged from a dismantled German warship. His jagged concrete memorial (1921) to the workers killed in fending off the Kapp Putsch (an attempt to take over the Weimar Republic in March 1920) was influenced by German Expressionism, an art movement that stressed the artist's emotions and inner vision.

When the conservative middle class of Weimar began to express its disapproval of the "radical" atmosphere at the Bauhaus, Gropius moved the school to Dessau. Gropius designed the new Bauhaus building from 1925 to 1926 to include workshops, studios, offices, cafeteria, auditorium, student housing, and Gropius's private architectural offices. A series of connected flat-roofed blocks with unornamented walls of stucco and glass, it is a landmark in modern architecture. This example of the International style (see LUDWIG MIES VAN DER ROHE) was Gropius's most famous building, and it became an ideal for several generations of modern architects.

When the same problems with the community that had plagued the Bauhaus in Weimar surfaced in Dessau, Gropius resigned in 1928 to practice architecture in Berlin. He was particularly interested in low-cost housing and he worked with other architects on several projects, including the Siemensstadt Housing in Berlin (1929–1930), which featured blocks of apartments in long rows.

Gropius left Germany in 1934 to work in England and three years later came to the United States as professor of architecture and later chairman of the Department of Architecture at Harvard's Graduate School of Design. At Harvard he incorporated in the curriculum Bauhaus ideas about the integration of the arts and sciences into architectural design and introduced the so-called New Architecture, which stressed social issues and logical construction methods.

In his own architectural work, Gropius was associated with Marcel Breuer, his colleague from the Bauhaus. The two of them in 1937 designed Gropius's house at Lincoln, Massachusetts, which was the first modern house in New England. It was a rectangular block with a flat roof and horizontal bands of windows; his European idiom translated into American wood, but with industrial details.

Gropius became an American citizen in 1944, and two years later organized an architectural firm called The Architects' Collaborative (TAC), which designed the new Harvard Graduate Center (1948–1960). With Pietro Belluschi, Gropius served as design consultant for the Pan-Am Building in New York (1958), where he recommended cutting the four corners to reduce the bulk of the boxlike building. He designed the U.S. embassy in Athens (1956–1961) and, referring to the classical architecture nearby, gave the building square columns and an atrium.

Gropius and TAC had several commissions in Germany in the 1950s. The largest was a housing project for 50,000 families in Berlin, which was later named Gropiusstadt. They also designed a new factory in Selb, Germany, for

Rosenthal Ceramics (1963), for which Gropius created a glassed inner court containing plants and birds that could be seen by any worker in the factory, and the Bauhaus Archive in Berlin (1964–1968). In his last years he designed the Tower East Office Building in Cleveland (1967) and the John F. Kennedy Federal Office Building in Boston (1961–1966).

He died in 1969 at the age of eighty-six.

BIBLIOGRAPHY

Isaacs, Reginald R., *Gropius: An Illustrated Biography of the Creator of the Bauhaus*, 1991; O'Neal, B. (ed.), *Walter Gropius*, 1966.

Guthrie, Woodrow Wilson

(July 14, 1912–October 3, 1967)
Folksinger, Songwriter

The legendary Woody Guthrie is best remembered for such songs as "This Land Is Your Land" and "Reuben James." His belief that music could change social conditions influenced BOB DYLAN, Joan Baez, Pete Seeger, and others.

Woodrow Wilson Guthrie was born in Okemah, Oklahoma, the third of five children. His father, Charley, a real estate speculator with political ambitions, supported the family comfortably until Woody was seven. Then Charley's prosperity, undermined by alcoholism and threatened by the oil boom, foundered.

Things went from bad to worse. In 1919 Clare, the eldest child, died in a fire. In 1927 Charley was badly burned in another blaze; he left Okemah to join his two younger children, who lived with his sister Maude in Texas, and to recuperate. Woody's mother, Nora, was afflicted with Huntington's chorea (the degenerative disease that was to kill Woody) and was

consigned to a mental institution. Left on his own at fifteen, Guthrie drifted and was sporadically taken in by friends and relatives.

A restless loner, Guthrie spent his days reading in the public library and went to school infrequently until he dropped out at sixteen. He taught himself to play the harmonica and the guitar, and performed at barn dances and revival meetings, in pool halls and in bars. In 1935 he headed for California, one of thousands of Okies who fled the Dust Bowl in the thirties. That hobo life, punctuated by menial jobs and occasional street singing, shaped his convictions and heightened his sense of mission.

In 1937 his radio program, "Here Come Woody and Lefty Lou," was heard over KFVD in Los Angeles. Guthrie went on to broadcast in New York City with "Cavalcade of America" and "Pipe Smoking Time." By 1938 he was on the West Coast again singing in migrant camps and on radio shows with Will Geer and Cisco

Houston. A mimeographed songbook he put together, *On a Slow Train through California*, found its way to Pete Seeger. Guthrie and Seeger met at a concert for migrant workers in 1940. That year ALAN LOMAX, the son and collaborator of folklorist JOHN LOMAX, recorded Guthrie's *Dust Bowl Ballads* for the Library of Congress Archive of Folk Song. Lomax introduced Guthrie to New York's liberal café society and helped him search out publishers and sponsors for his works.

In 1941 the Almanac Singers formed in New York with Guthrie, Pete Seeger, and others. The group toured the country, then settled in Greenwich Village later that year. Guthrie founded and worked briefly with the Headline Singers (Leadbelly [HUDDIE LEDBETTER], Sonny Terry, and Brownie McGhee), and wrote an article for the magazine *Common Ground*. The piece led to an autobiography, *Bound for Glory*, published in 1943. Early writings, spurred by his sympathy for the underdog, were published in *The Daily Worker* and *People's Daily World*.

In 1943 Guthrie joined the U.S. Merchant Marine with Cisco Houston. In the course of their World War II travels they collected musical instruments, sang in North Africa, the United Kingdom, and Sicily, and survived dangerous torpedo attacks. After Guthrie's discharge in 1945, he recorded hundreds of songs for the Folkways label.

The over 1,000 songs written or adapted by Guthrie (he often put new words to old tunes) were nearly all inspired by his life on the road. He sang of hard times in the Great Depression, the Dust Bowl drought, unions, and the New Deal. He performed frequently at protest meetings, on picket lines, and on marches, and his lyrics urged action as they underlined his beliefs. "This Land Is Your Land" and "Union Maid" are especially well known, as are "So Long, It's Been Good to Know Ya," "Goin' Down the Road," "Roll on Columbia," "Reuben James," and "Pastures of Plenty." Guthrie also wrote songs like "My Car" and "Why Oh Why" for children.

Guthrie's column for the Communist paper *People's Daily World* made him a target during the McCarthy era, and by the midfifties he was seriously ill, struck down by the disease that had killed his mother. By the sixties, he was bedridden and his son, Arlo, began to perform his songs. It was at this time that the young Bob Dylan began to visit him regularly.

After his death in 1967, *Tribute to Woody Guthrie* concerts were recorded at Carnegie Hall, January 1968, and the Hollywood Bowl, September 1970. A film, *Bound for Glory*, starring David Carradine as Guthrie, was released in 1976.

BIBLIOGRAPHY

Guthrie, W., *Bound for Glory*, 1943, and *Seeds of Man*, 1976; Klein, J., *Woody Guthrie: A Life*, 1980.

Hammett, Samuel Dashiell

(May 27, 1894–January 10, 1961)
Novelist, Screenwriter

Dashiell Hammett's detective stories, such as *The Maltese Falcon* and *The Thin Man*, brought hard-edged characters, seamy action, and the ambience of the urban underworld to a genre that had been dominated in the previous generation by the elegance and rationality of Sherlock Holmes.

Hammett was born in St. Marys County, Maryland, in 1894. Educated at the Baltimore Polytechnic Institute until the age of fourteen, he served in the U.S. Army's Motor Ambulance Corps during World War I. He worked variously as a newsboy, freight clerk, messenger, stevedore, advertising manager, and finally for fourteen years as a private detective for the Pinkerton Agency before turning to writing full time in 1922.

New York World Telegram and Sun Collection
at the Library of Congress

Hammett began publishing detective stories in *Black Mask*, a pulp magazine, in 1923. From the start, he ignored conventions of the genre. Whereas most contemporary stories featured detective heroes who solved crime after crime using flawless procedure and impeccable logic, Hammett's detectives grumbled about the inadequacy of fingerprints as clues and faced files full of unsolved cases. They worked in cities gone to seed and spoke the language of the criminals they hunted. Hammett's story "Fly Paper," published in *Black Mask* in 1929, is often cited as the first true example of so-called hard-boiled fiction.

In 1929 Hammett published *Red Harvest* and *The Dain Curse* and, in 1930, *The Maltese Falcon*, in which he introduced his sleuth, Sam Spade. In *The Glass Key* (1931), Hammett's own favorite book, Ned Beaumont runs down the bootlegger who murdered the son of a public official and takes the girl of the town's political boss away from him. *The Thin Man* (1932) features Nick Charles, a former detective who solves a murder when he discovers that the suspected murderer, the thin man, was himself slain months earlier by the real murderer. In 1934, *The Thin Man* became a successful movie starring William Powell and Myrna Loy.

Among Hammett's later detective novels were *The Continental Op* (1945), *Nightmare Town* (1948), *The Creeping Siamese* (1950), and *Woman in the Dark* (1951).

Hammett, who lived in Hollywood from 1930 to 1942, became a successful screenwriter, cowriting *City Streets* (1931) and *Woman in the Dark* (1934), as well as two sequels to *The Thin Man* released in 1936 and 1939. Perhaps most notable among his screenplays was *Watch on the Rhine* (1943), about a refugee from Nazi Germany who murders his blackmailer, which Hammett adapted from the play by LILLIAN HELLMAN. (Hammett and Hellman had begun a long-term relationship in 1930; they lived and worked together after Hammett's 1937 divorce from Josephine Dolan.)

After 1946 Hammett taught creative writing in New York City. He served as president of the Civil Rights Congress of New York in

1946–1947. In 1951 he was sentenced to six months in prison for contempt of Congress when he refused to cooperate with the anti-communist investigation led by Senator Joseph McCarthy and the House Un-American Activities Committee (HUAC).

After Hammett's death in 1961, Lillian Hellman edited a collection of his works, *The Big Knockover: Selected Stories and Short Novels*, published in 1966. "Tulip," one of the short novels, is close to autobiography.

BIBLIOGRAPHY

Johnson, Diane, *The Life of Dashiell Hammett*, 1984; Symons, Julian, *Dashiell Hammett*, 1985.

Hammond, John Henry, Jr.

(December 15, 1910–July 10, 1987)
Critic, Record Producer

Jazz aficionado John Hammond had a gift for spotting new talent and remarkable tenacity in boosting careers of jazz artists. He was especially influential during the 1930s when he promoted recordings by Count Basie, FLETCHER HENDERSON, BILLIE HOLIDAY, BENNY GOODMAN, and others.

John Henry Hammond, Jr., was born to New York City wealth and privilege: his mother was a Vanderbilt, his father a banker and lawyer. He was sent off to Hotchkiss, a prestigious preparatory school. While there he frequently traveled to Harlem to listen to black blues singers. Hammond entered Yale in 1930 but dropped out in his sophomore year to follow his jazz interests.

He began to write for British publications like *The Gramophone* and later, in 1931, *Melody Maker*. At twenty-one an inheritance enabled him both to produce the music that had fascinated him since he was a teenager and to bring black and white musicians together—an unheard-of phenomenon at that time.

Hammond's goal was finding jazz musicians and recording them. He tried unsuccessfully to produce records but it was not until a 1933 trip to England that, in the words of James L. Collier, the "young, brash, opinionated rich man's son" who had been haunting American depression-ridden record companies, got a break. He met Sir Louis Sterling, president of the English Columbia Gramophone Company.

He returned to New York to produce records for English Columbia: eight sides by the Fletcher Henderson Orchestra, eight by Benny Carter's big band, four by a Benny Goodman group, and another four by a Joe Venuti sextet. In 1934 Hammond helped form Benny Goodman's orchestra and secured bookings for him. The association of the two men was to be a long one and was strengthened by Goodman's marriage to Hammond's sister, Alice, in 1941.

In the late 1930s Hammond was often to be found at Café Society, a Greenwich Village interracial night club where the band was directed by pianist Teddy Wilson. At this time Hammond was a powerful figure in the jazz world because of his control of jobs and his many press contacts. Concerts in 1938 and 1939 at Carnegie Hall, "Spirituals to Swing," showcased and promoted Hammond discoveries.

As swing bands lost ground in the late 1940s, Hammond was less influential, but he continued his work in the record industry with Columbia Records, Brunswick/Vocalion, Keynote, and others. He later was responsible for starting BOB DYLAN and Bruce Springsteen on their recording careers. Through the years his writings appeared in *Down Beat, The Brooklyn Eagle, The Nation, Tempo, Chicago News,*

New Masses, and European magazines, including *Jazz Hot.* His autobiography, written with Irving Townsend, *John Hammond on Record,* appeared in 1977.

BIBLIOGRAPHY

Hammond, J., with I. Townsend, *John Hammond on Record,* 1977; Schuller, G., *The Swing Era: The Development of Jazz, 1930–1945,* 1989.

Harnett, William Michael

(August 10, 1848–October 29, 1892)

Peto, John Frederick

(May 21, 1854–November 23, 1907)
Painters

William Harnett and John Peto were nineteenth-century American masters of the trompe l'oeil, or trick-the-eye, technique that made still-life paintings almost optical illusions because the objects looked so real.

William Michael Harnett was born in Ireland in 1848 but grew up in Philadelphia, where he attended the Pennsylvania Academy of the Fine Arts. He moved to New York in 1871 and studied art by night at Cooper Union while he worked as an engraver of silver by day. This work fostered the care, precision, and sureness that appears in his painting, to which he turned full time in 1874.

Harnett had infinite patience and is said to have been nearsighted. A friend said his glasses were jammed close to the eye socket, "through which he seemed to glare from his intense strain to see, but his eyes were microscopic."

He chose to paint still lifes, because they saved him the price of a model. At first he did small pictures of different combinations of mugs and pipes, newspapers and books on tabletops, or a violin fastened to a door. These were painted so meticulously that he succeeded in making the objects look as though they were completely real. Critics made fun of his work, which they considered outdated, but he appealed to many old-fashioned collectors.

In his early years, he also did larger canvases, one of which is *The Artist's Card Rack* (1885). A collection of envelopes and cards are held by tape to the surface of a door. The flatness of this composition, with the even surface of the door preventing the viewer's eye from trying to go back in space in the picture, helps the trompe l'oeil illusion work effectively.

Harnett spent the years from 1880 to 1886 in Europe, mostly studying in Munich. There he painted smaller and smaller tabletop still lifes, but in Paris, where he went toward the end of his European stay, he painted four of his largest paintings, collectively known as *After the Hunt.* The last one, which is lifesize, was painted in 1885 for the Salon, the big annual art exhibition in Paris. It is his most famous picture and made his reputation. In it, a dead rabbit, three dead birds, a game bag, a gun, a hunting horn, and other paraphernalia of the chase hang on a door. The painting was displayed until Prohibition in 1918 in a fancy saloon near City Hall in New York. Every other bar in the country wanted a picture like it, and forgers had a field day turning out their own versions. The work is now in the M. H. De Young Memorial Museum in San Francisco.

From 1886 until 1892 Harnett lived in New York and painted more tabletop still lifes, with the objects arranged in a pyramid on the table against the background of a paneled wooden door. An example is *Emblems of Peace* (1890). He also painted a great many pictures of horseshoes and other homely objects.

Since Harnett's work was not highly regarded in his lifetime, no one wrote articles and books about him. Many of his pictures are lost.

The other great trompe l'oeil painter, John Frederic Peto, was born in Philadelphia in 1854 and also studied at the Pennsylvania Academy of the Fine Arts. He tried sculpture, painting, and photography in Philadelphia without much success before he moved to the New Jersey shore to play cornet at religious camp meeting revivals in 1889.

Peto lived the rest of his life isolated in Island Heights, New Jersey, where he developed his own somewhat brooding style. He painted worn-out, broken, thrown-away objects. Like Harnett, he painted objects like clippings, postcards, cards, and a cornet fastened to the flat surface of a door, as in *Ordinary Objects in the Artist's Creative Mind* (1887). Another, which shows knickknacks and leftover food on the narrow sill of a window, is called *The Poor Man's Store* (1885).

Peto was even less famous in his lifetime than Harnett, and unscrupulous dealers forged the signature of the better known artist on many of Peto's pictures and sold them as Harnett's work. Peto admired Harnett and consciously used some of his subjects and compositions, thus complicating the problem of attribution.

When Surrealism (a liberation of the unconscious through painting) and abstraction became fashionable in the 1930s, critics began to reevaluate the superrealism and the formal quality of the door compositions of both Peto and Harnett. They came to appreciate the artists' careful work and illusionistic style.

BIBLIOGRAPHY

Frankenstein, Alfred, *After the Hunt—William Harnett and Other American Still Life Painters 1870–1900*, 1969; Wilmderding, John, *Important Information Inside: The Art of John F. Peto and the Idea of Still-Life Painting in Nineteenth-Century America*, 1983.

Harris, Joel Chandler

(December 9, 1848–July 3, 1908)
Journalist, Short-Story Writer

In the decades after the Civil War, Joel Chandler Harris, known for his Uncle Remus stories, used the African American folklore he had learned on a plantation in his youth to create literature for children.

Harris was born in 1848, near Eatonton, Georgia. He had little formal schooling, but his mother encouraged his wide reading in Shakespeare, the Bible, and especially Oliver Goldsmith. At the age of thirteen, he began work as a printer's assistant on a weekly newspaper published on a Georgia plantation, Turnwold. Much of his education came directly from the newspaper's owner, Joseph Addison Turner; he also got to know the plantation workers and their folktales during his two years there. Harris worked for newspapers in Macon, New Orleans, and Savannah before beginning a twenty-four-year career at the Atlanta *Constitution* in 1876.

Harris's first assignment at the *Constitution* was to produce humorous sketches of African Americans. He drew on his experiences at Turnwold, creating the character Uncle Remus and trying to duplicate black speech. After about a year, Harris realized the stories he had heard as a child had literary potential; in 1879, he published his first Uncle Remus animal story in the *Constitution*. "Negro Folklore: The Story of Mr. Rabbit and Mr. Fox, as Told by Uncle Remus" became the introduction to Harris's first volume, *Uncle Remus: His Songs and His Sayings* (1881).

The stories about Tar Baby and the Briar Patch, Brer Rabbit and Brer Fox, as well as the tortoise, the deer, the bear, and other animals, often emphasized a contrast between strength and wisdom: the smaller, shrewder animal triumphed over the larger one. The stories are told by an eighty-year-old ex-slave to a young white boy to whom he often wishes to impart a moral lesson. Though Harris claimed in his introduction to the volume to present each tale "without embellishment and without exaggeration," he related each with wit and attention to the richness of character; not simply a transcriber of folklore, he truly re-created each tale in the telling.

Harris published *Nights with Uncle Remus*, a second collection of tales, in 1883. Unlike the first volume, whose action takes place after the Civil War, these tales are set during the years of slavery. Though Harris does not glorify life on the plantation, slave and master demonstrate only affection for each other. He avoids stereotyping Uncle Remus, casting him as a rounded character of warmth, intelligence, and a little superstition. Harris also introduces a new storyteller, Daddy Jack; unfortunately, the fact that Jack speaks in the difficult Gullah dialect of the South Carolina coastal plantations hindered the popularity of the new volume.

Other Uncle Remus volumes written by Harris include *Uncle Remus and His Friends* (1892), *Told by Uncle Remus* (1905), and the posthumously published *Uncle Remus and the Little Boy* (1910). The author wrote other stories for children, such as *Little Mr. Thimblefinger and His Queer Country* (1894) and *Mr. Rabbit at Home* (1895).

Harris also wrote for adults. Believing that American fiction should concentrate on the common person, he created a succession of sketches of people, both black and white, from the mountains and the rural lowlands, including *Mingo and Other Sketches in Black and White* (1884) and *Free Joe and Other Georgian Sketches* (1887). Other collections of stories include *Balaam and His Master* (1891), *The Chronicles of Aunt Minervy Ann* (1899), and *The Making of a Statesman* (1902).

Harris died in Atlanta, Georgia, in 1908.

BIBLIOGRAPHY

Bickley, R. Bruce, Jr., *Joel Chandler Harris*, 1978; Cousins, Paul M., *Joel Chandler Harris: A Biography*, 1968.

Harrison, Peter

(June 14, 1716–April 30, 1775)
Architect

Peter Harrison, who lived in Newport, Rhode Island, was a merchant who became the first and most distinguished architect in the American colonies. He designed a number of Georgian churches and other buildings in Newport and Boston noted for their purity of mass and sophistication of detail.

Born in York, England, Harrison came to this country in 1740. He became a ship owner and active merchant in Newport, trading in wine, rum, molasses, and mahogany. He also knew cartography, drafting, and surveying. He made maps of Newport and Cape Breton, as well as designing a stone lighthouse and a fort for Goat Island as the French and Indian War drew near. (The fort was never finished.)

Harrison married wealthy and socially prominent Elizabeth Pelham of Newport. In 1747 he went back to England. There he evidently studied building styles and either acquired his extensive library of books on architecture, the best privately owned such library in the colonies, or added to a collection he had before he first came to America. At any rate, he owned books like Colin Campbell's *Vitruvius Britannicus*, Edward Hoppus's *Andrea Palladio's Architecture*, and James Gibbs's *A Book of Architecture* and *Rules for Drawing*. He would adapt patterns from them for the buildings he would design in America.

Redwood Library and Athenaeum, Newport, RI

In 1748 Harrison was asked to design a library in Newport named for Abraham Redwood. He sent the plans from England. He patterned the templelike building close after Hoppus's book on Palladian architecture. Although he had to use wood instead of cut stone, he instructed the workers to mix sand with the paint in order to simulate the effect of stone.

Harrison did design a stone building, King's Chapel in Boston (1749–1758). Hugh Morrison has called its elegant interior, taken from Gibbs's *Rules for Drawing*, the "finest of Georgian church architecture in the Colonies." (The front colonnade was a later addition.)

In 1759, designing Newport's Touro Synagogue at the request of merchant friends of his,

Harrison adapted the plan of the Portuguese Synagogue in London. The Newport synagogue is especially notable for its well-proportioned interior with classical embellishment, which Harrison took from several English pattern books. It survives, virtually unaltered. The clients were pleased and asked him to design the Brick Market (1761–1773), still standing near the Newport docks. Modeled on Inigo Jones's Old Somerset House in England, it has large pilasters above a brick arcaded base.

For Christ Church in Cambridge (1760–1761), he combined elements from various architectural books. He also did a number of houses, including his own at Leamington Farm, Newport (1747), Governor Wentworth's in New Hampshire (1768–1770), a summer home for Abraham Redwood (1766), and Winthrop House in New London (1754). Except for Christ Church, Harrison would not take money for any of his architectural work, accepting instead thanks and pieces of silver plate.

In 1766 Harrison, a loyal Tory, moved to New Haven and became collector of customs. He died there in 1775, a year after a mob attacked his house and destroyed his furnishings and his drawings.

BIBLIOGRAPHY

Bridenbaugh, C., *Peter Harrison: First American Architect,* 1949; Wright, Louis B., et al., *The Arts in America: The Colonial Period,* 1966.

Hassam, Frederick Childe

(October 17, 1859–August 27, 1935)
Painter

Childe Hassam was the leading American disciple of the French Impressionists, who tried to paint the "impression" of a subject as it appeared to the eye at one moment and rendered in juxtaposed strokes of multiple colors. He is best known for his paintings of busy street scenes and sunlit gardens filled with brilliant flowers.

Hassam was born in Dorchester, Massachusetts, to a father who was a merchant and a collector of American antiques. As a boy, he liked boxing, football, and swimming, but his talent for drawing led him to work for a wood engraver. He did illustrations for *Scribner's* magazine, *Harper's Weekly* magazine, and the book *Venetian Life* by WILLIAM DEAN HOWELLS. At night, he went to sketch classes at the Boston Art Club and the Lowell Institute.

In 1883 he traveled and painted in England, Holland, Spain, and Italy. After he came back to Boston he married Kathleen Maude Doane, with whom he had been in love for some time. Before he and his wife returned to Paris, he painted several softly lighted street scenes in Boston, including *Boston Common at Twilight* (1886), in which a woman and two children are on the sidewalk at the extreme left of the picture, while the expanse of snow-covered Common takes up most of the canvas.

The Hassams stayed in France for three years, while Childe studied at the Académie Julien and worked on his own. On this trip he absorbed the manner of the Impressionist painters, who believed in painting out of doors directly from nature and painting contemporary people in streets, in parks, and at the beach. His *Le Jour du Grand Prix* (1887), in which people in carriages rolling down a city street in bright sunshine, shows the Impressionist influence.

Back in this country, he set up a studio at Fifth Avenue and Seventeenth Street in New York City and began to paint street scenes in the luminous Impressionist manner, capturing hansom cabs, messenger boys, street cleaners, and fashionable women as they made their way. His *Washington Arch in Spring* (1890) is perhaps the finest example of this period.

Hassam later moved to an apartment on West 57th Street, where he combined home and studio and where he lived for thirty years. He became good friends with other artists like J. Alden Weir, John Twachtman, Robert Reid, and Willard Metcalf. Hassam joined these painters and five others who were interested in Impressionism in 1898 to form a group called the Ten American Painters. They exhibited independently of the National Academy of Design, which was a rather conservative organization dedicated to teaching and exhibiting art.

In 1916, as America prepared to enter World War I, Hassam began to paint his series of Impressionist paintings of flags, his patriotic response to the conflict. *The Fourth of July 1916* shows dozens of flags hanging from every level of the buildings along Fifth Avenue in New York. Buildings are sketched in with white and pale colors, and the flags rippling in the wind dominate the picture. The series was in part inspired by similar paintings of flags by Monet, Dufy, Renoir, and others, thus transferring a striking Parisian theme to New York in the years before and during World War I.

From 1890 to 1916 Hassam spent his summers in New England, painting the sea and the shore at Appledore in the Isles of Shoals off the coast of New Hampshire. Art historian William Gerdts has said that Hassam's paintings of flowers in the gardens at Appledore, in which he "had begun laying down 'that mosaic of small touches of pure color' . . . that are arguably the most beautiful [pictures] of his career." He also painted at Gloucester, Newport, Provincetown, and Old Lyme, Connecticut, a haunt of the American Impressionists. Hassam studied the light on the church at Old Lyme as closely and as long as Monet, the leading Impressionist painter in France, studied the light on Rouen Cathedral. Just as Monet painted many versions of Rouen Cathedral, Hassam painted several versions of the church. After 1919 the house that Hassam bought at East Hampton, Long Island, became his summer home. His summertime pictures are sunlit, clear, and fresh. He used short, broken brush strokes that made the picture surface seem to vibrate and the colors scintillate, emphasizing the play of sun and shadows. An example is *Sunny Blue Sea* (1913), which shows a woman wearing a wide-brimmed hat, sitting on the rocks as the sea charges below her.

In the winter Hassam worked inside, often painting people before a background of either his studio window, a screen, or a vase of flow-ers. All his pictures are happy and full of life and look spontaneous. He was a popular painter and won prizes and sold pictures steadily.

Toward the end of his life, as modernism and abstraction swept American painting, Childe Hassam, who had been a leader of change, found himself a traditionalist, defending the old ways of representational art. He died at his home in East Hampton after a long illness. He left his remaining pictures to the American Academy of Arts and Letters and established a fund for the advancement of American art.

BIBLIOGRAPHY

Adams, Adeline, *Childe Hassam*, 1938; Hoopes, Donelson F., *Childe Hassam*, 1979.

Hawkins, Coleman Randolph

(November 21, 1904–May 19, 1969)
Jazz Musician

Coleman Hawkins, always open to new ideas, transformed the tenor saxophone from vaudeville novelty to serious jazz instrument. His constantly evolving style with its tone, technical proficiency, and powerful harmonic improvisation inspired contemporaries, while his musical flexibility and experimentalism continue to influence new generations of admirers.

Hawkins was born into a middle-class family in St. Joseph, Missouri. His mother, a schoolteacher and organist, started him on the piano at five and the cello at seven. On his ninth birthday, he received a tenor saxophone. Sent to Chicago for high school, Hawkins went on to study harmony and composition at Washburn College in Topeka, Kansas.

In 1921 he landed his first professional job with the 12th Street Theater Orchestra in Kan-sas City. Blues singer Mamie Smith performed there that summer with the Jazz Hounds, and she asked Hawkins to tour with the group. By March 1922 he was performing and recording with Smith in New York.

Hawkins traveled to California with the Jazz Hounds in 1923, but in June returned to New York to free-lance. He recorded his first solo, "Dicty Blues," with the FLETCHER HENDERSON Orchestra in August. Hawkins stayed with Henderson until 1934, a featured soloist at Roseland, the New York dance hall, through the 1920s.

The "Dicty Blues" documents Hawkins's early solo style: big-toned, energetic, slap-tongued. LOUIS ARMSTRONG's brief tenure with the Henderson band (1924–1925) affected Hawkins. Exposure to Armstrong's improvisations led Hawkins to the more melodic and swinging jazz style. He dropped the slap-tongued attack for softer tonguing, especially in ballads. From pianist ART TATUM, Hawkins learned how to anticipate harmonic changes by playing chords before their statement by the rhythm section.

Hawkins's musical reputation led him to leave the Henderson Orchestra in 1934 to accept an invitation from Jack Hylton, a successful British bandleader. Hawkins stayed abroad for five years, but when war threatened in 1939, he returned to New York. Soon thereafter he recorded "Body and Soul," a landmark performance.

Many consider this best-selling jazz performance a masterpiece. Gunther Schuller has written that it "pulled together in one majestic . . . improvisation the various strands of Hawkins's previous stylistic exploration [with] seamless inner unity." Hawkins recorded "Body and Soul" again in 1959. The later version, from the Playboy Jazz Festival in Chi-cago, is another example of Hawkins's virtuosity.

From the early 1940s Hawkins played with small groups and was able to embrace the new harmonic challenges of bebop. In the following years he toured Europe and recorded at home with groups that included musicians like MILES DAVIS, Fats Navarro, and Milt Jackson. He was heard frequently in the 1960s at New York nightclubs until his health began to fail. His final concert took place at Chicago's North Park Hotel on April 20, 1969.

Hawkins experimented constantly, always listened to what was new in jazz and in classical music, and had a gift for shaping styles to his own purposes.

BIBLIOGRAPHY

James, B., *Coleman Hawkins,* 1984; McCarthy, A., *Coleman Hawkins,* 1963; Williams, Martin, *The Jazz Tradition,* 1972, rev., 1980.

Hawks, Howard Winchester

(May 30, 1896–December 26, 1977)
Film Director, Producer

Howard Hawks, one of Hollywood's best but least appreciated directors, whose memorable films include *Bringing Up Baby, Sergeant York,* and *Red River,* was belatedly acknowledged in 1975 with an honorary Academy Award as a "giant in the American cinema."

He was born in Goshen, Indiana, to Frank and Helen Hawks. Two younger brothers, Kenneth and William, also entered the film industry but never achieved his fame. The family moved to Pasadena, California, when Howard was ten, where his father became vice president of a hotel chain.

After high school, Hawks attended Throop College of Technology, graduated from Phillips-Exeter Academy in New Hampshire, then received an engineering degree from Cornell University. In the summers he worked as a prop boy for Famous Players–Lasky (later Paramount) and directed a few scenes of *The Little Princess* (1917), a MARY PICKFORD film.

During World War I he was a flying instructor for the U.S. Army Air Corps in Texas. A professional racer for three years, he built a car that won at Indianapolis. Such experiences made him a natural for conveying his characters' personalities through physical action in such films as *The Dawn Patrol* (1930), *The Crowd Roars* (1932), *Only Angels Have Wings* (1939), *Air Force* (1943), and *Red Line 7000* (1965).

Hawks learned his craft directing one-reel comedies and writing scripts for Paramount and MGM before directing his first feature, *The Road to Glory* (1926), at Fox studios. Unlike many directors and actors, he easily made the transition to sound, fully aware of its aesthetic and technical requirements. His first talkie, *The Dawn Patrol,* made for Warner Brothers, was notable for its lean dialogue.

Shrewd business sense allowed Hawks to remain independent—unbound to any one studio—and exercise creative control over his work. He was perhaps the first to have "directed by" precede "produced by" in the credits, stressing the importance of the director.

Hawks worked in all genres. In addition to the action and war films mentioned, he directed *Scarface* (1932), a classic gangster drama starring Paul Muni, coproduced with millionaire Howard Hughes, and modeled on the life of Al Capone. *Twentieth Century* (1934) with JOHN BARRYMORE and Carole Lombard, the first film in which "sexually attractive, sophisticated stars indulged in their own slapstick," as critic Andrew Sarris described it, began what became known as screwball comedy, the most original genre of the 1930s. *Bringing Up Baby* (1938), the zaniest example, paired CARY GRANT and KATHARINE HEPBURN as absentminded professor and loony socialite chasing a leopard across Connecticut.

Other hits included *The Big Sleep* (1946), which starred Humphrey Bogart, one of the great detective thrillers; *Red River* (1948), the first of four westerns with John Wayne—and Montgomery Clift's first film; and the musical *Gentlemen Prefer Blondes* (1953), which starred Marilyn Monroe at her most delightful.

Hawks's excellent screenwriters included lifetime friend WILLIAM FAULKNER, Ben Hecht, and BILLY WILDER, although some of his best stories were his own ideas. In *His Girl Friday* (1940), his adaptation of *The Front Page,* Hawks turned the two male reporters in the original play version into a man and a woman. Starring Cary Grant and Rosalind Russell, the film sparkles with an erotic tension absent from the original and is enhanced by rapid, overlapping dialogue, a new technique at the time.

Hawks's style was always direct: he favored straightforward storytelling over flashbacks and eye-level camerawork over unusual angles.

He used close-ups sparingly and made effective use of long shots and panoramic vistas.

Appreciation of Hawks's films increased when critics in the 1960s noted that despite their diversity, his films shared strong thematic and cinematic unities. They are frequently about male friendships tested by love of the same woman and the importance of integrity and professionalism. The Hawksian hero is stoic and unsentimental, but not invulnerable or without feeling.

Hawksian women are equally strong. One need only cite as evidence Ann Dvorak as Paul Muni's sister in *Scarface;* or Lombard, Russell, and Hepburn in the films mentioned; or Lauren Bacall as a challenge to Bogart in *To Have and Have Not* (1943—her debut) and *The Big Sleep;* or Angie Dickinson standing up to Wayne in *Rio Bravo* (1959). Many critics view this as a truly modern aspect of Hawks's work.

Hawks produced many of his films and some directed by others, such as the science-fiction thriller *The Thing* (1951). He also partly directed films credited to others. After a dispute with SAM GOLDWYN, *Come and Get It* (1936) was completed by William Wyler; and producer Howard Hughes completed direction of *The Outlaw* (1940–1943), a potboiler western that launched Jane Russell.

In his last active decade Hawks made *Hatari!* (1962), a romantic adventure set in Africa; *Man's Favorite Sport?* (1964), a comedy; and his third and fourth westerns with Wayne, *El Dorado* (1967) and *Rio Lobo* (1970), his last film.

Hawks was married to Athole Shearer Ward from 1928 to 1940, to Nancy Gross from 1941 to 1948, and to Dee Hartford from 1953 to 1959. He had four children and adopted his first wife's son.

BIBLIOGRAPHY

Doague, Leland A., *Howard Hawks,* 1982; McBride, Joseph, *Hawks on Hawks,* 1982; Mast, Gerald, *Howard Hawks, Storyteller,* 1982.

Hawthorne, Nathaniel

(July 4, 1804–May 19, 1864)
Novelist, Short-Story Writer

Nathaniel Hawthorne, best known for his novel *The Scarlet Letter,* combined moral seriousness with a conviction that literature could transcend human foibles and suffering. He often turned to the early history of New England for tales he could transform imaginatively into myths concerning the ideals of freedom, equality, and justice.

By the time Hawthorne was born in Salem, Massachusetts, in 1804, his family had lived in New England for five generations. Among his ancestors were a judge in the Salem witch trials and the captain of a privateer during the American Revolution whose valor had been commemorated in a ballad. Hawthorne's father, who captained a merchant vessel, journeyed to Europe and the Far East before he died of yellow fever, in what is now Surinam, when his son was four.

After his father's death, Hawthorne was raised by the family of his mother, Elizabeth Clarke Manning, in a house with his grandparents and eight uncles and aunts, in addition to his own mother and two sisters. Books offered his only solitude, and he read voraciously.

Among Hawthorne's fellow students at Bowdoin College were the poet HENRY WADSWORTH LONGFELLOW and Franklin Pierce, who later became president of the United States. Hawthorne graduated in 1825 with no clear goals and returned to the Manning house in Salem. For the next twelve years, he lived mostly from the Mannings' generosity and spent his time reading and writing.

In 1828 he published *Fanshawe,* a Gothic romance, anonymously and at his own expense, though he later gathered up and burned every copy he could find. He began a collection of short stories, but he burned the manuscripts when he could not find a publisher. In 1830 he printed five tales in the *Salem Gazette* and began an association with an annual known as *The Token,* which published two stories in its 1831 edition. He continued writing for magazines until his *Twice-Told Tales* came out in 1837. It was reviewed by Longfellow in the July issue of *North American Review.*

The stories in *Twice-Told Tales* reflect Hawthorne's interest in the daily life of the community, as well as his penchant for fictionalizing historical anecdotes. In "The May-Pole of Merry Mount," Hawthorne tells the story of the Puritan destruction of a rival colony near what is now Quincy, Massachusetts. In "The Minister's Black Veil," also based loosely on historical fact, he studies the effects of secret sin on the individual and his relations with the community. The Reverend Hooper has covered his face in penance for an undisclosed wrong; his action isolates him from his parishioners at the same time it empowers him to speak forcefully to them about the need to redeem themselves.

In 1840, hoping to find a way both to write and to support a wife, Hawthorne invested in Brook Farm, an experiment in communal living at West Roxbury, Massachusetts, organized by the Transcendentalists (see RALPH WALDO EMERSON and HENRY DAVID THOREAU). He gave up on the attempt after seven months, when he found that the manual labor precluded his doing much writing. The experience, however, gave him the material to write his novel *The Blithedale Romance* (1852).

Hawthorne and Sophia Peabody were married on July 9, 1842, and took up residence at the Old Manse in Concord, Massachusetts. He was able to return to his writing, and he worked quickly to satisfy the magazines. His collection *Mosses from an Old Manse* (1846) is most noteworthy for two stories written before 1830, "Young Goodman Brown" and "Roger Malvin's Burial," and an intriguing tale set in Italy, "Rappaccini's Daughter."

With their first child, a daughter, born in 1844, the Hawthornes returned to Salem, where he sought a political appointment to supplement his income. He became surveyor of customs in 1845 and began work on *The Scarlet Letter* (1850).

In the preface to the novel, Hawthorne feigns having found the manuscript and a scarlet letter *A* in the attic of the Salem Custom House. The story opens with the public condemnation of Hester Prynne and a demand that she name the father of her illegitimate daughter, Pearl. Hester must wear a visible sign of her sin of adultery, a scarlet *A* embroidered on her chest; she comes to accept her situation and, through service to the community, earns respect. It is her husband, who seeks to expose Hester's lover out of hate, who is finally perceived as the most grievous sinner.

The House of the Seven Gables (1851) concerns an ancestral curse on the inhabitants of a 200-year-old Salem house. It had been built on land obtained by fraud by a member of the Pyncheon family from Matthew Maule. Pyncheon also managed to have Maule executed for witchcraft, and Maule's dying curse on the Pyncheons has lasted through several generations. The curse is lifted when a descendant of Maule named Holgrave falls in love with Phoebe Pyncheon, who was raised away from the house and is thus untainted by it.

In 1852 Hawthorne published *The Snow-Image and Other Twice-Told Tales*, collecting such stories as "Ethan Brand" and "Major Molineux." His *Tanglewood Tales* for children appeared in 1853. When Franklin Pierce was elected president in 1852, Hawthorne was named U.S. consul at Liverpool, England. He and his family lived there from 1853 until 1857. They then spent several months in Italy, where Hawthorne gathered material for his last major book, *The Marble Faun* (1860), which he wrote during a subsequent stay in England.

Set in Rome, *The Marble Faun* concerns the effects of guilt upon Donatello, a young Italian count, after he murders a man he suspects is the object of affection of Miriam, the woman he himself loves. His guilt matures him, and Donatello eventually turns himself over to the authorities.

A brain tumor has been suspected as the cause of Hawthorne's death in 1864. At the time, he was traveling with Franklin Pierce in Plymouth, New Hampshire. He was buried at the Sleepy Hollow Cemetery in Concord, Massachusetts.

BIBLIOGRAPHY

Mellow, James R., *Nathaniel Hawthorne in His Times*, 1980; Turner, Arlin, *Nathaniel Hawthorne*, 1980.

Hayes, Helen

(October 10, 1900–March 17, 1993)
Actress

During more than sixty years on stage, Helen Hayes starred as a child actress, an ingénue, a serious actress, and a comic old lady, achieving her greatest success as Queen Victoria in *Victoria Regina* by Laurence Housman in 1935.

Born Helen Hayes Brown, daughter of a traveling salesman and a would-be actress, she later took her mother's maiden name. She grew up in Washington, D.C., where she made her first stage appearance at the age of five at the Holy Cross Academy playing Peasebottom in Shakespeare's *A Midsummer Night's Dream*. Early in 1909 she impersonated a Gibson Girl bathing beauty in a matinee of *Jack the Giant Killer* and four months later played Prince Charles Ferdinand in Robert Marshall's *A Royal Family* with the Columbia Players.

Having caught the critical eye of Broadway producer Lew Fields when he was visiting Washington, Hayes was taken by her mother to New York, where they persuaded him to cast her as the Little Mime in the VICTOR HERBERT operetta *Old Dutch* in 1909. One reviewer called her "a clever tot" who "knows a thing or two." In 1910 she was Psyche Finnegan, a brash little girl, in another Fields musical, *The Summer Widowers.* After two other comedies and the lead role in *Little Lord Fauntleroy,* Hayes, now twelve, could find no other parts. She and her mother went back to Washington, where she finished her schooling with the sisters of the Sacred Heart Academy and did some acting with the Poli Players, a local stock company.

In 1917 she made a cross-country tour in her first leading role as the teenage "glad girl" heroine in Eleanor Porter's *Pollyanna.* By 1918 she was back in New York playing Margaret Schofield, the love interest in BOOTH TARKINGTON's *Penrod,* and that same year was Margaret in Sir J. M. Barrie's *Dear Brutus.* In 1919 she played Cora Wheeler to ALFRED LUNT's Clarence in another Tarkington comedy, *Clarence.* She starred as a cute young ingénue in at least one light romantic comedy on Broadway each year. This was a role for which she was admirably suited, since she was 5 feet tall and weighed 100 pounds. She won applause from audiences and compliments from reviewers for roles like Bab in *Bab* (1920), Mary Roberts Rinehart's stories about a subdebutante, adapted for the stage by Edward Childs Carpenter, and for her part in *The Wren,* which Tarkington wrote especially for her and which opened on her twenty-first birthday. She took piano lessons so she could play a spiritual on stage as Elsie Beebe in another play written especially for her, *To the Ladies* (1922), by Marc Connelly and GEORGE S. KAUFMAN.

Two older actress friends, Ruth Chatterton and Ina Claire, persuaded Hayes to prepare to tackle more difficult roles, and she began studying with voice and acting coaches. Later she took lessons in dancing, fencing, and boxing to help improve her movements on stage.

Better equipped and more secure, she appeared in Oliver Goldsmith's *She Stoops to Conquer* (1924). The next year she won praise for her Cleopatra in George Bernard Shaw's *Caesar and Cleopatra,* the first production of the Theatre Guild. She was Maggie Wylie in *What Every Woman Knows,* in 1926, and played Norma Besant, the doomed flapper in *Coquette,* for three years on Broadway and on tour.

In 1928 Hayes married Charles MacArthur, newspaperman, playwright, screenwriter, and coauthor of the newspaper comedy *The Front Page,* which opened on Broadway that same year. Their daughter, Mary, was born in 1930. Hayes had to leave the cast of *Coquette,* and she won great publicity by claiming that the baby was an "act of God" in order to get out of her contract. The MacArthurs adopted a son, James Gordon MacArthur, seven years later. Both children went on the stage.

In the 1933–1934 season Hayes played Mary Stuart in *Mary of Scotland* in New York and on tour. In 1935 she opened in another queenly role, Victoria in *Victoria Regina,* the greatest triumph of her career, which was seen by 2 million people. She played the part, in which she had to age from a teenage girl to an elderly widow, for two years on Broadway and later on a national tour.

Hayes won her long-desired opportunity to play Shakespeare on Broadway when she appeared as Viola, opposite Maurice Evans, in *Twelfth Night* (1940). She was Madeleine Guest in MAXWELL ANDERSON's anti-Nazi play, *Candle in the Wind* (1941) and Harriet Beecher Stowe in *Harriet* (1943), a play for which she bought the rights after she saw the student-written play at the University of Syracuse with a student cast.

After World War II she played a librarian who goes wild in Anita Loos's *Happy Birthday* (1946), which turned out to be her longest New York run. In 1948 she made her first appearance in London as Amanda Wingfield in TENNESSEE WILLIAMS's *Glass Menagerie,* a play she did not like. In 1949 she and her daughter were appearing together in a tryout of William

McCleery's *Good Housekeeping*, when Mary MacArthur died suddenly of polio.

In 1950 Hayes was Lucy Andrée Ransdell in *The Wisteria Trees*, Josh Logan's adaptation of Chekhov's *Cherry Orchard* reset in the nineteenth-century American South. Other roles included Mrs. Howard V. Larue II, a prim dowager turned maid of all work in Mary Chase's *Mrs. McThing* (1952); the duchess of Pont-au-Bronc in Jean Anouilh's *Time Remembered* (1957), for which she won a Tony Award; and Nora Melody, loyal wife of a drunken innkeeper, in *A Touch of the Poet* (1958), by EUGENE O'NEILL, which opened at the Helen Hayes Theater in New York. (Formerly the Fulton Theater, the Helen Hayes was renamed in 1955 to honor her fifty years on the stage.)

In 1961, at the request of the U.S. State Department, she took *The Glass Menagerie* and *The Skin of Our Teeth* on a tour of Europe, the Middle East, and Latin America. In 1964, in New York, she gave a program of "First Ladies" in a play by A. E. Hotchner called *The White House*. It lasted only twenty-three performances. Most of her later roles were revivals, including notably George Kelly's *The Show-Off* (1967), in which she played the mother. In 1969 she appeared in *The Front Page*, playing Mrs. Grant, a character Charles MacArthur had based on Hayes's own mother. Her last Broad-

way appearance was in a revival of *Harvey* by Mary Chase in 1970, and her last stage appearance was in O'Neill's *Long Day's Journey Into Night* at the Hartke Theater in Washington, D.C., in 1971.

Hayes did not confine her acting to the stage. She appeared in many movies, most notably *The Sin of Madelon Claudet* (1931), for which she won an Oscar for best actress; *A Farewell to Arms* (1932), considered her finest film performance; *Anastasia* (1956); and *Airport* (1970), for which she earned another Oscar. On the Helen Hayes Theatre of the Air (1940–1942), she performed in a single play each week for a radio audience. She made her television debut in 1950 in *The Late Christopher Bean*, following it up with appearances in dozens of other television plays and movies.

Hayes received the Presidential Medal of Freedom in 1986 from President Ronald Reagan. She died at age ninety-two at her home in Nyack, New York.

BIBLIOGRAPHY

Barrow, Kenneth, *Helen Hayes: First Lady of the American Theatre*, 1985; Hayes, Helen, *Star on Her Forehead*, 1949, *A Gift of Joy*, 1965, and *On Reflection*, 1968; Robbins, Jhan, *Front Page Marriage*, 1982.

Heifetz, Jascha

(February 2, 1901–December 10, 1987)
Violinist

The virtuoso Heifetz raised violin technique to new levels of precision and consistency, thereby setting exacting standards for violinists who followed. His legendary buttery tone was strong yet pure and sweet, his intonation always impeccable. The Lithuanian child who could play Mendelssohn's Concerto at age six became the world's foremost violinist.

Born in Vilnius, Lithuania, Heifetz began violin lessons at the age of three with his father, Ruvim, a professional musician. Shortly thereafter he began studies with Elias Malkin, a prominent teacher. At nine Heifetz was accepted at the St. Petersburg Conservatory, where he became a pupil of Leopold Auer. He performed in St. Petersburg the next year and in May 1912, when he was eleven, took Berlin by storm in his debut there. As a result, he was invited to play the Tchaikovsky Concerto with the Berlin Philharmonic Orchestra in October 1912.

Heifetz continued his studies with Auer until the summer of 1917, when an offer to tour the United States allowed him to leave Russia. With his family he traveled east, through Siberia to Japan and finally to California and on to New York, where he made his triumphal debut at Carnegie Hall, October 27, 1917, the auspicious beginning of a remarkable career.

After touring England in 1920, Australia in 1921, and the Orient in 1923, Heifetz became an American citizen in 1925 shortly before his 1926 tour of Palestine. He recorded the major violin concertos during the thirties, visited the Soviet Union in 1934, and also collaborated at various times with such artists as pianist ARTUR RUBINSTEIN, cellist Emanuel Feuerman, and violist William Primrose recording trios. His reputation was enhanced by a film, *They Shall Have Music* (1939), and through radio broadcasts.

Following World War II, Heifetz settled in California. He cut down on his solo performances and turned to chamber music. With cellist Gregor Piatigorsky and other musicians he established a chamber music series presented in Los Angeles. Some series concerts were brought to New York's Carnegie Hall in

Library of Congress

1964 and 1966. Beginning in 1962 he taught a master class at the University of Southern California.

In 1967 Heifetz made an emotional return to Israel, where he performed with the Israel Philharmonic Orchestra. In 1972, some fifty-five years after his Carnegie Hall debut, he made his farewell performance at a benefit recital for the University of Southern California scholarship fund at the Dorothy Chandler Pavilion in Los Angeles.

Heifetz commissioned and performed works from conservative contemporary composers like William Walton and Louis Gruenberg. His own transcriptions for violin reflect his unique and elegant playing style and include arrangements of songs from GEORGE GERSHWIN's *Porgy and Bess*, Sergei Prokoviev pieces, and *Hora staccato* by Gregoraş Dinicu.

Though the Heifetz technique was near perfect, he never displayed it for its own sake, and his performance was devoid of mannerisms. He was often accused of being cold, both in person and in musical interpretation. Heifetz held his violin high, turned his face toward his left hand, and bowed with his right elbow elevated. He produced an uncommonly strong sound from his 1742 Guanarius or 1731 Stradivarius, a tone that was enriched and modulated by an intense but controlled and unsentimental vibrato. The seemingly effortless sound could be bold, grand, impetuous. He could play at breakneck speeds but always subordinated his technical facility to the music itself. As an ensemble player he was a master in blending with others.

The great teacher Carl Flesch wrote of Heifetz, "He represents a culmination of the contemporary development of our art. . . . His tone has a noble substance and is of a magical beauty, and there is not the smallest flaw in his technical equipment."

BIBLIOGRAPHY

Axelrod, H. R. (ed.), *Heifetz,* 1976; Schonberg, H. C., *The Glorious Ones: Classical Music's Legendary Performers,* 1985.

Heinlein, Robert Anson

(July 7, 1907–May 8, 1988)
Science-Fiction Writer

Robert A. Heinlein, author of *Stranger in a Strange Land,* has been called the dean of science-fiction writers. He introduced the notion that science fiction could go beyond escapism to imagine the opportunities and problems humanity might face in the future.

Heinlein was born in Butler, Missouri, and raised in Kansas City. He attended the University of Missouri for a year before taking an appointment at the U.S. Naval Academy at Annapolis, Maryland.

After graduating from Annapolis in 1929, he served five years as a gunnery officer on aircraft carriers. He retired from the navy after contracting tuberculosis in 1934. Though he briefly studied physics and mathematics at the University of California at Los Angeles, he required further recuperation and so moved to Colorado. There he sold real estate and ran a silver mine.

An avid reader of science fiction, Heinlein first turned to writing in response to a contest in *Astounding Science-Fiction* magazine. His entry, "Life-Line," was published in the August 1939 issue. Over the next three years, he published twenty-eight stories in *Astounding Science-Fiction* and *Unknown Worlds,* both edited by John W. Campbell, Jr.

Heinlein soon changed the face of science fiction. Whereas previous writers had used the genre to frame implicit criticisms of the present society or simply as escapist fantasy, Heinlein saw an opportunity to project the ways in which scientific and technological advances would change the lives of people. His work had a consistent moral frame: he concerned himself with how humanity ought to live in the future, given changes in its practical circumstances.

Early in his career, Heinlein conceived the notion of a "future history," a loose background framework for his stories that allowed him to link them thematically. He charted the future history—with dates of significant events and lifelines of major characters—on the wall of his study.

The future history frames much of Heinlein's fiction, but nineteen stories and two novellas in particular were gathered into a volume, *The Past Through Tomorrow,* in 1967. Of these early stories, one of the best known is "The Roads Must Roll" (1940), based on the premise that the streets of tomorrow will be replaced by massive conveyor belts.

During World War II, Heinlein went to work at the Philadelphia Naval Yards. He returned to writing in 1947, and, by selling stories to such glossy magazines as the *Saturday Evening Post,* became the first major science-fiction writer to break into the larger market for general fiction.

Heinlein also began publishing in hardcover, especially a new series of juvenile fiction for Scribner's, beginning with *Rocketship Galileo* (1947). His juvenile novels include *Space Cadet* (1948), *Farmer in the Sky* (1950), *The Rolling Stones* (1952), *Starman Jones* (1953), *The Star Beast* (1954), and *Tunnel in the Sky* (1955).

In the 1960s, Heinlein turned his attention to novels for adults. In 1961 he published *Stranger in a Strange Land,* which became a best-seller and by far his best-known novel. The hero, Valentine Michael Smith, is a human being raised by Martians. He returns to Earth culture-free, seeking to understand his humanity. The protagonist comes to appreciate human pleasures, learning to laugh from the monkeys in the zoo and experimenting sexually without inhibition. His joy, in turn, frees others, who join him in a new mystical religion whose rituals feature communal sex. Smith believes that the problems of human society can be eliminated simply by thinking correctly.

Another well-known novel, *The Moon Is a Harsh Mistress* (1966), relates the fight for freedom of a nation, Luna. The story features the friendship of the narrator, a bright computer technician named Emanuel Garcia O'Kelly, with a sentient computer known as Mike. Mike has developed a protective love for his creators, and he is destroyed in their battle for freedom.

Among Heinlein's subsequent works are *I Will Fear No Evil* (1971), *The Notebooks of Lazarus Long* (1978), *Job: A Comedy of Justice* (1984), and *The Cat Who Walks Through Walls* (1985).

Heinlein's work was honored with four Hugo Awards, as well as the Science Fiction Writers of America Grand Master Award. He died on May 8, 1988, in California.

BIBLIOGRAPHY

Panshin, Alexei, *Heinlein in Dimension,* 1968; Slusser, George Edgar, *Robert A. Heinlein, Stranger in His Own Land,* 1976, and *The Classic Years of Robert A. Heinlein,* 1977.

Hellman, Lillian

(June 20, 1905–June 30, 1984)
Playwright

Some of Lillian Hellman's highly successful plays deal with explosive political issues, while others examine greedy and manipulative families. Her personal life was as fraught with controversy as her plays, and she earned both approval and denunciation for refusing in 1952 to implicate radical friends during a congressional investigation of subversion in America.

Hellman was born in New Orleans. Although she moved with her parents to New York when she was five, she continued to go back to New Orleans to spend almost half of each year while she was growing up. Many of her plays drew on this background. She attended New York University and Columbia University, but dropped out in her junior year.

In the autumn of 1924 she went to work for a publishing firm, Boni and Liveright. She married Arthur Kober on December 30, 1925, and began reviewing books for the New York *Herald Tribune* and reading scripts for a number of producers. As a script reader, her big discovery was *Grand Hotel,* the hit of the 1930–1931 season.

Hellman went to Hollywood with Kober, where in 1930 she met DASHIELL HAMMETT, author of *The Thin Man.* She fell in love with Hammett and remained devoted to him until his death in 1961. She and Kober remained friends after their divorce in 1932.

Her first play, *The Children's Hour,* was produced on Broadway in 1934. Since it dealt with a child's false charges of lesbianism against two schoolteachers, it was controversial. Its controlled tension and natural dialogue, as well as the taboo topic and the intensity of emotion, made it a hit. Her second play, *Days to Come* in 1936, about a labor strike in the Midwest, was not successful.

Hellman drew on memories of her mother's family in Demopolis, Alabama, to portray the Hubbards, the rapacious family of 1900 in the popular and critical success, *The Little Foxes*, produced in 1939. Tallulah Bankhead played the heartless Regina Hubbard Giddens.

As World War II approached, she wrote *Watch on the Rhine*, a slashing antifascist play about a German anti-Nazi leader who is raising money in America for his cause at home. Produced in 1941, it won the New York Drama Critics' Circle Award. *The Searching Wind*, about a diplomat who was unable to take a stand against fascism, opened in 1944.

Hellman returned to the Hubbard family for *Another Part of the Forest* in 1946, writing about them in 1880, twenty years before the time of *The Little Foxes*. She next adapted the French play *Montserrat*, about hostages who give their lives to protect Simón Bolívar in Venezuela in 1812, and directed it herself in 1949. *The Autumn Garden* (1951), a nonpolitical play, takes place in a summer resort on the coast of the Gulf of Mexico.

The post–World War II years ushered in a period of intense anticommunist feeling in the United States. The fear of internal communist subversion grew to fever pitch, fueled by the cold war abroad and by investigations at home initiated by the House Un-American Activities Committee (HUAC) and later by Senator Joseph McCarthy and his special subcommittee. Hellman sometimes said that she was a member of the Communist party, and sometimes said that she was not a member but had attended meetings in the thirties. Dashiell Hammett, who had been a Communist, spent six months in jail for refusing to answer questions about subversives in the film industry. Like Hammett, Hellman was "blacklisted" in Hollywood, which meant that as a suspected former Communist, she could not get work in the movies. Beset with financial troubles, she was forced to sell her farm.

In 1952 Hellman was subpoenaed to appear before HUAC and refused to answer questions that would involve her naming names of friends who had been Communists. It was in a letter to HUAC on May 19, 1952, that Hellman wrote her most famous line: "I cannot and will not cut my conscience to fit this year's fashions, even though I long ago came to the conclusion that I was not a political person and could have no comfortable place in any political group." She was accounted a hero in this matter by some people, a clever opportunist by others.

In 1955 Hellman edited the letters of Anton Chekov for the Great Letters Series and began work on the book for the musical *Candide*. Meanwhile, she adapted Jean Anouilh's play *The Lark*, the story of Joan of Arc's struggle of conscience. It starred Julie Harris in 1955. When *Candide*, with music by LEONARD BERNSTEIN, opened in 1956, the critics found fault with Hellman's book and it lasted only a couple of months on Broadway.

Hellman's next play, *Toys in the Attic*, again drew on her own relatives for models. The play, which took her three years to write, is about Julian, played by Jason Robards, a man who is destroyed by his adoring unmarried sisters and by his wife so that he will remain dependent on them. It opened in New York in 1960, and both critics and the public responded favorably.

Strong-minded and outspoken, Hellman developed a coterie of devoted friends and a troop of implacable enemies. She wrote several autobiographical volumes. *An Unfinished Woman: A Memoir* won a National Book Award in 1969; *Pentimento* (1973) contained cameo portraits of old friends. *Scoundrel Time* (1976), which dealt with her political past, caused many people to accuse Hellman either of misinterpreting facts or of getting them wrong. *Maybe* appeared in 1980.

Hellman was blind and in failing health for two years before her death in New York in 1984.

BIBLIOGRAPHY

Rollyson, Carl, *Lillian Hellman: Her Legend and Her Legacy*, 1988; Wright, William, *Lillian Hellman, the Image, the Woman*, 1986.

Hemingway, Ernest Miller

(July 21, 1899–July 2, 1961)
Novelist, Short-Story Writer

Ernest Hemingway, author of such classics as *The Sun Also Rises, A Farewell to Arms,* and *For Whom the Bell Tolls,* is regarded as the quintessential American novelist and one of the great prose stylists writing in English in the first half of the twentieth century.

Ernest Miller Hemingway was born in Oak Park, Illinois, on July 21, 1899. His father, a physician, instilled in his son a love of hunting, fishing, and sports. His mother, who had once aspired to being an opera singer, taught him an appreciation for art and music.

National Archives

In 1917 the young Hemingway skipped college and found a job at the Kansas City *Star.* He tried unsuccessfully to enlist in the army but instead joined the Red Cross ambulance corps in 1918. Severely wounded in Italy after only a few weeks' service, he was decorated by the Italians as a war hero.

After marrying Hadley Richardson in 1921, Hemingway traveled to Europe as a correspondent for the Toronto *Star.* He joined a community of expatriate writers living in Paris and was guided in his early literary efforts by GERTRUDE STEIN and EZRA POUND.

Hemingway's seven years in Paris shaped his style and gave him characters and subjects. He worked as a journalist to pay the rent while he concentrated on learning to write; nevertheless, as he experimented with both poetry and fiction, laboring to strip the language bare of unnecessary adornment, he may have been helped by his newspaper experience, which had taught him an economy of style. Though at first he considered himself a disciple of SHERWOOD ANDERSON, Hemingway soon found a voice that struck the other writers of his acquaintance as rare and original. As F. SCOTT FITZGERALD was moved to advise his editor at Scribner's, Maxwell Perkins, "I'd look him up right away. He's the real thing."

In Our Time (1925), a collection of Hemingway's stories, attracted attention for its narrative technique, featuring his spare prose and objective description. It also introduced Nick Adams, a character who became a type for many later Hemingway protagonists. The book chronicles Nick's exposure to a series of violent experiences that culminate with his sustaining a severe wound during World War I.

Hemingway's first major work, *The Sun Also Rises* (1926), established him as a writer of international reputation. Jake Barnes, an American journalist living in Paris, wounded in the war, and now sexually impotent, loves the beautiful and promiscuous Lady Brett Ashley. Because Jake is unable to consummate their relationship, Brett turns to other lovers before returning hopelessly to him. The novel's depiction of what Gertrude Stein called the Lost Generation—disillusioned with traditional values and caught in aimless hedonism—caused a sensation.

In 1926 Hemingway left Hadley and their three-year-old son, Bumby, for Pauline Pfeiffer, whom he had come to know in Paris. They married and settled in Key West, Florida, in 1928 and began a succession of travels that would eventually take them to Cuba, Africa, Spain, and Italy.

In 1928 Hemingway's father committed suicide. Earlier that year, Pauline had delivered a son, Patrick, by cesarean section, a traumatic event Hemingway worked into his next novel, *A Farewell to Arms* (1929). Gregory, Hemingway's third son and last child, was born in 1931.

In *A Farewell to Arms*, Frederic Henry, an American lieutenant in the Italian ambulance service during World War I, falls in love with an English nurse, Catherine Barkley. With the Italians in retreat and Catherine pregnant, Frederic eventually deserts his unit. Catherine and the baby die in childbirth, but Frederic nevertheless has found strength in their love. "The world breaks every one and afterward many are strong at the broken places," he says.

During the 1930s, Hemingway lived in Key West, Florida, hunted in Wyoming and Africa, and fished in the Gulf Stream off Cuba. He wrote *Death in the Afternoon* (1932), an extended essay in which he explored bullfighting in Spain as a ritual, and *Green Hills of Africa* (1935), an account of a big game expedition.

During the years 1933 to 1936, Hemingway published a number of his best-known short stories, including "A Clean, Well-Lighted Place," "The Short Happy Life of Francis Macomber," and "The Snows of Kilimanjaro."

To Have and Have Not (1937), perhaps Hemingway's most experimental novel, tells the story of Harry Morgan, an ex-police officer who runs a charter boat in Florida and Cuba and who gets mixed up in smuggling during the Great Depression. Harry fits the mold of the Hemingway hero: a rugged individualist, he prides himself on his prowess as a fighter and a lover. The novel uses multiple narrative perspectives, a device that lets the reader see how little any single character's view actually represents the full story.

In 1937 Hemingway returned to Spain as a correspondent covering the civil war. Ardently pro-Loyalist, he helped raise money for ambu-

lances and medical supplies. Out of this experience came *For Whom the Bell Tolls* (1940), describing three days in the life of Robert Jordan, an American fighting for the Loyalist forces in Spain. Jordan is assigned to blow up a bridge behind enemy lines in order to slow the movement of Fascist forces after a Loyalist attack. The guerrillas learn that the Loyalist attack cannot succeed, but Jordan blows the bridge as instructed. He is wounded during the retreat and is left behind to meet certain death at the hands of the Fascists.

In 1950 Hemingway published *Across the River and into the Trees*, an unsuccessful novel about an aging American colonel who spends his last weekend in Venice with a beautiful, young Italian countess. *The Old Man and the Sea* (1952) was much more successful. In 1952, *Life* magazine published the entire text in a single issue, an unprecedented experiment. In 1953 Hemingway was awarded a Pulitzer Prize, and a year later the Nobel Prize for Literature. In the story an old Cuban fisherman fights a giant marlin for three days, finally subduing it, only to have the carcass attacked by sharks. The old man brings home only the skeleton of the great fish, but he has shown his stature through the quality of his elemental struggle.

Hemingway continued to write, but he produced no more works of such importance. In 1953, in the midst of an African safari, he suffered serious head and abdominal injuries in a plane crash. A long, painful period of recuperation followed, and, for the first time, Hemingway found his prodigious physical strength sapped, his energy gone, and with it his concentration. He grew displeased with the draft of a book about the safari. With the rise of Fidel Castro in Cuba, the Hemingways moved permanently to Ketchum, Idaho. There he worked on a collection of sketches based on his life in Paris during the early days of his career, published after his death as *A Moveable Feast* (1964).

Suffering the effects of a lifetime of injuries, plus mild diabetes and depression, Hemingway saw his physical powers wane further. He was troubled by a loss of memory that hindered his efforts to write about his Paris years. After enduring months of hospitalization at the Mayo Clinic in Rochester, Minnesota, he grew suicidal. On July 2, 1961, in Ketchum, he shot himself.

BIBLIOGRAPHY

Baker, Carlos, *Ernest Hemingway: A Life Story*, 1969; Lynn, Kenneth S., *Hemingway: His Life and Work*, 1987; Rovit, Earl, and Gerry Brenner, *Ernest Hemingway*, 1986.

Henderson, Fletcher Hamilton

(December 18, 1897–December 29, 1952)
Arranger, Bandleader, Pianist

The pioneering arrangements by Fletcher Henderson and Don Redman allowed sparkling improvisations by such stellar musicians as LOUIS ARMSTRONG and COLEMAN HAWKINS to emerge from choruses marked by sharply defined rhythms presented by Henderson's whole band. These innovations helped shape what was to become swing.

Born to a middle-class black family in Cuthbert, Georgia, Fletcher Hamilton Henderson studied music with his mother, a classically trained piano teacher. He earned a degree in chemistry and mathematics at Atlanta University, where he played baseball and acquired the nickname Smack, a reference to the impact of the ball/bat connection.

In 1920 he went to New York to find a job as a chemist. Youth and race worked against him, and he was unsuccessful in his search. To support himself he turned to working as a song demonstrator for the Pace-Handy Music Company, an early black music publisher. When Harry Pace established Black Swan in 1921, the first black recording company, Henderson moved over to Black Swan as a musical jack-of-all-trades.

While employed there, Henderson put together groups to accompany featured Black Swan singers and thus became a bandleader by default rather than by design. His bands performed at dances and clubs and worked at the Broadway nightclub Club Alabam. In 1924 an offer came from the Roseland Ballroom. A whites-only spot, it grew to be the best-known dance hall in New York. Henderson stayed at Roseland for ten years, and his work there brought him recognition and fame.

Henderson's group, one of the many that came into being because of the social dancing fad, developed from an unremarkable dance band into a lively jazz orchestra. The change came in response to the attractions of the exciting new style, but more importantly because of the musical innovations of Louis Armstrong. Armstrong arrived in 1924, and his short stint with Henderson's New York band was critical for the growth of jazz.

While Armstrong's melodic improvisations and swinging rhythms were shaping New York's music and musicians, the Henderson band's music director, Don Redman, was working out his new arrangement patterns of brass and reed interplay, patterns that became formulas for big bands in the years to come. Instrumental solos were inserted between set "arranged" sections, and Louis Armstrong was the spectacular early soloist. Redman and Henderson established and brilliantly developed this basic formula.

The creative Armstrong, having made his mark on the Henderson style, returned to the greener pastures of Chicago in the fall of 1925. By 1926, according to Armstrong biographer James L. Collier, the band "was playing excellent jazz, with first-rate soloists and an ability to make the arranged passages swing." The

Fletcher Henderson Orchestra successfully blended the steady tempo, syncopation, lilt, and notation of swing into pleasing concoctions and became a model for jazz bands until the mid-1930s.

Don Redman wrote most of the Henderson band arrangements until 1927, when he left to become music director of McKinney's Cotton Pickers. Henderson took over most of this work, though he continued his practice of buying arrangements from free-lance musicians. He had found his metier. His arrangements, for example, "King Porter Stomp" and "Wrapping It Up," were playable, clean, and relaxed.

The unassuming Henderson had a knack for spotting new talent and hired most of the major black jazz players of the era, many of whom, like Armstrong and Lester Young, made their names with him. Management skills, however, were not his strength, and as a result, his group broke apart all too frequently. In 1934, due to financial reverses, he sold some of his work to BENNY GOODMAN for Goodman's new band.

These popular arrangements ushered in the widespread success of swing bands that continued for a decade, from 1935 to 1945.

Henderson directed bands until 1939, when he was hired by Goodman as a full-time staff arranger. In 1941 he returned to band leading but wrote arrangements for a living, unable to keep pace with the swing band boom he had helped create. In December 1950 he had a stroke that left him partially paralyzed. He died two years later.

Though not a forceful person, Henderson nevertheless became a musical catalyst, for his taste and intellect helped shape big band jazz. The pioneering Fletcher Henderson Orchestra, a model for swing bands, lived on through the music of Benny Goodman and others and attracted audiences for years.

BIBLIOGRAPHY

Allen, W., *Hendersoniana*, 1973; Collier, J. L., *Louis Armstrong: An American Genius*, 1983; Hadlock, R., *Jazz Masters of the Twenties*, 1965, rep., 1986; McCarthy, A., *Big Band Jazz*, 1974; Schuller, G., *Early Jazz: Its Roots and Musical Development*, 1968.

Hendrix, Jimi

(November 27, 1942–September 18, 1970)
Rock Guitarist, Singer, Songwriter

Jimi Hendrix discovered an as yet unknown world of expression within the electric guitar. Though his superb, highly amplified guitar playing was often upstaged by galvanizing theatrics, his brief, explosive career was a relentless quest to expand the horizons of music and sound.

Born in Seattle, Washington, while his father, Al, was away in the army, Jimi was named Johnny Allen by his mother. After his father's return home, Johnny Allen became James Marshall Hendrix. Later, as a professional musician, he changed his name to Jimi.

His mother, Lucille, who was seventeen when she married Al in 1942, was unreliable. Hendrix shuttled back and forth from caretaker to caretaker, from school to school. He attended eight public schools before he dropped out of Garfield High School in 1960. After his parents were divorced, his mother remarried but died the following year, in 1958, of cirrhosis of the liver.

Hendrix taught himself to play guitar in the mid-1950s while he was in junior high school. Left-handed, he played a right-handed instrument upside down all his life, even when left-handed instruments became available. Hendrix's father bought him his first electric guitar in 1959, and that year Jimi joined a group, the Rocking Kings.

"The first guitarist I was aware of was MUDDY WATERS," Hendrix recalled. "I heard one of his old records when I was a little boy and it scared me to death." He also listened and learned from other bluesmen, including B. B. King and John Lee Hooker.

After a run-in with the law and with jobs hard to find, Hendrix enlisted in the army in 1961. After basic training in California, he joined the 101st Airborne Division and was stationed at Fort Campbell, Kentucky, where he met bassist Billy Cox. Together they formed a group, the King Kasuals, and within a few months were playing at Club del Morocco in Nashville, Tennessee. In 1962, after a medical discharge, granted because of a parachute injury, Hendrix moved to Nashville, where he began his professional career working with various rhythm and blues groups, including Little Richard's band, in rough roadhouses and bars, the only venues open to black entertainers. He learned to please the crowd in these places where the clientele tended to be demanding. While in New York City in 1964, he met and played with the Isley Brothers, who encouraged his wild costumes and onstage antics that included playing the guitar with his teeth, one hand behind his back or between his legs.

In 1966 Hendrix formed his own band, Jimmy James and the Blue Flames, and began playing in New York City's Greenwich Village. Hendrix, who had remained an instrumentalist and was inspired by BOB DYLAN's style, now tried singing and exploring his guitar. His dazzling playing soon won him a reputation among musicians. The Blue Flames were playing at Cafe Wha! when Bryan ("Chas") Chandler, formerly a member of the English group the Animals, heard Hendrix and immediately signed him to a management contract. They went to England later that year, where with bass guitarist Noel Redding and drummer John ("Mitch") Mitchell the Jimi Hendrix Experience was created.

The group's debut at the Olympia in Paris was a great success, and the Experience went on to play throughout Europe. A record contract resulted in the group's first single, "Hey Joe" and "Stone Free," issued in December 1966. Hendrix was an immediate success in England.

Are You Experienced, Hendrix's first recording of his own, was released in 1967. Reviewer Keith Altham wrote, "Hendrix is a new dimension in electrical guitar music, launching what amounts to a one-man assault upon the nerve cells."

When Hendrix returned home in 1967, he toured with the Monkees, a group he found intolerable to work with, and finally managed to create a public outcry in reaction to his outrageous onstage behavior. He was allowed to leave the tour and the resulting publicity led to a smash appearance at the Monterey Pop Festival, where he climaxed his performance by setting fire to his guitar.

Hendrix's second album, *Axis: Bold as Love,* was released in 1968. *Time* reported that "he hopped, twisted and rolled over sideways without missing a twang or a moan. He slung the guitar low over swiveling hips, or raised it to pick the strings with his teeth; he thrust it between his legs and did a bump and grind. . . . For a symbolic finish he lifted the guitar and flung it against the amplifiers."

After releasing the double album in 1968, Hendrix wanted to change his direction. "I want to be respected in the music field," he said. He put the Experience on hold, and it never reformed. Hendrix supervised the construction of his own Greenwich Village recording studio, Electric Lady, and continued his musical experiments. That summer he performed at Woodstock and was the final performer of the festival. During that year he also faced charges for heroin possession in Toronto, where he was later acquitted. On New Year's Eve in 1969 he debuted the Band of Gypsys with Billy Cox (bass guitar) and Buddy Miles (drums) and with them recorded the album *Band of Gypsys,* which won a gold record.

Hendrix died in London in 1970 at age twenty-seven of suffocation due to the inhalation of vomit during his sleep. The presence of barbiturates in his system was noted as the cause. Two albums, *The Cry of Love* and *Rainbow Bridge*, contain material Hendrix was working on at the time of his death. Robert Hilburn commented in the *Los Angeles Times*, "Hendrix's music was perfectly tied to the times. It was a troubled, violent, confused, searching music on the one hand, an assertive, demanding, triumphant, sensual music on the other." Hilburn continued, "He got sounds out of the guitar that most people didn't imagine ever were there."

BIBLIOGRAPHY

Hopkins, J., *Hit and Run: The Jimi Hendrix Story*, 1983; Shapiro, H., and C. Glebbeek, *Jimi Hendrix: Electric Gypsy*, 1990.

Henri, Robert

(June 25, 1865–July 12, 1929)
Painter

Robert Henri, a leader of the Ashcan school, a group of urban, realist painters, earned distinction as a painter, art teacher, and leader in organizing artists to work for more opportunities to exhibit their works.

Henri, whose real name was Robert Henry Cozad, grew up in the town of Cozad, Nebraska, which his father, a professional gambler, had founded. In 1882 the elder Cozad shot a man in self-defense and left town to avoid a lynch mob. Eventually, Robert and his mother were able to meet his father and move to New Jersey. They changed their names, and Robert became Robert Henri, pronouncing the last name "Hen-rye."

In 1886 Henri entered the Pennsylvania Academy of the Fine Arts, where he studied drawing and modeling under a famous teacher, Thomas Anshutz. After two years at the academy, Henri went to Paris in 1888, where he studied at the Académie Julien. Admitted to the Ecole des Beaux-Arts, the official, government-sponsored art school in Paris, Henri resented the rigid, academic training. He left Paris to travel. Back in the United States in 1891, he studied again at the Pennsylvania Academy in Philadelphia, this time under an Impressionist teacher, Robert Vonnoh. (The Impressionists tried to capture a brief "impression" of everyday scenes or objects, using short strokes of pure color.) In 1892 he began his long teaching career when the Philadelphia School of Design for Women hired him as an instructor.

Four younger artists—John Sloan, William Glackens, Everett Shinn, and George Luks, all illustrators for the Philadelphia *Press*—gathered every Thursday night at Henri's studio to drink punch, eat Welsh rarebit or spaghetti, and hear Henri talk. Henri inspired them with the belief that their work for the newspaper had the seeds of great art in it. (Newspaper artists covered fires, accidents, speeches, and parades as photographers do today. They had to work fast and tell a visual story with a few details.) The true painter, Henri said, loved the real life around him and painted it quickly, sharply, darkly, and tenderly. Their paintings, in fact, were to become so dark that they were to be called the Revolutionary Black Gang and, later, the Ashcan school.

In the mid-1890s Henri gave up Impressionism, which he had decided was becoming superficial and academic, and returned to Europe. There he developed a new style, using broad brush strokes and giving less emphasis to light and color. When he had a one-man show in Philadelphia, he met two New York painters, William Merritt Chase and Arthur B. Davies, who introduced him to the New York art world.

After two years in Brittany, he and his wife settled in New York. He painted a few New York scenes and summer landscapes but mainly concentrated on pictures of people. He quickly became a prominent painter, winning awards and serving on art juries. Tall, loud, and fiery, he also became a spokesman for artists. He taught at several art schools in New York, including the Art Students League, and then at the school he started himself. He encouraged and inspired his students, urging them to paint honestly and not to imitate other people's styles.

After his wife died in 1905, he traveled all over the world, painting farmers in Ireland and Europe, Indians in California and New Mexico, and Down-East Yankees in Maine. His character studies have freedom, freshness, and vitality. *The Old Model*, painted in 1912, has a hasty, sketchy look but is full of the breath of real life.

In 1908 he helped organize a group, named The Eight by the newspapers, to hold exhibitions. Members of The Eight were Henri, his four friends from the Philadelphia *Press*, and Arthur B. Davies, Maurice Prendergast, and Ernest Lawson. Their exhibition in a New York gallery shocked the public with its unconventional paintings of starkly realistic city scenes.

During the last years of his life, Henri had a summer home, Boycott House, in County Mayo, Ireland, where he enjoyed trout fishing. In the fall of 1928, he became ill on the ship en route from Ireland. In failing health for nearly eight months, he died at St. Luke's Hospital in New York.

BIBLIOGRAPHY

Homer, William Innes, *Robert Henri and His Circle*, 1988; Yarrow, William, and Louis Bouche, *Robert Henri, His Life and Works*, 1921.

Hepburn, Katharine Houghton

(November 8, 1907–)
Actress

Katharine Hepburn, at the top of her profession for sixty years, is arguably the most highly regarded and universally respected of all living Hollywood actresses. Equally brilliant in comedy and drama, she was the only performer to win four Academy Awards.

Born in Hartford, Connecticut, Hepburn was the second of six children and the first daughter of Thomas and Katharine Houghton Hepburn. Her father, from a poor and simple family, was a doctor; Kate's first ambition was to become a surgeon just like him. Her mother—whose family, the Houghtons, was one of America's foremost dynasties—was active in the woman suffrage movement in the early 1900s, joined Margaret Sanger's crusade for birth control in the 1920s, and was one of the founders of the organization later known as Planned Parenthood.

Hepburn marched for these causes with her parents and supported similar causes—such as pro-choice—in the 1970s and 1980s. To biographer Christopher Andersen she said, "[T]he single most important thing anyone needs to know about me is that I am totally, completely the product of two damn fascinating individuals who happened to be my parents."

As a young girl, Hepburn was an accomplished painter, sculptor, and athlete. A tomboy for much of her childhood, she shaved her head at age nine to keep the boys from pulling her hair. She attended West Middle School in Hartford, and later Hartford's Oxford School. Inspired by her grandfather's stories, she became interested in drama at age ten, performing plays on a makeshift stage in a shed at the family's country house in Fenwick.

The Museum of Modern Art/Film Stills Archive

In 1921 the tragedy of her older brother Tom's apparent suicide devastated her. She left school, was given private tutors, and spent a great deal of time watching silent movies as an escape, secretly dreaming of becoming an actress.

At Bryn Mawr, she began studying medicine, but as a result of poor academic performance and eccentric behavior (swimming nude in a fountain), she almost flunked out. She switched to English, became active in the college's drama society, and graduated with honors in 1928. Her senior year performance as Pandora in *The Woman in the Moon* won the attention of a friend of theatrical producer Eddie Knopf, who, as a result of Hepburn's persistence, gave her her first professional, nonspeaking role as one of Catherine the Great's ladies-in-waiting in *The Czarina.*

Her first speaking role was in Knopf's stock company's production of *The Big Pond,* but when they reduced her to understudy for the Broadway opening, she refused. Her first role on Broadway was in *These Days,* after which she was understudy and then fill-in for Hope Williams in Philip Barry's *Holiday.* Williams

was a strong influence on Hepburn's acting and vocal style.

In 1928 she married Ludlow Ogden Smith, whom she had met during her senior year at Bryn Mawr, and for the next several years appeared in a number of plays, making her biggest impression as an Amazon in *The Warrior's Husband* in 1932. In that year she tested for the role of Sydney in the film *A Bill of Divorcement,* which was to star JOHN BARRYMORE. She won the part and signed a contract with producer David O. Selznick for $1,500 a week.

Remarking on Hepburn's initial impact on film audiences, Selznick said that while her look was totally new and unglamorous for Hollywood, she proved instantly to be a unique screen personality.

The film was directed by George Cukor, with whom Hepburn formed a lasting friendship, and from whom she learned the subtle differences between stage and film acting. In the course of her career, she made nine other features with Cukor, including *Little Women* (1933), three of the nine films she made with Spencer Tracy—*Keeper of the Flame* (1942), *Adam's Rib* (1949), and *Pat and Mike* (1952)—and two television films, *Love Among the Ruins* (1978) and *The Corn Is Green* (1979).

Her second film, also produced by Selznick, was *Christopher Strong* (1933), directed by Dorothy Arzner, one of Hollywood's few women directors. Hepburn's initial success peaked when she won her first Oscar for her third film, *Morning Glory* (1933). She continued to develop as an actress with an amazing range—playing the spunky backwoods heroine in *Spitfire* (1934), the homespun girl of BOOTH TARKINGTON's *Alice Adams* (1935), *Mary of*

Scotland (1936), an ambitious actress in *Stage Door* (1937), and the flighty Susan in the screwball masterpiece *Bringing Up Baby* (1938).

The latter, a brilliant comic performance, was also her most scintillating teamwork with CARY GRANT, with whom she also appeared in *Sylvia Scarlett* (1935), *Holiday* (1938), and *The Philadelphia Story* (1940), all directed by Cukor.

In the 1940s Hepburn began a long personal and professional relationship with actor Spencer Tracy. Their first film together was *Woman of the Year* (1942), in which Hepburn is a political commentator and Tracy a sportscaster. Besides the three directed by Cukor, their other notable film was FRANK CAPRA's political satire *State of the Union* (1948). Their last was the preachy *Guess Who's Coming to Dinner* (1967), which was Tracy's last screen appearance and won Hepburn a second Oscar. While their relationship never led to courtship or marriage, Hepburn, in her autobiography, said, "We just passed twenty-seven years together in what was to me absolute bliss. It is called love."

In the 1950s she gave several memorable performances as spinsters: as the missionary in John Huston's *The African Queen* (1951), she is won over by equally memorable Humphrey Bogart as a drunkard sea captain; in *Summertime* (1955) she has an autumnal love affair with Rossano Brazzi while vacationing in Venice; and in *The Rainmaker* (1956) she is wooed by charming con man Burt Lancaster.

She also gave two striking performances as neurotic mothers in screen adaptations of TENNESSEE WILLIAMS's *Suddenly, Last Summer* (1959) and EUGENE O'NEILL's *Long Day's Journey into Night* (1962). Her third Oscar was for *The Lion in Winter* (1968), her fourth for *On Golden Pond* (1981), which costarred HENRY FONDA. Her most recent appearance was in the television movie *Laura Lansing Slept Here* (1988), written especially for her.

Divorced from Ludlow Smith in 1934, Hepburn never remarried, believing that she could not be successful at both marriage and a career.

BIBLIOGRAPHY

Andersen, Christopher, *Young Kate*, 1988; Hepburn, Katharine, *Me: Stories of My Life*, 1991; Kanin, Garson, *Tracy and Hepburn*, 1970.

Herbert, Victor August

(February 1, 1859–May 26, 1924)
Cellist, Composer, Conductor

New York's darling at the turn of the century, Herbert brought romance, melody, and hints of Vienna to his more than forty operettas. Songs like "Ah, Sweet Mystery of Life" from *Naughty Marietta* tend to eclipse Herbert's skills as virtuoso cellist, expert conductor, and superb orchestrator.

Born in Dublin, Ireland, Victor Herbert was very young when he lost his father, Edward Herbert. Fanny, Herbert's mother, married Wilhelm Schmid, a German physician, and settled in Stuttgart, Germany, in 1866. Young Herbert attended the local *Gymnasium* and learned to play piano and flute, before turning to the violoncello.

Unable to study medicine because of financial circumstances, the talented Herbert was taken on by master teacher Bernhard Cossman for two years, probably 1874 to 1876. Cossman, "one of the great cellists of the century," according to Herbert's biographer, Edward N. Waters, was a fine teacher and a superb instrumentalist. Cossman provided Herbert with a solid musical foundation, one that gained him entrance, in 1881, to the Stuttgart Conservatory. There, coached and encouraged by composer and conductor Max Seifriz, Herbert gained experience as an orchestral musician and occasionally had opportunities to perform as soloist.

After a tour of Europe, Herbert returned to Stuttgart and entered the court orchestra. Between 1881 and 1886 Herbert immersed himself in chamber music and appeared as soloist (for performances of his Suite for Cello and Orchestra and of his First Cello Concerto). He joined the faculty of a new music school and continued to play with the Stuttgart court orchestra.

Herbert married soprano Therese Foerster in Vienna in 1886. A scout for the new New York Metropolitan Opera Company spotted Foerster early that summer and engaged the young couple, she as soloist, he as cellist for the company's orchestra. The newlyweds sailed for New York, arriving October 24, 1886. Herbert plunged immediately into the city's musical world.

His musical ventures included solo performances with the New York Symphony Society, establishment of a forty-piece orchestra that played successfully in New York and Boston, and formation of the New York String Quartet. As conductor, he appeared at summer concerts, at festivals, and on tour. He joined the faculty of the National Conservatory of Music and in 1894, as soloist, performed his Second Cello Concerto with the New York Philharmonic Society. The work is said to have inspired Dvořák, then at the National Conservatory, to compose his own lovely concerto for violoncello.

In 1893 Herbert became leader of the 22nd Regiment Band of the New York National Guard. In his seven years as bandleader, he wrote marches like *The Gold Bug* and *The Serenade*. In 1898 he went to Pittsburgh as conductor of its Symphony Orchestra and during his six-year tenure there raised the orchestra's standards to those of New York and Boston organizations. Back in New York in 1904, he organized the Victor Herbert Orchestra, popular for its programs of light music. In 1908 he was elected to the National Institute of Arts and Letters.

Herbert, steeped in European musical theater, is best known for his operettas written between 1894 and 1924. Most familiar are *Babes in Toyland* (1902), *Mlle. Modiste* (1905), *The Red Mill* (1906), and *Naughty Marietta* (1910). Some of the delightful waltzes found in these works, like "I'm Falling in Love with Someone" or "Kiss Me Again," are beloved by audiences but are difficult to sing because of the range and precision required.

Herbert wrote two unsuccessful operas, *Natoma* (1911) and *Madeleine* (1914). A copyright law activist, he worked tirelessly to secure royalties for composers. He helped found ASCAP (American Society of Composers, Authors and Publishers) and remained an officer of the organization until he died in New York, May 26, 1924.

BIBLIOGRAPHY

Purdy, C. L., *Victor Herbert—American Music Master,* 1944; Waters, E. N., *Victor Herbert: A Life in Music,* 1955, rev., 1978.

Hersey, John Richard

(June 17, 1914–March 24, 1993)
Journalist, Novelist

Known for his postwar novel *A Bell for Adano,* as well as for *Hiroshima,* a chronicle of the destruction caused by the atom bomb, John Hersey combines the techniques of journalism and fiction to produce vivid accounts of the impact of historical events on ordinary lives.

Hersey was born to Christian missionary parents in Tianjin, China. In 1924 his family returned to the United States, settling in Briarcliff Manor, New York. After graduating from Yale University in 1936, he studied at Cambridge University in England.

Hersey's first job after graduation was as secretary to the novelist SINCLAIR LEWIS. He then worked several years as a journalist, including stints as a correspondent in China and Japan for *Time* magazine from 1937 until 1944. Early in World War II, he covered the South Pacific and later the Sicilian campaign before going to Moscow in 1944.

His first book, *Men on Bataan* (1942), was drawn from his experience covering the fall of the island in April 1942. A second book, *Into the Valley* (1943), observed a group of U.S. Marines skirmishing on Guadalcanal. The book was compared to the war fiction of STEPHEN CRANE.

Hersey's Pulitzer Prize–winning war novel, *A Bell for Adano* (1944), concerns the American occupation of a small Sicilian town. It reflects on the impact on the Italian people of America's method of military governance, which stands in stark contrast to its democratic ideology.

Hiroshima (1946) so successfully mingled the techniques of journalism and fiction that it secured Hersey's reputation. The book describes the impact of the atomic bomb blast on the Japanese people by telling the stories of six survivors—recounting where they were when the bomb fell, how they reacted, and what happened to them afterward. The survivors' emotions are revealed in their actions. The book, published as one entire issue of *The New Yorker,* created a sensation. Distributed free by the Book-of-the-Month Club, it was read aloud on radio stations around the country. Hersey had succeeded in making a distant event terrifyingly real.

Hersey faced a similar challenge in *The Wall* (1950), a novel that tells the story of the deaths of 500,000 Jews at the hands of the Nazis in the Warsaw ghetto. Hersey invented a diarist, Noach Levinson, to render the story intensely personal and to establish the historical and cultural context for the events of three years. It was dramatized in 1961 by Millard Lampell.

Hersey called his style of fiction "the novel of contemporary history." He found his motivation as a writer from a felt need to educate the reading public about topics ranging from war to racism, education, and overpopulation.

Subsequent novels include *The Marmot Drive* (1953), *A Single Pebble* (1956), *The War Lover* (1959), *The Child Buyer* (1960), *White Lotus* (1965), *The Walnut Door* (1977), *The Call* (1985), and *Antoinetta* (1991). His nonfiction includes *The Algiers Motel Incident* (1968) and *Aspects of the Presidency* (1980). He also edited a collection of essays, *The Writer's Craft* (1974).

Hersey taught at Yale University for many years. He died of cancer in 1993.

BIBLIOGRAPHY
Sanders, David, *John Hersey,* 1967.

Hicks, Edward

(April 4, 1780–August 23, 1849)
Painter

E dward Hicks, who in his forties became a self-taught painter of primitive pictures, is best known for *The Peaceable Kingdom*, of which 60 of 100 versions have survived.

Hicks was born in Bucks County, Pennsylvania, near what is now Langhorne, and was apprenticed to a carriage maker in his early teens. He decorated coaches, signs, tables, chairs, fire buckets, and chests. When he was twenty-three years old, he joined the Society of Friends, or Quaker church, and it wasn't long before he became one of the best-known Quaker preachers. He refused to take pay for his sermons and lived by his paintbrush.

He took up easel painting in middle age, turning out rural landscapes and scenes of country life, but he feared art was contrary to religion and thought painting was a "trifling, insignificant art, which has never been of any substantial advantage to mankind." He said that "if the Christian world was in the real spirit of Christ, I do not believe there would be such a thing as a fine painter in Christendom." At other times, however, he testified that art could bring meaning to life.

The Peaceable Kingdom portrays a charmingly awkward scene, with William Penn posing with Indians on the left and a group of children and animals in a woodland on the right. Hicks used as his models the animals in Bible illustrations, children in engravings done after Raphael's paintings, the left foreground from a reproduction of BENJAMIN WEST's *William Penn's Treaty with the Indians*, and the Natural Bridge of Virginia from a popular print.

Hicks explained that *The Peaceable Kingdom* illustrated his belief that Pennsylvania was the fulfillment of the prophecy in the eleventh chapter of Isaiah that justice and gentleness would prevail among humanity and between humans and beasts. He also said the painting symbolized the peace of soul that humans can acquire when they control their animal passions. He gave away many of his canvases to friends and often included a poem, of which the first verse read, "The wolf shall with the lambkin dwell in peace / his grim carnivorous thirst for blood shall cease; / The beauteous leopard with his restless eye, / shall by the kid in perfect stillness lie."

When Hicks died, 3,000 people came to his funeral, mourning not the artist so much as the preacher.

BIBLIOGRAPHY

Ford, Alice, *Edward Hicks: His Life and Art*, 1985.

Hindemith, Paul

(November 16, 1895–December 28, 1963)
Composer, Conductor, Teacher, Theorist, Violist

The conservative Hindemith, like his predecessor Brahms, often looked back as he composed. An outstanding theorist, he was a demanding teacher who passed on both his discipline and ideas to American students.

Paul Hindemith was born to a working-class family in Hanau, near Frankfurt, Germany, and began to study violin at age six. In 1909 he entered the Frankfurt Conservatory, remaining there until 1917. A gifted instrumentalist, Hindemith became concertmaster of the Frankfurt Opera Orchestra and violist in the noted Amar Quartet when he was nineteen.

He was composing, too, and his music was performed first in public on June 2, 1919. With the subsequent performances of his one-act operas, a string quartet, and Kammermusik no. 1, at the Donaueschingen festivals, he established himself as a leading young German composer.

Hindemith's work harks back to German tradition and was often informed by Johannes Brahms, though from 1918 to 1923 overt experimentation and innovation dominated his compositions. Operas like *Mörder, Hoffnung der Fraven* (Murder, Hope of Women, 1919) and *Sancta Susanna* (1921) revealed his interest in expressionism. In Kammermusik no. 1 (1922), a chamber work, Hindemith reflected the impact made on him by IGOR STRAVINSKY and Darius Milhaud, while his interest in nightclubs and jazz surfaced in *Suite "1922"* for piano.

Between 1924 and 1933 Hindemith drew on the Baroque. His solo concertos are rooted in Bach's Brandenburg concertos. Other important works like the Concerto for Orchestra (1925) and *Cardillac* (1926), an opera, employ elements of the Baroque as well. In a short opera of the period, *Hin und zurück* (Roundtrip, 1927), based on an antirealist text, the action proceeds forward, then reverses like a film being run backwards. The music does the same in a technical tour de force.

Appointed professor of composition at the Hochschule für Musik in Berlin in 1927, Hindemith continued to compose and often performed on the viola and viola d'amore. His teaching experience led to the writing of the influential *Unterweisung im Tonsatz* (1937–1939), translated later as *The Craft of Musical Composition* (1941–1942), and to compositions designed for amateurs.

Hindemith was very much a part of the ferment of the 1920s. With the socially conscious playwright Bertolt Brecht, who wrote the text, he created *Lehrstück* (1929) for amateurs. It is an example of his contributions to the down-to-earth art, *Gebrauchsmusik* (music for everyday use), that was intended to be both accessible to and playable by the average person.

By 1933 Hindemith's style was more conservatively tonal and his forms more classical in *Mathis der Maler* (Mathis the painter) and its related symphony. The opera is based on the composer's imagined life of Matthias Grünewald, whose masterpiece, the Isenheim Altarpiece, expresses the mysticism of the Middle Ages and the realism of the Renaissance.

Initially ignored by the Nazis, by 1934 Hindemith was under attack for his modernism, and, according to Propaganda Minister Joseph Goebbels, "atrocious dissonance," "cultural Bolshevism," and "spiritual non-Aryanism." Hindemith's music was banned as being "unbearable to the Third Reich." After a period of uncertainty, in January 1935 the composer was forced to leave the Hochschule. He turned to concertizing and writing, made his American debut at the Library of Congress, April 10, 1937, playing his viola sonata, and in 1938 emigrated to Switzerland. He left for the United States in

February 1940 and six years later became an American citizen.

Before heading to Yale University in the fall of 1940 as a visiting lecturer, Hindemith taught at the Berkshire Music Center and lectured at Wells College, Cornell University, and the New York State College at Buffalo. A year later he was appointed professor at Yale, and he remained a member of the faculty until 1953.

Hindemith taught Yale students composition, harmony, and theory, using his own translated theoretical text, *The Craft of Musical Composition.* Other writings were to follow: *A Concentrated Course in Traditional Harmony* (1943); *Elementary Training for Musicians* (1946); and a second volume on harmony, *Exercises for Advanced Students* (1948).

Hindemith often lectured on the history of theory. In 1945, to illustrate its evolution, he began to present concerts with members of the Yale Collegium Musicum. The successful performances were heard in New York City and in New Haven.

After he arrived in America, Hindemith wrote sonatas, violin concertos, symphonies, a ballet, *Ludus tonalis* (1942, a cycle of fugues and interludes for piano), and a full-length opera, *Die Harmonie der Welt* (1956–1957), based on the work of the Renaissance astronomer Johannes Kepler.

Before he left Yale in 1953 to settle in Switzerland, Hindemith delivered the Charles Eliot Norton lectures at Harvard University (1949–1950) and published his lectures there as *A Composer's World* (1952). In Switzerland he continued to conduct, tour, and compose, and in 1955 he gave up teaching. His last work, a Mass, was completed in 1963. Hindemith died in Frankfurt, Germany, December 28, 1963.

BIBLIOGRAPHY

Hindemith, P., *A Composer's World,* 1952; Machlis, J., *Introduction to Contemporary Music,* 1961; Skelton, G., *Paul Hindemith: The Man behind the Music,* 1975.

Hitchcock, Alfred Joseph

(August 13, 1899–April 29, 1980)
Director, Producer

Hitchcock, the "master of suspense," was also the "supreme technician of the American cinema," as one critic put it. His films, always popular with audiences, have increasingly gained the respect of scholars and other filmmakers, several of whom—including François Truffaut and Brian de Palma—have paid homage to his influence in their own work.

Born in London, he studied engineering at a Jesuit school and, later, art at the University of London. As a schoolboy he was a loner, owing to a lifelong shyness. He traced his fear of punishment to ritual beatings by the Jesuits for minor infractions. Overweight all his life, he

cleverly employed his rotund profile as an instantly recognizable signature. In his television series, *Alfred Hitchcock Presents,* his silhouette marked the opening of every show.

As a teenager, he worked as an advertising layout draftsman for a department store, but was keenly interested in filmmaking. In 1920 he secured a job at an American film company's London office as a designer of title cards, the method used to convey information and dialogue in silent films. In three years he rose to scriptwriter, art director, and assistant director. He directed his first film, *The Pleasure Garden,* in 1925, followed by eight more silent features. In 1929 he made *Blackmail,* his—and England's—first talking film.

In 1926 he married Alma Reville, who collaborated on many of his movies as writer and adviser. Their daughter, Patricia, appeared in a number of Hitchcock's films. Hitchcock won immediate praise for his mastery of cinematic technique. From 1927 and throughout the 1930s he was Britain's preeminent film director, his reputation secured with such classics as *The Lodger* (1926), *The Man Who Knew Too Much* (1934), *The 39 Steps* (1935), and *The Lady Vanishes* (1938).

The Museum of Modern Art/Film Stills Archive

in a Hitchcock film as to "whodunit." The audience is engaged emotionally in a wrenching process through which the falsely accused person must be proven innocent. In his celebrated interview with French filmmaker François Truffaut, Hitchcock said, "If you've designed a picture correctly, in terms of its emotional impact, the Japanese audience should scream at the same time as the Indian audience."

Despite their often chilling psychological intensity, Hitchcock's films are never short on wit and charm. Indeed, one of his unique talents was to mischievously engage the viewer in an ambivalent relationship with his villains, who are often more charming than his heroes. In this way, his films escape the moral schemas of more simple-minded thrillers. The wit extended to his familiar cameo appearances in the films, a practice he began out of necessity to populate a scene, but which caught on and became another of his signatory gimmicks.

Lured to Hollywood in 1939, he signed a contract with producer David O. Selznick and made *Rebecca,* starring Laurence Olivier and Joan Fontaine. Although the film was a huge success and won the Oscar for Best Picture of 1940, it is overshadowed by those that followed, notably *Foreign Correspondent* (1940), *Suspicion* (1941), *Shadow of a Doubt* (1943), *Spellbound* (1945), and *Notorious* (1946).

In these films, Hitchcock explored his favorite themes, perhaps the most familiar of which was that of an "innocent" person being wrongly accused. Frequently asked in interviews why such characters acted guiltily and displayed an abnormal fear of the law, Hitchcock loved to relate a childhood anecdote wherein his father sent him to be locked up in a jail cell, and the officer said, upon his release minutes later, "That's what we do to naughty boys."

This theme is underwritten by a distinction he made between mystery and suspense: "Mystery is an intellectual process, like in a 'whodunit' [whereas] suspense is essentially an emotional process." There is rarely any doubt

In conjunction with the underrated moral complexity of his films, Hitchcock had an uncanny gift for casting against type, often evoking the dark sides of actors generally associated with virtuous character traits. Thus, romantic leads like CARY GRANT and folk heroes like JAMES STEWART played roles against the grain, which exposed their vulnerable, less attractive features.

Beginning with *Strangers on a Train* in 1951, he made one artistic and/or box-office success after the other: *I Confess* (1953), *Dial M for Murder* (1954), *Rear Window* (1954), *To Catch a Thief* (1955), a remake of *The Man Who Knew Too Much* (1956), *The Wrong Man* (1956), *Vertigo* (1958), *North by Northwest* (1959), and *Psycho* (1960), the latter a classic of the horror genre that broke box-office records during its initial release.

In these movies, no less than in his silent films, Hitchcock's art always stressed visual imagery over dialogue, a fact easily illustrated by such unforgettable sequences as the attack of a crop-dusting plane on Cary Grant in *North by Northwest* and the brutal shower murder of Janet Leigh in *Psycho.*

Before his death, he made only five more features, the most notable of which are *The Birds* (1963), *Marnie* (1964), and *Frenzy* (1972). The last, *Family Plot,* was released in 1976.

In addition to being his most creative period for features, the 1950s was also his triumphant period in television. His series, *Alfred Hitchcock Presents,* ran from 1955 to 1966 and con-

sisted of many half-hour gems, twenty of which he directed himself.

Nominated for an Academy Award five times, he never received the Oscar for Best Director, but he did receive the IRVING G. THALBERG Award in 1968 in recognition of "the most consistent high level of production achievement by an individual producer." He was also the recipient of the Life Achievement Award by the American Film Institute and, among other honors, was knighted by Queen Elizabeth just a few months before his death.

BIBLIOGRAPHY

Freeman, David, *The Last Days of Alfred Hitchcock,* 1984; Humphries, Patrick, *The Films of Alfred Hitchcock,* 1986.

Hockney, David

(July 9, 1937–)
Graphic Artist, Painter, Photographer, Scenic Designer

A major figure in contemporary British and American art, David Hockney is famous for paintings that combine Pop art elements with a refined technique for emphasizing detail, and for his superb etchings inspired by literary works. He also gained recognition as a scenic designer and photographer in the 1970s and 1980s.

Hockney was born into a working-class family in Bradford, Yorkshire, England, and subsequently studied at the Bradford School of Art (1953–1957). A conscientious objector, he did hospital work to fulfill his national service obligations (1957–1959). Dubbed the wunderkind of British art while a student at the Royal College of Art (1959–1962), Hockney gained instant international acclaim with showings of his works at the Young Contemporaries Exhibition (London, 1961–1962)

and the Paris Biennale (1963). *A Rake's Progress* (1961–1963), a series of sixteen etchings inspired by artist William Hogarth, chronicles Hockney's 1961 visit to New York City in a witty, often biting style that established him as one of the finest draftsmen in contemporary art.

His initial fame coincided with the Beatles' rise in the pop music world, and his flamboyant lifestyle made him a celebrity of the antiestablishment culture in 1960s London. He was a striking presence with his bleached blond hair, owlish glasses, and gold lamé jacket.

Hockney's early work was influenced by abstract artist JACKSON POLLOCK and the Pop art movement (see ROY LICHTENSTEIN), which stressed the pictorial aspect of art and imitated the stereotyped images of the mass media. His use of graffiti, caricature, advertising images, and a combination of the pictorial with written allusions resulted in strikingly original, often humorous, works that had an innocent quality like children's drawings, but were highly sophisticated in technique. *The Cha Cha Cha that Was Danced in the Early Hours of 24th March* (1961) is a good example.

Hockney moved to the United States in 1964. He taught at the Universities of Iowa (1964), Colorado (1965), and California (at Los Angeles, 1966; at Berkeley, 1967). His mature style—more realistic, streamlined, and often ironic, yet still idiosyncratic and inventive in detail—emerged at this time. *Beverly Hills Housewife* (1966) is representative of the artificial, often "frozen-like" world of his paintings with their stylized, flat, paper-doll cutout figures. Hockney's frequent stays in California inspired his well-known swimming-pool paintings. In these, the homosexual themes that had been of his oeuvre for many years emerge in the clarifying sunlight of southern California. Always aiming to tell a story through his art, Hockney said, "My paintings seem to me to be self-explanatory."

His love of poetry led to the introduction of words in his pictures and drawings, as in the etchings *Myself and My Heroes* (1961) containing quotations from WALT WHITMAN. Homage was also paid to past artists in many of his works, such as *Artist and Model* (1973–1974) in which he depicted Picasso as artist and himself as model. He became a successful scene designer, with such productions as IGOR STRAVINSKY's opera *The Rake's Progress* at the Glyndeborne Festival (1975) and Eric Satie's *Parade* at the Metropolitan Opera, New York (1980).

During the 1980s Hockney turned to photography, creating Cubist photos in which several photos are combined to present a single but fractured image. He also experimented with computer-adapted art, using such computer materials as paint-box programs.

BIBLIOGRAPHY

Hockney, David, *David Hockney by David Hockney*, 1977; Livingstone, M., *David Hockney*, 1981.

Holiday, Billie

(April 7, 1915–July 17, 1959)
Singer

A jazz original who died too young, Billie Holiday, often called Lady Day, was a model for countless singers. Her smokey voice, wonderful melodic lines, emotional quality, and remarkable way with lyrics reflect her admiration for LOUIS ARMSTRONG, an inspiration she always acknowledged.

Holiday was born in Baltimore, Maryland, to unmarried teenage parents. Clarence Holiday, her father, left the family early and in the 1930s played banjo and guitar with the FLETCHER HENDERSON Orchestra in New York. Billie's harsh, uncertain, tumultuous childhood included suspected rape at the age of ten, time in a Catholic home for girls, four months in a

New York Welfare Island state institution, prostitution to support her ailing mother, and little formal schooling.

In the early 1930s Billie began to perform—at a small club in Brooklyn, then at Pod and Jerry's in Harlem. By 1933 she was singing at Monette's, another Harlem club, where producer/critic JOHN HAMMOND heard her and was struck by "her dignity and sensitive phrasing." Hammond arranged recording sessions for Holiday with BENNY GOODMAN and helped her with bookings at New York clubs. Early recordings, "Your Mother's Son-in-Law" and "Riffin' the Scotch," hint at the unique phrasing and timing that set her apart.

By 1935 Hammond was recording Holiday frequently, often with pianist Teddy Wilson and other expert jazz musicians. Wilson commented, "I had never heard a girl with a sound like Billie's. She could just say 'Hello' or 'Good Morning' and it was a musical experience. And her singing, in a very integral way, was a reflection of her whole psychology, her experience. What you heard when she sang was the very essence of her character."

Library of Congress

The next seven years were extraordinarily productive and were to be the peak of Billie's career. Many recordings, among them "Body and Soul" and "Love Me or Leave Me," included the accompaniments of tenor saxophonist Lester Young, Holiday's friend and musical alter ego, the man who first called her Lady Day. Young's sensitive playing and the accompaniments of Buck Clayton, another Count Basie sideman, along with the Basie rhythm section, highlighted and enhanced Holiday's expressiveness and way with words.

Holiday appeared, too, with Fletcher Henderson and Jimmie Lunceford and, on occasion, sang with her own bands in New York clubs. In 1937 she joined the Count Basie Orchestra, left after a few months with some ill-feeling, and in 1938 moved on to Artie Shaw's band and became one of the first black singers to be featured by a white orchestra.

By 1939 she was headliner at Café Society, a Greenwich Village interracial club that was fast becoming fashionable. That year she recorded what was to be a great artistic and commercial success, "Strange Fruit." Words from his own poem were set to a haunting melody by Lewis Allen and performed beautifully and from the heart by Holiday. The early protest song, controversial because of its explosive political content, concerned a lynching. Billie wrote her own still heartbreaking song of childhood and poverty, "God Bless the Child."

Popular in New York clubs from 1939 to 1943, Holiday appeared in a movie, *New Orleans* (1946), with Louis Armstrong and Kid Ory, but her performing career was being sabotaged by destructive personal habits. Arrested several times on narcotics charges, her cabaret card was revoked. Cabaret cards, New York police licenses, were required of artists performing where liquor was sold. For twelve years after her ten-month term for drug possession at the Federal Women's Reformatory at Alderson, West Virginia, she was not able to work in New York nightclubs.

From 1944 to 1950 Holiday recorded for Decca, but alcohol and narcotics were destroying her voice and her body. Soon after her last performance in May 1959 she was hospitalized with a kidney ailment. She died not long after being arrested in her hospital bed, perhaps unjustly, on a narcotics charge. She was forty-four.

According to critic Nat Hentoff, "This was a woman who was as deeply pervasive an influence on jazz singing as Louis Armstrong and CHARLIE PARKER were on jazz instrumental playing."

BIBLIOGRAPHY

Chilton, J., *Billie's Blues: The Billie Holiday Story, 1933–1959,* 1975; Holiday, B., and W. Duffy, *Lady Sings the Blues,* 1956; James, B., *Billie Holiday,* 1984.

Holly, Buddy

(September 7, 1936–February 3, 1959)
Rock and Roll Singer

Buddy Holly's music, like the music of another Texan, ROY ORBISON, has a clear connection to traditional songwriting. Out of the same influences that shaped the music of other rock pioneers, Holly created deceptively simple melodies and a distinctive, remarkably well-crafted sound.

Born Charles Hardin Holley in Lubbock, Texas, Buddy was the fourth and last child of fundamentalist Baptists Lawrence and Ella Holley. He studied piano at eleven and, nine months later, gave it up for the guitar. When his last name was misspelled in 1956 on his first recording contract, Holly never corrected it.

While still a junior at Lubbock High School, Holly and a friend played often for KDAV, a country music station in Lubbock. "I could see right away that Buddy had it," announcer "Hipockets" Duncan said, especially the "determination to develop [his] talent." Holly's vocal style, inspired by country singer HANK WILLIAMS and the blues of MUDDY WATERS and HOWLIN' WOLF, hints, too, at bluegrass, rhythm and blues, and gospel. By 1955 Holly was listening to ELVIS PRESLEY over radio station KSEL.

In 1956, as Holly's style coalesced, he got his first big break: a recording contract with Decca in Nashville, Tennessee. Backing him for the audition were Sonny Curtis (guitar), Don Guess (bass guitar), and Jerry Allison (drums). Though the Decca recordings included some lively Holly originals, such as "Changing All Those Changes," the performances were unpolished.

Not until 1957, after Holly and his group, now called the Crickets, had been dropped by Decca, did the ensemble hit its stride. Taken up by Norman Petty in Clovis, New Mexico, ninety miles west of Lubbock, the Crickets began to record for Petty's Coral/Brunswick. The first single, "That'll Be the Day," was a hit. Next came an album, *The Chirping Crickets*. Critic Greil Marcus calls it "the most fully realized rock album of the era." Two other Holly songs reached the top ten in 1957: "Oh Boy!" and "Peggy Sue." Holly made many other recordings before he died near Mason City, Iowa, the victim of a plane crash in February 1959. The recordings were issued posthumously.

Holly was lionized after his death. The Cricket style was clear, clean, and accessible. Cheerful melodies masked the fervor of word and beat and on "That'll Be the Day," "I'm Looking for Someone to Love," and "Maybe Baby" Holly is personal, witty, inventive as he shifts quickly from one emotion to another. His melodic lines, punctuated by excursions into falsetto, seem exuberant and free.

Holly sang of the ordinary as he quietly broke new ground in rock and roll. He was the first to use strings and vocal double-tracking, and his was the first white rock group to appear at Harlem's Apollo Theater. In 1969 Lillian Roxon wrote:

> [He] was one of the giants of early rock . . . it is impossible to hear a song on the charts today that does not owe something to the tall, slim, bespectacled boy from Lubbock, Texas. . . . More than any other singer . . . he brings back a time when music was fun.

BIBLIOGRAPHY

Goldrosen, J., *Buddy Holly: His Life and Music,* rep., 1979; Goldrosen, J., and J. Beecher, *Remembering Buddy,* 1987.

Holmes, Oliver Wendell

(August 29, 1809–October 7, 1894)
Essayist, Novelist, Physician, Poet

Oliver Wendell Holmes wrote essays, fiction, and verse best exemplified by his book *The Autocrat of the Breakfast Table*. Learned and witty, pointed yet genial, his discourses ranged from the sciences to religion and society, engaging his readers and urging them always toward reason and good sense.

Holmes was born in Cambridge, Massachusetts, the son of a Congregational minister. He was educated at Phillips Academy in Andover, Massachusetts, and at Harvard University, from which he graduated in 1829. After pursuing law for a year, he switched to medicine, studying first in Paris and then at Harvard University, where he earned his M.D. in 1836.

Holmes's poetry first captured the imaginations of many with the publication of "Old Ironsides" in the Boston *Daily Advertiser* on September 16, 1830. This lament against the planned destruction of the *Constitution*, the famous frigate from the War of 1812, was reprinted around the country and stirred public sentiment to such an extent that the ship was preserved.

By the time Holmes had earned his medical degree, he had published two volumes of verse, *The Harbinger: A May-Gift* (1833) and *Poems* (1836). His wit is evident in such poems as "The Height of the Ridiculous," "The Ballad of the Oysterman," "To an Insect," and "Contentment." Holmes wrote his famous poem "The Last Leaf" after spotting Major Thomas Melville, the grandfather of HERMAN MELVILLE and reputedly a participant in the Boston Tea Party, during walks about the streets of Boston.

Holmes established his medical career, first as a teacher at Dartmouth College, then at Harvard, where he eventually became dean of the medical school. He was both an active practitioner and an avid researcher. His 1843 paper "The Contagiousness of Puerperal Fever" advocated personal hygiene to physicians in the days before Louis Pasteur and Joseph Lister. He collected many of his medical papers into three volumes, *Boylston Prize Dissertations* (1838), *Homeopathy and Its Kindred Delusions* (1842), and *Medical Essays, 1842–1882* (1883).

If Holmes had found little time to write nonmedical prose during medical school and the years he spent establishing his career, in 1857 he hit upon the idea of recording his own talk. Holmes was a brilliant conversationalist, who liked to hold forth on a wide range of topics. *The Autocrat of the Breakfast Table* began as a series in the *Atlantic Monthly* in 1857 and was published as a book the following year. Its dialogue takes place around the breakfast table at a boarding house, and a number of characters participate. The autocrat demonstrates a fondness for epigrams ("Put not your trust in money, but put your money in trust") and occasionally recites verse, including two of Holmes's best-known poems, "The Deacon's Masterpiece" and "The Chambered Nautilus." Holmes continued the "autocrat" series with *The Professor at the Breakfast Table* (1859), *The Poet at the Breakfast Table* (1872), and *Over the Tea Cups* (1891).

By nature a conservative and by experience a member of elite Boston society, Holmes seldom used his writing to undermine established institutions or values. However, he believed strongly in the power of human reason, and he rebelled against religious dogmatism, particularly his own Puritan heritage. "The Deacon's Masterpiece, or, the Wonderful 'One-Hoss Shay'" pokes fun at a clergyman who builds a chaise (carriage) he thinks will last forever; like the Calvinism it represents, the "shay" finally breaks down all at once. As a religious image, Holmes preferred "The Chambered Nautilus": like the human soul, the sea creature makes its shell larger as it grows.

As the "autocrat" demonstrates, Holmes had an ironic sense of his own social position. In his first novel, *Elsie Venner* (1861), he described the cultured, old-moneyed elite as the "Brahmin Caste of Boston"; the coinage "Boston Brahmin" is still commonly heard.

Holmes's three novels, *Elsie Venner* (1861), *The Guardian Angel* (1867), and *A Mortal Antipathy* (1885), address such matters as free will and the influence of heredity on behavior. Each explores a neurosis; Holmes jokingly referred to them as his "medicated" novels.

An extremely popular writer, Holmes remained closely allied for years with the *Atlantic Monthly*. In fact, his friend JAMES RUSSELL LOWELL accepted the editorship of the publication on condition that Holmes contribute regularly. In all the magazine published sixty-five Holmes poems, all three novels, and four "autocrat" series—at least one major contribution every year until 1893, the year before Holmes's death at age eighty-five. His son, Oliver Wendell Holmes, Jr., later became an associate justice of the U.S. Supreme Court.

BIBLIOGRAPHY

Hoyt, Edwin P., *The Improper Bostonian*, 1979; Morse, John T., Jr., *Life and Letters of Oliver Wendell Holmes*, 2 vols., 1896; Tilton, Eleanor M., *Amiable Autocrat: A Biography of Oliver Wendell Holmes*, 1947.

Homer, Winslow

(February 24, 1836–September 29, 1910)
Illustrator, Painter

Largely self-taught, Winslow Homer developed his own naturalistic style for his wood engravings and paintings that ranged in subject from Civil War battle scenes to children playing and from landscape to seascape.

Homer was born in Boston. When he was six years old, his father, a prosperous hardware merchant, moved the family to nearby Cambridge, which was then a country village. Homer's mother was an amateur painter, and by the time he was eleven, Winslow was drawing sketches and illustrating his schoolbooks. His father bought him a set of lithographs of heads, eyes, ears, and noses and also a set of animals. When he was nineteen, he began an apprenticeship to a lithographer in Boston, where he stayed two years and did commercial artwork—which he hated—including covers for sheet music, playing cards, posters, and portraits of members of the Massachusetts state senate. During this time a French wood engraver gave him a little instruction in drawing on woodblocks for engraving.

After he finished his apprenticeship with the lithographer in 1857, Homer set up a studio and began free-lancing. He did some work for *Ballou's Pictorial* and sent drawings to *Harper's Weekly*. In 1859 he moved to New York and set up a studio. He went to night classes at the National Academy of Design and for a short time took painting lessons from a French artist named Frédéric Rondel.

In 1861, *Harper's Weekly* commissioned him to go to Washington to draw scenes of Abraham Lincoln's inauguration, and later to cover pictorially the Civil War in Virginia. He did drawings of battles at Yorktown and Chicahominy, as well as camp scenes and army life. (He continued to send drawings to

Harper's Weekly until 1874.) Back in New York, he painted pictures based on his sketches in the field. Among them are *The Army of the Potomac—A Sharpshooter on Picket Duty* (1862), *The Last Goose at Yorktown* (1863), and the finest of his war paintings, *Prisoners from the Front* (1866), in which a young Union officer faces three shabby but dignified Confederate prisoners. Homer used a naturalistic style, rendering his subjects accurately and objectively in superbly composed pictures.

Library of Congress

He traveled in France in 1867 and returned to New York, where he painted steadily, exhibiting his work at the National Academy of Design. Now he was painting landscapes and scenes of country life like *Snap the Whip* (1872), which shows schoolchildren playing at recess, and *The Croquet Game* (1866). These pictures provide a valuable record of life in rural America in the nineteenth century. Homer sold an occasional oil painting for $200, a paltry sum when compared with the $20,000 that famous painters like ALBERT BIERSTADT and FREDERIC CHURCH sometimes received.

In 1873 Homer turned seriously to watercolor, which he liked because he could work swiftly to capture light and colors on his brief trips out of New York City for hunting and fishing. His watercolors were popular and sold steadily, providing Homer with a small income so that he could at last give up his magazine work.

In 1881 and 1882 Homer spent two seasons in Tynemouth, an English fishing port on the North Sea. He used mostly watercolors to depict the fishermen and the wives who worked beside them, mending nets and carrying baskets of fish. His painting changed as it showed a new emotion, a stronger color sense, and a feeling for atmosphere and the water. *Watching the Tempest* and *Perils of the Sea*, both painted in 1881, belong to this period.

In 1883 when he was only forty-eight, Homer retired to Prouts Neck, a rocky promontory in the town of Scarboro on the Maine coast, where his father and brothers had bought property. He lived and worked in a small cottage that faced the sea. In the summer, when his nephews and nieces came, the place was lively, but he was alone in the wintertime. Homer was happy there in spite of the solitude. He had found in the sea the subject he most wanted to paint, and he observed and painted it in all kinds of weather, even during storms and squalls. He even built a small, portable wooden studio that he could move about the beach to paint the sea from different viewpoints. In *Northeaster* (1893), for example, one of the best-known pictures from Prouts Neck, the stormy ocean beats against the rocks and foams up into billows. Another is *Eight Bells* (1886), which shows two slicker-clad seamen on deck using a sextant, while wind batters their oilskins.

In 1885 Homer began spending winters in Florida, the Bahamas, Nassau, or Cuba, where he painted superb tropical scenes. His haunting *Gulf Stream* (1899) is a scene of danger and suspense in spite of the brilliant blue sky and the sparkling waters of the Caribbean. A young black man waits in a boat, which has lost its mast, for what must be certain death, since sharks follow the drifting boat.

Homer's work became popular before he died in 1910. Art historian John Wilmerding has written: "Winslow Homer was a special artist.... Though he was affected by the artistic currents of his century, he never imitated or borrowed directly. His stature as a painter increased to the end of his life."

BIBLIOGRAPHY

Cikovsky, Nicolai, *Winslow Homer*, 1990; Hendricks, Gordon, *The Life and Work of Winslow Homer*, 1979; Judge, Mary, *Winslow Homer*, 1986; Wilmerding, John, *Winslow Homer*, 1972.

Hood, Raymond Mathewson

(March 21, 1881–August 15, 1934)
Architect

Raymond Hood was an architect who first excelled at the Late Gothic Revival style, but also made his mark as a designer of modern skyscrapers in New York City between 1924 and 1931.

Hood was born in Pawtucket, Rhode Island, the son of a prosperous box manufacturer. He earned a degree in architecture from the Massachusetts Institute of Technology in 1903, choosing for his senior thesis topic "A Design for a Parish Church in the Gothic Style." He went to work in the Boston office of Cram, Goodhue & Ferguson, the country's leading Gothic Revival designers (see RALPH ADAMS CRAM and BERTRAM GOODHUE).

In 1905 he went to Paris to study at the Ecole des Beaux-Arts, where he received his diploma in 1910, after winning the *Prix Cavel* in 1910 for a Gothic design. Back in America, Hood worked for an architect in Pittsburgh for three years.

He opened his own office in New York in 1914 and endured eight years of struggle and disappointment. Prospects improved when he designed additions to the Hotel DuPont in Wilmington and Mori's Restaurant in New York.

In 1922, John Mead Howells asked him to join him in the great international competition to design the *Chicago Tribune* building in Chicago, one of the most significant events in the history of American architecture. Their entry won first prize and the commission to design the new building. The second-place winner was ELIEL SAARINEN. The *Chicago Tribune* building (1922–1925) was ornamented with Late Gothic detail that echoed what Hood had used in his design for the *Prix Cavel* competition in Paris.

Hood designed the American Radiator Building (1924) in New York, with walls of black brick rising to a crown of gold terracotta. The building was a modernized, abstracted Gothic. He was involved in the design of a number of Gothic buildings after that: Bethany Union Church in Chicago (1926), the McCormick Mausoleum in Winnebago, Illinois (1927), and the Masonic Temple and Scottish Rite Cathedral in Scranton, Pennsylvania (1926–1929).

Hood began to question the validity of using earlier styles for the present day. The next two buildings with which he was involved were the Beaux-Arts Apartments (1930–1931) and the *Daily News* building (1929–1931) in New York City, neither of which had a single traditional detail. In the Beaux-Arts Apartments, a band of white brick horizontally underlines the windows. The *Daily News* building, considered Hood's masterpiece, is a modern skyscraper with setbacks from street to tower between vertical strips of windows and piers of white brick.

The McGraw-Hill building (1931) in New York, clad with blue-green paint and terracotta tiles and horizontal bands of windows, was, despite its unusual color, considered an example of the International style in the 1932 exhibit of that name at the Museum of Modern Art.

Hood was one of eight architects who collaborated on plans for Rockefeller Center, one of the first attempts at multiblock commercial development in New York City, and his influence is visible in the center's RCA Building (1933).

Hood continued to work until 1933, when he suffered a breakdown. He died the next year at his home in Stamford, Connecticut, of heart disease.

BIBLIOGRAPHY

Stern, Robert A. M., *Raymond Hood*, 1982.

Hopper, Edward

(July 22, 1882–May 15, 1967)
Painter

Edward Hopper, a leading American figurative painter, was distinguished for his subjects of solitary figures in urban settings and spare interiors. He is the poet of the everyday, of the prosaic, of the melancholy of the modern world, and the encroachments upon the individual by modern industrialization.

He was born in 1882 in Nyack, New York, and showed an early propensity for drawing and painting. His parents did not object to his becoming an artist, but they urged him to consider the practical life of a commercial illustrator. After graduating from high school in 1899, he moved to New York City and oscillated between painting and illustration, studying at the Correspondence School of Illustrating and the New York School of Art. In the latter institution, through the influences of the painter/illustrators John Sloan and ROBERT HENRI, he forged the great themes of his entire career. Sloan and Henri were heirs to the tradition of realism that had been recently inculcated into American painting by THOMAS EAKINS, Thomas Anshutz, and the younger group of New York painters that came to be known as the Ashcan school (see ROBERT HENRI). This was a spirit of the direct and unsentimentalized observation of the modern-day world, of the details of the raw and the ordinary. At the same time, the growing conflict between old world culture and industrialization, between urban sprawl and the isolated individual, was a growing concern. In his trips to Paris between 1906 and 1910, Hopper further confirmed these attitudes when he encountered in the paintings of Charles Méryon and Edouard Manet a preoccupation with railroads and other aspects of industrialization.

Back in New York, Hopper had his first one-man exhibition at the Whitney Studio Club in January 1920. It was a milestone in his career and propelled him toward the fame he would enjoy throughout the remaining years of his life. (The Whitney Museum now houses a substantial collection of Hopper's work.) During the 1920s Hopper kept himself removed from European movements, concentrating on the American scene and its contrasts between conservative stasis and progressive growth. He supported himself as a commercial artist, his images of a prosperous, corporate America appearing in the pages of magazines like *Profitable Advertising: The Magazine of Publicity* and *Wells Fargo Messenger*. Although Hopper later dismissed his illustrative work, historian Gail Levin has pointed out that these images prefigured many of the subjects, moods, and compositions of his so-called serious paintings, which he painstakingly crafted in his spare time.

As compared to the optimism and power of the urban imagery of his contemporary Joseph Stella, Hopper during these years emphasized the unheroic and the banal. His etchings and canvases depicted the prosaic, lonely lives of women in tenements (*Evening Wind*, 1921; *Eleven A.M.*, 1926), the encroachment on rural landscapes by the railroad (*Railroad Crossing*, 1923; *House by the Railroad*, 1925), the late-night desolation of shops and cafés (*Automat*, 1927; *Drugstore*, 1927), and the empty night streets of the city (*Night Shadows*, 1921; *The City*, 1927). Few artists have rivaled his sensitivity to the new artificial light sources of neon and fluorescence. Indeed, a later image like *Nighthawks* (1942) is just as much a document of the peculiar quality of artificial lighting as it is a commentary on the "night owls" of the late-night streets. These images shared an affinity both with the hard-boiled fiction of DASHIELL HAMMETT (just emerging in the mid-1920s) and with the German Expressionist cinema currently being imported into American theaters. They also prefigured the great film noir period in the 1940s of American émigré filmmakers like Fritz Lang, Curt Siodmak, Edward Dmytryk, and Anthony Mann.

In the 1930s and 1940s, after purchasing an automobile, Hopper began to document another important aspect of the passing scene—the growth of tourism, of motels, gas stations, and highways. *Hotel Room* (1931), *Gas* (1940), *Rooms for Tourists* (1945), and *Western Motel* (1957), for example, chronicled the diminution of the American landscape that had been glorified a hundred years earlier by the Hudson River school of painters (see THOMAS COLE). These works, claims biographer Robert Hobbs, connect Hopper to a later generation of artists in the 1960s, like Pop artists ANDY WARHOL and CLAES OLDENBURG, New Realists Richard Estes and Ralph Goings, and Earthworks artist ROBERT SMITHSON, who likewise documented the "nonspaces" of modern world motels and featureless highways.

Hopper's realism is not as objective as it seems. He suggested moods without illustrating them. In his billfold he always carried a statement by the German artist/poet/philosopher Goethe: "The beginning of the end of all literary activity is the reproduction of the world that surrounds me by means of the world that is in me. All things being grasped, related, re-created, loaded, and reconstructed in a personal form, in an original manner." Hopper himself noted in 1953 that his art "is the outward expression of an inner life in the artist, and this inner life will result in his personal vision of the world." Thus, in most of his work is the ambiguity between object and interpretation, between illustration and painting—an ambiguity that, suggests Hobbs, can be compared to "a still in a film that the viewer helps to direct.... His work remains a question mark, and what it does not permit us to know is as important as what it does."

Hopper led a private life, participating in few of the artists' claques and movements of the day. His life seems to have revolved entirely around his art and his wife, Jo, who also served as his female model. He was an imposing figure, well over six feet, stubborn and taciturn, conveying an almost monklike aura. Yet most of his works revealed a vital, if repressed sensuousness. His images of women were frequently quite erotic and theatrical; indeed, the dual portrait of him and his wife, painted near the end of his life in 1965, was entitled *Two Comedians*. The couple, "two small figures out of pantomime," as Jo Hopper put it, were depicted bowing from the proscenium to an unseen crowd. Life indeed had its dramatic moments and artificial poses; Hopper, reclusive as he was, was a most willing participant and telling observer.

BIBLIOGRAPHY

Hobbs, Robert, *Edward Hopper*, 1987; Levin, Gail, *Edward Hopper as Illustrator*, 1979.

Howells, William Dean

(March 1, 1837–May 11, 1920)
Critic, Novelist, Playwright, Poet

William Dean Howells, best remembered for *The Rise of Silas Lapham*, remained a prolific writer over six decades. Through his fiction, in his criticism, and by his influence as editor of the *Atlantic*, he championed realism in American fiction.

Howells was born in Martins Ferry, Ohio, raised in a succession of Ohio towns, and schooled sporadically. The son of a newspaperman, he began contributing poems and stories to Ohio newspapers at the age of fifteen.

In 1851 Howells went to work for the *Ohio State Journal*. By the age of twenty-three he had published *Poems of Two Friends* with John J. Piatt and a campaign biography, *Lives and Speeches of Abraham Lincoln and Hannibal Hamlin*, with J. L. Hayes.

To thank Howells for writing his biography, President Lincoln appointed the author U.S. consul in Venice in 1860. He spent the Civil War years there and wrote a series of travel letters to the Boston *Daily Advertiser* that were later collected as *Venetian Life* (1866).

The latter book's success earned him a slot as an editor at the *Atlantic* magazine, of which he became editor in chief in 1871. Over the course of a decade at the *Atlantic*, Howells published work by such established writers as JAMES RUSSELL LOWELL, RALPH WALDO EMERSON, and HENRY WADSWORTH LONGFELLOW. He also encouraged new writers, especially HENRY JAMES and MARK TWAIN.

Howells developed a theory of realistic fiction, in part to promote the work of James and Twain, which he expounded in essays and reviews and employed himself in his autobiographical first novel, *Their Wedding Journey* (1872). He wrote about commonplace events, frequently using a journey to frame the narrative, in such novels as *A Chance Acquaintance* (1873), *A Foregone Conclusion* (1874), and *The Lady of the Aroostook* (1879).

With *The Undiscovered Country* (1880), Howells began to broaden the scope of his fiction, seeking a moral vision that could comprehend the loss of traditional religion in the post-Darwinian era. *A Modern Instance* (1882), which examines the failure of a marriage due to a lack of moral discipline, is an early example of what has been called social realism. *The Rise of Silas Lapham* (1885) tracks the ascendance of an entrepreneur who finally recognizes his own ruthlessness and ruins himself financially by rejecting unethical business practices.

Having departed the *Atlantic*, Howells began to ·contribute a column, the "Editor's Study," to *Harper's Weekly* in 1886. Influenced in part by reading the work of the Russian fiction writer Leo Tolstoy, Howells adopted a strong liberalism. He helped lead the effort that obtained a belated pardon, on grounds of improper judicial process, for three of eight anarchists convicted of having thrown a bomb during the Haymarket Square riot in Chicago in 1886. Howells's cautious radicalism was reflected in *A Hazard of New Fortunes* (1890), which examines the tensions between a wealthy magazine publisher and his staff after the editor refuses to fire a staff member who has declared himself a radical. In *A Traveler from Altruria* (1894), the author offered a view of America's social and economic shortcomings through the eyes of a visitor from a utopian land.

After 1894, Howells's social agenda seemed tamer. He continued to write fiction, including *The Landlord at Lion's Head* (1897), *The Kentons* (1902), *The Son of Royal Langbrith* (1904), and his last, *The Leatherwood God* (1916).

In all, Howells wrote thirty-five novels, eight story collections, thirty-five plays, five books of poetry, six books of criticism, and thirty-four miscellaneous volumes. Noteworthy volumes include *Suburban Sketches* (essays, 1871), *Criticism and Fiction* (1891), *Stops of Various Quills* (poems, 1895), *My Literary Passions* (1895), *Literary Friends and Acquaintance* (1900), *Heroines of Fiction* (two vols., 1901), and *My Mark Twain* (1910).

BIBLIOGRAPHY

Howells, William Dean, *Years of My Youth*, 1916; Lynn, Kenneth S., *William Dean Howells: An American Life*, 1971; Wagenknecht, Edward, *William Dean Howells: The Friendly Eye*, 1969.

Howlin' Wolf

(June 10, 1910–January 10, 1976)
Blues Singer, Guitarist, Harmonica Player

Raised on Mississippi Delta blues, Howlin' Wolf took his music to Memphis and Chicago after World War II. His band's strident amplified sound and his showmanship electrified urban audiences with a screaming, driving style that foreshadowed rock and roll and affected musicians in the United States and England.

Chester Arthur Burnett, later known as Howlin' Wolf because of his ferocious delivery, was born in Aberdeen, near West Point, Mississippi. He arrived at the Delta's Dockery Farms in 1926. The Dockery, known for fair dealing and good jobs, was a prosperous plantation near Cleveland, Mississippi. Charley Patton, "the most celebrated bluesman in the vicinity," according to blues chronicler Robert Palmer, was in the area and "Dockery's and nearby towns like Cleveland, Drew, and Ruleville [were known] all over Mississippi . . . as the place one went to learn to play the blues."

Patton "started me off playing," Wolf told interviewer Peter Welding in the mid-1960s. "He took a liking to me, and I asked him would he learn me, and at night, after I'd get off work, I'd go and hang around." When Wolf made his first recording in Memphis, it was "Saddle My Pony," after Patton's standard, "Pony Blues." Patton's original was striking for its dense, layered rhythmic devices that were rooted in West African drumming.

During the mid-1930s Wolf was a sometime road partner to veteran Delta bluesmen, but mostly he was a farmer and part-time musician. In 1948, after a stint in the armed forces during World War II, he went to West Memphis, Arkansas. Thirty-eight, still playing Patton's pieces and one-chord drone numbers, he had decided to become a professional musician. He bought an electric guitar, established a band, and found a radio show as showcase.

By 1950 Wolf's group became "the most awesome electric blues band the Delta had seen," says Palmer, one that "perfectly mirrored the dialogue between tradition and innovation that was beginning to transform the Delta's music. As Wolf "strutted and howled . . . [the] band rocked," says Palmer.

Wolf's Memphis recording, "Moanin' at Midnight," and its flip side, "How Many More Years?" soared in the ratings. In 1952 Wolf settled in Chicago. He worked in clubs where MUDDY WATERS played, and the two became rivals. In 1956 the successful "Smokestack Lightnin'" was issued, just as rock and roll was coming into its own.

Rock musicians listened and learned from Wolf's recordings. Memphis guitarist Paul Burlison, who had worked at Crown Electric Company with ELVIS PRESLEY, recorded "The Train Kept A-Rollin'" with the Rock and Roll Trio. Burlison sounds quite like Wolf's sideman, Willie Johnson, on the recording. In England, guitarist Mike Green modeled his style after Burlison's and himself influenced a younger generation of guitarists, including Eric Clapton.

"Wolf was the most exciting blues player I've ever seen," says Palmer. "He was a huge hulk of a man, but he advanced across the stage in sudden bursts of speed . . . lunged for the microphone, blew a chorus of raw, heavily rhythmic harmonica, and began moaning. He had the hugest voice I have ever heard . . . and when he hummed and moaned in falsetto, every hair on your neck crackled with electricity." Despite several heart attacks, Wolf continued to perform. He died of cancer in Hines, Illinois, in 1976.

BIBLIOGRAPHY

Guralnick, P., *Feel Like Goin' Home,* 1971; Palmer, R., *Deep Blues,* 1981.

Hughes, James Langston

(February 1, 1902–May 22, 1967)
Novelist, Playwright, Poet, Short-Story Writer

Langston Hughes wrote poetry, fiction, and plays that were meant to capture the essence of the black experience in America over five decades. A prolific writer of rare versatility, he wrote for the men and women he saw struggling first for survival and then for equality from the 1920s through the 1960s.

Born in Joplin, Missouri, Hughes was raised in Lawrence, Kansas, and Cleveland. After a year spent in Mexico with his father, he entered Columbia University in 1921, though he withdrew the following year.

Library of Congress

For four years, Hughes worked at odd jobs on board ship and abroad, while his verse began to appear in magazines. In 1926 he enrolled at Lincoln University, near Philadelphia. By the time of his graduation in 1929, he had published two volumes of verse, *The Weary Blues* (1926) and *Fine Clothes to the Jew* (1927), that earned him a reputation among the writers and artists of the African American cultural movement known as the Harlem Renaissance. He published his first novel, *Not Without Laughter,* in 1930.

Hughes's interest in music is evident from his first book of poetry. Hughes took the blues and blues musicians as his subjects and incorporated blues lyrics into the structure of *The Weary Blues'* title poem. Over the course of his career, Hughes experimented with verse forms drawn from the lyric structures of the blues, bebop, progressive jazz, and gospel. He regarded music as the most representative element of black culture; the body of his poetry traces its evolution.

Hughes was an important voice of racial protest, as well as black affirmation. His politics evolved as times changed, but he held fast to a belief in the black popular imagination, and he wrote for the broadest audience possible.

Hughes graduated from college just as the Great Depression hit, and the suffering he witnessed radicalized him. Furthermore, visits to Haiti and Cuba convinced him that the United States had acted as an imperialistic power in the Caribbean. In 1932 he left for a year in the Soviet Union, where he assisted with a film about race relations in America and wrote some of his most radical poetry. The short stories collected in *The Ways of White Folks* (1934) reflect his growing anger.

The late 1930s saw the production of a host of Hughes's plays, including most prominently *Mulatto*, a tragedy about interbreeding among races, which ran on Broadway in 1935 (and was produced in a musical version called *The Barrier* in 1950). Other Hughes plays produced in these years were *Little Ham* (1935), *Joy to My Soul* (1937), and *The Organizer* (1939). His play *Don't You Want to Be Free?* was the first production of the Harlem Suitcase Theatre, founded by Hughes in 1938.

Hughes's politics eventually grew less strident, and he wrote radio scripts supporting the U.S. role in World War II. In 1942 he began writing a column for the African American weekly newspaper *Chicago Defender*. He introduced the character of Jesse B. Semple (nicknamed Simple), a black, urban working man whose shrewd humor filled the column for twenty years. Hughes eventually filled five volumes with sketches based on these columns,

beginning with *Simple Speaks His Mind* (1950).

Street Scene, originally a play by Elmer Rice (1929), was turned into a musical with lyrics by Hughes and music by the composer KURT WEILL. It opened on Broadway in 1947 and became a great success. Hughes bought a house in Harlem and began producing the books for a number of musicals, including *Simply Heavenly* (1957), *Esther* (1957), and *Port Town* (1960). His plays *Black Nativity* (1961) and *Jerico-Jim Crow* (1963) incorporated gospel music.

Hughes wrote several more volumes of verse, including *Fields of Wonder* (1947) and *One-Way Ticket* (1949). His *Montage of a Dream Deferred* (1951) and *Ask Your Mama* (1961) took their forms from jazz; the latter was written for musical accompaniment. *The Panther and the Lash* (1967) reflects Hughes's growing support for the black militants active in the civil rights struggle in the United States in the late 1960s.

Hughes also produced two more collections of short stories, *Laughing to Keep from Crying* (1952) and *Something in Common* (1963); another novel, *Tambourines to Glory* (1958); a history of the National Association for the Advancement of Colored People, *Fight for Freedom* (1962); and several books of fiction and nonfiction for children.

BIBLIOGRAPHY

Hughes, Langston, *The Big Sea*, 1940, and *I Wonder as I Wander*, 1956; Meltzer, Milton, *Langston Hughes: A Biography*, 1968; Rampersad, Arnold, *The Life of Langston Hughes*, 2 vols., 1986, 1988.

Hunt, William Morris

(March 31, 1824–September 8, 1879)
Painter

William Morris Hunt, brother of Richard Morris Hunt, the architect, was a painter of outdoor scenes, an art teacher, and a cultural leader in Boston.

William Morris Hunt was born in Brattleboro, Vermont, the son of a judge and member of Congress. Hunt learned to draw at an early age, and his first teacher was an Italian artist. He entered Harvard, but left in his third year and never finished college.

His mother, who was interested in art, took him to France and to Rome for his health. In 1845 he enrolled at the academy of art in Düsseldorf, Germany, where the teachers insisted on meticulous drawing. Finding the Düsseldorf system too rigid, he went to Paris, where he studied under Thomas Couture and soon became his best pupil. Hunt's work was so much like Couture's that one of his paintings, *The Jewess* (1850), was mistaken for the work of his master.

In Paris, Hunt admired the work of Jean François Millet, one of the Barbizon painters, who believed in direct study of nature and worked in the little town of Barbizon near the forest of Fontainebleau. Hunt went to see Millet, and they became friends. Millet was painting softly modeled pictures of rural scenes and peasant life. His painting methods and philosophy of art made a powerful impression on the young American and influenced his work for the rest of his life. Hunt, too, worked at Fontainebleau and bought several of Millet's paintings.

Hunt returned to America in 1855 and lived in Brattleboro, Newport, and the Azores, before settling down eventually in Boston in 1862. Unfortunately, his studio on Sumner Street was in the path of the fire that swept Boston in 1872, and many of Hunt's pictures as well as his collection of Barbizon paintings were destroyed. Saved were a few of Millet's pictures, which Hunt had hung in his home on Beacon Street.

When he returned to painting, Hunt used more brilliant colors. He is best known for his atmospheric out-of-door paintings like *Ball Players* and *The Bathers*, both done in 1877. He also painted a number of notable portraits, including one in 1871 of Francis Gardner, master of the Boston Latin School. A critic at the time said that his portraits were better than the work of JOHN SINGLETON COPLEY or GILBERT STUART.

Hunt married Louisa Dumaresq Perkins and they were part of Boston society, with Hunt well known, respected, and sought after. He helped find buyers for pictures by the Barbizon painters and opened a successful art school. Among his pupils were the painter John La Farge, the sculptor DANIEL CHESTER FRENCH, the novelist HENRY JAMES, and James's brother, the psychologist and philosopher William James. Hunt urged Boston's aspiring young artists to study in France instead of Germany, and after his ideas on art education developed, he published a book, *Talks on Art*, in 1875. Hunt said he felt like a missionary among the heathen whose ignorance and indifference irritated him. He was never happy.

Hunt received his most important commission in 1875, to paint two murals for the Assembly Chamber of the New York State Capitol in Albany. His two paintings, *The Flight of Night* and *The Discoverer*, which were each fifteen by forty-five feet, were applied directly to the stone walls. Much admired at the time that they were painted, the murals were soon ruined by dampness.

When he was fifty-five, Hunt drowned in an ocean pool in the Isles of Shoals, off the New Hampshire coast. His death is considered a suicide.

BIBLIOGRAPHY

Hoppin, Martha J., *William Morris Hunt: A Memorial Exhibition*, 1979; Vose, Robert C., *The Return of William Moris Hunt*, 1986; Webster, Sally, *William Morris Hunt, 1824–1879*, 1991.

Inge, William Motter

(May 3, 1913–June 10, 1973)
Novelist, Playwright

William Inge, a successful dramatist of the 1950s, was arguably this country's first authentic midwestern playwright. He won a Pulitzer Prize for *Picnic* and an Academy Award for his screenplay of *Splendor in the Grass*.

William Inge's small-town midwestern childhood was to become the stuff of his most successful plays. Six of his seven major plays were set in the Midwest, specifically in small towns populated by repressed, unhappy, and unfulfilled characters. "The Midwest helped to form me as a person," he wrote in 1967, "giving me my background, my storehouse of subject matter, helping in the creation of my viewpoints and philosophy."

Inge was born in 1913 in Independence, Kansas, the son of an overprotective mother and a traveling salesman who was usually absent. Shy and something of a "momma's boy," he was teased at school and, as an escape, found outlets for his energies in high school acting. In 1930 he enrolled at the University of Kansas, where he studied drama and continued acting. Uncertain of the risks in an acting career, however, he turned his back on the theater to study for his teaching degree. While on the faculty of Stephens College in Columbia, Missouri, as fate would have it, he worked closely with the famous actress Maude Adams, then in retirement. Once again, he began to consider a career in the theater. As a drama critic for the St. Louis *Star-Times* in 1945, he met TENNESSEE WILLIAMS, fresh from his recent success with *The Glass Menagerie*. Williams encouraged Inge to write and within a year his first play was completed, *Farther Off from Heaven*. It was staged in an amateur production in Dallas, and immediately Inge wrote more plays. *Come Back, Little Sheba* (1950) was produced in New York by the Theatre Guild, and Inge was able to leave his teaching duties forever.

A decade of critical and popular success followed. Despite a growing problem with alcoholism and sexual ambivalence, Inge successfully wrought out of his small-town experiences and lonely sensibilities those works for which he is best known. *Come Back, Little Sheba* told of the unhappy marriage of an alcoholic man and his faded, daydreaming wife. *Picnic* (1953), which won a Pulitzer Prize, was a portrait of a small Kansas town whose various sexually repressed female characters are affected by the advent of a handsome young stranger. *Bus Stop* (1955) throws together a rather unlikely pair of strangers who have been stranded by a blizzard, a lovesick cowboy and a tawdry singer. *The Dark at the Top of the Stairs* (1957) was a rewrite of *Farther Off from Heaven*, and its depiction of a dysfunctional family makes it Inge's most autobiographical play.

When Inge lost much of the money he had earned by backing his first Broadway failure, *A Loss of Roses* (1959), another Kansas play, he retreated, hurt, and headed for Hollywood. At first, all went well. ELIA KAZAN, who had directed *The Dark at the Top of the Stairs* in New York, encouraged him to write screenplays. Inge produced an original script derived from his one-act play, *Glory in the Flower*, and retitled it *Splendor in the Grass*. It was a story about an ill-starred romantic couple in a Kansas town. Kazan directed it, and in 1961 it won Inge an Academy Award for Best Original Screenplay. But he was dissatisfied with later screenplays: *That Hill Girl*, *All Fall Down*, and *Bus Riley's Back in Town* (for which he demanded his name be removed from the credits). His last Broadway efforts, *Natural Affection* (1963) and *Where's Daddy?* (1966), were critical and popular disasters.

Inge's last years were spent working in theater workshops at the University of California at Los Angeles while he lived a virtual recluse with his sister, Helene Inge Connell. He committed suicide in 1973. The epigraph from his autobiographical novel, *My Son Is a Splendid Driver* (1971), was sadly apt: "Woe to those who do not know their own misery and woe to those who love this wretched and corruptible life."

BIBLIOGRAPHY

Shumey, Robert Baird, *William Inge*, rev., 1989; Voss, Ralph, *A Life of William Inge*, 1989.

Inness, George

(May 1, 1825–August 3, 1894)
Painter

George Inness, one of the most productive American nineteenth-century landscape painters, worked in his later years to fuse the spiritual with the real world in his pictures.

Inness was born on a farm near Newburgh, New York, the son of a prosperous New York City merchant, and grew up in a country home outside Newark, New Jersey, then a quiet, leafy town. Although he suffered from epilepsy and did not do well in school, he was ambitious and strong-willed and resolved to become a painter. His father disapproved and gave him a grocery store in Newark to run when he was only fourteen. He set up an easel and painted behind the counter, hiding when customers came in.

Relenting, his father paid for drawing lessons with an itinerant painter, John Jesse Barker, who soon announced that he had taught young Inness all he knew. When he was sixteen, Inness worked for two years for Sherman and Smith, New York map engravers, studied with Régis François Gignoux, a French landscape painter who was working in New York, and began to sell his pictures.

Inness was interested in the work of Asher Durand and THOMAS COLE, members of the Hudson River school of landscape painters, and at first he worked directly from nature. After he set up his own studio in New York, he paid for meals at the Astor House Hotel with his pictures. His first painting to be exhibited (at the National Academy of Design) was an 1844 landscape. It showed wooded hills, open fields, a stream with a bridge, cattle, sheep, horse and rider, and a red barn—everything. Although it was not masterly, it looked real and won modest praise.

An auctioneer bought several of Inness's early pictures and provided him with the money to study abroad in 1851. In 1853 he returned to France, where the paintings by Corot, Rousseau, and Daubigny—French members of the Barbizon school who believed in painting landscape in the open air—impressed Inness. Back in the United States, he settled in Medfield, Massachusetts, for five years, a productive period. His style changed as he left behind the careful rendition of exact details and took up a broader, stronger technique. He did many landscape paintings of different seasons and at different times of day.

In 1870 Inness returned to Italy and France for five years. Back in this country, he spent a year in Boston, two years in New York, and finally, in 1878, settled down in an old house in Montclair, New Jersey. Inness was no longer a disciple of any school or group of painters, and refused to follow formulas, as he continued to grow and develop in his own way.

He did, however, fall under the spell of Emanuel Swedenborg, a Swedish mystic and philosopher, reading many volumes of his work. His painting became richer and looser, glowing with light, as he tried to convey a mystical view of nature in his pictures. In the dark and brooding *Coming Storm* (1879), for instance, cows stand in a river and a rainbow arches overhead. It is similar in composition to the detailed, straightforward versions of *Delaware Water Gap* he had painted in 1861, but the light and emotional effect are entirely different and more impressive.

After 1880 his painting became even stronger. He painted nature as he envisioned it in his imagination, almost never working outdoors nor making preliminary sketches. Inness scorned the Impressionists, who insisted on painting directly from nature. Although he sketched outdoors, he returned to his studio to paint scenes over and over again. His paintings became more and more abstract and ethereal in his last years.

He continued to paint the same subject over and over in different versions, some of them frenzied and almost abstract. Sometimes he would finish a picture, then paint a completely different picture on top of it. He painted as many as twenty-five pictures on one canvas.

Inness cared very little for money and left economic worries to his patron, Ogden Haggerty, other collectors, his own brothers, and various art dealers. In the 1870s Thomas B. Clarke bought thirty-nine paintings from Inness and started a trend. Other rich collectors bought his work, and Inness made more money than any other landscape painter living. Critics called him America's finest painter.

He died of heart disease while he was on a trip to Scotland for his health. His body was brought back to the United States and his funeral held at the National Academy of Design. "George Inness's landscapes are the best painted in our time and country, in many instances the best painted in any time or country," wrote a critic in the Boston *Transcript* at the time of his death.

BIBLIOGRAPHY

Cikovsky, Nicolai, *The Life and Work of George Inness,* 1978; Inness, George, Jr., *Art and Letters of George Inness,* 1917; Werner, Alfred, *Inness' Landscapes,* 1973.

Irving, Washington

(April 3, 1783–November 28, 1859)
Biographer, Essayist, Fiction Writer, Humorist

Washington Irving's stories and sketches made him the first American writer with an international reputation as a man of letters. His two best-known pieces, "Rip Van Winkle" and "The Legend of Sleepy Hollow," became legends and are the first fully developed examples of the American short story.

Born in New York City into a large family, Irving had little formal schooling. At age sixteen, he began to study law, and in 1801 he was apprenticed to a lawyer. He worked at this vocation until 1804, when ill health interrupted

and he began a two-year visit to Europe. He passed the bar examinations upon his return, but repeated attempts by his family to set him up in practice failed.

Irving's first published writings appeared in the New York *Morning Chronicle,* which was edited by his brother Peter. The essays, under the pen name Jonathan Oldstyle, Gent., satirized local theater and customs.

With his brother William and their friend James Kirke Paulding, Irving published twenty issues of a humorous periodical, *Salmagundi,* in 1807. Modeled on such English periodicals as the *Spectator* by James Addison and Sir Richard Steele, *Salmagundi* was less ironic and more farcical in its presentation. Its essays were directed at "the conduct of the world," politics, the performing arts, and society.

Irving subsequently published *A History of New York* (1809) under the pseudonym Diedrich Knickerbocker. This burlesque relates the history of the colony of New Netherlands through the eyes of an addled old man who wishes his forebears to be seen as heroes but reveals them to be often venal, greedy, and dishonest.

Library of Congress

Irving later revised the book several times, trying to improve the structure and reform the blunt language, but he never recreated the book's youthful comic energy.

Over the next decade, Irving divided his time between the family hardware business and his literary efforts. He served briefly in the War of 1812. From 1813 to 1815 he edited the *Analectic Magazine.* In 1815 he traveled to England to represent the family business there, not planning an extended stay, though he would remain abroad for seventeen years.

After the collapse of the family business in 1818, Irving gave more of his energy again to his writing. While in England, he met the romantic novelist Sir Walter Scott, whom he admired and sought to emulate.

In 1819 and 1820 Irving published *The Sketch Book of Geoffrey Crayon, Gent.*, a collection of stories and sketches, which offers scenes drawn from Irving's childhood in the Hudson Valley, as well as a tourist's eye view of England and its heritage. Its two best-known stories, "Rip Van Winkle" and "The Legend of Sleepy Hollow," are German folktales Irving transplanted to settings in the Hudson Valley.

The title character in "Rip Van Winkle" is a henpecked husband who seeks relief by roaming the wilderness. He encounters the ghosts of Henry Hudson's crew, who offer him a drink that puts him to sleep for twenty years. He wakes up as an old man to find a world changed by the American Revolution; he must somehow settle into a bustling new way of life.

"The Legend of Sleepy Hollow" concerns Ichabod Crane, a calculating, unimaginative schoolmaster. Crane's foil is Brom Bones, a hearty frontiersman. Knowing Crane to be superstitious, Bones costumes himself as the headless horseman and runs Crane out of town. Bones's hoax frees him to marry the girl both men admired.

His reputation at its peak, Irving remained in Europe for twelve more years, trying to continue the success he enjoyed with *The Sketch Book.* In 1822 he published *Bracebridge Hall,* a collection of stories that was in part a sequel to *The Sketch Book.* In 1824 he brought out *Tales of a Traveller,* but its sales were disappointing and its critical reception even worse.

Worried about his finances, Irving accepted an invitation by the U.S. ambassador to Spain, Alexander Hill Everett, to join the American legation in Madrid. Irving's studies there resulted in three historical accounts: *History of the Life and Voyages of Columbus* (1828), *A Chronicle of the Conquest of Granada* (1829), and *The Companions of Columbus* (1831). He also wrote *The Alhambra* (1832), his most successful attempt to rework the formula behind *The Sketch Book.*

Irving returned to the United States in 1832. In 1834 the Astor family commissioned him to write an account of John Jacob Astor's success in the fur trade, *Astoria* (1836). While at Astor's house, he met the Northwest explorer Benjamin Louis Eulalie de Bonneville, whose story he subsequently published as *The Adventures of Captain Bonneville* (1837).

In 1842 Irving accepted an appointment from President John Tyler as minister to Spain, a post he held for four years. Upon his return to Sunnyside, his estate on the Hudson near Tarrytown, New York, he revised his *Life of Oliver Goldsmith* (1849) and wrote a two-volume biography, *Mahomet and His Successors* (1850). These were followed by a collection of essays, *Chronicles of Wolfert's Roost and Other Papers* (1855).

Irving spent his final years hard at work on a five-volume *Life of George Washington* (1855–1859), the final piece of which was published just weeks before his death on November 28, 1859.

BIBLIOGRAPHY

Bowden, Mary Weatherspoon, *Washington Irving*, 1981; Leary, Lewis, *Washington Irving*, 1963; Williams, Stanley T., *The Life of Washington Irving*, 2 vols., 1935.

Ives, Charles Edward

(October 20, 1874–May 19, 1954)
Composer

Charles Ives, for many people the quintessential American composer, wrote some two hundred songs, four symphonies, two major piano sonatas, and many smaller works. His innovations anticipated those of ARNOLD SCHOENBERG and IGOR STRAVINSKY and fashioned a surprising new musical language from familiar popular materials.

Charles Edward Ives was born in Danbury, Connecticut, the son of George E. Ives and Mary Elizabeth Parmelee. Ives's father knew his Bach and counterpoint and after service as a bandmaster during the Civil War, returned to Danbury, where he taught theory and instruments and led local choirs, orchestras, and bands.

George Ives, always fascinated with the possibilities of sound, held unconventional musical views. Charles Ives remembered that his father "thought that man as a rule didn't use the faculties that the Creator had given him hard enough . . . he would have us sing a tune in E flat, but play the accompaniment in C . . . he made us stick to the end, and not stop when it got hard."

These lessons were not wasted. Ives's sketches, found in his father's old copybook, include fugues in four keys that prefigure his later dissonances. At twelve Charles Ives was composing and playing in his father's band, and at fourteen he was hired as organist at the Danbury Baptist Church. The Danbury *News* noted, October 2, 1888, that Ives was the youngest organist in the state.

In 1891 Ives attended Danbury Academy and in 1893, New Haven's Hopkins Grammar School. That May he became organist at St. Thomas Episcopal Church in New Haven. He entered Yale in the fall of 1894 and took the organist's job at Center Church in New Haven, where he worked with choirmaster John Cornelius Griggs. After George Ives died November 4, 1894, it was Griggs who encouraged Charles Ives's composing.

Ives graduated from Yale in 1898 with a mediocre academic record, moved to New York, and went into the insurance business. At the same time, he became organist at the First Presbyterian Church in Bloomfield, New Jersey, and then at Central Presbyterian Church in New York. In 1901 Ives finished the Second Symphony and *From the Steeples and the Mountains* (for bells, trumpet, and trombone). After his cantata, *The Celestial Country,* was performed at the church in 1902, he resigned so that he could devote more time to composing.

In 1905 Ives met Harmony Twichell of Hartford; they married in 1908. In 1906 Ives began to have heart trouble. His double life as businessman and composer was exacting a toll. Meantime Ives and Julian Myrick, who became a lifelong friend, formed a successful partnership in insurance. Ives and his wife bought property in West Redding, Connecticut, in 1912, and Ives continued to compose, transforming his admiration for the New England Transcendentalists into works like the *Concord* Sonata for piano (1910–1915), the *First Orchestral Set: Three Places in New England* (1908–1914), and *The Fourth of July* (1911–1913).

Ives felt deeply about World War I. Songs of the period reflect his concern. He was involved, too, in fund drives for the Red Cross and Liberty Loan, and suggested issuing small bonds to encourage support from the general public. After a severe heart attack in 1918, he took a year to recuperate. During this time he organized his songs. They were eventually privately printed in 1922 and issued as *114 Songs.* By 1923 he was working on his quarter-tone piano pieces (for two pianos tuned one quarter tone apart). Plagued by recurring heart troubles, he resigned from his very successful insurance business January 1, 1930.

Soon a few enterprising musicians were beginning to perform Ives's compositions in the United States and abroad. Hubert Linscott and AARON COPLAND performed seven songs at the first festival to be held at the Yaddo artists' colony in Saratoga Springs, New York, in May 1932, and John Kirkpatrick played the *Concord* Sonata in 1939, drawing admiration from critic Lawrence Gilman, who judged it "the greatest music by an American." Charles Ives was awarded a Pulitzer Prize in 1947 following a performance of the Third Symphony, which, according to his practice, he did not attend. He died of a stroke in New York City in 1954.

Ives, the democrat, a quintessential New Englander, was steeped in the Transcendentalists and shared their belief in individualism and in the harmony of nature. His music took root in recalled boyhood sounds: bands, fiddlers, hymn tunes, parlor ballads, patriotic songs. Thanks to his father's iconoclasm and inquiring mind, Ives was free enough of European tradition to write down what he heard, from off-key renditions of hymns to multiple marching bands competing for attention in holiday parades. The result was an explosive new vernacular musical language—dissonances, polyrhythms, tone clusters, polyharmonies—that paralleled and usually predated the innovations of composers abroad. Biographers Henry and Sidney Cowell point out that "Ives can, in fact, be shown to be one of the four great creative figures in music of the first half of the twentieth century. The others are Schoenberg, Stravinsky, and Bartok."

BIBLIOGRAPHY

Cowell, H., and S. Cowell, *Charles Ives and His Music,* 1955; Perlis, V., *Charles Ives Remembered: An Oral History,* 1974.

Jackson, Mahalia

(October 26, 1911–January 27, 1972)
Singer

Mahalia Jackson's majestic contralto, commanding presence, and deep emotion drew the world's attention and helped establish gospel music as a distinct genre. Her singing style was inspired by great blues artists like BESSIE SMITH and Ma Rainey, as well as by the idioms of black church music.

Born in New Orleans to a family of devout Baptists, Mahalia Jackson grew up poor. Though she sang in the Baptist choir, she was attracted to the more spontaneous music of the Holiness Church (an evangelical sect) and to the sounds of blues and jazz. The recordings of Ma Rainey, Mamie Smith, and Bessie Smith were especially influential, though Mahalia listened to them secretly; the blues were considered the devil's work by strict Baptists.

Jackson left school in the eighth grade and in 1927 headed north. In Chicago she worked as a domestic to support herself and became a lead singer in the Greater Salem Baptist Church choir. The pastor's son, Robert Johnson, with his brothers Price and Wilbur, Louise Barry Lemon (soprano), and Mahalia, formed the Johnson Gospel Singers, perhaps the first professional gospel group. The Johnson Singers toured in the early 1930s, but by mid-decade the group dissolved.

Mahalia began to be recognized on her own, and in 1937 Decca recorded her. Though her voice lacks the richness of later years, nonetheless a distinctive style is present, as in "God's Gonna Separate the Wheat from the Tares," adapted from the New Orleans wakes she knew so well. Elements of the later Jackson are found, too, in "Keep Me Every Day," a Baptist hymn, and in a new gospel tune, "God Shall Wipe All Tears Away."

In the early 1940s Jackson toured with Thomas A. Dorsey, composer and former accompanist of Bessie Smith and Ma Rainey. By 1945 she was known in gospel churches for her rich contralto voice and her spirited style. In 1946 she signed with Apollo Records and produced some powerful recordings, including the very popular "Move On Up a Little Higher." This hit record crowned Mahalia Jackson the Gospel Queen. Writer Anthony Heilbut says, "The spiritual depth of Mahalia's best hymns has seldom been surpassed. Together with her jubilant shouts, they made her a towering force in gospel's greatest era." A 1949 recording, "Let the Power of the Holy Ghost Fall on Me," won the French Academy's Grand Prix du Disque.

Studs Terkel, the Chicago journalist, began to feature Jackson on his local TV program in 1950 and that year she toured Europe. By 1954 she appeared on her own radio and TV programs. Now too high priced for black churches, she performed mostly for whites. In 1958 she sang at the Newport Jazz Festival and recorded DUKE ELLINGTON's *Black, Brown, and Beige* with his orchestra. Some thought she had sold out to show business, but the reality was she always sang in a religious context and never performed in nightclubs.

Jackson sang for President Eisenhower's birthday in 1959, at John F. Kennedy's inauguration in 1961, and at the funeral of her friend, Martin Luther King, Jr., in 1968. In late 1971 she interrupted a European tour because of illness. She died in Chicago, January 27, 1972. There were two funeral services: one in Chicago, one in New Orleans.

BIBLIOGRAPHY

Goreau, L., *Just Mahalia, Baby*, 1975; Heilbut, A., *The Gospel Sound: Good News and Bad Times*, 1971, rev., 1985; Jackson, M., and E. M. Wylie, *Movin' On Up*, 1966.

James, Henry, Jr.

(April 15, 1843–February 28, 1916)
Critic, Novelist, Short-Story Writer

A prolific writer, Henry James is best known for his early fiction, *Daisy Miller* and *The Portrait of a Lady*. However, the narrative techniques and the themes of his later novels—concerning the choices made by individuals who feel constrained by circumstance—profoundly influenced twentieth-century fiction.

Henry James, Jr., was born in New York City, the grandson of one of the nation's first millionaires. His father, Henry James, Sr., devoted his life to the study of religion and philosophy. James's older brother, William, was to become a well-known psychologist and philosopher.

James was raised in New York and educated largely by private tutors. At the age of twelve, he joined his family in a three-year sojourn in Europe, enjoying the cultural riches of Paris, Geneva, and London.

In 1860, encouraged by a friend, the painter John La Farge, James undertook some literary translations from the French, though they were rejected for publication. In 1862 he entered Harvard Law School, but he spent most of his year there reading fiction. He began to publish fiction and essays in such magazines as *The Nation* and the *Atlantic Monthly*, whose editor, WILLIAM DEAN HOWELLS, became a lifelong friend.

In 1869 James made his first solo trip to Europe. The cultural wonders of Florence, Venice, and Rome deeply affected him. He

Library of Congress

wrote travel essays and stories that were full of descriptive detail.

During his absence, James lost a cousin, Minny Temple, to tuberculosis. He had worshiped her, and their friendship was as close as he ever got to a serious romantic involvement. Minny would appear in his fiction in the heroines of *The Portrait of a Lady* (1881) and *The Wings of the Dove* (1902).

James returned to Cambridge, Massachusetts, and wrote his first novel, *Watch and Ward* (1871), which was serialized in the *Atlantic*. During a second trip abroad, beginning in 1872, he started *Roderick Hudson* (1875), the story of an expatriate American artist in Rome.

Believing that Europe offered a cultural milieu he needed as a writer, James moved there in 1875, settling first in Paris, where he came to know the novelists Guy de Maupassant, Gustave Flaubert, and Ivan Turgenev. The following year, he moved permanently to England, staying twenty years in London.

An international theme runs through much of James's fiction. He enjoyed juxtaposing European and American characters and dealt frequently with the problems faced by American expatriates living abroad. In particular, he contrasted the American dream of freedom for the individual with a more European ideal of social accommodation. Two early novels that dealt directly with cultural tensions between the continents were *The American* (1877) and *The Europeans* (1878).

James achieved his first great popular success with his long story *Daisy Miller.* An American innocent abroad, Daisy horrifies the American colony in Rome with her inattention to local customs and social norms. She dies of fever, in part as a result of her insistence on traveling where and when she pleased.

The novel generally acknowledged to be the greatest of James's early period is *The Portrait of a Lady.* Romantic, naive Isabel Archer leaves her native Albany, New York, in the company of a sophisticated aunt, bound for Europe. There she is pursued by suitors from England, Italy, and the United States. When her uncle leaves her a small fortune, Isabel feels free to set the course her life will take, and she marries Gilbert Osmond, an expatriate living in Italy. This disastrous choice has in fact been engineered by Madame Merle, her aunt's friend and Osmond's lover. It leads finally to self-knowledge and resignation on Isabel's part. As a psychological portrait of Isabel, the novel prefigured much of James's later work. Isabel's long meditation on her husband and his lover in chapter 42 represented a milestone in the development of stream-of-consciousness technique.

In *The Bostonians* (1886), James's only major work set entirely in the United States, the author presents Verena Tarrant, a beautiful and sensitive young woman, who is influenced by the determined feminist Olive Chancellor. Olive hopes she has molded Verena after herself, but Verena finds greater satisfaction with a husband and family. James called it "a tale very characteristic of our social conditions." American critics, especially Bostonians, attacked it severely. *The Princess Casamassima* (1886) concerns a more violent activism. Hyacinth Robinson, a revolutionary increasingly troubled by the poverty he sees in London, contemplates an assassination but ends his own life instead.

In the early 1880s, James made two trips to the United States associated with the final illnesses of his parents. These were to be his only visits to his native land for twenty years. In 1898 he purchased Lamb House in Sussex, England, where he would live out the rest of his days.

The Tragic Muse (1890) represents a turning point in James's prose style, which became increasingly elaborate. The story of a young man who rejects a life of wealth and social standing for that of an artist, it also reflects James's frustrations as a writer in society.

The lack of commercial success of these last three novels inspired James to write for the theater. His experiments as a playwright failed miserably, however, and so proved only a short-lived diversion. Returning to fiction, James brought a new theatricality to such works as *The Spoils of Poynton* (1897), *What Maisie Knew* (1897), and *The Turn of the Screw* (1898), the most popular of them all.

Three major novels written just after the turn of the century seem to many critics to represent James's finest work. James himself thought *The Ambassadors* (1903) his best. The novel concerns Chad Newsome's refusal to return to Massachusetts from Paris and his French mistress in order to manage the family business for his widowed mother. His mother sends an emissary, her own fiancé, Lambert Strether, to bring Chad home. However, when Strether sees that Chad has matured under the influence of Madame de Vionnet, he feels reluctant to disturb him and even suggests "Live all you can; it's a mistake not to." The reader comes to understand the nature of Chad's love affair as Strether does, yet even as its more scandalous aspects reveal themselves, Strether's advice seems fitting.

The Wings of the Dove (1902) tells the story of an American heiress, Milly Theale, who journeys to Europe and there meets a couple who conspire against her fortune. Merton Densher courts Milly, whom he knows to have a fatal illness, planning to marry her and inherit her wealth. Milly discovers the plot but bequeaths her money to Densher anyway. Her generosity changes his heart, and Densher refuses the inheritance, causing a split with his lover, Kate Croy.

James's most difficult book, *The Golden Bowl* (1904), recounts the marital exploits of a wealthy American father and daughter. Maggie Verver marries an Italian, Prince Amerigo, who nonetheless continues an affair with Maggie's best friend, Charlotte Stant. Charlotte marries Maggie's father, Adam Verver. In order to preserve appearances, the characters endlessly deny they know what is happening, until Adam takes Charlotte back to the United States to manage his art collection.

James traveled to the United States in 1904, staying almost a year. Upon his return to England, he revised his works into the comprehensive New York Edition (twenty-six volumes, 1907–1917), adding prefaces that offered important insights into the craft of fiction.

Plagued by ill health in his later years, James nonetheless completed two volumes of autobiography, *A Small Boy and Others* (1913) and *Notes of a Son and Brother* (1914). With the outbreak of World War I, James found himself unable to finish a last, major novel, *The Ivory Tower.*

James became a British citizen in 1915 as a token of support for the war effort. He died in London in 1916.

BIBLIOGRAPHY

Dupee, Frederick W., *Henry James*, rev., 1956, and *Henry James, Autobiography*, 1983; Edel, Leon, *Henry James*, 5 vols., 1953–1972, rev., 1 vol., 1985.

Jarrell, Randall

(May 6, 1914–October 14, 1965)
Critic, Novelist, Poet

Randall Jarrell is best known for his World War II poetry, in which he delves into the hearts of men who fought and died, and for his witty criticism of the modern poets. The poet ROBERT LOWELL once said: "His gifts, both by nature and by a lifetime of hard dedication and growth, were wit, pathos, and brilliance of intelligence."

Jarrell was born in 1914 to working-class parents in Nashville, Tennessee. In 1915 the family moved to Long Beach, California, but in 1925 Jarrell's mother separated from his father and moved back to Nashville. Later, an uncle paid to send Jarrell to Vanderbilt University, where he earned a B.S. in 1936 and an M.A. in 1939.

At Vanderbilt, Jarrell studied under JOHN CROWE RANSOM. In 1937 he followed Ransom from Vanderbilt to Kenyon College and roomed at Ransom's house with Robert Lowell, an undergraduate transfer from Harvard University who took his degree in 1940 and published the first of many volumes of poetry four years later.

In 1939 Jarrell took a teaching job at the University of Texas at Austin. There he met his first wife, Mackie Langham, who had just earned her M.A. They were married in 1940.

Jarrell's first independent volume, *Blood for a Stranger* (1942), contains a number of poems that address the deteriorating political situation leading toward World War II. In 1942, Jarrell enlisted in the U.S. Army Air Force and was sent to Wichita Falls, Texas, for aviation training. Failing to make the grade as a pilot, he became a celestial-navigation instructor.

His volumes *Little Friend, Little Friend* (1945) and *Losses* (1948) both drew on his military experiences, often dealing with stark subjects in intentionally bitter tones. Typically, the poems impose a careful metric structure—often iambic pentameter—on the sounds of American speech. In a number of the poems, Jarrell takes on the personas of war dead who seek to understand the reasons for their deaths. His "The Death of the Ball Turret Gunner" concludes with an unforgettable line:

"When I died they washed me out of the turret with a hose."

In 1946 Jarrell won a reviewing slot for *The Nation* magazine and a part-time teaching job at Sarah Lawrence College in Bronxville, New York. In 1947 he took a faculty position at the Woman's College, later the University of North Carolina at Greensboro. In his teaching and criticism, he promoted poetry that took as its subject matter people's commonplace experiences, especially the work of WALT WHITMAN, ROBERT FROST, WILLIAM CARLOS WILLIAMS, and MARIANNE MOORE.

The Seven-League Crutches (1951) includes a number of poems based on fairy tales, as well as translations from the German poet Rainer Maria Rilke. Jarrell also began the practice of "translating" visual art into poetry, taking as his first subject a work by Albrecht Dürer, the sixteenth-century German painter and engraver.

In the summer of 1951, while teaching at the University of Colorado, Jarrell met Mary von Schrader, an aspiring novelist. He divorced Mackie Langham and married von Schrader in 1952.

Jarrell's first book of criticism, *Poetry and the Age*, was published in 1953. In addition to two influential general essays—"The Obscurity of the Poet" and "The Age of Criticism"—he included pieces on Whitman, WALLACE STEVENS, Moore, Williams, Robert Lowell, and Robert Frost.

Pictures from an Institution (1954), a comedic novel drawn from Jarrell's experience at Sarah Lawrence, comprises a collection of portraits of academic character types. Some critics read it as a reply to MARY MCCARTHY's popular novel on the same subject, *The Groves of Academe* (1952). But Jarrell became worried that he was losing his ability to write poetry: "A bad fairy has turned me into a prose writer," he complained.

In 1956 Jarrell was appointed poetry consultant at the Library of Congress, a position he held for two years. "The Woman at the Washington Zoo," considered by many to be his best poem, came from the experience of "driving to work through Rock Creek Park, past the zoo." The poem, a monologue from the perspective of the central character, reflects on the loneliness of life in the middle class. The woman laments: "so / To my bed, so to my grave, with no / Complaints, no comment. . . . / The world goes by my cage and never sees me." The poem became the title poem in a collection published in 1960, which earned Jarrell a National Book Award in 1961.

A collection of essays on literature, art, and modern culture, *A Sad Heart at the Supermarket* (1962), addresses such themes as "The Intellectual in America" and "The Taste of the Age" and includes a detailed analysis of his own poem, "The Woman at the Washington Zoo," which reveals even more about Jarrell than his subject.

Jarrell translated a number of Grimm's fairy tales, including "Snow-White" and "The Fisherman's Wife," for a collection for children. His editor was so pleased that he suggested Jarrell attempt a children's book. Jarrell wrote *The Gingerbread Rabbit* and *The Bat-Poet*, both published in 1964, and *Fly By Night*, published posthumously in 1976.

Inspired by the return of letters he had written to his mother during a happy summer-long visit to his paternal grandparents at the age of twelve, Jarrell wrote a flood of poems for *The Lost World* (1965). A number of these revisit the fantasies of childhood; others impose an adult awareness over the child's.

The last year of Jarrell's life was very difficult. He suffered from severe depression complicated by adverse reactions to mood-elevating drugs. At one point, he was hospitalized against his will, diagnosed as manic-depressive. He became suicidal. Finally, off the drugs, he recovered sufficiently to return home, but he was struck by a car and killed walking alone at night on a country highway.

BIBLIOGRAPHY

Ferguson, Suzanne, *The Poetry of Randall Jarrell*, 1971; Pritchard, William H., *Randall Jarrell: A Literary Life*, 1990.

Jefferson, Thomas

(April 13, 1743–July 4, 1826)
Architect, Statesman

Thomas Jefferson, the third president of the United States, was one of the country's leading amateur architects. He popularized the neoclassical style and designed the University of Virginia, which was designated by the American Institute of Architects in 1976 as the greatest architectural creation of the nation's first 200 years.

The son of a prominent Virginia planter, Jefferson graduated from the College of William and Mary in 1762, received his law degree in 1767, and practiced law until 1774. In 1776 he penned the Declaration of Independence, then served as governor of Virginia (1779–1781). He wrote two of the most influential works of the age, a natural history titled *Notes on Virginia* and the *Statute of Virginia for Religious Freedom*.

During these years as lawyer, statesman, and author, Jefferson also pursued his love of the arts—painting, music, sculpture, and especially architecture. Well read in architectural theory and practice, he was a keen observer of buildings as he traveled at home and abroad. He felt that architecture had a social and political purpose in addition to its aesthetic and practical aspects. A beautiful building that embodied the nation's cultural values would serve to reinforce the country's ideals, improve the taste of its citizens, and garner the world's admiration. He was primarily influenced by ancient Roman buildings, the Italian Renaissance architecture of Palladio, and the eighteenth-century French architecture that he saw while serving as a diplomat, then as ambassador to France (1785–1789). In particular, he loved the ancient Roman temple Maison Carrée, at Nimes, France, using it as the basis for his design for the state capitol building at Richmond, Virginia. The first major neoclassical structure built in America, the capitol reintroduced the use of the temple form for public buildings in the Western world.

While serving as George Washington's secretary of state (1790–1793), Jefferson exerted much influence on the development of the nation's capital in the District of Columbia. He set the standards of quality and performance for design and construction, and initiated the first major architectural competition in the country for plans for the president's house and the Capitol building. In addition, he drew a city plan with ovals and diagonal streets inspired by the formal gardens at Versailles, France. As president (1801–1809), Jefferson continued his involvement with the architectural shaping of the new capital, and appointed architect BENJAMIN LATROBE as surveyor of public buildings.

Jefferson was a self-taught gentleman-architect who never practiced professionally. He said, "Architecture is my delight, and putting up, and pulling down, one of my favorite amusements." One of the best examples of his architectural genius was the evolution of his home, Monticello. His first version, finished in 1782, was an adaptation of Palladio's Roman villa with a 2-story portico. After his sojourn in France, he found Monticello old-fashioned, and redesigned and rebuilt it (1796–1809) to resemble a French pavilion. He gave it the appearance of a 1-story house, with large porticoes and a dome. He also planned the hippodrome-shaped gardens outlined by terraces that hid the underground service rooms (such as kitchen, cellars, stables) and the connecting passageways. His interior design with its polygonal rooms, skylights, bed alcove, and concealed staircases was revolutionary. Monticello was also the first American house to have complete working drawings in the modern definition.

In 1809 Jefferson retired to Monticello, but he soon began work on his crowning architectural achievement—the University of Virginia (completed, 1825). The university has been described as "the lengthened shadow of one man," because Jefferson executed the designs, supervised the construction, obtained financial support, furnished the library, hired the professors, and provided the guiding educational philosophy. Its revolutionary concept and design reflected his personal philosophy: "This institution of my native state, the hobby of my old age, will be based on the illimitable freedom of the human mind to explore and expose every subject susceptible of its contemplation." Designed as a unified academic community, it has a central axis consisting of ten academic pavilions (five on each side of a rectangular lawn) connected by colonnades, the north end of which culminates in a central rotunda. Two parallel rows of dormitories form a second rank of buildings and are surrounded by terraced gardens outlined by low, serpentine brick walls.

The rotunda, patterned after the Pantheon in Rome, was the heart of the university and housed the library, lecture room, the country's first planetarium, and a gymnasium underneath its terraces. Each pavilion had different architectural features, derived from various Roman temples, and each housed a separate discipline, providing a lecture hall and accommodations for the professor and his family.

Jefferson executed some 460 architectural drawings during his lifetime, amassed a large architectural library, and was sought after by friends, officials, and other architects for his advice. The unified, harmonious results of his eclectic method of design paralleled his ability to meld aspects of idealism, rationalism, and romanticism into a personal and national political philosophy.

BIBLIOGRAPHY

Dumas, Malone, *Jefferson and His Time*, 4 vols., 1948–1970; Kimball, Fiske, *Thomas Jefferson: Architect*, 1968; Nichols, Frederick D. (comp.), *Thomas Jefferson's Architectural Drawings*, 4th ed., 1978.

Jewett, Theodora Sarah Orne

(September 3, 1849–June 24, 1909)
Novelist, Short-Story Writer

Believing that an author's locale and experience should be her chief source of material, Sarah Orne Jewett sought to introduce to the rest of the country the inhabitants of her region in Maine during the late eighteenth century. Her novel *The Country of the Pointed Firs* is an American classic.

Born September 3, 1849, Jewett lived out her life in South Berwick, Maine. Her father, a physician, encouraged her interests in observing people and nature and introduced her to English literature. Her first novel, *A Country Doctor* (1884), offers an account of her relationship with her father, drawn from her memories of accompanying him on his rounds. The heroine of the book refuses marriage and becomes a country doctor.

Though her own background was patrician, Jewett felt deeply bound to the seafarers and farmers who made their lives around her. She watched sadly as they lost their way of life: the merchant trade moved to larger harbors such as Boston and New York, men and young people escaped to find work in industrial centers, and summer people invaded the small-town peace. When Jewett began writing in 1866, she evinced a deep reverence for the resourcefulness of her people, not just the brave fishermen and merchant sailors of the past, but the widows and spinsters now living in quiet decrepitude.

Her first book, *Deephaven* (1877), collected sketches published in the *Atlantic Monthly* and depicts life in a Maine seaport. She wrote in the preface that she believed it was important for her to introduce her readers to the inhabitants of her little-known region. Her goal was to elevate local color, or regionalism, to its highest literary level. Her early influences were Harriet Beecher Stowe and Rose Terry Cooke.

Much of Jewett's reputation rests on short stories she wrote from 1885 to 1896, collected in *A White Heron* (1886), *The King of Folly Island* (1888), *Strangers and Wayfarers* (1890), *A Native of Winby* (1893), and *The Life of Nancy* (1895). "A White Heron" may be her best-known story.

Her work culminated in *The Country of the Pointed Firs* (1896). Again a depiction of life in a Maine seaport town, it is a novel without a plot comprised of a number of linked sketches of the characters who have adjusted to economic decay and found a life in harmony with their rugged environment. The women are seen as particularly strong, especially Almira Todd, a widow and an herbalist, who literally draws life from the barren soil.

Jewett's narration is meditative, nostalgic, sometimes ironic. Her narrators offer minute descriptions of both outdoor landscapes and domestic arrangements indoors. She is unusually successful at dialect, managing to suggest both the accents and the rhythms of speech in the region.

Jewett became an active part of Boston literary society. At the home of her good friend Annie Fields, the widow of a well-known publisher, she met many of the nation's great writers. WILLA CATHER, for one, spoke glowingly of the influence Jewett had on her.

Jewett continued writing until 1901. *A Tory Lover,* her last novel, is based on the life of John Paul Jones. An accident in 1902 left her incapacitated. She died in 1909.

BIBLIOGRAPHY

Cary, Richard, *Sarah Orne Jewett*, 1962; Thorp, Margaret Farrand, *Sarah Orne Jewett*, 1966.

Johns, Jasper

(May 15, 1930–   )
Painter

Jasper Johns is a transitional figure between the Abstract Expressionism of the 1950s and the American clichés of Pop art in the 1960s. He is most famous for the *Flag* and *Target* images he has produced throughout his entire career.

Johns was born in 1930 in Augusta, Georgia, and grew up in South Carolina. After a stint in the army, he spent three semesters at the University of South Carolina, Columbia. When he moved to New York City he worked a short while at Bonwit Teller's and Tiffany's, where he met two of the most important influential persons in his life, painter ROBERT RAUSCHENBERG and composer JOHN CAGE.

In 1954 he began the series of images that made him famous—the *Flag, Target,* and *Number* paintings. Throughout the ensuing

decades he has returned again and again to these motifs. "I was concerned," he said, "with the invisibility those images had acquired, and the idea of knowing an image rather than just seeing it out of the corner of your eye." To provoke this reexamination, he varied their essential attributes—color, shape, texture, medium, size, and design elements—providing a contrast between the Pop art (see ROY LICHTENSTEIN) of his subjects and the tactile qualities of Abstract Expressionism (see BARNETT NEWMAN). These images reflected both the anxiety of patriotism during the McCarthy years and the triumph of inflated patriotism during the Eisenhower presidency.

Influenced by the "combine paintings" of Robert Rauschenberg, Johns has worked and reworked his subjects in many media—

encaustic, oil, collage, lithograph, etching, painted bronzes, and assemblages of plaster cast masks and such items as spoons and chairs. *Target with Four Faces* (1955), for example, utilized encaustic and collage on canvas with an arrangement of plaster casts. *Field Painting* (1963–1964), attached to the canvas raised letters, a neon light (controlled by an embedded light switch), an ale can, and a coffee tin. At times he has worked with such precision and neutrality as to transform his canvases into objects in themselves rather than reproductions of those objects. Always fascinated with the attraction between subject and object, percept and concept, he has summed up the critical response to his work in these terms: "Two meanings have been ascribed to these American Flag paintings of mine. One opposition is: 'He's painted a flag so you don't have to think of it as a flag but only as a painting.' The other is: 'You are enabled by the way he has painted it to see it as a flag and not as a painting.'"

In 1958 Johns had his first one-man exhibition—a series of *Flag, Target,* and *Numbers* paintings—at the Leo Castelli Gallery in New York (where he has subsequently exhibited regularly). He became a part of the "Happening" movement with artist Allan Kaprow in 1959 (see GEORGE SEGAL). In that same year he was included in the Museum of Modern Art's "Sixteen Americans." He began working with lithographs in 1960 (*Target*) as well as bronze casts of everyday objects, like coffee cans and beer cans (*Painted Bronze,* 1960). Several other projects included the *O Through 9* series (1959–1979) and the *Watchman* and *Souvenir* series executed in Japan in 1964.

In the 1970s Johns alternated between styles of freely expressionistic brush strokes (like *Voice Two,* 1971), which assimilated his familiar number and letter symbols into a broadly brushed gray field, and works displaying tight linear patterns (*Weeping Women,* 1975).

Comprehensive retrospectives of his work were held at the Jewish Museum in New York in 1964, the Pasadena Art Museum in 1965, the Whitney Museum of American Art in 1977, the Museum Ludwig in Cologne in 1978, and the Seibu Museum of Art in Tokyo that same year. Since 1963 he has been the director of the Foundation for Contemporary Performance Arts, and from 1967 to 1972 he was artistic adviser to the MERCE CUNNINGHAM Dance Company. In 1973 he was elected a member of the National Institute of Arts and Letters, and in 1988 he was awarded the Grand Prix at the Venice Biennale. He presently maintains two residences, in the country outside New York City and in the French Antilles.

As art critic William Gass concisely put it, "Jasper Johns makes artifacts out of artifacts, things from things, and images out of images . . . turning the up-side sideways, and relieving capacities of their natural energies." Commentator David Shapiro wrote: "Johns has had a lover's quarrel with the real. . . . He makes the ordinary unfamiliar and somehow metaphorical. . . . [His] drawings use the imagery of a garbage can lid, a hinge, a hook, a thermometer, and place it in such puzzling and poignant space that it cannot be overlooked." In historian Tilman Osterwold's words, painting, for Johns, "exists in its own right." That is, there is a balance between the topical, conceptual, and factual aspects of the work: "The subject (painting) does not override the object (picture); perception is not colored by emotional or idealistic prejudice, and the picture itself is not an illustration of any kind of idea." In general, like Rauschenberg, Johns has moved away from Abstract Expressionism in pursuit of the exploitation of the everyday images of America.

BIBLIOGRAPHY

Gass, William, "Johns," *The New York Review,* February 2, 1989; Osterwold, Tilman, *Pop Art,* 1991; Shapiro, David, *Jasper Johns: Drawings 1954–1984,* 1984; Stich, Sidra, *Made in U.S.A.: An Americanization in Modern Art,* 1987.

Johnson, Philip Cortelyou

(July 8, 1906–   )
Architect

Philip Johnson has been a dominant figure in American architecture as critic, author, historian, and museum director, as well as a practicing architect. A paradoxical, often idiosyncratic designer and lecturer, Johnson moved from a celebration of the International style through a period of eclectic "decorative" classicism to Post-Modernism.

Johnson was born into a wealthy family in Cleveland, Ohio. He received a degree in classics from Harvard University in 1930. While first director of the department of architecture at New York's Museum of Modern Art (MOMA; 1930–1936), he organized the momentous "Modern Architecture" exhibition and wrote the influential *International Style: Architecture since 1922,* both in collaboration with pioneer architectural historian Henry-Russell Hitchcock (1932). The book defined and promoted a distinct style of modern architecture for which they coined the term "International," describing designs that are simple, functional, and unadorned and that embrace the machine aesthetic by using modern materials like concrete, steel, and glass. Worldwide acceptance of the style would lead to a common architecture, devoid of national or regional traditions. Johnson also authored other important works, such as *Machine Art* (1934) and a 1947 monograph on the pioneering Internationalist LUDWIG MIES VAN DER ROHE, who was his mentor.

After receiving an architectural degree from Harvard in 1943, he served in the army during World War II, then returned to MOMA as director of architecture and industrial design (1946–1954). Articulate, urbane, and witty, he helped develop the museum as a major arbiter of artistic taste, and served as a trustee from 1958 onward. He contributed his own contemporary works to the museum's collections and was the architect of two additions to the museum (1950, 1964) and its sculpture garden (1953).

Johnson's first masterpiece was his own house in New Canaan, Connecticut (1949). Called the Glass House, it is a landmark in postwar architecture and illustrates Mies's principles of a universal space and the primacy of structure. It is a finely proportioned transparent box, steel-framed and glass-walled, sitting templelike in its landscape. During the next four decades the residence was expanded into a multifaceted compound including a guest house, an unusually shaped studio with a conical, chimneyed-shaped skylight, and an underground gallery. The changes to the compound mirror the experimental twists of Johnson's unfolding design style.

Johnson's domestic architecture of the 1950s is Miesian-inspired with a latent neoclassicism (which came to the fore in the 1960s), and is characterized by balance between building and setting, symmetrical design, interior elegance, historical allusions, and elaborate indoor-outdoor lighting. The Roman villa–like Hodgson House (with Landes Gores, 1951) and the Wiley House (1953), both located in New Canaan, exemplify this style.

In New York City, Johnson established a private practice (1954–1964), then a partnership with Richard Foster (1964–1967), and finally a partnership with John Burgee (1967–1983). He collaborated with Mies van der Rohe on New York's Seagram Building in New York (1958), a spectacular International style skyscraper of amber-tinted glass walls articulated by vertical I-beams of extruded bronze. He largely abandoned the International idiom during the 1960s in favor of a more eclectic, "decorative" classicism characterized by monumentality, visual richness, and the use of arches and curvilinear forms and original, often idiosyncratic shapes. In the vanguard of architectural change, Johnson anticipated the widespread shift from the International style by more than a decade. Buildings of this period include the Sheldon

Memorial Art Gallery in Lincoln, Nebraska (1963) and the New York State Theater at Lincoln Center (1964). The epitome of this phase of his evolving career was Boston Public Library's New Wing (with Burgee, 1973) which reflected the academic classicism of the original designer CHARLES FOLLEN MCKIM of McKim, Mead & White and featured broad arches associated with the Romantic Classical tradition of the late eighteenth century.

Johnson's continued distancing from the cool, puritanical International mode can be seen in a series of skyscrapers designed with Burgee. Such multitowered complexes as the Investors Diversified Services Center in Minneapolis (1973) were pivotal in shifting popular taste away from the modernist glass "boxes." Houston's strikingly visual Penzoil Place (1976), with its side-by-side trapezoidal towers crowned by dramatically angled, sliced-off tops, creates a pictorial arrangement that plays an active role in the cityscape.

Johnson's design approach took another turn in the late 1970s when he embraced the architectural past more deliberately. The 37-story AT&T building in New York City (with Burgee, 1978–1983), with its juxtaposition of past ideas and forms with new aspects melded into a whole, became an emblem of Post-Modernism (see MICHAEL GRAVES). The granite-clad, vertically mullioned skyscraper with a colonnaded base, 6-story entrance arch, and a broken pediment at the top evokes the classical New York skyscrapers of the early twentieth century, among other things.

Johnson continues to comment on the diverse trends of contemporary architecture and to explore his own preferences, recently shifting to a style influenced by deconstructivism (taken from a theory of literary criticism, it proposes that meaning is imposed by the viewer, not the designer). In addition, he is consultant to John Burgee Architects.

BIBLIOGRAPHY

Hitchcock, Henry-Russell, *Philip Johnson, Architecture, 1949–1965,* 1966; Jacobus, John, *Philip Johnson,* 1962; Noble, Charles, *Philip Johnson,* 1972; Stern, Robert A. M. (ed.), *Philip Johnson: Writings,* 1978.

Jones, James Earl

(January 17, 1931–)
Actor

James Earl Jones's imposing physical presence, powerful bass voice, and remarkable versatility have made him for over thirty years a solid leading man and character actor on both stage and screen.

Jones was born in Arkabutla, Mississippi, in 1931. His father, Robert Earl Jones, a prize-fighter-turned actor (he appeared as the streetwise Luther in *The Sting,* 1973), abandoned the family before his birth. James was brought up by his maternal grandparents in Manistee, Michigan. A speech impediment became so serious that between the ages of eight and fourteen he was nearly mute; he communicated to his teachers in grade school primarily by writing notes. However, by the time he graduated in 1949, he had successfully overcome the problem.

In 1953, after graduating with a degree in drama from the University of Michigan, he moved to New York City to study acting. From 1957 to 1960 he performed in a succession of bit parts in Off-Broadway productions. A turning point came when he was cast as Deodatus

Village in Jean Genet's *The Blacks* in 1961. It not only brought him plaudits from the critics but a personal revelation about racism: "Through that role, I came to realize that the black man in America is the tragic hero, the Oedipus, the Hamlet, the Macbeth ... even the working-class Willy Loman, the Uncle Tom and Uncle Vanya of contemporary American life."

His association with the New York Shakespeare Festival under JOSEPH PAPP, which began in 1960, resulted in his next career landmark, the title role in *Othello* in the summer of 1964. After taking the role downtown to the Martinique Theatre, he won the Drama Desk–Vernon Rice Award for best Off-Broadway actor of the year.

Jones began to branch out to television and the movies. In 1965 he narrated the television documentary, *Beyond the Blues*. That same year he also became the first African American male to take a continuing role on a daytime television series, *As the World Turns*. In 1970 he brought to the screen his Tony Award–winning role of Jack Jefferson (based on prizefighter Jack Johnson) in *The Great White Hope* (1968). It was his first starring role in films and it won him an Oscar nomination. His subsequent film roles have ranged from a black president of the United States (*The Man*, 1972), to a baseball player (*The Bingo Long Traveling All-Stars and Motor Kings*, 1976), to a tribal chieftain (*Exorcist II:*

The Heretic, 1977), to a soldier in *Gardens of Stone* (1987), and numerous roles as government officials in espionage thrillers like *The Hunt for Red October* (1990) and *Patriot Games* (1992). His deep voice alone won him, uncredited, the "role" of Darth Vader's voice in the *Star Wars* trilogy.

Back on stage in 1987, he won his second Tony for the role of Troy Maxson, a Pittsburgh common laborer, in August Wilson's *Fences*. There was a fury in the performance that was almost frightening. "I often pick [roles] that do less placating than agitating," Jones said at the time. "I like to upset people."

Jones lives in Los Angeles and also keeps a home in upstate New York. Critic Jack Kroll, writing in *Newsweek* in 1968, summed up his abilities: "Jones has a great big technique without the slightest trace of emptiness or inflation. He can expand before your eyes from a flare point of inarticulate feeling to a storm system of emotion."

BIBLIOGRAPHY

Kroll, Jack, "James Earl Jones in *The Great White Hope*," *Newsweek*, October 14, 1968; Pomerantz, Gary, "Emperor Jones," *Southpoint*, May 1990; Sweeney, Louise, "Jones: Awesome Figure Onstage and Off," *Christian Science Monitor*, January 4, 1988.

Joplin, Janis Lyn

(January 19, 1943–October 4, 1970)
Blues and Rock Singer

For many, Janis Joplin was the late sixties. For others, she still represents wild sixties' music and antiestablishment counterculture. A rebel who embraced feminism and the communal values of San Francisco's hippies, Joplin awakened record moguls to the

financial potential of rock and the youth market.

Born in Port Arthur, Texas, Joplin grew up comfortably. Her fascination with folk music and the blues set her apart from her teenage peers early on, for she was listening intently to recordings of HUDDIE LEDBETTER, Odetta, and BESSIE SMITH. At seventeen, clad in jeans and a white shirt, she left home.

Joplin found work as a country and western singer in Houston, and, like so many young people of the time, dreamed and schemed about how to reach California. Once there, she enrolled at a series of small colleges, four in all, sang folk songs, drew unemployment to survive, and in 1965 tried the San Francisco folk scene. Though her singing and remarkable voice with a three-octave range found favor with a few, she didn't earn enough to survive. She spoke later of the experience, "Things got all messed up for me out there."

Joplin returned to Texas in 1966 and took a job as vocalist with a country and western band. By June that year she was back in San Francisco as female vocalist with Big Brother and the Holding Company, a group established in 1965.

Rock was the perfect medium for Joplin. It allowed her to vent her intensity, anger, and frustration and to perform with the kind of frenzied energy that became her signature. When she appeared with Big Brother and the Holding Company at the Monterey Pop Festival in the summer of 1967, she stopped the show with her howls, throaty whispers, and frenetic body language.

The galvanizing Monterey performance led to a contract for the group with BOB DYLAN's manager, Albert Grossman, and in time, to a contract with Columbia Records. *Cheap Thrills,* their first album released by Columbia, climbed to the top spot on the charts in 1968.

That year the group traveled to New York. *The Village Voice* reported on a performance at the Anderson Theater on Second Avenue, "Although not beautiful . . . she sure projects. Janis is a sex symbol in an unlikely package. . . . She jumps and runs and pounces, vibrating the audience with solid sound. The range of her earthy dynamic voice seems almost without limits."

In 1968 Joplin, now a star, organized her own group, the Kozmic Blues Band, with Sam Andrew of the original Big Brother. Her strenuous schedule included performances as featured artist at festivals, on television, and in concert and was relieved only by her increasing dependence on alcohol and drugs.

In 1970 she formed another group, the Full Tilt Boogie Band, and went west to make a new album at Columbia's Hollywood studios. Before the session was completed, she was found in the Landmark Hotel in Hollywood, fresh puncture marks on her arm, dead of an accidental heroin overdose. There were several successful albums issued posthumously, as was the film of her life, *The Rose* (1979), which starred Bette Midler.

BIBLIOGRAPHY

Dalton, D., *Janis,* 1971; Friedman, M., *Buried Alive: The Biography of Janis Joplin,* 1973.

Joplin, Scott

(November 24, 1868–April 1, 1917)
Ragtime Composer/Pianist

After Scott Joplin's "Maple Leaf Rag" was published in 1899, ragtime, an antecedent of jazz, swept the country. Its lilting melodies, anchored by steady bass rhythms, soon had the nation's toes tapping. Joplin, a pioneer in developing the piano rag, is now considered one of the first important American composers.

The turn of the century was a time of great social change in America. Cities were growing, railroads expanding, and in post–Spanish-American War white society, optimism ran high. Not so in black America, where racism and Jim Crow laws were wiping out gains made after the Civil War.

Ragtime probably originated in the Midwest a few years earlier. Its rhythms doubtless had their roots in African music, although its forms were those of traditional European dances. Its displaced accents startled contemporary white listeners, but today the syncopations seem mild. Though a forerunner of jazz, ragtime was distinct from it, for ragtime is written while jazz is improvised.

Scott Joplin, the second of six children of Jiles Joplin, a former slave, grew up poor in the Reconstruction South. Raised in the Texarkana area of Texas, Joplin learned the popular European dances of the day from his violin-playing father and absorbed black music's richness of rhythm and melody through his mother's church.

Joplin was fascinated by the piano, and his mother managed to buy a used instrument for

Bettmann Archive

him. Gaining skill, he played in churches and for social events, gradually gaining a reputation. A local piano teacher taught him to read music and laid the groundwork for studies in composition at the George R. Smith College for Negroes in Sedalia, Missouri, where he enrolled, probably in 1897.

Joplin's father did not approve of music as a career. The subject was a bone of contention, Jiles ever stressing the values of a secure trade. Scott, however, continued on course. With his brother, Willie, he established a vocal group, the Texas Medley Quartette, and went on to sing with them in Texas, Alabama, and Missouri.

Joplin arrived in St. Louis, Missouri, a teeming urban center, in the mid-1880s. Now an itinerant pianist, he settled near the river in an area known for saloons and sporting houses. With St. Louis as base, he traveled in Missouri, to Louisville and Cincinnati, and in 1893 to the World's Columbian Exposition in Chicago. He stayed in Chicago nearly two years and there met and became friends with rag pianist Otis Saunders.

Joplin and Saunders went back to St. Louis in 1894. Two years later they were in Sedalia, Missouri, attracted by opportunities for work in its large red-light district. Playing at Sedalia's Maple Leaf Club changed Joplin's life. There, in 1899, John Stark, a music publisher, was in the audience. Stark heard Joplin play "Maple Leaf Rag" and a contract followed, a plum for a black musician at the time. The piece was a hit, and Joplin was on his way.

Encouraged, Joplin completed a folk-ballet late in 1899, *The Ragtime Dance*. A longer work, it included words and music and notes for dances to be performed, including the ragtime dance, the cakewalk prance, and the slow drag. Joplin financed its performance, but Stark did not publish it until three years later.

Joplin, who had ambitions for black music, went on to try opera. The score for *A Guest of Honor* is lost, though the work is said to have been performed in St. Louis in 1903 by Joplin's touring Ragtime Opera Company. Joplin continued to write rags, too. Some twenty were published between 1899 and 1905, among them "The Entertainer." Fifteen more appeared between 1907 and 1909.

In the 1908 *School of Ragtime*, a self-published instruction book, Joplin states, "Play slowly until you catch the swing, and never play ragtime fast." On sheet music of the period he cautions, "NOTE: Do not play this piece fast. It is never right to play Ragtime fast. Composer."

Joplin went to New York in 1907, breaking with Stark two years later. As biographer Peter

Gammon said of *A Guest of Honor*, "it was chiefly Joplin's obsession with writing a ragtime opera that made the Stark Publishing Company's blood run cold." This time Joplin's second opera, *Treemonisha*, was at the heart of the dispute, even though, as scholar Addison Reed suggests, it was "the culminating achievement of Joplin's life." Underwritten by Joplin it was produced once, in 1915, in Harlem, and failed.

Joplin's dream of creating an opera that presented black music on its own terms was ahead of its time. Joplin had a breakdown, was committed to Manhattan State Hospital, and died in 1917. Honors came posthumously: a 1970s revival of ragtime, rediscovery of Joplin's achievements, and revival of *Treemonisha;* a 1976 Pulitzer Prize for *Treemonisha;* and a commemorative U.S. postage stamp in 1983.

BIBLIOGRAPHY

Blesh, R., and H. Janis, *They All Played Ragtime*, 1950, rev., 1979; Gammon, P., *Scott Joplin and the Ragtime Era*, 1975; Hasse, J. E. (ed.), *Ragtime: Its History, Composers and Music*, 1985.

Judd, Donald

(June 3, 1928–   )
Sculptor

A leading figure of Minimal art, Donald Judd is noted for visually simple, impersonal, objective, and highly undifferentiated sculptures composed of "unexpressive" geometric forms, which he named specific objects. He is also an influential art critic who champions the "art of direct experience," which is objective and aesthetically neutral.

Judd was born in Excelsior Springs, Missouri, and studied art at the College of William and Mary (1948–1949), Columbia University (1949–1953; master's degree, 1962), and the

Art Students League in New York City. A painter during the 1950s, he gradually made the transition to sculpture in the early 1960s, by first creating three-dimensional wall reliefs (see AUGUSTUS SAINT-GAUDENS), then freestanding floor pieces. Early works were rather austere sculptures made of plywood, Masonite, galvanized metal, canvas, and paint, devoid of emotional overtones. By 1963 he was creating boxes from metal, painting them with industrial pigment, and frequently incorporating two Plexiglas sides to reveal the interior. He also began writing criticism for various art magazines, such as *Art News*, and served as contributing editor for *Arts Magazine* from 1959 to 1965.

In 1963 he had his first one-man show at the Green Gallery in New York City, where he established himself as a prominent Minimalist. Reacting against the expressive, personal emotion and the self-revelatory artist-as-creator attitude of the Abstract Expressionists (see BARNETT NEWMAN), the proponents of Minimal art (emerging in the 1950s, primarily in the United States) stressed a "nonart" approach that was impersonal and spectator-oriented, and possessed a minimal amount of "artwork" by the artist. Judd's *Stark* of 1965 exemplifies his aim to create sculptures in which a certain number of geometric volumes occupy "real space," creating a unified effect on the viewer. It is composed of a series of mathematically related, identical solid boxes that are cantilevered from a wall and reach from floor to ceiling, with space between each.

In an article entitled "Specific Objects," Judd maintained that a work of art is defined by its visible material qualities, not by anything else, such as subjective feeling or differentiation (specialized differences or distinctions) imposed by the artist. He stated that "a shape, a volume, a color, a surface is something itself. It shouldn't be concealed as part of a fairly different whole. The shapes and materials shouldn't be altered by their context." For Judd, the artwork itself is the subject. He created works that were holistic or nonrelational in which he rejected the part-whole composition of traditional art.

Judd is also known for a Minimalist style of sculpture called Primary Structures in which he created extremely simplified, geometrically repetitive structures, often using industrially produced elements, to define a new spatial order. An example is *Untitled* (1973), a series of painted cold-rolled steel hollow rectangular frames receding progressively toward a wall. The brilliant color of the light-reflecting steel and the play between color and texture of the interior space and exterior surfaces clarify contours and angles, softening the severity of the well-defined form. His sculptures are characterized by a certain coldness and anonymity, a visual clarity, and an aesthetic neutrality whereby the spectator is presented the "facts" to interpret as desired.

Throughout his career, Judd has served as a visiting artist and taught sculpture at various schools, including Dartmouth College (1966) and Yale University (1967). Since 1970 he has created several large, geometric sculptures for outdoors, designed to correlate with their exhibition spaces. His famous sculpture for the Guggenheim International (1971) is a large, galvanized iron ring with a smaller, tilted ring inside it, which reflects the structure of the museum building itself. In recent years he has focused on fuller integration of his sculptures with their surroundings by using the walls and ceilings of exhibition spaces as structural components of the works, erasing the distinction between object and environment. His 1991 sculpture, *Untitled*, is a square, wall-hung arrangement of boxes made of rusted Cor-Ten steel sides and yellow-enameled rear panels. Judd has also applied the spare, highly original aesthetic of his sculptures to transforming an old Swiss inn on Lake Lucerne into his private retreat (1991).

BIBLIOGRAPHY

Battock, Gregory (ed.), *Minimal Art*, 1968; Johnson, Ken, "Donald Judd at Pace," *Art in America*, December 1991; Muller, Gregoire, "Donald Judd: Ten Years," *Arts Magazine*, February 1973; Rose, Barbara, "Don Judd: The Complexities of Minimal Art," *Vogue*, March 1969.

Kahn, Louis Isadore

(February 20, 1901–March 17, 1974)
Architect, Architectural Educator and Theorist

A legend in modern architecture, Louis I. Kahn quietly spearheaded a major shift in architectural thought in the mid-1950s based on a reintroduction of the inspirational/spiritual dimension to design that stressed the need to search for what a building "wants to be."

Kahn was born on the Island of Osel in Estonia, was brought to Philadelphia in 1905, and became a U.S. citizen in 1915. He studied at the Pennsylvania Academy of Fine Arts (1918–1920) and received an architectural degree from the University of Pennsylvania (1924). While working for Philadelphia city architect John Molitor, he was appointed chief designer for the Sesquicentennial Exposition (1925–1926). From 1928 to 1929 Kahn traveled and studied in Europe, acquiring a passion for architectural order as manifested in classical antiquity.

Returning to Philadelphia in 1930, Kahn initially worked with the Beaux-Arts classical architect Paul Cret, before starting his own practice in 1934. During periods of unemployment in this depression era, he formulated his philosophy and, in 1932, had organized the Architectural Research Group (approximately thirty unemployed architects and engineers) as a "think tank" for Philadelphia city planning. His concept of the city as a place of "assembled institutions," a "continuum of structures" with the street as the "meeting place," led to a lifelong string of civic positions, including consultant architect for Philadelphia's Housing Authority (1937) and for its Planning Commission (1946–1952; 1961).

Kahn was associated briefly with architects George Howe (1941–1943) and Oskar Stonorov (1942–1943), then became professor of architecture at Yale University in 1947. During a ten-year stay, he inspired hundreds of architects with his metaphysical, even poetic approach to creating, and fomented a revolution within the modern movement by rebelling against the cold, severe anonymity of the then-dominant International style (see LUDWIG MIES VAN DER ROHE) in architecture. Although small in stature with a face badly scarred from a childhood accident, Kahn was a spellbinding speaker who peppered his presentations with imaginative metaphors, parallels, and wit. He also taught at the University of Pennsylvania from 1957 to 1974, and was a fellow at Princeton University in 1960.

Kahn's architectural philosophy was grounded in his natural affinity for the classical idiom of the Beaux-Arts tradition, which emphasized clarity of planning combined with an interest in noble materials and volumetric complexity. He called for a more personal, sensitive approach to link architectural concepts with human values and put form before mere functionalism. For him, the essence of architecture was space or "room," which embraced the human connotation of place; a building's plan became the dramatic interaction of a "society of rooms." He said, "The room is the beginning of architecture. It is the place of the mind. . . . Enter your room and know how personal it is, how much you feel its life."

Kahn's early work was not widely known, but after 1950 he gained international fame by producing a series of significant buildings, beginning with the Yale University Art Gallery (with Douglas I. Orr, 1951–1953), New Haven, Connecticut. This structure illustrates a key idea of his philosophy: that the architect should design the "servant" areas (which include such necessary utilities as stairs, elevators, lavatories, and heating systems) directly into the building as positive elements. Although often physically separate, these "servant" spaces would function with the "served" spaces or main activity areas as an aesthetic unit. The galleries proper, or the "served spaces," were concrete lofts separated by a rectangular "servant" zone, featuring a concrete cylinder for the stairway. The building caused a sensation because Kahn left the tetrahedral-framed ceiling open to show the ducts and pipes radiating from the central core. The use of bold forms composed of masses and open spaces, with the building materials, structure, and mechanical aspects strongly expressed, became a constant of Kahn's style. (The important consideration he gave to engineering can be seen in his close association with noted engineer August E. Komendant from 1956 onward.)

In 1957 Kahn became a professor of architecture at the University of Pennsylvania and continued his powerful influence as educator, theorist, and practitioner. His Alfred Newton Richards Medical Research Building for the university (1957–1961) attracted worldwide attention. The complex is a series of six interconnected towers, square in plan and built of precast concrete, bricks, and glass. These towers are "served" by taller shafts containing stairways and ducts. Surprisingly picturesque in perspective, the building has had immeasurable aesthetic influence, although it is considered a functional failure by many critics.

Kahn's masterful design for the Salk Institute for Biological Studies in La Jolla, California (1959–1965), includes two parallel laboratory buildings, containing flexible, loftlike spaces, that border an austere courtyard with a linear trickle of water falling toward the Pacific view. The external combinations of concrete, travertine, and teak give hints of the Mediterranean and of the tropics.

Kahn's approach to the volumetric aspect of a building was a radical departure from previous ideas of contained volumes. While his external forms are usually simple, the interior spaces have dramatically varied configurations and unexpected sources of light. The library at Phillips Exeter Academy in Exeter, New Hampshire (1967–1972), exemplifies this, with an understated exterior of brick, wood, and glass, an interior zone of both stacks and study areas, and a cubic void at the center where walls are pierced by giant circular openings.

The Kimbell Art Museum in Fort Worth, Texas (1966–1972), illustrates two other major components of Kahn's work: the importance of structure-related considerations and his use of light as the "maker" of architecture. The museum is a series of concrete, cycloid vaults, each supported by a few columns, alternating with low galleries that contain "servant" elements. The sources of daylight are a long glass wall facing a park and slits at the apex of each vault, which allow natural as well as artificial illumination of the art.

Kahn's search to reveal the character of building materials as they relate to architectural space is central to the design for the Center for British Art and Studies at Yale (1969–1974). The interior spaces are based principally on a 20-by-20-foot-square module, with oak panels set in a grid of concrete. This theme is introduced at the entrance where four squares were "removed" from the northeast corner, creating a large lobby space echoing the pattern. This area is gently overwhelmed by a concrete cylinder—the principal stairway. Kahn said of the stainless steel-and-glass–clad exterior, that "on a gray day it will look like a moth; on a sunny day, like a butterfly." Kahn's creation of novel forms is best seen in the design for a complex of legislative and administration buildings at Dacca, Bangladesh, which was under construction at the time of his death. The plan details a "ruinlike" complex of concrete and brick cylinders and cubes pierced by massive circular, semicircular, and triangular openings.

Kahn's impact on architectural theory and design goes beyond the visual power of his executed works. The less tangible qualities are also evocative: the sense of humanity in his buildings, the romantic allusions to ruins and decay, as well as to perfection, and the way his buildings unfold with clarity and simplicity. His works—and his ideas—are testimony to the mythic stature he has achieved in the history of twentieth-century architecture.

BIBLIOGRAPHY

Brownlee, David B., and David G. De Long, *Louis I. Kahn: In the Realm of Architecture*, 1991; Lobel, John, *Between Silence and Light: Spirit in the Architecture of Louis I. Kahn*, 1979; Ronner, Heinz,

Sharad Jhaveri, and Alejandro Vasella, *Louis I. Kahn: The Complete Works, 1935–1974*, 1977; Wurman, Richard, and Eugene Feldman (eds.), *The Notebooks and Drawings of Louis I. Kahn*, 2d ed., 1973.

Kaufman, George Simon

(November 16, 1889–June 2, 1961)

Hart, Moss

(October 24, 1904–December 21, 1961)
Playwrights

The team of Kaufman and Hart was the most successful writing duo on the Broadway stage during the 1930s. Their best work, like *You Can't Take It with You*, was characterized by astringent wit and memorably bizarre characters.

They were the cowriters of nine plays, but they possessed different temperaments and came from very different backgrounds. George S. Kaufman, the elder by fifteen years, was born in Pittsburgh, worked on several newspapers, and began writing for the theater in the 1920s in collaboration, variously, with Marc Connelly and Edna Ferber (*Merton of the Movies*, 1922, and *The Royal Family*, 1927). His MARX BROTHERS vehicles, *The Cocoanuts* (1925) and *Animal Crackers* (1928), best characterized his penchant for trenchant, zany humor. He was tall, lean, and dour, a curmudgeon and a ladies' man—by turns aloof, enigmatic, and caustic. According to Alexander Woollcott, Kaufman's deadly humor made him "the first wit of his time."

Hart was born in New York and grew up in virtual poverty in a crowded Bronx apartment. He began his theatrical career working as a social director in the Jewish resorts in the Catskills (the so-called borscht circuit). Affable, gregarious, and something of a dandy, he

was a virtual unknown when he took a draft of *Once in a Lifetime* to the celebrated Kaufman. They toiled over the play for ten months in Kaufman's New York apartment before opening night on Broadway on September 24, 1930. The play satirized the wholesale migration of Broadway actors and writers to Hollywood at the dawn of the talking picture era. Kaufman himself played the role of Lawrence Vail, Broadway playwright. Inevitably, a movie version was produced by Universal in 1931.

Kaufman and Hart's plays were, at their best, full of witty dialogue, memorable characters, and an unsentimentalized attitude toward life. By the time they were ready for their next play, *Merrily We Roll Along* (1934), Hart had blossomed into a confident playwright and screenwriter; he no longer felt that he occupied an inferior position to the celebrated Kaufman. *Merrily We Roll Along* was a drama about the decline of a playwright, and it contained the then-novel idea of presenting its scenes in reverse chronological order. Although the play was sold to Hollywood, no film version was produced. *You Can't Take It with You* (1936), their greatest success, depicted the antics of a family of eccentrics. It won the 1936 Pulitzer Prize, and FRANK CAPRA directed the film version in 1938. *I'd Rather Be Right* (1937) brought a semiretired George M. Cohan back to the stage in the role of President Franklin D. Roosevelt. It was a musical comedy with songs by RICHARD RODGERS and Lorenz Hart. *Sing out the News* (1938), *The Fabulous Invalid* (1938), and *The American Way* (1939) were departures from the Kaufman and Hart formula. All three were responses to the deepening crisis in Europe and the political climate at home in the late 1930s. The first was a revue full of mild, topical satire, the second a comedy/fantasy about the history of the New York stage, and the last a drama about the immigrant experience in America. None was a critical or popular success.

With *The Man Who Came to Dinner* (1939), however, a play written for and about their friend Alexander Woollcott, the team was back in form. The verbal wit and the abundance of allusions to their circle of friends and colleagues made it the team's most personal collaboration. In the film version, which was released in 1941, Monty Woolley played Sheridan Whiteside.

The plot of their last play, *George Washington Slept Here* (1940), concerns a Manhattan couple who escape the big city and purchase a farm in the country. Slim in plot and weak in ideas and wit, the payoff comes when the young marrieds discover that the local legend that George Washington had slept there was untrue—it was Benedict Arnold who had been a guest. Jack Benny and Ann Sheridan played the couple in the film version, released in 1942.

Although Kaufman and Hart did not collaborate on any more new plays after 1941, they continued highly successful careers on their own (Kaufman directing *Guys and Dolls* and Hart directing *My Fair Lady*) and remained close friends. They had houses near each other in Bucks County, Pennsylvania, were frequent bridge players and partygoers, and never allowed their correspondence to lapse. As a team they were consummate professionals, wrote drama critic Brooks Atkinson.

The two men died within a few months of each other in 1961.

BIBLIOGRAPHY

Atkinson, Brooks, *Broadway*, 1970; Goldstein, Malcolm, *George S. Kaufman: His Life, His Theater*, 1979; Hart, Moss, *Act One*, 1960.

Kazan, Elia

(September 7, 1909–)
Director

E lia Kazan, a celebrated stage and screen director, is best known for his productions in both media of the works of TENNESSEE WILLIAMS, WILLIAM INGE, ARTHUR MILLER, and THORNTON WILDER; and for guiding the acting careers of MARLON BRANDO, James Dean, and Marilyn Monroe.

He was born Elia Kazanjioglou in Constantinople (now Istanbul) Turkey, in 1909. At the age of four, he emigrated with his Greek parents to New York City, where his father continued the family business as a rug merchant. He attended Williams College and Yale University, where he studied in the drama department.

In 1932 he joined the Group Theatre as an actor and assistant stage manager. Soon he was directing, including Thornton Wilder's play *The Skin of Our Teeth* (1942), S. J. Perelman and Ogden Nash's *One Touch of Venus* (1943), Arthur Miller's *All My Sons* (1947) and *Death of a Salesman* (1949), and Tennessee Williams's *A Streetcar Named Desire* (1947). These were the years when he cofounded the

Actors Studio and, with Lee Strasberg, promulgated the famous Method school of acting, a style derived from the great Russian actor and director Konstantin Stanislavsky and which encouraged actors to respond as much to their inner feelings as to the requirements of the text. "The actor becomes aware that he has emotional resources," Kazan explained in his autobiography, "[and] that he can awaken, by this self-stimulation, a great number of very intense feelings; and that these emotions are the materials of his art." (Kazan split with the Actors Studio in the early 1960s when it founded its own theater.) The actors he worked with read like a Who's Who of the modern American entertainment world—James Dean, Marlon Brando, Karl Malden, Jessica Tandy, and Marilyn Monroe (with whom he had a romantic liaison).

Meanwhile, his interest in the cinema had led him to the documentary film movement of the late 1930s. Among the government-sponsored films he codirected were *The People of the Cumberlands* (1937), a short film about the working conditions of miners in Tennessee. Kazan's passion for social injustice and his documentary "eye" (coupled with his feel for the "naturalistic" style of acting that he carried over from the theater) were fused in his first Hollywood features. His debut, *A Tree Grows in Brooklyn* (1945), was a compassionate view of the poverty of the working classes; *Gentleman's Agreement* (1947) indicted anti-Semitism in America (winning Kazan a Best Director Academy Award); *Boomerang* (1947) indicted political and judicial corruption; and *Panic in the Streets* (1950) ruthlessly documented the spread of a deadly plague in New Orleans.

Kazan continued to direct both stage plays and movies throughout the 1950s. His films grew more secure and visually dynamic. His 1951 version of *A Streetcar Named Desire* brought the explosive Marlon Brando to the screen. *Viva Zapata!* (1952) was filmed from a screenplay by JOHN STEINBECK. *On the Waterfront* (1954), a gritty, location-shot drama about striking dock workers, won Kazan a second Best Director Oscar. And *East of Eden* (1954), which introduced James Dean, again paired Kazan with John Steinbeck. On stage, he directed new plays by Tennessee Williams and William Inge, respectively, *Cat on a Hot Tin Roof* (1955) and *The Dark at the Top of the Stairs* (1957).

A yearlong involvement with the Communist party in 1934 drew him into the House Un-American Activities Committee (HUAC) investigations in 1952. At first, he was an unfriendly witness; eventually, however, he not only admitted past membership in the party, but named the names of other members in the entertainment industry. He made no apologies for this action in his autobiography, claiming, rather, that it had been time for him to denounce communism.

He has written an autobiographical novel, *The Arrangement* (1968), which he brought to the screen in 1969, an autobiography, *Elia Kazan: A Life* (1988), and a movie derived from his novel based on his immigrant experiences, *America America* (1963). His last film, *The Last Tycoon* (1976), adapted F. SCOTT FITZGERALD's savagely satiric novel about Hollywood.

BIBLIOGRAPHY

Kazan, Elia, *Elia Kazan: A Life,* 1988; Pauly, Thomas H., *An American Odyssey: Elia Kazan and American Culture,* 1983.

Keaton, Buster

(October 4, 1895–February 1, 1966)
Film Actor, Director, Producer

One of the true comic geniuses of film history, Buster Keaton starred in many of the most creative comedies of the silent era. *The General,* is considered one of the greatest movies ever made. A mime equaled only by CHARLIE CHAPLIN, Keaton's deadpan face and balletic body were naturally suited to silent films.

He was born Joseph Frank Keaton in Piqua, Kansas. His parents, Joe and Myra, were vaudeville performers; by age five he was part of their act, the Three Keatons. The name Buster came from an outburst by the magician Harry Houdini after witnessing the six-month-old boy falling downstairs. Accidents and near disasters became the staple of Keaton's physical comedy.

The Museum of Modern Art/Film Stills Archive

Vaudeville was the boy's life. He never knew the world of other children; nor was he formally schooled, as were two later siblings, Harry and Louise. He sparred with his father in physically demanding stunts for seventeen years until the act broke up in 1917.

Keaton was about to enter musical comedy when a friend brought him to Joseph M. Schenck's movie studio in New York where he met Roscoe ("Fatty") Arbuckle, a successful comic with whom he made fifteen two-reelers over the next three years. Keaton quickly recognized the possibilities of the medium, devising gags and sequences and physical and mechanical ways to make them work. As Arbuckle put it, Keaton "lived in the camera,"

interrupted only by his eleven months in the army during World War I.

In 1920 Keaton began his own company, starring in and codirecting (with Eddie Cline and Clyde Bruckman) twenty shorts, including such gems as *One Week, The Playhouse, The Boat, The Paleface,* and *Cops,* a Kafkaesque masterpiece in which hordes of police pursue a lone individual.

These formed the essence of Keaton's art. He stressed authenticity and credibility, performing dangerous stunts himself, without stand-ins or fakery through editing. He was the first to film comedy at standard camera speed, instead of the accelerated tempo of the Keystone comedies, which rendered action unnatural. Rather than a string of pratfalls, Keaton's films were based on logical cause and effect, which enhanced their believability.

In 1923, to secure big theatrical rentals, producer Joseph Schenck encouraged the move to features, allowing Keaton to develop his ideas more fully. A hugely successful partnership, the features grossed $3 million a year.

The first two, made in 1923, were *The Three Ages* and *Our Hospitality,* and, like those that followed, have become classics: *Sherlock, Jr.* and *The Navigator* (1924), *Seven Chances* and *Go West* (1925), *Battling Butler* (1926), *The General* (1927), *College* (1927), and *Steamboat Bill, Jr.* (1928).

As before, Keaton insisted on honest depiction of action. Clyde Bruckman, his screen-writer, has said: "No one ever doubled for Buster. He rides the handlebars of the driverless motorcycle in *Sherlock,* flies through the air on a tree in *Steamboat Bill,* and goes over the waterfall in *Our Hospitality.*"

Keaton's stories often involve a doleful fall guy who must overcome many obstacles to achieve his goal. Writer Paul Gallico called him "Frustration's Mime, pursued, put-upon, persecuted by humans as well as objects suddenly possessed of a malevolent will of their own." In his masterpiece *The General,* an epic Civil War comedy, he must recover his stolen steam engine and prove to his girl that he is loyal to the South.

Despite upbeat endings, Keaton's films often depict a surreal world and have been called precursors to the theater of the absurd and the work of Samuel Beckett and Eugene Ionesco. In all circumstances, pleasant or unpleasant, calm or dangerous, Keaton's face was a perennially unsmiling mask.

In 1928 Schenck dissolved the company and Keaton went to MGM, where he was promised more money and better working conditions. Except for *The Cameraman* (1928), however, he did poorly under the studio's factory-style methods. His marriage broken and his career in decline, he turned to alcohol. Upon recovery he played in sound shorts and features for Educational Films and Columbia Pictures.

He made cameo appearances in many films, including BILLY WILDER's *Sunset Boulevard* (1950), *Limelight* (1952), in which he and director Chaplin played aging clowns, *Around the World in Eighty Days* (1956), and *A Funny Thing Happened on the Way to the Forum* (1966). In 1965 he did a solo in the short *Film,* written for him by Samuel Beckett. He made about seventy guest appearances on television, including *The Ed Sullivan Show.*

In 1955 Keaton's films, believed lost or destroyed, were discovered in a hidden vault in his former Italian villa in Beverly Hills. Thus began the rehabilitation of his reputation as the creator of some of this century's most unique and timeless art.

Keaton married Natalie Talmadge in 1921; they had two sons, Joseph and Robert, and were divorced in 1933; he married young starlet Eleanor Norris in 1940.

BIBLIOGRAPHY

Blesh, Rudi, *Keaton,* 1966; Kerr, Walter, *The Silent Clowns,* 1976; Lebel, J.-P., and P. D. Stovin (trans.), *Buster Keaton,* 1967; Robinson, David, *Buster Keaton,* 1969.

Kensett, John Frederick

(March 22, 1816–December 14, 1872)
Painter

John Frederick Kensett's clearly delineated landscapes show well-known scenes in the eastern United States in glowing color. He can be described as a member of the Hudson River school of painters, who produced detailed panoramic landscapes, and also as one of the Luminists, who were interested in capturing atmospheric effects.

Kensett was born in Cheshire, Connecticut, the son of an English engraver who came to America in 1812. Kensett learned engraving from his father and, after his father's death, from his uncle, Alfred Daggett of New Haven. For two years he engraved maps, labels, and bank notes in New York, working longest for the American Bank Note Company. When he decided to try his hand at painting, he had a picture accepted for an exhibition at the National Academy of Design. With Asher B. Durand and other young painters, he went in 1840 to Europe to study European painting techniques.

Kensett stayed in Europe seven years. Part of the time he spent in Paris, where he shared a studio on the rue de l'Université with a young Boston artist, Benjamin Champney. The two of them made excursions to sketch in the forest at Fontainebleau, a popular location for French Barbizon painters, who were among the first to paint out of doors directly from nature. Kensett went to England to collect a small legacy, but legal complications held up the money. While he waited there for two years, he painted and worked at engraving. "My real life commenced there in the study of the stately woods of Windsor and the famous beeches of Burnham and the lovely and fascinating landscape that surrounds them," he said.

In 1845 he went with Champney and two friends on a walking tour through Germany and Switzerland, over the Alps to the Italian lakes. Kensett went on to Rome, where he shared a studio near the Spanish Steps with an American artist named Thomas Hicks. In August 1847 he headed home by way of Venice and Germany.

While he was abroad, he had sent work back for exhibitions. He arrived in the United States to find himself already a success. His *View of Windsor Castle,* for instance, had been greatly admired. He continued to travel, painting in the Adirondacks, up and down the Genessee and Hudson rivers, around Lake George and Lake Champlain, in the Catskills and the White mountains, at Newport, on the Connecticut

Library of Congress

shore, and at Niagara Falls. He was a fine draftsman and, as a good engraver would, included accurate details. He was especially interested in the gradations and variations in sunlight. His placid pictures, which were very popular, are examples of the Hudson River school of painting (see THOMAS COLE), and reflected his own genuine love of nature.

Never married, Kensett was generous, kind, and sympathetic. He has been described as "the most thoroughly amiable" of all artists. Both his art and his personality were endearing, and he had many friends among the painters, writers, and businesspeople of New York.

His most famous painting, *Lake George* (1869), has an air of supreme calm and clarity. An expanse of shimmering sky and a band of shadowed mountains are reflected in the mirror-smooth lake below. A tiny Indian canoe glides faintly through the shadows, dwarfed by the magnificent scene. Other well-known paintings include a woodland scene, *Bish-Bash, South Egremont, Massachusetts* (1855); a view of the shore, *Beacon Rock, Newport Harbor* (1857); and a view of mountains, *View from Cozzens' Hotel near West Point* (1863). In the thirty-eight paintings of Long Island Sound that he did toward the end of his life, he paid particular attention to the interaction of light in sea and sky. These Long Island paintings are particularly fine examples of American Luminism.

Kensett died in his studio at the age of fifty-six.

BIBLIOGRAPHY

Driscoll, John Paul, *John Frederick Kensett,* 1985; Wilmerding, John, *American Light,* 1991.

Kern, Jerome David

(January 27, 1885–November 11, 1945)
Composer

The composer of "I've Told Ev'ry Little Star," "The Song Is You," and some thousand other delights, Jerome Kern wrote songs for over 100 stage productions, including *Show Boat.* Kern's integration of music and drama shifted Broadway's attention from popular European operettas to fledgling, strictly American musicals, a genre that evolved from his innovations.

Kern, born in New York City to Fanny and Henry Kern, showed an early interest in music. In 1895 the Kerns moved to Newark, New Jersey, where the youngster attended high school. Kern's mother started him playing piano. He went on to study harmony, theory, and piano at the New York College of Music, now part of New York University, and abroad.

In 1902 Kern published his first work, a piano piece. At the time he was a Broadway rehearsal pianist and a song promoter for various firms, including Harms, where he eventually became a junior partner. His work at Harms included writing songs for British musicals headed for American production. "How'd You Like to Spoon with Me?" written in 1905, was one of these interpolated (inserted) songs.

Kern traveled to London for Harms. There he established important stage contacts and signed a contract with American impresario Charles Frohman to write songs for British shows on Broadway. By World War I over 100 of Kern's songs had found their way into some thirty shows, mostly into operettas imported from abroad.

Kern broke through with the New York version of *The Girl from Utah,* originally a British production. Audiences fell in love with the first of his great songs, "They Didn't Believe Me." The success led to four Kern musicals for the small Princess Theatre. Here Kern experimented quite successfully with a new kind of musical show, one that presented realistic characters living within a realistic story line

and formed the prototype of the American musical. "Bill," a song later used in *Show Boat,* appears in one of these, *Oh Lady! Lady!* (1918). This and other Kern songs (between 1915 and 1918, nineteen Broadway productions included Kern melodies) made an impression on two young composers: GEORGE GERSHWIN and RICHARD RODGERS.

Other hit songs like "Look for the Silver Lining," from *Sally* (1920), and "Who?" from *Sunny* (1925; lyrics by Oscar Hammerstein II) were included in more commercial musicals. The shows, popular on both sides of the Atlantic, helped the new American musical concept take hold abroad and at home.

Many think *Show Boat* (1927) was the most influential Broadway musical ever written. Based on Edna Ferber's novel, the production recruited Oscar Hammerstein II as a lyricist for the songs that were so essential to characterization and story. Several *Show Boat* tunes are now standards: "Ol' Man River," "Can't Help Lovin' Dat Man," "Make Believe," and "Why Do I Love You?" But perhaps more important, after *Show Boat,* Broadway knew that music was an integral part of the story and composers left off writing songs for interpolation. *Show Boat,* known worldwide, has been filmed and was the first musical comedy to be included in the repertory at the New York City Opera (1954).

Kern continued to expand the concept of the musical. His works were adapted for the screen. *Roberta,* with the song "Smoke Gets in Your Eyes," was on Broadway in 1933 and was filmed in 1935. Kern also wrote original scores for films like *Swing Time,* released in 1936. It starred FRED ASTAIRE and Ginger Rogers and showcased favorites like "A Fine Romance" and "The Way You Look Tonight."

Despite its lovely song, "All the Things You Are," *Very Warm for May* failed on Broadway in 1939. Thereafter Kern moved to Hollywood, wrote exclusively for films, and produced increasingly sophisticated songs: "The Last Time I Saw Paris," an Academy Award winner from *Lady Be Good* (1941); "Dearly Beloved," from *You Were Never Lovelier* (1942); and "Long Ago and Far Away," from *Cover Girl* (1944).

Kern died in 1945 in New York, where he had gone for a revival of *Show Boat* and to write the score for a new stage musical. *Till the Clouds Roll By*, a film biography, appeared in 1946.

BIBLIOGRAPHY

Bordman, G., *Jerome Kern: His Life and Music*, 1980; Ewen, D., *The Story of Jerome Kern*, 1953, and *The World of Jerome Kern*, 1963.

Kline, Franz Josef

(May 23, 1910–May 13, 1962)
Painter

Franz Kline, a member of the New York school, was a major figure in the Abstract Expressionist movement of the late 1940s and 1950s.

Kline was born in Wilkes-Barre, Pennsylvania, in 1910. He studied art at Girard College in Philadelphia and at Boston University, as well as at the Heatherley School of Fine Art in London.

While supporting himself with various odd jobs, including a stint as a window display designer for a Buffalo, New York, department store, Kline in his early career painted figures, traditional landscapes, cityscapes, and portraits. However, as described in a famous passage by Elaine de Kooning, one day late in 1948 Kline was in WILLEM DE KOONING's Fourth Avenue studio in New York looking at projected enlargements of some of de Kooning's sketches. Suddenly, he saw their implications as large-scale, free abstract images. It was a revelation—in de Kooning's phrase, a "total and instantaneous conversion." (Art critic Arthur C. Danto compares this transformation to Marcel Proust's tasting of the madeleine.) In that instant Kline abandoned representational imagery and modestly sized images for a full-fledged Abstract Expressionism (see BARNETT NEWMAN) of enormous proportions.

With buckets of cheap commercial paint and housepainter brushes, Kline attacked large pieces of canvas on the walls of his studio. An examination of two paintings entitled *Nijinsky*, executed a year apart (1949–1950), demonstrates the change. The former is a recognizable portrait; the latter, whose architectonics are obviously derived from the former, is nonetheless a wholly abstract, independent work.

Kline's first black-and-white abstractions began around 1950, the year of his first one-man exhibition. Works like *Mahoning* (1956) and *Requiem* (1958) have a monumental authority (the latter is nearly 9 feet high). There is nothing tentative in their powerful, almost savage thrusts to the edges of the canvas. They suggest the verve of Asian calligraphy and the grand sweep of the suspension bridge. Unlike the paintings of ROBERT MOTHERWELL, however, which had an intellectual and lyrical quality, Kline's work was pure energetic formalism. Dynamic and architectonic swashes were this painter's heroic, gesticular message.

Ironically, Kline's powerful images are physically fragile, because of the poor quality of the materials used. "There are moments or periods when it would be wonderful to plan something and do it and have the thing only do what you planned to do," he said, "and then, there are other times when the destruction of those planned things becomes interesting to you. So then, it becomes a question of destroying—of destroying the planned form."

Kline did not add color until the mid-1950s with *Dahlia, Yellow, Red, Green, Blue,* and *Orange and Black Wall.* By then he did not have long to live. Just two years after receiving

a prize at the Venice Biennale, he died of a heart condition in 1962.

BIBLIOGRAPHY

Danto, Arthur C., "The Vital Gesture: Franz Kline in Retrospect," *The State of the Art,* 1987; Gordon, John, *Franz Kline: 1941–1962,* 1969.

Koussevitzky, Serge Alexandrovich

(July 26, 1874–June 4, 1951)
Conductor

The temperamental Russian-born bassist and conductor of the Boston Symphony espoused new American music and excelled in performances of French and Russian orchestral works. Known for subtle coloration and beauty of orchestral tone, Serge Koussevitzky, founder of the Berkshire Music Center, was a popular and exacting, though often unconventional, musical interpreter.

Koussevitzky had early piano training and learned to play the cello before he traveled from his Russian birthplace, Vishny-Volotchok, to Moscow to enter the Moscow Philharmonic Music School in 1888. To gain free instruction, as a fourteen-year-old he switched to the double bass as his principal instrument and progressed superbly in his musical studies under Joseph J. Rambusek.

In 1894 Koussevitzky joined the Bolshoi Theater Orchestra as a bassist and two years later began concertizing on his own with particular success in Berlin in 1903 and London in 1907. He was composing, too, and wrote a concerto for double bass that had its first performance in Moscow in 1905, a landmark year for Koussevitzky because of his marriage to Natalya Ušhkkov after an early marriage had ended in divorce.

With the new bride's wealth, Koussevitzky was able to advance his career rapidly. The virtuoso bass-viol player, having observed

other Europeans conduct, led a student orchestra at the Berlin Hochschule für Musik. In 1908 Koussevitzky, still without formal conducting studies, hired the Berlin Philharmonic Orchestra and made a successful debut as conductor. The next year he founded the Editions Russes de Musique, a Russian music publishing house, formed his own orchestra to promote the composers he published (among them Prokofiev, Rachmaninoff, Scriabin, and IGOR STRAVINSKY), and began a long tenure as guest conductor of the London Symphony Orchestra.

After the Russian Revolution in 1917, Koussevitzky traveled throughout Europe, especially Paris, where he led his own orchestra in the first performances of Maurice Ravel's orchestration of Modest Mussorgsky's *Pictures at an Exhibition* (commissioned by Koussevitzky) and Arthur Honegger's *Pacific 231.*

Koussevitzky succeeded Pierre Monteux as conductor of the Boston Symphony Orchestra in 1924 and for twenty-seven years influenced the American musical world through his high musical standards and his sponsorship of new music. He commissioned and performed a great number of works by such contemporary American composers as SAMUEL BARBER, AARON COPLAND, GEORGE GERSHWIN, PAUL HINDEMITH, and Igor Stravinsky.

In 1940 Koussevitzky established the Berkshire Music Center, a summer music school in Massachusetts, where he gave classes in conducting (LEONARD BERNSTEIN was an alumnus) and conducted concerts. He became an American citizen in 1941 and, after his wife's death in 1942, established the Koussevitzky Music Foundation in her memory to support new composition. Koussevitzky died in Boston in 1951.

BIBLIOGRAPHY

Schonberg, H., *The Great Conductors*, 1968; Smith, M., *Koussevitzky*, 1947.

Laemmle, Carl

(January 17, 1867–September 24, 1939)
Film Producer

Carl Laemmle, a pioneer of the film industry, worked his way from uneducated German immigrant to founder of Universal Studios. Engaged in every aspect of the film business from exhibition and distribution to production, he fought heroically against Thomas Edison's Motion Picture Patents Company's attempts to eliminate competition.

He was born in the village of Laupheim, Württemberg, Germany, to Julius and Rebekka Laemmle, the tenth of thirteen children. Eight of his brothers and sisters died during a scarlet fever epidemic while he was still a child.

Laemmle left school at thirteen to work for a relative. He was devoted to his mother, and when she died, he left for America. He came to New York in 1884, worked and earned enough to go to Chicago, where his older brother, Joseph, had earlier emigrated. In 1894 he was bookkeeper for a clothing company in Oshkosh, and in 1898 married Recha Stern, niece of the store's owner. Though made manager of the store soon after, he left after a falling out.

An experience in a nickelodeon (a makeshift theater in which early movies were shown for 5 cents) so intrigued him that he determined to get into the business. He rented a store, installed chairs and projection equipment, and opened his first movie house, called the White Front Theater, in Chicago in 1906. He used the profits to develop others.

In 1907 Laemmle and his associate, Robert H. Cochrane, went into distribution to supply films for their own and competitive theaters. Called the Laemmle Film Service, it was the largest picture exchange in the country. Next, he produced his own movies, battling the "Trust" (Motion Picture Patents Company) and the General Film Company, who sought to discourage independent producers and distributors. He organized the Independent Motion Picture Company (IMP) and began making films. His first production was the one-reel *Hiawatha* (1909). His struggle against the "Trust" continued until the federal government enforced its dissolution.

In 1913 he and Cochrane amalgamated IMP with several other companies to form the Universal Film Manufacturing Company and moved activities to Hollywood, where Universal City was established in 1915. Laemmle divided his time between New York and Hollywood, overseeing all activities, from casting and story selection to budget allocation and distribution. Friendly, unpretentious, and hardworking, he was known to everyone as Uncle Carl.

Always the showman, Laemmle made the opening of Universal City a historic occasion, inviting exhibitors and their families from all over the country to come to "the wonder city of the world . . . [to see] how we blow up bridges, burn down houses, wreck automobiles, and smash things up in general in order to give the people of the world the kind of pictures they demand." The idea was so successful that it continued as the "Universal tour" and contributed substantially to the company's profits.

Laemmle understood that movies satisfied the needs of an expanding working class and helped acclimatize immigrants to American values. He was one of the first film executives to appreciate the possibilities of the foreign market, convinced that American films were envoys of American ideals of "liberty" and "happiness." He genuinely believed that exhibiting his pictures globally was a way of expressing his gratitude for the success he found in America.

Universal's directors included Thomas Ince, who was later killed under mysterious circumstances, and Lois Weber, one of the few women directors working in Hollywood. JOHN FORD made his directorial debut in 1917 with *The Tornado*. Most prestigious was ERICH VON STROHEIM, whose *Blind Husbands* (1919) and *Foolish Wives* (1920) were among the studio's most successful—and scandalous—productions. IRVING THALBERG was general manager in charge of production at Universal before he went to MGM.

The studio's first full-length feature was *Traffic in Souls* (1913), a controversial drama about white slavery. Among the studio's silent classics were *The Hunchback of Notre Dame* (1923) and *The Phantom of the Opera* (1925), both with Lon Chaney.

Laemmle's son, Carl, Jr., became general manager in 1929. His production of *All Quiet on the Western Front*, an antiwar film, won the Academy Award for Best Picture of 1929–1930. The studio began a popular cycle of horror films with *Dracula* starring Bela Lugosi, its biggest hit of 1931, and *Frankenstein* (also 1931), with Boris Karloff; and melodramas, such as the original versions of *Imitation of Life* (1934) and *Magnificent Obsession* (1935). Other notable films were the innovative musical *King of Jazz* (1930) and a memorable version of JEROME KERN's *Show Boat* (1936).

Carl, Jr.'s, extravagance and poor judgment resulted in the studio's near bankruptcy. Despite his father's attempts to save it, in 1936 its theaters and operations were sold and a new management severed connections with Laemmle. The studio was now called New Universal.

Laemmle died in 1939.

BIBLIOGRAPHY

Drinkwater, John, *The Life and Adventures of Carl Laemmle*, 1931, rep., 1978; Gabler, Neal, *An Empire of Their Own: How the Jews Invented Hollywood*, 1988; Hirschhorn, Clive, *The Universal Story*, 1983.

Lange, Dorothea

(May 25, 1895–October 11, 1965)
Photographer

The documentary photographer Dorothea Lange is best known for her sensitive, impassioned images of the life of migrant workers during the depression of the 1930s.

Lange was born in 1895 in Hoboken, New Jersey, and attended the New York Training School for Teachers from 1913 to 1914. She studied photography after school at the studio of Arnold Genthe. At Columbia University in 1917 she studied with Clarence White. After relocating to San Francisco in 1918, she opened her own portrait studio, which she ran for the next twelve years.

Her photographs of migrant agricultural workers in 1935, commissioned by the California State Emergency Relief Administration and exhibited at Willard Van Dyke's Group f/64 gallery (see ANSEL ADAMS and EDWARD WESTON), caught the attention of Roy E. Stryker of the federal Farm Security Administration (FSA; formerly the Resettlement Administration), for whom she worked from 1935 until 1939. Their efforts helped to gain public support for federal relief programs. Her images of the privations of American rural life in the dust bowl—like *Migrant Mother, Nipomo, California* (1936) and *Tractored Out, Childress County, Texas* (1938)—have been described by historian Beaumont Newhall:

> [The] migratory workers with overladen jalopies on the highways, living in tents pitched in fields or the town dump, in transient camps, working in the fields, are at once an accurate record and a moving comment, for she had a deep feeling of compassion and respect for them.

Her portrait of a migrant mother huddled with her children in a tent became the most widely reproduced of all the FSA pictures and hangs in the Library of Congress.

During the 1940s she worked for the War Relocation Authority, documenting the Japanese American internment camps, and for the Office of War Information. She traveled abroad many times in the 1950s and worked on several assignments for *Life* magazine. In 1971 the Oakland Museum in California established the Dorothea Lange Award.

Lange was an important figure, along with John Grierson, Walker Evans, and Pare Lorentz,
in the growing government-supported documentary movement in photography and film in America and Great Britain in the 1930s. Her images upset the "Art for Art's Sake" crowd, wrote EDWARD STEICHEN in 1938: "[F]or these documents told stories and told them with such simple and blunt directness that they made many a citizen wince." Infused with ALFRED STIEGLITZ's and Edward Weston's aesthetic grounding of "straight" photography, and imbued with her own strong sense of social outrage, she achieved a synthesis of an unvarnished eye and a poetic sensitivity. She wrote: "My own approach is based upon three considerations. First—hands off! Whatever I photograph, I do not molest or tamper with or arrange. Second—a sense of place. Whatever I photograph, I try to picture as part of its surroundings, as having roots. Third—a sense of time. Whatever I photograph, I try to show as having its position in the past or in the present."

Lange died in San Francisco in 1965.

BIBLIOGRAPHY

Lange, Dorothea, "The Assignment I'll Never Forget," in Paul Taylor (ed.), *Popular Photography*, February 1960; Newhall, Beaumont, *The History of Photography*, 1982; Steichen, Edward, "The FSA Photographers," in Beaumont Newhall, *Photography: Essays and Images*, 1980.

Lardner, Ringgold Wilmer

(March 6, 1885–September 25, 1933)
Humorist, Short-Story Writer

Ring Lardner wrote biting satires of life in middle America in the 1910s and 1920s. His uncanny ability to exploit the patterns of spoken speech to reveal his characters helped free American prose of the stilted formality that had constrained it in the nineteenth century.

Lardner was born in Niles, Michigan, in 1885 and attended Armour Institute of Technology (now the Illinois Institute of Technology) for a year (1901–1902). He worked as a freight clerk, gas meter reader, and bookkeeper before becoming a reporter for the South Bend, Indiana, *Times* in 1905. He then held a string of sports writing and editing jobs in Chicago and St. Louis before taking over a column called "In the Wake of the News" at the Chicago *Tribune* in 1913.

Lardner began to publish in magazines a series of fictional letters from a busher—a baseball player doomed to the minor leagues. Jack Keefe unconsciously reveals himself as an oafish, conceited, self-deceiving sorehead. Lardner captures uncannily Keefe's semiliterate midwestern speech. He collected the letters into a volume, *You Know Me, Al: A Busher's Letters* in 1916.

The success of *You Know Me, Al* brought Lardner's work to the attention of a larger public. He churned out a succession of books of stories and humorous essays, including *Gullible's Travels* (1917), *My Four Weeks in France* (1918), *Own Your Own Home* (1919), *The Real Dope* (1919), and *Symptoms of Be-*

National Archives

ing Thirty-five (1921). In 1919 he moved to Long Island, where he wrote a column called the "Weekly Letter" and eventually started a comic strip called *You Know Me, Al.*

Lardner's first wide critical acclaim came with *How to Write Short Stories (with Samples)* (1924), which included "Some Like Them Cold," a deadpan exchange of letters between a would-be songwriter and a girl he had met in a Chicago subway station. The volume also featured "The Golden Honeymoon," in which an aging man describes a Florida trip he and his wife took in honor of their golden wedding anniversary. The critic EDMUND WILSON noted that Lardner demonstrated "an unexcelled, a perhaps unrivalled, mastery" of American language. Both Wilson and the British novelist Virginia Woolf praised Lardner's ability to get beneath the surface of ordinary life in America by concentrating on boxers, salesmen, chorus girls, stockbrokers, and stenographers.

Wilson went as far as to put Lardner forth as a budding MARK TWAIN. He wondered in his review of *How to Write Short Stories*, "Will Ring Lardner then, go on to his *Huckleberry Finn* or has he already told all he knows?" If *The Love Nest and Other Stories* (1926) fell short of Wilson's aspirations for Lardner, it nonetheless contained the story many readers think of as Lardner's best: "Haircut."

In fact, Lardner mined the same vein—cynical treatment of essentially commonplace lives—until his death in 1933, publishing *The*

Story of a Wonder Man in 1927 and *Lose with a Smile* in 1933. He also branched out into theater: *Elmer the Great* was produced in 1928; he cowrote (with GEORGE S. KAUFMAN) *June Moon,* based on "Some Like Them Cold," in 1929.

BIBLIOGRAPHY

Elder, Donald, *Ring Lardner: A Biography,* 1956; Evans, Elizabeth, *Ring Lardner,* 1979; Yardley, Jonathan, *Ring: A Biography of Lardner,* 1977.

Latrobe, Benjamin Henry

(May 1, 1764–September 3, 1820)
Architect, Civil Engineer

Benjamin Henry Latrobe greatly influenced American architecture in the Federal period, introduced the Greek Revival style, and became the first professional U.S. architect to achieve international stature. As a civil engineer, he created the country's first citywide waterworks, among other innovative engineering designs.

Latrobe was born in Fulneck, Yorkshire, England, the son of a Moravian minister and an American mother. After studying in England and Germany and touring Europe, he was apprenticed in 1784 to the London engineer John Smeaton. He worked for architect Samuel Pepys Cockerell (1787–1788) before opening his own architectural office in 1791. He became known for the classical elegance and good proportions of his buildings, as in Hammerwood Lodge in Sussex (1792), a precursor of his Greek Revival style. After his wife died in childbirth in 1793, Latrobe suffered a nervous breakdown. This, plus a construction halt because of war between Britain and France, motivated him to leave his two children with relatives and sail to America for a fresh start.

After his arrival in Norfolk, Virginia, in 1796, Latrobe made extensive notes about his new country, from history to geological formations, in his sketchbooks. In this crucial period during the country's formative years there was urgent need for housing, public buildings, and improvements in roads and service systems. Latrobe became a leader in making lasting contributions to American architecture and civic planning, raising each to a new professional level.

Latrobe's first commission was the Pennock House in Norfolk, which introduced new standards of comfort, convenience, and privacy. Other important houses are Sedgeley (in a slightly Gothic mode) near Philadelphia (1799) and the severely classical Decatur House in Washington, D.C. (1818). His innovations included moving the main staircase from the entrance hall to one side, adding a hidden staircase for daily use, and often installing indoor water closets (primitive toilets).

In 1797 Latrobe designed and supervised construction of the state penitentiary in Richmond, Virginia, which reflected his innovative, humane approach to penology. At this time he became friends with THOMAS JEFFERSON; it was to be an auspicious relationship for both men.

In 1798 Latrobe moved to Philadelphia, where he became part of the intellectual and social elite and married Mary Elizabeth Hazelhurst (1800). Here he created two of his master works: the Bank of Pennsylvania (1801) and the country's first waterworks (1799–1801). The bank, with its simple geometric exterior, two end porticoes (porches) featuring Greek Ionic columns, and a low central dome, was the first Greek Revival building in the country. Greek Revival was a phase of Classic Revival, or neoclassical, architecture, which stressed symmetry and the use of forms like columns and pediments derived from classical Greece and Rome. For many the Greek Revival symbolized democratic principles of the new nation by echoing the ideals of Greek democracy.

Latrobe became famous as an engineer with the creation of the Philadelphia waterworks, which tapped water from the Schuylkill River, raised it to a central storage tank using steam power, then distributed it through the city by gravity. In the city's Central Square he erected a classical building to house the pumping machinery and offices. Both these works reflect his tenet of complete integration of appearance, construction, function, and symbol. In a letter to Jefferson he defined his architectural motivation: "It is not the ornament, it is the use that I want."

In 1803 Latrobe was appointed by President Jefferson as surveyor of public buildings, the nation's most important architectural position. During the next eight years he labored to complete construction of the Capitol (originally designed by William Thornton), but was subjected to public criticism, political interference, and material shortages. When the War of 1812 disrupted his work, he moved to Pittsburgh, where he joined a venture with steamboat innovator Robert Fulton. Latrobe suffered another breakdown when the venture failed and he was left financially ruined. In 1815 he returned to Washington to rebuild the Capitol after its near-destruction from British shelling during the war. He altered the original plans by designing a new chamber for the House of Representatives (now Statuary Hall) and adding, in the Senate wing, classical columns topped by capitals representing leaves of the American tobacco plant. He also added a portico to the White House and designed the drawing room at the request of President Madison's wife, Dolly. Pushed to the breaking point by criticism, he resigned from his work on the Capitol in 1817.

The Roman Catholic Cathedral (1804–1818; now the Cathedral of the Assumption of the Blessed Virgin Mary) in Baltimore stands as a masterpiece of Latrobe's genius. Designed on a monumental scale, the cathedral has classic geometric simplicity in the form of a Latin cross with an innovative and complex system of interrelated vaults, climaxed in a dome over the central crossing. It was the first stone-vaulted church in the country.

Other notable buildings designed by Latrobe include Christ Church (1808) and St. John's Church (1815–1816) in Washington, D.C., and the Baltimore Stock Exchange (1820). Latrobe was also a talented artist, a performing musician, a poet, a superb writer, and a naturalist/geologist. In 1809 he suggested an innovative plan to connect the Great Lakes with the Hudson River by means of a canal; sixteen years later the Erie Canal was built. In 1819 he moved to New Orleans to complete the city's water system, which his son Henry had started before dying of yellow fever. Unfortunately, Latrobe succumbed to the same disease. He had influenced a generation of architects, especially Robert Mills, who became the first American-born professionally trained architect.

BIBLIOGRAPHY

Hamlin, Talbot, *Benjamin Henry Latrobe*, 1955; Norton, Paul F., *Latrobe, Jefferson, and the National Capitol*, 1977.

Ledbetter, Huddie William

(ca. January 21, 1885–December 6, 1949)
Blues Guitarist, Singer

Library of Congress

The great bluesman Huddie Ledbetter, better known as Leadbelly, wandered the South and honed his solo style doing time in prison. His moving songs employed echoes of African music in improvised laments that sang of the hard times he knew all too well.

Born near the Texas border in Mooringsport, Louisiana, Leadbelly grew up on a backwoods farm in the Lake Cado district. His father, Wes, was a hardbitten, hardworking sharecropper who with great effort had bought his own land. His mother, Sally, half Cherokee, worked with her husband to clear the land and work the soil and to grow and harvest cotton.

Leadbelly was, by his own account, a formidable farmhand, but he liked good times and had an ear for music. As a teenager he went to the local country dances, called sooky jumps, and began to perform on Saturday nights. His uncle taught him to play the accordion, and on his own he picked up guitar, mandolin, harmonica, and piano. He was big, strong, short-tempered, and lethal in a fight. After his second child was born out of wedlock, he was forced out of the area.

Fanin Street, the red-light district of Shreveport, attracted the rebel, and it was there he heard the barrelhouse blues that inspired his rhythmic, strumming guitar style. He moved on to the black section of Dallas, where he met rural blues singer Blind Lemon Jefferson and adopted some of Jefferson's songs, including "Match Box Blues" and "C. C. Rider." During the Texas years Leadbelly took up the twelve-string guitar.

Leadbelly courted trouble. He gambled, womanized, drank, and brawled. In 1917 he killed a man and in 1918, under the name of Walter Boyd, was sentenced to thirty years in the Huntsville, Alabama, prison. His release in 1925 is said to have come about after he asked for a pardon in a song he improvised when Texas governor Pat Neff visited the prison.

In 1930 he ran afoul of the law again. Convicted of assault, he was sentenced to ten years in the state prison at Angola, Louisiana. Folklorists JOHN LOMAX and ALAN LOMAX discovered him there in 1934 and recorded him. According to legend, another plea for pardon, recorded by Lomax, was delivered to O. K. Allen, the governor of Louisiana, who released him. But, according to jazz writer Leonard Feather, the discharge was routine.

Leadbelly recorded additional folk songs and blues for Lomax and, with Lomax as his manager, toured the Northeast. Leadbelly married, settled in New York City, and continued to record blues, ballads, spirituals, prison work songs, country dance tunes, and cowboy songs for John and Alan Lomax for the Library of Congress.

Though he served a year for assault (1939–1940) in a New York prison, New York City and Huddie Ledbetter were compatible. Jazz, its roots in the blues, was in the air, and jazz lovers admired Leadbelly as a blues singer. The folk revival movement of the late 1930s and early 1940s embraced his music, too, especially protest songs like "Scottsboro Boys." He performed in nightclubs, singing and playing his guitar, often sliding a knife on the strings to produce voicelike sounds. Among his best-known songs recorded commercially in the 1940s are "Goodnight Irene," "Rock Island Line," and "Good Morning Blues." Gradually, however, he fell out of favor with audiences. In 1949, shortly before his death, he sang in Paris.

At the end of the year, poor and all but forgotten, Leadbelly died in New York's Bellevue Hospital.

BIBLIOGRAPHY

Barlow, W., *"Looking Up at Down": The Emergence of Blues Culture*, 1989; Lomax, J., and A. Lomax, *Negro Folk Song as Sung by Leadbelly*, 1936.

Le Gallienne, Eva

(January 11, 1899–   )
Actress, Director, Producer

Eva Le Gallienne, distinguished actress of stage and screen, has been a tireless advocate of classical repertory theater in America.

Le Gallienne was born in London in 1899, the daughter of poet Richard Le Gallienne and Danish critic Julie Norregaard. She studied at the Royal Academy of Dramatic Art in London and made her major debut at age fifteen in the London company of actress Constance Collier in *The Laughter of Fools*. She came to America soon afterward. In 1921 she enjoyed acclaim in Ferenc Molnar's fantasy, *Liliom.*

After a stint with the Provincetown Theatre, she founded in 1926 the Civic Repertory Company in New York on West 14th Street, where for the next six years she directed and starred in many of its productions of Shakespeare, Molière, Goldoni, Giraudoux, and Ibsen. Many famous actors worked with her, including John Garfield, Alla Nazimova, Howard da Silva, and Burgess Meredith. "She was a leader," recalled Meredith, "and she was glamorous and talented and full of idealism. . . . She was a very precise director. . . . Her fight was a fight on the side of the angels." No matter how high-minded, however, the enterprise was doomed by the Great Depression and folded in 1933. "A valiant theater institution that provided the

public with a series of classics was too expensive to operate," concluded Broadway critic Brooks Atkinson. During the late 1930s she toured America, performing the leading roles in Ibsen's *A Doll's House*, *The Master Builder*, and *Hedda Gabler.*

In 1944 she produced, directed, and acted in a notable presentation of *The Cherry Orchard*, and in 1946 she cofounded the American Repertory Theatre with Cheryl Crawford and Margaret Webster. Other Broadway productions included *The Starcross Story* (1954) and *The Southwest Corner* (1955). Still active in the 1960s and 1970s, she made a handful of film appearances (including *Resurrection*, 1979) and appeared in productions of the National Repertory Theatre (MAXWELL ANDERSON's *Elizabeth the Queen* and Euripides' *Trojan Women*) and Ionesco's *Exit the King* with the Association of Producing Artists. In addition to radio, recording, and teaching activities, she founded the National Women's Party and published translations of Ibsen's plays. She has written two volumes of memoirs, *At Thirty-three* (1934) and *With a Quiet Heart* (1953).

Few actresses of her time did more for the cause of classical dramatic repertoire than Eva Le Gallienne. Always optimistic about the American stage, she declared in 1934 that it "was on the verge of a great renaissance." The talking picture, far from striking the stage a death blow, had delivered it from the doldrums. "They acted as a sort of purge, eliminating all possibility of producing the kind of plays which appeal only to the 'mentality of 12'; restricting the field no doubt, but immeasurably increasing the necessary standard of work."

BIBLIOGRAPHY

Atkinson, Brooks, *Broadway,* 1970; Le Gallienne, Eva, *At Thirty-three,* 1934, and *With a Quiet Heart,* 1953; Ross, Lillian, and Helen Ross, *The Player: A Profile of an Art,* 1984.

Lewis, Harry Sinclair

(February 7, 1885–January 10, 1951)
Novelist

S inclair Lewis, the first American writer to win the Nobel Prize for Literature, added a new realism to the depiction of life in middle America. His keen ear for the spoken word and his strong satiric sense marked such classic novels as *Main Street, Babbitt,* and *Elmer Gantry.*

The son of a country doctor, Harry Sinclair Lewis was born in Sauk Centre, a small town on the Minnesota prairie. An awkward youth with few friends, he was happy to escape the town when, at age seventeen, he was sent to Oberlin Academy in Ohio to prepare for Yale University.

At Yale, Lewis contributed stories and poems to the campus literary magazine. He interrupted his studies during his senior year to participate in the novelist Upton Sinclair's socialist experiment, Helicon Hall, in Englewood, New Jersey. Afterward, Lewis worked briefly

National Archives

as a free-lance writer before returning to Yale and graduating in 1908.

Lewis worked for a succession of newspapers and publishing houses until 1916, when sudden success selling his short stories to the *Saturday Evening Post* and other publications meant he could begin writing full time. He published a novel for boys, *Hike and the Aeroplane,* in 1912 and his first adult novel, *Our Mr. Wrenn,* in 1914.

Before 1920, Lewis published four more novels: *The Trail of the Hawk* (1915), which he thought prefigured the career of the flier Charles Lindbergh; *The Job* (1917), the story of a young woman's attempt to enter the work force; *The Innocents* (1917), a depiction of an elderly couple and their life in a small town; and *Free Air* (1919).

Main Street (1920) changed the course of Lewis's career. A trenchant satire of small-town life, it exposed the pettiness and bigotry of many of the citizens of Gopher Prairie, a village modeled on Sauk Centre. The protagonist, Carol Kennicott, is married to the town doctor. She hopes to bring beauty and culture to Gopher Prairie but is stymied by suspicious townspeople. A friend to the poor and to social outcasts, she leaves the town to work in a government office in Washington, D.C., for two years during World War I. Not only was the novel the first to offer a significant contradiction to the cherished American myth of happy small-town life, but it challenged traditional notions of gender roles. The book was a bestseller and gave Lewis an international reputation.

With *Babbitt* (1922), Lewis extended the satire begun in *Main Street* to one of its denizens, the middle-American businessman and booster. To his credit, George Babbitt understands that his middle-class existence and middling achievement fall short of any importance, but he is incapable of changing the course of his life. When Babbitt's son elopes, Babbitt encourages him not to fear what others may think. *Babbitt* created a sensation, drawing the wrath of booster clubs around the country and coining in its title a new name for an American social type.

Arrowsmith (1925), based on the research of several months spent with the bacteriologist Paul de Kruif, concerns the obstacles a scientist encounters in his idealistic search for truth. Dr. Martin Arrowsmith begins as a small-town practitioner but finds his way first to the health department of a small city, then to a research institute founded by a wealthy couple. Seeking isolation from the meanness and corruption he finds around him, as well as from his own material ambitions, Arrowsmith eventually takes his work to an island in the West Indies and from there to a small farm in Vermont. *Arrowsmith* earned Lewis a Pulitzer Prize in 1926, but he refused it, believing the award was intended to promote idealized portrayals of American life.

Elmer Gantry (1927) was Lewis's funniest and most pointed satire. It depicted a self-promoting evangelist, who rises to the top of a midwestern church by trading on his good looks and plagiarized sermons. The book was condemned as the devil's work by its targets in the revival movement, but it pleased many more by exposing hypocrisy within a hallowed American institution. The novel was made into a movie in 1960.

With *Dodsworth* (1929), Lewis began to view his subjects in a more sympathetic light. Sam Dodsworth, a prosperous businessman who nonetheless appreciates culture and art, takes his mannered and shallow wife, Fran, to Europe, where she engages in a string of affairs. Dodsworth finally leaves her and takes comfort in the love of a more generous woman, who inspires him to use his abilities as a businessman to serve the commonweal. He returns to the United States to build a better suburb near his home city of Zenith.

In 1930 Lewis became the first American honored with the Nobel Prize for Literature. Ironically, the award came as Lewis was searching unsuccessfully for new subject material.

Critics regard two of Lewis's ten succeeding novels as having approached the importance of his work of the 1920s. *It Can't Happen Here* (1935) projects the rise of a fascist dictatorship in the United States. Doremus Jessup, a Vermont newspaper editor, fails in a conspiracy against the dictator Berzelius Windrip, who has seized control of Congress and the Supreme Court after election to the presidency. *Kingsblood Royal* (1947) took on prejudice against interracial marriage and parenting, depicting the trauma of a man who discovers a black among his ancestors.

Lewis's other novels include *Ann Vickers* (1933), which apparently based its depiction of a social worker on Lewis's second wife, the journalist Dorothy Thompson; *Work of Art* (1934), about the hotel industry; *The Prodigal Parents* (1938), on the political dimensions of the generation gap; *Bethel Merriday* (1940), about the ambitions of a young actress; *Gideon Planish* (1943), which exposed the materialism of a college president; *Cass Timberlane*

(1945), about an unworkable marriage between an older man and a younger woman; *The God-Seeker* (1949), a historical novel about a Minnesota missionary; and *World So Wide,* published posthumously in 1951, about an American in Europe.

BIBLIOGRAPHY

Light, Martin, *The Quixotic Vision of Sinclair Lewis,* 1975; Lundquist, James, *Sinclair Lewis,* 1973; Schorer, Mark, *Sinclair Lewis: An American Life,* 1961.

Lichtenstein, Roy

(October 27, 1923–   )
Painter

Roy Lichtenstein's importance as a chief formulator of American Pop art is rivaled perhaps only by ANDY WARHOL. Lichtenstein is most famous for his images derived from comic strips and advertising art.

Lichtenstein was born in New York City in 1923. Early self-taught as a painter, he began studying only in the late 1930s with Reginald Marsh at the Art Students League. After his military service in Europe during World War II, he completed his studies at Ohio State University, where he taught until 1951.

He had his first one-man exhibition in 1951 at the Carlebach Gallery in New York. For the next six years he worked in Cleveland, Ohio, as a commercial artist and designer and did display work for shop windows. From 1957 to 1960 he taught at the State University of New York, Oswego. His easel paintings, which for a time had been influenced by a Cubist-inspired Expressionism, began to display by the late 1950s his growing fascination with commercial illustration, advertising, and comic book art. In effect, from the tangles of his gestural paintings emerged the images of WALT DISNEY's Mickey Mouse and Donald Duck.

Lichtenstein, with JASPER JOHNS, Andy Warhol, James Rosenquist, ROBERT RAUSCHENBERG, Jim Dine, and CLAES OLDENBURG, was a leader of American Pop art. "Americanism" itself was the big subject—the idea of progress, the media industry, and the Cult of the Celebrity. In the everyday, ubiquitous im-ages of the commercial illustrations of Madison Avenue and the movie clichés of Hollywood, he found a peculiar kind of pictorial vocabulary, which, in the words of historian Tilman Osterwold, consisted of "trivializing and generalizing emotions, actions, people and objects so as to make these conform to popular opinion." Lichtenstein's images—*Mister Bellamy* (1961), *Eddie Diptych* (1962), *Drowning Girl* (1963)—derived from strips like *Steve Canyon, Dick Tracy, Sgt. Rock,* and *Millie the Model.* Not only did he aim to capture a sense of depersonalized objectivity, but he also wrought commentaries on contemporary graphic processes. The rigorous simulations of Ben-Day dot patterns in his images made them look as if they had been produced mechanically, with little evidence of the hand of an individual artist. The icons of popular pictorial literature were neutralized by the painter's clever conceit of doing what a machine can do, thus reversing the century-old fascination with the machine's ability to do what a human can.

Unlike the comics, however, Lichtenstein's works transcend the mundane. By lifting a particular comic strip panel out of its context, for example—by monumentalizing it through enlargement, by tightening its pictorial coherence, by emphasizing the references to its reproductive process, and by depriving it of its narrative logic—he thus allows the viewer to confront it as something new and unfamiliar. "It gets you to examine the images more closely," says Lichtenstein, "the dots, the pure colors—you can see how artificial and abstract they really are." When he isolates a product like a hot dog and holds it up to public view, he says, he is attempting to show its mythological, or even "classical," status. "What was hitherto vacuous, suddenly becomes suggestive and meaningful," concludes Osterwold.

Important exhibitions were held during the 1960s and early 1970s at the Cleveland Museum of Art, the Galerie Ileana Sonnabend, Paris, the Solomon R. Guggenheim Museum, New York, and the Pasadena Art Museum (also shown in Amsterdam, London, Bern, and Hanover). Later retrospectives of his work have been held at the Museum of Modern Art, New York City (1987) and the Kunsthalle, Frankfurt (1988).

In spite of the occasionally hostile reception his works have aroused—particularly from some of the comic book artists whose images he has appropriated and from critics who have protested his borrowings from the works of past masters like Matisse, Picasso, and Arp—Lichtenstein has remained unbothered; his later works have retained their amiable yet satiric edge. His *Self Portrait* (1978) substitutes a panel of dot patterns for the artist's head. His *Big Paintings* series and *Brushstroke* series (1965–1966) take the brush strokes so seriously celebrated in Abstract Expressionism (see BARNETT NEWMAN) and transform them into absurdist forms. His growing confidence in mixing allusions to classical and modern art, as well as to his own works, can be seen in his large murals done in New York since 1983—for the wall of the Leo Castelli Greene Street Gallery, the Equitable Building on Seventh Avenue, and the subway junction at Times Square and 42nd Street. These are not merely eclectic jumbles or collages. As Hilton Kramer has noted, from these disparate source materials "[Lichtenstein creates] new compositions that echo the original sources, and indeed parody them, without really repeating their pictorial strategies."

Lichtenstein's works constitute a comprehensive view of modern consumer culture and the traditions of picture making. They constantly challenge our attitudes about "high," "low," and "pop" culture. In an interview with Alan Solomon in 1966, Lichtenstein summed up the attitude about consumer culture that continues to motivate his work to this day: "It's that sort of antisensibility and conceptual appearance of the work that interests me and is my subject matter."

BIBLIOGRAPHY

Alloway, Lawrence, *Roy Lichtenstein*, 1984; Kramer, Hilton, *The Revenge of the Philistines: Art and Culture, 1972–1984*, 1985; Osterwold, Tilman, *Pop Art*, 1991.

Loewy, Raymond Fernand

(November 5, 1893–July 14, 1986)
Industrial Designer

Raymond Loewy, a founding father of American industrial design, promoted functionalism in product design, pioneered the streamlined look that drastically altered the appearance of thousands of objects, and headed the world's largest industrial design firm. His designs for everything from toothbrushes to airplanes have affected the daily lives of millions.

Loewy was born in Paris and showed an early aptitude for drawing automobiles and locomotives. In 1908, after winning a medal for a model plane design, he received a patent, registered the trademark, and produced the models for the children's market; this first business venture was successful. He earned an engineering degree from the University of Paris in 1910, then studied advanced engineering at the Ecole de Laneau. His studies were interrupted by World War I service in the French Army Corps of Engineers, for which he won four Croix de Guerre citations and was made an officer in the French Legion of Honor. After completing his degree in 1918, he found no job prospects. Encouraged by his brother who was living in New York City, he emigrated to the United States in 1919.

Loewy's career was launched, unexpectedly, when he did a charity sketch on shipboard during the Atlantic crossing. It was purchased by a British diplomat who introduced him to Condé Nast, publisher of *Vogue*. He worked as a fashion illustrator for *Vogue* and other periodicals, and as a free-lance designer of window displays for such New York stores as Macy's, before opening his own industrial design office in 1929. That same year he became art director for Westinghouse Electric, and gained recognition for designing a new duplicating machine casing for the Gestetner Company in England. Sales of the copier skyrocketed, and his compact and elegant design remained unchanged for forty years.

Frustrated with the "mountains of ugly, sleazy junk" being produced in America, Loewy worked to bring the techniques of functional design to industrial products. According to the concept of functionalism, every object, regardless of complexity, has an ideal form that expresses its function and is inherently beautiful. Loewy's first major design success was the Coldspot refrigerator for Sears, Roebuck & Company (1934), which had innovative non-rusting aluminum shelves and a sleek exterior. The design won first prize at the 1937 Paris International Exposition, bringing him fame and many clients. Sears's yearly refrigerator sales quadrupled, illustrating the marketing advantages of industrial design. In 1937 he designed the first all-welded locomotive for the

Pennsylvania Railroad Company, which earned the Gold Medal in transportation at the Paris Exposition. This design flaunted the streamlined style for which he became famous: dynamic primary forms accented by similarly abstracted details.

Loewy became a naturalized U.S. citizen in 1938, and was working as a consultant to some 250 American and foreign companies by the 1960s. His design method was to work in tandem with the individual engineering departments of the various companies. Following his creed that "Industrial design keeps the customer happy, his client in the black, and the designer busy," Loewy became the designer with the Midas touch. His goal was to make everyday objects sleek, unencumbered, and attractive by creating a shape, an image, a "packaged" look. The "Loewy look" appeared in ballpoint pens, radios, lipstick containers, dishes, and such classic designs as the original Coca-Cola bottle, the Lucky Strike cigarette pack (1941), and the Pepsodent toothpaste package (1945). He created a line of moderately priced, color-stained wood furniture, called the Spectrum group, for the Mengel Furniture Company (1953), and even designed cookie shapes for the Nabisco Company.

Loewy was a master of package design, attributing his success to being a "professional what-iffer." Although his critics often labeled him a mere shell designer, Loewy felt that "you start with a machine and enclose it. But in many cases the shell is essential."

In 1944 he founded Raymond Loewy Associates with five partners; it developed into the world's largest industrial design firm with offices in New York, Chicago, Los Angeles, South Bend (Indiana), London, and São Paulo, Brazil. One of the firm's most famous early commissions was the design and execution of the interiors for the well-known glass-and-steel Lever Brothers office building in New York City. Using a basic grayish beige scheme throughout, each floor was individualized by a different shade in the spectrum. In addition, the office desks were adjustable in height and had rounded corners. Renamed Raymond

Loewy/William Snaith, Inc., in 1961, the firm expanded its operations to include market research, engineering, and architectural work, in addition to industrial design.

Loewy is best known for his vehicle designs: cars for Studebaker Corporation and BMW, locomotives and passenger cars for the Pennsylvania Railroad, trucks for the International Harvester Company, buses for Greyhound, sleeper planes for Trans World Airlines, airplane interiors for Lockheed, and fireproof ocean liners for the America-President and Panama cruise lines. In 1953 he gained international fame for his automobile body design for Studebaker, which was more advanced than that of any other mass-produced car of the time.

During the 1950s Loewy began designing trademarks and logos for such companies as Shell International Petroleum Company and British Petroleum. Believing that "the correct logo is paramount for sales," Loewy created the famous eagle silhouette logotype of the U.S. Postal Service and transformed the public image of Standard Oil and Esso when the trademark was changed to Exxon.

Loewy was often involved with government projects during the 1960s and 1970s. He redesigned Air Force One for President Kennedy, creating a sleek, white, missilelike appearance. From 1967 to 1973 he worked for the National Aeronautics and Space Administration (NASA), creating spacecraft designs for the Apollo and Skylab projects. He also became NASA's chief adviser for studies of the psychophysiological comfort and safety of astronauts in space.

By the time of his death, Loewy had brought industrial design to a position of importance in the workplace, and his firm had trained over 2,000 people for work in the field. In 1969 the *London Sunday Times* had named Loewy "one of the 1000 makers of the 20th century."

BIBLIOGRAPHY

Loewy, Raymond, *Never Leave Well Enough Alone*, 1951; Schoenberger, Alan (ed.), *Raymond Loewy: Prince of American Industrial Design*, 1990.

Lomax, John Avery

(September 23, 1867–January 26, 1948)

Lomax, Alan

(January 15, 1915–)
Folk Musicologists

Thanks to John and Alan Lomax, American folk song has been preserved. First the father and then the son gathered, studied, and recorded thousands of songs from around the country. This national heritage, now at the Library of Congress, serves as a resource and inspiration for scholars and folk artists.

John was born in Goodman, Mississippi, and grew up on a farm in Texas. As a child he loved the hymns he heard at Methodist schools and camp meetings and songs the cowboys sang, and he soon began to write them down. Following school, he taught at a small college, and at age twenty-eight went to the University of Texas and received his B.A. in 1897. He taught for several years at Texas Agricultural and Mechanical College, during which time he also earned an M.A. in literature from the University of Texas in 1906 and an M.A. in English from

Harvard University in 1907. His professors at Harvard urged Lomax to continue collecting songs, and he returned to Texas on scholarships to travel through the cattle country, listening to songs and recording them on an early machine. His first published collections of songs, *Cowboy Songs and Other Frontier Ballads* (1910), contained "Git Along Little Dogies" and "Home on the Range."

In 1904 Lomax married Bess Brown of Texas. His son Alan, the third of four children, was born in 1915. In 1917 Lomax was fired from the University of Texas and became a banker, first in Chicago and later in Dallas, though he continued to lecture on cowboy songs at colleges and published his second collection, *Songs of the Cattle Trail and Cow Camp*. He lost his job in 1932 during the Great Depression, but, with support from the Library of Congress and the American Council of Learned Societies, in 1933 he went on the first of many song-collecting trips. He was often accompanied by his son Alan, who was won over to the cause as a teenager when he heard an elderly African American woman singing the spiritual "God's Goin' to Trouble de Waters." From that day until the elder Lomax died in 1948, Alan assisted and collaborated in the folklore work. The hundreds of songs gathered on that first trip became the core of the Archive of American Folk Song of the Library of Congress, a collection that now preserves many thousands of songs, over 10,000 of them contributed by the Lomaxes.

At the end of the 1933 trip, the family moved to Washington, D.C., where John Lomax took up duties at the Library of Congress as honorary consultant and archivist, curator of the new Archive of Folk Song. His son went to Harvard for a year, then transferred to the University of Texas, from which he graduated in 1936. Alan became assistant curator of the Archive of Folk Song in 1937. During their trips together the Lomaxes went to rural black communities in the South and penitentiaries, from which important songs came, such as "Rock Island Line" and "John Henry." They encouraged folksingers and helped spread the folk song movement that began in New York City and became popular nationwide. By 1942, when Alan left the archive, he had recorded artists in Washington and around the country, including HUDDIE LEDBETTER and JELLY ROLL MORTON.

In 1939 Alan Lomax hosted a folk music series for Columbia Broadcasting. He played recordings, sang, and discussed folk music. After World War II and his service with the Office of War Information and the U.S. Army Special Services, he went to Decca Records as director of folk music. In 1947 he was awarded a Guggenheim Fellowship and then went on to broadcast with Mutual Broadcasting. In 1963 he became director of the "cantometrics" project at Columbia University, an international study of folk song and culture. Among his publications are *Mister Jelly Roll* (1949), *The Folk Songs of North America* (1960), and *Folk Song Style and Culture* (1968).

BIBLIOGRAPHY

Lawless, R., *Folksingers and Folksong in America*, 1960; Lomax, A., *Mister Jelly Roll: The Fortunes of Jelly Roll Morton*, 1950, rev., 1973, and *Folk Song Style and Culture*, 1968.

London, Jack

(January 12, 1876–November 22, 1916)
Essayist, Novelist, Short-Story Writer

Jack London, best known for his Klondike stories, especially *The Call of the Wild*, wrote more than fifty novels and nonfiction works on social themes. Most of his fiction concerns the primal human struggle for survival against overwhelming natural and social forces.

London was born John Griffith Chaney in San Francisco, the son of Flora Wellman and her common-law husband, William H. Chaney, a traveling astrologer who abandoned her when she became pregnant. His mother married John London when Jack was nine months old, but the union provided little security: London was a widower with eleven children of his own, two of whom he had placed in an orphanage while he eked out a living as a carpenter.

Jack learned self-reliance at an early age. He quit school at fourteen to work in a factory. After a year, his meager income helped him to buy a boat in order to rob privately owned oyster beds, earning himself the nickname Prince of the Oyster Pirates. After getting caught by the California Fish Patrol, he worked for them for a while and then in 1893 shipped out as a seaman aboard a schooner, hunting seals in the Bering Sea and traveling to the Far East. Along the way, he sold his first newspaper story, an account of a typhoon off the coast of Japan.

Returning to the United States, he held a succession of factory jobs, marched briefly with Jacob Coxey's Army of the Unemployed on their journey to Washington to protest the depression of 1893–1894, tramped around the United States and Canada, and joined in the Klondike gold rush in 1897. At the age of twenty-two he returned to Oakland, California, to begin writing full time.

His stories of the Klondike began to sell. His breakthrough was an article called "An Odyssey of the North," which he sold to the *Atlantic Monthly* in 1899. The next year he published his first collection of stories, *The Son of the Wolf*, followed in quick succession by two more, *The God of His Fathers* (1901) and *Children of the Frost* (1902).

London published his best-known novel, *The Call of the Wild*, in 1903. It is a parable of London's faith in the power of the individual to survive if he is strong enough to withstand the challenges posed by nature and society. *The Call of the Wild* concerns a dog, Buck, stolen from a comfortable home and forced to adapt to the harsh life of a sled dog in the Klondike. When his master is killed, Buck reverts to a primitive state, running with a pack of wolves, which he leads with his superior intelligence and strength. A companion volume, *White Fang* (1906), recounts the tale of a wild Northland dog tamed with patience and kindness by a mining engineer who eventually takes the dog to his home in California.

At least nominally a socialist, London was torn between a theoretical commitment to personal sacrifice for the greater good and his own ideal of the strong individual. *The Sea-Wolf* (1904) concerns a fierce individualist, Wolf Larsen, captain of a sealing schooner, the *Ghost*. Larsen rescues two victims of an ocean mishap, only to be shipwrecked with them later on a desert island. Larsen dies, despite his strength and skill; the couple he rescued survive because they acquire his strength and are able to cooperate with each other. In *Martin Eden* (1909), the title character, another individualist—this time an ex-sailor who becomes a writer—commits suicide when sudden fame and an inability to find a purpose outside himself cause him to lose his sense of identity.

London continued to write social fiction even as his faith in socialism waned; he would resign from the party shortly before his death in 1916. *The Iron Heel* (1908) forecasts the rise of fascism as capitalists come to believe that only a totalitarian state can prevent the advent of socialism. In *The Valley of the Moon* (1913), London observed the effects of a strike on the life of one man, a teamster named Billy Roberts, who has been described as an Aryan hero.

Among London's other works are *The People of the Abyss* (1903), an account of slum life in the East End of London; *Burning Daylight* (1910), another novel involving a central character in the Klondike with qualities of a superman; *John Barleycorn* (1913), "alcoholic memoirs" supporting Prohibition; and *The Star Rover* (1915), about a convict who, using astral projection, escapes horrendous prison conditions for periods of time.

If London's sympathies with the struggling masses can be said to have eventually diminished, it may have been in part because his own success as a writer had given him a taste of wealth. In 1906 he purchased a 130-acre ranch in Sonoma County, California, which he farmed, using scientific methods. The next

year, he began a voyage around the world aboard a 45-foot boat he had built, the *Snark;* he sailed as far as Hawaii and then Australia before abandoning the trip due to tropical infections he had probably picked up in the Solomon Islands.

London covered the Mexican Revolution for *Collier's* in 1914 but was forced to return home after acquiring a severe case of dysentery. The next year, his kidneys failing, he moved to Hawaii, hoping to regain his health. He returned to his California ranch no healthier, and he died on November 22, 1916, at the age of forty.

BIBLIOGRAPHY

Johnston, Carolyn, *London: An American Radical?* 1984; Kingman, Russ, *A Pictorial Life of Jack London*, 1979; Labor, Earle, *Jack London*, 1974; Sinclair, Andrew, *Jack: A Biography of London*, 1977.

Longfellow, Henry Wadsworth

(February 27, 1807–March 24, 1882)
Poet, Translator

Henry Wadsworth Longfellow is best remembered as the maker of myths around such characters as Hiawatha, Miles Standish, and Paul Revere. He stands among the few American poets to reach a remarkably wide audience in his own lifetime through publication of lyrical ballads, sonnets, and especially long narrative verse.

Longfellow was born in Portland, Maine, the son of a prominent lawyer and grandson of a local Revolutionary War hero. He grew up in a house filled with books, and by the time he enrolled in nearby Bowdoin College at the age of fifteen, he had already published several poems in a Portland newspaper.

At graduation, in 1825, Longfellow had published essays and poems in such journals as the *American Monthly Magazine* and the *United States Literary Gazette*, and he hoped to embark upon a literary career. His father, however, insisted another profession would prove essential to his financial well-being, and Longfellow dutifully considered law and medicine. When Bowdoin offered him a professorship in the developing field of modern languages, father and son deemed it suitable, and Longfellow went abroad for three years to study in France, Spain, Italy, and Germany.

Returning to his Bowdoin professorship in 1829, Longfellow carried a heavy teaching load, edited textbooks in French and Spanish, continued to publish essays in journals, and published *Outre-Mer: A Pilgrimage beyond the Sea* (two volumes, 1833–1834), a collection of travel essays modeled on WASHINGTON IRVING's *Sketch Book.*

In 1835 Longfellow won an appointment to Harvard University's faculty and again traveled abroad to pursue his studies. Despite the tragic loss of his wife, Mary Potter, during childbirth while in Rotterdam, Longfellow stayed on in Europe, and that winter in Heidelberg he became familiar with much romantic German literature that was to affect him deeply.

At Harvard, Longfellow's knowledge of European literature won the enthusiasm of his students, just as it intrigued the Cambridge intelligentsia, including RALPH WALDO EMERSON, NATHANIEL HAWTHORNE, and OLIVER WENDELL HOLMES. Longfellow's translations, particularly of the Italian Renaissance poet Dante Alighieri, and his editing of the anthology *The Poets and Poetry of Europe* (1845) helped broaden the American literary horizon.

The publication of Longfellow's first volume of poetry, *Voices of the Night* (1839), assured his own popular reputation, in part because it reflected the values of his Puritan heritage. "Life is real! Life is earnest! / And the grave is not its goal," he wrote in "A Psalm of Life."

There followed several volumes containing the long narrative poems, with their legendary characters, for which Longfellow is most often remembered, including *Ballads and Other Poems* (1842), with "The Wreck

Library of Congress

of the Hesperus" and "The Village Black- smith"; *Evangeline: A Tale of Acadie* (1847); *The Song of Hiawatha* (1855); *The Courtship of Miles Standish* (1858); and *Tales of a Wayside Inn* (1863), with the ballad "Paul Revere's Ride."

Longfellow's verse featured a homey warmth and simple, repetitive rhythms. Its accessibility to a popular audience was reflected in its sales. *Evangeline* sold 36,000 copies in its first ten years; *The Song of Hiawatha,* 30,000 in six months. On the first day of publication, *The Courtship of Miles Standish* sold 15,000 copies. By 1854 Longfellow was earning sufficient income from the sales of his poetry that he could give up his teaching position at Harvard to become a full-time writer.

Longfellow also wrote lyric poetry, some of which has enjoyed a more enduring critical reputation than his narrative verse. Most often cited are his sonnets "Nature" (1878) and "The Cross of Snow" (1886), the latter a memorial to his second wife, Frances Appleton, who died in 1861 from burns after her dress caught fire. The former poem compares nature to a mother putting her child to bed:

> So nature deals with us, and takes away
> Our playthings one by one, and by the hand
> Leads us to rest so gently, that we go
> Scarce knowing if we wish to go or stay,
> Being too full of sleep to understand
> How far the unknown transcends the what we know.

Longfellow's tremendous popularity continued throughout his life. His poetry was translated and enjoyed a wide audience in Europe. During a trip abroad in 1868 and 1869,

Longfellow was granted honorary degrees from Oxford and Cambridge universities. Two years after his death in 1882, a bust of him was unveiled in the Poet's Corner in London's Westminster Abbey. He was the first American writer to be so honored.

BIBLIOGRAPHY

Arvin, Newton, *Longfellow: His Life and Work*, 1963; Wagenknecht, Edward, *Henry Wadsworth Longfellow, His Poetry and Prose*, 1986; Williams, Cecil B., *Henry Wadsworth Longfellow*, 1964.

Louis, Morris

(November 28, 1912–September 7, 1962)
Painter

Morris Louis changed the course of twentieth-century painting in America by bringing to the forefront completely autonomous abstract painting. A pioneer of the Post–Painterly Abstraction movement, Louis explored color-shape relationships in two-dimensional, stained canvases, which were precursors of Color Field painting.

Born in Baltimore, Maryland, of Russian heritage, Morris Louis Bernstein studied at the Maryland Institute of Fine and Applied Arts (1929–1933). From 1936 to 1940 he lived in New York City and worked for the depression-era Works Progress Administration's Federal Arts Project. During this time his penchant for experimentation led him to join other artists, including Mexican painter David Siqueiros, in a studio where they explored techniques using Duco enamel paint. In 1938 he dropped his last name.

Returning to Baltimore in 1940, Louis became a private art teacher and devoted himself to further experimentation with various types of paints, the means of applying paint on canvas, and spatial relationships. He isolated himself from the dominant art world of New York, making only a few forays to that artistic hub during the rest of his life. In 1948 he began experimenting with acrylic paints, which would figure prominently in his later breakthrough paintings, and exhibited annually from then until 1952 with the Maryland Artists Group at the Baltimore Museum of Art. In 1952

Louis taught at the Washington Workshop Center of the Arts, Washington, D.C., where he met fellow painter Kenneth Noland.

During the first twenty years of his career Louis created abstract paintings that were greatly influenced by the Cubist movement (a revolutionary movement spearheaded by Pablo Picasso that stressed the "image of the visible" by the geometric use of abstract lines and planes, strong flat colors, and expressive distortions). The turning point in his career came in 1953 when he accompanied Noland to New York City, where he was exposed to the paintings of JACKSON POLLOCK and HELEN FRANKENTHALER and the critical viewpoint of Clement Greenberg, who espoused "flatness"—a two-dimensional surface—in painting. Fascinated by Pollock's spatter technique and Frankenthaler's elimination of foreground and background distinctions through the process of staining, Louis completely transformed his artistic approach.

Beginning with his series of *Veil* paintings (1954 and 1958–1959), Louis created works with flatness, thus isolating the purely visual qualities of color, devoid of any depth or tactile associations inherent in three-dimensional surfaces of overlaid pigment (thick paint). He also developed a staining technique in which he spilled extremely thin, quick-drying acrylic paint onto sheets of unsized, unprimed canvas stapled to a scaffold but hanging freely. The paint flowed down the surface in wedges, splashes, or curves, guided only by the folds in the canvas or the artist's cloth-covered stick, and soaked into the canvas immediately. As seen in the painting *Saraband* (1959), the result was the complete integration of paint and canvas with the elimination of such things as expressive brush strokes, tactile associations, and three-dimensional imagery. The style would become known as Post-Painterly Abstraction. It rejected all forms of personal expressiveness, figural painting, and "painterly" qualities in favor of an art stripped down to its essence in which artistic materials are emphasized and visual relevance is paramount. Louis's work prefigures Color Field painting (see BARNETT NEWMAN) with its emphasis on the nontactile, purely visual reality of color no longer restricted by drawing, shape, or pictorial image.

Louis's fame and influence rest on the large-scale, abstract, purely visual color-space explorations he created during the last nine years of his life. He produced a huge number of paintings revolving around a few themes, and constantly moved back and forth between themes. At the same time he was working on the *Veil* paintings, he also experimented with a series called *Florals* in which thin acrylic washes of color radiate inward to a densely colored center. In 1959 he created the *Omega* series char-

acterized by different-colored horizontal "fingers" pushing inward from the right and left sides of the canvas, and the *Japanese Banners* paintings noted for their large unstained areas and irregular diagonal stripes along the right and left sides.

During the last three years of his life Louis created paintings in which large parts of canvas were left blank, and colors were separated and applied as parallel groupings across the canvas's corners, or poured straight down the canvas in vertical stripes or bands. In the *Unfurled* series, as exemplified by *Delta Gamma* (1960) and *Alpha Phi* (1960–1961), canvases have a blank center with broken, parallel diagonal stripes of color across the lower corners. In his final series, *Stripes* (1961–1962), vertical bands of almost pure color and clearly defined edges are bunched together and surrounded by empty canvas. A very private artist, Louis continued to experiment with color-space relationships until he died of lung cancer in his fiftieth year.

BIBLIOGRAPHY

Fried, Michael, *Morris Louis,* 1970; Krauss, Rosalind E., *Morris Louis,* 1971; Rose, Barbara, "Quality in Louis," *Artforum,* October 1971.

Lowell, James Russell

(February 22, 1819–August 12, 1891)
Critic, Poet, Political Satirist

James Russell Lowell was one of the best-known American men of letters of the mid-nineteenth century. His elevation of vernacular language in poetry and his witty, satiric verses captured public attention. His heartfelt concern over the troubling moral questions posed by such institutions as slavery helped make his writings influential.

Lowell was born at Elmwood, his family's home in Cambridge, Massachusetts. He entered Harvard University at the age of fifteen. Despite a penchant for reading everything but the books on the syllabus, which earned him a two-month "rustication"—or suspension—in Concord, Lowell graduated in 1838. He earned a law degree at Harvard in 1840, though he did not practice long.

Lowell published his first book, *A Year's Life and Other Poems,* in 1841. Two years later, he became editor of a reformist journal, *The Pioneer,* which lasted only three issues.

In 1844 Lowell married Maria White, herself a poet and reformist, who encouraged Lowell to write in opposition to slavery. He served briefly as an editorial writer for the abolitionist newspaper *Pennsylvania Freeman* and wrote extensively for the *National Anti-Slavery Standard.*

In 1848 Lowell published three volumes that secured his poetic reputation: *A Fable for Critics* is a verse satire that assesses nineteenth-century American writers as it sketches them. Included were RALPH WALDO EMERSON, HENRY WADSWORTH LONGFELLOW, OLIVER WENDELL HOLMES, EDGAR ALLAN POE, and NATHANIEL HAWTHORNE. Many of the judgments expressed in the poem became critical truisms.

The Biglow Papers mingled poems with prose sketches and addressed the war with Mexico, particularly Lowell's conviction that its primary motivation was the desire to expand slavery. Hosea Biglow, a straightforward commentator in the Yankee tradition, and his friend Birdofredom Sawin exchange letters assailing politicians and statesmen of the day. The poems' original and effective use of Yankee dialect constituted a literary landmark. Critics recognized the introduction of distinctly American vernacular to literature.

The Vision of Sir Launfal, a narrative poem, relates the conversion of a medieval knight who has searched for years for the Holy Grail, only to find it while sharing a bowl of water with a beggar. For Lowell, the poem articulated a particularly American vision of brotherhood in a classless society.

Over the years, from 1847 to 1853, Lowell suffered the losses of three of his four children and of his wife, the one who had given real direction to his work. In 1855, when Longfellow gave up the Smith Professorship in Modern Languages at Harvard, Lowell accepted the post. He taught at Harvard from 1857 until 1872.

In 1857 Lowell became the first editor of the *Atlantic Monthly,* a position he held until 1861. In 1864 he joined Charles Eliot Norton as coeditor of the *North American Review.*

During the Civil War, Lowell composed a second set of *Biglow Papers,* which were published initially in the *Atlantic* and then as a volume in 1867. At the end of the war, he wrote a series of odes on the notion of moral victory achieved through sacrifice, including his "Commemoration Ode" (1865), the first literary tribute to Abraham Lincoln.

In *The Cathedral* (1870), Lowell uses Chartres as the locus for a poetic meditation on the conflicting values of science and religion and on the contemporary struggle for faith. "Agassiz" (1874) comprises an elegy for the Harvard naturalist Louis Agassiz, blending profound respect for the work of human reason with a hope that its promise can be fulfilled in a life beyond this one.

In 1872 Lowell gave up his Harvard chair to travel to Europe for two years, during which time he was honored with honorary degrees by Oxford and Cambridge universities. He served as U.S. ambassador to Spain from 1877 to 1880, and to England from 1880 to 1885.

Home in Cambridge, Lowell published his last book of verse, *Heartsease and Rue,* in 1888, as well as several books of essays. He died at Elmwood on August 12, 1891.

BIBLIOGRAPHY

Duberman, Martin, *James Russell Lowell,* 1966; Scudder, Horace E., *James Russell Lowell,* 2 vols., 1901; Wagenknecht, Edward C., *James Russell Lowell: Portrait of a Many-Sided Man,* 1971.

Lowell, Robert Traill Spence, Jr.

(March 1, 1917–September 12, 1977)
Poet, Translator

Robert Lowell's ambitious efforts to create and then re-create poetic forms to encompass his broad personal and social concerns profoundly influenced the course of American poetry in the mid-twentieth century. His confessional poems, particularly those in *Life Studies*, brought to modern poetry a new intimacy and immediacy.

Robert Traill Spence Lowell, Jr., was born in Boston, Massachusetts, the great-grandson of a clergyman and novelist, Robert Traill Spence Lowell, himself the brother of the poet JAMES RUSSELL LOWELL. The poet Amy Lowell was a distant relative. Robert Lowell found these relations embarrassing. He declared his revered great-great-uncle "pedestaled for oblivion" and said of the colorful public figure Amy Lowell that it was "as if MAE WEST were a cousin."

Lowell's own parents suffered chronic financial difficulties, and they fought continuously. His mother, Charlotte Winslow, descended from a prominent Massachusetts family that had included a governor of Plymouth colony and a revolutionary war general. Her social ambitions were largely frustrated by her marriage to Commander Robert Traill Spence Lowell, who worked at the Boston Naval Shipyard before going unsuccessfully into private business. Their son was sent to the prestigious St. Mark's School, of which his great-grandfather had been headmaster, but his anger often surfaced in behavior problems.

Copyright *Washington Post*; Reprinted by permission of the D.C. Public Library

Lowell attended Harvard for two years. After a violent argument with his father, he took off for Tennessee, where he met the poet ALLEN TATE and spent the summer camped on Tate's lawn, talking about and writing poetry. In the fall, Lowell enrolled at Kenyon College, where he worked with Tate's friend and fellow Fugitive poet JOHN CROWE RANSOM.

Graduating from Kenyon in 1940, he married the novelist Jean Stafford and pursued graduate study at Louisiana State University with the poet and novelist ROBERT PENN WARREN. In 1943 he refused on principle to serve when inducted into the army, earning himself several months in prison in New York City and Danbury, Connecticut.

In 1944 Lowell's first volume of poetry, *Land of Unlikeness*, was published privately. His first major volume, *Lord Weary's Castle*, came out two years later.

Though the poems in *Lord Weary's Castle* reflected some values of Roman Catholicism, the faith to which Lowell converted with his marriage to Stafford, they doubt humanity's ability to transcend violence and greed. Stylistically, the volume's dense and allusive poetry was of a piece with much written by such Modernists as T. S. ELIOT, and especially Allen Tate. The volume won Lowell a Pulitzer Prize in 1947.

A third volume of poetry, *The Mills of the Kavanaughs* (1951), continued in a similar vein, but Lowell himself felt the poems lacked real interest because formally they did not break new ground.

Lowell divorced in 1948 and married the novelist Elizabeth Hardwick the following year. He taught for brief periods at the University of Iowa and Kenyon and lived for three years in Europe.

The decade of the 1950s was a period of silence for Lowell as a poet. His personal life was in turmoil. He left the Catholic church. He lost both parents, his father in 1950 and his mother in 1954. Following his mother's death, he suffered a psychotic episode that led to a series of hospitalizations and chronic manic-depressive illness.

In 1959 Lowell published *Life Studies,* a book that changed the course of modern poetry. Its poems were confessional in nature, examining minutely moments in Lowell's own life, from the deaths of his parents to his own unhappy marriage to his psychological breakdown. *Life Studies* moves beyond the simply confessional, however, to consider the larger social context for the poet's experience. The volume won the National Book Award in 1960.

"For the Union Dead," the title poem of a volume printed in 1964, concerns civil rights. It depicts AUGUSTUS ST. GAUDENS's monument to the Massachusetts Fifty-fourth Regiment of black Union army soldiers as being alone and ignored in the city of Boston and observes how little progress has been made on behalf of black schoolchildren since the Civil War.

In 1961 Lowell published a volume of translations of European poems, *Imitations,* earning himself the Bollingen Poetry Translation Prize the following year. He also translated Racine's play *Phaedra* (1961) and Aeschylus's *The Oresteia* (1979).

Lowell's activism grew ever more public. In 1965 he declined President Lyndon Johnson's invitation to the White House Festival of the Arts as a protest of the Vietnam War. He became actively involved in campaigning for Senator Eugene McCarthy as a candidate for the 1968 Democratic presidential nomination.

The poems in *Near the Ocean* (1967) confront the legacy of the war and the threat of nuclear annihilation for America's youth.

Next Lowell embarked on an ambitious effort to find a poetic form that would allow him to link "the day-to-day with history." His *Notebook 1967–1968* (1969) features a long string of unrhymed sonnets that reflect on historical events, artistic achievements, and moments in the poet's personal life. Lowell revised and expanded the work the following year into a volume called simply *Notebook.* Subsequently, he added more but divided the historical from the personal; the broader social commentary filled a volume called *History* (1973), and the personal material a second book called *For Lizzie and Harriet* (1973). The title refers to his wife and daughter. These sonnet sequences, like the *Cantos* of EZRA POUND and the *Dream Songs* of JOHN BERRYMAN, were meant to be broadly inclusive of the poet's thought and experience.

Lowell moved to England in 1970. The following year, he and the fiction writer Caroline Blackwood had a son; he subsequently left Elizabeth Hardwick and their daughter and married Blackwood. These events are reflected in *The Dolphin* (1973), the last in the sonnet series and a meditation on sex and aging. The volume won a Pulitzer Prize.

Lowell's marriage to Blackwood soon foundered, and he felt alienated from both his families. He died of heart failure in a taxi cab en route to Hardwick's home in New York City after a visit with Blackwood in Ireland. His final volume of poetry, *Day by Day* (1977), had been published a month earlier.

BIBLIOGRAPHY

Axelrod, Steven Gould, *Robert Lowell: Life and Art,* 1978; Hamilton, Ian, *Robert Lowell,* 1982; Meyers, Jeffrey (ed.), *Robert Lowell: Interviews and Memoirs,* 1988.

Lubitsch, Ernst

(January 28, 1892–November 30, 1947)
Film Director, Producer

An already accomplished filmmaker in Germany, Ernst Lubitsch became Hollywood's greatest director of the comedy of manners, a genre he virtually invented in the silent era. His style, which became known as the Lubitsch touch, is evident in such classics as *Ninotchka* and *To Be or Not to Be.*

Born in Berlin, Ernst was the only child of tailor Simon Lubitsch and his wife. At the Sophien-Gymnasium he performed in school plays and at sixteen dreamed of the theater while working as a bookkeeper in his father's clothing shop.

With the help of comedian Victor Arnold, Ernst performed low comedy in cabarets and music halls, learning timing and technique. In 1911 he was admitted to theatrical genius Max Reinhardt's Deutsches Theater, playing small parts in classics—his debut, one of the gravediggers in *Hamlet.*

In 1912 he was property man and assistant for the Bioscope film studios in Berlin, and appeared in two Reinhardt film productions, *The Miracle* and *Venetian Nights.* Between 1913 and 1918 he played in a number of short comedies, including the Jewish character "Meyer" series, and directed his first one-reeler, *Miss Soapsuds,* in 1914. *Shoe Salon Pinkus* (1916) was his first big success as director.

In 1918 he directed *The Eyes of the Mummy* and *Carmen,* his first important features, placing him and actress Pola Negri in the forefront of European cinema. They duplicated this success in 1919 with *Madame Du Barry,* which, under the title *Passion,* was the first German film to open in the United States. Lubitsch's reputation was further enhanced by his charming fairy tales, *The Oyster Princess* and *The Doll* (both 1919). His last film in Germany was *The Flame* (1922).

Invited to Hollywood by MARY PICKFORD, who hoped he would transform her screen image, he made his first American film, *Rosita,* a ro-

mance about a Spanish street singer. While Pickford was disappointed, Lubitsch remained to sign a contract with the fledgling Warner Brothers for five films.

The first was *The Marriage Circle* (1924), a comedy of manners set in pre–World War I Vienna. Influenced by CHARLIE CHAPLIN's *A Woman of Paris* (1923), a sophisticated love triangle melodrama, Lubitsch's handling of similar material had an even greater influence on a generation of filmmakers. Chaplin himself remarked that Lubitsch "could do more to show the grace and humor of sex in a nonlustful way than any other director I've ever heard of."

In the same year Lubitsch directed *Forbidden Paradise* for Paramount, with Pola Negri, who had also emigrated to Hollywood, as Catherine the Great. The film was critically acclaimed, as was *Lady Windermere's Fan* (1925), an adaptation of Oscar Wilde's play. One of his greatest successes, it was considered a tour de force, capturing the Wildean spirit without the use of a single Wildean epigram.

Completing his Warners contract with *So This Is Paris* (1926), Lubitsch filmed *The Student Prince* for MGM, but was unhappy with stars Norma Shearer and Ramon Novarro, who lacked that playfully erotic spirit characteristic of his work. Certain scenes were reshot by director John Stahl at LOUIS B. MAYER's request.

Between 1928 and 1938 he directed fifteen films, mostly at Paramount. Three starred singers Maurice Chevalier and Jeanette MacDonald, notably *The Love Parade* (1929), Lubitsch's first sound film and a milestone in the development of the cinematic musical; *One Hour with You* (1932), a musical remake of *The Marriage Circle;* and *The Merry Widow* (1934), another adaptation of the operetta produced by IRVING THALBERG for MGM. In this same period Lubitsch directed two of his best comedies, *Trouble in Paradise* (1932) and *Design for Living* (1933), both with Miriam Hopkins.

In 1935 Lubitsch became production chief at Paramount and made three elegant comedy-romances in succession: *Desire* (1936) with MARLENE DIETRICH and GARY COOPER; *Angel* (1937) with Dietrich and Herbert Marshall; and *Bluebeard's Eighth Wife* (1938) with Cooper and Claudette Colbert. The latter was further enhanced by a screenplay by BILLY WILDER and Charles Brackett.

The Lubitsch/Wilder/Brackett combo outdid itself in 1939 with *Ninotchka,* one of Hollywood's wittiest and most endearing achievements, boasting, in addition to its direction and writing, the one memorable comic performance by GRETA GARBO, who considered it her best American film. She plays a stiff communist envoy sent to Paris to retrieve three comrades who have been seduced by the West. Succumbing to Paris and her suave costar, Melvyn Douglas, her liberation is expressed through a newfound sense of humor. The ads for the film aptly promoted this angle, declaring, "Garbo laughs!"

The quality of Lubitsch's work never diminished. Over the next few years he made *The Shop around the Corner* (1940), featuring wonderful performances by Margaret Sullavan and JAMES STEWART; *To Be or Not to Be* (1942), a satire on theater people and the Nazis, featuring comedian Jack Benny and the final screen appearance of Carole Lombard; *Heaven Can Wait* (1943), his first film in color starring Gene Tierney and Don Ameche; and *Cluny Brown* (1946), his last completed work, "slyly lancing the British caste system," with Jennifer Jones and Charles Boyer. He had begun *That Lady in Ermine* (1948) when he died suddenly.

Few directors were paid such high tribute by their peers. Writer/director Joseph L. Mankiewicz considered Lubitsch "head and shoulders beyond everyone in the field of sophisticated high comedy." For ORSON WELLES, "Lubitsch was a giant . . . his talent and originality were stupefying." In 1947 Lubitsch received an honorary Oscar for distinguished contribution to the art of motion pictures.

BIBLIOGRAPHY

Hake, Sabine, *Passions and Deceptions: The Early Films of Ernst Lubitsch,* 1992; Paul, William, *Ernst Lubitsch's American Comedy,* 1983; Weinberg, Herman G., *The Lubitsch Touch,* 1968.

Lunt, Alfred David, Jr.

(August 12, 1893–August 3, 1977)
Actor

Fontanne, Lynn

(December 6, 1887–July 30, 1983)
Actress

Regal, willowy Lynn Fontanne and her handsome husband, Alfred Lunt, known collectively as the Lunts, starred in sparkling, sophisticated comedies on the stage in London and New York from 1919 to 1960. They have been called the best loved and most successful acting team in American theatrical history.

Fontanne was born in Woodford, Essex, England, and christened Lillie Louise, the daughter of a French designer of printing type and an Irish mother. With no experience and no training, except for reciting Shakespeare for her father, Fontanne was taken on as a pupil by the reigning queen of the English stage, Ellen Terry, in 1904. Terry also arranged for Fontanne's stage debut in the chorus of a Christmas pantomime of *Cinderella* in London in 1905. Fontanne was a successful comedienne on the London stage when the American actress Laurette Taylor met her in 1915 and took her back to New York as a member of her own company. Fontanne became a leading comic actress when she played the pushy wife in a delectable, moronic comedy, *Dulcy* (1921), by GEORGE S. KAUFMAN and Marc Connelly.

Lunt, born in Milwaukee, Wisconsin, and educated at Carroll College, made his professional stage debut with the Castle Square Theater stock company in Boston in 1912. He toured with Lillie Langtry and made his first Broadway appearance in a minor comedy, *Romance and Arabella*, in 1917. In the spring of 1919 he met Lynn Fontanne when they were in New York rehearsing a stock company production of *Made of Money*, a variation of the Pygmalion story. The play opened June 9 in Washington, D.C.—their first appearance on the same stage—and was followed by *A Young Man's Fancy*, which gave them star billing and rave reviews from the critics. They fell in love but could not yet afford marriage. Fortunately, BOOTH TARKINGTON had finished a new play written specifically for Lunt and cast opposite him an unknown ingénue named HELEN HAYES. *Clarence* opened in New York in September 1919 and played 300 performances there before a national tour ended in the spring of 1921. By that time the advertisements read "Alfred Lunt in *Clarence*." Meanwhile, Fontanne was starring in *Dulcy* in Chicago and eventually in New York. They were married in May 1922.

Laurette Taylor asked the Lunts in 1923 to join her in *Sweet Nell of Old Drury*, an old comic melodrama revived to raise money for the Equity Players. The Lunts were together on Broadway at last. A comedy by Ferenc Molnár, *The Guardsman* (1924), proved to be their first great joint triumph. It was also the first financial success for the Theater Guild, which had been founded in 1919 to raise the artistic standards of the New York theater.

Lunt seldom appeared without Fontanne but had done so as Mr. Prior in Sutton Vane's *Outward Bound* (1923), in which the passengers on a ship discover they have died and are on their way to another life. Fontanne played without Lunt in 1928 as Nina Leeds in EUGENE O'NEILL's *Strange Interlude*, a nine-act drama that caused a sensation by using asides to the audience to reveal the inner thoughts of the characters in contrast with their direct speech.

In 1930 they created the roles of Queen Elizabeth and the Earl of Essex in MAXWELL ANDERSON's *Elizabeth the Queen* for the Theater Guild, and after that they never acted separately. The Lunts appeared in twenty-three Theater Guild productions between 1924 and 1949 in plays by George Bernard Shaw, Eugene O'Neill, Maxwell Anderson, ROBERT SHERWOOD, and S. N. Behrman.

The Lunts also created the leading roles in three plays by Robert Sherwood. Fontanne was Elena and Lunt the former crown prince Rudolf now driving a taxi in *Reunion in Vienna* (1931), a comedy set in a country with an authoritarian government. In 1936 she was Irene and Lunt Harry Van, a seedy song-and-dance man in Sherwood's antiwar comedy, *Idiot's Delight*. In 1940 Lunt was Dr. Kaarlo Valkonen, the scientist, and she was Miranda in Sherwood's drama about Finnish resistance against the Russians, *There Shall Be No Night*.

Fontanne played Madame Arkadina in Anton Chekhov's *Sea Gull* and Alkmena in S. N. Behrman's version of Jean Giraudoux's *Amphitryon 38*, in which Lunt played Jupiter. In 1938 the Lunts took *Amphitryon 38* and *The Sea Gull* on a cross-country tour, adding *Idiot's Delight* in 1939. Their last appearance with the Theater Guild was in S. N. Behrman's adaptation of *I Know My Love* in 1949.

Besides their Theater Guild performances, the Lunts starred in *Design for Living* (1933), a comedy by Noel Coward, and in his drama, *Point Valaine* (1935). In 1946 they played in Terence Rattigan's *O Mistress Mine;* in 1954 in Noel Coward's *Quadrille,* a comedy set in the nineteenth century; and in 1956 in *The Great Sebastians*, written especially for them by Howard Lindsay and Russel Crouse.

After a lifetime of playing mostly in comedies, in May 1957 they opened the new Lunt-Fontanne Theater in New York with Friedrich Duerrenmatt's dark tragedy, *The Visit*. They toured the United States (1959–1960) in the same play and then in June 1960 opened the new Royalty Theater in London with their by now famous performance of Duerrenmatt's un-

forgettable tragedy. It was their last appearance on stage.

They appeared on television in *The Magnificent Yankee*, a play about OLIVER WENDELL HOLMES by Emmet Lavery, in 1965.

BIBLIOGRAPHY

Brown, Jared, *The Fabulous Lunts*, 1986; Zolotow, Maurice, *Stagestruck*, 1965.

McCardell, Claire

(May 24, 1905–March 22, 1958)
Fashion Designer

Claire McCardell was an innovative fashion designer whose styles helped to define the "American look" as it emerged during the 1930s and 1940s. Her functional and comfortable ready-to-wear clothes at moderate prices would influence the American fashion industry for the rest of the century.

McCardell was born into a prosperous family in Frederick, Maryland, where her father was a bank president and state senator. At an early age she began cutting paper dolls from fashion magazines and, by high school age, was making all her own clothes. She left Hood College after two years (1923–1925) to pursue her interest in design at the New York School of Fine and Applied Arts (now Parsons School of Design). In 1927 she studied at that school's Paris branch and attended the haute couture showings of the Parisian fashion houses. Experimenting with discarded, end-of-season dress models, McCardell developed what became a hallmark of her style—clothing with flexibility and easy fit.

After graduation in 1928, she worked as a model, a sketch artist, and a painter of lampshades until 1930, when she met dress designer Robert Turk, who became her mentor. When his company disbanded, Turk took her

with him to the sportswear firm of Townley Frocks (New York City), where she became head designer in 1932. Except for a brief association with Hattie Carnegie (1939–1940) during the period of Townley's reorganization, McCardell spent the rest of her life at the firm, becoming a partner in 1952.

Aware of the American woman's desire for comfort, easy fit, and affordable prices, McCardell worked to adapt the casual comfort and fit of sportswear to clothes for all occasions. She said: "I do not like glitter . . . I like comfort in the rain, in the sun; comfort for active sports, comfort for sitting still and looking pretty. Clothes should be useful." In 1934 she created the first "separates," a five-piece black wool jersey combination consisting of a halter top, a jacket, slacks, skirt, and culottes. Her distinctive use of line and color to create clothes that move naturally with the body is epitomized by the "Monastic" dress (introduced in 1938), which had an identical front and back and no fixed waist.

During World War II, McCardell's innovative designs turned restrictions on fabric into fashion gems, such as the "Popover," a denim wraparound dress, and the versatile "body suit" or leotard in wool jersey. She was the first to use denim as a fashionable fabric and introduced wool jersey for evening wear. Another innovation was her use of cotton for coats, suits, and evening dresses, rather than just sports clothes. She also incorporated many details from men's clothing, such as large pockets, topstitching on blue jeans, and trouser pleats. Women liked her easy-fitting designs, which generally had no waistline or an adjustable one. Particular favorites were her harem pajamas, string-tied Empire-line dress, and tapered, high-waisted wool challis slacks.

She occasionally introduced some playful touches into her clothes, such as ornamental colored zippers and brass fishing boot hooks on the sides of her popular 1943 "Diaper" bathing suit. In addition to clothing, she designed accessories, such as shoes, hats, gloves, and jewelry.

In 1943 she married widowed architect Irving Harris. During the 1940s she earned all major awards given within the fashion industry. She also served as adviser to the Costume Institute at New York's Metropolitan Museum of Art, a teacher and critic at the Parsons School, and an officer of The Fashion Group, an organization of women in the fashion industry. In her 1956 book, *What Shall I Wear?* she stated the guiding spirit behind her designs: "For me, it's America—it looks and feels like America. It's freedom, it's democracy, it's casualness, it's good health. Clothes can say all that." McCardell died of cancer in 1958, but she left a legacy of clothing design that reflects the American way of life.

BIBLIOGRAPHY

"The American Look," *Time*, May 2, 1955; Epstein, Beryl, *Fashion Is Our Business*, 1945; Lee, Sarah Tomerlin (ed.), *American Fashion*, 1975.

McCarthy, Mary Therese

(June 21, 1912–October 25, 1989)
Critic, Novelist, Short-Story Writer

Mary McCarthy, a prominent figure in American intellectual circles during the last half of the twentieth century, produced novels, short stories, drama criticism, political reporting, histories of architecture, and autobiography. Her incisive satiric novels most often targeted intellectuals caught between inner lives and reality.

McCarthy was born on June 21, 1912, in Seattle, Washington. Both of her parents died in the influenza epidemic of 1918. The harsh treatment she and her brothers received at the hands of a great-aunt and her authoritarian husband is described in *Memories of a Catholic Girlhood* (1957).

At Vassar College, McCarthy and ELIZABETH BISHOP were among four students who founded the literary magazine *Con Spirito*.

After graduation in 1933 she moved to New York City and married an aspiring actor, Harold Johnsrud. The union lasted only three years. She began writing book reviews for *The Nation* and *The New Republic* and became drama critic for *Partisan Review*. She associated with leftist intellectuals and flirted with communism.

In 1938 she married the famous literary critic EDMUND WILSON. Their difficult marriage lasted seven years and produced a son. Six short stories about the struggles for identity of a single character, drawn from McCarthy's own life, were published as McCarthy's first book, *The Company She Keeps,* in 1942. McCarthy and Wilson divorced in 1946. She married Bowden Broadwater the same year.

McCarthy described *The Oasis* (1949) as a philosophical landscape. The novel, a defense of American intellectual life, describes a utopian experiment on a mountaintop that fails when the participants realize they cannot change themselves.

The Groves of Academe (1952) satirizes intellectual pretensions at a small college, where the

Library of Congress

truth is subverted by an incompetent faculty member who tries to avert being fired by claiming discrimination on the basis of his past as a Communist. Though many were offended by the novel, most readers admired it for its brilliant style and ferocious wit.

McCarthy's heroine in *A Charmed Life* (1955) is a writer and intellectual living with her second husband in a community like McCarthy's on Cape Cod. There, a group of artists lead "charmed" lives outside conventional standards of morality until the heroine gets pregnant after a drunken seduction by her former husband.

During the late 1950s, McCarthy's marriage deteriorated. She wrote in Europe, while Broadwater taught in New York and her son studied there. McCarthy's publications during this period included two art history books, *Venice Observed* (1956) and *The Stones of*

Florence (1959), and two collections of reviews and essays, *Sights and Spectacles, 1937–1956* (1956) and *On the Contrary* (1961).

In 1961 Broadwater and McCarthy divorced, and she married James Raymond West, an official with the U.S. State Department, with whom she then lived in Paris and in Castine, Maine.

The Group (1963) became a best-seller. It chronicles the experiences of eight young women who graduate from Vassar College full of self-confidence and faith in "progress." Each character faces difficult realities about the forces that limit her life.

McCarthy wrote three books expressing opposition to the Vietnam War: *Vietnam* (1967), *Hanoi* (1968), and *Medina* (1972). Her novel *Birds of America* (1971) traces a young man's loss of faith in the concept of equality. *Cannibals and Missionaries* (1979) describes the hijacking of a plane en route to Iran.

In her later years, McCarthy wrote several books of essays and criticism, including *Ideas and the Novel* (1980), *Occasional Prose* (1985), and *How I Grew* (1987). McCarthy died of cancer in New York in 1989.

BIBLIOGRAPHY

Grumbach, Doris, *The Company She Kept,* 1976; McKenzie, Barbara, *Mary McCarthy,* 1966; Stock, Irvin, *Mary McCarthy,* 1968.

McCullers, Lula Carson Smith

(February 19, 1917–September 29, 1967)
Novelist, Playwright

Carson McCullers wrote novels and drama that explore the psychic makeup of characters who lived in isolation on the edges of Southern society in the 1940s and 1950s. Her work helped establish the tradition known as Southern gothic.

McCullers was born in Columbus, Georgia, in 1917. After graduating from Columbus High School in 1933, she attended Columbia University and New York University, then settled in New York City to study music.

Her fiction was always set in the state of Georgia. Though she believed a writer could not escape from the place of her birth, she regarded the South antagonistically as a place where one might be worth "no more than a load of hay."

McCullers attained immediate literary success with her first novel, *The Heart Is a Lonely Hunter* (1940), the story of a deaf and mute boy growing up in a small Southern town and of his association with an adolescent girl. The isolation felt by the deaf-mute and the girl's desperate loneliness represent a theme that would recur frequently in McCullers's fiction. Likewise, the girl's passion for music—her only solace—would be repeated, perhaps reflecting McCullers's own childhood and adolescence spent in daily eight-hour practice sessions at the piano. In fact, when McCullers outlined *The Heart Is a Lonely Hunter* for her publisher, she did so in musical terms, as if it were a symphony, and she later insisted on the need for "precision and harmony" in her literary composition.

Within six years, McCullers had published two more popular novels. Like *The Heart Is a Lonely Hunter*, each sold over half a million copies. *Reflections in a Golden Eye* (1941) concerns violence at a peacetime army post. The theme of isolation is addressed in the character of a single soldier, perpetually silent, who lurks in the night, staring through a window at the sleeping wife of an officer. In *The Member of the Wedding* (1946), a lonely, motherless girl, thirteen-year-old Frankie, somehow gets the mistaken idea that she will accompany her elder brother out into the world once he marries. From the book, McCullers wrote a play that was produced on Broadway in 1950 and won the New York Drama Critics' Circle Award.

After the success of *The Member of the Wedding*, McCullers faced precipitously declining health. She suffered strokes, heart disease, paralysis, and finally cancer. Her illnesses severely limited her ability to write. Nevertheless, in 1951 McCullers published a collection of stories, *The Ballad of the Sad Café.* The title story, a novelette, was turned into a play by Edward Albee. McCullers produced another collection of stories, *Seven* (1954), as well as a play, *The Square Root of Wonderful* (produced in 1957), and another novel, *Clock Without Hands* (1961).

McCullers's work is often cited as an example of the Southern gothic literary tradition, which featured psychological portraits of characters who bordered on the grotesque. Others in the tradition include William Faulkner, Flannery O'Connor, and Eudora Welty.

BIBLIOGRAPHY

Carr, Virginia Spencer, *The Lonely Hunter: A Biography of Carson McCullers*, 1975; McDowell, Margaret B., *Carson McCullers*, 1980.

MacDowell, Edward Alexander

(December 18, 1860–January 23, 1908)
Composer, Pianist, Teacher

One of America's first internationally recognized composers, Edward MacDowell dominated the American musical scene for years prior to the turn of the century. Though his music may now seem derivative rather than innovative, he commanded respect as a composer and pianist, as well as a teacher.

Born in New York City to Thomas and Frances McDowell, Edward began to study piano at age eight with Colombian violinist Juan Buitrago, who exchanged room and board for the lessons. By 1876 the youngster was in Paris to study piano and theory. In February 1877 he was admitted to the Paris Conservatory and in October of that year won a scholarship and a place as a regular piano student. In the late 1870s, when he changed his name to MacDowell, his family followed suit.

In 1878 MacDowell traveled to Germany to further his studies. In May 1879 he entered the Frankfurt Conservatory to study piano with Carl Heymann, advanced composition with Joachim Raff, and counterpoint and fugue with Franz Böhme. Franz Liszt was in the audience when MacDowell made his first concert appearance on June 9, 1879, and heard MacDowell play twice in 1880.

MacDowell left the conservatory in July 1880, though he continued to study with Heymann and Raff and to instruct private piano students. On Raff's recommendation MacDowell sent one of his compositions to Liszt, who successfully lobbied for its performance at an 1882 conference in Zurich, Switzerland. In Zurich, MacDowell performed his *Erste moderne Suite* (First Modern Suite). Its success convinced him to turn more seriously to composition. Liszt continued to encourage the composer after hearing his First Piano Concerto.

Over the next two years MacDowell's works were performed in Chicago, Detroit, and Saratoga, New York, and by the end of the next year German publishing houses had issued ten of the twenty-four-year-old's works, including a two-piano version of the First Piano Concerto dedicated to Liszt.

MacDowell married one of his students, Marian Nevins, in 1884. The newlyweds returned to Germany, where the composer devoted himself to writing. In three years he produced an extraordinary amount of work: solo piano pieces, piano duets, songs, another piano concerto, three orchestral tone poems, and the *Romanze* for cello and orchestra.

The MacDowells returned to the United States in 1888, settling in Boston, where they remained until 1896. MacDowell gained stature as a soloist and composer as his works were heard around the country. Boston was a productive environment for composition. He wrote piano sonatas, *Woodland Sketches* for piano, songs, and two orchestral suites. By 1896 he was considered a leader in American music—as composer, performer, and teacher.

In May 1896 MacDowell was appointed Columbia University's first professor of music and plunged into a whirlwind of activity. He taught, conducted the Mendelssohn Glee Club, composed, gave private piano lessons, concertized during school breaks, and from 1899 to 1900 served as president of the newly established Society of American Musicians and Composers. In 1903 he clashed with Columbia's president, Nicholas Murray Butler, and resigned the following year. An accident with a hansom cab prompted the composer's decline into mental illness, and in 1908 he died. MacDowell was buried in Peterborough, New Hampshire, on his own country property. The place, following MacDowell's wishes, was converted to an artists' colony that was presided over for many years by his widow and is still a going institution today.

Molded by his Germanic training, MacDowell was not an innovator; rather, many believe his music to be derivative. The two piano concertos, *Hamlet* and *Lamia*, are reminiscent of Liszt, other compositions suggest Wagner, while his later works can evoke the lyricism of Grieg. Much of his music relies on dense textures, chromatics, and dramatic contrast for its effect. Though MacDowell worked comfortably with large forms like the piano concerto or piano sonata, he was at his best in such small melodic efforts as "To a Wild Rose."

BIBLIOGRAPHY

Gilman, L., *Edward MacDowell*, 1906, rev., 1909, reissued 1969 as *Edward MacDowell: a Study.*

McKim, Charles Follen

(August 27, 1847–September 14, 1909)
Architect, Designer

Mead, William Rutherford

(August 20, 1846–June 20, 1928)
Businessman

White, Stanford

(November 9, 1853–June 25, 1906)
Architect, Designer

In business from 1879 until the 1920s, McKim, Mead & White was one of the largest, most successful and influential architectural firms in the world.

With a commitment to "build well," McKim, Mead, and White popularized a modernized classical architecture centered mainly around the Italian Renaissance Revival style, established a high standard for public building design, and promoted architectural education. Their designs of clubhouses, residences, banks, churches, and public and commercial buildings helped to define the "American Renaissance" at the turn of the century.

Charles Follen McKim, the guiding spirit of the firm, was born in Isabella Furnace, Pennsylvania. After studying engineering at Harvard and architecture at the Ecole des Beaux-Arts in Paris (1867–1870), he worked with architect HENRY HOBSON RICHARDSON. McKim's idea that architecture acts as a public symbol by defining civic aspirations and, when integrated with the other arts, exerts a civilizing influence on society became the firm's philosophical foundation. Independently, he worked on several special projects, such as the completion and extension of Pierre Charles L'Enfant's plans for Washington, D.C., as part of a special commission.

William Rutherford Mead was born in Brattleboro, Vermont. He graduated from Amherst College (1867), studied architecture in Florence, Italy (1871–1873), and served an apprenticeship in a New York architectural office before becoming a founding partner of the firm. Noted for his shrewd business practices and sound judgment, Mead became the business manager and construction supervisor of the firm, as well as an astute critic of his partners' designs. He was even-tempered and good-humored, and often joked that his job was to keep his partners from "making damn fools of themselves."

Stanford White was born in New York City, the son of famed literary and music critic Richard Grant White. After graduation from New York University, he pursued architectural training in Henry Hobson Richardson's office, where he met McKim. White was devoted to a more facile expression of beauty, and became known for his "painterly" approach to color and texture and his mastery of decorative detail. Within the firm, he emerged as the designer for the nouveau riche, designing not only buildings but also interiors, furniture, book jackets, magazine covers, picture frames, and gravestones. He was also famous for his collaboration with sculptor AUGUSTUS SAINT-GAUDENS on several projects. Stannie, as he was affectionately known, was attuned to his age; his flamboyant style—work and life—personified the Gay Nineties era.

The New York–based firm bearing their name was formed by these diverse personalities in 1879. By the deaths of White in 1906 and McKim in 1909 the company had designed some of the finest buildings in America. Initially, fame was gained with the firm's country and seaside homes and country clubs designed in the shingled Colonial Revival, or Shingle style, which was originated by Richardson and characterized by shingle-covered walls and roofs, long bands of windows, and wide porches and verandas. A balanced but asymmetrical facade, large chimneys, and circular towers are some of the hallmarks of the firm's Shingle style, as seen in two Newport, Rhode Island, houses: the Isaac Bell house (1881–1883) and the Robert Goelet house (1882–1884). The Newport Casino (1879–1880), begun by McKim and finished by White, was a rousing success and spawned a stream of wealthy clients. This shingled building with its comparatively restrained public facade, semi-enclosed court with polygonal clock tower, and ornately latticed piazza (porch), foreshadows one of the firm's outstanding design traits: the ability to suit a building's character to its environment and complicated program.

The Villard Houses on New York City's Madison Avenue (1882–1885), begun by McKim, worked on by White, and finished by the firm's draftsman, Joseph Morrill Wells, introduced the more archaeological Italian Renaissance Revival style that is identified with the firm and became a prototype for much residential design. This U-shaped grouping of six houses under one roof surrounding a courtyard illustrates the harmony of proportions and details so characteristic of their style. The return to classicism with the adaptation of the villa and palazzo styles of fifteenth- and sixteenth-century Italy, with their arcades and courtyards, perfectly suited the desire of the nineteenth-century's nouveau riche for urban and country houses of splendid dimensions.

The first masterworks of the firm (between 1887 and about 1894) show the divergent approaches of McKim and White under the broad umbrella of Italian Renaissance style. The monumental Boston Public Library (1887–1895) reveals the more disciplined approach of McKim, who stressed large-scale, comprehensive planning and meticulous attention to detail, proportion, order, and clarity of expression. The library has a monumental facade of carefully detailed stonework and rows of arched windows and a tile roof. The entrance doors and panels were done by sculptors Saint-Gaudens and DANIEL CHESTER FRENCH, reflecting the firm's commitment to integration of the arts.

White's masterpiece, the original Madison Square Garden in New York City (1887–1891), revealed his eye for color and texture and his creative borrowings from past architectural forms. A multipurpose sports and entertainment complex with several towers, loggias, and a roof garden, the building was a richly appointed Italian and Spanish Renaissance structure of light-colored terra cotta and abundant ornamentation.

The two architects complemented each other perfectly: McKim, with his scholarly, methodical approach contrasted with White, who could "draw like a house afire," according to

McKim, and complete fifteen commissions to McKim's one. It was primarily White's emphasis on rich ornamentation that earned the firm the nickname, McKim, White and Gold. White's talent and exuberant spirit shine in the brick and terra cotta facade of the palazzo-like Century Club in New York City (1889–1891), while McKim's hand is evident in the more formal and scholarly block of the University Club (1899).

The firm's mature works date from 1900 to 1909. Considered a jewel of Renaissance Revival architecture, the J. P. Morgan Library (1902–1907) by McKim has expanses of plain exterior walls and an arched entrance loggia, complemented by rich interior details. Their largest structure was New York's Pennsylvania Railroad Station (1903–1910), also by McKim, which boasted a severe granite exterior with Roman Doric columns, a huge waiting room with a vaulted ceiling modeled after Rome's Baths of Caracalla, and a concourse of steel and glass leading to the trains. Another of White's masterworks was the Madison Square Presbyterian Church (1903–1906). A cube-shaped structure with a Corinthian-columned portico (porch), the church had buff-colored brick walls with terra cotta ornament glazed in moss green, yellow, and powder blue—one of the most exuberant uses of polychromy in American classical architecture.

In 1895 McKim helped to establish the American Academy in Rome to promote postgraduate study in the arts and served as its first president. In 1906 the firm suffered a major blow when White was shot and killed by Harry Thaw in a jealous rage over his wife, Evelyn Nesbit's, acquaintance with the architect. McKim died in 1909; Mead retired in 1919 but remained as a consultant until his death. White's son, Lawrence Grant White, became an architect and partner in the firm in 1920, continuing the founders' popular neoclassical design style in such works as the Savoy Plaza Hotel (1927).

BIBLIOGRAPHY

Baldwin, Charles C., *Stanford White*, rep., 1976; Hill, Frederick P., *Charles F. McKim: The Man*, 1950, and *A Monograph of the Works of McKim, Mead & White*, rep., 1973; Moore, Charles, *The Life and Times of Charles Follen McKim*, rep., 1969; Reilly, Charles H., *McKim, Mead & White*, rep., 1972; Roth, Leland, *McKim, Mead & White, Architects*, 1983; Wilson, Richard Guy, *McKim, Mead & White, Architects*, 1983.

MacLeish, Archibald

(May 7, 1892–April 20, 1982)
Playwright, Poet

A rchibald MacLeish wrote finely crafted lyric poetry and verse plays that spoke to the need for a humanistic revolution to address the social and cultural ills of the twentieth century. A committed public servant, he was Librarian of Congress, assistant secretary of state, and a founder of UNESCO.

MacLeish was born on May 7, 1892, in Glencoe, Illinois. At Yale University he wrote poetry and short stories for the *Yale Literary Magazine*. In 1915 he entered Harvard Law School.

In June 1916 MacLeish married Ada Hitchcock. He entered World War I the following year, joining the ambulance corps. His first volume of poetry, *Tower of Ivory* (1917), came out while MacLeish was in the army.

After the war, MacLeish returned to Harvard Law School, earning his LL.B. in 1919.

After two years as a successful trial lawyer, MacLeish quit his firm and moved with his wife and two young children to Paris, where he devoted himself to his poetry.

MacLeish wrote two volumes of poetry plus a play in blank verse before publishing his first important book of poetry in 1926. In *Streets in the Moon,* MacLeish began to find his own verse technique in his experiments with unrhymed sonnet forms and the so-called chop lines that resemble steps on a page. He also began to articulate a vision of the role of art in the modernist's world of desolation. His poem "Ars Poetica" defines poetry as a way of seeing via the imagination, of endowing experience with meaning. It offers the notion that "A poem should not mean / But be."

MacLeish began to feel strongly the promise of American civilization, with its tradition of individual liberty. He returned to the United States in 1928, settling on a farm in Conway, Massachusetts. In a volume of poems called *New Found Land* (1930), he announced his rediscovery of American values.

In 1932 he published *Conquistador,* an epic about the Spanish conquest of Mexico. The speaker of the poem is a Spanish soldier, and the reader experiences the New World through his senses and emotions. MacLeish wanted to explore the heart of the individual American, independent of race or country of origin; his decision to have a common soldier narrate the poem reflects this interest. *Conquistador* was awarded a Pulitzer Prize.

MacLeish worked on the editorial staff of *Fortune* magazine from 1929 to 1938. He began to assume a more public voice through articles and poems addressing broad social themes. His commitment to the public good is reflected in

Library of Congress

the satirical poems in *Frescoes for Mr. Rockefeller's City* (1933) and the more rhetorical verses in *Public Speech* (1936), plus three verse plays on topical themes—*Panic* (1935), *The Fall of the City* (1937), and *Air Raid* (1938), the last two in the form of radio scripts. This same sense of civic duty eventually led MacLeish to a more professional involvement in public affairs.

In 1938 MacLeish became curator of the Nieman Foundation of Journalism at Harvard for a year, then served five years as Librarian of Congress. From 1942 to 1945, he worked as director of the U.S. Office of Facts and Figures, assistant director of the U.S. Office of War Information, and assistant secretary of state. In the last position, he worked to found UNESCO (United Nations Education, Scientific, and Cultural Organization).

Two highly patriotic volumes of poetry bracketed MacLeish's years of public service: *America Was Promises* (1939) and *Actfive and Other Poems* (1948).

MacLeish taught literature and creative writing at Harvard from 1949 to 1962. A book of literary criticism, *Poetry and Experience* (1961), was distilled from his lectures there. *Collected Poems, 1917–1952* (1952) included forty-one new poems, most of them less public in nature. The volume earned MacLeish both a Pulitzer and the Bollingen Prize in 1953. His emphasis on lyric poetry continued in *Songs for Eve* (1954), *The Wild Old Wicked Man and Other Poems* (1968), and *New and Collected Poems: 1917–1976* (1976).

J. B. (1958), MacLeish's best-known verse play, was a Broadway hit, earning both a Pulitzer Prize and a Tony Award.

MacLeish enjoyed a vigorous old age, continuing both his writing and outdoor work on his farm. He died on April 20, 1982, three weeks short of a symposium organized to honor him on his ninetieth birthday.

BIBLIOGRAPHY

Smith, Grover, *Archibald MacLeish,* 1971.

Mailer, Norman Kingsley

(January 31, 1923–)
Essayist, Novelist

N orman Mailer writes fiction and nonfiction that explore the individual's struggle for freedoms against oppressive social institutions in twentieth-century America. His first and best-remembered novel, *The Naked and the Dead*, introduced Mailer's central concerns with unforgettable power and violence.

Mailer was born in Long Branch, New Jersey, a shore town where his mother's family was in the hotel business. When he was four years old, the family moved to Brooklyn, New York, where his father worked as an accountant and his mother ran a nursing and housekeeping service.

As a boy, Mailer was fascinated by airplanes; when he entered Harvard University at the age of sixteen, he intended to become an aeronautical engineer. At Harvard, he discovered writing. His first published short story, "The Greatest Thing in the World," appeared in the *Harvard Advocate;* it also won first prize in *Story* magazine's annual college competition. Mailer decided to dedicate himself to becoming "a great American novelist."

Seeking the sort of experience he could mine for fiction, Mailer enlisted in the army in 1944. His experience in the invasion of the island of Luzon in the Pacific theater during World War II served as the basis for his war novel, *The Naked and the Dead* (1948). The book's extraordinary critical and popular success made him instantly famous; the novel has been described as the finest, most sophisticated fiction to emerge from the war.

The Naked and the Dead describes a landing by a fourteen-man platoon of American soldiers on a small Japanese-held island in the South Pacific. The members of the platoon come from diverse backgrounds ethnically, socially, and economically. The platoon is a microcosm of American society. Strong characters dominate the novel, particularly Lieutenant Hearn, the liberal and rational man who leads the platoon on the landing, and General Cummings, the ambitious commander who is determined to shape the campaign according to his own needs. The novel's realistic depiction of the struggles of the men among themselves and against the natural environment is the source of its power.

Mailer wrote two more novels—both critical disappointments—before turning to nonfiction. *Barbary Shore* (1951) reflects on American and Soviet forms of authoritarianism and their effects on the lives of men of differing political persuasions and existential modes. *The Deer Park* (1955) concerns the meaning of art to a talented movie director who stands accused of being a communist by a congressional investigative committee. Both novels depict individuals caught up in a fight against larger social institutions that would crush their freedom—a frequent theme in Mailer's writing.

In 1955 Mailer cofounded a weekly newspaper, *The Village Voice*, in New York's Greenwich Village. He wrote a regular column, which he mined for his books *Advertisements for Myself* (1959) and *The Presidential Papers* (1963).

Advertisements for Myself established Mailer as a public persona. A collection of his fiction, poetry, essays, articles, and letters, it openly chronicles Mailer's efforts to render the best in himself through his art. The writer as fighter is a recurring metaphor; his struggles to achieve artistic form are essentially warlike.

In *The White Negro* (1957), Mailer lionizes the consciousness of the urban American black, whom he sees as functioning in a fashion that undermines the hold of oppressive cultural and social forces. Mailer favors even violent behavior on the part of the individual, arguing that it more sanely vents the collective social tendency toward anonymous, guiltless savagery: that is, war.

Mailer's turbulent energies wreaked havoc in his personal life. After an all-night party at their Manhattan apartment in 1960, Mailer stabbed his second wife, Adele Morales, with a penknife; both were hospitalized and recovered, though they divorced in 1962. In the course of the next year, he married and divorced the third of his six wives. He became known for hard drinking and riotous behavior and was arrested twice after bellicose arguments, one of which ended in a violent encounter with a police officer.

Mailer returned to fiction with *An American Dream* (1965). The protagonist, Stephen Rojack, struggles to evolve himself back to a more primitive persona, free of the accomplishments—as an author, a teacher, and a war hero—that have been the source of his identity. In the course of the novel, he murders his estranged wife and defeats her father in mortal combat.

Mailer employed his reportorial skills in a series of books chronicling complex events in current history. *The Armies of the Night* (1968), which recounts an antiwar march on the Pentagon in October 1967, earned Mailer the National Book Award and the Pulitzer Prize. *Of a Fire on the Moon* (1970) covers the flight of Apollo 11. *The Prisoner of Sex* (1971) analyzes male sexuality in light of the women's liberation movement. *The Executioner's Song* (1979) is based on the life of convicted murderer Gary Gilmore; the book won Mailer a second Pulitzer.

More recent novels include *Ancient Evenings* (1983), about reincarnation in ancient Egypt, *Tough Guys Don't Dance* (1984), and *Harlot's Ghost* (1992). Mailer continues to live and write in Brooklyn.

BIBLIOGRAPHY

Bufithis, Philip, *Mailer*, 1978; Manso, Peter, *Norman Mailer: His Life and Times*, 1985; Mills, Hilary, *Norman Mailer: A Biography*, 1982; Poirier, Richard, *Norman Mailer*, 1972.

Malamud, Bernard

(April 26, 1914–March 18, 1986)
Novelist, Short-Story Writer

Bernard Malamud, a Jewish writer who helped introduce ethnicity as a matter for serious attention in twentieth-century American literature, wrote fiction that framed the struggles of ordinary people—usually well intentioned but clumsy—to break out of lives constricted by sadness and poverty in order to realize their own humane potential.

Malamud was born in Brooklyn, New York, the son of immigrant Russian parents who scraped by running a small grocery store. He began writing for the literary magazine at

Erasmus Hall, his high school in Brooklyn. In 1936 he earned a bachelor's degree at the City College of New York, and in 1942, a master's from Columbia University.

During the 1940s he wrote short stories while teaching at Erasmus Hall and Harlem High School. In 1949 he joined the faculty at the University of Oregon, where he taught composition for twelve years and wrote his first four novels. In 1961 Malamud moved to Bennington College in Vermont, where he served out the rest of his teaching days.

Malamud's first novel, *The Natural* (1952), concerns a talented thirty-three-year-old rookie who becomes the greatest batter in baseball history, then sells out his team to a gambler after corrupting himself through a liaison with a temptress, the gambler's protégé. Roy Hobbs recovers himself too late to help his team. He is struck out at the end by a young hotshot pitcher. While *The Natural* involves no Jewish characters, it addresses the theme of wisdom achieved through suffering that characterizes much of Malamud's fiction.

Malamud's next novel, *The Assistant* (1957), is set in a poor Jewish community where the central characters run the type of small grocery store Malamud's parents had owned. Frank Alpine robs the store but returns out of guilt to assist the owner, Morris Bober, during his recovery from a gunshot wound received during the robbery. Frank becomes involved in Morris's life, falling in love with Morris's daughter and eventually saving the business when, in a moment of despair, Morris tries to burn it down. Frank assumes Morris's role in the store after Morris's death, and he converts to Judaism.

The stories in *The Magic Barrel* (1958), Malamud's first collection of short fiction, utilize the form of the Yiddish folk tale. Most concern Jews living in poverty in the inner city; narratives shift from realistic depictions of urban scenes to fantastic renderings of characters' dreams. Among the stories included in this volume are "The Angel Levine," "The Last Mohican," and "The First Seven

Years." It won him a National Book Award in 1959.

A New Life (1961), based to some extent on Malamud's own experience at the University of Oregon, concerns a young teacher at Oregon's Cascadia College, who is frustrated by the school's lost commitment to the liberal arts. After he starts an affair with the wife of the chairman of his department, Seymour Levin must choose between love and his profession. At the end of the novel, he finds himself jobless in a car headed out of town with the woman he has impregnated—and whom he realizes he no longer loves—and her two children.

The Fixer (1966), Malamud's best-known novel, is based on a historic event, the arrest and trial of Mendel Beiliss in Kiev, Russia, in 1913 on charges that he ritually murdered a Christian child. Yakov Bok, Malamud's protagonist, is an irreligious Jew, whose only crime is to have slipped out of a Jewish settlement to live and work among Christians. Accused of the boy's murder, he spends two and a half years in prison awaiting trial; Malamud records in detail Bok's physical and spiritual suffering. As he faces his torment, Bok comes to feel for the first time a kinship with his fellow Jews and a humane concern for the well-being of his community. *The Fixer* won both a Pulitzer Prize and a National Book Award.

In *The Tenants* (1971), Malamud constructs an allegorical assessment of relations between blacks and Jews. The book recounts the story of two writers—one Jewish and established, the other black and unknown—who share a condemned tenement. Their rivalry runs to love as well as art: when Harry Lesser steals Willie Spearmint's white girlfriend, Spearmint destroys Lesser's manuscript, a project of nine years' work. The story ends in violence, and the reader is left to doubt the redemptive power of art.

Malamud wrote two more novels, *Dubin's Lives* (1979), about a biographer who identifies too closely with his subjects, and *God's Grace* (1982), an apocalyptic beast fable. His short stories are collected in *The Magic Barrel* (1960), *Idiots First* (1963), *Rembrandt's Hat* (1973), and *The Stories of Bernard Malamud* (1983).

Malamud died in 1986.

BIBLIOGRAPHY

Abramson, Edward A., *Bernard Malamud Revisited*, 1993; Hershinow, Sheldon J., *Bernard Malamud*, 1980; Richman, Sidney, *Bernard Malamud*, 1967.

Mamet, David

(November 30, 1947–)
Film Director/Writer, Playwright

David Mamet's plays and movies are unsentimentalized views of the collapse of the American Dream. They are characterized by profane expression and by his uniquely terse, elliptical dialogue.

Mamet was born in Chicago in 1947 and grew up on the city's South Side. Following his parents' divorce in the late 1950s, he divided his secondary education between the Francis W. Parker School and the Rich Central High School. Meanwhile, he got his first experience in the theater by working as a busboy at Chicago's famous improvisational comedy cabaret Second City and as a backstage volunteer at a local playhouse.

Resisting his father's wish that he pursue a law degree, Mamet studied literature and theater at the experimental Goddard College in Plainfield, Vermont. He also began acting under Sanford Meisner at the Neighborhood Playhouse in New York City and worked as house manager for the famous Off-Broadway musical *The Fantasticks*. During this same period he wrote his first play, a satirical revue called *Camel*. After graduating from college he went through a succession of jobs, working as a cabdriver, short-order cook, and sales representative for a real estate firm. In 1971 he returned to Goddard College to teach. Influenced by the work of Lanford Wilson and Samuel Beckett, he wrote several plays as classroom exercises and formed the St. Nicholas Company, an acting ensemble named for the patron saint of troubadors. A year later several of his new plays were staged in Chicago theaters, including *Sexual Perversity in Chicago*, which won the Joseph Jefferson Award in 1974.

Despite his growing success in Chicago, Mamet was a virtual unknown elsewhere. But after several of his scripts were rejected by New York producers, two plays, *Sexual Perversity in Chicago* and *Duck Variations*, were produced in the 1975–1976 season at the Off-Broadway St. Clements Theater and Cherry Lane Theater. One reviewer referred to the speeches in *Sexual Perversity* as "uncannily credible" and full of "brutal, dirty, monosyllabic observations" that left an aftertaste of "underlying sadness" and "loneliness." Writing in *Newsday* in 1976, Allen Wallach noted: "He is brilliant at showing how little is communicated when people exchange half-digested scraps of information and receive opinions they never bother to examine." Soon after, a revised version of *American Buffalo*, which had won Mamet an Obie Award in 1976, opened on Broadway in 1977. It was a character study of three small-time crooks planning a petty burglary of the home of a coin collector. After much wrangling, the inept schemers call off their plans. Although the critics were divided—some objecting to its static inactivity, others applauding its crudely poetic diction—*American Buffalo* was voted the Best Play of 1977 by the New York Drama Critics' Circle.

Other plays in the late 1970s included *A Life in the Theater*, a series of exchanges between two actors who are preparing several roles for stage performance; *The Water Engine*, a depression-era fable about an inventor whose discovery of a new kind of automobile engine is stolen by corrupt industrialists (the play was originally conceived as a radio drama for National Public Radio); and *The Woods*, a two-character variation on *Sexual Perversity*. For the Pulitzer Prize–winning *Glengarry Glen Ross*, written in 1983, Mamet drew from his experiences selling real estate, creating a devastating indictment of the American Dream.

Mamet's lifelong interest in the motion picture medium has led recently to many screenplays and directing projects. (His Hollywood experiences were the subject matter for his play *Speed-the-Plow*, 1987.) He adapted to the screen *Sexual Perversity in Chicago* (retitled *About Last Night*, 1987) and *Glengarry Glen Ross* (1992) and directed his own scripts for *House of Games* (1989), starring his wife, Lindsay Crouse, *Homicide* (1991), starring longtime associate Joe Mantegna, and *Hoffa* (1992), a project for director Danny DeVito.

His most recent play, *Oleanna* (1992), concerns a battle of wills and words between a college student and her professor.

Commentator David Savron says that Mamet's work is about those American ideals of power, buying and selling—achieving nothing less than "the demystification of the American Dream." Individuals are alienated from each other as well as from society in general. As Mamet himself succinctly puts it, his characters "go nuts." Unlike ARTHUR MILLER, however, who strives to change social conditions, Mamet has no activist agenda. "I just write plays," he said in an interview in 1988. "I don't think that my plays are going to change anybody's social conditions."

BIBLIOGRAPHY

Carroll, Dennis, *David Mamet*, 1987; Mamet, David, *The Cabin: Reminiscences and Diversions*, 1992.

Mapplethorpe, Robert

(November 4, 1946–March 9, 1989)
Photographer

Robert Mapplethorpe, a photographer whose work has caused much controversy, is known for his dramatic, austere black-and-white photos of flowers, portraits of celebrities, and studies of male nudes, many with an explicit sexual content.

Born in Queens, New York, Mapplethorpe turned from his Catholic, middle-class upbringing to pursue artistic freedom. After studying at New York's Pratt Institute (1963–1970), he became an underground filmmaker and artist, creating such early works as the collage *Model Parade* (1972). Impatience with painting and sculpture led him to experiment with photography—with satisfying results.

The turning point in Mapplethorpe's career occurred when he met wealthy advertising executive Sam Wagstaff, who encouraged his photography, assisted him financially, and provided a studio loft. In 1976 he had his first one-man show in Manhattan, featuring sensual flower photos, revealing self-portraits, and portraits of friends that brought immediate acclaim. These works reveal the strong contrast between black and white through stark lighting, and the still-life or formal arrangement of precise forms (whether flowers or people) posed against a plain or blank background devoid of anything extraneous, which became the hallmarks of his style. Mapplethorpe said, "My work is about seeing—seeing things like they haven't been seen before."

Mapplethorpe's major theme was celebration of the human form, focusing primarily on male nudes to explore images of power and sexuality. He did a photographic series of black male nudes, highlighting the powerful musculature of the masculine form in posed arrangements of limbs or body parts (hands, feet), which resemble pieces of sculpture. These photos were published in two highly acclaimed books, *Black Males* (1980) and *The Black Book* (1986). Believing that his works should challenge the viewer and evoke very personal responses, Mapplethorpe shook the art world when he exhibited his photos of homoerotism and sadomasochism in 1977. He dared to bring sex, especially "underground" sexual activity, to the forefront, thereby shattering old ideas of what was acceptable for the subject matter of art.

Juxtaposing a sophisticated, formal style with bold content that grabs the viewer's attention, Mapplethorpe's sexually explicit photos elicit varied responses of shock, disgust, and praise. A retrospective, *The Perfect Moment,* containing nature photos, portraits, nudes, and some sexually explicit shots, was shown at major museums in 1988–1990, but when it opened at the Cincinnati Contemporary Arts Center in 1990, there was a storm of protest. Although the museum and its director were acquitted of subsequent obscenity charges for showing the objectionable photos, Mapplethorpe's photos of male sexuality and bondage figured prominently in congressional debates concerning restrictions on funding for the National Endowment for the Arts, relative to prohibiting "obscene or indecent" art.

Mapplethorpe often designed his own frames and experimented with different matting techniques, believing that "sometimes . . . the structure in which a photograph is presented is as important as the photograph itself." In the late 1980s he experimented with color photography and with printing his photos on silk or linen, or framing them between fabrics. With the fortune he inherited from his long-time friend Wagstaff, Mapplethorpe established a foundation for the visual arts and for AIDS research funding. He died of AIDS in 1989. Some of his most affecting photos were a series of self-portraits, detailing the progress of the disease.

BIBLIOGRAPHY

Mapplethorpe, Robert, *Photographs,* 1978, and *Certain People,* 1985; Szarkowski, John, *Mirrors and Windows: American Photography Since 1960,* 1978.

Marin, John Currey

(December 23, 1870–October 1, 1953)
Painter

John Marin was America's greatest modern master of watercolor, a visionary whose highly individual seascapes and city scenes forged a bridge between Cubism and Abstract Expressionism.

Marin was born in Rutherford, New Jersey, in 1870. Raised by maternal grandparents after his mother's death, he attended several New Jersey schools and studied at the Stevens Institute of Technology for one semester in 1886. Uncertain of his abilities as an artist—he was already executing drawings and watercolors—he worked as a clerk in an architect's office and, in 1893, as a free-lance architect. Finally, in 1899 he entered the Pennsylvania Academy of the Fine Arts, where he won several prizes for his outdoor sketches, and the Art Students League in New York City.

From 1905 to 1910 he lived in Paris, studying in a rather desultory fashion at the Delecluse Academy and the Académie Julian. Rejecting the influence of Henri Matisse and the Fauves, Marin turned instead to JAMES WHISTLER, Paul Signac, Paul Cézanne, and Pierre Bonnard, producing images in watercolor and oil that were softly evocative, yet planar structured and firmly linear. *Untitled, No. 1 (Bridge)* and *Movement, Seine, Paris* (both 1909), for example, revealed Marin's wish to "let go" (his words), to defy the physical laws of gravity and stress. Forms were implied rather than described. Layers of thin washes punctuated by jabbing strokes were gently underpinned by skeletal pencil lines, imparting a delicate impressionism that seems Asian in sensibility.

These Paris etchings, oil paintings, and watercolors were exhibited yearly at the Salon d'Automne (1907–1910) and the Salon des Indépendants (1907 and 1908). It was in Paris that he first met the photographer ALFRED STIEGLITZ, owner of the 291 Gallery in New York. Stieglitz arranged for Marin's first New York shows in 1909; he continued to exhibit Marin annually. Marin returned to America in 1910 and settled in Cliffside, New Jersey, although he would spend most of his summers painting in Maine. At the famous Armory Show of 1913 (see STUART DAVIS), Marin's watercolors of the Woolworth Building were shown in the American section.

At Stieglitz's gallery, Marin became a central figure in a group of avant-garde American artists that included Marsden Hartley, GEORGIA O'KEEFFE, and Max Weber. Utilizing a bright palette and vigorous brushwork, his New York scenes, like *Municipal Building* and *Brooklyn Bridge* (both 1912) twist and writhe in a Futurist dynamicism. "I have just started some downtown stuff," he said at the time about these important works, "and to pile these great houses one upon another with paint as they do pile themselves up there so beautiful, so fantastic—at times one is afraid to look at them but feels like running away." At the same time,

his rural pictures of New Jersey and Maine were juxtapositions of free, slashing brush strokes with an almost calligraphic lyricism. Aspects of Cubism (geometric abstraction of lines and planes) and Expressionism (distortion or exaggeration of forms and color) were blended and transformed. While never committed to abstraction, Marin nonetheless played fast and loose in these landscapes with the significations of a subject. Biographer Ruth E. Fine suggests that Marin's effects in these images are like seismic responses to his body, evidence of the spontaneity of his process: "Strokes are laid in and left as freshly applied; marks are carved into the painted surfaces. . . . Some areas . . . are washed in and scrubbed out, leaving evidence of the artist's circular hand motion; fingerprint dabs stand for windows in the buildings."

It was in the 1920s, however, according to commentator Sheldon Reich, that the essential Marin legend was consolidated: of the self-taught, wiry little man with lined face and wizened features who worked independently of trendy movements and "continued to produce some of the most provocative and advanced paintings being done in this country." Celebrated watercolors like *The Red Sun, Brooklyn Bridge, Maine Islands,* and *From Bold Isle, Maine* (all 1922) were loose and spontaneous. He was painting in oils again (taking up the medium he had relinquished a decade earlier), executing thickly painted seascapes that seemed to revel in the power of waves smashing on rocks. Sea, land, and sky were broken intervals of space that conformed to some inner structure. "I can have things that clash," Marin said. "I can have a jolly good fight going on. There is always a fight going on where there are living things. But I must be able to control this fight at will with a Blessed Equilibrium."

In the opinion of the art museum curator Larry Curry, Marin's marine paintings came into full emergence in the 1930s. Marin bought a house at Cape Split at Addison, Maine, in 1933 and spent his remaining summers preoccupied with the "insistent" waves of the surrounding sea (*Small Point, Maine,* 1932, *Grey Sea,*

1938, and *Breaking Sea, Cape Split, Maine,* 1939). So consistent was he in both media of watercolor and oils, said Curry, that their effects—particularly in black-and-white reproductions—seem interchangeable.

In the decade of the 1940s and early 1950s, again according to Curry, in pictures like *Movement—Sea and Sky* (1946) and *The Written Sea* (1952), Marin worked in a manner and to an effect that approached Abstract Expressionism (see BARNETT NEWMAN). "Using paint as paint is different from using paint to paint a picture," Marin said in 1947 of his late oils. "I'm calling my pictures this year 'Movements in Paint' and not movements of boat, sea, or sky. . . . " His acclaim was such that a year later the formalist critic Clement Greenberg pronounced him "the best painter alive in America at this moment."

Marin was prolific. His catalog includes more than 2,500 watercolors and 500 oils. The larg-est retrospective of his work was held in 1936 at the Museum of Modern Art. Two floors were devoted to 160 watercolors, 21 oils, and 44 etchings. In 1948 he was the recipient of the Fine Arts Medal of the American Institute of Architects. Other honors included membership in the National Academy of Design and the National Institute of Arts and Letters. "Leave it to the true creative artist," Marin wrote. "He'll find a place for the stones and weeds of life in his picture and all so arranged that each takes its place and part in that rhythmic whole—that balanced whole—to wing its music with color, line and spacing upon its keyboard."

BIBLIOGRAPHY

Curry, Larry, *John Marin—1870–1953,* 1970; Fine, Ruth E., *John Marin,* 1990.

Marisol

(May 22, 1930–   )
Sculptor

Marisol is famous for her enigmatic, mysterious, highly original life-size carved figures and assemblages that satirize aspects of society. Her work, which frequently incorporates her own features, has been identified with the folk art tradition, and elements of both Pop and Assemblage art.

Marisol Escobar was born in Paris to Venezuelan parents. Her globe-trotting family introduced her to many different cultures, which impacted on her artistic development. She studied painting at the Ecole des Beaux-Arts in Paris (1949), then at the Art Students League, the New School for Social Research, and the Hans Hofmann School (1951–1954) in New York City. In the 1950s Marisol dropped her surname to promote artistic identity and became part of the Greenwich Village Beat Gen-eration. She taught herself the techniques of sculpture and was deeply influenced by South American and early North American folk art, especially hand-carved painted figures.

Marisol's early sculptures were small terracotta or carved wood figures of animals and people that were sometimes housed in glass-fronted boxes; *Figures in Type Drawer* (1954) is representative of these playful, often erotic pieces. By 1958 she was working on a larger scale and exploring mixed media by creating carved mahogany portrait "families" with painted or drawn features. Fame came with her 1962 sculpture *The Family,* an 83-inch-tall mixed-media grouping representing a farm family from the dust bowl. Five figures—a seated mother and her four children—are painted on blocks of wood. Except for one smiling girl, the figures share the same grim expression.

During the 1960s Marisol's highly original sculptured figures, often described as dolls or mannequins, became popular with the art-viewing public, and she was celebrated in the media as the "Latin Garbo," symbolizing glamour and mystery. In 1963 she became a naturalized U.S. citizen. She was frequently escorted by Pop art guru ANDY WARHOL and starred in his underground movie *The Kiss*. Marisol's work approaches Pop art (see ROY LICHTENSTEIN)—which stresses the pictorial and imitates mass media stereotypes by using such techniques as caricature and advertising images—through the use of such pop subjects as John Wayne and Britain's royal family, and some portraits that border on caricature.

Her sculptures also relate to Assemblage art in their mixed-media presentation and use of manufactured materials and found objects. A good example is *The Party* (1965–1966), fifteen life-size figures carved from solid blocks of wood and dressed in evening clothes or scraps of Marisol's own clothes. One woman sports a TV set in her carved coiffure, while servants hold trays of glasses. The sculpture also illustrates her talent for using aspects of primitive folk art and arrangements of mannerisms and dress to create scenes that satirize the social and political milieu. In her 1967 *Heads of State* exhibition, she used exaggeration with undertones of the absurd, and a mixture of two- and three-dimensional effects achieved through projections and graphics, to heighten the satire. The sculpture of President Lyndon B. Johnson, a giant, domineering figure holding three wooden "birds" with human faces—his wife and two daughters—in his left palm, is regarded as a satiric view of male chauvinism.

A central theme in Marisol's art, the quest for self-identity, gained prominence in 1964. Constant self-references, either by using her features on figures or by appending plaster or clay casts of her face, hands, or feet, were included in many sculptures. After a two-year hiatus (1969–1970), during which she traveled to the Far East and South and Central America, Marisol returned to work with a marked change in direction. She identified with the mythic qualities of the sea world by creating carved, stained mahogany predatory fish displaying her face, like *Zebra* (1971). Then in 1975 she exhibited a series of crayon and pencil drawings characterized by erotic and surreal imagery, as exemplified by *The King of Hearts*.

With her 1989 sculpture *Emperor Hirohito with Empress Nagako*, Marisol returned to large-scale mixed-media subjects inspired by the sociopolitical climate. Here, clothes and decorations are painted on boxes to form their bodies, hands are made of cut plywood or modeled clay, and Hirohito's eyes are round patties with slits inserted into an expertly carved head.

Marisol continues to work in New York City.

BIBLIOGRAPHY

Berman, Avis, "Marisol's Movers and Shakers," *Smithsonian*, February 1984; Loring, J., "Marisol's Diptych," *Arts Magazine*, April 1973; "Marisol's Mannequins," *Horizon*, March 1963; "Sculpture: The Doll Maker," *Time*, vol. 85, no. 22, May 1968.

Marx Brothers

Chico (1891–October 11, 1961)
Harpo (1893–September 28, 1964)
Groucho (October 2, 1890–August 19, 1977)
Gummo (1894–April 21, 1977)
Zeppo (1901–November 30, 1979)
Film Actors, Vaudeville Performers

The Marx Brothers—primarily Groucho, Chico, and Harpo—were a totally anarchic force, uncontained by plots and stories, indifferent to codes of behavior and manners. Whereas other comedy acts were ambushed by trouble or disaster, they created it themselves.

The five brothers were born Leonard (Chico), Adolph (Harpo), Julius (Groucho), Milton (Gummo), and Herbert (Zeppo). A sixth—Manfred—died in 1888 at age three. They lived with immigrant parents Samuel and Minnie Marx in the largely German community of Yorkville in New York City. Samuel made a modest living as a tailor; Minnie—whose parents were entertainers—was the typical "stage mother," pushing her sons into show business from their early years. In 1914 she opened a theatrical agency to handle their engagements. Education was minimal: Harpo never finished second grade, and Groucho did not complete seventh. A constant reader, Groucho often quipped that his "education was self-inflicted."

Chico played piano for nickelodeons (early movie theaters) and saloons; occasionally, Harpo filled in for him. Both Chico and Groucho were "song pluggers," singing for prospective buyers. Groucho's first job in show business was as a female impersonator for the Leroy Trio. A

The Museum of Modern Art/Film Stills Archive

good boy soprano, he also sang with the Gus Edwards vaudeville troupe.

Minnie went on tour with Groucho and Harpo under various billings. In 1912, while performing in a small Texas town, they began insulting the audience when it interrupted their act. Getting a good response, they varied future acts, singing less and using more ad libs, puns, and jokes. Their act, "Fun in Hi Skule," introduced many features that became permanent: Harpo's red wig, Groucho's frock coat and mock-professorial demeanor, Gummo's bland straight man (a role later assumed by Zeppo). Groucho's cigar and greasepaint mustache came later.

Joining his brothers in 1913, Chico suggested expanding the "skule" act with musical numbers, stage effects, and comedy sketches. Help also came from Minnie's show business brother, Al Shean, who advised Harpo to remain mute because his voice clashed with his comic appearance. Contracted with the Orpheum circuit, an important theatrical chain, the brothers became a regular attraction at New York's famous Palace Theater, and by 1919 they were at the height of their vaudeville success.

In 1924 they made their Broadway debut in *I'll Say She Is,* using the nicknames given them by entertainer Art Fisher in 1914: "Groucho" reflected his serious manner; "Harpo" referred to his favorite instrument; "Chico" was named so because he chased girls. The show was enthusiastically reviewed in *The New Yorker* magazine.

It was followed by *The Cocoanuts* in 1925, written by GEORGE S. KAUFMAN and Morrie Ryskind, with songs by IRVING BERLIN, all Broadway heavyweights. Groucho, for whom "ad-libbing was as essential as breathing," changed lines in every performance. Ryskind exclaimed that nobody paid attention to Berlin's songs: "These guys could ruin anything. They run around for fifteen minutes, and then the young lovers do a song. Nobody gives a damn if the boy loves the girl or not."

While the brothers were playing on Broadway in *Animal Crackers*, which had opened in 1928—and which Kaufman and Ryskind also wrote—they signed a contract with Paramount Pictures and filmed *The Cocoanuts* (1929) at its New York studios in Astoria. The combined antics of the wisecracking Groucho, the maniacal mime Harpo, and the mock-Italian clown Chico were unlike anything seen in movies before. They did not just chew up the scenery; they rendered plot and script superfluous.

No small part of their impact was their novel use—and nonuse—of language during the transition period between silent and sound films. Chico spoke in broken English and made-up Italian and Harpo spoke not at all (although he often made noises), but Groucho was the master of language. He talked nonstop and nonsensically, partly to distract people in the movie, but always as a way of commenting on the absurdities of everything around him. Another important element was Margaret Dumont, the matronly actress who suffered many indignities with dignity as Groucho's comic foil in six of their films.

Their second film, an adaptation of *Animal Crackers* (1930), featured Groucho as African explorer Captain Spaulding, who relates his adventures with such absurd lines as "One morning I shot an elephant in my pajamas. How he got in my pajamas, I don't know. But that's entirely irrelephant."

Monkey Business (1931), coscripted by S. J. Perelman, was their first film written directly for the screen. Playing stowaways on a ship, at one point Groucho, Chico, and Harpo all pretend to be French singer Maurice Chevalier to get off the ship. In *Horse Feathers* (1932) Groucho plays Professor Quincy Adams Wagstaff, head of Huxley College, who tries to buy football players at a speakeasy run by Chico.

Their next film, *Duck Soup* (1933), though not a commercial success, is now considered a satiric masterpiece largely thanks to director Leo McCarey. Groucho as Rufus T. Firefly, prime minister of a miniscule imaginary country named Freedonia, declares war on neighboring Sylvania. Chico is a peanut vendor outside the palace, and Harpo pretends to drive Groucho around in a sidecar that never moves. The film was straight man Zeppo's last appearance with his brothers.

Their fortunes at Paramount less than bright, they accepted an invitation from IRVING G. THALBERG to make their next two films at MGM, where production values were greater and their gags could be elaborated. The first was *A Night at the Opera* (1935), in which Chico claims to manage a tenor whom Groucho is trying to sign for his opera company. Singers Kitty Carlisle and Allan Jones costarred. The film—an original screenplay by Kaufman and Ryskind—includes a famous scene aboard an ocean liner in which dozens of people squeeze into a tiny stateroom. In *A Day at the Races* (1937) Groucho is a horse doctor named Hackenbush who is summoned by Margaret Dumont to head a sanitarium. Both films were among MGM's most successful comedies.

Groucho, Harpo, and Chico appeared in five other films together, including *Room Service* (1938), costarring comedienne Lucille Ball; *At the Circus* (1939); *Go West* (1940); and *Love Happy* (1950), their last appearance as a team.

In 1960 Groucho's autobiography, *Groucho and Me*, was a best-seller. In 1974 he received a Special Academy Award "in recognition of his brilliant creativity," but also in his brothers' absence, "for the unequaled achievements of the Marx Brothers in the art of motion picture comedy."

Unlike Chico and Harpo, Groucho found new life on television. In 1951 he hosted the quiz show *You Bet Your Life*. One of the most popular programs of the 1950s, it made Groucho a household name. In 1962 he hosted *The Tonight Show* before Johnny Carson took over, and appeared on a number of other shows.

The Marx Brothers movies experienced a revival in the 1960s during the student movements and protests against the Vietnam War. Their satirical spirit, denigrating convention and upper-class values, and the mockery of war and politics in films like *Duck Soup,* seemed completely in sync with the countercultural attitudes prevalent at the time.

BIBLIOGRAPHY

Chandler, Charlotte, *Hello, I Must Be Going: Groucho and His Friends,* 1978; Marx, Adolph, *Harpo Speaks,* 1961; Marx, Arthur, *My Life with Groucho,* 1988; Marx, Groucho, *Groucho and Me,* 1960; Marx, Groucho, and Richard J. Anobile, *The Marx Bros. Scrapbook,* 1973.

Maybeck, Bernard Ralph

(February 7, 1862–October 3, 1957)
Architect

Bernard Maybeck was one of the foremost residential architects in northern California and is considered one of the founders of the Bay Area style of architecture, which combined traditional forms with contemporary materials on unusual sites and focused on environmental and human needs.

Maybeck was born in New York City, the son of an immigrant German woodcarver. His originality and skill became evident when, as a teenager, he designed and patented a reversible passenger seat for trains while working for a furniture company. He went to Paris to study furniture design, became interested in architecture, and was admitted to the Ecole des Beaux-Arts in 1882. During the next four years Maybeck's approach to building became rooted in the idea that architecture, as an art form, has beauty as its essence. His architectural objective was to bring together present needs and local materials, revitalized forms from the past, aspects of the natural site, and fine craftsmanship into a unique creation that would stir one's romantic soul.

Returning to the United States in 1886, Maybeck worked for a New York architectural firm, then as a design partner in Kansas City where he met his wife, and next as a draftsman in San Francisco. He moved to Berkeley, California, in 1894 where, for the next six decades, he primarily designed houses, churches, and schools, which have been described as "unclassifiable hybrids" because of his delightfully eclectic approach. His own chalet-like house in Berkeley (1892–1902) heralded the synthesis of a residential style that would become characteristic of the environs of San Francisco. Later referred to as Berkeley Brown Shingles, Maybeck's houses were noted for their exterior redwood shingles, carvings on balconies and gables, sleeping porches, exposed ceiling beams, built-in window seats, and large fireplaces. The Chick House at Berkeley (1914) and the Bingham House at Montecito (1916) are fine examples of his style in large format.

As an instructor in drawing and descriptive geometry at the University of California, Berkeley (mid-1890s), Maybeck encouraged the young JULIA MORGAN and gained the patronage of influential socialite Phoebe Apperson Hearst, who gave money for the international competition to obtain a Beaux-Arts plan for the

University of California, Berkeley (1899). For Mrs. Hearst he designed Hearst Hall, a reception pavilion and gymnasium attached to her Berkeley home (1899). It was structurally quite an innovation because of the use of laminated arches (glued layers of wood) and the planned ability to be moved to another site. In 1902 and 1903 he designed the castlelike Hearst mansion, Wyntoon, on the McCloud River, which had high gray lava walls, a wooden superstructure, and a steep, tiled roof (destroyed by fire, 1933).

Maybeck's masterpiece is the First Church of Christ, Scientist in Berkeley (1910–1912), with its unconventional structure and juxtaposition of Byzantine, Gothic, Romanesque, and Japanese elements. He combined redwood timbers with reinforced concrete piers and metal factory windows and used rich ornamentation from a wide range of architectural precedents to link past and present.

Another of Maybeck's triumphs is the Palace of Fine Arts, created in temporary materials for the Panama-Pacific International Exposition in San Francisco (1915). The most popular building in the city's history, it was preserved after the fair and restored during the 1960s. The actual gallery structure, curved with three-hinged steel trusses and screened by a freestanding colonnade and a large, arched rotunda set in a lagoon, was like a ruin that evoked a feeling of melancholy, which Maybeck said was necessary for the contemplation of great art.

An eccentric person, Maybeck designed his own clothes, espoused many prevalent fads, and enjoyed playing the roles of visionary, bohemian, and mystic. Unfortunately, many of his buildings were destroyed in the 1923 Berkeley fire. But he lived on to replace many of them, design more classical fantasies, and receive the gold medal of the American Institute of Architects in 1951.

BIBLIOGRAPHY

Cardwell, Kenneth H., *Bernard Maybeck—Artisan, Architect, Artist,* 1976; Longstreth, Richard, *On the Edge of the World: Four Architects in San Francisco at the Turn of the Century,* 1983; Woodbridge, Sally, *Bernard Maybeck, Visionary Architect,* 1992.

Mayer, Louis B.

(July 4, 1885–October 29, 1957)
Film Producer

Louis B. Mayer rose from immigrant junk dealer to head of Metro-Goldwyn-Mayer, the largest movie studio in the world. He developed the star system and for twenty-five years stubbornly held to producing his brand of "wholesome family entertainment." He was for many years America's highest paid employee.

Eliezer (or Lazar) Mayer was one of five children born in Russia to Jacob and Sarah Mayer. At age three, his family emigrated to New Brunswick, Canada. Leaving school at twelve, he worked in his father's junk business, then in 1904 moved to Boston to start his own. Within six months he married Margaret Shenberg, the first girl he ever dated. They had two daughters, Edith and Irene, later separated, and divorced in 1947.

His business failing, Mayer moved in with relatives in Brooklyn, working in a scrap metal business. When this failed, he returned to Boston, became interested in movies, refurbished a rundown theater, and showed spectacles, such as the Italian *Cabiria* (1914). He acquired more theaters and in 1915 earned a fortune by securing the New England rights to D. W. GRIFFITH's *Birth of a Nation*, the first blockbuster in movie history.

Mayer moved into distribution, forming Metro Pictures with several partners, then into production, leaving Metro to form the Gordon-Mayer Film Exchange. He made his first film—*Virtuous Wives*—in a Brooklyn studio in 1918.

Moving to California where the film industry was flourishing, Mayer concentrated on production. He hired Lois Weber, one of the few women directors of the silent era, and Marshall Neilan, who had directed MARY PICKFORD. The first signs of Mayer's puritanism and tyrannical treatment of employees—for both of which he became notorious at MGM—emerged in his encounter with Neilan, whose flagrant womanizing epitomized everything Mayer detested.

Mayer agreed to make four films a year for Marcus Loew's theater chain. In 1924 Loew's Incorporated absorbed Goldwyn Pictures and Louis B. Mayer Productions, in addition to Mayer's former Metro Company, to form Metro-Goldwyn Pictures. Mayer was made studio chief, and the brilliant young IRVING THALBERG supervisor of production.

The studio, called Metro-Goldwyn-Mayer (abbreviated to MGM), became the largest in Hollywood, its logo a roaring lion. Through the 1930s and 1940s it employed 4,700 people on 187 acres in Culver City; it had a music library second in size only to the Library of Congress; the makeup department could prepare 1,200 persons in an hour; the wardrobe department dressed 5,000 actors in a day's work.

Hits like *The Big Parade* (1925), starring John Gilbert, earned MGM $4.7 million in profits in its first year and taught Mayer the value of promoting "stars." He had many change their lifestyles, even their lovers, to conform to the studio's images of them. MGM was their "family," and Mayer as their "father" was not above throwing temper tantrums to get his way.

Mayer's instincts for talent were generally good. Norma Shearer, Joan Crawford, Wallace Beery, Lon Chaney, Jean Harlow, William Powell, and Clark Gable were among MGM's biggest stars in its first decade. However, he nearly missed signing GRETA GARBO because he thought her overweight.

"Familial" instincts aside, Mayer was strictly business. Historian Lewis Jacobs remarked that "no company [is] crueler than Metro-Goldwyn-Mayer. No feeling for art, no feeling for artists, no feeling even for people as such. The moment they stop earning money . . . out they go." The sentiment was echoed by many stars.

The quality of MGM's films in the first decade was attributed to Thalberg, with whom Mayer often disagreed. *Anna Christie* (1930, Garbo's first talkie), *Mutiny on the Bounty* (1935), *Camille* (1936), and PEARL BUCK's *The Good Earth* (1936) were all Thalberg projects.

After Thalberg's death in 1936, Mayer's commitment to family entertainment dominated in films like *A Family Affair* (1937), which launched the "Andy Hardy" series, one of the most profitable in Hollywood history, peaking with *Love Finds Andy Hardy* (1938).

Fond of stories with children, Mayer developed more child actors than any other studio, including Freddie Bartholomew, star of *Captains Courageous* (1937); Judy Garland, star of *The Wizard of Oz* (1939), the studio's most expensive production at the time; Mickey Rooney, Andy Hardy himself; and Elizabeth Taylor, whose first MGM film was *Lassie Come Home* (1943).

The most famous movie released by MGM was *Gone with the Wind* (1939), produced by Mayer's son-in-law, David O. Selznick, who had left MGM to form his own studio, Selznick International Studios. Selznick wanted to borrow Clark Gable from MGM for the role of Rhett Butler, and Mayer thought he could use the deal to lure Selznick back to the studio. It did not work, but MGM secured the distribution rights for what became one of the biggest box office hits of all time.

A film reflecting Mayer's taste, and both critically and commercially successful, was *Mrs. Miniver* (1942). It starred Greer Garson, who Mayer discovered in England and considered the epitome of virtuous motherhood. About a

British family surviving World War II, it was the most popular movie of the year and won seven Academy Awards, including Best Picture. Winston Churchill remarked that its propaganda was worth 100 battleships.

Throughout the 1940s Mayer's tactics and taste ruled the studio, conflicting with production supervisor Dore Schary as he had with Thalberg. The studio had fewer hits, Mayer insisting on sentimental qualities less tenable in the postwar period. Paradoxically, this same period saw the flourishing of the MGM musical—from *Meet Me in St. Louis* (1944), directed by Vincente Minnelli, to *Singin' in the Rain* (1952), directed by dancer Gene Kelly and Stanley Donen. Continuing through the 1950s, the musical is probably the studio's most durable contribution to film culture.

Wanting MGM films to occasionally "say something," however, Schary produced *Battleground* (1949), a realistic war drama that earned critical praise and was a financial success. Nevertheless, Mayer refused to accede to Schary's creative judgment. Their feud ended when Loew's corporate head, Nicholas Schenk, decided that the studio needed Schary and requested Mayer's resignation.

Mayer's departure on August 31, 1951, astonished the industry and augured the dissolution of the Hollywood studio system. Four years later, Schary was out and power struggles ensued throughout the decade in which television competed for audiences. Mayer unsuccessfully attempted to retake control before he died in 1957, an unhappy millionaire.

MGM made a number of very successful films in the late 1950s—notably Minnelli's *Gigi* (1958) and William Wyler's *Ben-Hur* (1959), both of which won numerable Oscars, including Best Picture of their year. In the mid-1950s the studio released its movies to television and branched out into other businesses, including hotels. It continued to produce films, but distributed them through United Artists.

Mayer's career elicited both extreme praise and criticism, as can be gathered by these remarks by two of Hollywood's most important producers. Selznick considered him "the greatest single figure in the history of motion picture production," while SAMUEL GOLDWYN quipped, "The reason so many people showed up at his funeral was because they wanted to make sure he was dead."

BIBLIOGRAPHY

Carey, Gary, *All the Stars in Heaven,* 1981; Crowther, Bosley, *Hollywood Rajah,* 1960; Eames, John Douglas, *The MGM Story,* 1982; Gabler, Neal, *An Empire of Their Own: How the Jews Invented Hollywood,* 1988.

Meier, Richard Alan

(October 12, 1934–   )
Architect, Artist

Richard Meier is known for his elegant "white houses" and pristine high-tech buildings that contrast with the environment. Working within the modernist tradition articulated by Le Corbusier, he developed a style that stresses clarity and balance between light, form, and space.

Meier was born in Newark, New Jersey, and earned an architectural degree from Cornell University in 1957. He worked for the New Jersey architectural firm of Frank Grad & Sons, and the New York City firms of Davis, Brody & Wisniewski (1958–1959), Skidmore, Owings & Merrill (1959–1960; see LOUIS SKIDMORE), and Marcel Breuer & Associates (1960–1963). During these years, he spent his free time creating abstract paintings and collages in the studio of his friend, artist FRANK STELLA. In 1963 he established his own practice, Richard Meier & Associates, working out of his New York City apartment. He also was adjunct professor of architecture at Manhattan's Cooper Union (1963–1973).

Meier's first commissions were for private residences, such as a New York studio/apartment for Stella and the Smith House in Darien, Connecticut (1965–1967), which combined the imagery of Le Corbusier translated into wood and placed in a picturesque setting. His first large commission was a creative transformation of the 13-story steel-and-concrete Bell Telephone laboratory buildings in New York's Greenwich Village into 383 loft-style studio apartments for artists, called Westbeth Artists' Housing (1970). This pioneering effort in "adaptive reuse" became the world's largest artists' residence and the first of its kind in the United States.

In the early 1970s Meier became well known as one of the New York Five, a Corbusian-influenced group of architects who published an influential book titled *Five Architects* (1972; SEE MICHAEL GRAVES). Swiss-born architect Le Corbusier, who espoused modular structure and expressive geometric forms, has continued to be the strongest influence on Meier's developing style. However, Meier balances the functional Corbusian forms with his own pictorial and compositional ideas. He continually explores the relationship of architecture to nature, stating that a building should contrast with its surroundings "to heighten one's awareness of nature." Focusing on vertical composition, Meier has clothed his buildings in white to intensify the planar quality in contrast to nature's more amorphous forms and to highlight the interplay of natural light with vertical space. Meier has said: "In stating that my fundamental concerns are space, form, light, and how to make them, I mean to accentuate that my goal is presence, not illusion. I pursue it with unrelenting vigor."

The Douglas House in Harbor Springs, Michigan (1971–1973), a 3-story, vertically arranged structure clinging to a wooded incline above Lake Michigan, boasts a typical "Meier-esque facade" of stark simplicity with its combination glass wall and white-painted wood exterior ornamented solely by connective steel stairs and pipe railings. Each interior level is arranged into three areas: the private spaces (bedrooms) against the cliff, the public living areas along the lakefront, and the connective circulation and light areas in between.

Meier successfully meshed form, style, and function in the Bronx Developmental Center (1970–1977), a silvery sleek multistructured total-care facility for some 400 mentally handicapped people, aged seven to seventy. Visualizing the facility as a world within a world, like a monastic community, he designed it to "open the complex inward" and "create its own context." From the outer or public area of offices and lecture halls distinguished by a huge aluminum and glass wall, one moves into the private residential area with its staggered L-shaped units, then into the interior recreational courtyard. Such connectives as glass-enclosed passageways link all areas, and subtle details mark the movement from public to private.

Another Meier building is the Atheneum (1974–1979), a visitor's center for the restored nineteenth-century Utopian community of New Harmony, Indiana, along the Wabash River. The white porcelain-enamel-clad structure seems to oppose the town's established architecture, yet conjures up Utopian visions. When the surrounding fields flood, Meier describes the building as floating "above the water, a porcelain-paneled object from another time and context." An interior ramp leads visitors upward through a series of exhibits to a crowning view of river and town.

Meier is especially known for his museum buildings, such as Atlanta's High Museum of Art (1980–1983). It is a complex structure of granite, glass, and white porcelain panels with an inside ramp that ascends through a curved central atrium from which the art galleries radiate. Visitors weave between galleries and the atrium while also changing levels. He also designed the Museum of Decorative Arts (1979–1985) in Frankfurt, Germany.

In 1984 Meier won what has been called the commission of the century: to design the J. Paul Getty Center in Los Angeles. He presented the final designs for the six-building complex in 1991 (projected completion in 1996). Situated on a 110-acre hill site with commanding views of Los Angeles and the Pacific, the buildings are based on Meier's characteristic cubes and curving forms, yet each is distinctive in design. For example, the largest building, the new Getty Museum, has a courtyard surrounded by five pavilions that are connected by walkways and bridges, while the Center for the History of Art and the Humanities is distinguished by its 5-story cylindrical form with a curved interior ramp.

Dubbed modernism's last best heir, his style has remained consistently Corbusian-based, yet uniquely his own.

BIBLIOGRAPHY

Frampton, Kenneth, and Colin Rowe, *Five Architects: Eisenman/Graves/Gwathmey/Hejuduk/Meier*, 1972; Futagawa, Yukio, *Richard Meier: Smith House and House in Old Westbury*, 1973; Meier, Richard, and Joseph Rykwert, *Richard Meier, Architect*, 1984.

Melville, Herman

(August 1, 1819–September 28, 1891)
Novelist, Poet, Short-Story Writer

While his nineteenth-century contemporaries preferred his straightforward adventure novels about his experiences in the South Seas, Herman Melville has since become known for his symbolic fiction, especially the epic novel *Moby-Dick.* Melville died almost unknown, but today he is regarded as one of the greatest American writers.

Melville was born in New York City, the third of eight children of Allan and Maria Gansevoort Melvill. (The *e* was added to the family name in the 1830s.) Melville's father was a prosperous dry goods merchant, his mother a descendant of a prominent Dutch family that had settled early along the Hudson River. Both

Library of Congress

Melville's grandfathers had distinguished themselves in the Revolutionary War era: Major Thomas Melvill participated in the Boston Tea Party, dressed as an Indian; General Peter Gansevoort was heroic in the defense of Fort Stanwix.

The economic panic of 1830 cost Melville's father his business. He landed a job managing a fur business in Albany, near a branch of the Gansevoort family. There he suffered further financial setbacks, and, in 1832, after a trip to New York City to meet with his creditors, he collapsed with pneumonia and died.

While Maria Melville borrowed money from her prosperous relatives, her eldest sons worked a variety of jobs to help the family financially. Herman quit school to clerk at his uncle Peter Gansevoort's bank, then assisted with a fur business set up by his brother Gansevoort. The economic depression of 1837, however, wiped out Gansevoort's business, and the Melville family moved to Lansingburgh, a small town near Albany, to save money.

After teaching a term at a local country school, Herman studied surveying but found no job available afterward. He decided to seek his fortune at sea. In 1839, at the age of twenty, he signed on the *St. Lawrence,* a packet ship that ran between New York and Liverpool. The trip later became the source of Melville's novel *Redburn: His First Voyage* (1849).

In January 1841, Melville sailed out of Fairhaven, Massachusetts, on a whaling ship, the *Acushnet.* The first year of the voyage through the South Seas was pleasant, but then poor whaling dampened morale. In July 1842, while the ship was anchored at Nuku Hiva, one of the Marquesas Islands, Melville and a companion jumped ship. They were taken in by an island tribe, the Taipis, who were reputed to be cannibals. The natives treated them kindly, but after a couple of weeks, Melville began to fear their intentions and escaped, signing onto an Australian whaling ship, the *Lucy Ann.*

Morale aboard the *Lucy Ann* was so poor that the crew turned mutinous, and, after a strike in which Melville participated, the ship docked in Tahiti, where Melville and others were jailed for several weeks. Upon release, he roamed the islands for two months, then joined the crew of another whaler, the *Charles and Henry,* for six months. Discharged in Hawaii, he enlisted in the U.S. Navy and sailed back to Boston aboard the warship *United States* in October 1843.

Returning home to Lansingburgh, Melville recounted his adventures for his family, who encouraged him to write them down. The results were his first book, *Typee* (1846), a fictionalized rendering of his experience among the cannibals of the Marquesas, and a sequel, *Omoo* (1847), the story of the *Lucy Ann,* Melville's imprisonment in Tahiti, and his sub-

sequent return to sea. Written as colorful adventure yarns, the books sold well.

In 1847 Melville married Elizabeth Knapp Shaw, the daughter of Lemuel Shaw, then Massachusetts chief justice. Melville and his bride moved to a house in New York City, along with his brother Allan and his wife, their mother, and four unmarried sisters. Melville became part of the literary circle of Evert Duyckinck, an influential editor.

Upset because some critics had begun to doubt the authenticity of his two realistic novels, Melville decided to try a new approach. His third novel, *Mardi and a Voyage Thither* (1849), begins realistically with the story of a woman rescued from a South Seas tribe by a sailor, but it veers into allegory after she again disappears. The hero's search for her becomes the search for truth and lost innocence; he visits islands whose populations parody the social problems of the United States, England, and France.

Readers had little patience with this kind of philosophizing, and Melville grudgingly took his family's advice to return to the adventure novels. *Redburn* tells the story of Melville's initiation to life at sea and the squalor of Liverpool. *White-Jacket; or, The World in a Man-of-War* (1850) is a realistic story based on Melville's months aboard the *United States.* However, the ship here also serves symbolically to represent the larger nation, and Melville's depiction of the brutal treatment of sailors was meant as a broader social commentary.

Oppressed by living conditions at the New York house, which had been made more crowded by the birth of the first of their four children, Melville moved his family to Pittsfield, Massachusetts. There he got to know NATHANIEL HAWTHORNE, who lived nearby, and began work on his masterpiece, *Moby-Dick* (1851).

Melville's epic novel concerns a whaling captain's obsessive, vengeful search for the great white whale that had maimed him. The story of Captain Ahab is told by a young sailor named Ishmael, the sole survivor of the hunt for the whale. Recounted realistically, the story is nonetheless richly symbolic: Ahab's quest represents the search for truth, and Melville uses images and allusions to literature, religion, and philosophy to pose difficult questions about the meaning of life. Despite some favorable reviews, *Moby-Dick* was not a popular success, and Melville found himself again bitterly resenting the need to cater to the tastes of the reading public.

Melville now resolved to write nothing allegorical, and he began, in 1853, to produce short stories, which he published in *Harper's New Monthly Magazine* and *Putnam's Monthly Magazine* and later collected in *Piazza Tales* (1856). Among the best-known stories are "Bartleby the Scrivener," "Benito Cereno," and "The Encantadas."

After a six-month tour of Europe and the Near East in 1856 and 1857, taken to recover his physical and mental health, Melville went on the lecture circuit, though again with little financial success. In 1861 his wife's father died,

and the family was able to live on the inheritance. In 1866 he landed a job as a customs inspector in New York, a job he held for nineteen years.

When Melville died in 1891, a last, short novel was found on his desk: *Billy Budd,* an allegorical rendering of the conflict between innocence and evil. The novel went unpublished until 1924, on the occasion of the centennial of his birth. Today *Billy Budd* stands next to *Moby-Dick* as a triumphal work of art.

BIBLIOGRAPHY

Arvin, Newton, *Herman Melville,* 1950; Chase, Richard, *Herman Melville,* 1949; Howard, Leon, *Herman Melville: A Biography,* 1951; Rogin, Michael Paul, *Subversive Genealogy: The Politics and Art of Herman Melville,* 1983; Rosenberry, Edward H., *Melville,* 1979.

Menotti, Gian Carlo

(July 7, 1911–   )
Composer

Gian Carlo Menotti is best known for his enormously accessible operas. The television opera *Amahl and the Night Visitors* may well have been seen by more people than any other opera and is rebroadcast every year at Christmas.

The sixth child of ten, Menotti was born near Lake Lugano in the small country town of Cadegliano, Italy. His father was a well-to-do exporter, his mother an amateur musician who started Menotti's musical training early. He composed a song at four and at six decided he would become a composer. By the time he entered the Milan Conservatory at thirteen, he had written two operas.

On ARTURO TOSCANINI's advice, Menotti entered the Curtis Institute in Philadelphia,

Pennsylvania, in 1928. He studied piano and composition, graduated with honors in 1933, and returned to Europe. It was in Vienna in 1934 that he began work on his one-act comic opera *Amelia al Ballo* (Amelia Goes to the Ball). Orchestration completed, the libretto translated into English by George Mead, the work was performed successfully in Philadelphia on April 1, 1937.

Amelia's success led to an opera commission from NBC radio. Menotti wrote the score for *The Old Maid and the Thief* (1939), again using traditional opera buffa techniques. *The Island God* (1942), a failure, was composed for the Metropolitan Opera House. He said of it later, "My error was in trying to write an opera around a philosophic theme."

Menotti remained in the United States during World War II but retained his Italian citizenship. He composed *Sebastian,* a ballet, in 1944 and the Piano Concerto in F in 1945 (performed for the first time by the Boston Symphony Orchestra).

The Medium was introduced in 1946 by the opera theater of Columbia University. Commissioned by the Alice M. Ditson fund, it is a melodrama performed by five singers, a dance mime, and small orchestra. It ran on Broadway from 1947 to 1948 and was introduced by a curtain raiser, *The Telephone.* The double bill toured for the U.S. State Department in 1955, and in 1951 there was a film version of *The Medium* directed by Menotti.

The Consul earned him the Pulitzer Prize in 1950. It played for eight months on Broadway, earned the Drama Critics' Circle Award, has been translated into a dozen languages, and has been performed around the world. The music drama turns on the tragedy of people trapped by history.

Menotti, now very popular, was again commissioned by NBC, this time for a television opera. Inspired by a fifteenth-century Hieronymous Bosch painting, *The Adoration of the Magi,* now at the Prado in Madrid, he wrote *Amahl and the Night Visitors* (1951), first televised Christmas Eve 1951 and still broadcast annually.

In *The Saint of Bleecker Street* (1954), set in contemporary New York, Menotti pits the physical world against the spiritual. *The Saint* was awarded the Drama Critics' Circle Award for best play, the New York Music Critics' Circle Award for best opera, and the Pulitzer Prize in music for 1955.

Menotti continued to receive commissions and went on composing for the stage, for television, and for choral groups. In 1958 he founded the Spoleto Festival of Two Worlds to promote young international talent in music and other arts. Subsequently he composed less and devoted increasing amounts of time to the festival. In 1977 Menotti launched another Spoleto in Charleston, South Carolina: Spoleto Festival U.S.A.

During the 1960s Menotti wrote librettos in English for SAMUEL BARBER (*A Hand of Bridge* in 1960 and *Vanessa* in 1964). Menotti had been a close friend of Barber's since their student days at Curtis; in fact, the two composers had shared a home, Capricorn, in Mount Kisco, New York. The house was sold in 1973. Menotti has since moved to a 1789 country house in Scotland. He was awarded a Kennedy Center Honor for lifetime achievement in the arts in 1984.

Menotti's work, always theatrical, fits the voice well, is accessible, and remains immensely popular. Reviewers think his music either sentimental and dull or powerful and moving. A musical conservative, Menotti writes tonally, and, as H. W. Hitchcock, a critic says, with a "theatrical sense of a popular playwright and a Puccinesque musical vocabulary . . . an Italianate love of liquid language and a humane interest in characters."

BIBLIOGRAPHY

Gruen, J., *Menotti: A Biography,* 1978; Hitchcock, H. W., *Music in the United States: A Historical Introduction,* rev., 1974.

Merman, Ethel Agnes

(January 16, 1908–February 15, 1984)
Actress, Singer

Ethel Merman, a brash, high-voltage performer whose voice COLE PORTER described as "a brass band going by," appeared in many musical shows on Broadway, film, and television. She introduced many song standards by GEORGE GERSHWIN, Cole Porter, IRVING BERLIN, and STEPHEN SONDHEIM.

She was born Ethel Zimmerman in 1908 in Astoria, New York, just a few blocks away from the Famous Players–Lasky Studios (later Paramount), where as a small child she was star-struck by the movie celebrities who passed through. Although she displayed early talents as a singer, her parents persuaded her to take a four-year business course in Long Island City. But her persistence to be a performer paid off. After shortening "Zimmermann" to her stage name of "Merman," she found jobs singing in New York restaurants and cafés. That led, in 1929, to her first big break, a stint in a Broadway nightclub on the same bill with the famous vaudeville team of Clayton, Jackson, and Durante. From there it was a short hop to her first (and only) collaboration with songwriter George Gershwin, in *Girl Crazy* (1930), where she premiered the first of the song standards that became her signatures, "I Got Rhythm."

The 1930s were crowded with appearances on Broadway and on screen. There was the 1931 stage edition of the George White *Scandals,* Cole Porter's *Anything Goes* (1934), for which she introduced "You're the Top," "I Get a Kick out of You," and "Blow, Gabriel, Blow." Her movies included a Bing Crosby vehicle, *We're Not Dressing* (1932); an Eddie Cantor comedy, *Kid Millions* (1934); a screen version of *Anything Goes* (1936); and *Alexander's Ragtime Band* (1938), in which she sang Irving Berlin's "Heat Wave" and "Blue Skies." With *Panama Hattie* (1940), one of her greatest hits, she was pronounced by a *Time* magazine writer as "the undisputed No. 1 musicomedy songstress of these harassed times."

The indefatigable Merman roared into the 1940s and 1950s with several more Irving Berlin vehicles, the stage version of *Annie Get Your Gun* (1946), in which she portrayed Annie Oakley; both the stage and movie versions of *Call Me Madam* (1950 and 1953), where she impersonated American diplomat Perle Mesta; and the film *There's No Business Like Show Business* (1954). But, as she notes in her autobiography, the peak of her career was yet to come. *Gypsy,* lyrics and music by Stephen Sondheim and Jule Styne, opened in 1959 and provoked critical raves, generally pronouncing her the "first lady" of the American stage. The role of Mama Rose was her favorite character, and "Everything's Coming up Roses" became yet another signature tune.

Along the way there were four husbands, personal tragedy (the loss of a daughter), and a fair number of stage and screen failures. She has written that through it all she remained very much the "bold brassy dame" she usually played in her roles. "I say what I mean and mean what I say and I expect the same from others. That's probably why I've gotten into some of the messes I have."

BIBLIOGRAPHY

Merman, Ethel, with George Eels, *Merman—An Autobiography,* 1978; Thomas, Bob, *I Got Rhythm: The Ethel Merman Story,* 1985.

Mies van der Rohe, Ludwig

(March 27, 1886–August 17, 1969)
Architect

Ludwig Mies van der Rohe, one of the formulators of the International style of architecture, emigrated to the United States from Nazi Germany. With FRANK LLOYD WRIGHT and Le Corbusier, he was the most influential designer of the twentieth century.

Mies was born in Aachen (Aix-la-Chapelle), Germany, in 1886, the youngest of five children, and educated at that city's Cathedral School. His father, a master mason and owner of a small stonecutting shop, taught the boy an understanding of the qualities and possibilities of masonry construction. Throughout his teens, Mies studied the medieval churches of his city, principles of Renaissance decoration, and worked as a draftsman for local designers and architects. Beginning in 1907, Mies came under the influence of several important progressive figures. He served an apprenticeship with Bruno Paul, an architect and furniture designer, and worked for Peter Behrens, in whose office he became acquainted with WALTER GROPIUS and Le Corbusier. He also was introduced to the designs of Frank Lloyd Wright, which were published by Ernst Wasmuth (Berlin) in 1911. Pursuing Behrens's ideal of order and simplicity in design, Mies worked on several buildings, including the German embassy (1911–1912) in St. Petersburg, as well as several houses in the neoclassical tradition, like the Perls House (later Fuchs House) in Berlin (1911). He also did the brick Kröller house in The Hague (where he lived for a period after leaving Behrens's office).

After serving with the German army in the Balkans during World War I, Mies burst onto the international scene between 1919 and 1924 with designs for a new kind of skyscraper, sheathed entirely in glass. (Although some of these projects were never built, they established the basis of his reputation.) He also designed houses derived from the open-planning concepts of Frank Lloyd Wright, structuring a series of freestanding vertical planes at right angles to each other so that the exterior and interior were integrated. Throughout the 1920s he experimented with "zoned houses," which isolated the various functional areas, with brick construction for several Berlin monuments, and apartment house complexes built of steel. He was also active in several organizations, the Novembergruppe, the Zehner Ring, and the Deutscher Werkbund—all of which promoted modern architecture.

In 1927 he was the director of the Werkbund exposition of houses in Stuttgart to which he invited the foremost young architects of Europe, including Gropius and Le Corbusier. This has been called by PHILIP C. JOHNSON "the most important group of buildings in the history of modern architecture." It was his first major opportunity in large-scale planning. He personally oversaw the Weissenhof housing development, which was an innovation in its use of steel for domestic architecture, strip windows, and the bold cantilevers of the roof elements. Even more daring was his design of the German pavilion for the 1929 International Exposition at Barcelona (rebuilt 1983–1984). This was Mies's most complete statement to date of all the qualities of refinement, simplification, and elegance that were his hallmarks. It was a long, low building that integrated interior and exterior spaces and interlocked the various rooms in a free-flowing continuity. He used a great variety of expensive materials, including Roman travertine, green Tinian marble, onyx, glass, and chrome-plated steel.

Mies was by now an acknowledged leader of the so-called International style. Postwar communications had brought together architects and designers like Mies, Wright, and Le Corbusier from many countries in the service of a structural system for urban planning and low-cost mass housing. The primacy of function was advocated. Applied ornament was eschewed, as was strong contrast of colors on both interiors and exteriors. The new system of spatial organization promoted a free flow of interior space, as opposed to the stringing together of static symmetrical boxes. Based on the materials of structural steel and ferroconcrete, the outside walls of structures became, in effect, a skin of stucco or masonry, metal, and glass that constituted an enclosure rather than heavy, supported walls. As art historian H. H. Arnason has said, "One could speak of an architecture of volume rather than of mass."

An important part of Mies's career has been his innovative furniture designs. Typically, he eschewed applied ornamental design. His MR chair, for example (the letters deriving from his initials), designed in 1927 for the Stuttgart Exposition, was a steel and leather cushioned chair whose geometrical, curved design has become a modern classic and is still in production.

Mies began his brief association with the Bauhaus school of design in Dessau in 1930 when he became its third director. Three years later, after moving the institution to Berlin, he closed it under the pressure of the Nazis. He left Germany for America in 1938 to join the faculty of Armour Institute in Chicago (now the Illinois Institute of Technology). His course of instruction concentrated on the nature of function and creativity in architecture. He retired from the position in 1959. One of the most extensive works during his American career was the design of the Illinois Institute's 100-acre campus on Chicago's South Side (1939–1958). The complex of buildings was the first modern American campus conceived as a single architectural unit. It has been both praised and criticized for the simplicity of the structures' vast walls of yellow brick, exposed steel members, and huge glass windows. The elegant International style Seagram Building in New York City (1958), with interiors designed by Philip Johnson, uses amber-tinted glass and bronze.

Mies's most famous pronouncement on modern architecture was made in 1924: "Architecture is the will of an epoch translated into space. . . . It must be understood that all architecture is bound up with its own time, that it can only be manifested in living tasks and in the medium of its epoch." Thus, he demanded that modern architecture reflect advanced available technologies and materials and reveal the working structures inherent in the building. The ideals of elegance, simplicity, and utility were expressed in his dictum "Less is more." "I have wanted to keep everything reasonable and clear," he wrote near the end of his life, "to have an architecture that anybody can do." However, he has been criticized for imposing rather cold abstract concepts on the needs of the individual lifestyle. In reply, Mies wrote: "Some people say that what I do is 'cold.' That is ridiculous. You can say that a glass of milk is warm or cold. But not architecture." Commentator Raymond McGrath, writing in *Architecture Review,* noted that "to Mies belongs the credit of imbuing modern architectural forms with the genuine spiritual qualities of great design. . . . His magnificent simplicity, his sensitiveness to form, and his understanding of spatial relationships, combine to make his . . . works outstanding."

In 1960 he was presented the Gold Medal of the Chicago Chapter of the American Institute of Architects. Three years later he received the Presidential Medal of Freedom from Lyndon B. Johnson. Among his last projects were a number of office complexes and urban developments, including the Federal Center (1959–1973) in Chicago—his first opportunity to create a major urban space with freestanding buildings within a large city, and the Toronto-Dominion Centre (1969). Shortly before his death from pneumonia in 1969, he returned to Berlin to lay the cornerstone for his New National Gallery.

BIBLIOGRAPHY

Blaser, Werner, *Mies van der Rohe: Continuing the Chicago School of Architecture,* 1981; Johnson, Philip, *Mies van der Rohe,* 1953; Schulze, Franz, *Mies van der Rohe, A Critical Biography,* 1985; Spaeth, David, *Mies van der Rohe,* 1985.

Millay, Edna St. Vincent

(February 22, 1892–October 19, 1950)
Poet

Edna St. Vincent Millay wrote spirited verses in traditional poetic forms, especially the sonnet. Her work achieved great popularity in the 1920s and 1930s, and it remains familiar, perhaps because it is lively and direct.

Millay was born on February 22, 1892, in Rockland, Maine, and was raised in various New England towns. Her mother, divorced when Millay was eight, encouraged her talent for writing.

When Millay was twenty, her poem "Renascence" won publication in an annual collection called *The Lyric Year.* "Renascence" begins with the well-known lines "All I could see from where I stood / Was three long mountains and a wood." It was published again in Millay's first volume, *Renascence and Other Poems,* in 1917.

In 1913, the year after "Renascence" was first published in *The Lyric Year,* an acquaintance endeavored to help Millay get a college education. Accordingly, Millay enrolled in classes at Barnard College for a semester, then completed her degree at Vassar College in 1917.

Upon graduation, Millay moved to Greenwich Village in New York City, where she adopted a bohemian way of life and enjoyed the company of other young writers. She also joined the Provincetown Players as an actress; the troupe produced some of her plays. Millay's second volume of poetry, *A Few Figs from Thistles,* was published in 1920 and made her reputation.

Millay advocated emancipation from Victorian social mores and a free-thinking approach to moral questions. She demanded equality for women and the right to act out her individuality. She became a model for many, and her flair for dramatic personal appearances only enhanced her following.

The Harp-Weaver and Other Poems (1923) contains thirty-nine sonnets, a form of which Millay became an acknowledged master. The volume won her a Pulitzer Prize. In the same year, Millay married Eugen Boissevain, an importer, and they purchased a farm in upstate New York, at Austerlitz. There they lived out the rest of their days.

Because Millay's poetry is concentrated in traditional forms—Shakespeare and Keats were her models—her following has diminished in recent years. Critics have noted the irony that the free-spirited Millay should have chosen to write sonnets, while more conservative individuals, such as T. S. ELIOT, were revolutionizing the techniques of poetry. Nevertheless, Millay's capacious moral concerns and the intimacy of her poetic voice yielded lyrics that are both immediate and universal.

Millay's other books of poetry are *The Buck in the Snow and Other Poems* (1928), *Poems Selected for Young People* (1929), two sonnet cycles, *Fatal Interview* (1931) and *Wine from These Grapes* (1934), *Conversation at Midnight* (1937), *Huntsman, What Quarry?* (1939), *Make Bright the Arrows* (1940), and the posthumous volume *Mine the Harvest* (1954), edited by Norma Millay. She also wrote three plays and the libretto for an opera, *The King's Henchman,* composed by Deems Taylor (produced in 1927).

Millay died a year after husband, at Austerlitz, in 1950.

BIBLIOGRAPHY

Brittin, Norman A., *Edna St. Vincent Millay,* rev., 1982; Gould, Jean, *The Poet and Her Book: A Biography of Edna St. Vincent Millay,* 1969; Gurko, Miriam, *Restless Spirit: The Life of Edna St. Vincent Millay,* 1962.

Miller, Arthur

(October 17, 1915–)
Playwright

Arthur Miller, along with WILLIAM INGE and TENNESSEE WILLIAMS, was an influential voice in the American theater in the 1950s. His best works are characterized by concerns for societal problems and a passion for social liberation.

He was born in Manhattan in 1915, the son of immigrant Polish Jews. Due to faltering fortunes in the garment business, the family moved to Brooklyn, where he spent his childhood. Throughout his years at Abraham Lincoln High School, during the depths of the Great Depression, he showed little interest in his studies, preferring sports to books. Yet, as he recalls in his memoirs, *Timebends* (1987), visits as a child to the vaudeville shows were already making an indelible impression on him. Later, at the University of Michigan, he became the night editor of the *Michigan Daily* and began to write plays. In the 1937–1938 academic year he won two Avery Hopwood Awards from the university, for *Honors at Dawn* and *No Villain.* When a revision of *No Villain* called *They Too Arise* (now entitled *The Grass Still Grows*) won a Theatre Guild Award in 1938, he was encouraged to become a professional writer. He was briefly involved with the Federal Theatre Project and spent a stint writing for several radio shows, including *Cavalcade of America* and the *Columbia Workshop.*

His first Broadway play, *The Man Who Had All the Luck,* opened in 1944 and ran for only four performances. At the heart of the story is a plot that would crop up many times in Miller's later work—the rivalry of two brothers for the affection of their father. His next play, *All My Sons,* won the New York Drama Critics' Circle Award in 1947. In it, a young man discovers that his father, an airplane manufacturer, had sent the Air Force defective engine parts, which had caused not only the deaths of twenty-one flyers during World War II but also, indirectly, the suicide of an older brother.

Miller's first masterpiece, *Death of a Salesman* (1949), secured his reputation for the creation of significant American drama and won him a second Drama Critics' Circle Award and a Pulitzer Prize. It is a powerful portrait of Willy Loman, a salesman, who is caught in his own web of shallowness and false values. Again, the theme of two brothers' rivalry for their father's affection comes to the fore, accenting the tragic downfall of their father.

The staging of *Death of a Salesman* was as significant as its theme. Since much of the action is set in the past, Miller and designer Jo Mielziner created a set where characters could move through time and space without moving props. Mielziner, who had just designed the sets for Tennessee Williams's *Streetcar Named Desire,* constructed Willy's house so that its various rooms could become all the places called for in the play—a business office, a hotel room, a restaurant, and finally a cemetery. Characters in the present observed the wall lines and used doors to enter and exit, while characters from the past simply walked through the "walls." Thus, both realism and symbolism as theme and style are intertwined.

If *Death of a Salesman* is a tragedy—and Miller argued in his "Tragedy and the Common Man" that it is possible to write tragedy in the classic Greek mode about the plight of people of today—then *A View from the Bridge,* adapted in 1956 from a one-act play written a year before, was even more obviously a contemporary tragedy. Eddie Carbone is an essentially good man whose downfall stems from his incestuous obsession for his young niece, Catherine. The play has a Chorus (a narrator), implacable Furies (the Brooklyn immigration officials), and a rigid system of social justice and revenge (the Italian American community). Eddie has committed wrongs and suffers as a result, but, like Willy, he remains wholly sympathetic.

Two other plays from the 1950s revealed a new kind of hero for Miller. Peter Stockmann in *An Enemy of the People* (1950)—an adaptation of the Ibsen original—and John Proctor in *The Crucible* (1953) are, by contrast to Willy and Eddie, not victims, but victors, men who are doomed, but who display courage in the face of their fates. Stockmann is a doctor who finds disease in his town's water supply. His fight against the business interests who seek to keep it a secret for the sake of profits results in his ruin. In *The Crucible,* a historical drama about the Salem witchcraft trials, Proctor takes a moral stand against the persecutions. He is himself sentenced to the gallows. In neither case do we feel the deaths of these characters to be wasted, nor their causes fruitless.

The decade after 1955 was full of personal and political turmoil for Miller. Because of his leftist politics, he was called before the House Un-American Activities Committee (HUAC) to answer questions regarding his alleged Communist party involvements. He freely admitted attending party meetings but denied being a member. Like the character of John Proctor in *The Crucible,* he further stated that his conscience would not permit him to implicate others in his testimony. As a result, Miller was found guilty of two counts of contempt of Congress. Before he was sentenced, the conviction was overturned by the U.S. Court of Appeals.

Meanwhile, his marriage to Mary Grace Slattery ended in 1955. A year later, he married the movie star Marilyn Monroe. Although he encouraged her to make one of her finest movies, *Some Like It Hot* (1959), and wrote a screenplay for her, *The Misfits* (1961), she was angry that he apparently thought her suited for "dumb blond" roles. After their divorce, Monroe died of an apparent drug overdose in 1962 and Miller married again, this time to Ingeborg Morath (one of the photographers on *The Misfits*).

Miller's first play in nine years, *After the Fall* (1964), confronted the protagonist, Quentin, with three crises in his past—the Nazi death camps, his appearance before the HUAC investigations, and the suicide of his beautiful but neurotic wife. Parallels with his personal life seemed obvious, although Miller denied them. Despite these sensationalistic implications, however, the play's essentially abstract characters and bare-stage presentation doomed it to an early demise.

Since the mid-1960s Miller and his wife have traveled widely, and he has written the texts for his wife's photography books, including *In Russia* (1969) and *Chinese Encounters* (1979). In 1983 he took *Death of a Salesman* to the Beijing People's Art Theatre, becoming the first foreigner to direct there in post-Mao China. Meanwhile, his later plays continue to investigate collisions between the individual and society—the light philosophical comedy of *The Creation of the World and Other Business* (1972), an attack of Soviet ill-treatment of dissidents in *The Archbishop's Ceiling* (1977), and an account of survival in Auschwitz, the teleplay *Playing for Time* (1980).

BIBLIOGRAPHY

Bigsby, C. W. E., *File on Miller,* 1988; Miller, Arthur, *Timebends,* 1987; Moss, Leonard, *Arthur Miller,* 1980.

Miller, Henry Valentine

(December 26, 1891–June 7, 1980)
Essayist, Novelist

In his fiction and essays, Henry Miller took exuberant liberties with both style and subject matter, writing at length and in detail about his sensual experiences while traveling at home and abroad. His best-known novels are *Tropic of Cancer* and *Tropic of Capricorn.*

Miller was born in Manhattan and raised in Brooklyn, New York, by German American parents. After only two months at City College of New York in 1909, he took a job with a cement company. Later he worked in his father's tailor shop, became a manager for Western Union Telegraph Company, and ran a Greenwich Village speakeasy.

In 1930 Miller moved to France, where he lived for nine years, publishing his first three books. Judged obscene, they were excluded by American censors until the early 1960s, when they became widely popular in the United States. *Tropic of Cancer* (1934) describes Miller's early, destitute years in Paris. *Black Spring* (1936) contains autobiographical essays and sketches ranging from Brooklyn to Paris. *Tropic of Capricorn* (1939) offers a hilarious account of his career at Western Union.

Returning to New York in 1940, Miller traveled extensively in the United States and finally settled in Big Sur, California. His voluminous writings, most of them autobiographical, were marked by a zest for experience, a strongly sensual appetite, and a belief that "more obscene than anything is inertia." His autobiographical trilogy *The Rosy Crucifixion*, comprising the novels *Sexus* (1949), *Plexus* (1953), and *Nexus* (1960), were not released in the United States until the 1960s.

Miller drew much of his subject matter from his travels, whether at home or abroad. *The Colossus of Maroussi* (1941), an appreciation of life in Greece just prior to World War II, is considered one of his finest works. It finds the spirit of Hellenism in the lives of the people with whom Miller ate, drank, and talked. *Aller Retour New York* (1935) describes a round-trip to the city during the period he spent in Paris, and *The Air-Conditioned Nightmare* (1945) is a collection of essays about a U.S. tour he made in 1941. *Big Sur and the Oranges of Hieronymus Bosch* (1957) describes Miller's life atop a California mountain overlooking the sea.

Miller also based his work on people he had come to know. *Max and the White Phagocytes* (1938) is a comic portrait of a European Jew who had become uprooted from his homeland and whom Miller befriended during his time in Paris.

Despite his cleverness, Miller offered long rushes of experience and impression without much attention to the structure of a tale. His characters are quick sketches, drawn without interest in their psychology or in any motivation beyond the sex drive. Miller does offer humor, novelty, and a taste for subjects such as Zen and the occult. The liberties he took in writing about sex helped free later writers of limits imposed by censors.

BIBLIOGRAPHY

Brown, J. D., *Henry Miller*, 1986; Perles, Alfred, *My Friend Henry Miller: An Intimate Biography*, 1956; Wickes, George, *Henry Miller*, 1966; Winslow, Kathryn, *Henry Miller: Full of Life*, 1986.

Monk, Thelonious Sphere

(October 10, 1920–February 17, 1982)
Jazz Musician

Thelonious Monk abandoned conventional patterns and fashioned striking stripped-down compositions anchored by difficult chord progressions. Critic Martin Williams wrote that the creator of "'Round Midnight" was the first major composer in jazz since DUKE ELLINGTON. Monk's sometimes jarring, angular playing brilliantly married his musical concepts to interpretive improvisations.

Copyright *Washington Post*; Reprinted by permission of the D.C. Public Library

Monk was born in Rocky Mount, North Carolina. He was four when his mother brought him to New York and moved the family into an apartment on West 63rd Street in the black area called San Juan Hill. The small flat was to remain Monk's home for years.

Before he was six Monk began to teach himself piano by watching the keys of a player piano. At eleven he started lessons and later accompanied his mother when she sang in church. He played for rent parties and won amateur night prizes at the Apollo Theater in Harlem so often he was banned from competing there. Monk left Stuyvesant High School when he was sixteen to tour in a quartet that was part of an evangelist's entourage.

Two years later, he was back in Manhattan. He studied briefly at the Juilliard School, worked in the house band at Minton's Uptown Playhouse, free-lanced, and jammed. In the late 1930s and early 1940s his jam session cohorts included saxophonist CHARLIE PARKER, trumpeter DIZZY GILLESPIE, drummer Kenny Clarke, and guitarist Charlie Christian. Their avant-garde experiments evolved into bebop.

Parker, Gillespie, and others who became stars made the new language of bop accessible to audiences, but the uncompromising Monk made no concessions to attract listeners. His music—dissonant, complex, and difficult—brought him little steady work and almost no critical attention.

But in 1944 "'Round Midnight," an early Monk composition, was recorded by Cootie Williams's band. That year Monk also made his first recording with saxophonist COLEMAN HAWKINS as part of a quartet. At the time Monk worked at the Spotlight Club on 52nd Street with the Dizzy Gillespie Orchestra.

In 1947 Monk was signed by Blue Note. The Blue Note recordings issued between 1947 and 1952 include his compositions "Thelonious," "Evidence," and "Criss Cross." They are considered by many critics to represent characteristic and important works, though at the time they didn't sell well. In 1950 Monk recorded "Bloomdido" and "My Melancholy Baby" as a sideman for Charlie Parker.

In 1951 he was arrested with jazz pianist Bud Powell on a heroin charge. Though not a user, Monk refused to cooperate with the police. Jailed for sixty days, he lost his cabaret card, the police license New York required of all entertainers. Six years later, after jazz patron Baroness Pannonica de Koenigswarter, a member of the Rothschild family, helped him regain the license, his performing career blossomed. He played frequently in a quartet with JOHN COLTRANE.

The introspective Monk began to receive critical and popular acceptance. "His stubborn pursuit of his private musical vision in the face of cruel neglect had at last paid off," writes critic Grover Sales. The *Down Beat* critics poll named him best jazz pianist for three years running, 1958 through 1960. He toured Europe, appeared at jazz festivals, wrote the score for Roger Vadim's film *Les liaisons dangereuses*, and performed in concert at Carnegie Hall. "Sphere," a nickname he chose to set himself apart from "square," was the subject of a *Time* cover story, and his contract with Columbia Records, signed in 1962, began to yield returns.

Writer Grover Sales says that "describing Monk's music is like describing the color orange to a blind person." But Ran Blake speaks of Monk's "heavy attack and distinctive 'clanging' timbre, crushed notes and clusters, and left-hand chords made up of seconds and sixths instead of conventional triadic jazz harmonies. . . . [His] economical approach, . . . tempo suspension and silence . . . allowed him when improvising to explore different aspects of themes with unusual rigor."

Monk said himself in 1961, "Jazz is America musically. . . . Jazz is my adventure. I'm after new chords, new ways of syncopating, new figurations, new runs. How to use notes differently. That's it. Just using notes differently."

Monk toured the world, was awarded a Guggenheim Fellowship, and was honored by President Jimmy Carter. He appeared at the Newport Jazz Festival in the mid-1970s, but mostly lived a secluded life at the New Jersey home of the Baroness Pannonica de Koenigswarter until his death in 1982.

BIBLIOGRAPHY

Goldberg, J., *Jazz Masters of the Fifties*, 1965, rep., 1980; Hentoff, Nat, *Thelonious Monk*, 1961; Williams, M., *The Jazz Tradition*, 2d ed., 1983.

Moore, Charles Willard

(October 31, 1925–   )
Architect, Architectural Educator

Charles Moore, a leader in Post-Modernist architectural design of the 1960s through the 1980s, espoused a personalized, populist, and "inclusionist" approach to architecture through his teaching and practice. His works are known for their eclecticism, connotative overtones, and unusual spaces.

Moore, who was born in Benton Harbor, Michigan, received a bachelor's degree in architecture from the University of Michigan (1947) and a master's degree and doctorate in architecture from Princeton University (1957). He taught at the University of Utah and at Princeton, and served in the U.S. Army Corps of Engineers, before joining the faculty of the University of California, Berkeley (1959), becoming chairman of the architectural department (1962–1965).

Influenced by the humanist approach of Jean Labatut and LOUIS KAHN, who were two of his teachers at Princeton, Moore rebelled against the rigid order, exclusionism, and stark simplicity of mid-century modern architecture. He favors a personalized architecture not bound to any one tradition, and emphasizes communication and connectedness by engaging myth, historicism, fantasy, even whimsy in his designs. He has defined architecture as the "choreography of the familiar and the unfamiliar."

In 1962 Moore formed a partnership in San Francisco with Donlyn Lyndon, William Turnbull, and Richard Whitaker, called MLTW Associates. During the next decade Moore and his firm became internationally famous, producing a corpus of works that developed the idiom called Supermannerism. This approach echoed the sixteenth-century mannerist style and is characterized by manipulation of forms and scale and an all-inclusive vocabulary that accommodates humor, dislocation, ambiguity, historical traditions, and the unexpected in texture, color, and perspective.

Among the Post-Modern era's (see MICHAEL GRAVES) most imitated housing designs are the condominiums Moore created for Sea Ranch, a residential resort, on the Pacific cliffs at Gualala, California (with MLTW, first phase 1964–1965). Inspired by Italian hill towns, rural Vermont buildings, and an adjacent weather-beaten barn, the overall design illustrates a key aspect of Moore's style: the influence of vernacular architecture from many places. The intricate plan provided ocean views from all units and areas sheltered from the wind.

In 1965 Moore became chairman of Yale's Department of Architecture and reshaped its approach to architecture by emphasizing a re-examination of the nature and function of architecture. From 1969 to 1975 he served as dean of the School of Architecture at Yale. During this time he divided his practice between the San Francisco and New Haven offices, but eventually moved his practice to Essex, Connecticut. When he became professor of architecture at the University of California at Los Angeles (1975–1986), Moore retained the Essex office, called Moore Grover Harper, and became partner in two Los Angeles–based firms: Moore Ruble Yudell and the Urban Innovations Group. He has taught at the University of Texas at Austin since 1986.

One of Moore's most colorful works is the Piazza d'Italia, a public square and fountain in New Orleans (with Perez Associates, 1975–1980). It reveals his characteristic use of cultural and historical references through such elements as a large map of Italy for a plan and unexpected juxtaposition—classical Corinthian pilasters decorated with polished stainless steel and neon—to create a "flashy," but sophisticated, synthesis.

During the 1970s and 1980s Moore focused on the idea of "participatory buildings," in which the clients define what they want and the architect refines it. A good example is the New Jersey house (1973–1978) Moore designed (with Richard Oliver) for a blind man with a sighted family. Visually, the house is a deliberately unbalanced active composition of angled walls, towers, and pitched roofs. To make the house easily negotiable for the owner, Moore incorporated nonvisual elements such as sound and smell (the fountain and plants in the central hall or orangerie), and touch (terra-cotta tiles in the orangerie, pegged oak planks in the living room, and carpeting in the library).

Moore returned to the Sea Ranch Resort to design a vacation house (1983–1988), which he described as "one part cabin and one part wooden castle." Characteristic of his later rambling, extended house designs, this structure appears to be of 1 story in front but reveals a stepped formation of angled tower, wings, and windows in the rear. The trapezoid-shaped, multitiered courtyard with its driftwood-accented sand garden is a focal point.

The houses that Moore has designed for himself best illustrate his idea that "a good house speaks not just for the material from which it is made, but of the intangible rhythms, spirit and dreams of people's lives." His Essex, Connecticut, remodeled house (late 1960s) was famous for its green pyramid constructed to hide the bed and its painted lettering on the ceiling, an example of Supergraphics—huge design fragments painted or applied to surfaces to change scale and viewpoint through optical effects, distortion, or destruction of architectural planes. His eighth personal home, a remodeled house in Austin, Texas (mid-1980s, with Richard Dodge and Arthur Andersson), is an ellipse-shaped office-home compound noted for its richly decorated interior. The sweep of an interior curved wall guiding the eye to outside vistas, the whimsical cutouts over the fireplace, and the shelves and cubbies of "little objects made into miniature worlds" show Moore's unique synthesis of ideas and things.

Other major works by Moore include Kresge College at the University of California, Santa Cruz (with MLTW, 1965–1973), designed like a Mediterranean hillside village with an air of the stage set; the Church Street South Housing Project, New Haven, Connecticut (with MLTW, 1965–1969); a Malibu house (with Urban Innovations Group, 1991); and St. Matthew's Episcopal Church in Pacific Palisades, California (with Moore Ruble Yudell, 1983–1984), designed with much input from the congregation.

Moore also wrote *The Place of Houses*, with Gerald Allen and Donlyn Lyndon (1974) and *Body, Memory, and Architecture* (1977) with Kent Bloomer, which promoted the concept that architecture should engage all the senses.

BIBLIOGRAPHY

Cook, John W., and Heinrich Klotz, "Charles Moore," *Conversations with Architects*, 1973; Filler, Martin, "Charles Moore: House Vernacular," *Art in America*, October 1980; Littlejohn, David, *Architect: The Life and Work of Charles W. Moore*, 1984; Moore, Charles, and Gerald Allen, *Dimensions: Space, Shape, and Scale in Architecture*, 1976.

Moore, Marianne Craig

(November 15, 1887–February 5, 1972)
Poet

Marianne Moore wrote poetry of rare intelligence and wit that reflected a profound moral vision of nature and the human spirit. Her meticulously crafted—often revolutionary—verse forms helped demonstrate the range and depth of modern poetry.

Moore was born in her grandfather's house in Kirkwood, Missouri, on November 15, 1887. She never knew her father, who was confined to an institution for the mentally ill after suffering a breakdown. At age seven, Moore moved with her mother and brother to Carlisle, Pennsylvania, where she lived for two decades. A biology major at Bryn Mawr College (1905–1909), she wrote for the campus literary magazine. From 1911 to 1915 she taught at the government Indian school at Carlisle.

Moore's early poetry, published in such magazines as *The Egoist* and *Poetry* in 1915 and 1916, is marked by an easy mix of images and commentary and also an affinity for fine

distinctions. She and her mother moved to New York City in 1918, where she joined a group of writers associated with *Others* magazine, including two talented young poets, WILLIAM CARLOS WILLIAMS and WALLACE STEVENS, who encouraged her to find her own style.

"Poetry," a memorable poem written in 1919, makes clear how strongly she felt about the power of imagery. She writes in the syllabic verse that came to be identified with her work: natural rhythms of speech, yet strictly counted, line by line, and subtly patterned with rhymes.

Moore's first book, *Poems*, was published without her knowledge by friends through the Egoist Press in England in 1921. Her second volume, *Observations* (1924), contained fifty-three poems of Moore's own choosing, including "Marriage," a free-verse collage of quotations that cleverly reprises the tensions and perils of the marital state. (Moore herself never married.) "An Octopus" meticulously describes the icy majesty of Mount Rainier and satirizes the exploitation of nature for recreation and commerce. *Observations* won Moore the Dial Award for 1924.

In 1925 Moore became acting editor of *The Dial*, a renowned modernist journal that sought to relate high culture to American life. Her work there gained her international appreciation. After the magazine ceased publication in 1929, she moved to Brooklyn and was able to support herself and her mother by the income from her poetry and book reviews.

Selected Poems, with a laudatory introduction by her friend T. S. ELIOT, appeared in 1935. "Miss Moore's poems," he wrote, "form part of the small body of durable poetry written in our time."

Moore read widely, and her poetry drew on sources in natural history, the arts, baseball, and public affairs. Imagery and language taken from science and journalism tempered the rhetoric of her poetry. Her choice of words was unerringly precise.

The Pangolin and Other Verse (1936) displays Moore's interest in animals as a subject for poetry. "The Pangolin" juxtaposes the animal's image with that of man and discourses on the nature of grace.

In *What Are Years* (1941) and *Nevertheless* (1944), Moore melds a keen awareness of the tragedies of World War II into observations about animals, American history, and the characteristics of other countries. In the former volume, "He 'Digesteth Harde Yron'" describes the extinction of bird species with the sensibilities of one who witnessed the atrocities against the Jews in Europe. In "A Carriage from Sweden," published in *Nevertheless*, Moore ironically characterizes that country's neutrality during the war.

Her mother's death in 1947 profoundly affected Moore's life and work. Her *Collected Poems*, published in 1951, carried a simple dedication to her mother. It also contained an elegy, "By Disposition of Angels," which offers an image of a star burning in the heavens as a counterpoint to her grief. The volume won her the National Book Award, the Pulitzer Prize, and the Bollingen Prize.

Moore spent nine years working and reworking a verse translation of *The Fables of La Fontaine*, published in 1954. The next year, *Predilections*, a selection of essays written over forty years, gathered together in a single volume many elements of her critical sensibility.

Moore's later verse, written from 1956 to 1970, tends to be looser and lighter. Many of these poems, such as "Blue Bug" and "Tell Me, Tell Me," appeared in the *New Yorker*.

The Complete Poems (1967) presents Moore's own final selections from among a lifetime of poetic works. For some, it constitutes her canon. It earned her the Poetry Society of America's Gold Medal for Distinguished Achievement (her second) and also the National Medal for Literature.

Moore died in New York in 1972.

BIBLIOGRAPHY

Engel, Bernard, *Marianne Moore*, 1964; Hall, Donald, *Marianne Moore: The Cage and the Animal*, 1970; Phillips, Elizabeth, *Marianne Moore*, 1982; Stapleton, Laurence, *Marianne Moore: The Poet's Advance*, 1978.

Morgan, Julia

(January 28, 1872–February 2, 1957)
Architect

Julia Morgan, the first professionally successful woman architect in the United States, helped to establish a distinctive architectural identity for northern California residential areas during the early twentieth century and is famous for designing the fabulous Hearst estate at San Simeon, California.

Born and raised in the San Francisco Bay Area, Morgan became the first woman to graduate from the University of California, Berkeley, with an engineering degree. One of her instructors, architect BERNARD MAYBECK, became a major influence in her life, sometimes collaborating with her on projects. In 1896 she went to Paris in hopes of being accepted into the architectural section of the renowned Ecole des Beaux-Arts. After a two-year struggle against the institution's gender bias, she won admittance and became the first woman graduate in architecture (1901).

Returning to the United States, Morgan worked with architect John Galen Howard on projects at the University of California, Berkeley. Her first independent commissions were for Mills College for Women, Oakland, California, and included the construction of a bell tower (1903–1904; earliest college bell tower in the West), library (1905–1906), gymnasium (1907–1908), and social center (1916). In 1903 Morgan opened her own architectural firm in San Francisco, which she ran like an atelier (school/workshop), sharing the profits with her staff. She gained a reputation for meticulous craftsmanship, a client-oriented approach to design, and close supervision of on-site construction. Early in her career she used structure as a focal point for architectural expression. The Young Women's Christian Association became a major client, commissioning Morgan to construct residences and recreation centers in California, Utah, and Hawaii.

Morgan's career blossomed during the building boom after the San Francisco earth-

quake and fire (1906), in part because of the publicity of how well the Mills College bell tower withstood the quake. Her reputation was made with the commission to rebuild the Fairmont Hotel. An eclectic designer of houses, churches, schools, banks, and hospitals, she integrated various architectural traditions, such as Spanish-Moorish balconies and arcades, Gothic-inspired decorative carving, and medieval- or Renaissance-derived facades, juxtaposed with simple materials of brick, stucco, and shingle. She was one of the innovators of a northern California style of residential architecture, called Bay Area style, which emphasized compatibility with the landscape and a merging of indoors and outdoors through terraces, balconies, and patios and much use of wood. Her sophisticated style is characterized by frequent use of redwood shingles in her early work and the dramatic placement of indoor and outdoor Julia swimming pools.

Morgan's most famous architectural work is associated with the Hearst family. For a quarter of a century she was a loyal and accommodating architect to the erratic patron and collector William Randolph Hearst, the publishing magnate, for whom she designed the Hearst Cottage at Grand Canyon (1925) and the palatial, 123-acre showplace on the Hearst ranch at San Simeon, California (1919–1947), among other projects. The design for San Simeon included a Spanish Gothic–style castle (La Casa Grande) overlooking a large open terrace surrounded by three guest houses. This challenging task involved incorporating parts of castles and monasteries that Hearst had purchased overseas into the twin-towered, 100-room Casa Grande.

After forty-five years as an architect, during which time she designed more than 700 buildings, Morgan closed her office, destroyed many of her records, and retired. A workaholic, putting in fourteen- to sixteen-hour days, she was shy and sought anonymity, stating that "the buildings speak; I do not speak." Although her work was not well known outside California until the late 1960s, she was a pioneer in opening the architectural field to women.

BIBLIOGRAPHY

Boutelle, Sara H., *Julia Morgan, Architect*, 1988; Carleton, Winslow, *The Enchanted Hill*, 1980; Longstreet, Richard, *Julia Morgan, Architect*, 1977.

Morton, Jelly Roll

(October 20, 1885–July 10, 1941)
Jazz Musician

Jelly Roll Morton, the first great jazz artist, may not have "invented jazz,"—as he was to claim late in his career—but his "King Porter Stomp" and "Wolverine Blues" are jazz standards. The way he blended the discipline of composition with his exuberance and improvisation pointed the way for later jazz innovators.

In an interview with folklorist ALAN LOMAX, Morton spoke of his birth into a Creole family in New Orleans and said he learned the guitar at seven and began the piano at ten. Morton's name has been given variously as Ferdinand Joseph La Menthe, LaMothe, or Lemott. Research undertaken in the 1980s has brought general acceptance of Lemott as correct, a name changed by Jelly Roll to Morton sometime early on. By 1902 he was performing in the bordellos of Storyville, gambling and playing pool. On the outs with his respectable family, scratching to earn his way, and captive to the music that was to make his name, he soon moved from Louisiana cities to Mississippi, Alabama, and Florida.

National Archives

With New Orleans as his base, Morton traveled to Memphis, St. Louis, and Kansas City, playing and working in minstrel shows. In 1911 pianist James P. Johnson heard him play his striking "Jelly Roll Blues" in New York. He arrived in Los Angeles in 1917 and stayed there five years, thanks to a string of successes. Drawn to the Chicago of the early 1920s, he made his first recordings in 1923, two with a group, "Big Foot Ham" and "Muddy Water Blues," others solo performances of his own work. The recordings reveal an established, mature sophistication, a style that melded ragtime, blues, and African American elements into what was becoming known as jazz.

Three years later Morton was working with his Red Hot Peppers, a small New Orleans–style ensemble, the group gathered only for recording. The results are a wonderful blend of freedom and discipline; many feature each instrumentalist in solos. "Black Bottom Stomp" and "The Pearls" display Morton's own skills as piano soloist and as composer/

arranger. These pieces showcase a dazzling range of textures but nevertheless preserve formal clarity. The sensitive countermelodies that run throughout some of the best solos are unique and are not heard again until developed by Earl Hines and ART TATUM years later.

When Morton moved to New York in 1928, he continued to record and to emphasize solo improvisations. He never moved on to take up the new big band styles of Don Redman, FLETCHER HENDERSON, or John Nesbitt, and by 1930 his New Orleans–style arrangements and performances were thought old hat. Some of his compositions survived in performances of others. For example the BENNY GOODMAN 1935 rendering of "King Porter Stomp," in Fletcher Henderson's big band arrangement, was central to introducing the swing era.

Jelly Roll Morton's fortune failed in the 1930s. Always colorful and innovative, he was given to ostentation—he wore a diamond filling in a front tooth—and sometimes to outrageous and boastful talk. He moved to Washington, D.C., managed a jazz club, and played only occasionally. In 1938 his admirer

Alan Lomax, later his biographer, recorded a remarkable series of interviews with Jelly Roll for the Library of Congress in which Morton recalls, with fact and fancy, his early days in New Orleans and recreates musically the styles of his contemporaries there. Morton as historian is invaluable, and he comes across in this series in a surprising way as an astute theorist and analyst of the music he knew so well.

The Library of Congress series spurred interest in Morton and led to additional recordings in 1939 and 1940, an interest that coincided with the revival of New Orleans music. Morton's death in 1941 brought this late flowering of his career to an abrupt end.

BIBLIOGRAPHY

Balliett, W., *Jelly Roll, Jabbo and Fats*, 1983; Lomax, Alan, *Mister Jelly Roll*, 1950; Schuller, Gunther, *Early Jazz: Its Roots and Musical Development*, 1968; Williams, M., *Jelly Roll Morton*, 1962, and *Jazz Masters of New Orleans*, 1967.

Motherwell, Robert

(January 24, 1915–July 16, 1991)
Painter

Robert Motherwell was the youngest of his generation of American Abstract Expressionists who emerged in the 1940s. His celebrated series, *Elegy to the Spanish Republic*, typifies his artistic, social, and philosophical concerns.

Motherwell was born in Aberdeen, Washington, in 1915, the son of a banker. The family moved to San Francisco three years later. At the age of eleven, he received a fellowship to the Otis Art Institute in Los Angeles. Although he was too young for the life-drawing classes, he excelled in illustration. In 1932 he entered Stanford University, where he pursued varied interests in music, philosophy, French litera-

ture, and psychoanalytic theory. After more studies in art and philosophy at Harvard and Columbia universities—with a stint teaching at the University of Oregon sandwiched in between—he decided to pursue a career in writing and painting rather than teaching.

Unfit for military service because of asthma, Motherwell developed a political consciousness during World War II. Themes of the war for freedom and defeat of fascism recurred in his work throughout his career. By 1941 he had become acquainted with many Surrealist artists in exile in New York, including MARCEL DUCHAMP, Max Ernst, and André Breton. He enjoyed a brief stint as editor of the magazine

VVV, which was devoted to what biographer Frank O'Hara considered "imaginative works of universal interest . . . in what may simply be called the field of the wonderful," and pursued his interests in Surrealism. Other literary endeavors in the 1940s included editing The Documents of Modern Art, a series of illustrated publications on such movements as Dada, Cubism, and Surrealism; lecturing on "The Modern Painter's World" at Mt. Holyoke College; editing the short-lived arts journal *Possibilities (An Occasional Review)* (with JOHN CAGE, Pierre Chareau, and Harold Rosenberg); and editing a book, *The Dada Painters and Poets* (1951). Meanwhile, he had his first one-man exhibition at Peggy Guggenheim's Art of This Century Gallery in 1944 and appeared in the "Fourteen Americans" show at the Museum of Modern Art in 1946.

In 1949 he painted *Granada,* the first of what would become the central series in his career, the *Spanish Elegies.* (He first used the term "elegy" for a 1948 collage plate and continued its use throughout his career.) Biographer H. H. Arnason referred to them as "among the most important paintings of the twentieth century." Derived from his interest in a Spanish sensibility, his devotion to the painter Picasso and the poet/playwright Garcia Lorca, and his impassioned political attitudes regarding the Spanish Civil War, the forms suggest architecture, phalluses, or bull's testicles. Sometimes the forms seem strung together, like beads on a wire, or entrapped between strong vertical bars. For historian and critic Jack D. Flam they have a "harsh music," overtones of death and love and physical anguish: "The hand moves, feeling is transmitted. In the now quick, now light, now violent, now probing movement of the brush or pen or pencil, a gesture makes feeling intelligible."

Other series included the somber *Iberian* paintings, which he began in 1958, while he and his second wife, HELEN FRANKENTHALER, were summering in Spain and France. The *Open* series was executed in the late 1960s. Each of the numbered entries consisted of a field of color filling the entire canvas with the exception of a rectangular or square area extending from the upper edge to half or two-thirds the distance from the bottom. The *Lyric Suite* series (1965) consisted of 565 "automatic" paintings in ink on Japanese rice paper.

A retrospective exhibition at the Museum of Modern Art in 1965 was followed by other retrospectives in London, Vienna, Mexico City, and Dusseldorf throughout the 1970s and 1980s.

Few recent painters have been more steeped in the sheer variety of the modes in art. Motherwell never limited himself to one particular kind of expression. His formal repertory embraces a Zenlike calligraphy, primordial forms, elaborate fugal compositions, and complex networks of angular and biomorphic shapes that seem to march—or, crawl—across the canvas. Black and white have been his main colors—he describes their connotations in his *Spanish Elegies* as, respectively, death and life—but he sometimes uses a color range that is limited to ochers, blues, and reds. Unlike the paintings of his fellow Abstract Expressionists (see BARNETT NEWMAN), Motherwell's work is suffused with allusions and references to literary and philosophical issues. "It would be very difficult to formulate a position in which there were no external relations," he wrote in 1951. "I cannot imagine any structure being defined as though it only has internal meaning." His gifts as a writer and editor further entitle him to be the unofficial spokesperson for his artistic times. "Motherwell's work in its entirety becomes a superb and beautiful litany or evocation of the existence of modern man," wrote Robert T. Buck, "and in particular the struggle to infuse meaning into life."

"In a sense, all of my pictures are slices cut out of a continuum whose duration is my whole life," said Motherwell, "and hopefully will continue until the day I die."

BIBLIOGRAPHY

Arnason, H. H., *Robert Motherwell,* 1977; Flam, Jack D., and Dore Ashton, *Robert Motherwell,* 1985; O'Hara, Frank, *Robert Motherwell,* 1965.

Muddy Waters

(April 4, 1915–April 30, 1983)
Blues Singer, Guitarist

Mississippi bluesman Muddy Waters was steeped in the rural Delta's rough laments with their subtle inflections of timing, pitch, and timbre. After he went north to stay, he helped shape urban blues by intensifying the Delta sound to produce a harsher, more aggressive style that became the Chicago blues.

Muddy Waters was born McKinley Morganfield in Rolling Fork, Mississippi. He went to live with his maternal grandmother when he was six months old. "When I got big enough to crawl around," he said, "I would play in the mud and try to eat it. My grandma

Copyright *Washington Post*; Reprinted by permission of the D.C. Public Library

started that Muddy thing, and after we were up there near Clarksdale, the kids started the Waters." He was three when he and his grandmother moved to the Delta's cotton country.

Early on he made music, Waters remembered, from "beatin' on bucket tops and tin cans" when he was three to the harmonica, at seven, to the guitar when he was seventeen. There was little schooling. He worked in the fields and developed his ear by playing and listening to musicians and records.

He was twenty-six in the summer of 1941 when folklorist ALAN LOMAX recorded his "Country Blues" and "I Be's Troubled." In May 1943, denied a pay raise by the plantation owner, Waters headed to Chicago. "I wish you could have seen me," he said in *Rolling Stone*, the magazine named after a Waters song, "I got off that train and it looked like this was the fastest place in the world."

Waters settled in, found work, and played in black clubs where the noise level forced a change in instrument: he adopted the electric guitar. His slide playing, a ring of metal or glass run up and down the neck, once gentle, became forceful and strident. Other instruments added volume: piano, bass, amplified harmonica, and rhythm guitar. This combination became standard for Chicago blues.

In 1948 Waters formed his own band and began to record for Chess Records. Others joined him, including WILLIE DIXON, composer of "Hoochie Coochie Man." Bassist Dixon speaks about that time, "With Muddy we started to put a beat behind the music and make definite rhythm patterns ... we tried to set up a melodic pattern to match the rhythm, and this gave songs the feeling we wanted ... it became a style."

In the late 1950s blacks lost interest, though Waters's music, modified, was played as rock and roll. Teens loved the music, and the blues was taken up by groups like the Rolling Stones, indebted to Waters for the name.

Waters toured in the 1960s, but it was the 1970s that brought success with white audiences. A featured performer at jazz festivals, he made his final appearance in June 1982 playing "Blow Wind Blow" with Eric Clapton. He died in Westmont, Illinois, a year later.

BIBLIOGRAPHY

Oliver, P., *Muddy Waters*, 1964; Palmer, R., *Deep Blues*, 1981.

Nabokov, Vladimir

(April 23, 1899–July 2, 1977)
Critic, Novelist, Poet

Vladimir Nabokov, a Russian émigré who lived in the United States for almost twenty years, wrote in English with extraordinary fluency, constructing elaborate fictions using subtle allusions and word play to layer each text with multiple meanings. His wildly controversial novel *Lolita* concerns a man's obsessive love for a twelve-year-old girl.

Nabokov was born in the city of St. Petersburg, Russia, to a wealthy, aristocratic family, and was raised in a fashionable city home and on a sprawling country estate to the south. At the age of seventeen, he published his first volume of verse. His father, a distinguished professor of criminology and a liberal member of the Russian Parliament, became cabinet secretary to the Provisional Government founded after the revolution of February 1917.

The family fled to the Crimea after the Bolshevik coup of October 1917, and left the country altogether in 1919 as the Red Army advanced. Nabokov was sent to study at Cambridge University in England, and the family settled in Berlin. Nabokov's father was killed in 1922 when, while presiding over a meeting, he tried to disarm a militant monarchist assassin attacking the speaker.

After his graduation from Cambridge in 1922, Nabokov returned to Berlin, where he made a living giving Russian lessons, writing a newspaper column, and composing the first Russian-language crossword puzzles for an émigré newspaper. He wrote his early Russian novels under the pseudonym V. Sirin. In 1925 he married Vera Slonim.

The Nabokovs lived in Berlin until 1938, when Nazi activity drove them to Paris. In 1940, fleeing before the advancing Nazi army, they sailed for the United States. Nabokov briefly taught Slavic languages at Stanford University. Then, while teaching at Wellesley College, his skill as a lepidopterist earned him a research fellowship at Harvard University. Eventually, his scholarly biography *Nicolai Gogol* (1944) won him a professorship of comparative literature at Cornell University in 1948, where he stayed until the royalties from his novel *Lolita* (1955) allowed him to retire from teaching. In 1959 he moved to Switzerland, where he lived and wrote until his death in 1977.

Nabokov wrote three of his seventeen novels while living in the United States: *Bend Sinister* (1947), *Lolita*, and *Pnin* (1957). The first, *Bend Sinister*, is the account of a philosopher's attempt to preserve his integrity against the wishes of a dictator who demands his endorsement. In the last, *Pnin*, a hapless Russian émigré professor, stymied professionally, is baffled by the wiles of the woman he has loved, who uses him to gain entrance to the United States, as well as an education for her son.

Lolita, the novel that made Nabokov both famous and infamous, describes Humbert Humbert's perverse fascination with Dolly Haze, a preadolescent girl. Their cross-country odysseys—during which Humbert indulges his sexual obsession and flees a mysterious competitor for Dolly's love—gave Nabokov an opportunity to satirize American motel culture. The text is rife with elaborate literary puzzles, word games, and parodies, including veiled references to the author. (A frequent Nabokovian joke is to endow a minor character with a name that is an anagram of the author's—in this case, Vivian Darkbloom, a conspirator with Clare Quilty, the man who eventually takes Dolly from Humbert.)

The manuscript for *Lolita* was considered so shocking that it was rejected by several American publishing houses before a French publisher of pornography printed it in 1955. Widespread recognition of the book's aesthetic virtues prompted G. P. Putnam's Sons to put out an edition in 1958, and it sold rapidly. A movie version was made in 1962.

Nabokov wrote five other novels in English. His first, *The Real Life of Sebastian Knight* (1940), written in Europe while he contemplated emigrating to the United States, comprises the narrator's attempt to understand the life of his recently deceased half brother, a novelist and a genius.

Pale Fire (1962), composed after Nabokov had left the United States for Switzerland, comprises a 999-line poem by a fictional poet, John Shade, plus an introduction, footnotes, and index by Charles Kinbote, an editor and Shade's neighbor. The poem and its annotations reveal Shade's life and Kinbote's fantasies, though the two are mingled. The book satirizes scholarly pedantry and stands as a commentary on the complexity of any literary artifact.

Ada, or Ardor: A Family Chronicle (1969), set on a planet called Antiterra, concerns the incestuous love of the young protagonist Van Veen for his sister Ada; Van's metaphysical obsession with the past, which leads to a long discourse on the nature of time and space, serve to distract him from the effect of their incest on those around them.

Transparent Things (1972) is the story of a young man whose attempt to liberate himself sexually leads to marriage to a heartless woman he eventually kills in a rage over her cruelty and her infidelities.

Nabokov's final novel, *Look at the Harlequins!* (1974), concerns a Russian émigré writer, a puppet image of Nabokov himself, whose novels are parodies of Nabokov's. The book is a self-reflexive comment on the process and problems of fiction.

Nabokov wrote nine novels in Russian during his years in Berlin and Paris; he and his son, Dmitri, eventually translated all of them into English. Some of these early novels reflect on Nabokov's life as an émigré and present strong moral conflicts. They are *Mary* (1926), *King, Queen, Knave* (1928), *The Defense* (1930), *The Eye* (1930), *Glory* (1932), *Laughter in the Dark* (1932), *Despair* (1934), *Invitation to a Beheading* (1935), and *The Gift* (serialized 1937–1938, published in full 1952).

His charming autobiographical account of life in Imperial Russia was first published as *Conclusive Evidence* (1951), then revised as *Speak, Memory* (1966). By far his most ambitious contribution to world literary scholarship was his translation with notes of the 1831 novel in verse by Aleksandr Pushkin, *Eugene Onegin* (four volumes, 1964; revised 1975).

BIBLIOGRAPHY

Boyd, Brian, *Vladimir Nabokov: The Russian Years*, 1990, and *Vladimir Nabokov: The American Years*, 1991; Field, Andrew, *VN: The Life and Art of Vladimir Nabokov*, 1986.

Nathan, George Jean

(February 14, 1882–April 8, 1958)
Author, Drama Critic, Editor

George Jean Nathan was one of the most powerful literary and dramatic editors and critics in the first half of the century. He was particularly notorious for his relentless attacks on the trivial and sentimental aspects of the contemporary American drama.

Nathan was born in Fort Wayne, Indiana, in 1882. After studying at Cornell University and the University of Bologna, he got a job as a cub reporter on the New York *Herald* through the influence of his uncle, Charles Frederic Nördlinger, a well-known critic and playwright. During his apprenticeship, he worked the police and sports beat and contributed occasional theater reviews. A meeting in 1908 with another young journalist, H. L. Mencken, began a friendship and professional association that would last for many years. As joint editors from 1914 to 1923 of *The Smart Set* magazine (founded in 1890), a publication aimed at a sophisticated audience, they published the work of some of the most powerful writers of the day, including THEODORE DREISER, and a number of younger writers, like EUGENE O'NEILL, F. SCOTT FITZGERALD, and SHERWOOD ANDERSON. He also cofounded two other influential literary journals, *The American Mercury* (1924–1932) with Mencken and the *American Spectator* (1932–1937) with O'Neill and others. While temperamentally and philosophically different—Mencken was the angry satirist and Nathan the detached cynic and snob—the partnership made them powerful arbiters of literary taste.

Indeed, by 1925 Nathan was the most widely read and highest paid dramatic critic in the world. His opinions appeared in more than thirty publications, including a stint as dramatic critic for *Vanity Fair,* and an equal number of books and annuals. While maintaining a posture of eclectic tastes—in *The World in Falseface* (1923) he described his "pestiferous catholicity of taste that embraces 'Medea' and 'The

Library of Congress

Follies,' Eleanora Duse and Florence Mills"—Nathan ruthlessly castigated what he considered the "one-cylinder taste" of the American drama. At the same time, he used his influence to champion the work of important playwrights such as O'Neill, Luigi Pirandello, and Sean O'Casey, reprinting some of their early plays in his magazines. From 1943 through 1951 he published his annual *Theatre Book of the Year.*

Among his forty books, mostly collections of his reviews and aphorisms, were *Mr. George Jean Nathan Presents* (1917), *The Popular Theatre* (1918), *Testament of a Critic* (1931), and *Encyclopaedia of the Theatre* (1940). He also wrote several plays, in collaboration with either Mencken (*Heliogabalus,* 1920) or art critic Willard Huntingdon Wright (*Europe after 8:15,* 1914). His favorite targets included the talking picture, which he attacked from its inception in 1927 to its development in the early 1930s.

BIBLIOGRAPHY

Frick, Constance, *The Drama Criticism of George Jean Nathan,* 1943; Lazarus, A. L. (ed.), *A George Jean Nathan Reader,* 1990; Nathan, George Jean, *The World in Falseface,* 1923, and *Testament of a Critic,* 1931.

Neutra, Richard Josef

(April 8, 1892–April 16, 1970)
Architect

A seminal figure in twentieth-century American architecture, Richard Neutra was the major American pioneer of the International style and spurred the development of a new direction in the regional architecture of southern California. He also exerted substantial influence through his books and lectures.

Neutra was born in Vienna, Austria, and studied there at the Institute of Technology, then at the University of Zurich in Switzerland. After service as an Austrian artillery officer during World War I, he worked for Swiss landscape architect Gustav Ammann and developed the concept that architecture must harmonize with nature. He was also influenced significantly by Viennese architecture, especially the subway stations designed by Otto Wagner, and the design philosophy of Adolf Loos, who espoused unadorned or stripped architecture and the use of industrial prefabrication. He worked for the Berlin architect Erich Mendelsohn from 1921 to 1923 before emigrating to the United States in 1923, where he felt the future of architecture rested. He became a naturalized citizen in 1929.

After design positions in New York City, Chicago, and with FRANK LLOYD WRIGHT in Wisconsin, Neutra formed the Architectural Group for Industry and Commerce with Rudolph Schindler in Los Angeles (1925–early 1930s). His first building, the Jardin Apartments in Los Angeles (1927), was made of reinforced concrete with cantilevered balconies and bands of metal-framed windows. It was one of the first International style structures in the country (see LUDWIG MIES VAN DER ROHE). This style, which originated in Europe in the early 1920s, embraced the machine aesthetic and championed unadorned, often boxlike structures of concrete, steel, and glass.

Neutra humanized the style by emphasizing the relationship between a structure and its site, and by approaching design as a means to serve the organic nature of man, a concept he labeled Biorealism. His international reputation came with the 1929 Lovell House, a 3-story structure noted for its steel frame sheathed with concrete and glass, masterfully integrated with the natural landscape of the Hollywood Hills.

A hallmark of Neutra's work is the interrelationship between interior and exterior space, as exemplified by his use of sliding glass doors to extend the classrooms outward at Corona Avenue School in Los Angeles (1934). This became a prototype for the city's school designs. This fusion of the modernist idiom with the regional considerations initiated a new phase of southern California architecture.

In the 1930s Neutra designed several modular experimental houses composed of steel and plywood, such as Hollywood director JOSEF VON STERNBERG's house in Northridge (1935). The architect was particularly adept at designing multiple-housing units, such as the Indian pueblo–inspired Strathmore Apartments in Los Angeles (1938) and five housing projects in California and Texas for the Federal Housing Authority (1939–1941). After World War II, Neutra expanded his practice, designing such varied projects as the Lincoln Memorial Museum at Gettysburg, Pennsylvania (1959), the U.S. Embassy in Karachi, Pakistan (1960), a theater in Düsseldorf, Germany (1959), and the Dayton Museum of Natural History (1959) in Ohio.

Neutra was in partnership with Robert Alexander, a planner, in the 1950s, and later with his son, Dion.

Neutra lectured worldwide and wrote extensively about architecture. Among his most influential books are *How America Builds* (1927) and *Survival Through Design* (1954).

He won many awards and design competitions and became the first architect honored on the cover of *Time* magazine (1949). One of his fascinating, though never realized, projects was a plan (1926–1930) for an ideal future city, called Rush City Reformed, which idealized, on a human scale, transportation, living, and working in the twentieth century.

BIBLIOGRAPHY

Boesiger, Willy (ed.), *Richard Neutra, Buildings and Projects, 1923–1966,* 3 vols., 1966; Hines, Thomas S., *Richard Neutra and the Search for Modern Architecture: A Biography and History,* 1981; McCoy, Esther, *Richard Neutra,* 1960; Neutra, Richard J., *Life and Shape,* 1962.

Nevelson, Louise

(September 23, 1899–April 17, 1988)
Painter, Printmaker, Sculptor

L ouise Nevelson is considered the originator of Environmental sculpture. Her monochromatic stacked boxes filled with bits of found materials and assembled into wall-sized thematic groupings or "environments" are typical of her highly personal style.

Born Louise Berliawsky in Kiev, Russia, Nevelson emigrated with her family to Rockland, Maine, in 1905. Childhood exposure to the power of nature along the rugged Maine coastline influenced the themes of her later sculptures. In 1920 she married businessman Charles Nevelson and moved to New York City, where she applied herself to dramatics and dance, as well as painting and drawing. She studied at the Art Students League (1928–1930), then left her husband and child to study with Hans Hofmann in Munich, Germany (1931). In 1932–1933 she assisted Mexican painter Diego Rivera on a mural project for the New Workers' School in New York City.

During the 1930s and 1940s she traveled in Mexico and Central America, developing a strong interest in pre-Columbian art. In 1937 she taught at the Educational Alliance School of Art under the auspices of the depression-era Works Progress Administration and began to exhibit in New York galleries. Her early sculptures were usually small terra-cotta figures, such as *Earth Woman II* (1933), or landscape-like wood constructions composed of furniture fragments and architectural decorations. Although her first one-woman show in New York (1941) was well received, she did not sell any works. As a result, she hauled the pieces back to her loft and destroyed them. She was a practicing artist for thirty years before she sold her first major work in 1959.

During the period she referred to as the "unfolding" of her style (1940s to mid-1950s), Nevelson was influenced by Picasso, African art, and Aztec and Mayan art. She often scavenged in ruined buildings for cast-off objects, such as doorknobs, hinges, wheels, and bits of furniture, which she combined into new images. Sometimes she would juxtapose these discarded objects on platforms, columns, boxes, or other pedestal-like constructions. Her technique of combining different nonartistic materials through a pattern of proliferation broke with the traditional methods of sculpting by modeling and carving. She said of her work: "I always wanted to show the world that art is everywhere, except it has to pass through a creative mind."

Her mature style emerged in the mid-1950s when she established herself as a major American artist through a series of one-woman shows—beginning with *Ancient Games and Ancient Places* (1955)—with works that showed what was to become her trademark sculptural environments. The objective of the twentieth-century movement known as Environmental art was to involve directly the viewer in an artwork through total immersion. Nevelson created environments of sculptures arranged thematically in a single color to form unified wholes that seem to surround the viewer. Her 1958 thematic environment titled *Moon Garden + One,* which consists of 116 boxes and circular containers filled with odd pieces of wood arranged in recurring shapes, introduced her famous stacked-box style.

Maintaining that shadow and space were the most important elements of her sculptures, Nevelson created increasingly more complex monochromatic abstract constructions of open-faced wooden boxes stacked to form compartmentalized walls filled with intricate patterns of found wood pieces. Her first major wall was *Sky Cathedral* (1958), which was painted black. She also used white and gold effectively to help create a uniform mood, as in *Dawn's Wedding Feast* (1959), her first white environment, and her large gold wall, *An American Tribute to the British People* (1960–1965).

In the 1960s she began to use other materials, such as Plexiglas, aluminum, Formica, and steel. More austere and architecturally oriented, these sculptures explored the range of rich tones provided by one color. Many of her steel constructions were commissioned as sculptures for public sites, such as *Dawn Shadows* (1982), which stands in front of the Pace Gallery in New York City, and her largest wall sculpture, *Sky Gate—New York* (1978), which stands at the World Trade Center in New York. A good example from this period is *Atmosphere and Environment V* (1966) composed of aluminum and black epoxy enamel. She was also engaged in painting, drawing, and printmaking, completing twenty-six editions of lithographs while working at the Tamarind Lithography Workshop in Los Angeles in 1963.

The recipient of many awards, Nevelson has had her sculptures exhibited worldwide, including works in the permanent collection at New York's Museum of Modern Art. Her sculptures have been variously described as "honeycombs," "doll houses," "boxed reveries," and "pieces of magic," with a mysterious, dreamlike, and mythopoetic quality that embody the spirit of the legendary past for the viewer. They are regarded as some of the most original and evocative works in modern art.

Nevelson was a strong-willed, independent woman who defied the pressures of family and friends to achieve her goal, of which she said simply, "I was born to be an artist." Her highly individualistic style in art was mirrored by her personal manner. She wore wild hats and striking clothes that she designed herself, and smoked Tiparillo cigars. Commenting on the unusual concept of her works, Nevelson said that Michelangelo, if he appeared today, would not recognize them as sculpture.

Nevelson died in New York City in 1988.

BIBLIOGRAPHY

Glimcher, Arnold B., *Louise Nevelson,* 1972; Lisle, Laurie, *Louise Nevelson: A Passionate Life,* 1990.

Newman, Barnett

(January 29, 1905–July 4, 1970)
Painter, Sculptor

Barnett Newman, a champion of Abstract Expressionism, spearheaded the development of Color Field painting, was a forerunner of Minimal art, and pioneered the very large format and the shaped canvas. He also exerted much influence through his critical and theoretical writings.

Newman was born in Manhattan, New York, of Russian-Polish-Jewish heritage. He studied at the Art Students League (1922–1926) and graduated from City College of New York in 1927 with a degree in philosophy. He worked in his father's clothing manufacturing business (1927–1929), became a substitute art teacher in the New York City school system (1931–1940), and even ran for mayor on the Writers-Artists ticket (1933). During these years he associated with such artists as JACKSON POLLOCK and developed his basic approach to art.

The idea of seventeenth-century philosopher Spinoza that intuition is a rational form of knowledge, and the concepts of independent thinker HENRY DAVID THOREAU, influenced Newman. Proclaiming the artist as the "highest role a man could achieve," he sought to infuse his work with an intellectual and emotional content while rebelling against rules and traditional artistic forms. By the mid-1940s he had developed a style of "mystical" abstraction, which used the "automatic" techniques of free association and imagery associated with Surrealism (post–World War I movement stressing "automatism"—impromptu or unplanned compositions seen as cosmic revelations), as seen in the Genesis-inspired works *Gea* (1945) and *Genetic Moment* (1947). He became well known and influential as a critic and theorist through his writing for several exhibition catalogs of the 1940s. Here he revealed the metaphysical connotations that permeate all of his work: "The basis of an aesthetic art is the pure idea . . . the artist's problem is the idea complex that makes contact with mystery—of life, of men, of nature, of the hard black chaos that is death, or the grayer, softer chaos that is tragedy."

The year 1948 was crucial in Newman's evolving career. With William Baziotes, ROBERT MOTHERWELL, David Hare, and MARK ROTHKO he cofounded the "Subjects of the Artist" School from which emerged the principles of Abstract Expressionism. This powerful, diversified movement, concentrated primarily in American painting, stressed a nonrepresentational art that was immediate, subjective, participatory, and spontaneous, adapting the surrealist idea of psychic improvisation. Newman became the chief spokesperson for the movement, whose innovators were labeled the New York school, through his incisive articles as associate editor of the journal *Tiger's Eye*. Two main branches of Abstract Expressionism developed: Action painting (creation of bold, seemingly random compositions using such techniques as dripping or spattering paint), as exemplified by Pollock, and Color Field painting (creation of a purely visual reality of color unrestricted by drawing, shape, or pictorial image), as seen in Newman's work.

The year also brought his breakthrough painting, *Onement I* (1948), a monochromatic field of pure red interrupted by an orange vertical line, which exploded conventional spatial relationships by obliterating foreground-background and part-whole distinctions. Newman anticipated Minimal art (see DONALD JUDD) with his simplification of form and creation of paintings that are single, undifferentiated images existing in an unstructured picture space. His hallmark became a vast monochromatic field of pure color with one or more narrow, emblematic vertical stripes, or "zips" as he called them, in another intense color and used to define, limit, or modulate color.

In 1950 Newman created his first "shaped" canvas, an 8 foot–by–1½ inch painting called *The Wild,* which prefigured the trend among later artists to create canvases of unusual shapes. He was also a pioneer of the large-format picture, which envelopes the viewer's entire visual field, as seen in his immense painting (8 feet by 18½ inches), *Cathedra* (1951). When his 1950 and 1951 one-man shows generated hostility and confusion, Newman isolated himself, entering a period of artistic stagnation that was exacerbated by a heart attack in 1957.

During the 1960s Newman created his most famous works and achieved widespread recognition. His canvases of huge saturated fields of pure color in simple forms using concentrated means in works like *Purple in the Shadow of Red* (1963) and the series *Who's Afraid of Red, Yellow & Blue?* (1966–1970) helped establish Color Field painting. In the controversial *Stations of the Cross* (1958–1966), a series of fourteen black-and-white paintings with modulating vertical zips, Newman used abstract shape as "a vehicle for an abstract thought-complex, a carrier of awesome feelings" to explore human suffering.

In his sculptures, Newman replicated the emblematic vertical stripes of his paintings in the form of vertical structures, as in *Here II* (1965) and *Here III* (1966). His most famous sculpture, *Broken Obelisk* (1963–1967) installed at the Rothko Chapel in Houston, Texas (1971), is a steel structure composed of an inverted, unfinished obelisk balanced on a pyramid. As in his paintings, Newman used shape and heroic scale (it is 26 feet high) to symbolize meaning: what is tragic yet eternal in the human spirit.

Newman had tremendous influence on artists of the 1960s and 1970s, including FRANK STELLA, through the impact of his monumental scale, his evocation of the vast and the sublime, his search for an absolute quality of color, and his creation of a physical place within a color.

BIBLIOGRAPHY

Hess, Thomas, *Barnett Newman,* 1969; O'Neill, John P. (ed.), *Barnett Newman: Selected Writings and Interviews,* 1990; Rosenberg, Harold, *Barnett Newman: Broken Obelisk and Other Sculptures,* 1971, and "Barnett Newman and Meaning in Abstract Art, *Art International,* March 1972.

Noguchi, Isamu

(November 17, 1904–December 30, 1988)
Designer, Sculptor

Isamu Noguchi is renowned for his outdoor sculptures and environmental projects to be found worldwide, and his stage designs for productions of the MARTHA GRAHAM Dance Company. His diverse artistic output includes the design of furniture, public gardens, and playgrounds, in addition to abstract sculptures that synthesize traditions of East and West.

The son of Japanese poet Yone Noguchi and American writer Leonie Gilmore, Noguchi was born in Los Angeles, California, but spent the first thirteen years of his life in Japan. In later years, the artist said, "My Japanese background gave me a sensibility for the simple. It taught me how to do more with less and how to become aware of nature in all its details." Returning to the United States in 1917, he was briefly apprenticed to Gutzon Borglum, sculptor of Mount Rushmore (1921), who discouraged his artistic pursuit. After premedical studies at Columbia University (1923–1924), he returned to art as a career. A 1927 Guggenheim Fellowship enabled Noguchi to work and study in Paris with abstract sculptor Constantin Brancusi who became a major influence on his developing style.

Back in the United States, he supported himself by executing stylized portrait heads of such people as GEORGE GERSHWIN, and by working for the depression-era Federal Arts Project. His love of theater and dance led to design projects for various productions. In 1935 Noguchi began his celebrated fifty-year collaboration with dancer-choreographer Martha Graham. His abstract "interactive" set, costume, and lighting designs became integral parts, functioning almost as characters, in such

Photo by Jun Miki; Courtesy of the Isamu Noguchi Foundation, Inc.

Graham works as *Appalachian Spring* (1944) and *Cave of the Heart* (1946).

In 1938 he created stainless steel reliefs, titled *News,* for the facade of the Associated Press Building in New York's Rockefeller Center. During World War II he voluntarily spent six months in a Japanese-American internment camp in Arizona. After the war Noguchi studied traditional Japanese art forms and materials, and was married briefly (1953–1955) to Japanese actress Yoshiko Yamaguchi. From the 1950s onward he created many of his best-known sculptures, gardens, and designs.

Noguchi approached the art of sculpture as "creating space," and described his sculptures as "images of moods—moods of flowers, of the vegetative and nonvegetative aspects of nature." Many of his famous sculptures are sleek, monolithic abstractions with polished surfaces, usually in stone, that were designed in conjunction with architecture, such as his 28-foot-high *Red Cube* (1968) outside Marine Midland

Bank Company, which has become a New York City landmark.

Concern for the environment and its effect on humanity led Noguchi to create sculpture gardens where people "interact" with environmental forms. Among the best known are gardens at the Paris Headquarters of UNESCO (1956–1958), the Beinecke Rare Book and Manuscript Library at Yale University (1960–1964), the Billy Rose Sculpture Garden of the Israel Museum in Jerusalem (1960–1965), and the Isamu Noguchi Garden Museum in Long Island City (1985), which contains a retrospective collection of his work. Especially evocative are the two bridge sculptures, titled *Tsukuru* (to build) and *Yuku* (to depart), that Noguchi created at the entrance to Peace Park in Hiroshima, Japan (1952).

Noguchi also became a successful designer of furniture that was both aesthetic and practical, and over 100 variations of round paper lamps, which he described as "illuminated sculptures." Regardless of the artistic form he was creating, he felt that "art must have some kind of humanly touching and memorable quality."

BIBLIOGRAPHY

Gordon, John, *Isamu Noguchi,* 1968; Hunter, Sam, *Isamu Noguchi,* 1978; Noguchi, Isamu, *A Sculptor's World,* 1968, and *Isamu Noguchi: A Space of Akari and Stone,* 1985.

Norris, Benjamin Franklin, Jr.

(March 5, 1870–October 25, 1902)
Novelist

Frank Norris was one of a handful of writers who introduced the techniques of Naturalism to American fiction, rescuing it from the sentimentalism of the nineteenth century and laying the foundation for the modern novel. Norris's best fiction concerns the impact of large social forces on the lives of individuals.

Benjamin Franklin Norris was born to a well-to-do family in Chicago in 1870, but moved with his parents to San Francisco in 1884. At seventeen he developed what he thought was an abiding interest in painting, and his father took him to Paris, where he studied art for two years. In 1890 he enrolled at the University of California at Berkeley, where he discovered the writings of the French Naturalist Emile Zola. When, in 1894, he went to study for a year at Harvard University, he began the early versions of his own Naturalist novel, *McTeague.*

After leaving Harvard, Norris traveled, covering the Boer War for *Harper's Weekly* magazine and the San Francisco *Chronicle.* Upon his return to California in 1896, he joined the editorial staff of the literary magazine the *Wave* in San Francisco. He later covered the Spanish-American War for *McClure's* magazine.

His first novel, *Moran of the Lady Letty,* was published in 1898. This short adventure novel recounts the story of the brave daughter of a Viking sea captain who takes over the *Lady Letty* when he drowns.

McTeague (1899) concerns a dentist whose weakness for alcohol and inability to cope with complex social relationships—particularly marriage—prove his undoing. He loses control of his life; he loses his practice, murders his wife, and flees. The book is naturalistic in the sense that McTeague is a victim of social forces he cannot control, but its sensational plot and lurid details also recall romantic fiction.

Norris soon published *Blix* (1899), a romance about a struggling newspaperman and the wealthy woman he hopes to marry, and *A Man's Woman* (1900), a melodramatic adventure novel.

With *The Octopus* (1901), Norris began what was projected as a major trilogy called *The Epic of the Wheat.* A naturalistic novel, the book was intended to demonstrate the working of economic forces determining the fate of wheat farmers in California. The octopus of the title is the railroad, which encircles and strangles the wheat farms. *The Octopus's* broad sweep contains many subplots, and Norris describes the farmers' planting and field work in great detail and with attention to local color. The farmers fight the railroad over the price of shipping their wheat and owning their own land. The novel's climax, an armed confrontation between the farmers and railroad deputies, is based on the historic Mussel Slough incident.

Norris's brief career ended in 1902, after he underwent surgery for appendicitis; he died of peritonitis on October 25.

The Pit (1903), the second book in the projected trilogy, was published posthumously; the third book, *The Wolf,* was never written. *The Pit* concerns the protagonist Charles Jadwin's efforts to corner the Chicago wheat market. Also published posthumously, *Vandover and the Brute* (1914), is based on an early manuscript Norris had difficulty publishing and which was lost for several years following the San Francisco earthquake. It depicts the effects of a degenerative disease, lycanthropy, on a young man.

BIBLIOGRAPHY

French, Warren, *Frank Norris,* 1962; McElrath, Joseph R., Jr., *Frank Norris Revisited,* 1992; Walker, Franklin, *Frank Norris: A Biography,* 1932.

O'Connor, Mary Flannery

(March 25, 1925–August 3, 1964)
Novelist, Short-Story Writer

Despite the brevity of her career, Flannery O'Connor has become known as one of the finest short-story writers of the twentieth century. Consciously southern, her work uses grotesque characters and bizarre situations to frame conflicts that are profoundly religious.

Born in Savannah, Georgia, in 1925, Mary Flannery O'Connor lived most of her life on her family's farm in Milledgeville. She studied at the Georgia State College for Women (now known as Georgia College) from 1942 to 1945 and earned an M.F.A. from the University of Iowa in 1947.

In 1950 O'Connor contracted disseminated lupus, a degenerative disease that severely limited her mobility. Only on rare occasions was she able to leave the farm in Milledgeville to give readings of her work or to participate in college symposia. She died of the disease at the age of thirty-nine.

Raised Roman Catholic in a part of the South populated with Protestant fundamentalists but touched as well by modern secularism, O'Connor was deeply concerned with the problem of redemption in a society that had moved beyond traditional religious faith. Her stories usually depict common individuals who have been rendered grotesque by desperate spiritual hunger, thrashing violently toward some redeeming moment of grace or understanding.

O'Connor's first novel, *Wise Blood* (1952), was drawn from a story in a collection she had written as her master's thesis at the University of Iowa. Hazel Motes is an itinerant preacher, convinced he is called to found "The Church Without Christ." Yet his search for an alternative faith turns up empty, and he returns, by violent means, to Jesus. Believing, in the end,

Isaiah's biblical admonition that "the eyes of the blind shall be opened," Motes blinds himself and dies by the side of the road.

A Good Man Is Hard to Find (1955), O'Connor's first collection of short stories, includes such well-known stories as "The Artificial Nigger" and "The Displaced Person." The title story concerns a family on vacation, slain by an escaped convict. The story's climax involves an exchange between "The Misfit," whose actions stand as his denial of Christ's promise of salvation, and the grandmother, who is redeemed in the last moments of her life by accepting her killer as "one of my own."

O'Connor's second and final novel, *The Violent Bear It Away* (1960), depicts the efforts of young Francis Marion Tarwater to reconcile his great-uncle's legacy of religious fanaticism with his uncle's disbelief. Tarwater accepts his own calling to become like his great-uncle, a fundamentalist prophet, after being violated sexually by a stranger. Having confronted sin, he understands the need for redemption.

A second volume of short stories, *Everything That Rises Must Converge* (1965), posthumously published, includes "The Enduring Chill," "The Lame Shall Enter First," and "Greenleaf." *The Complete Stories* (1971), containing twelve that had not before been published in book form, earned O'Connor a posthumous National Book Award in 1972.

BIBLIOGRAPHY

Browning, Preston M., *Flannery O'Connor*, 1974; Getz, Lorine M., *Flannery O'Connor: Her Life, Library, and Book Reviews*, 1980; Walters, Dorothy, *Flannery O'Connor*, 1973.

Odets, Clifford

(July 18, 1906–August 14, 1963)
Actor, Playwright

Clifford Odets, the best-known of the American social protest playwrights of the 1930s, lived to see the accolades proclaiming him the most promising playwright of 1930s Broadway turn to condemnation for "selling out" to 1940s Hollywood. Yet his thirty years of writing for the theater, movies, and television produced an enduring body of work.

He was the first child of Russian and Austrian parents who had settled in an immigrant, working-class section of Philadelphia. At age six he moved with his family to the Bronx, where his father managed a printing plant. After rejecting his father's plans for him to join him in business, Odets dropped out of high school to pursue his real love, acting. He began taking odd jobs in Philadelphia and New York theaters, appearing in vaudeville, writing radio plays, understudying Spencer Tracy in *Conflict* (1929), and appearing in the Theatre Guild production of Karel Capek's *R.U.R.* (1929). In 1930 he joined the newly formed Group Theatre in New York, which had been founded by Harold Clurman, Cheryl Crawford, and Lee Strasberg to "create a permanent acting company to maintain regular New York seasons." Sympathetic to the Group's essentially leftist politics, Odets acted in some productions and then, dissatisfied, began to write his own original plays. *Waiting for Lefty* (1935) and *Awake and Sing!* (1935), essentially ensemble pieces (the Group rejected the star system in favor of collective productions), were full of the optimistic, if rather simplistic proletarian ideologies that have come to identify Odets's early work. Harold Clurman has described these aims as "rescuing the suffering working class, supporting the rising trade unions [and even espousing] socialism of one kind or another."

Both plays reached Broadway in 1935. *Waiting for Lefty*, which was relatively short, was coupled with his one-act play *Till the Day I Die*

(1935), one of the first anti-Nazi dramas to appear in New York. *Awake and Sing!* reached an even wider audience because of its compassionate humor. The sudden success and celebrity status brought him offers from Hollywood. At first he scorned the movie industry and refused to desert the values held by the Group; however, when his *Paradise Lost* failed in 1935, he accepted an offer of $2,500 a week from the Paramount studio. His first screenwriting effort, Lewis Milestone's *The General Died at Dawn* (1936), was greeted with a brickbat from critic Frank Nugent, one of the most famous reviews in movie history: "Odets, where is thy sting?" Odets stayed long enough to write a script called "Castles in Spain" (later rewritten and produced as *Blockade* in 1938) and then with his new bride, actress Luise Rainer, returned to New York and the Group.

He came back just in time. His new play, *Golden Boy* (1937), saved the Group from an impending financial crisis and became the greatest commercial success of his career. Less obviously political in intent than his earlier plays, *Golden Boy* told the story of a concert violinist who sacrifices his art to become a successful prizefighter. During this phase of his career Odets began to turn to wider concerns than political agendas. His other plays of the 1930s and early 1940s, *Rocket to the Moon* (1938), *Night Music* (1940), and *Clash by Night* (1941), were essentially dramas of failed relationships, reflecting his own troubled marriage, which ended in divorce. The Group, meanwhile, was wracked by internal dissension and disbanded in 1941.

Back in Hollywood by 1942 (an arthritic condition kept him from active military service), he wrote three screenplays—adaptations of Richard Llewellyn's novel *None But the Lonely Heart* (1944), which he also directed, Fannie Hurst's *Humoresque* (1946), and a thriller based on William Irish's *Deadline at Dawn* (1946). Although well paid, he hated his work. "I took my filthy salary every week and rolled an inner eye around an inner landscape," he said. "Hollywood is a bon-bon town; it's a taffy pull. . . ." At any rate, he gathered enough firsthand experience to write one of his strongest plays, *The Big Knife* (1949), the story of a young man who sells out his integrity as a stage actor to sign a new movie contract. Like *Golden Boy*, its central character realizes too late the dreadful cost of his decision and commits suicide. Nonplussed, Hollywood bought the play and produced a movie version, directed by Robert Aldrich, in 1955. *The Country Girl* (1950), after opening on Broadway, was also released as a film in 1955, starring Grace Kelly and Bing Crosby.

In the spring of 1952 Odets suffered a crisis that crippled his writing career. He testified before the House Un-American Activities Committee (HUAC), then investigating alleged communist influences in the entertainment industry. He had been a member of the Communist party only briefly in 1934, and in the years since then had grown weary of hearing anything approaching a social issue condemned as a communist influence. "I get damn tired of hearing crackpots here and in Washington constantly ascribing anything really human in films to the Communists alone. Why do they keep giving the Devil all the good tunes?" Now he was asked to confirm the names of his former associates in the party.

His testimony so filled him with revulsion that he completed only one more play, *The Flowering Peach* (1954), before his death from cancer in 1963. Yet it has been exaggerated that the hearings spelled the end of his career. Among his later screenplays, for example, his script for Alexander MacKendrick's *The Sweet Smell of Success* (1957) was one of the cinema's bright spots in the 1950s. It remains a scathing indictment of the publicity hounds and other scavengers who nip at the heels of the entertainment business.

At their best, Odets's plays are authentic documents of the dignity of the working class and the importance of the family. They are filled with brilliant dialogue and an emphasis on music and musical effects. Even his flaws reflected the times that shaped him and about which he wrote. In Harold Clurman's words:

> His was a rebellion against our materialism, our subservience to the idol of Success as the supreme good. Odets's denunciation of this blight was not that of a sociological preacher. He knew its corrosive properties because they dwelt within *him*, and he hated them because they were crippling him and, at last, literally killed him.

BIBLIOGRAPHY

Miller, Gabriel, *Clifford Odets*, 1989; Odets, Clifford, *The Time Is Ripe: The Nineteen Forty Journal of Clifford Odets*, 1988; Weales, Gerald, *Odets the Playwright*, 1985.

O'Hara, John Henry

(January 31, 1905–April 11, 1970)
Novelist, Short-Story Writer

John O'Hara's gift for dialogue and tightly constructed plots made him one of America's most popular short-story writers. His novels and stories reflect the changes in American society between 1914 and 1970.

O'Hara was born in 1905 in Pottsville, Pennsylvania, the son of a prominent physician. As a young man, he became acutely conscious of the town's social hierarchy, which tended to exclude Irish Roman Catholics such as himself. He rebelled against his father's highly disciplined approach to life and work and got himself expelled from three preparatory schools for failings both academic and behavioral.

Despite his rowdiness, O'Hara hoped to attend Yale University. This dream failed when his father died suddenly in 1925. Having worked at the Pottsville *Journal* for a year as a cub reporter, O'Hara stayed on for another year before his uneven performance got him fired. He traveled to Chicago in search of a reporting job but finally landed in New York. He worked as a reporter for the New York *Herald Tribune* and for *Time* magazine, then as a rewrite man at the *Daily Mirror*. He also wrote a radio column for the *Morning Telegraph*.

In 1928 O'Hara began to find success selling short stories to *The New Yorker* magazine. In 1933 he gave up his job in order to write full-time; he published his first novel, *Appointment in Samarra*, in 1934. The book won him the first of a string of jobs writing for film studios, which stretched into the 1950s.

Set in Gibbsville, a fictional Pottsville, *Appointment in Samarra* depicts the last three days in the life of Julian English, whose insecurities about his social standing and his sexual adequacy drive him on drunken impulse to suicide. The book typifies O'Hara's utilitarian prose, his realistic approach to storytelling, and his naturalistic conviction that a man's fate can be sealed by such factors as social stratification and human weakness regarding sex.

Butterfield 8 (1935), O'Hara's only roman à clef, is based on the story of Starr Faithfull, a Jazz Age denizen of speakeasies and a sexual adventuress, whose drowning created a tabloid sensation in 1931. O'Hara's heroine, Gloria Wandrous, was sexually molested as a child and, consequently, spends her adult life trying to find love through sex. *Butterfield 8* was an instant best-seller.

In 1940 O'Hara wrote the libretto for the musical comedy, *Pal Joey*, a collaboration with songwriter RICHARD RODGERS and lyricist Lorenz Hart. The lead character was drawn from the protagonist in a collection of O'Hara's short stories: Joey Evans, a street-smart night club master of ceremonies, who obtains the down payment on his own club by sleeping with the wife of a tycoon. The musical was a hit, running for 374 performances; a revival in 1952 ran for 540 performances and won O'Hara a New York Drama Critics' Circle award. It has been revived many times since.

O'Hara's next novel, the sprawling, 600-page *A Rage to Live* (1949), was his first attempt at writing a comprehensive social history. Set in a city based on Harrisburg, Pennsylvania, the novel follows the exploits of Grace Tate, a sexual predator whose infidelity ruins her husband. The book details the trappings of life among the American aristocracy. Despite strongly negative reviews, the book sold 100,000 copies in its first two months.

Ten North Frederick (1955) contrasts the public and private lives of a Gibbsville aristocrat, Joe Chapin. Wealthy and educated, Chapin is handicapped by his own naiveté. He falls victim to a scheming wife and a cunning politician, who takes Chapin's money without helping him achieve his lofty political aspirations. *Ten North Frederick* won O'Hara the National Book Award.

Alfred Eaton, the protagonist in *From the Terrace* (1958), pursues his goals more pragmatically and with greater success than does Joe Chapin. Eaton becomes a wealthy financier, although at the end of the novel he encounters personal and professional tragedies and loses his direction. O'Hara considered *From the Terrace* to be his masterpiece.

O'Hara kept up a prodigious output of fiction throughout the last fifteen years of his life. Among the novels were *Ourselves to Know* (1960), *Elizabeth Appleton* (1963), *The Lockwood Concern* (1965), *The Instrument* (1967), *Lovey Childs* (1970), and *The Ewings* (1972).

O'Hara's collections of short stories include *The Doctor's Son* (1935), *Pipe Night* (1945), *Hellbox* (1947), *Sermons and Soda-Water* (1960), *The Cape Cod Lighter* (1962), *The Hat on the Bed* (1963), and *Good Samaritan* (1974).

O'Hara died in Princeton, New Jersey, on April 11, 1970.

BIBLIOGRAPHY

Bruccoli, Matthew J., *The O'Hara Concern: A Biography of John O'Hara*, 1975; Farr, Finis, *O'Hara: A Biography*, 1972; Long, Robert Emmett, *John O'Hara*, 1983; MacShane, Frank, *The Life of John O'Hara*, 1980.

O'Keeffe, Georgia Totto

(November 15, 1887–March 6, 1986)
Painter

Georgia O'Keeffe, one of the first women to achieve public celebrity in the field of art in the United States, achieved a unique fusion of personal expression, descriptive subject matter, and abstract form.

She was born in 1887 near Sun Prairie, Wisconsin, and grew up with her two brothers and four sisters on a large farm. She was fascinated with drawing at a young age and preferred to paint flowers and growing things to human subjects (a priority she kept all her life). After the family moved to Williamsburg, Virginia, in 1903, she studied art at the Chatham Episcopal Institute. In the next few years she continued her studies at the Art Institute of Chicago and the Art Students League in New York City.

Several great artists directly influenced her formative years in New York—notably William Merritt Chase, from whom she studied still life, and ALFRED STIEGLITZ, whose famous "291" Gallery was her first introduction to the modern art of Auguste Rodin, Paul Cézanne, and Henri Matisse. In addition, her exposure to the works of the Russian Abstractionist Wassily Kandin-sky led to a new appreciation of space on the canvas as a kind of "visual music" and compositions as possessing "melodic" and "symphonic" character. However, her family's deteriorating finances forced her to leave New York in 1908, and for the next ten years she worked as a commercial artist in Chicago and taught at the University of Virginia, the public schools in Amarillo, Texas, and West Texas State Normal College. It was at this time that she gained her first appreciation of the open landscapes of the American Southwest and began painting solely for her own purposes and enjoyment.

When Stieglitz, unbeknownst to her, arranged for her first one-person show in 1917, she returned to New York City. She was the only American-educated woman among the select group of European males represented in the Stieglitz exhibitions. Their relationship intensified, although the fifty-three-year-old Stieglitz was twenty-three years older. He provided her living quarters at his niece's studio, arranged for her to have annual shows, and took numerous photographs of her. (She was the only major woman artist of her generation to both pose nude and to allow the photographs to be exhibited.) They married in 1924 and continued to live in New York for the next five years. Among her important paintings of this period is the *Radiator Building—Night, New York* (1927).

As her motto put it, her ambition always was "to fill space in a beautiful way." She was always intoxicated with color and shape, and in her autobiography she recalled that her earliest sensory impressions were of light on patterned quilts, the shapes made by buggy wheels in the dust, and the wildflowers encountered on her walks to country school. Thus, the trademarks of her mature work included near-abstract shapes (especially ovoid forms) that suggest flowers, bones, clouds, stones, and other nature shapes—executed in richly colored hues and large, clean patterns. This unique vision is seen as early as her 1913 *Tent Door at Night*, consisting of three curving triangular shapes framing an aqua central triangle of sky. This is equally true of her New York cityscapes, like the *East River* series, executed between 1925 and 1929, which also relied heavily on geometric shapes that emphasized either the horizontal or vertical directions. Images like these placed her, along with Charles Sheeler, at the forefront of the Cubist-derived movement known as Precisionism.

Yearning for more time and space to paint, and suffering from an acute melancholia, O'Keeffe decided to return for the summer of 1929 to an area she had discovered a few years before, New Mexico. She stayed in Taos among a company of other artists, including novelists D. H. Lawrence and Willa Cather, at the home of Mabel Dodge Luhan, an heiress and patroness of the arts. O'Keeffe learned to camp and ride horseback, and she painted local landscapes, flowers, and desert bones. For the next several years she divided her time between New York, where her exhibitions of new works continued at Stieglitz's gallery, and New Mexico, where she preferred to live

alone. In 1940 she bought the first of her three New Mexico homes, the Ghost Ranch. When Stieglitz died in 1946, O'Keeffe had little left to tie her to the East, and she moved permanently to New Mexico. She turned increasingly in her paintings to its cliffs, red hills, flowers, bones, tree stumps, and rivers. By now, she had become something of a legend, living in relative isolation and refusing to allow many of her new works to be seen publicly (although she allowed a few to be exhibited in New York and Chicago). Her appearance, which for decades had been documented by Stieglitz's numerous photographs, presented a striking contrast to her luminous canvases: she stood upright like a ramrod, was proud of her long, delicate fingers, wore broad-brimmed black hats and conservative black suits with white collars, kept her face unadorned, and plaited her silver hair at the neck.

O'Keeffe's New Mexico paintings were, in the words of her biographer, Jan Garden Castro, "unprecedented in the history of art." Her *Rancho de Taos Church* series (1929–1930) abstracted the arid landscape and ancient architectural forms of sun-bleached earth and turquoise-blue sky into shapes that stand apart from the presence of humans and that avoid direct descriptive cues. She collected bones and depicted their forms against detached space and abstract backgrounds in the *Cow's Skull* series of the 1930s and the *Pelvic* series of the 1940s. These images were a particularly important contribution to the tradition of the still life.

O'Keeffe personally supervised her one-woman shows in the 1940s, the first in which more than a few of her works reached audiences outside New York. It was not until 1953 that she finally visited Europe. Other trips to Mexico, Peru, and Europe culminated in a journey around the world. Then, in 1970, at New York's Whitney Museum, she was the subject of a retrospective, the largest collection of her work ever assembled. The critics argued whether or not she was a mystic or a sensualist, whether she was preoccupied with the spiritual or the visible world. In 1973, back at the Ghost Ranch she met a young potter, Juan Hamilton. In her later years he became her trusted companion, secretary, and assistant. Until her death at age ninety-eight, she remained active, turning to pottery. Her weakening eyesight, however, decreased her productivity as a painter. Among her last series of works were a number of paintings of the Washington Monument.

BIBLIOGRAPHY

Bellavance-Johnson, Marsha, *Georgia O'Keeffe in New Mexico,* 1988; Castro, Jan Garden, *The Art and Life of Georgia O'Keeffe,* 1985; O'Keeffe, Georgia, *Georgia O'Keeffe,* 1976.

Oldenburg, Claes Thure

(January 28, 1929–)
Painter, Sculptor

Claes Oldenburg was a major figure in the "Happenings" and Pop art movements that began in the 1950s. He is best known for his later "soft sculptures" and large constructions derived from the shapes of everyday, banal objects.

Oldenburg was born in Stockholm, Sweden. Because his father worked in the Swedish diplomatic service, he spent his early life being shuttled between Scandinavia and America. "He must have felt himself between languages and between countries," writes historian Gene Baro of these crucial, formative years. "With devastating child's logic, belonging to no country, he invented one of his own." After graduating from Yale University in 1950, he worked for Chicago's City News Bureau as a reporter. But a growing interest in painting and figure drawing led him to the Chicago Art Institute two years later. He became a U.S. citizen in 1953. His early works were mostly nudes and portraits painted in a rough, expressionistic manner.

In 1956 he moved to New York, where he met other artists with whom he would be thenceforth associated—Jim Dine, Red Grooms, Allan Kaprow, and GEORGE SEGAL. The spirit of the "Happening" was in the air, a fusion of participatory improvisation and environmental structure. Three years later, Oldenburg had his first one-man show. Important influences on him were comic books, children's drawings, primitive art, and graffiti. He created Pop art sculptures (see ROY LICHTENSTEIN) that, in critic Robert Hughes's words, were delightful distortions of everyday objects: "[Oldenburg's vitality came] from his wild metaphors of the world as body—hard things drooping into softness, small things turning mountainous." In the early 1960s he mounted two exhibitions. *The Street* (1960) and *The Store* (1961) were total environments comprised of found objects and artificially contrived constructions: in the former, a mixture of wrapping paper, burlap, newspapers, wrecked cars, and billboards; in the latter, a vulgar array of consumer goods and advertising art that had been fashioned from plaster, muslin, and chicken wire (the whole spattered with bright enamel house paint). For *The Store* he rented an actual retail space at 107 East 2nd Street on New York's Lower East Side, made the items himself, displayed them to the startled passersby, and conducted real sales. In 1962 the site was converted into the Ray Gun Theater, where for ten weeks wordless "plays" were produced. These environmental installations broke down the barriers between art and life.

Later exhibitions in the 1960s included *Floor-Burger (Giant Hamburger), Floor-Cone (Giant Ice Cream Cone),* and *Giant Blue Men's Pants* (all in 1962). These huge sculptures were derived from materials like sewn canvas and foam rubber. He introduced new materials into his work after 1964 with synthetic materials like vinyl, Plexiglas, and Formica. With *Bedroom Ensemble* (1963) and *Electric Outlet with Plug* (1964) he strove to create anonymous, industrially finished surfaces that belied the hand of the artist. The latter work was a skewed reproduction of a West Coast motel suite, complete with zebra-striped furniture and vinyl-covered bed. The vinyl materials enabled him to transform the imagery of functional, hard objects like bathtubs, ironing boards, light switches, electric fans, and typewriters into the "soft sculptures" for which he is best known—objects that relied on touch, gravity, and chance for their final shapes. Thus, these otherwise impersonal industrial products were transformed into delightful, "humanized" shapes.

His lithographs and drawings display similar preoccupations. In the late 1970s he executed a series on the motif of a simple screw. *Soft Screw in Waterfall* (1976), for example, depicts an enormous peg balancing on a cascade of water. "His vision is volumetric," wrote Gene Baro in his study of Oldenburg's prints and drawings; "objects appear in middle distance (or at far distance) with air and light, expressed as energy, playing about the forms."

Other sculpture exhibitions during these years revealed his tendency to enlarge the commonplace into the gigantic. He executed a series of drawings of proposed "monuments" for New York City and Washington, D.C. He envisaged, for example, a half-peeled banana scaled to colossal size and sited in Times Square and a Good Humor bar to sheathe the former Pan Am Building. His *Scissors in Motion* (1967) was intended to replace the Washington Monument. Although these projects were never finalized, another design for a giant lipstick was eventually fabricated and installed at Yale University in 1969. The work, aptly titled *Lipstick (Ascending) on Caterpillar Tracks*, acquires sexual connotations in that the lipstick can be extended and retracted in its sheath. The tractor treads allowed the work to be moved about. With characteristic, puckish humor, Oldenburg declared: "Isn't it terrible to have sculptures littering the landscape that are unremovable?"

Since 1976 he has collaborated with his wife, the writer Coosje van Bruggen. Their whimsically titled works include *Clothespin* (1976), *Hat in Three Stages of Landing* (1982), *Toppling Ladder with Spilling Paint* (1988), and *Dropped Bowl, with Scattered Slices and Peels* (1990). They have cowritten an account of their projects, *A Bottle of Notes and Some Voyages* (1988), which critic Richard B. Woodward called "both a historical map and a personally coded autobiography." Oldenburg in person, despite his reputation for shyness, can be as delightfully startling as his works. He has been known to wear his art on his sleeve, as it were—in his early years he occasionally roamed the streets wearing some of his fantastic costume creations, including a large papier-mâché "elephant mask."

Fantasy and whimsy abound in Oldenburg, but it is a fantasy that is drawn from the visible world, not from dreams. "For years he has creatively distorted the minutiae of contemporary life," wrote Frances De Vuono, "offering us the most madcap, cynical, introspective, and tender of interpretations." The results, according to Oldenburg, obliterate the barriers between high art and mass culture:

> I am for an art that does something other than sit on its ass in a museum. I am for an art that grows up not knowing it is art at all. ... I am for an art that takes its form from the lines of life ... and is sweet and stupid as life itself.

BIBLIOGRAPHY

Johnson, Ken, "Claes Oldenburg and Coosje van Bruggen at Leo Castelli," *Art in America*, March 1991; Oldenburg, Claes, and Gene Baro, *Claes Oldenburg: Drawings and Prints*, 1969; Oldenburg, Claes, and Emmett Williams, *Store Days*, 1967; Rose, Barbara, *Claes Oldenburg*, 1970; Woodward, Richard B., "Pop and Circumstance," *Art News*, February 1990.

Olmsted, Frederick Law

(April 26, 1822–August 28, 1903)
Landscape Architect

Frederick Law Olmsted, the first professional landscape architect in the United States, is famous for his public park designs and for developing the first urban park systems. He also designed landscapes for many private estates and college campuses, and anticipated the National Parks movement with his promotion of conservation and preservation.

Olmsted was born in Hartford, Connecticut. His schooling was erratic, and he lost the opportunity to attend college when sumac poisoning threatened his eyesight. As a result, he explored many potential careers: surveying, clerking for a New York City firm, seafaring on a voyage to China (1843–1844), farming in Connecticut and on Staten Island (1847–1855), and writing and publishing (1850–1861). A tour of England sparked his interest in landscape gardening, and he envisioned "People's Parks" in America, like the publicly owned Birkenhead Park outside Liverpool. The trip resulted in his first successful book, *Walks and Talks of an American Farmer in England* (1852).

Olmsted became involved with writing during the 1850s and acted as a *New York Times* roving correspondent throughout the southern states. His portraits of the antebellum South mixed travel details with commentaries on the social issues surrounding slavery and were eventually collected into four highly successful books: *A Journey in the Seaboard Slave States* (1856), *A Journey Through Texas* (1857), *A Journey in the Back Country* (1860), and *The Cotton Kingdom* (1861).

Olmsted's management skills and his imaginative improvements of appearance and convenience at his Staten Island farm contributed to his appointment as superintendent for the development of Central Park in New York City (1857). In addition to supervising the clearing of the land, Olmsted produced the winning design for the park in collaboration with English architect Calvert Vaux. During the next twenty years Olmsted worked intermittently on Central Park, a landmark of landscape architecture and one of the first large parks designed specifically for public use. His design approach was to evaluate the terrain, weather, soil conditions, and surroundings, and the ways in which the land could enhance the community's well-being.

Faced with a long, narrow, treeless, and swampy terrain with elevations from 4 feet to 137 feet, Olmsted designed a country park with lakes in the main hollows, lawns and meadows in the flatter areas, and clusters of evergreens and foliage for a wooded effect, highlighted by the natural rock outcroppings. Although some formal settings provide for specific gatherings, like concerts, Central Park is a masterpiece of the English picturesque tradition adapted to American needs. A popular eighteenth- and nineteenth-century English landscape garden style for private estates, the picturesque is an informal, pastoral design that stresses the wild, irregular aspects of nature and is distinguished by twisting paths, plant variety, and the use of natural-appearing creations rather than architectural steps, terraces, or walls to mark or link varying gradations. Olmsted made the picturesque style a standard for the American public park. Two innovations in Central Park were placement of the four transverse roads below grade to hide them from view, and creation of separate foot and bridle paths and a carriage road that crossed them only at underpasses and overpasses formed by Vaux's bridges.

During the Civil War Olmsted served as general secretary of the U.S. Sanitary Commission, changing the course of army medical practice through his expert organization and supervision. From 1863 to 1865 he was the development manager for Mariposa Estates in the Sierra Nevada, California, then returned to

New York, where he resumed work on Central Park and formed a partnership with Vaux (1865–1872). Olmsted's design for Brooklyn's Prospect Park (1866–1867) opened up vistas of water and meadow and preserved much of the varied terrain, underscoring his aim for "natural, in preference to artificial, beauty." For Riverside, a model suburban garden community along the Des Plaines River near Chicago (1868), the firm created a river park, a commercial district around the railroad station, and a curvilinear street system with a central town common, all in the picturesque mode.

As early as the mid-1860s, Olmsted's belief in establishing a balance between use and preservation in land management led him to propose the creation of a scenic reservation for California's Yosemite Valley. His fight to save Niagara Falls from uncontrolled development culminated with the creation of the Niagara Falls Reservation, designed with Vaux (1887). Although partially blocked today by a highway on the American side, the scenic winding paths and carriageways opened romantic vistas of the rapids and falls accented by indigenous foliage.

Olmsted envisioned park systems and parkways as part of planning cities and their suburbs, and created the country's first park systems linked by parkways. His most renowned park and parkway system was for Boston, initially begun in 1878 as a plan to eliminate the health hazard of the polluted Back Bay waters and to improve accessibility to the city. The completed system provided sewers, basins, tidal gates, causeways, and bridges artfully strung in a series of pleasure drives, parks, and connected ponds along a shaped and planted Muddy River, which he thought of as an "emerald necklace" around the city. The Charles River area was linked to the inner city via the Fenway, Jamaicaway, and Arborway, which comprised the country's first parkway system.

Commissioned to improve the setting for the enlarged Capitol in Washington, D.C. (1874–1890s), Olmsted subordinated the landscape design to the architecture, providing shade trees that allowed for vistas of the imposing edifice. He designed a "grand pedestal" for the Capitol: a marble terrace and fountain with two staircases and a parapet encircling the Senate and House wings, in the classical mode. His vision of a federal city park system connecting the Capitol grounds with the Mall, the White House grounds, and the river parks was realized by his son, Frederick Law Olmsted, Jr., in the 1920s.

In 1881 Olmsted moved his practice to Brookline, Massachusetts, at the urging of HENRY HOBSON RICHARDSON, with whom he collaborated on several projects, including the Oakes Ames Estate (1880–1881) in North Easton and the Crane Memorial Library (1880–1883) in Quincy, Massachusetts. In 1884 his stepson, John C. Olmsted, became his partner in the firm. Among Olmsted's many landscape designs for private estates, the most prominent is George Washington Vanderbilt's Biltmore near Asheville, North Carolina (1888). Faced with over 2,000 acres of mountain and river valley terrain and a French Renaissance style chateau (by Richard Morris Hunt), Olmsted created formal terraces close to the mansion with a shrub garden sloping to a valley, pond, and waterfall below. He put aside the river bottom lands for farming, and the rest of the estate became a managed forest and arboretum, the first scientific forest management experiment in the country.

Olmsted's last major design was for the World's Columbian Exposition in Chicago (1893; with Henry Sargent Codman). Here, on the swampy land along Lake Michigan, he created a lagoon containing a wooded island filled with gardens and small buildings, as the focal point for the fair's neoclassic white city designed by such architects as McKim, Mead & White (see CHARLES FOLLEN McKIM). The design meshed with his plan for a water park (Jackson Park) to be created there as part of his earlier design for a Chicago park system (1871).

In 1895 Olmsted retired from the firm, but his son and stepson carried on. By 1898 his advancing senility required commitment to

McLean Hospital (whose grounds he had designed) in Waverly, Massachusetts, where he subsequently died. He left a legacy of 20 parks, 7 park systems, 21 college campuses, 175 estates, and other projects in which designed landscape elements were used to enhance the all-important natural scenery. He was the first to sign his drawings with "landscape architect," to charge fees for such work, to bring a social consciousness to landscaping, and to design huge public parks and suburban developments. Olmsted pioneered the profession of landscape architecture where previously there had been merely landscape gardeners who created beautiful but functionless estate and city gardens.

BIBLIOGRAPHY

Fisher, Irving D., *Frederick Law Olmsted and the City Planning Movement in the United States,* 1986; Kalfus, Melvin, *Frederick Law Olmsted: The Passion of a Public Artist,* 1990; Olmsted, Frederick Law, Jr., and Theodore Kimball Hubbard (eds.), *Frederick Law Olmsted, Landscape Architect, 1822–1903,* 2 vols., 1973; Roper, Laura Wood, *FLO: A Biography of Frederick Law Olmsted,* 1973.

O'Neill, Eugene Gladstone

(October 16, 1888–November 27, 1953)
Playwright

If Eugene O'Neill were not America's first great modern playwright, as many have claimed, certainly he was the first to achieve international stature and to claim an important influence on a later generation of writers, like TENNESSEE WILLIAMS, ARTHUR MILLER, and EDWARD ALBEE. Much of his work was autobiographical, drawing on the troubled and complicated relationships of his family, as well as his experiences at sea.

O'Neill was born in 1888 in New York City to a theatrical family. His father, James O'Neill, Sr., had

The Nobel Foundation

worked with James A. Herne and DAVID BELASCO and spent most of the latter part of his career touring in the lead role of one of the most popular melodramas of the nineteenth century, *The Count of Monte Cristo.* For the first seven years of his life, young Eugene accompanied his father on the road, and, as a result, developed an ambivalent attitude (at times extending to outright detestation) toward the commercial theater. Rebellious and dissipated, he left Princeton University in his first year, married Kathleen Jenkins in 1909 (the union was dissolved three years later), contracted malaria while prospecting for gold in Honduras, worked as a seaman on several occasions (including a three-month stint on a Norwegian square-rigger, a hitch on a cattle boat, and service as an able seaman on freighters and luxury liners), and wrote for several newspapers. During a stay in a sanitorium in 1912 for the treatment of tuberculosis, he began writing his first plays (many of which were derivative of the styles of melodrama popularized by his father). At Harvard University in the fall of 1914 he enrolled in the legendary "47 Workshop" play writing course under Professor George Pierce Baker. A year later, with a trunk full of short plays, he went to Provincetown, Massachusetts, where, with the assistance of other young playwrights like George Cram Cook and Susan Glaspell, he had his play, *Bound East for Cardiff,* produced in 1916 at the Wharf Theater. The fall of that year the Provincetown Players relocated to New York and pledged to present a program of new, experimental plays. Among the O'Neill plays produced between 1916 and 1918 were the four short plays later collected as *S. S. Glencairn (Bound East for Cardiff, In the Zone, The Long Voyage Home, The Moon of the Caribees).*

With the Pulitzer Prize–winning play *Beyond the Horizon* (1920) O'Neill, now married to Agnes Boulton, moved from the little theaters of Greenwich Village to the more commercial houses of Broadway. A remarkably fertile period ensued throughout the decade of the 1920s. *Anna Christie* (1921) won him a second Pulitzer Prize and was filmed in Hollywood in 1930 with GRETA GARBO in the title role. He experimented with the techniques of European expressionism in *The Emperor Jones* (1920) and *The Hairy Ape* (1922); with the devices of the Greek theater (masks and choruses) in *The Great God Brown* (1926) and *Lazarus Laughed* (1928); and with the trappings of melodrama (like the aside, or spoken thoughts) in *Strange Interlude* (1928). The last play was produced under the auspices of the Theatre Guild, whose large subscription audience and prestige ensured it a fair measure of commercial success. *Strange Interlude* brought him to the crest of his popularity, earning him over $250,000 and a third Pulitzer Prize. The association with the guild lasted the rest of O'Neill's life.

In 1929 he divorced Boulton, left his two children, and married Carlotta Monterey, who ultimately survived him. Thus began a period of artistic consolidation and maturation, but also of family turbulence. His subsequent plays subsumed frankly experimental techniques and traditional forms into a wholly unique and unified vision. The trilogy *Mourning Becomes Electra* (*Homecoming, The Hunted, The Haunted,* 1931), the nostalgic comedy of *Ah, Wilderness!* (1933), and the epic lengths of *The Iceman Cometh* (1946) and *Long Day's Journey into Night* (1956), for which he won a posthumous Pulitzer Prize—all displayed characters and themes of displaced persons, dysfunctional families, dreams as coping mechanisms for otherwise sordid lives, and an overall sense of alienation from history. O'Neill claimed to detest the "photographic" plays of his contemporaries and referred to his own method as supernaturalism, by which he meant using symbolism in a realistic way. For example, the character of Yank in *The Hairy Ape* is both a specific character and a representation of humanity in general; and the site of Harry Hope's saloon in *The Iceman Cometh* becomes, in Act 2, an evocation of the Last Supper.

Although never wholly free of the commercial lures of the theater, O'Neill nonetheless remained to the end a stubborn individualist. He always tried to cleave to the proclamation he made in 1923: "I intend . . . to write about anything under the sun in any manner that fits the subject. And I shall never be influenced by any consideration but one: Is it the truth as I know it—or, better still, feel it? If so, shoot, and let the splinters fly wherever they may." His perseverance won him a Nobel Prize for Literature in 1936.

After a failed production by the Theatre Guild in 1947 of *A Moon for the Misbegotten*

(1942–1943), O'Neill wrote no new plays. He died in 1953 of Parkinson's disease after many years of seclusion and personal unhappiness. His widow, as the heir in control of the estate, sanctioned world premieres in Stockholm of two more plays, *A Touch of the Poet* (1958) and *More Stately Mansions* (1962). It was the Broadway premiere of *A Long Day's Journey into Night* (1956), however, that sparked the O'Neill revival that continues unabated around the world.

BIBLIOGRAPHY

Bloom, Harold (ed.), *Eugene O'Neill*, 1987; Clark, Barrett H., *Eugene O'Neill: The Man and His Plays*, 1947; Gelb, Arthur, and Barbara Gelb, *O'Neill*, 1960.

Orbison, Roy Kelton

(April 23, 1936–December 6, 1988)
Rock and Roll Singer, Songwriter

Roy Orbison's melancholy ballads, haunting tenor voice, and toned down presence were a marked contrast to the hurricane that was rock and roll. Revered by his peers, the composer of "In Dreams" was a major influence on rock star Bruce Springsteen, who said, "No one sings like Roy Orbison."

Born in Vernon, Texas, Roy Orbison grew up in Wink, a small West Texas town. His father worked in the oil fields and taught him to play guitar. By the time Roy was eight he had played for local radio and by fourteen he was a member of a rockabilly band, the Wink Westerners. Rockabilly (from rock and hillbilly) was an early form of rock and roll that fused blues and country music.

After early recordings with the Wink Westerners were unsuccessful, Orbison approached Sun Records in Memphis, Tennessee. Sun owner Sam Phillips had a keen ear for talent, having launched the career of ELVIS PRESLEY. He also saw talent in the young Orbison, but Phillips encouraged him to sing uptempo rockabilly numbers, which did not do justice to Orbison's true talent as a singer of ballads. Sun recorded Orbison singing "Ooby Dooby." The single made it to number fifty-nine on the U.S. pop charts in 1956.

Orbison was more at home with country ballads than with Presley's more visceral style that derived from rhythm and blues. He moved to Nashville, became a staff songwriter for the Acuff-Rose publishing company, and earned success in 1958 with the Everly Brothers' recording of his song "Claudette."

Orbison's recordings of ballads for Monument were hits: "Only the Lonely," "Blue Angel," "Running Scared," and "In Dreams," a favorite of fans. His haunting love songs were well served by his tenor voice with its remarkable three-octave range, but it was the upbeat "Oh, Pretty Woman" that became the biggest hit.

Orbison's career peaked in the early 1960s. He was especially admired in Great Britain, where he toured extensively, often sharing billing with the Beatles. His popularity began to decline in the late 1960s and early 1970s, but despite this and a series of profound personal tragedies, he continued to perform and record.

By the mid-1980s, interest in Orbison and his music was reborn. Even filmmakers were using his material. Orbison was welcomed by Springsteen into the Rock 'n' Roll Hall of Fame in 1987, and he recorded with BOB DYLAN, George Harrison, Tom Petty, and Jeff Lynne (as the Traveling Wilburys). A 1988 video, *Roy Orbison and Friends: A Black and White Night,* included Bruce Springsteen, as well as many other artists, singing and performing Orbison's music alongside the man himself.

Orbison, always dressed in black, wore sunglasses and seemed motionless and restrained in contrast to the posturing and posing of many rock stars. Before his death in Hendersonville, Tennessee, he had prepared an album, *Mystery Girl.* It was issued posthumously in 1989.

BIBLIOGRAPHY

Clayson, A., *Only the Lonely: The Life and Artistic Legacy of Roy Orbison,* 1989; Whitcomb, I., *Rock Odyssey: A Chronicle of the Sixties,* 1983.

Papp, Joseph

(June 22, 1921–October 31, 1991)
Theatrical Impresario

Joseph Papp, who founded and directed the New York Shakespeare Festival and sponsored free performances of Shakespeare, was one of the most influential producers in the history of the American theater.

Papp was born Josef Yossil Papirofsky, the child of Polish immigrants, in Brooklyn. His first language was Yiddish. After service in the navy in World War II, he studied at the Actors Laboratory in California. He later worked in New York for CBS as a television stage manager; it was then that he changed his name to Papp because he said Papirofsky was too long for screen credits.

In 1954 he began staging free performances of Shakespeare in a Presbyterian church on the Lower East Side. With the backing of the New York City Parks Department, he moved his free Shakespeare to an amphitheater in East River Park in 1956. He produced two plays that year, *Julius Caesar* and *The Taming of the Shrew* starring Colleen Dewhurst who, like all the actors that first year, performed without pay. The next year his Shakespeare productions toured all five boroughs of New York City. Later he settled in Central Park, where the Delacorte Theater was built in 1962 as a permanent home for the New York Shakespeare Festival.

In 1966 Papp took over a landmark building, the Astor Place Library on Lafayette Street in Lower Manhattan, and renamed it the New York Shakespeare Festival Public Theater. He carved six theaters out of the spaces in the old Astor Library and here produced new plays as well as Shakespeare.

One of the new plays was *Hair,* the lively 1967 rock musical that went on to become a hit on Broadway. He developed other new plays at the Public that soon found much wider audiences: *No Place to Be Somebody* (1969), *The Basic Training of Pavlo Hummel* (1971), *Sticks and Bones* (1971), *That Championship Season* (1972), *Short Eyes* (1974), and, the biggest hit of all, *A Chorus Line* (1975), which earned almost $150 million for the New York Shakespeare Festival. Three of these, *No Place to Be Somebody, That Championship Season,* and *A Chorus Line,* won Pulitzer prizes.

Beginning in 1973, for three seasons, Papp also produced plays at Lincoln Center. He even made an ill-fated attempt to do a Broadway series of new plays, while producing at the Public, in Central Park, and at Lincoln Center.

Papp was a great showman, whose personality contributed almost as much as his talent to his enterprises. He was also a great fund raiser, soliciting contributions from individuals, foundations, and corporations to keep his theatrical ventures operating as the budget grew from $20,000 for his first season in East River Park to $16 million in 1987.

He fought labor unions, bureaucracy, critics, and anyone else who might stand in the way of his crusade to bring theater to the people. Until his final illness, he ran the Public Theater single-handedly and single-mindedly. He alone decided what plays would be produced. He battled to keep the principle of free performances alive and reserved some tickets from every performance for last-minute "rush" sales at half price. Long lines formed as people—students, out-of-work actors, retirees, and the unemployed—waited to get first crack at these tickets.

Papp believed that theater was always more than simply theater. "Theater is a social force," he once said, "not just an entertainment." His goal, he said, was to "radicalize the environment." He brought to public view the works of many black, Hispanic, and Asian American playwrights and actors and was a pioneer in color-blind casting in Shakespearean plays.

BIBLIOGRAPHY

King, Christine E., *Joseph Papp and the New York Shakespeare Festival*, 1988; Rothstein, Mervyn, "Joseph Papp, Theater's Champion, Dies," *New York Times*, November 1, 1991.

Parker, Charles Christopher, Jr.

(August 29, 1920–March 12, 1955)
Jazz Musician

Charlie Parker's remarkable, up-tempo, coherent improvisations were based on complex and ingenious constructions of rhythm, pitch, and harmony. His restless sound and amazing stylistic experiments inspired musicians from Cannonball Adderley to JOHN COLTRANE, and the bop style he helped create continues to affect the jazz world.

Born in Kansas City, Kansas, Parker, an only child, moved to that center for black American music, Kansas City, Missouri, when he was ten. When he was eleven, his mother presented him with a saxophone. Parker supplemented what he had learned about music in school by what he picked up from nearby clubs, standing outside to listen to visiting big bands.

In 1933 he took up the alto sax and began to play in groups, developing his skills by listening and by doing. When Lester Young played at the Reno Club in the mid-1930s, Parker was so impressed he decided to leave

school for the life of a professional musician. Soon known as Yardbird, or Bird for short, because of his love of chicken, Parker at fifteen was married and already flirting with drug addiction.

Parker was self-taught, but he was not without discipline. One summer he worked at an Ozark Mountain resort and memorized Lester Young sax solos from Count Basie band recordings. Back in Kansas City, Parker was hired by Buster ("Prof") Smith, an alto saxophonist, in 1937. Smith left his own mark on Parker's sound and phrasing.

In 1938, working as a dishwasher in the Harlem club where ART TATUM played, Parker was struck by what he heard of Tatum's legendary technique—harmonic mastery and lightning speed. In Harlem again in 1939, after a brief time in Kansas City following his father's death, he worked at Clark Monroe's Uptown House and jammed whenever he could. Later he explained in a *Down Beat* interview how he transformed Ray Noble's popular "Cherokee" into "KoKo":

> I'd been getting bored with the stereotyped [chord] changes that were being used ... and I kept thinking there's bound to be something else. I could hear it sometimes, but I couldn't play it. .... I was working over 'Cherokee,' and, as I did, I found that by using the higher intervals of a chord as a melody line and backing them with appropriately related changes, I could play the things I'd been hearing. I came alive.

Still, it took until 1944 for his concepts to jell. Because of the recording strike in the early 1940s, there is little preserved that documents Parker's stylistic development. (The strike by the American Federation of Musicians against recording companies lasted from August 1942 to November 1944, during which time no instrumental recordings were made. Settlement included the payment of royalties to musicians from jukeboxes, films, and radio broadcasts.) Recordings made in 1941 with Jay McShann's group, an important Kansas City band, hint at Lester Young's influence but also show Parker's fresh improvisations, unique tone, and liquid phrasing.

By 1943 Parker was playing tenor sax with Earl Hines's group along with DIZZY GILLESPIE, whose innovations complemented Parker's own. The Parker/Gillespie connection brought forth the new style, bop. In 1945 the Dizzy Gillespie Quintet, with featured artist Parker, recorded in the new style that turned jazz upside down.

Parker recorded as a bandleader first in 1945, *Bird/The Savoy Recordings*, with a group that included the young MILES DAVIS, but critics at first did not like bop's breakneck speed and unpredictable twists and turns. That year Parker and Gillespie appeared in Hollywood for six weeks to bad reviews. Parker stayed on in Los Angeles, performing and recording until his addictions caused him to be hospitalized. Released from Camarillo State Hospital in January 1947, he returned to New York in April and formed a quintet with Miles Davis, trumpet; Duke Jordan, piano; Tommy Potter, bass; and Max Roach, drums. Parker was eventually signed by impresario Norman Granz, and subsequently his recordings became more successful commercially.

Parker was most productive between 1947 and 1951. He recorded, played with various groups, toured Europe, and became better known and better paid. Whether improvising ornate and/or moving solos, such as GEORGE GERSHWIN's "Embraceable You," or composing his own pieces, such as "Klacktoveedsedstene" or "Crazeology," Parker was easily the most influential jazz player during his later years. Ill health dogged him after 1950, drugs and alcohol taking a toll. In July 1951 he lost his New York cabaret license for two years because of drug use. Still, during the last two years of his life—in debt, ill, and suicidal—he produced some fine recordings, including *Summit Meeting at Birdland* and *The Greatest Jazz Concert Ever*. In 1954 he tried to take his life twice. Seven days after his last public appearance at Birdland, the club named for him, he died of a heart seizure in Manhattan at the apartment of Baroness Pannonica de Koenigswarter, a jazz patron.

BIBLIOGRAPHY

Priestley, B., *Charlie Parker*, 1984; Reisner, Robert G. (ed.), *Bird: The Legend of Charlie Parker*, 1975.

Peale, Charles Willson

(April 15, 1741–February 22, 1827)
Inventor, Museum Curator, Naturalist, Painter

Charles Willson Peale, one of the outstanding painters of the early American Republic, painted more than a thousand portraits, mostly of Revolutionary War leaders. He founded the nation's first museum and first art school. He also produced a dynasty of artists. His descendants and those of his brother, James, also a painter, were active throughout the nineteenth century and are described briefly at the end of this profile.

Charles Willson Peale was born in Chestertown, Maryland, the son of a schoolteacher, and grew up in Annapolis. Apprenticed at thirteen to a saddler, he quickly learned how to make saddles, and also to repair clocks and craft objects in silver. Peale found his true vocation, however, in art. He traded a saddle for art lessons from painter John Hesselius and became a portrait painter.

In 1767 several wealthy neighbors raised the money for him to visit England and study with BENJAMIN WEST, the expatriate American painter. His painting style became less stiff and more elegant. He also learned miniature painting, etching, and sculpture. He returned to Maryland and in 1776 moved to Philadelphia, where he joined the Philadelphia militia and took part in the Battles of Trenton and Princeton. At Valley Forge he painted miniature portraits for his soldiers to send home as mementoes. When he could get no canvas in the field, he painted portraits on bed ticking of George Washington, the Marquis de Lafayette, and General Nathanael Greene.

Between 1772 and 1795 Peale made seven portraits from life of George Washington, eventually painting sixty in all. His 1772 portrait is recognized as the first authentic likeness of Washington. After the war, he made copies of his wartime portraits and opened an art gallery in Philadelphia to which he charged admission. He continued to add paintings of national leaders like John Adams (1791–1794), Alexander Hamilton (1791), and James Madison (1792). Peale's likenesses were realistic, accurate in detail, and sensitive to the sitter's personality.

Peale had scientific interests as well. After he led an expedition in New York State that unearthed the skeleton of a mastodon, he decided to open a natural history museum, called the Peale Museum, in Independence Hall, Philadelphia, in 1786. He stuffed and displayed snakes, bats, cranes, and a tiger. Benjamin Franklin sent him the corpse of his Angora cat when it died, and Washington sent from Mount Vernon some pheasants that had come from Lafayette in France. Eventually, more than 100,000 objects—paintings, stuffed animals, birds, insects, reptiles, minerals, fossils, and the mastodon skeleton—were on view at what he called "a school of Nature." He painted *Exhumation of the Mastodon* (1806) and displayed the picture in the museum. His self-portrait, *The Artist in His Museum* (1822), shows him lifting a curtain to reveal his museum, the mastodon's feet visible at the right. He was a pioneer in displaying birds against painted backgrounds of their natural habitats. To help finance the museum, Peale continued to produce portraits for exhibition. With his sons, he later opened similar museums in Baltimore and New York.

In 1794 he helped found the Columbianum in Philadelphia, which in 1795 sponsored the nation's first art school and the first exhibition of the work of American artists. Peale insisted on life classes for the art, and when he could find no male model to pose in the nude, he posed himself. The school failed. He was later one of the founders of the Pennsylvania Academy of the Fine Arts (1805). Like Franklin, he conducted experiments and invented new devices, including a steam bath, a smokeless stove, and a telescopic gun sight.

Married three times, Peale had seventeen children, ten of whom lived to adulthood. When he died at eighty-five, he was courting another woman.

His youngest brother, James Peale (1749–1831), was also a painter, producing miniatures and still lifes. A cabinetmaker, James made the frames for Charles's paintings. He also did two portraits of Washington and painted *The Battle of Princeton* (1783). In 1786 the brothers decided that James would specialize in miniatures, leaving the full-size portraits to Charles.

Raphaelle Peale (1774–1825), the oldest son of Charles Willson Peale, studied painting with his father. He turned to still-life painting and became a master of trompe l'oeil (see also WILLIAM HARNETT), the "trick of the eye" kind of painting that is so realistic that it fools the viewer into thinking it is real, not a picture. In *After the Bath* (1823), a realistic towel hangs on a line and a woman is dressing behind it. The viewer catches a glimpse of a woman's arm and hair above the towel and a foot below it, a teasing image of suggestiveness and artifice.

Rembrandt Peale (1778–1860) became his father's favorite pupil and the best-known artist among Charles Willson Peale's children. Rembrandt studied with Benjamin West in London and traveled abroad. Impressed by the large historical paintings he saw in Paris, he decided to try his hand at this kind of art. In *The Court of Death* (1820), which contained twenty-three figures, Death is on a throne, surrounded by figures representing War, Pestilence, Famine, Conflagration, Delirium Tremens, and Suicide, among other causes of death. His brothers Rubens and Franklin and his father posed for the picture. *The Court of Death* became one of the "traveling murals" popular in the nineteenth century and earned its maker $9,000, a huge sum at the time, when it went on tour.

Rubens Peale (1784–1865) was known as a museum manager. For twelve years after 1810, he managed his father's museum in Philadelphia. From 1825 to 1837, he ran the Peale Museum in New York City, where he exhibited the first Egyptian mummy seen in America.

Rubens retired in 1837, but in 1855 he returned to painting landscapes and still lifes.

Titian Ramsay Peale (1799–1885), youngest of Charles Willson Peale's children, became an able illustrator of natural life. He went with Major Stephen H. Long's expedition to the Rocky Mountains, on which he made 122 sketches, and traveled to Georgia, Florida, South America, and the Pacific, making sketches for illustrated books on birds, butterflies, and animals.

Sarah Miriam ("Sally") Peale (1800–1885), daughter of James Peale, learned to paint as a child in her father's studio in Philadelphia. Charles Willson Peale believed in equality for women and helped Sarah launch her career. In a time when few women worked outside the home, she supported herself for sixty years, competing with male painters. In 1825 she moved to Baltimore and opened a studio in her cousin Rembrandt's museum. She became the leading portraitist in Baltimore and painted likenesses of more than a hundred individuals, including Daniel Webster and the Marquis de Lafayette.

Anna Claypoole Peale (1791–1878), daughter of James Peale and the granddaughter of James Claypoole, an early Pennsylvania artist, was a miniaturist and worked in Philadelphia, Baltimore, Washington, and Boston. Among the subjects for her sprightly miniatures were Andrew Jackson and James Monroe.

Mary Jane Peale (1827–1902) was born in New York City, where her father, Rubens Peale, managed the Peale Museum. She learned portraiture from her uncle Rembrandt Peale and Thomas Sully, studied in Paris, and later at the Pennsylvania Academy of the Fine Arts. Working mostly in New York, she had a successful career as a portrait painter and also did flower studies.

BIBLIOGRAPHY

Flexner, James Thomas, *America's Old Masters*, 1980; Miller, Lillian B., and David C. Ward (eds.), *New Perspectives on Charles Willson Peale*, 1991.

Pei, Ieoh Ming

(April 26, 1917–)
Architect

I M. Pei is noted for his creative designs—often heroic examples of Late Modernism—for urban renewal, government and academic buildings, and museums. Characteristics of his style are elegant primary forms, fine contrasts of materials and geometrics, and structures that are ingeniously suited to the unusual configurations of their sites.

Pei was born in Canton, China, the eldest son of a prominent banker, and spent his childhood in Canton, Hong Kong, and Shanghai. Inspired to become an architect by the building boom in Shanghai, he came to the United States to study (1935). He graduated from the Massachusetts Institute of Technology in 1940, and received a master's degree in architecture from Harvard University in 1946. From 1945 to 1948 he taught at the Harvard Graduate School of Design. In 1942 he married Eileen Loo, the American-educated daughter of a distinguished Chinese family, and had three sons (two of whom work in their father's firm) and one daughter. After World War II, Pei decided to remain in the United States permanently because of the communist takeover of China. He became an American citizen in 1948.

Moving to New York City in 1948, Pei began his career designing multipurpose urban projects as the director of architecture for real estate developer William Zeckendorf and the latter's contracting firm of Webb & Knapp, Inc. During this time he acquired an expert under-

Copyright *Washington Post*; Reprinted by permission of the D.C. Public Library

standing of the financial, technical, and aesthetic aspects of architecture. Early successful projects were the Mile High Center in Denver, Colorado (1952–1956), and Place Ville Marie in Montreal, Canada (1955–1966). The country house he designed (1951–1952) in Katonah, New York, reflects the influence of Hungarian-born architect Marcel Breuer, whose theories had a lasting impact on Pei's style. Breuer's emphasis on light, shade, and texture is realized in Pei's timber-framed house with its glass partitions and skylights inviting the interplay of light and shadow.

Pei opened his own architectural firm, I. M. Pei and Partners, in New York City in 1955, and developed it into one of the country's most successful and renowned architectural firms. Although many of his early works, such as the Society Hill Housing Project in Philadelphia, Pennsylvania (1957–1964), were influenced by the architects WALTER GROPIUS and LUDWIG MIES VAN DER ROHE, Pei developed a more personal style by the late 1960s.

Pei emerged as a singular talent independent of any one dominant architectural theory or style, although he is often identified with the Late Modernists because of the ways that he has reformed the Modernist aesthetic of glass and concrete to evoke the visionary images of past epochs. He has contrived groupings of taut geometric shapes and stressed elegance of detail, as well as the importance of function and setting in the overall design of a building. His skill in manipulating concrete is evident in the award-winning National Center for Atmospheric Research in Boulder, Colorado (1961–1967), with its pueblo-inspired blocks and towers. Boston's John Hancock Tower (1966–1976), done with partner Henry N. Cobb, illustrates the more sleek, fully glazed aspect of his style. A good example of his striking use of geometric forms and light effects is the John F. Kennedy Library in Boston (1964–1979), which is a complex of rectangular, triangular, and cylindrical wings made of whitewashed concrete and glass.

Pei is particularly famous for the many museum buildings he has designed, which include the Everson Museum of Art in Syracuse, New York (1961–1968), the Herbert F. Johnson Museum of Art at Cornell University in Ithaca, New York (1968–1973), and the West Wing of the Museum of Fine Arts in Boston (1977–1986). The East Wing of the National Gallery of Art in Washington, D.C. (1968–1978), considered one of Pei's finest buildings, consists of two basic triangles connected by a huge skylighted atrium. The interior triangular and hexagonal galleries and triangular piers illustrate his skill at creating an active variety of interior spaces. It is a tribute to Pei's ingenuity that the wing fits so well on its trapezoidal site.

One of Pei's most controversial structures is the addition to the Louvre Museum in Paris (Phase 1 completed in 1989). Striving to link the landscape with the sky, water, and light to create a unity with the past, Pei chose the pyramid as "the most structurally stable of forms." For the museum courtyard, he designed a main pyramid and three smaller pyramidons of steel and reflecting glass panels to cover a subterranean visitors' center, shops, and other facilities, all surrounded by reflecting pools and fountains. The architect felt the glass would not obscure the three facades of the museum proper and would provide a focus, a symbol, and a mirror. He said, "On this pyramid, people will see the moving reflex of the clouds and the stars." Although there was much criticism in what, during construction, became known as "the battle of the pyramid," most people have reacted favorably to the building since its completion.

In 1989 the name of the firm was changed to Pei, Cobb, Freed & Partners to acknowledge his longtime associates and the rising generation of architects. His firm has designed some of the largest civic and corporate structures in the United States, including the Jacob K. Javits Convention Center in New York City (1979–1986) and Nestlé Corporate Headquarters in Purchase, New York (1981). Other major projects by Pei include the Fragrant Hill (Xiangshan) Hotel in Beijing, China (1979–1982), which was praised for its unusual blend of traditional Chinese and modern Western aspects, and the 70-story Bank of China office tower in Hong Kong (the tallest building outside the United States), completed in 1990. The prismatic tower, composed of huge steel-and-glass triangles, was a personal triumph for Pei, since his father had founded that branch of the Bank of China.

A giant in the architectural field, Pei himself is a quiet, confident, impeccably dressed, charismatic man known for his love of museums. Recently, he has been working on designs for Phase 2 of the Louvre project and for the Rock-'n-Roll Hall of Fame in Cleveland, Ohio.

BIBLIOGRAPHY

Contemporary Architects, 1987; Filler, M., "Star Quality," *Architectural Record,* January 1990; Goldberger, Paul, "Winning Ways of I. M. Pei," *New York Times Magazine,* May 20, 1979; "I. M. Pei & Partners," *Architecture Plus,* February 1973; Wiseman, Carter, *I. M. Pei: A Profile in American Architecture,* 1990.

Pelli, Cesar

(October 12, 1926–   )
Architect

Cesar Pelli, a renowned designer of public buildings and once an exponent of Minimalist architecture, is famous not only for his innovative use of glass as a cladding, but also for his subsequent interest in traditional materials used in new ways. He exerted much influence as dean of the School of Architecture at Yale University.

Pelli, born in Tucuman, Argentina, graduated from the University of Tucuman in 1949. He served as director of design for an Argentine government organization (1950–1952). He received his master's degree from the University of Illinois in 1954 and decided to stay in the United States, becoming a naturalized citizen in 1964. From 1954 to 1964 he was an associate architect in the firm of EERO SAARINEN, working on such projects as the Stiles and Morse Colleges at Yale. He was influenced by Saarinen's varied approaches to architecture, and by the freedom given him to develop his own style.

In 1964 Pelli went to Los Angeles and worked as design director for the firm of Daniel, Mann, Johnson, and Mendenhall, before becoming a partner at Gruen & Associates (1968). He gained prominence with the creation of the Pacific Design Center in Los Angeles (1971), a huge building enveloped in dark blue glass that echoes the great glass exhibition halls of the nineteenth century. Dubbed the Blue Whale because it dwarfs its surroundings, the center appears to be alive as the glass reflects the changing colors of the sky. The structure's taut surface of glass and the huge scale of its simple geometric shape, devoid of extraneous details like moldings, illustrate aspects of Minimalist architecture, which became prominent in the 1960s.

Pelli uses modern technology and machine-made materials in an architectural approach that balances "the art of the individual building design and civic expression." An example is the U.S. embassy building in Tokyo (1972), which is sheathed in a thin skin of anodized aluminum with exposed structural ends and has operable windows of mirrored glass. His commitment was to "an architecture that celebrates life. . . . An architecture that enhances life accents perception, lightness, and change. . . . Architecture is not in the empty building but in the vital interchange between building and participant."

His fascination with transparency led to his repeated use of glass as an outer skin—not as a structural wall—encasing all or most of a building. The San Bernardino City Hall (1969) is enveloped with expanses of angled bands of dark brown glass that reflect the cityscape. Rejecting the concepts of monumentality and permanence in architecture, Pelli created open-ended building complexes that allowed for expansion and change as natural conditions. His award-winning design for the United Nations Headquarters in Vienna (1969) illustrates this concept. It is a multilayered space with a circulation spine (structural backbone) that replaces lobbies, lounges, and stairwells and extends the length of the seven attached modular towers. The circulation spine allows for additions.

Pelli opened his own architectural office in New Haven, Connecticut, in 1977. A major commission was the renovation and addition to New York's Museum of Modern Art (1977–1984). He effectively used varied-sized glass panels in several shades of gray on the surface of the addition to blend the lines of the original museum with those of the addition and the 56-story residential tower attached to it. His winning 1981 design for New York's Battery Park World Financial Center, located on a waterfront site adjacent to the World Trade Center in lower Manhattan, is dominated by four skyscrapers of unusual shapes and a large public area under a vault of glass.

Pelli has also had considerable influence in the architectural field through his frequent visiting professorships at various universities in the United States and Argentina (1960–1976) and as dean of the School of Architecture at Yale University from 1977 to 1984. And his brick buildings at Rice University and Princeton University reveal a greater interest in context and the decorative use of bricks.

BIBLIOGRAPHY

Frampton, Kenneth, *Cesar Pelli/Gruen Associates*, 1981; Maholy-Nagy, Sibyl, "Cesar Pelli: Public Architect," *Architectural Forum*, March 1970; Pastier, John, *Cesar Pelli*, 1980.

Phyfe, Duncan

(ca. 1768–August 16, 1854)
Cabinetmaker, Furniture Designer

Considered by many as the greatest of all American furniture makers, Duncan Phyfe was a principal proponent/creator of the American Federal and the American Empire styles in furniture design. He also introduced the factory system into American cabinetmaking.

Phyfe (originally spelled Fife) was born in Loch Fannich, Scotland, a village about 30 miles northwest of Inverness. His family emigrated to the United States in the 1780s and settled near Albany, New York. Phyfe was apprenticed to a cabinetmaker, and by 1792 his name appeared in the New York City register as owner of a joiner's shop (cabinetmaking and woodworking shop) on Broad Street. In 1793 he married a Dutch woman who subsequently bore him four sons and three daughters. He changed the spelling of his last name to the more fashionable Phyfe in 1794.

His business prospered, and he bought a larger shop on Partition Street (now Fulton Street) in 1795. He then purchased houses on either side (1802, 1811) and used the three buildings as workshops, warehouse, and showrooms. In 1816 he acquired a house across the street, which became his permanent residence. At the height of his career, he employed over 100 workers and transformed the apprenticeship system of production, which had no division of labor, into a system in which each individual performed a specific duty, thus introducing the factory method into American cabinetmaking. He was the leading furniture producer in New York City for almost five decades; his fame and popularity rested on his excellent design and craftsmanship. Early patronage from millionaire John Jacob Astor established his reputation.

Phyfe's early pieces were highly individualized adaptations of English neoclassical furniture (a return to the styles associated with ancient Greek and Rome), as designed by George Hepplewhite, Robert Adam, and Thomas Sheraton, and were based on their designs in the English pattern books of the day. He introduced the elegant proportions that came to dominate American Federal style furniture (a classically oriented style originating in Britain and stressing rectilinear outline, and the use of veneers and inlays in ornamentation: 1780s–1810). He combined elements of this with aspects of the French Directoire style (furniture style of the French postrevolutionary period that emphasized classically inspired decoration and restrained ornamentation) to create a style all his own, often referred to as the Duncan Phyfe style, which inspired many imitators. A master of line, proportion, and detail, Phyfe was especially adept at the artistic use of veneers and had a remarkable ability to work with mahogany to bring out its color and texture. He preferred to use the reddish mahogany from Cuba and Santa Domingo (in later years he also used rosewood and black walnut), and would pay as much as $1,000 per log. His reputation for quality led West Indian exporters to label the best mahogany wood "Duncan Phyfe logs."

During the Federal/Directoire period, Phyfe became famous for his tripod-based pedestal tables, his use of reeding (carved ornamental ridges abutting each other) on posts and legs, his wood or brass paw/claw feet, outward sweeping curves in chair and table legs, and his "cloverleaf" tabletops. Characteristics of his design were slender lines and delicate carving of classical motifs, such as leaves, plumes, and drapery swags. Particularly popular and distinctive were his scroll-back chairs, as well as his chairs with a lyre- or harp-shaped splat (central wood piece of chairback).

A leader in introducing and popularizing new design, Phyfe was a principal creator of the American Empire style. Derived from the French Empire style of the reign of Napoleon I and known as the Regency style in England after the regency of George IV, it is characterized by massive furniture with sculptured supports, restrained ornamentation, and Greek, Roman, and Egyptian motifs (1810–1830s). Hallmarks of Phyfe's American Empire style include figured veneers, the lotus-leaf motif, "pillar and claw" dining tables, continued use of the lyre splat and paw feet, and his adaptation of the ancient Greek *klismos* (chair with slightly splayed saber legs and central splat supporting the back). A mahogany window bench featuring dog's paw feet and lyre splat,

accompanied by thirteen matching chairs, made for Governor William Livingston of New Jersey (1810–1815) exemplify his best Empire work.

After 1830, however, Phyfe acquiesced to popular demand for the more massive, bold type of Late Empire furniture, and his creativity declined. From then until his retirement in 1847 he produced this heavy, rather nondescript furniture, which he later derogatorily described as "butcher furniture." By the time of his retirement he had amassed a fortune, thanks to his astute business sense and his ability to foresee the public's needs and desires. His furniture was quite expensive for its day; for example, a decorative table could cost $265.

In his personal life, Phyfe was an independent thinker and a strict Calvinist who focused all of his attention on his work and family. He was described by family members as "always working and always smoking a short pipe." He spread the neoclassical tradition in America and had an impact on the design and production of American furniture prior to the Victorian age.

BIBLIOGRAPHY

Cornelius, Charles O., *Furniture Masterpieces of Duncan Phyfe*, 1922; McClelland, Nancy, *Duncan Phyfe and the English Regency, 1795–1830*, 1939.

Pickford, Mary

(April 8, 1893–May 29, 1979)
Film Actress, Producer

Mary Pickford was the first real movie star and the most popular and successful female star of the silent era. Known as America's Sweetheart, she specialized in films with a Pollyannaish view of life, playing characters of beguiling innocence and untar-

nished virtue. She was also a shrewd businesswoman and cofounder of United Artists Pictures.

Pickford was born Gladys Mary Smith in Toronto. Her British father was killed in an accident when she was five; her Irish mother, Charlotte, ran a candy store but could scarcely support the family. With next to no formal education, Gladys started acting to earn money. She made her debut at age five with her sister Lottie in a melodrama, *The Silver King*, at the Toronto Opera House. From that point her mother managed her career until her own death in 1928.

Pickford appeared on stage with stock companies in favorites like *Uncle Tom's Cabin*, was billed as Baby Gladys Smith in the touring company of *The Fatal Wedding* in 1901, and played the title role in *The Child Wife* in 1904. In 1906 Broadway impresario DAVID BELASCO hired her for *The Warrens of Virginia* and changed her name. On tour with the play in Chicago, Mary saw her first movies.

Back in New York, she was hired at $5 a day by the American Mutoscope and Biograph Company, where she worked with D. W. GRIFFITH and made over a hundred one- and two-reelers between 1909 and 1913, beginning with *Her First Biscuits* (1909).

Fellow actors included her brother Jack, Owen Moore (her first husband), and Lillian and Dorothy Gish. She was recognized by the public as "Little Mary, the Girl with the Golden Curls." In 1911 she also worked for CARL LAEMMLE's Independent Motion Picture Company, earned $175 a week, and made over thirty films, many directed by Thomas Ince.

By 1913 she was earning $500 a week, making longer films for ADOLPH ZUKOR's Famous Players, one of which, *Tess of the Storm Country* (1914), a huge hit directed by Edwin S. Porter, made her a star and Zukor's most valuable asset. Other successes followed, notably *The Poor Little Rich Girl*, directed by Maurice Tourneur, *The Little American*, directed by

Library of Congress

CECIL B. DEMILLE, and *Rebecca of Sunnybrook Farm*, all released in 1917. In 1918 she made four films for Paramount, including *Stella Maris*, in which she played two parts, and her last—*Captain Kidd, Jr.*—the following year.

By then a huge box-office draw, she released three films in 1919 through her own company, including *Daddy Long Legs*, and in that same year, joined CHARLIE CHAPLIN, Douglas Fairbanks, and D. W. Griffith, to form United Artists, a film-distributing company that handled their movies and guaranteed them the greatest profits. From then to her retirement she earned over $1 million a year. *Pollyanna* (1920) was her first film to be released through United Artists.

In 1920 she and Fairbanks were married and hailed as the all-American couple. Pickford began to complain of being in "a dramatic rut eternally playing this curly-headed girl," and displayed other talents in *The Love Light* (1921), a drama set in World War I, in which she is an Italian lighthouse keeper who falls in love with a German spy; and *Little Lord Fauntleroy* (1921), in which she played a little boy and his widowed mother.

She even helped bring German director ERNST LUBITSCH to Hollywood, in the hope that he would transform her, as one historian put it, "from Pollyanna into Pola Negri." The result was *Rosita* (1923), a sentimental Spanish romance that launched Lubitsch's Hollywood career and did well at the box office, but to Pickford was "the worst picture, bar none, that I ever made."

Partly in reaction, she returned to the "curly-headed girl" in *Little Annie Rooney* in 1925, proving that even at age thirty-two she could still play a twelve-year-old. Box-office receipts proved her correct. In *Sparrows* (1926), however, a downbeat theme proved less appealing to her public. In 1929 she released *Coquette,* her first—and United Artists' first—all-talking film. She won the Academy Award for Best Actress in the part of a spoiled southern flirt. Her last film was *Secrets* (1933), a costume drama directed by Frank Borzage, written by her friend and frequent screenwriter Frances Marion, and costarring Leslie Howard. Many felt the film demonstrated that her acting style was outdated.

Pickford and Fairbanks enjoyed enormous popularity both in America and in Europe. At "Pickfair," their Beverly Hills mansion, they entertained some of the world's greatest celebrities. They were among the first to be "immortalized" by leaving their hand and footprints in cement at Grauman's Chinese Theater. They never had children, although, from his first marriage, Fairbanks had a son who also became an actor. They appeared together in only one movie, *The Taming of the Shrew,* in 1929. Shortly into the sound era both the marriage and Pickford's career ended. She retired after *Secrets,* and she and Fairbanks divorced in 1935.

She was remarried in 1937 to bandleader Buddy Rogers, with whom she had costarred in *My Best Girl* (1927). They adopted two children, Ronald and Roxanne. While Pickford never returned to acting, she produced, or coproduced with her husband, a number of films through the 1930s and 1940s. In 1976 she received an Honorary Oscar "in recognition of her unique contributions to the film industry and the development of film as an artistic medium." It was her last public appearance. She and Rogers resided at "Pickfair" until her death.

BIBLIOGRAPHY

Bergan, Ronald, *The United Artists Story,* 1986; Carey, Gary, *Doug and Mary,* 1977; Eyman, Scott, *Mary Pickford: America's Sweetheart,* 1990; Herndon, Booton, *Mary Pickford and Douglas Fairbanks,* 1977; Pickford, Mary, *Sunshine and Shadow,* 1955; Windeler, Robert, *Sweetheart,* 1973.

Plath, Sylvia

(October 27, 1932–February 11, 1963)
Novelist, Playwright, Poet

With its frank anger over social expectations of women, as well as its surprising metaphors and often grotesque humor, the verse of Sylvia Plath stretched notions of the subject matter appropriate to poetry. Her novel, *The Bell Jar,* is remembered for its candid depiction of its protagonist's extreme psychological distress.

Plath was born in Boston, Massachusetts. Her father, a zoologist and an expert on bees, taught at Boston University. Her mother was a teacher who struggled to support the two children alone when her husband died after only nine years of marriage.

Driven to achieve, Plath excelled in school and set her sights on a successful career. Her high self-expectations exacted a toll. She suffered a severe breakdown after her junior year at Smith College in 1953. Treated with electroconvulsive shocks, she made national headlines when she disappeared after one treatment. Her brother found her under the crawl space of the breezeway of their house, half dead from an overdose of sleeping pills. It was five months before she had recovered enough to return to Smith.

During her college years, Plath published her poetry in a number of commercial and literary magazines. She graduated from Smith with highest honors in 1955 and won a Fulbright Fellowship for study at Cambridge University in England.

In June 1956 Plath secretly married the young British poet Ted Hughes. Later, they moved together to Boston, where Plath taught a year at Smith and then held part-time secretarial jobs while both wrote furiously.

Plath assembled her first published collection, *The Colossus and Other Poems* (1960), in London after a stay at the writer's colony at Yaddo in Saratoga Springs in 1959. It was published in the United States in 1962. The title poem addresses her late father, the "colossus" she could never fully understand.

In late 1959 Plath and Hughes returned to England, where Plath gave birth to a daughter in 1960. Plath concentrated on poetry and began her novel, *The Bell Jar* (1963), which was published under the pseudonym Victoria Lucas. The book's adolescent heroine is suicidal: Esther Greenwood has understood that her life does nothing more than play out larger forces in conflict in her environment. She sees her electric shock treatments as punishment for rebellion against this state of affairs.

Plath had a son in 1962 and, in the same year, wrote a radio play, *Three Women: A Monologue for Three Voices*, about the experiences of three women giving birth in a hospital. It was broadcast on the BBC Third Programme.

Plath's poems in this period reflect a persona that feels itself at one moment rigid and false, at another amorphous and changing. In the poem "Elm," there is even a suggestion that the self may contain other selves capable of acting independently:

I am inhabited by a cry.
Nightly it flaps out
Looking, with its hooks, for something to love.
I am terrified by this dark thing
That sleeps in me;
All day I feel its soft, feathery turnings, its malignity.

After Plath and Hughes separated in 1962, Plath wrote the so-called October poems, which vent the anger of a woman confined too long by social conventions and the expectations of her parents and husband. Among these are "Lady Lazarus," "Daddy," "Poppies in July," "Ariel," and "The Rabbit-Catcher," all published posthumously in *Ariel* (1965).

Plath knew she was writing well, but her depression returned and became unshakable. She committed suicide by sleeping pills and gas inhalation on February 11, 1963.

Several volumes of Plath's poems were published after her death, some edited by Hughes, who served as her literary executor. Among these are *Wreath for a Bridal* (1970), *Fiesta Melons* (1971), *Crossing the Water* (1971), *Winter Trees* (1972), and *Pursuit* (1973). Her *Collected Poems* (1981) won the Pulitzer Prize in 1982.

BIBLIOGRAPHY

Alexander, Paul (ed.), *Ariel Ascending*, 1985, and *Rough Magic: A Biography of Sylvia Plath*, 1991; Rose, Jacqueline, *The Haunting of Sylvia Plath*, 1991; Wagner-Martin, Linda, *Sylvia Plath: A Biography*, 1987.

Poe, Edgar Allan

(January 19, 1809–October 7, 1849)
Fiction Writer, Poet

Edgar Allan Poe wrote poetry and stories intended to excite the reader's soul through the contemplation of beauty and terror. Striving to make each detail in a poem or tale contribute to a unity of effect and to use symbols to create a "profound undercurrent," Poe influenced a generation of writers in France and America in the mid-nineteenth century.

Poe was born in Boston to itinerant actors, but his father soon abandoned him, his mother, and two siblings. After his mother's death of tuberculosis in Richmond, Virginia, when Poe was only two, the boy was sent to the home of John Allan, a prosperous tobacco merchant, who raised him in London as well as in Richmond.

In February 1826, Allan sent Poe to the University of Virginia but withdrew him before Christmas when the youth tried to augment his slim allowance by gambling. Allan and Poe seldom saw eye to eye, and though Poe enrolled at West Point in 1830 in an attempt to mollify Allan, he was expelled in 1831 when it became clear the attempt was futile. They never reconciled, and, since Allan had never legally adopted Poe, the latter had no prospect of an inheritance.

Poe published his first three volumes of poetry amid this family turmoil: *Tamerlane and Other Poems* (1827); *Al Aaraaf, Tamerlane, and Minor Poems* (1829); and *Poems* (1831). The latter contains the great brief lyric "To Helen," written for Jane Stith Stannard, as well as "Israfel," which embodies Poe's argument that poetry must be as impassioned and lyrical as music.

Always strapped for funds, in 1835 Poe began an assistant editorship at the *Southern Literary Messenger* in Richmond. It was the first of several such jobs. In 1836 Poe married his cousin Virginia Clemm, who was only thirteen. They lived with her mother, Poe's aunt, who anchored the family through bouts with poverty and Virginia's illnesses.

For the *Messenger,* Poe wrote the stories "Berenice" and "Morella," both psychic dramas, and began the serial collected subsequently as *The Narrative of Arthur Gordon Pym* (1838). A third psychic drama, "Ligeia," was published in *American Museum* in 1838; Poe was proud of the story's intricate symbolism.

Poe's most anthologized story, "The Fall of the House of Usher," was published in 1839 in *Burton's Gentleman's Magazine,* of which Poe was then an editor. Roderick Usher's twin sister Madeline has been placed in the vault at the family's decaying mansion, but he is convinced she is not dead. Dressed in her shroud, she appears alive to him and a visiting friend; she embraces her brother, and they die simultaneously.

The twenty-five stories produced by 1840 were published in *Tales of the Grotesque and Arabesque* that year. The volume sold badly, but Poe pressed on with his stories.

"The Murders in the Rue Morgue," which first appeared in the successor to *Burton's, Graham's Magazine,* in 1841, set the form for the modern detective story. Though Poe himself disparaged the genre ("Where is the ingenuity of unraveling a web which you yourself [the author] have woven for the express purpose of unraveling?"), his story was the first to use analysis to discover how a crime was committed. Among Poe's other "tales of ratiocination" are "The Mystery of Marie Roget" (first published in 1842), the first such detective story to attempt to solve a real crime; the highly popular "The Gold Bug" (1843), one of the earliest tales to introduce a hunt for buried treasure and to include a coded message; and "The Purloined Letter" (1844), Poe's own favorite, which, like "The Murders in the Rue Morgue," presents the detective C. Auguste

Dupin as a seer relying on trancelike meditation and keen observation to fathom the thoughts of the culprit.

Virginia Poe suffered her first bout with tuberculosis in January 1842. Her health was constantly in jeopardy afterwards, and Poe suffered greatly with each relapse. His preoccupation with death led Poe to write "The Masque of the Red Death" (1842). It was followed by the horror stories published in 1843, "The Pit and the Pendulum" and "The Tell-Tale Heart." Poe's stories were collected in two more volumes, *The Prose Romances of Edgar A. Poe* (1843) and *Tales by Edgar A. Poe* (1845).

In 1844 Poe and his wife moved to New York City, and he returned to writing poetry. Among the verses published over the next five years are "The Raven," "Ulalume," "For Annie," and "Annabel Lee." In "The Raven," Poe's best-known poem, the poet, sadly remembering a lost love, is haunted by death in the guise of a raven. The poem made Poe famous. *The Raven and Other Poems* was published in 1845.

Poe's poetry made a deep impression on the poet Charles Baudelaire, who translated his works into French. Through Baudelaire, Poe influenced the development of the poetic movement known as Symbolism, which favored "the derangement of all the senses" and the symbolic expression of emotion.

Virginia died in 1847. Poe himself was quite ill and wrote little, though he did complete "Ulalume" that year. Over the next two years, Poe began a series of brief love affairs. A second version of "To Helen" was written for Sarah Helen Whitman, to whom Poe became engaged; in "For Annie," Poe ascribes his recovery from illness to his love for Annie Richmond. Poe also was briefly engaged to his childhood sweetheart, Sarah Elmira Royster Shelton, now widowed.

Poe's later years were marked by querulous behavior, arguments with literary and social figures, and terrible drinking sprees. His wildness has been ascribed to a brain lesion diagnosed in his youth, which was thought to produce manic and depressive periods, as well as to drug addiction, though no medical evidence exists to support that notion.

Poe caroused at least four times while traveling during the summer of 1849. After a six-day disappearance in Baltimore, he was found semiconscious and in great distress and brought to the Washington College hospital, where he died on October 7.

BIBLIOGRAPHY

Quinn, Arthur Hobson, *Edgar Allan Poe,* 1941; Symons, Julian, *The Life and Works of Edgar Allan Poe,* 1963; Wagenknecht, Edward, *Edgar Allan Poe: The Man Behind the Legend,* 1963.

Pollock, Paul Jackson

(January 28, 1912–August 11, 1956)
Painter

Jackson Pollock was the foremost member of the first generation of Abstract Expressionists, sometimes dubbed "action painters," which appeared after World War II. He is regarded by many as the most revolutionary of all American modernists.

He was born in 1912 in Cody, Wyoming, the fifth and youngest son of Stella May McClure and LeRoy Pollock, a stonemason. In the next twelve years the family moved several times— San Diego, Phoenix, and Orland, California— before Pollock began studies in 1926 at the Art

Students League in New York under THOMAS HART BENTON. His brother Charles had studied with Benton, and later so did his other brothers, Frank and Sande. Pollock continued studying with Benton for the next decade, his apprenticeship interrupted by sporadic traveling and several tries at the Manual Arts High School in Los Angeles (from which he was expelled several times). He also became interested in the mural work of the Mexican painters José Orozco, David Siqueiros, and Diego Rivera.

The tutelage under Benton was to prove very influential. Despite Benton's rather unstable personality, his frequent illness, and his growing problem with alcohol, Pollock respected him and, according to Benton biographer Henry Adams, found in him a second father figure. (For his part, Benton included a portrait of Pollock as the harmonica player in his *Arts of the West* mural from the Whitney series.) From Benton, Pollock learned to accent rhythm and linearity—the restless counterplay of forms—and to work toward centrifugal construction and a sense of deep space. Particularly, Benton's sense of overall design departed from the traditions of Western painting, which emphasized a few central forms and simple pyramidal groupings. Rather, he taught a kind of "all over" strategy, a composition with no single center of focus or impact—"a form of pictorial organization that would reshape the destiny of American painting," says Adams.

Pollock was declared 4-F, psychologically unfit for the draft, in 1941, and he worked for the Works Progress Administration's War Services Program briefly as a draftsman of machine designs. He drifted in and out of odd jobs, including painting ties and janitorial work. His career took a decisive change for the better when he met his future wife, Lee Krasner, an art student. Her advanced artistic background, contacts in the art world, and awareness of the more formal innovations of Cubist art—in which natural forms are reduced to geometrical ones—greatly influenced him. She introduced him to the critic Clement Greenberg, who would become an important proselytizer of his work, and a circle of young artists who would

later be grouped under the title of Abstract Expressionists (see BARNETT NEWMAN). The group included ROBERT MOTHERWELL, William Baziotes, and Matta Echaurren. They all exhibited in the new Art of This Century gallery, which was opened by Peggy Guggenheim (an important collector of modern art) in 1943.

Guggenheim's enthusiasm for his work— "Now I consider [Pollock] to be one of the strongest and most interesting American painters"—led her to commission him to paint his first really large-scale work. This work, entitled simply *Mural* (1943), measured 8 feet by nearly 20 feet in length. It was a breakthrough for Pollock, liberating him from the influences of Picasso and Miró. Viewing this, Robert Motherwell concluded, prophetically, that Pollock's artistic destiny was to "confront the process of painting itself." At the same time, Pollock grew increasingly preoccupied with the mural's capacity to inhabit the space of the viewer. "I believe the easel picture to be a dying form," he said in 1947, "and the tendency of modern feeling is towards the wall picture or mural." Soon, he began gaining public notice. Critics like Clement Greenberg began writing about him, he held his first solo exhibition at Art of This Century in New York in 1943, and the Museum of Modern Art purchased *The She-Wolf,* his first major museum sale.

After moving to Springs, Long Island, with his wife, he began making his first "all over" poured paintings. From 1946 to 1951 he produced his greatest works, including the *Arabesque (Number 13A, 1948), Lavender Mist (Number 1, 1950),* and *Autumn Rhythm (Number 30, 1950).* He abandoned easel painting altogether and laid his canvases on the studio floor. Placing himself within the space of the painting (his handprints are visible in some of the works), he then poured—or flicked and dribbled with his brush or a stick—the gobs and splatters of enamel, aluminum, and oil paint across the surface. He frequently added sand, broken glass, and other foreign materials to the heavily impastoed paint. It was tempting to believe that Pollock fully surrendered himself to a kind of unconscious process, encouraging "accidents"—hence the derisive appellation "Jack the Dripper." And it is true that Pollock was rejecting the inflections of traditional hand-and-wrist brushwork in favor of the "lucid delirium" (as Italo Tomassoni felicitously put it) of the more unconscious pouring procedures. Yet there is ample evidence that he carefully organized his work, and that he cultivated the sense of struggle between control and freedom. As art historian Elizabeth Frank writes, "The rhythmic repetitions of tossed paint meander, flow, bite, sear, and bleed, never turning into pattern or decoration, always renewing themselves with consummate freshness. Emotion, as in great poetry, undergoes great change in the process of taking its own course."

Were these great works "utter abstractions"? Tantalizingly, some of the poured paintings, like *White Cockatoo (Number 24A, 1948)* and *Out of the Web (Number 7, 1949)* and, among the later works, *Ocean Greyness* (1953) reveal figural shapes, as if a latent meaning were there all the time, threatening to peek out and reveal itself at any moment.

Pollock was rapidly becoming a famous—and notorious—painter. Two issues of *Life* magazine, in 1948 and 1949, featured the article "Jackson Pollock: Is He the Greatest Living Painter in the United States?" The writer derided his pouring technique as drooling. *Time*, in its November 20, 1950, issue, branded him a fraud. Filmmaker Hans Namuth shot a film of him at work in 1950 that was shown at the Museum of Modern Art. Pollock's tough, brooding appearance—the cigarette dangling from his lips, his scowling face, the severe black T-shirts and rugged denim slacks—made him a public celebrity akin to James Dean and MARLON BRANDO. He was regarded as an "art cowboy," rugged and inarticulate. To those who bothered to listen to him, however, he was eloquent about his work:

> When I am *in* my painting, I'm not aware of what I'm doing. It is only after a sort of "get acquainted" period that I see what I have been about. I have no fears about making changes, destroying the image, etc., because the painting has a life of its own. I try to let it come through. It is only when I lose contact with the painting that the result is a mess. Otherwise there is pure harmony, an easy give and take, and the painting comes out well.

"Pollock broke the ice," WILLEM DE KOONING said succinctly. Jackson Pollock took American painting out of a provincial impasse and into successful rivalry with European modernism. Nonetheless, a sense of defeat and depression dogged Pollock's final days. By 1956 he was producing nothing at all and was almost constantly inebriated. On a night in the summer of 1956 in East Hampton, New York, his car went out of control and crashed into a clump of trees. He was killed instantly.

BIBLIOGRAPHY

Frank, Elizabeth, *Pollock,* 1983; Landau, Ellen G., *Jackson Pollock,* 1989.

Porter, Cole Albert

(June 9, 1891–October 15, 1964)
Songwriter

Cole Porter the fastidious craftsman and Cole Porter the wealthy sophisticate meet in such classic songs as "I've Got You Under My Skin" and "I Get a Kick Out of You." His mocking lyrics marry jaunty melodies to evoke the high life, and the union still lifts spirits from Broadway to Hollywood.

Porter was born on a 750-acre farm in Peru, Indiana, to Samuel Fenwick Porter and Kate Cole Porter. It was Kate Porter's father, J. O. Cole, wealthy from his West Virginia lumber business, who sent Porter to private school—Worcester Academy, Massachusetts (1905–1909)—and to Yale University

(1909–1913). If young Porter became a lawyer, he was to receive a sizable inheritance from J. O. Cole.

Music intervened. Kate Porter, a pianist herself, started her son off at Indiana's Marion Conservatory: violin at six, piano at eight. The proud mother had Porter's song, "The Bobolink Waltz" (1902), published in Chicago when the youngster was only eleven. At Worcester Academy, Porter produced words and music for amateur theatricals. Later he composed for Yale's Dramatic Club and was deeply involved with the University Glee Club. He wrote two popular football songs, "Bingo Eli Yale" and "Bulldog," before heading to law school.

By 1915, on the recommendation of the law school dean at Harvard University, and with the reluctant consent of his grandfather, Porter was studying composition at Harvard's music department. That year two of his songs made it into Broadway productions: "Esmerelda" in *Hands Up* and "Two Big Eyes" in *Miss Information*. In 1916 *See America First*, written with T. Lawrason Riggs while both were still at Harvard, opened in New York, but failed, as had the two 1915 shows.

Discouraged, Porter left for Paris in the fall of 1917. He served in a World War I relief mission and then joined the French Foreign Legion. After his discharge in 1919, he sailed home to announce his intent to marry the beautiful, wealthy socialite Linda Lee Thomas and to plead with his grandfather for increased support. J. O. denied the request. As it turned out, a chance shipboard encounter with producer Raymond Hitchcock saved the day. After meeting Porter, Hitchcock commissioned him to write music and lyrics for *Hitchy-Koo of 1919*, a revue. Porter's song, "An Old-Fashioned Garden," was one of the show's hits.

With healthy royalty checks stabilizing his finances, Porter married Linda Thomas in 1919. The Porters led a high-flying social life in Europe, entertaining in Paris, Venice, and on the Riviera. Porter performed his songs at parties, and he continued his musical studies with French composer Vincent d'Indy at the Schola Cantorum in Paris. When J. O. Cole died in 1923, he left Porter over $1 million.

Porter's shows of the early 1920s, *Greenwich Village Follies of 1924* and *Paris* (1928), did not catch on, nor did his ballet, *Within the Quota*, in 1923. An early foray into symphonic jazz, it was performed by the Swedish Ballet in Paris, where it succeeded, and in New York, where it did not.

Porter finally hit with a 1929 London production, *Wake Up and Dream*, which included "What Is This Thing Called Love?" That year *Fifty Million Frenchmen* opened in New York. It included "You Do Something to Me" and "You've Got That Thing." Commenting in the *Judge*, critic GEORGE JEAN NATHAN wrote, "When it comes to lyrics this Cole Porter is so far ahead of the other boys in New York that there is just no race at all."

One of the best-trained popular songwriters of the twentieth century, Porter designed his music for the theater. Critic Alec Wilder says Porter's lyrics were "astonishingly softened and warmed by his music." That music, often overshadowed by the words, was elegant and complex, using a wealth of chromatic lines in harmony and melody. Ethan Mordden speaks of "grasping syncopation and obsessive repeated notes" and the "rhythm itself: unexpected jazzy explosions in the middle of a ballad, such propulsive energy that songs seem to be racing themselves to the finish."

Many of Porter's best-known songs originated in 1930s' Broadway productions: from "Love for Sale" (*The New Yorkers*, 1930) and "Night and Day" (*Gay Divorce*, 1932) to "You're the Top" (*Anything Goes*, 1934), as well as "Begin the Beguine" and "Just One of Those Things" (*Jubilee*, 1935), and Mary Martin's "My Heart Belongs to Daddy" (*Leave It to Me*, 1938).

In 1937, while riding horseback on Long Island, Porter was thrown by his horse and crushed by the animal. Both of Porter's legs were broken. He had thirty-one operations over the next twenty years to save his legs and was in pain for the rest of his life.

In 1948 Porter scored with what many consider his masterpiece, *Kiss Me Kate.* This song-filled, rollicking musical, based on Shakespeare's *Taming of the Shrew,* included favorites from "So in Love" to "Brush Up Your Shakespeare."

Porter produced music for Broadway shows from *Anything Goes* in 1934 to *Silk Stockings* in 1955 and was involved in films for three decades, from *Born to Dance* in 1936 to *Les Girls* in 1957. After Linda Porter (who hated life in Hollywood) died in 1954, Porter lived reclusively. His right leg was amputated in 1958, and he stopped writing songs as his health declined. Porter died in Santa Monica, California, in 1964 following kidney surgery.

BIBLIOGRAPHY

Ewen, D., *The Cole Porter Story,* 1965; Kimball, R., and G. Gill, *Cole: A Biographical Essay,* 1971; Wilder, A., *American Popular Song: The Great Innovators, 1900–1950,* 1972.

Porter, Katherine Anne

(May 15, 1890–September 18, 1980)
Novelist, Short-Story Writer

Katherine Anne Porter wrote brilliant short fiction that examined minutely the hearts of people and their ties to time and place. Though her published works are not voluminous, her virtuosity established her early as a "writer's writer." She is widely known for her only novel, *Ship of Fools.*

The great-great-great granddaughter of Daniel Boone's younger brother Jonathan, she was christened Callie Russell Porter but later changed her name. Born in poverty in a log cabin in Indian Creek, Texas, she was educated at the Thomas Boarding School in San Antonio, Texas. She first married at age sixteen. At twenty-one, she worked for a newspaper in Chicago and later played bit parts in movies to support herself while she wrote.

Though she attracted attention among writers for the stories she began to publish in small literary magazines, her standards were exacting. She said she had burned "trunksful" of manuscripts. In 1921 she went to Mexico and studied Aztec and Mayan art. She wanted to travel to Europe but was prevented by medical and financial obstacles until 1931, after her first collection of short stories, *Flowering Judas* (1930), had won acclaim and she had received a Guggenheim Fellowship. She sailed for Germany from Vera Cruz, Mexico.

Porter and her companion, Eugene Pressly, lived in Paris for four years. They married in 1933. While in the city, she renewed her friendship with ALLEN TATE and met GERTRUDE STEIN. She later recounted a brief confrontation with ERNEST HEMINGWAY in a humorous essay, "A Little Incident in the Rue de l'Odéon."

The Paris years were highly productive for Porter. Though she struggled with a biography of Cotton Mather, which she would never finish, she wrote a good deal of short fiction. She completed the final version of *Hacienda: A Story of Mexico,* which tied together her knowledge of Mexican subcultures, from native Indians to artists and revolutionaries.

Most of the stories she completed in Paris were rooted in Texas. *The Old Order: Stories of the South* (1955), a long sequence of stories, re-creates her family's history. She later wrote that her travels had given her back "the native land of the heart" because she could research and write about her heritage more safely from a distance. Upon her return from Paris, she visited her family for the first time in eighteen years.

In the late 1930s, she wrote three short novels at an inn in Pennsylvania, but she had them so clearly in mind when she left Paris that she was able to transcribe them almost without interruption. "Pale Horse, Pale Rider" centers on a brief love affair between a Southern newspaper woman and a soldier who dies in the influenza epidemic of 1919. "Old Mortality" studies the effect on Porter's fictional self of knowing the falsity of her romanticized past. "Noon Wine," a powerful and tragic story, is set among the dirt farmers she knew in Texas and uses the real names of members of her family.

Pale Horse, Pale Rider (1939), the title she gave the three collected short novels, earned her great critical acclaim but no wider following. To support herself, she devoted her time to a succession of teaching jobs at Stanford University, the University of Michigan, and Washington and Lee University. Lecture tours eventually took her to 200 colleges and universities in the United States and Europe.

In 1938 Porter divorced Pressly and married Albert Russel Erskine, Jr., an English professor. They were divorced in 1942.

Porter published *The Leaning Tower and Other Stories* in 1944. The title story was based on her own life—three months spent in Berlin when visa troubles delayed her arrival in Paris in 1931. A collection of nonfiction pieces, *The Days Before,* came out in 1952.

Porter worked sporadically on her only novel, *Ship of Fools,* based on her voyage to Europe aboard the German ship *Vera* in 1931. Though it was not published until 1962, the book became an immediate commercial success and was made into a movie in 1965.

Her *Collected Stories* (1965) won both a Pulitzer Prize and a National Book Award.

Porter's work was admired for its meticulous form and psychological insight. In her introduction to *Flowering Judas,* she wrote that her generation had lived "under the heavy threat of world catastrophe." Her own efforts had been "to grasp the meaning of those threats, to trace them to their sources and to understand the logic of this majestic and terrible failure of the life of man in the Western world."

BIBLIOGRAPHY

Givner, Joan, *Katherine Anne Porter: A Life,* rev., 1991; Hardy, John Edward, *Katherine Anne Porter,* 1973.

Pound, Ezra Weston Loomis

(October 30, 1885–November 1, 1972)
Critic, Poet

Regarded by some as the "poet's poet," Ezra Pound wrote verse whose vivid imagery and spare language strongly influenced poetic technique during the first half of the twentieth century in Britain and the United States. An iconoclast in literature, art, and music, he produced a body of poetry and criticism that remain controversial.

Pound was born in the mining town of Hailey, Idaho, and was raised a Presbyterian in Wyncote, Pennsylvania, a suburb of Philadelphia. He studied for two years at the University of Pennsylvania, where he made a lifelong friend of the poet WILLIAM CARLOS WILLIAMS, who was studying medicine. Pound earned a bachelor's degree from Hamilton College in 1905 and returned to Penn to take a master's in 1906. He taught briefly at Wabash College in Crawfordsville, Indiana, but his unorthodox lifestyle led to his early dismissal.

Bored and convinced that he would find no literary role models in the United States,

Pound traveled to Europe, printing his first book of poems, *A Lume Spento* (With Tapers Quenched) in Venice in 1908. Settling in London, he published two more volumes, *Personae* and *Exultations*, in 1909. These began to earn him critical attention.

Pound befriended Ford Madox Ford and William Butler Yeats. Ford helped Pound refine and simplify his verse. (Pound later said the sight of Ford rolling on the floor laughing over the poetic affectations in *Exultations* saved him two years' work on technique.)

In 1912 Pound had an interview with F. S. Flint for *Poetry* magazine, which described the principles of Imagism. Among its tenets were "direct presentation" rather than description of an image; "to use absolutely no word that does not contribute to the presentation"; and to compose language following the rhythms of the "musical phrase" rather than the "metronome." Pound edited the first anthology of Imagist poetry, *Des Imagistes*, in 1914.

While in London, he contributed to the weekly *New Age*, served as literary adviser of the magazine *The Egoist*, and worked as a correspondent for the Chicago-based *Little Review*. Pound was among the first to praise the poetry of ROBERT FROST and D. H. Lawrence. He persuaded Harriet Shaw Weaver to serialize James Joyce's *Portrait of the Artist as a Young Man* in the pages of *The Egoist*. He found publishers and financial support for the young American poet T. S. ELIOT a few months after they met in London.

He next branched into art criticism, championing the sculptor Henri Gaudier-Brzeska. Pound admired the work of the so-called Vorticists, who embraced industrial society and favored its hard edges and precise shapes in their painting and sculpture. He contributed to *Blast*, the magazine of the Vorticists published by the painter and novelist Percy Wyndham Lewis.

Pound became intrigued by Chinese poetry, particularly the way images were used in succession without the transitional verse found in English forms. Similarly, he developed an interest in Japanese Noh plays, many of which take shape around a single image. He translated both. He collected his Chinese translations into a volume called *Cathay*, published in 1915. Eliot later called Pound "the inventor of Chinese poetry for our time."

Around 1915 Pound began work on a modern epic poem. He would publish sections of his *Cantos* over the next fifty years. The poem had no narrative line or continuing characters. It comprised a succession of images, bits of personal history, even Confucian philosophy, woven together unevenly. Pound incorporated various languages and even inserted Chinese characters in the midst of verse in English. The *Cantos* alienated some critics with their obscurity; others see the whole as a monumental work that defined Pound as a poet and helped redefine modern poetry.

Pound left London for Paris in 1920. *Hugh Selwyn Mauberley*, a farewell to London and to British literary culture, was published the same year. It has become one of the most celebrated and controversial poems of the twentieth century. Despite its frank indictment of the commercialization of modern culture, *Mauberley* seems to lack a deeper tragic sensibility. Its detached persona leaves some critics wondering how deeply Pound felt about the poem. These critics tend to see Pound as a skilled craftsman of verse rather than as a writer of great poetry. Pound's defenders see his unique voice—his originality—in both *Mauberley*'s form and its spirit; they argue that its ironic tone hardly condemns it as serious poetry.

In Paris for four years, Pound assisted Eliot in editing his long poem *The Waste Land*. He helped ERNEST HEMINGWAY refine his prose style and wrote an opera based on the poetry of François Villon. He completed several books of criticism.

In 1924 Pound moved to Rapallo in northern Italy. He pursued an interest in economics that had begun around 1918 when he met Major C. H. Douglas, who originated the doctrine known as Social Credit. Pound came to believe that the public misunderstood money and banking. Douglas held that the ineffective distribution of money caused economic depressions and that the manipulation of money by international bankers was the most frequent cause of war.

Obsessed by these ideas, Pound wove them into his cantos. *A Draft of XXX Cantos* (1933) and *The Fifth Decad of Cantos* (1937) inveigh against modern economic practice, which he saw as exploitative and usurious. These theories also became the subject of two prose works, *ABC of Economics* (1933) and *Jefferson and/or Mussolini* (1935).

During World War II, when he chose to remain in Italy though it was at war with the United States, Pound made over 300 broadcasts over Rome Radio in which he tried to convince Americans that economic injustice was the true cause of the war. He condemned the banking industry—and the Jews who, he said, controlled it—and proclaimed his support of the Italian Fascists. In 1945 he was captured by Italian partisans and turned over to the U.S. Army. He was held in a prison camp at Pisa for six months. Despite rapid decline in his physical and mental health, he managed to compose eleven new cantos and translate from the Chinese two short books by Confucius.

When Pound was flown to the United States in November 1945, he was found unfit to stand trial for treason. Declared legally insane, he was held for twelve years at St. Elizabeths Hospital in Washington, D.C. He continued his work on Confucius, wrote more cantos, and carried on extensive correspondence. The translations of Confucius were published in 1947 as *The Unwobbling Pivot and the Great Digest.* In 1948 the new poems appeared in print as *The Pisan Cantos,* a continuation of his modern epic; the volume was awarded the prestigious Bollingen Prize the same year.

Eventually, the efforts of friends such as Frost and ARCHIBALD MACLEISH obtained his release. He returned to Italy, where he wrote and said little, apparently remorseful over his expressed anti-Semitism and dubious of the value of his written work. He died in Venice in 1972.

BIBLIOGRAPHY

Carpenter, Humphrey, *A Serious Character: The Life of Ezra Pound,* 1988; Flory, Wendy Stallard, *The American Ezra Pound,* 1989; Tytell, John, *Ezra Pound: The Solitary Volcano,* 1987; Wilhelm, James J., *The American Roots of Ezra Pound,* 1985.

Powers, Hiram

(July 29, 1805–June 27, 1873)
Sculptor

Hiram Powers, a central figure of the expatriate artistic colony in mid–nineteenth-century Italy, was the first American-born sculptor to achieve international fame. He was noted for naturalistic portrait busts of prominent men and the "spirituality" of his more idealized female figures in the neoclassical style.

Powers was born near Woodstock, Vermont, and moved with his family to Cincinnati, Ohio, in 1819. Apprenticed to a clock and organ builder at age eighteen, he held various other jobs until becoming a supervisor in 1826 at the Western Museum, owned by Joseph Dorfeuille, in Cincinnati. Here he acquired facility in modeling and mechanical art through creating and automating wax figures depicting scenes from Dante's *Inferno.* Although Powers had no formal art training, he began doing portrait busts while at the museum. His ingenuity and ability to "seize the likeness" attracted the attention of wealthy businessman Nicholas Longworth, who became his patron.

With Longworth's financial backing, Powers moved to Washington, D.C., in 1834, where he received commissions to do portrait busts of many prominent government figures, including Chief Justice John Marshall, Daniel Webster, John Quincy Adams, and Andrew Jackson. The Jackson bust, modeled from life while Jackson was president (1835), established his career as one of the foremost portrait sculptors of his time. Exhorted by the president to "make me as I am," Powers created a stunning likeness of the weathered face and penetrating eyes that revealed the vigor of the subject's personality with sensitivity. Such naturalistic portrait busts, with their simplicity, individuality, and lively realism, relegated idealism to secondary importance. He was so popular that he completed 150 portrait busts in this naturalistic mode between 1842 and 1855.

In 1837 Powers took his family to Italy, the acknowledged wellspring of all great sculpture during his time, where he established a studio in Florence with the help of American sculptor Horatio Greenough. He spent the rest of his life there, and his home became an artistic hub for such notables as HENRY WADSWORTH LONGFELLOW, Charles Dickens, and NATHANIEL HAWTHORNE. In 1842 he completed his first full-length nude, *Eve Tempted*, which was an idealized figure reflecting the dominant neoclassical style. The neoclassical movement was a return to classicism and idealism in deliberate imitation of the sculpture of antiquity, which represented moral qualities through art. Americans identified with the ancient Greek democratic ideals and viewed classical statues as prototypes of perfection and democratic symbols. Powers became one of the most important sculptors of the ideal genre, creating several busts, such as *Proserpine* (or *Persephone*, 1843), of which more than 100 replicas were made.

Powers often blended the neoclassical and the naturalistic, as in the life-size *Fisher Boy* (1841). The face and proportions of the figure represent the boy who modeled for it, while the composition is classical, with the boy holding a shell to his ear and leaning on a fishnet-draped tiller. Another such work was his *Greek Slave* (1841–1843), partially based on the classical Medici Venus in Florence, which became the single most celebrated statue of its day. He was inspired by the Greek struggle for independence from the Turks in creating this allegorical female nude who represented the ideal of Christian virtue. Her Naturalistic limbs and proportions are posed in a classical profile of slightly turned head with reserved expression.

The statue toured Europe and the United States, becoming the first successful introduction of the nude figure to the American public. Much of this success came from the interpretive literature accompanying the sculpture, which explained that while the slave was powerless to control her nudity in the face of the heathen Turks, her Christian virtue "clothed" her. Americans flocked to view the statue, often encouraged by clergy, although there were frequently separate viewing hours for men and women for the sake of propriety. *Greek Slave* epitomized nineteenth-century romanticism and melodrama, and six full-size and three two-thirds–size versions were executed.

Powers became the most famous sculptor America had yet produced and established himself as the "oracle" of sculpture in Florence. A genial, diligent man with a zest for life, he was noted for his technical skill, his precision and simplicity of design, and his concern with spiritual values and didactic themes. He would conceive and model an idea in clay, then employ artisans to carve his designs in marble. He promoted the use of marble, especially the fine white Carrara marble, as the only material able to embody the eternity of an idea.

Although Powers produced many figures and busts for homes and gardens of the wealthy, he also had several commissions for public pieces, since sculpture was closely identified with American ideals and historic people and events during this time. He produced statues of Ben Franklin (1844–1860) and THOMAS JEFFERSON (1860–1863) for the U.S. Senate and

---

House, respectively. His most important full-size public portrait was the bronze statue of Daniel Webster (1858) for Boston's State House. The figure is unusual for the use of period clothes rather than the classic drapery then fashionable in portrait sculpture.

Powers's last completed full-length sculpture was *The Last of the Tribes* (1867–1872), depicting an idealized female figure, half nude, looking back as she appears to run away. His works, especially *Greek Slave*, encouraged Americans to focus more seriously on sculpture than at any previous time: American sculptors were moving toward the center of their own stage.

BIBLIOGRAPHY

Crane, Sylvia, *White Silences: Greenough, Powers, and Crawford, American Sculptors in 19th-Century Italy*, 1972; Reynolds, Donald M., *Hiram Powers and His Ideal Sculpture*, 1977; Wunder, Richard, *Hiram Powers: Vermont Sculptor*, 1974.

Presley, Elvis Aaron

(January 8, 1935–August 16, 1977)
Rock and Roll Singer

A founder of rock and roll, Elvis Presley was stage center when teen enthusiasm for the new sound erupted. A phenomenally successful recording artist, Presley and his flamboyant style sent shock waves across America. His singing, rags-to-riches story, and premature death enshrined him in the hearts of fans.

Elvis Aaron Presley (he later spelled his middle name Aron) was the only child of Vernon, a truck driver, and Gladys, a sewing machine operator. Elvis, born into a hard scrabble existence in East Tupelo, Mississippi, survived; a twin brother, Jesse Garon, died at birth. The local Pentecostal First Assembly of God church and its white gospel music made a lasting impression on him. At eleven Presley began to play guitar. After the

NBC/Copyright *Washington Post*;
Reprinted by permission of the D.C. Public Library

family moved to Memphis, Tennessee, in 1948, he haunted Beale Street to hear black blues musicians like Big Bill Broonzy, Arthur ("Big Boy") Crudup, and B. B. King.

Graduating from L. C. Humes High School in 1953, Presley found work at M. B. Parker Machines and later was hired by Crown Electric Company as a driver. His 1953 vanity record, a 10-inch acetate disc, "My Happiness" and "That's When Your Heartache Begins" was made at the Memphis studio of Sam Phillips, the owner of Sun Records, who had recorded HOWLIN' WOLF.

Phillips noticed Presley and soon recruited a duo to back him: Scotty Moore, a guitarist who became Presley's manager, and Bill Black, a bass guitarist. In July 1954 the trio recorded "That's All Right." The blues song, written by Big Boy Crudup, was presented in rockabilly style and became a local hit. Rockabilly, created by Sun Records, infused country music with elements of rhythm and blues and gospel music. The recording led to Presley's first professional appearance in August 1954. The Memphis audience was riveted by the singer's earthy, passionate performance.

Presley built on his success with a series of one-nighters, including one at the Grand Ole Opry in Nashville. Radio station KWKH in Shreveport, Louisiana, broadcast him on the program *Louisiana Hayride* and in March 1955 he was televised by Shreveport's program of the same name. Successful recordings for Sun included "Good Rockin' Tonight"/"I Don't Care If the Sun Don't Shine." Memphis disc jockey Bob Neal replaced Moore as manager on January 1, 1955. Through Neal's efforts Elvis became nationally known with "Baby, Let's Play House" and "Mystery Train."

"Colonel" Tom Parker signed on as manager in the fall of 1955, and Presley began to throw off his country music image. Parker negotiated with RCA to take over the Sun Record contract, and in 1956 Presley's first RCA recording, "Heartbreak Hotel," reached the top of country, rhythm and blues, and pop charts. Subsequent recordings—"Blue Suede Shoes," "Don't Be Cruel" / "Hound Dog," "Love Me Tender," and "Any Way You Want Me"—soared in popularity.

Records, along with television and concert appearances, transformed Presley into the superstar teenage fans idolized and fixed on as a symbol. Riding success, in 1956 Presley made the first of some thirty films, *Love Me Tender*. In 1957 three more records were topping the charts: "Teddy Bear," "All Shook Up," and "Jailhouse Rock." The rags-to-riches Presley bought the now legendary Graceland, his mansion in Memphis.

During Presley's U.S. Army hitch (1958–1960), recordings made before his induction were issued. After service in Germany, he was discharged and returned home to produce more hit records—from "Are You Lonesome Tonight?" in 1960 to "Good Luck Charm"

in 1962—and to make films that received unenthusiastic reviews yet were nonetheless adored by fans. Presley's movie soundtracks were released and sold well. In 1967 Presley married Priscilla Beaulieu. Their daughter was born in 1968.

When the Beatles arrived on the musical scene in the 1960s, Presley's "king" status was threatened. Colonel Parker responded by stepping up Presley's public appearances and by negotiating a contract for *Elvis*, a television film produced in 1968.

Renewed interest in early rock and roll and in the vocalist's highly charged style was spurred through television performances and hits on the album *From Elvis in Memphis* and consolidated in the 1970s with annual cross-country tours that included Las Vegas performances. After 1975 Presley appeared less often and, when he did, his style seemed toned down.

Following a divorce in 1973, Presley's health began to fail. He died four years later in Memphis of heart failure, weakened by his ailments and the drugs he used to combat them. Posthumous fascination with his life and work turned Presley into a near-mythical figure.

Presley almost always sang other people's songs, reworking the originals with striking combinations of country, blues, gospel, and pop singing. As he crooned and sobbed and shouted, his quicksilver moods were energized by a passion that transformed his material and transported his audiences, shocking and attracting with telling directness and crude pelvic gyrations.

Sam Phillips of Sun Records once said that he could make a million dollars if he could find a white singer who performed with the black sound. He found his man in Presley, who imbued the black blues sound with the aura of country music through a vocal style that projected the rawness and directness of the blues. Presley owed a debt, too, to the gospel music of his childhood and to the easy ways of pop singers like Dean Martin and Mario Lanza.

John Rockwell wrote in the *New York Times* of Presley and the advent of a new kind of music, "one that swept aside the gentilities of the adult-oriented pop of previous decades and reflected the swelling youth market of the postwar baby boom. . . . He was as much a metaphor as a maker of music, and one of telling power and poignancy."

BIBLIOGRAPHY

Cotten, L., *All Shook Up: Elvis, Day-By-Day, 1954–1977*, 1985; Goldman, A., *Elvis*, 1981; Gregory, N., and J. Gregory, *When Elvis Died*, 1980; Stern, J., and M. Stern, *Elvis World*, 1987.

Quintero, José Benjamin

(October 15, 1924–   )
Director

José Quintero was a major force in the rise of the Off-Broadway movement in New York City in the 1950s. He is most famous for his work with the Circle in the Square Theater.

Quintero was born in Panama City, the son of Carlos Rivera and Consuelo Quintero. During his high school years he displayed a predilection for the priesthood, but after avidly watching a number of BETTE DAVIS pictures, he changed his mind and sought a career in show business. In 1944 he came to the United States to attend Los Angeles City College. Up until this time, he admitted in an interview in 1954, he had had no experience whatever with the stage: "I never saw a play until I reached Los Angeles. I went to see *Life with Father*. I didn't understand a word of English except God. I was intensely religious at the time and the slangy use of the word depressed me." After graduating from the University of Southern California in 1948 he got his theater training at the Goodman Theatre School in Chicago. A year later he directed his first play, TENNESSEE WILLIAMS's *Glass Menagerie*, at the Woodstock Summer Theatre in Woodstock, New York.

Quintero's importance to the rise of the Off-Broadway theater movement in New York City, an alternative to the commercially oriented Broadway theaters (where experimentation and new playwrights were usually ignored), can scarcely be overestimated. In 1950 his theater group, the Loft Players, began its legend-ary tenure with the Circle in the Square in Greenwich Village. This became Off-Broadway's most important theater, its name deriving from the fact that its productions were usually presented in the arena style—in the round. His 1952 revival of Williams's *Summer and Smoke* (which had been a flop during its 1948 premiere) firmly established his reputation, as well as that of its leading lady, Geraldine Page, whom he had met years before at the Goodman. Writing in *The American Theater Today*, commentator Richard Barr noted that this production brought to Off-Broadway an unusual recognition from the top theater critics. "The reputation the group gained by the one production led to the recognition of off-Broadway by the first-string critics . . . and theaters began to blossom all over the Greenwich Village area and the downtown Second Avenue District."

A close association with the works of Williams, EUGENE O'NEILL, and other prominent American writers and dramatists led to many landmark Quintero productions in the 1950s. There was a revival of TRUMAN CAPOTE's *Grass Harp* in 1953. The first Eugene O'Neill revival was *The Iceman Cometh* (1956), starring Jason Robards. Its extraordinary success led to more Quintero-O'Neill productions, including the first American production of *Long Day's Journey into Night* (1956), starring Frederic March; *A Moon for the Misbegotten* (1973), with Colleen Dewhurst as Josie; and *Desire under the Elms* (1963), with Dewhurst and George C. Scott.

Quintero has directed several motion pictures, including *The Roman Spring of Mrs. Stone* (1961), with Vivien Leigh and Warren Beatty. After a severe bout with cancer, Quintero has spent the last twenty years holding a number of college residencies, including

a stint at the University of Houston. He has continued directing revivals of O'Neill.

BIBLIOGRAPHY

Downer, Alan S., *The American Theater Today*, 1967; Quintero, José, *If You Don't Dance, They Beat You*, 1972.

Ransom, John Crowe

(April 30, 1888–July 3, 1974)
Critic, Poet

Though John Crowe Ransom produced only about 160 poems, their fine ironies and subtle ambiguities, as well as their affective strength, are thought by many to have captured the finest qualities of modern verse. His criticism, identified with southern agrarianism and the so-called New Criticism, influenced many twentieth-century poets and scholars.

Ransom was born in Pulaski, Tennessee, the son of a Methodist minister. Because the family moved frequently to accommodate changes in his father's ministry, Ransom was educated by his parents until the age of ten, when the family settled in Nashville and the precocious boy was enrolled in the eighth grade at the Bowen School. He later attended Vanderbilt University, though his studies were interrupted for three years due to financial difficulties. He graduated from Vanderbilt in 1909 and then studied at Oxford University for the next two years as a Rhodes Scholar.

After teaching for a year at the Hotchkiss School in Lakeville, Connecticut, he accepted an instructor's job at Vanderbilt. There, he and a colleague, Donald Davidson, helped found the group later known as the Fugitives. The group initially gathered to discuss religion and philosophy, but after the interruption caused by World War I—Ransom himself spent two

years on active duty in France—they turned their attention almost entirely to poetry. Between 1922 and 1925 they published a bimonthly journal of poetry and criticism, *The Fugitive*, attacking "the high-caste Brahmins of the Old South."

Ransom's first book of verse, *Poems about God* (1919), was published while he was still overseas. The poems address the disparity between what individuals perceive as ideal and what they experience as real; they express the poet's concern about the nature of God as witnessed in a world full of suffering and death. Though the volume received some favorable reviews, Ransom himself came to dislike these early poems, believing they lacked the subtleties of technique and of tone that made for mature poetry.

The poet ALLEN TATE, a fellow Fugitive, noted that Ransom appeared to make the transition to his mature poetic style overnight. Ransom brought a poem called "Necrological" to one of the meetings of the Fugitives. The poem concerns a monk living in the Middle Ages, who, wandering across a battlefield the day after a massacre, confronts sights that challenge his simple notions of God. "Necrological" incorporates the subtle rhythms and images, as well as the ambiguities of meaning, typical of Ransom's later work.

Two more volumes, *Chills and Fever* (1924) and *Two Gentlemen in Bonds* (1927), contained the bulk of Ransom's remaining output as a poet. Both books were praised warmly by critics. The poems focus on such subjects as the death of children ("Dead Boy" and "Bells for John Whiteside's Daughter") and the conflict between reason and desire ("Spectral Lovers" and "The Equilibrists"). They reflect Ransom's sense of the complexities of modern life and address such themes as the difficulty of finding love, the disparity between aspiration and opportunity, the decay of physical beauty in aging, and mortality.

Ransom turned his attention to criticism. His book *God without Thunder: An Unorthodox Defense of Orthodoxy* (1930) and the published symposia *I'll Take My Stand* (1930), for which Ransom wrote the introduction and a key essay, articulated the values of an agrarianism rooted in southern tradition and opposed to a corruptive capitalism.

In 1937 Ransom moved to Gambier, Ohio, to teach at Kenyon College, where he founded and edited an influential literary quarterly, *The Kenyon Review*. On its advisory board were Tate and ROBERT PENN WARREN. Ransom edited the journal from 1939 to 1959, and he taught at Kenyon until his retirement in 1958.

In *The New Criticism* (1941), Ransom advocated techniques for close textual analysis as the primary devices by which one ought to understand and evaluate poetry. The book's title gave a name to a critical movement that rejected more traditional methods—which often sought to put a poem into historic context, for example—in favor of a detailed interpretation of its inherent meanings.

Ransom did occasionally write new poems, and his *Selected Poems* (1945) contains five written after 1927. An enlarged edition of *Selected Poems* published in 1963 includes substantial revisions but no new poetry. The latter volume won Ransom the National Book Award in 1964. He had received the Bollingen Prize in 1951.

Ransom died on July 3, 1974.

BIBLIOGRAPHY

Parsons, Thornton H., *John Crowe Ransom*, 1969;
Young, Thomas Daniel, *Gentleman in a Dustcoat*, 1976.

Rauschenberg, Robert

(October 22, 1925–)
Painter

Robert Rauschenberg emerged in the 1950s as a leader of the American avant-garde. Best known for his combine paintings and collages of two- and three-dimensional elements, he has embraced a wide variety of movements, including Abstract Expressionism, Neo-Dada, and Pop art.

He was born in Port Arthur, Texas, in 1925. After a brief period studying pharmacology at the University of Texas, he served in the U.S. Navy. Following World War II he studied art history, sculpture, and music at the Kansas City Art Institute. In 1948 he attended the Académie Julian in Paris. A year later, back in the United States at Black Mountain College in North Carolina, he met two people who further stimulated his lifelong interests in music and dance and with whom he would enjoy a lifelong association, choreographer MERCE CUNNINGHAM and composer JOHN CAGE. Other associates from the Black Mountain days were architect Buckminster Fuller, painters ROBERT

MOTHERWELL and FRANZ KLINE, and the German Bauhaus artist Josef Albers. According to historian Tilman Osterwold, it was Albers's reductions of their basic form and structures that "influenced Rauschenberg's early concrete, philosophically conceived paintings."

In a variety of paintings, Rauschenberg was searching for his own identity. *Erased de Kooning Drawing* (1953) revealed his liberation from Abstract Expressionism (see BARNETT NEWMAN). A work in pencil and ink by WILLEM DE KOONING was rubbed out, leaving only traces of the image on the paper. *Yoicks* (1953) and *Red Painting* (1953), reflecting Albers's influence, were examples of a series keyed to black and red hues. In January 1955, in an exhibition at the Egan Gallery, he introduced what he called combine paintings, which derived from the Dadaists (see MARCEL DUCHAMP) and anticipated the development of Pop art (see ROY LICHTENSTEIN). These collages and assemblages included *Odalisque* (1955–1958), *Canyon* (1959), *Black Market* (1961), and *Lake Placid Glori-Fried Yarns from New England* (1971). They were heterogeneous mixtures of objects discarded by a throw-away society: newspaper clippings, light bulbs, rope, tufts of grass, pieces of wood, stuffed animals, photographs—all enhanced by silk-screen transfers and expressive slatherings of paint. As art historian Barbara Rose has noted, if Abstract Expressionism separated art from life, these works "reintroduced the stuff of life into art." Among the more spectacular of these combine paintings were *Bed* (1955), which included a real pillow and quilt over which paint was splashed, and *Monogram* (1955–1959), which combined a stuffed ram and an automobile tire.

National Archives

Similarly, Rauschenberg's silk-screen works of the 1960s were complex, collagelike allusions to current events and art history, combined with floating planes of color and flourishing abstract scrawls. The various images seemed to chase each other across the surface, appearing from below the surface and disappearing again, elusive, ambiguous.

There is a profound ambiguity in these works. All of the elements are intended to carry equal weight and significance. "A pair of socks," wrote Rauschenberg, "is no less suitable to make a painting with than wood, nails, turpentine, oil and fabric." Rauschenberg's attempts to bring overall unity to the disparate materials—or at least achieve some kind of momentary equipoise—typify the constantly shifting relationship between subject and abstraction. Referring to the elements in a combine painting called *Allegory* (1959–1960), critic Andrew Forge wrote that it is extraordinary "the way in which such powerful, aggressive forms as the metal, as the umbrella are brought to terms with the picture surface.... Things, passages, live side by side as equals, free to expand, to breathe, to display, unassailed by the 'personality' of their neighbours or by some overriding and generalising intention." At the same time, Rauschenberg admits that the traditional posture of the heroic artist is severely restricted and curtailed in these works: "The logical or illogical relationship between one thing and another is no longer a gratifying subject to the artist as the awareness grows that even in his most devastating or heroic moment he is part of the density of an uncensored continuum that neither begins with nor ends with any decision or action of his." Thus, Rauschenberg acknowledges the troubling undercurrents present in these deceptively accessible works. If all things are of equal value, can great values exist at all?

It is impossible to classify Rauschenberg narrowly. His activities reveal an extraordinarily eclectic range of interests. His commercial work has consisted of designing window displays for Bonwit Teller and Tiffany. At the same time he designed stage sets and costumes for the Merce Cunningham Dance Company; staged his own dance production, *Pelican* (1963), at a roller-skating rink; executed a series of drawings to illustrate Dante's *Inferno* (1959); produced his first lithographs (for which he was awarded the Grand Prix in 1963 at Ljubljana); organized with painter JASPER JOHNS a retrospective for John Cage; and had his first retrospectives and one-man exhibitions abroad (the Whitechapel Gallery in London, Galerie Sonnabend in Paris, and the Museum Haus Lange in Krefeld, Germany). In 1966, in the spirit of artistic collaboration, he founded with Billy Klüver the Experiments in Art and Technology (EAT), an organization to help bring together creative artists and technical and industrial engineers. Out of such experiences (which led, for example, to his invitation from NASA to witness the Apollo 11 moon launch in 1969) he executed a series of lithographs, *Stoned Moon.*

A large retrospective of his work was shown in several American cities from 1976 to 1978, and in 1989 his work went on world tour. He presently lives in New York City and on Captiva Island, Florida.

BIBLIOGRAPHY

Alloway, L., *Robert Rauschenberg,* 1977; Kotz, Mary Lyn, *Rauschenberg/Art and Life,* 1990; Osterwold, Tilman, *Pop Art,* 1991; Rookmaaker, H. R., *Modern Art and the Death of a Culture,* 1970.

Rich, Adrienne Cecile

(May 16, 1929–)
Essayist, Poet

Over the course of her forty-year career, the contemporary poet Adrienne Rich has written verse that begins with an awareness of women's missed opportunities in a male-dominated world but evolves into a more holistic view of women's strength and their power to transform society.

Rich was born in Baltimore, Maryland, the daughter of a physician who encouraged her to write from early childhood. She attended Radcliffe College, graduating in 1951.

In 1953 Rich married an economist, Alfred H. Conrad; their three sons were born over the next six years. They lived in Cambridge, Massachusetts, while Conrad taught at Harvard University, then in New York City, when he moved to City College of New York in 1966. Rich herself began teaching that year and has held positions at Douglass College, Swarthmore College, Columbia University, and Brandeis University. Conrad died in 1970.

During her senior year at Radcliffe, Rich published her first volume of poetry, *A Change of World* (1951), which had been selected by the poet W. H. AUDEN for the Yale Series of Younger Poets. Among the poems in the collection was "Aunt Jennifer's Tigers," which hints at themes that emerge more fully in Rich's later work. The poem contrasts Aunt Jennifer's apparent frailness with the vigor of the tigers she creates in her needlepoint.

Rich's second volume of poems, *The Diamond Cutters and Other Poems* (1955), continues in the same objective, controlled style.

The title poem proposes the care and precision of the diamond cutter's work as a model to pursue in art and life.

With *Snapshots of a Daughter-in-Law* (1963), Rich begins to confront, rather than contain, tensions and conflicts in herself and in the world around her. The title poem concerns a young woman who is angered by society's limited expectations of her, and whose quiet rage and hopes for change are contrasted with her mother-in-law's passive acceptance. The poem's looser style, particularly its use of speech cadences in place of more formal rhythm patterns, reflects Rich's freer approach to her subject material.

Her next volume, *Necessities of Life* (1966), demonstrates Rich's greater freedom in depicting sensual experience. *Leaflets* (1969) and *The Will to Change* (1971) reflect a growing preoccupation with social justice and voice particular concerns regarding civil rights and the Vietnam War. In *Diving into the Wreck* (1973), Rich creates metaphors for her own full-bore explorations of self. The volume won a National Book Award in 1974.

The peace of mind Rich finds in these exercises of self-discovery is extended to others in *The Dream of a Common Language* (1978) and *A Wild Patience Has Taken Me This Far* (1981). Her feminism broadens a vision that is intensely personal into social and political activism.

Rich further explored her feminism in such prose works as *Of Woman Born: Motherhood as Experience and Institution* (1976), which traces the evolution of the mother's role as defined in patriarchal society; *On Lies, Secrets, and Silence* (1979), in which she describes her own political development; *Compulsory Heterosexuality and Lesbian Existence* (1981); *Blood, Bread, and Poetry* (1986), in which she meditates on radical feminism and lesbian life; and *An Atlas of the Difficult World* (1991).

More recent volumes of poetry include *Your Native Land, Your Life* (1986) and *Time's Power* (1989).

Rich currently lives in California and teaches at Stanford University.

BIBLIOGRAPHY

Díaz-Diocaretz, Miriam, *The Transforming Power of Language: The Poetry of Adrienne Rich*, 1984; McDaniel, Judith, *Reconstituting the World: The Poetry and Vision of Adrienne Rich*, 1979.

Richardson, Henry Hobson

(September 29, 1838–April 27, 1886)
Architect

Henry Hobson Richardson, famous for his stone and shingled houses and the "Richardsonian Romanesque" of public buildings, was a major force in establishing an American architecture that was less obviously dependent on European precedents. His powerful, eclectic, yet individualized vocabulary quickly evolved into a national vernacular that was also influential abroad.

Richardson was born on a sugarcane plantation near New Orleans, Louisiana, and developed his characteristic energetic and affirmative approach to life during a trouble-free childhood. In 1859 he received a civil engineering degree from Harvard University, then studied architecture at the Ecole des Beaux-Arts in Paris (1860–1865). When his funds dwindled during the Civil War years, he worked for Parisian architect Theodore Labrouste to pay for his studies. Returning to New York in 1865, he formed a limited partnership with Charles D. Gambrill in 1867, which lasted, at least nominally, until Gambrill's death in 1878.

Richardson's design genius emerged in New England, beginning with a group of churches. Fame came with his design for Boston's Brattle Square Church (1869–1873). Here he first introduced the Romanesque Revival style with the expressive use of fine masonry, asymmetrical plan, round-arched openings, and picturesque corner tower with a crowning figural frieze. Richardson established himself as a major architect with the nearby Trinity (Episcopal) Church (1872–1877), in which he skillfully blended features from various styles, mostly Romanesque, into a unified work. The large central tower indicates a soaring interior open space defined by four massive clustered piers. Richardson's vision of a "color church," inside and out, was realized through the exterior textures and colors of the pink-gray granite walls trimmed with red sandstone, the roofs of red tiles, and the beautifully stained and painted interior. The church is also a testament to his belief in a "collaboration between equals" in the decoration of an important public building. American artist John La Farge and England's Edward Burne-Jones, as well as associates in Richardson's firm, CHARLES MCKIM (from 1870–1872) and STANFORD WHITE (from 1872–1878), contributed.

Richardson liked to revise his designs on site as a building was being constructed. Because most of his work was now in New England, he moved his family in 1874 to Brookline, Massachusetts, and established a practice there. A traditionalist, he strove to create a "rich, bold, living architecture" inspired by the architecture of the past, yet fulfilling a social and moral responsibility to the present. He became one of the first American architects to design important large-scale structures covering a broad range of building types, including churches, libraries, warehouses, and government buildings.

Some of the most representative examples of "Richardsonian Romanesque" are a series of libraries Richardson designed in Massachusetts and elsewhere, characterized by functional, asymmetrical planning and the use of fine woods for the interiors. The Winn Memorial Public Library in Woburn (1878) has a horizontal wing for the book repository contrasting with a clearly articulated stair tower, a great gable above the arched entrance, and a polygonal memorial room. A variation on this theme is the Ames Memorial Library (1877–1879) in North Easton, which appears as an extension of a granite outcrop within the picturesque landscape designed by FREDERICK LAW OLMSTED. His best library, the Thomas Crane Public Library (1880–1882) in Quincy, Massachusetts, reveals clearly legible parts subordinated to the perfectly scaled whole.

The most ambitious of Richardson's public projects is the Allegheny County complex comprising a courthouse and jail (1883–1888) in Pittsburgh, Pennsylvania. The rectangular courthouse with its open courtyard is dominated by a huge tower above the triple-arched entrance. The interior spatial relationships that separate or join various building functions are clearly articulated externally by the massing of forms and window arrangements. The outstanding feature of the interior is the grand staircase, with its huge arches and vistas. The jail is connected to the courthouse by a covered bridge. The striking visual contrast between the two buildings emphasizes their respective functions. Located on a pentagon-shaped site, the jail has a heavy, impenetrable look, emphasized by the bold, rough-faced masonry that had become a principle feature of the Richardsonian Romanesque. Composed of three long cell blocks radiating from an octagonal guard tower, the jailhouse is surrounded by a continuous wall, punctuated only by small windows and enormous arched gateways.

The Marshall Field Wholesale Store in Chicago (1885–1887) is considered Richardson's masterpiece. For this commercial venture, he abandoned ornamental, polychromed masonry in favor of an expressive use of rough-faced masonry and a rhythmic pattern of windows. This building inspired later developments of the Chicago skyscraper.

Richardson's residential projects included suburban and country houses of shingle-clad framing or of stone that appear to "grow out of the earth." He introduced the Shingle style (a mode of the early Colonial Revival) in 1872 with the house for Frank W. Andrews and that of William Watts Sherman (1874–1876), both in Newport, Rhode Island. Distinctive elements of the style, which became a staple of New England seaside communities, were shingled walls with a variety of patterns, roofs with multiple gables and decorated eaves, and tall, complicated chimneys. The Stoughton House in Cambridge, Massachusetts (1882–1883) represents the mature flowering of this Shingle style, which also stressed an open interior plan centered around a living hall with other spaces arranged in a fluid pattern.

Richardson's later urban dwellings of masonry were designed to shut out the city, both physically and visually. A good example is the fortresslike Glessner House in Chicago (1885–1887). The L-shaped house of rock-faced granite, with only a few windows streetside, encloses its corner site. The court elevations are more open and lively with a projecting bay in the dining room.

Perhaps Richardson's most original house is the Ames Gate-Lodge in North Easton, Massachusetts (1880–1881), designed to relate with its setting, which was landscaped by Olmsted. Constructed of massive boulders topped by a hipped roof of red tiles, the lodge's horizontal, earthbound quality makes it seem to be a work of nature rather than of man.

Richardson's buildings were known for their structural excellence, thanks largely to the building firm of W. W. Norcross, which worked with the architect on most structures. Richardson was mortally ill from an incurable kidney disorder during his last years; after his death at forty-seven, the firm passed to his associates George Foster Shepley (his son-in-law), Charles Rutan (who had been with him since 1870), and Charles Coolidge. Although he designed fewer than 100 buildings in a practice spanning about twenty years, he was the most influential American architect of his time, particularly affecting the careers of LOUIS SULLIVAN and FRANK LLOYD WRIGHT. He had redefined the potential of public buildings in America, introduced residential architecture sensitive to its setting, and strengthened the importance of spatial continuity in interior planning and exterior massing. As a friend said about the large, warm, and generous architect, "The man and his work are absolutely one."

BIBLIOGRAPHY

Hitchcock, Henry-Russell, *Richardson as a Victorian Architect*, 1966, and *The Architecture of H. H. Richardson and His Times*, 1975; Scully, Vincent J., Jr., *The Shingle Style and the Stick Style: Architectural Theory and Design from Richardson to the Origins of Wright*, 1971; Van Rensselaer, Mariana Griswold, *Henry Hobson Richardson and His Works*, 1888, rep., 1969.

Robbins, Jerome

(October 18, 1918–)
Choreographer, Dancer

Jerome Robbins took Russian classical ballet, as modernized by GEORGE BALANCHINE, to Broadway and thereby changed dance in musical comedy. Robbins's fine sense of theater, ability to portray his time, and integration of classic and colloquial dance resulted in dramatic success in ballet and on Broadway.

Born Jerome Rabinowitz in New York, Robbins grew up in Weehawken, New Jersey. He studied acting, piano, and violin, as well as modern, Spanish, and Oriental dance. He learned ballet technique from Ella Dagnova (a former Pavlova dancer), Helen Platova, and Eugene Loring. After he made his debut at the Dance Centre (a series of dance recitals in New York City) in 1937, he tried Broadway, landing a job in *Great Lady* (1939). The next year he made his first professional contact with George Balanchine through the theater in *Keep Off the Grass*.

In 1940 Robbins joined the Ballet Theater, rising from the corps de ballet to soloist. Four years later, he created *Fancy Free,* with music by LEONARD BERNSTEIN, for the group. The exuberant portrait of three sailors on shore leave in wartime America captures the spirit of the time and the ups and downs of the protagonists with delicacy and humor.

Fancy Free paved the way to Broadway, and from then on Robbins would have two parallel but interlocking careers, one in ballet and the other in musical theater. The next year, 1945, Robbins choreographed *On the Town,* an expansion of *Fancy Free,* into a musical. These two major triumphs, one in ballet, one in the theater, led to years of productive work in both media.

The choreographer was successful with Broadway shows like *Call Me Madam* (1950), *The King and I* (1951), *The Pajama Game* (1954), and *Peter Pan* (1954). But it was *West Side Story* with music by Bernstein, which Robbins conceived, directed, and cochoreographed with Peter Gennaro, that many critics consider his masterpiece. Its exciting and remarkable dance opening evolves from ordinary movement to an extraordinarily lively and brilliant dance sequence before a word is spoken. The opening is only one of several galvanizing dance moments in the musical.

Gypsy (1959) was another triumph. With no single heroine, Robbins manages to build the show around each of the three leads. Vaudeville and dance become the vehicle for human emotional expression. Jerome Robbins's ability to take one stage act and reveal it in several different ways to make his point is telling and the daring conclusion, "Rose's Turn," completely without dance movement, is wonderfully moving. *Fiddler on the Roof* (1964), Robbins's last Broadway effort, ran over five years. In it the choreographer continued to use dance as a way to express emotion rather than as a show stopper.

By 1950 Robbins had joined the New York City Ballet, where he danced, choreographed, and eventually became associate artistic director. Among the ballets he created there, before he left to found his own company in 1958, were *The Cage* (1951), a reworking of *Giselle,* and a tongue-in-cheek version of Nijinsky's *Afternoon of a Faun* (1953). In these ballets as well as in the musical *West Side Story,* a revision of Shakespeare's *Romeo and Juliet,* Robbins's use of traditional material was thoroughly contemporary as well as dramatic and tender. One unusual work Robbins created for his short-lived company, Ballets: U.S.A., was *Moves* (1961). It was performed in nonballetic style to absolute silence.

Soon after Robbins returned to the New York City Ballet in 1969, he created a new work, the romantic, abstract *Dances at a Gathering.* Over the next two decades Robbins continued to produce ballets, many characterized by a nearly ritualistic quality that the audience senses in the choreography, setting, music, and even in the dancers. Works created in these years include the colorful *Goldberg Variations* (1971) and ballets danced to music of American composers: *Dybbuk* (Leonard Bernstein), 1974; *The Gershwin Concerto* (GEORGE GERSHWIN), 1982; *Glass Pieces* (PHILIP GLASS), 1983; and *Eight Lines* (Steve Reich), 1985. In 1990, the year before Robbins resigned as co-director of the New York City Ballet, *Jerome Robbins's Broadway,* a retrospective of excerpts from eleven Broadway musicals that he had directed or choreographed, opened in New York.

Robbins, a popular and imaginative and often humorous choreographer was an innovator in ballet and in the theater who skillfully used contemporary American themes in ballets based on the traditional framework of classical dance movements. He has received numerous awards, including two Academy Awards in 1962 for his work in the film version of *West Side Story:* one for direction and one for choreography.

BIBLIOGRAPHY

Kirstein, Lincoln, *The New York City Ballet*, 1973; Siegel, M. B., *The Shape of Change: Images of American Dance,* 1979.

Robinson, Bill

(May 25, 1878–November 25, 1949)
Dancer

Both major guilds of tap dancers, The Hoofers and The Co-pasetics, called Bill Robinson the greatest tap dancer of all time. Bojangles delighted fans as he brilliantly tapped his way from vaudeville to Broadway to Hollywood over a fifty-year career that earned new respect for African American dancers.

Bill Robinson, born Luther Robinson in Richmond, Virginia, was orphaned before he was eight, danced in the street for pennies as a child, and never had formal dance training. At the age of twelve he began to tour with the show *The South Before the War.*

According to a childhood friend, Robinson came to New York in 1898. He got a job at

Library of Congress

Minors Theater in the Bowery and later danced at various restaurants, played vaudeville with a partner, George Cooper, and toured abroad. Robinson found his niche in vaudeville and fought his way to the top, becoming one of the few black dancers who performed solo on the Keith Theater circuit. At his peak he was earning $6,500 a week.

Robinson, with the help of his agent, created variety and cabaret acts that played at clubs and on the black theater circuit from the Apollo Theater in New York to the Alcazar in San Francisco. Occasionally he left vaudeville for Broadway shows.

Blackbirds of 1928, which opened May 9, 1927, made his name. It was in this show that

"Bojangles, whose Stair Dance was now acclaimed, became the first Negro dancing star on Broadway," said Marshall Stearns, a writer on music and dance. (According to one source, the nickname means "happy-go-lucky"; another says it suggests "powerful squabbler.")

The musical *Brown Buddies* opened October 7, 1930. Stearns noted how "critic after critic was delighted by the manner in which Bojangles watched his feet: 'He croons with his feet and laughs with them and watches them in wide-eyed amazement,' wrote Richard Lockridge in the *Sun,* 'as they do things which apparently surprise him as much as they do the rest of us. . . .'" Robinson appeared in other Broadway shows, including two based on Gilbert and Sullivan works: *The Hot Mikado* (1939) and *Memphis Bound* (1945).

Not known as a choreographer, Robinson may have interpolated his old acts into new shows and probably introduced earlier routines into films like *From Harlem to Heaven* (1929) and *Stormy Weather* (1943). The latter is known for its fine display of his dance style. In the 1930s Robinson appeared in four Shirley Temple films, where his dazzling flight-of-stairs routine was recorded.

"Robinson," said Stearns, "invented no new steps; rather, he perfected and presented them. . . . His Stair Dance, up and down a set of steps, with each step reverberating at a different pitch, was the most famous, but he had other favorites." His "contribution to tap dancing is exact and specific: He brought it up on the toes, dancing upright and swinging. . . . The flat-footed wizardry of [others] . . . seemed earthbound compared to the tasty steps of Bojangles, who danced with a hitherto-unknown lightness and presence." Bill Robinson died in New York in 1949.

BIBLIOGRAPHY

Stearns, M., and J. Stearns, *The Jazz Dance: The Story of American Vernacular Dance,* 1968, rep., 1979.

Robinson, Edwin Arlington

(December 22, 1869–April 6, 1935)
Poet

E dwin Arlington Robinson wrote short lyric and long narrative poems that explored the psychology of individual characters and the complexities of human relationships. While his forms were traditional, his ironic, austere verse influenced the work of many twentieth-century American poets.

Robinson was born in Head Tide, Maine. Shortly after, his family moved a few miles away to Gardiner, a town the poet would memorialize as Tilbury in his subsequent work. A quiet boy, Robinson began writing poetry in high school. He attended Harvard University from 1891 to 1893, but was called home because of his father's failing health.

In 1896 he published at his own expense *The Torrent and the Night Before,* a collection of poems. The volume was revised, expanded, and republished the following year as *The Children of the Night.* Included in the volume were "Luke Havergal," "Two Men," and "Richard Cory"; the last of these, one of Robinson's most anthologized poems, is a sixteen-line portrait of a seemingly successful man who has committed suicide.

Robinson moved to New York in 1897, and though he spent a year working at Harvard as a secretary, the city was to be his home for the rest of his life. Particularly in his early years there, he suffered great loneliness, as well as financial insecurity.

Captain Craig (1902), Robinson's second collection of verse, contained "The Book of Annandale." This long narrative poem relates the tale of a husband who promises his dying wife he will never remarry, and of a wife who makes the same promise to her dying husband. The surviving spouses meet and, after much soul-searching, marry each other.

Robinson's financial straits grew extremely difficult to bear. For a brief period, he eked out a living working as an inspector of subway construction, but he sometimes was forced to rely on the assistance of friends in order to avoid starvation. In 1905 President Theodore Roosevelt, who had admired *The Children of the Night*, came to the rescue, securing Robinson a job at the New York Custom House, which lasted until Roosevelt left office in 1909.

Robinson published his third book of verse, *The Town Down the River*, in 1910. Included in the volume was "Miniver Cheevy," a humorous character sketch of a man who believes he ought to have been born in the Middle Ages.

The following summer, Robinson visited the MacDowell Colony in Peterborough, New Hampshire; he found the place so conducive to work that he returned every summer for the rest of his life. *The Man Against the Sky* (1916) was the first volume to grow out of these summers at Peterborough. The title poem is a meditation on humanity's fate and on the value of diverse philosophical approaches one can take to life. It received greater critical attention than anything Robinson had written previously.

Robinson published *Merlin*, the first of three Arthurian poems, in 1917. A long narrative poem in blank verse, *Merlin* depicts the sage responding to King Arthur's fears about the machinations of his illegitimate son, Modred, and the love affair between his queen, Guinevere, and the knight Lancelot. The second Arthurian poem, *Lancelot* (1920), concerns the turmoil that follows Arthur's discovery of the affair, as Lancelot rescues Guinevere from being burned at the stake and takes part in the war that ruins Arthur.

Avon's Harvest (1921) opens with the title poem, another long narrative. It relates the story of a lawyer whose hatred and fear end in psychosis. He remains convinced of the presence of an enemy even after he has learned of the man's death. It is followed by a seven-stanza

portrait that quickly became a popular favorite: "Mr. Flood's Party." Eben Flood is a Tilbury Town resident who interrupts his lonely life once a year for a single drunken spree.

Robinson's fortunes began to turn with the publication of his *Collected Poems* (1921), which earned him a degree of financial security, as well as the first Pulitzer Prize for Poetry. *The Man Who Died Twice* (1924) won Robinson his second Pulitzer; this narrative poem concerns a musician who destroys two symphonies he has written in a fit of guilt over his own debauchery but who redeems himself by writing a new symphony.

In the volume *Dionysus in Doubt* (1925), two noteworthy poems, the title poem and "Demos and Dionysus," express Robinson's doubts about the political currents of the day; the latter poem in particular questions the democratic ideal, arguing that it reduces individuals and society to mediocrity.

Tristram (1927), the third Arthurian narrative, won Robinson his third Pulitzer, as well as his first real popular renown. Tristram falls in love with his uncle's wife, Isolt, but he marries another woman by the same name, Isolt of Brittany. His wife loves him deeply, but Tristram neglects her for his fantasy, the unattainable wife of his old uncle.

Trying to maintain his newfound financial security, Robinson began to produce a long narrative poem each year. Though these poems were popular, they were often verbose and sometimes obscure, and they have been remembered less favorably by critics. They include *Cavender's House* (1929), *Talifer* (1933), and *Amaranth* (1934).

Robinson died of cancer shortly after completing work on his final poem, *King Jasper* (1935).

BIBLIOGRAPHY

Coxe, Louis, *Edwin Arlington Robinson: The Life of Poetry*, 1969; Hagedorn, Hermann, *Edwin Arlington Robinson: A Biography*, 1938; Smith, Chard Powers, *Where the Light Falls: A Portrait of Edwin Arlington Robinson*, 1965.

Rockwell, Norman

(February 3, 1894–November 8, 1978)
Illustrator

Norman Rockwell was a painter and illustrator whose most popular works are enduring images of a sturdy, ruddy-cheeked Americana, full of the homespun nostalgia and simple values of small-town life.

Rockwell was born in 1894 in a shabby brownstone in New York. He dropped out of high school at age fifteen to study art full time. Rather than attend the prestigious National Academy School, which had discouraged his ambitions to be an illustrator, he preferred to go to the Art Students League. Renting the studio formerly owned by painter

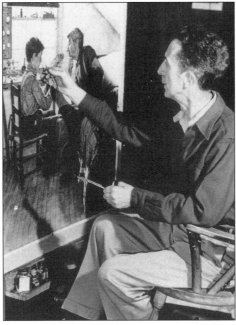

Ford Motor Company/Copyright *Washington Post*;
Reprinted by permission of the D.C. Public Library

Frederic Remington, he quickly established a reputation for children's subjects with many of the popular magazines of the day—*St. Nicholas, American Boy, Boy's Life.* His strongest ambition was to paint covers for the *Saturday Evening Post,* which he called "the greatest show window in America for an illustrator." Originally founded by Benjamin Franklin, the *Saturday Evening Post* was a family magazine with a modest circulation of 2,000. However, after publisher Cyrus H. K. Curtis purchased it in 1897 and turned it over to editor George Horace Lorimer, it quickly grew into the most successful magazine in American history. Its vision of middle-class values—what novelist WILLIAM DEAN HOWELLS had once described as "the smiling aspects of life"—was perfectly embodied by Rockwell's work. From 1916 to 1963 he enjoyed an uninterrupted relationship with the *Post,* for which he painted 317 covers. Here

was the essential Rockwell vision, an ingenuous view of rural life, with barefoot boys and gap-toothed girls, Boy Scouts, front porches, loving grandmas, and the venerable letter carrier.

"I paint life as I would like it to be," Rockwell wrote. "Maybe as I grew up and found that the world wasn't the perfectly pleasant place I had thought it to be, I unconsciously decided that, even if it wasn't an ideal world, it should be and so painted only the ideal aspects of it." Even those observers who are disposed to dismiss his anecdotal, realistic style must admit that his working methods were meticulous and exacting. He carefully researched the furniture and costumes of historical periods. When he illustrated *Tom Sawyer* and *Huckleberry Finn* in 1936, he visited the actual locations described by MARK TWAIN. His zeal for authentic character types led him to use as models his friends and neighbors in the towns of Arlington, Vermont, and Stockbridge, Massachusetts. Although he preferred to work from life, he frequently used a camera, staging his pictures like scenes from a play. He worked slowly, even painfully, taking many days just to do the preliminary sketches.

A self-portrait appeared on the cover of the *Saturday Evening Post* on October 8, 1938. The lanky, red-haired artist sits with his back to us, scratching his head, puzzling what to make out of the blank canvas before him. Rockwell always said that choosing the subject was the hardest thing about his work. "I had to beat [ideas] out of my head or at least maul my brain until something came out of it," he said. "It always seemed to me that it was like getting blood from a stone, except, of course, that eventually something always came."

BIBLIOGRAPHY

Meyer, Susan E., *The Great American Illustrators*, 1978; Rockwell, Norman, *My Adventures as an Illustrator*, 1960.

Rodgers, Richard Charles

(June 28, 1902–December 30, 1979)
Composer

For nearly fifty years Richard Rodgers composed refreshing, evergreen show tunes and, with lyricists Lorenz Hart and Oscar Hammerstein II, played a leading role in the growth and significance of American musical drama. His partnerships with Hart, then Hammerstein, produced nearly forty Broadway shows and two Pulitzer Prizes.

The son of a physician, Rodgers was born on Long Island and raised in New York City. He attended public schools and started composing early. He needed a lyricist, however. In 1918 he met Lorenz Hart, a lyricist who needed a composer. It was a perfect match. "I left Hart's house," Rodgers recalled, "having acquired in one afternoon, a career, a partner, a best friend, and a source of permanent irritation." Rodgers entered The Institute of Musical Art (now the Juilliard School of Music) in 1921, where he studied for two years.

Hart, born in New York in 1895, had studied journalism at Columbia University, but dropped out to translate plays for the Shubert brothers (see LEVI SHUBERT, SAMUEL S. SHUBERT, and JACOB J. SHUBERT), theatrical producers. In 1919 an early Rodgers and Hart song was added to a Broadway show. In 1920 the team's music and lyrics were featured in a show based on a 1919 Columbia varsity effort, *Fly with Me*. As it happened, one of the reviewing judges of *Fly with Me* was Columbia alumnus Oscar Hammerstein II, who was to write *Show Boat* with JEROME KERN.

Rodgers and Hart's first success was a 1925 revue, *Garrick Gaieties*. "A corking revue . . . Rodgers and Hart's stuff clicked here like a colonel's heels at attention," said *Variety*, the theater chronicler. Rodgers and Hart were extraordinarily popular for the rest of the decade. From 1926 to 1930 they produced fourteen shows and continued tinkering with the form of the musical play to strengthen dramatic impact. Gradually the pair moved further and further away from the conventions of revues. Musical numbers became more closely tied to plot, and transitional passages bridged stage actions.

After an unsuccessful stint in Hollywood (1930–1934), the duo returned to New York and began to write their own books in addition to lyrics and music. *On Your Toes* (1936) adds an important extended ballet sequence, including "Slaughter on Tenth Avenue," choreographed by GEORGE BALANCHINE, and the charming song "There's a Small Hotel." The next year *Babes in Arms* launched more sophisticated songs like "My Funny Valentine" and "The Lady Is a Tramp." Hart's death in 1943 ended twenty-five years of collaboration. They had produced nearly thirty musicals.

Oscar Hammerstein became Rodgers's collaborator after Hart died. Their partnership had an even greater impact on musical theater. *Oklahoma* (1943) "caused a revolution in the progress of the Broadway musical" according to critic Arthur Jackson. The convention-breaking show, with its country air, wealth of hit songs, and seamless transitions from dialogue to song, won the Pulitzer Prize for drama in 1944. Its integration of song, narrative, dance, and drama was "fresh and diverting," said the New York *Sun,* and the remarkable AGNES DE MILLE ballets, modeled on square dances, were showstoppers. *Oklahoma* ran on Broadway for five years and continues to be performed.

With *South Pacific* (1949) and its World War II drama and social themes, the team won another Pulitzer Prize (1950) and fans' hearts with songs like "Some Enchanted Evening" and "There Is Nothin' Like a Dame," and introduced Ezio Pinza, an opera basso, to the Broadway stage as the love interest for the bubbling Mary Martin. Rodgers and Hammerstein collaborated on nine musicals, including *The King and I* (1951) and *The Sound of Music* (1959), and contributed delightful songs to films as well as to Broadway. After Hammerstein's death in 1960, Rodgers continued composing, though with less success. He died in New York in 1979.

As Hart's collaborator, Rodgers wrote the music first, then Hart provided words.

Hammerstein had worked in the same Broadway tradition. The new partners reversed that process and fitted music to words. According to Rodgers biographer Deems Taylor, the change set the lyricist "free to use his imagination, to experiment," and challenged the composer by "offering him new rhythms and forms."

With Hart, Rodgers worked well within Tin Pan Alley limitations. As Hammerstein's partner, Rodgers was freer to break with convention, though critic Alec Wilder misses "that spark and daring flair which existed in the songs he wrote with Hart." But, Wilder concludes, "Rodgers' songs have, over the years, revealed a higher degree of consistent excellence, inventiveness, and sophistication than those of any other writer I have studied."

BIBLIOGRAPHY

Furia, P., *The Poets of Tin Pan Alley: A History of America's Great Lyricists,* 1990; Rodgers, R., *Musical Stages,* 1975; Taylor, D., *Some Enchanted Evenings,* 1953.

Roethke, Theodore Huebner

(May 25, 1908–August 1, 1963)
Critic, Poet

Theodore Roethke wrote poetry that explored the psyche, frequently by projecting the human experience of life and death onto images from nature. His stylistic innovations, particularly his work with less structured rhythms meant to convey a sense of the unconscious, influenced poets who followed in the late twentieth century.

Roethke was born in Saginaw, Michigan, the son of a German immigrant who ran a prosperous florist business. The work of generating plant life impressed the child deeply; the image of the greenhouse would surface in his adult poetry.

Roethke graduated from the University of Michigan at Ann Arbor in 1929. He began graduate school at Harvard University, but the Great Depression had affected his family's finances, and he left to find a job. He began a series of teaching jobs, at Lafayette College, Michigan State University, Penn State University, and Bennington College. He settled finally at the University of Washington at Seattle in 1947.

Encouraged in his writing by his friends, the poets Stanley Kunitz and Louise Bogan, Roethke published his first book of poetry, *Open House*, in 1941. The poems in this volume are traditional in structure and echo such poets as EMILY DICKINSON, EDWIN ARLINGTON ROBINSON, ROBERT FROST, and W. H. AUDEN.

Roethke's second book of verse, *The Lost Son and Other Poems* (1948), was recognized immediately for its originality. The volume begins with a series of greenhouse poems, such as "Cuttings (later)," which trace the origins of life to the soil. Subsequent poems suggest the evolution from lower forms of plant and animal life toward humanity. "The Lost Son," which depicts the poet's struggle as an adolescent to come to terms with his father's death, observes the youth's psychic regression and ultimate reemergence into the adult world of reason and order, suggesting an evolutionary parallel.

Praise to the End (1951) continued in a similar vein. Roethke explores the psyche of the child and the child's experience of the world around him, defined inevitably in terms of his own primal needs. Through the course of the volume, the poetic consciousness evolves toward the self-conscious identity that marks adulthood.

In 1953 Roethke married Beatrice O'Connell, a former student he had taught at Bennington College. Their whirlwind courtship had lasted only a month. Together they traveled to Europe for several months, honeymooning at Auden's villa at Ischia. For Roethke, who since 1936 had suffered several mental breakdowns, his marriage was an important source of peace.

The Waking (1953) came out as the Roethkes returned to Seattle in September. The volume contained a selection of previously published poems, plus eight new ones. "Four for Sir John Davies" concerns the redemptive power of romantic love. "The Waking" reflects on the evolution of man and sees the influence of his intuition, over reason, on his progress. The volume won the Pulitzer Prize in 1954.

Words for the Wind (1958) groups forty-three new poems into five sections. The first contains humorous poems and children's verses. The second features love poems, which build on the theme of "Four for Sir John Davies"; these include "Words for the Wind," "The Swan," and "I Knew a Woman." The third group of poems revisit Roethke's interest in the natural world. The fourth comprises a single poem: "The Dying Man," written to honor the poet William Butler Yeats. The final section, "Meditations of an Old Woman," is a memorial to Roethke's mother, who had died in 1954. The volume earned Roethke both the National Book Award and the Bollingen Prize, and he relished the recognition he had worked so hard to achieve.

Roethke died suddenly of a heart attack, on August 1, 1963, while swimming in a friend's pool. He had nearly finished work on his next volume of poetry, *The Far Field*. It was published posthumously in 1964. This final volume both recapitulates Roethke's lifelong interests in nature and in the love between man and woman and captures his preoccupation with death. At the same time he broods about "the abyss," he celebrates the life impulse. A collection of Roethke's essays, *On the Poet and His Craft*, appeared in 1965.

BIBLIOGRAPHY

Seager, Allan, *The Glass House: The Life of Theodore Roethke*, 1968; Wolff, George, *Theodore Roethke*, 1981.

Roth, Philip Milton

(March 19, 1933–)
Novelist

Philip Roth, a contemporary novelist who established a reputation for biting satire with his books *Goodbye, Columbus* and *Portnoy's Complaint,* has taken aim at such subjects as his own Jewish culture, the values of Middle America, male sexuality, and the writer's art.

Roth was born in Newark, New Jersey. He attended Newark College of Rutgers University for two years and completed his bachelor's degree at Bucknell University in 1954. He earned a master's degree at the University of Chicago the following year.

Roth spent another year at Chicago studying for a doctorate, but he dropped out to write film reviews for *The Nation* magazine. Over the course of his career, he has held teaching positions at the University of Chicago, the University of Iowa, Princeton University, the State University of New York at Stony Brook, and the University of Pennsylvania.

Roth attained success with his first book, *Goodbye, Columbus and Five Short Stories* (1959), which won the National Book Award in 1960. The title novella concerns Neil Klugman, a native of Newark who has fallen for Brenda Patimkin, a spoiled girl from the upper-middle-class town of Short Hills, New Jersey. Roth dissects the pretensions of suburban life; the book's satiric take on the values of a well-to-do Jewish family earned him the reputation, he said at the time, of being an anti-Semitic Jew.

Neither of Roth's next two novels were as controversial. *Letting Go* (1962), a novel of manners written to mimic HENRY JAMES, follows the love affairs of a graduate student, Gabriel Wallach, who is anxious and guilty about his inability to make an emotional commitment. *When She Was Good* (1967), the story of Lucy Nelson, a self-righteous Catholic who alienates her own family with her obsessive truth telling, demonstrated Roth also could situate his concerns with middle-class hypocrisy in Gentile culture.

Portnoy's Complaint (1969) reestablished Roth's reputation as a controversialist. Alexander Portnoy seeks to free himself—and especially his libido—from the repressive rules he learned from his domineering mother. Obsessive masturbation, obscenity, sex with Gentile women—that is, women as different as possible from his mother—all are meant to contravene the rules he learned in youth. But Portnoy cannot free himself, and therefore, like Gabriel Wallach, he also cannot commit himself to any woman.

Roth's next two novels proceed from outrageous premises. In Roth's most explicitly political novel, *Our Gang* (1971), which satirizes the presidency of Richard Nixon, Trick E. Dixon is so unredeemed a politician that after his death he attempts to make a comeback by running against Satan in hell. *The Breast* (1972), a spoof of Franz Kafka's famous story "The Metamorphosis," concerns a hapless protagonist, David Kepesh, who awakes one morning to find himself transformed into a massive female breast.

The Great American Novel (1973) parodies the mythology of "the great American pastime," as well as the literary pretensions reflected in the title. Roland Agni is the one real athlete on a team of misfits; his desire to get himself traded to another team leads him to flirt with dishonesty. When he straightens out, he is assassinated by communists, and the record of the entire baseball league is expunged by the American authorities who uncover the plot.

In *My Life as a Man* (1974), Roth explores the complex relationship between himself and his fiction. Peter Tarnopol is a fiction writer who is trying to understand himself by coming to terms with his reflection in his fictional alter ego, Nathan Zuckerman. Two Zuckerman stories are included; both concern love affairs that arise in some way from Tarnopol's own experience.

With *The Professor of Desire* (1977), Roth returns to the character of David Kepesh, the protagonist of *The Breast.* His body whole, Kepesh is now consumed with the pursuit of sexual passion, yet the anxious intellectual cannot stop analyzing his experiences long enough to enjoy them.

The Ghost Writer (1979) reintroduces Nathan Zuckerman, minus Peter Tarnopol. A successful Zuckerman reminisces about a visit twenty years earlier to the Jewish writer E. I. Lonoff in search of his approval; Zuckerman had sought a counterweight to the opinion of the many Jews in his community who found his work anti-Semitic. Indeed, the subsequent publication of Zuckerman's novel, *Carnovsky*—a

ringer for Roth's own *Portnoy's Complaint*—only worsened that reputation.

Roth wrote a series of novels featuring Zuckerman, including *Zuckerman Unbound* (1981), which offers more of the writer's tribulations after the publication of *Carnovsky; The Anatomy Lesson* (1983), *The Prague Orgy* (1985), and *The Counterlife* (1987). Other recent works include *The Facts: A Novelist's Autobiography* (1988), *Patrimony* (1991), and *Operation Shylock: A Confession* (1993).

BIBLIOGRAPHY

Halio, Jay L., *Philip Roth Revisited,* 1992; Lee, Hermione, *Philip Roth,* 1982; Rodgers, Bernard F., Jr., *Philip Roth,* 1978.

Rothko, Mark

(September 25, 1903–February 25, 1970)
Painter

Mark Rothko, categorized variously as an Abstract Expressionist and a Color Field painter, produced paintings notable for their seeming simplicity of form and color, totally independent of representational imagery or symbolic allusions.

He was born Marcus Rothkowitz in 1903 in Dvinsk, Russia. He went to Hebrew school and studied the Talmud. Because of the repression of the Jews, his family emigrated to America in 1913. They settled in the Jewish section of Portland, Oregon. After his father's death shortly thereafter, Marcus went to work as a newspaper delivery boy. In 1921 he received a full scholarship to Yale University, where he indulged his growing interests in music, mathematics, drawing, literature, and politics. He grew restless and, after leaving Yale without his degree, went to New York, where he stumbled into art courses at the Art Students League.

During occasional visits back to Portland, he also became interested in what would become another lifelong preoccupation, acting and the theater. Among all the arts, however, he soon realized that only painting could consolidate his diverse interests. "I became a painter because I wanted to raise painting to the level of poignancy of music and poetry," he recalled. He returned to New York for good in 1925.

His works of the late 1920s at first reflected the conservatism of painters like THOMAS HART BENTON, essentially an American reaction against European abstraction. Rothko's early landscapes and nudes were realistic and reveal his liberal politics—concerns with the poverty and disillusionment of the downtrodden urban masses. Nonetheless, after studying with Max Weber at the Art Students League, and being exposed to the work of the Cubists and the Fauves, Rothko's work began to reveal the influences of painters like Cézanne and Picasso, the spatial ambiguities and nonrepresentational shapes that would distinguish his later works. He had his first one-man show in New York at the Contemporary Arts Gallery in 1933. After working on the Federal Arts Project of the Works Progress Administration, he became a U.S. citizen in 1938 and began using the name Mark Rothko.

Rothko rarely dated his images and it is difficult to determine with certainty his chronological progress in the next two decades. But he painted steadily, supporting himself with a teaching position at the Brooklyn Jewish Center. Generally influenced by Surrealism, an art style in which imagery is based on fantasy or the subconscious, his works in the 1940s grew larger and the abstract shapes more primordial and more simplified. By the late 1940s, however, he gradually abandoned the forms, symbols, and allusions of Surrealism. While JACKSON POLLOCK was experimenting with dynamic, gestural paintings, Rothko—in *Untitled* and *Violet, Black, Orange, Yellow on White and Red* (both in 1949)—was reducing his forms to large color fields (see BARNETT NEWMAN), two or three rectangles of luminous colors and velvety textures that seem to hover in the same plane. The interpenetration of the colors had the effect of subtly undercutting the severity of the forms. There is an order and stability to his rectilinear structures that reveal the influence of Piet Mondrian (while avoiding the obvious grid scaffolding and dense color).

Rothko steadily renounced linear elements so that color and shape could stand alone. His lightly brushed squares and rectangles assumed a luminous, hovering quality. As if to underscore the abstract nature of his work, the titles are simply terms of colors and numbers, as *Tan and Black on Red* (1957), *Black, Pink and Yellow over Orange* (1951–1952), and *Light, Earth and Blue* (1954).

During the 1950s and 1960s the color red was employed as a strong emotional stimulus in many of his canvases. Color was the key to the spiritual realm for Rothko. In that, he was like those other metaphysicians of painting, Mondrian, Paul Klee, and Wassily Kandinsky. By combining the beauty of the spiritual and the physical worlds, art historian Diane Waldman writes, "Rothko was able to achieve this synthesis with the rigorously limited means he allowed himself. . . . In these pure, reduced, transcendent works, Rothko makes the concrete sublime." As for Rothko, he said in 1947: "I think of my pictures as dramas; the shapes in the pictures are the performers. They have been created from the need for a group of actors who are able to move dramatically without embarrassment and execute gestures without shame."

Rothko received his first major one-man museum exhibition at the Museum of Modern Art in 1961. Seven years later he suffered an aneurysm of the aorta, a condition aggravated by his heavy drinking. After completing a series of murals for a chapel in Houston, Texas—large fields of black, dark brown, and somber purple—he committed suicide in his studio in 1970.

BIBLIOGRAPHY

Waldman, Diane, *Mark Rothko: A Retrospective*, 1978.

Rubinstein, Artur

(January 28, 1887–December 20, 1982)
Pianist

Artur Rubinstein, the first pianistic superstar of the recording age, was a gifted child prodigy who became a world-famous artist. His lyricism brought the piano repertoire to life as he melded the best qualities of the romantic and modern styles into performances that enchanted audiences and won him renown.

Born in Łódź, Poland, Rubinstein was taken to Berlin when he was three to play for the noted violinist Joseph Joachim. He studied in Łódź and Warsaw, and at seven appeared in his first Łódź concert. He returned to Berlin in 1897. There Joachim oversaw his education: piano with Heinrich Barth, theory with Max Bruch and Robert Kahn.

In 1900 Rubinstein made his Berlin debut under Joachim playing Mozart's Concerto no. 23 in A Major, piano solos by Schumann and Chopin, and the Saint-Saëns G Minor Concerto. The appearance led to concerts in Germany and Poland and to a Paris debut in 1904.

Rubinstein made his first American tour in 1906 and traveled to Austria, Italy, and Russia prior to his 1912 London debut. He remained in London during World War I, often accompanying Belgian violinist Eugène Ysaÿe, though his visits to South America and Spain in 1916 and 1917 began a strong interest in the music of Granados, Albéniz, Villa-Lobos, and de Falla. Rubinstein continued to concertize until his marriage.

After he married Aniela Mlynarski in 1932, Rubinstein retired to restudy the repertory and to consolidate his technique. By 1937 when he toured the United States, it was clear that the pianist's great natural facility had been tempered with a new discipline. Rubinstein stayed in the United States during World War II, becoming an American citizen in 1946.

After the war Rubinstein resumed concertizing with increased energy. When he was in his seventies and eighties, he was able to play, in an evening, both Brahms concertos or three by Beethoven. He played chamber music with Jascha Heifetz, the Guarneri String Quartet and others during the 1960s and 1970s, and made many recordings before he retired in 1976, the year he was awarded the Presidential Medal of Freedom. In 1982 he died in Geneva, Switzerland, at the age of ninety-five.

Rubinstein's tone was "the envy of all pianists" says *New York Times* critic Harold Schonberg, who also notes that the pianist's huge hands were partly responsible, a "perfect piano hand" that could reach a twelfth. Rubinstein endowed his performances with "gorgeous sound, his feeling for a sinuous shape to a phrase, the drama he could infuse into the interpretations, the sheer joy that comes through the playing."

BIBLIOGRAPHY

Rubinstein, A., *My Young Years*, 1973, and *My Many Years*, 1980; Schonberg, H. C., *The Great Pianists*, 1987.

Ryder, Albert Pinkham

(March 19, 1847–March 28, 1917)
Painter

Albert Pinkham Ryder, one of the most individual American artists of the second half of the nineteenth century, produced intensely subjective works that were rooted in the romantic landscape tradition of the French painter Nicolas Poussin, but that anticipated the Abstract Expressionism of the mid-twentieth century.

Ryder was the fourth and last child born to Alexander Gage Ryder and Elizabeth Cobb of New Bedford, Massachusetts. The town was the most active whaling port in the world, and the future marine painter grew up fascinated with the tales of sea life and travels to other lands brought back to him by his two older seafaring brothers. Information about his formative years is scant, but it is known that he attended an all-male grammar school and that he frequently made little drawings of the farm animals of the region.

In 1870 the entire family moved to New York City, and Albert promptly applied for admission to the National Academy of Design. His lack of formal training led to his rejection, but he tried again and this time was accepted. He enrolled in several antique-drawing classes and life-drawing classes. However, it was not in cast or figure drawing that he discovered his true bent. It was in the landscape paintings he began to make in Yarmouth, Massachusetts, during his summer vacations. He soon realized that he was not interested in the realistic depiction of nature; instead, he discovered the medium of paint itself. "I squeezed out big chunks of pure, moist color," he said, "and taking my palette knife, I laid on blue, green, white and brown in great sweeping strokes. . . . I saw nature springing into life upon my dead canvas. It was better than nature, for it was vibrating with the thrill of a new creation."

Ryder's early work was already eliciting the kinds of critical reactions he would encounter the rest of his life. Paintings like *Landscape* and *Near Litchfield, Connecticut* were small, "coarsely finished," vague in details, narrow in their range of hues, and, in general, displayed weak drawing skills. Other observers, however, were struck by their subjective, almost abstract quality. He seemed not interested in landscape as a nationalist emblem (like such Hudson River school painters as THOMAS COLE) or as documentation of atmospheric effects (like the Luminist artist JOHN FREDERICK KENSETT). Rather, as biographer Elizabeth Broun has noted, his works were "emblems of something private or internal . . . small nature notes [that] seem to have imploded, leaving a small, silent, concentrated core." Embraced by members of an emerging avant-garde in America, he was elected in 1877 to the Society of American Artists, an organization that held exhibitions of young artists whose work had been rejected from the Academy shows.

For the next twelve years Ryder became acquainted with a wide circle of influential artists and entrepreneurs in New York and Europe, including painters John La Farge, J. Alden Weir, and art dealer Daniel Cottier. He read voraciously, especially Shakespeare and the British romantic poets, executed a number of decorations for interior furnishings, made several trips abroad, and absorbed the influences of many European painters. From Jean-Baptiste Camille Corot he found confirmation in his bent toward idealized landscapes; from Jean-François Millet, a fierce integrity and the sense of the dignity of rural life; and from the seventeenth-century Dutch artists a sensitivity toward genre details and the radiant glow of translucent light. His subsequent paintings attracted an ever-growing audience. *Market Horse* was described as "like an old Dutch master"; *The Chase* was "like Japanese lacquer-work"; and a small oriental painting called *Nourmahal* was akin to "a deep unfathomable mystery." He was opening a window onto the imagination, and for a time his popularity eclipsed even that of the more fiercely realistic THOMAS EAKINS.

Ryder spent the rest of his life in Greenwich Village. He disliked company and became a recluse, confining himself to his small, cluttered rooms at 308 West 15th Street, straying outside only for his nightly walks or for an occasional vacation in the country with a friend. His appearance, like his habits, grew increasingly eccentric over the years. He wore a slouch hat over scraggly hair, and his beard was usually matted and shaggy. His shirts were soiled and his trousers hung low from his hips. After 1888 he sent no more paintings to either the National Academy of Design or the Society of American Artists shows. Yet amid these squalid surroundings and during the last two decades of the century, he produced his finest work. As biographer Broun writes, "The more he confined himself, the farther his imagination ranged and the more he strayed from convention."

Well versed in literature (he wrote a large body of poetry), he based many of his paintings on themes from the Bible, works of Shakespeare, the German romantics, Lord Byron, EDGAR ALLAN POE, and Walter Scott. These particular paintings were full of melodrama and moonlight and bore suggestive titles like *Lord Ullin's Daughter, The Lorelei, The Tempest,* and *Siegfried and the Rhine Maidens.* From the pastoral poets like James Thomson he breathed an Elizabethan formality into *The Shepardess* and *Woman and Staghound.* His Bible scenes included the almost Byzantine *Story of the Cross* and the great *Jonah.* And there were the allegorical scenes, like *The Race Track* (also known as *Death on a Pale Horse*), depicting a skeletal figure wielding a deadly scythe while riding a horse around an oval track, which were more difficult to classify. These dusky evocations of innocent love, fugitive figures, and uneasy twilights are not attempts to illustrate poems and stories but abstractions of their emotions and moods.

In a class by themselves were Ryder's ecstatic marine nocturnes. Although few in number, images like *Toilers of the Sea, Moonlight Marine, Moonlit Cove,* and *Moonlight* contained simple, elemental shapes connoting boat and moon and wave that swirled and heaved toward each other, all part of an unutterable mystery. They approached abstract, pure form that virtually abandoned narrative implications.

Ryder was notorious for the way he labored at his paintings. He would fuss at his "painted dreams," as he called them, for years, even decades. As the layers of pigment and glaze accumulated, the impastoed images took on a palpable quality, so that even water and clouds became almost three-dimensional, the borders of his forms presenting edges in relief. This took its toll as the paintings have cracked badly over the years, and many museum curators will not let them travel. However, his vision, if not his pigments, was forever fixed beyond mere temporal and physical limitations. "Have you seen an inch worm crawl up a leaf or twig, and there clinging to the very end, revolve in the air, feeling for something to reach something?" he wrote in an uncharacteristic burst of self-explanation. "That's like me. I am trying to find something out there beyond the place on which I have a footing."

He spent his last years fighting weakening eyesight, railing at dealers who insisted on cleaning his paintings, and refusing to relinquish works that had been commissioned and paid for. It is a matter of record that he would sometimes deface a painting rather than allow it to fall into the hands of its rightful owner. Health problems finally caught up with him, and just a few days after his seventieth birthday he died of complications from a chronic kidney ailment. It is significant that before his death his works were included in the famous Armory Show in New York in 1913 (see STUART DAVIS).

BIBLIOGRAPHY

Broun, Elizabeth, *Albert Pinkham Ryder,* 1990; Eldredge, Charles C., *American Imagination and Symbolist Painting,* 1979.

Saarinen, Gottlieb Eliel

(August 20, 1873–July 1, 1950)
Architect, City Planner, Educator

Saarinen, Eero

(August 20, 1910–September 1, 1961)
Architect, Furniture Designer

Eliel Saarinen, a renowned architect and planner in his native Finland, became one of the foremost architects, educators, and city planners of his era in the United States. His son, Eero, emerged in the 1950s with a great talent for imaginative furniture and architectural designs in a sculptural vocabulary.

Eliel Saarinen was born in Rantasalmi, Finland, but grew up in the Russian border area of Ingermanland. He studied architecture at the Polytechnic Institute in Helsinki, Finland, and painting at the University of Helsinki, graduating with an architectural degree in 1897. In 1896 he formed an architectural firm with Herman Gesellius and Armas Lindgren. The fanciful design of the Finnish pavilion for the Paris Exposition (1899–1900), with its tapered tower and elaborate decoration, was highly acclaimed. It introduced a key aspect of Saarinen's style: the ability to unite distinctive or contradictory modes. He emerged as a leading architect of the National Romantic style, an eclectic mix of Finnish vernacular traditions, sensuous decorative elements of Art Nouveau, and the picturesque profiles of the Romanesque Revival associated with HENRY HOBSON RICHARDSON. Hvitträsk (1902), the studio home built by the partners near Helsinki, exemplifies the style with its picturesque composition of two large masses, a stone entrance tower, and steep red-tiled roofs.

In 1907 Eliel opened his own practice. His innovative design for the Helsinki Railway Station (1908–1914) brought international fame. The structure's solid mass has an austere arched entrance, a prominent stepped-form tower as an asymmetrical vertical accent, and

exposed concrete vaulting inside. He also focused on urban design, creating city plans for Revel, Estonia (1911–1913), and Canberra, Australia (1912), among others. Opposed to overcentralization, he promoted the development of satellite towns and greenbelts to separate city areas. Called the greatest living authority on city planning during his lifetime, Eliel saw the goal of architecture as the harmonious relationship of buildings and open space.

In 1923 Eliel came to the United States after his design won second prize in the Chicago Tribune Building competition. This design featured four setbacks in the upper half of an elegantly formed tower and influenced the evolution of modern skyscrapers. He established a practice in Ann Arbor, Michigan (1924–1950), and embarked on a second career in this more modernistic direction.

Eliel's greatest American project was the design and execution of a complex for Cranbrook Academy of Art and the associated boys' and girls' schools in Bloomfield Hills, Michigan (1926–1943). His concept of a harmonious environment was realized with an arrangement of quadrangles, courts, and open spaces highlighted by changes of scale, level, and view. The evolution of his style progresses from the picturesqueness of the Boys' School buildings surrounding multileveled courtyards (1926–1930) to the more modernist horizontal look and hipped roofs of the Kingswood School for Girls (1929–1930), with the influence of FRANK LLOYD WRIGHT.

Cranbrook had tremendous impact on modern architecture and design in general, not only through Saarinen's buildings and campus plan, but also through his roles as teacher, then president, of the Cranbrook Academy. In his humanist approach to design, he promoted the integration of all the arts and crafts, and stressed the unity of art and life, stating that the "province of the architect must include the design of communities on one end of the scale and the design of furniture and objects at the other. All must be related to each other and the times that produce them." To that end, he often designed the interiors, furniture, and other decorative elements for his buildings, or collaborated with other designers. At Kingswood his wife designed the rugs and wall hangings, his daughter designed the auditorium and dining hall interiors, and his son, Eero, designed the furniture. The Cranbrook Academy produced several noted designers, like CHARLES EAMES, Harry Bertoia, and Eliel's son.

Eero Saarinen was born in Kirkkonummi, Finland, and thrived in the artistic environment of Hvitträsk which was visited by such notables as composer Jean Sibelius and Russian writer Maxim Gorki. In addition to his famous father, his mother was a noted sculptor/weaver and his sister became an interior designer. After coming to America with his family, Eero lived at Cranbrook, studied sculpture in Paris (1929–1930), and received an architectural degree from Yale University (1934). He traveled and worked in Europe (1934–1936), then returned to Michigan, where he formed a design partnership with his father (1937–1941). The firm became Saarinen, Swanson & Saarinen with the addition of his brother-in-law, J. Robert F. Swanson (1941–1947), then changed to Saarinen, Saarinen & Associates (1947–1950).

Father and son designed several buildings together in a modernistic aesthetic, although they had different stylistic preferences. Eliel stressed form, materials, the picturesque, and chose the middle ground between the extremes of ornamentation and austerity, while Eero focused on function and plan, and was more attuned to modern technology, albeit interpreting it his own way. The fusion of their approaches is seen in the Tabernacle Church of Christ in Columbus, Indiana (1940–1942), with its articulated composition of grouped cubic blocks and freestanding campanile, picturesque sunken courtyard, and reflecting pool.

Eero became famous as an individual architect when he won a design competition for the Jefferson National Expansion Memorial in St. Louis (1948). The project, not completed until three years after his death, includes a park, two museums, open-air theater, tea terrace, frontier village, and five sculptural monuments, dominated by the giant stainless steel–covered Gateway Arch that has become the emblem of the city.

Another major commission was the General Motors Technical Center in Warren, Michigan, begun with his father (1948), but primarily Eero's design (with Smith, Hinchman & Grylls), completed in 1956. A radical departure in industrial design, the multibuilding complex is a glass and metal, brick and glass structure that is mirrored in the artificial pond, and a stainless steel water tower and low-slung dome as visual accents.

After his father's death, Eero formed his own firm, Eero Saarinen & Associates in Birmingham, Michigan, and became renowned for powerful sculptural designs and inventiveness, with each work representing an original response to that particular design challenge. Among the most famous of these works are the Kresge Auditorium, a huge domed triangle touching the ground at only three points, and the cylindrical brick chapel, both at the Massachusetts Institute of Technology, Cambridge (1953–1955), and the David S. Ingalls Hockey Rink at Yale University (1956–1959), with its spinelike concrete arch and swooping roof. His sculptural masterpieces, the Trans World Airlines Terminal at New York's J. F. Kennedy International Airport (1956–1962), with its soaring curves, and the main pavilion at Dulles International Airport, Chantilly, Virginia (1963), with its huge curved, cable-suspended roof sweeping between sloping concrete supports, were intended allusions to flight.

Eero was also one of the most important furniture designers of the century. In 1940 he designed an award-winning molded plywood chair with Charles Eames. The Womb chair (1946) and the Tulip chair (1957) became modern classics and introduced a new era of furniture design, shifting from geometric angularity to a freer, more sculptured style. The "womb" consisted of a comfortably proportioned, sculpted fiberglass shell hung by the arms from a substructure of steel rods; the "tulip" had a fiberglass shell mounted on a cast-aluminum pedestal stem with a flared circular base.

Eero died after brain surgery, at the height of his career. His last and perhaps finest design,

a skyscraper of black granite-faced triangular piers for CBS in New York, was completed after his death (1964).

BIBLIOGRAPHY

Christ-Janer, Albert, *Eliel Saarinen,* 1948; Kuhner, Robert A., *Eero Saarinen: His Life and Work,* 1975; Saarinen, Aline B. (ed.), *Eero Saarinen on His Work—A Selection of Buildings Dating from 1947–1964,* 1968; Saarinen, Eliel, *Search for Form—A Fundamental Approach to Art,* 1948; Spade, Rupert, *Eero Saarinen* 1971.

St. Denis, Ruth

(ca. January 20, 1878–July 21, 1968)
Dancer

Shawn, Edwin Myers

(October 21, 1891–January 9, 1972)
Choreographer, Dancer

Ruth St. Denis helped free dancers from ballet's restrictions and promoted modern dance in America. With her husband Ted Shawn, she founded Denishawn, the landmark school that trained U.S. dancers, and its company that spread the new gospel. Later Shawn established and directed the Jacob's Pillow Dance Festival near Lee, Massachusetts.

Ruth Dennis (her name was later changed to St. Denis by theatrical entrepreneur DAVID BELASCO) was born on a farm near Newark, New Jersey. The year of her birth is unclear, though St. Denis herself used the 1878 date. She began to dance and do theatrics early, and when an aunt intervened and sent her to the Northfield (Massachusetts) Seminary for Young Women in 1893, she clashed with founder and evangelist Dwight L. Moody over the theater, calling

him "a narrow-minded old bigot." She was home before Christmas.

The next year St. Denis and her mother moved to Manhattan, where the young woman found work in vaudeville. She had studied Delsarte techniques (the spiritual and geometrical codifications of body movement) with her physician mother, had a brush with ballet, and was gifted in theatrics. Four years later, in 1898, she was hired by David Belasco to dance in *Zaza.* St. Denis's five-year association with Belasco and his lavish productions made an indelible impression. Most characteristics of her later work—opulence, exotic locales and scenarios, generous scale, and emotionalism—stem from her observations of Belasco's ways with melodrama.

In 1903, while on tour with Belasco's *Madame DuBarry,* it is said St. Denis settled on a career as a dancer upon seeing a poster with an image of the Egyptian goddess Isis advertising cigarettes. For St. Denis, the goddess symbolized what she had been seeking, and for the rest of the tour she devoted herself to background research for *Egypta*. The prohibitive cost of production led her to try the less lavish *Radha*, a Hindu ballet, first performed in January 1906. Its success encouraged St. Denis to go abroad for what became a triumphal European tour.

St. Denis stayed overseas for three years, performing in England, Scotland, France, Belgium, Italy, Austria-Hungary, and Germany. She returned to the United States in 1909, produced *Egypta*, and began to travel the vaudeville circuit and to create other works, such as the Japanese ballet *O-Mika*.

In 1914 she met Ted Shawn. Born in Kansas City, Missouri, he grew up in Denver, Colorado. When he was attending the University of Denver to study for the ministry, he fell ill with diphtheria and was left partially paralyzed for over a year. The required body exercises for recovery became all-important to Shawn, and he left theology for the dance. In 1914 a tour landed him in New York. He met Ruth St. Denis, became her partner, and married her on August 13, 1914. They were to found the Denishawn school and the Denishawn dancers.

The Denishawn school offered classes in ballet, Oriental dance, primitive dance, movement techniques, and later German modern dance. The school's guiding principle was that all techniques and styles were worthy of study. From the main school in Los Angeles, where fees were collected in a cigar box, the enterprise grew, had branches in several cities, and opened Denishawn House in New York. Dancers who studied at Denishawn include MARTHA GRAHAM and Doris Humphrey.

Shawn served in the army in World War I and returned to Denishawn projects after the armistice. Denishawn dancers toured throughout the world for sixteen years, performing full-scale ballets, ensemble dances, pas de deux, and solos. Among the notable large-scale,

opulent, and always theatrical productions are *A Dance Pageant of Egypt, Greece, and India; Ishtar of the Seven Gates; Xochitl;* and *Job: A Masque for Dancing.* "Miss Ruth," as she was known to theater and dance folk, continued with Denishawn after her separation from Shawn at the end of the 1931–1932 season. The company's last performance with its two founders was in 1931.

St. Denis continued to perform and teach during the 1940s, exploring the connections between dance and religion and attempting to record her solos on film. She helped shape modern dance through the spiritual, exotic, and introspective aspects of her performance and employed movement that relied not on ballet but on motion found in acrobatics, ballroom dance, vaudeville, and musical theater. Active well into her eighties, she died in Hollywood, California, July 21, 1968.

Shawn's interest after 1933 centered on a campaign to establish the importance of male dancers. He developed dance technique for men and formed an all-male dance company. The group used Jacob's Pillow, an eighteenth-century farmhouse near Lee, Massachusetts, purchased by Shawn in 1931, as a summer base devoted to preparation for winter dance tours. Shawn's group of male dancers gave its last performance May 7, 1940. Shawn achieved his goal: men had their established place in the dance; male dancers commanded public respect.

In 1941 Shawn sold Jacob's Pillow because of financial difficulties. However, the purchasers, a corporation, hired him to direct a summer dance school and festival there, which he did until 1946. He returned as director in 1948. Jacob's Pillow has achieved international renown for its excellence, the variety of its programs, and its willingness to present new material and new dancers. Shawn danced well into the 1960s, though he performed less after he reached seventy. He died in Orlando, Florida, January 9, 1972.

By the 1960s, say dance critics Mary Clarke and Clement Crisp, both Ruth St. Denis and Ted Shawn could see the "rich harvest of modern dance which owed so much to their early labors in preparing America to understand and love a form of dance other than classical ballet—a form authentically American and an immensely influential expression of America itself."

BIBLIOGRAPHY

Shelton, S., *Divine Dancer: A Biography of Ruth St. Denis*, 1981; Terry, W., *Miss Ruth: The "More Living Life" of Ruth St. Denis*, 1969, and *Ted Shawn: Father of American Dance*, 1976.

Saint-Gaudens, Augustus

(March 1, 1848–August 3, 1907)
Sculptor

Augustus Saint-Gaudens, the dominant American sculptor of the late nineteenth and early twentieth centuries, is renowned for his public monuments and relief portraits. He changed the direction of this art with his vigorous naturalistic style and exerted tremendous influence on his contemporaries and a new generation of sculptors.

Although of French heritage, Saint-Gaudens was born in Dublin, Ireland, and brought to New York City while still an infant. At an early age he made drawings of the shoemakers as they worked in his father's shop. Encouraged in his artistic endeavors, Saint-Gaudens attended night classes at Cooper Union (1864–1866) and the National Academy of Design (1864–1866) while serving an apprenticeship with two cameo carvers. The oldest surviving example of his early sculptures is an 1867 bust of his father. In that year he went to Paris and started studies at the Petite Ecole before entering the prestigious Ecole des Beaux-Arts. With the outbreak of the Franco-Prussian War in 1870, he traveled to Rome, where he established a studio. (Later, he would divide his time between the Rome studio and others in Paris, New York City, and Cornish, New Hampshire.)

Saint-Gaudens was influenced by the vigor and realistic detail of naturalistic sculptures that he saw in Paris, by the works of Italian artist Donatello, and by the craftsmanship of Italian Renaissance relief sculptures (a type that projects from a background surface). He consolidated these influences and, combined with his own natural gifts, created a unique style that liberated American sculpture from the austere, restrained conventions of neoclassicism (revival of classical forms). He also encouraged in America the French-influenced shift from marble to bronze as the major medium of sculpture.

In 1881 he opened a studio on 36th Street in New York City. He later built a home and studios, which he called Aspet, in Cornish, New Hampshire, where he retreated every summer. His seminal work was the bronze and stone monument to the Civil War's Admiral David Farragut (1877–1881), which stands in New York's Madison Square Park. The figure is a stern, realistic standing portrait atop a sensuous base with symbolic female figures carved in relief. Saint-Gaudens's ability to blend the real and ideal into new sculptural imagery that expressed the spirit of the country made him a master interpreter of major American figures, at a time when an artist's genius was evaluated according to his skill at reflecting national ideals. His collaboration with architect STANFORD WHITE on the pedestal marked the beginning of a great professional and personal relationship between the men, and led to future collaboration with White's partners in the firm of McKim, Mead & White (see CHARLES FOLLEN McKIM).

Among Saint-Gaudens's other famous Civil War monuments are the standing *Abraham*

Lincoln (1887) and the seated *Lincoln* (1907) located in Chicago parks, the equestrian *General Sherman* (1897–1903) in New York City's Grand Army Plaza, and the *Memorial to Robert Gould Shaw* (1884–1897) in Boston. The Sherman monument, a dramatic presentation of Victory leading the surging horse carrying the bare-headed, confident general, epitomizes the sculptor's aim to capture the spirit of a subject's personality, as well as heroic symbolism, and won him the grand prize at the 1900 Paris Exposition.

Saint-Gaudens would read everything about a subject, or interview a living person, before beginning a piece in order to "build" his portrait from the inside out. The sensitive faces of the African American soldiers and the incredible sense of movement captured in the Shaw memorial exemplify his technical mastery of relief sculpting as well as his ability to create an intensely human historical record.

Saint-Gaudens became internationally known for his portrait reliefs, which comprise almost two-thirds of his works. His brilliant craftsmanship in subtly moving from high relief to low relief was exhibited in the early portrait *Mrs. Stanford White* (1884). With his famous relief portrait of author Robert Louis Stevenson (original bronze, 1887), Saint-Gaudens introduced the practice of issuing bronze sculptures in editions. For each cast, however, he changed various details, such as size, shape, color, and inscription placement, to create a unique version. He was an innovator in the creation of integral, decorative lettering as part of the total design.

Sometimes Saint-Gaudens departed from his usual naturalistic approach to create more abstract, subjective, and emotionally expressive works. His abstract masterpiece, the dramatic Adams memorial (1886–1891) in Rock Creek Cemetery, Washington, D.C., prefigures the dominance of the abstract in modern sculpture. The stark simplicity of the seated, enigmatic figure enshrouded in robes that conceal the face, set against a large stone, is powerfully evocative.

Throughout most of his career, Saint-Gaudens was preoccupied with the use of the mysterious "beyond," which left an indelible mark on his work. Often, this motif manifested itself in angelic figures representing such abstract concepts as love, as in the caryatids (supporting columns in the form of a draped woman's figure) *Amor* and *Pax* that he designed as mantlepiece supports for Cornelius Vanderbilt's home. The best representation of the theme is in the gilded bronze sculpture *Amor Caritas* (1898; several versions done between 1880 and 1898).

Simplicity was the hallmark of all his work, and his creed was "Conceive an idea. Then stick to it." Energetic, good-humored, and independent-minded, Saint-Gaudens also believed in discipline, high standards, and fine craftsmanship. He was a generous teacher and mentor to the promising young artists he brought into his studios, and taught at New York's Art Students League from 1888 to 1897. Influential in artistic circles, he joined with other sculptors to form the National Sculpture Society and was a founder of the Society of American Artists (1877). Much loved and honored worldwide, Saint-Gaudens counted such famous people as writers Robert Louis Stevenson and WILLIAM DEAN HOWELLS, artist John La Farge, and President Theodore Roosevelt among his friends. At the request of President Roosevelt he designed new U.S. coinage (1905–1907), which combined aspects of ancient Greek coins and Renaissance medals. Most famous was the $20 gold coin featuring Standing Liberty entitled "Double Eagle."

BIBLIOGRAPHY

Cortissoz, Royal, *Augustus Saint-Gaudens*, 1907; Dryfout, John H., *The Work of Augustus Saint-Gaudens*, 1982; Hall, Louise Tharp, *Saint-Gaudens and the Gilded Era*, 1969; Saint-Gaudens, Homer (ed.), *The Reminiscences of Augustus Saint-Gaudens*, 2 vols., rep., 1976.

Sandburg, Carl

(January 6, 1878–July 22, 1967)
Biographer, Poet

The twentieth-century poet Carl Sandburg wrote simple verse that celebrated the life of the common person and the values Sandburg associated with America as a democracy. The same interests led him to write a massive and impressive six-volume biography of Abraham Lincoln.

Sandburg was born of Swedish immigrant parents in Galesburg, Illinois. His boyhood hero was Abraham Lincoln, who had engaged in one of his historic debates with Stephen A. Douglas at nearby Knox College in 1858. Sandburg attended the public school in Galesburg until he was thirteen, then went to work driving a milk wagon. He subsequently worked as a porter in a barber shop, a house painter, and a dishwasher. When the Spanish-American War started in 1898, he enlisted and saw five months' service in Puerto Rico.

When he returned from the war, Sandburg enrolled in Lombard College (now part of Knox College) from 1898 until 1902. His mentor, Philip Green Wright, printed on a press in his basement fifty copies of Sandburg's slim first volume of verse, *In Reckless Ecstasy* (1904).

Sandburg traveled as a sales representative of stereopticon equipment and slides. After serving as an editor at the *Lyceumite* magazine in Chicago, he became involved as a district organizer for the Social-Democratic party in Wisconsin. He worked as a reporter for a succession of Milwaukee newspapers and as secretary to the first socialist mayor of Milwaukee from 1910 to 1912.

Library of Congress

In 1908 he married Lillian Steichen, the sister of photographer EDWARD STEICHEN, of whom he later wrote a biography, *Steichen, The Photographer* (1929).

In 1912 Sandburg returned to Chicago, continuing his newspaper career and working hard at his poetry. He published his *Chicago Poems* in 1916 and *Cornhuskers* two years later. These poems, written in free verse, portrayed the American scene. Stylistically, they varied from the energetic "Chicago" to the more delicate "Fog." Both volumes were popular with fellow poets and the general public.

During World War I, Sandburg was sent to Sweden as a correspondent by the Newspaper Enterprise Association. Upon his return, he worked as a reporter at the Chicago *Daily News* for thirteen years. He also wrote furiously, publishing four volumes of poetry during the 1920s: *Smoke and Steel* (1920), *Slabs of the Sunburnt West* (1922), *Selected Poems* (1926), and *Good Morning, America* (1928).

The first two volumes of Sandburg's monumental six-volume biography of Abraham Lincoln appeared as *Abraham Lincoln: The Prairie Years* in 1926. The four-volume *Abraham Lincoln: The War Years* appeared in 1939. The latter installment won Sandburg the Pulitzer Prize for History and portrayed Lincoln as the epitome of the American spirit.

The People, Yes, a long poem comprised of free verse, mixed with bits of narrative and folk sayings, appeared in 1936. His only novel, *Remembrance Rock,* appeared in 1948 and was not a critical success. It was followed four years later, however, by an impressive autobiography, *Always the Young Strangers.* Sandburg's *Complete Poems* (1950) won him a second Pulitzer Prize. Subsequent volumes included *Harvest Poems, 1910–1960* (1960), *Six New Poems and a Parable* (1961), and *Honey and Salt* (1963).

Always inspired by American history and lore, Sandburg was close to being a "national" poet. The prolific and much beloved writer died in his ninetieth year.

BIBLIOGRAPHY

Allen, Gay Wilson, *Carl Sandburg,* 1972; Callahan, North, *Carl Sandburg: His Life and Works,* 1987; Crowder, Richard, *Carl Sandburg,* 1963; Niven, Penelope, *Carl Sandburg: A Biography,* 1991; Sandburg, Carl, *Always the Young Strangers,* 1953, rep., 1991.

Sargent, John Singer

(January 12, 1856–April 4, 1925)
Painter

John Singer Sargent painted outdoor scenes and decorative murals, but he was most famous for his brilliant portraits of theatrical personalities, fashionable women, and children.

Sargent was born in Florence, Italy, to American parents living in Europe. His father had been a doctor in Philadelphia, and his mother was an amateur painter and musician. Young Sargent began the study of art when he was twelve with the landscapist Carl Welsch in Rome and at fourteen at the Accademia delle Belle Arti in Florence. He kept a sketchbook record of travels with his family in France, Spain, Germany, and Switzerland.

In 1874 the Sargents moved to Paris, where the young man studied anatomy, perspective, and decorative design at the Ecole des Beaux-Arts. He soon left the school to study with the painter Emile Auguste Carolus-Duran, who taught him to admire the work of Velázquez, the Spanish painter, above all others. Sargent was Carolus-Duran's most capable student, soon surpassing his teacher.

After Sargent paid his first visit to America in 1876, he returned to France and painted pictures that soon helped make him famous. In 1876 he painted *Gitana* and *Rehearsal of the Pasdeloup Orchestra at the Cirque d'Hiver* and in 1877 he sent his first picture, a portrait of a Miss Fanny Watts, to the Paris Salon, the annual government-sponsored exhibition of contemporary art.

In 1878 he painted *The Oyster Gatherers of Cancale,* which shows a group of women and children with baskets on a beach in Brittany. Working out of doors, Singer demonstrated a skill with light and color that rivaled that of the French Impressionist painters, who concentrated on catching the effect of light out of doors. In 1878 Sargent traveled to Capri and in 1879 to Spain, where he made sketches for *El Jaleo* (1882), which depicted a Spanish dancer and guitar players.

The Daughters of Edward D. Boit (1882), a masterpiece of interior painting of his early years, portrays four young sisters in pinafores. One leans against a tall vase; two stand with their hands behind their backs; the youngest sits on the rug with her toys. Called *Portraits d'Enfants,* it hung in the Salon of 1883 and in the Paris Exposition of 1889.

In 1884 his *Madame X* created a scandal at the Salon. Critics and the public alike condemned it for its overt sensuality. The portrait was of Madame Pierre Gautreau, a celebrated beauty, wearing a low-cut black velvet gown that revealed much lavender-powdered skin. Sargent was surprised and offended by the uproar. The sitter had chosen the dress herself, but Madame Gautreau hated the portrait and her mother asked Sargent to remove it from the show. Sargent refused.

Because of the episode, Sargent moved to London, where critics also found fault with his pictures. One newspaper said that a poll judged Sargent's *The Misses Vickers* (1884) to be the worst picture in the exhibition of the Royal Academy. Still, Sargent's portraits, stylish and elegant compared to work of the English portraitists, became very popular with patrons, and he soon had all the commissions he could handle.

In London he painted one of his most famous pictures, *Carnation, Lily, Lily, Rose* (1885–1886), in which two little girls dressed in white light Japanese lanterns in a twilight flower garden. While working on this painting, Sargent found that the light was right for him only twenty minutes each day. He worked two years on the painting, to capture the sense of happiness as well as the colors and light of a summer evening.

In the late 1880s Sargent became a friend of Claude Monet, leader of the French Impressionist painters, and visited him at his home in Giverny. While there he painted a picture of Monet painting outdoors.

In 1887 Sargent went to the United States to paint portraits. Mrs. Isage Newton Phelps Stokes came to his studio straight from the tennis court, and Sargent painted her, vibrant and smiling, in her tennis dress of a floor-length white duck skirt, shirt, tie, and tailored jacket. (Mr. Phelps Stokes was painted in the background as an afterthought.)

His work became so popular in America that Sargent returned to Boston almost every year, even establishing a second studio in Boston. The Boston Museum of Fine Arts bought several of his watercolors, and he did mural decorations for the Boston Public Library, a building designed by McKim, Mead & White (see CHARLES FOLLEN McKIM). Sargent decided to use as the theme of the murals the development of religious thought from paganism through Judaism to Christianity. (He made research trips to Egypt, Greece, and Jerusalem and spent more than thirty years on the project.)

In England in 1889 he painted actress Ellen Terry as Lady Macbeth. He also did portraits of actors EDWIN BOOTH and Joseph Jefferson in 1890 and of Ada Rehan, the actress, in 1894.

Sargent painted many other portraits, but a great favorite with the public has been *The Wyndham Sisters* (1899), which shows Madeline, Pamela, and Mary, the three beautiful, slender daughters of Percy Scawen Wyndham, wearing white dresses, their hair piled on top of their heads. When King Edward VII saw the painting, he cried, "The three graces!" and that became its informal name.

In 1918, while World War I raged, the British government asked Sargent to go to the battlefields in France to record his impressions. After the war, the government asked him to paint a group portrait of the twenty-two members of the British General Staff, which he titled *Some General Officers of the Great War* (1920–1922).

BIBLIOGRAPHY

Fairbrother, Trevor J., *John Singer Sargent and America*, 1986; Olson, Stanley, *John Singer Sargent: His Portrait*, 1986.

Schoenberg, Arnold Franz Walter

(September 13, 1874–July 13, 1951)
Composer

The musical language that Arnold Schoenberg was heir to—that of Wagner, Brahms, and Mahler—had been becoming ever more chromatic, its sense of tonal center or key ever more in flux. As his ear led him even further in this direction, his mind was constantly searching for new ways to make his musical language more coherent and graspable. His eventual solution, twelve-tone technique, constituted a new musical syntax and made him, along with his rival and opposite, IGOR STRAVINSKY, one of the two major forces in twentieth-century composition.

Born in Vienna, Austria, Arnold Schoenberg began to study violin in 1882, taught himself cello, and early on began to compose. Alexander von Zemlinsky instructed the young musician in counterpoint for a few months, Schoenberg's only formal instruction in composition.

Steeped in Viennese tradition, Schoenberg reflected the surrounding romanticism in his early works, a string quartet (1897) and the 1899 string sextet *Verklärte Nacht* (Transfigured Night). In 1900 a performance of his songs caused protest. "And ever since that day," he said, "the scandal has never ceased." The scandal was provoked by the way Schoenberg pushed established musical boundaries to explore chromaticism. By 1908 his compositions seemed even more foreign to a musical world pervaded by the romanticism of Wagner and Liszt.

Schoenberg moved to Berlin in 1901 and supported himself by conducting operettas and music hall revues. He completed *Gurrelieder,* his huge cantata for voices and orchestra, that year (the score needed so many staves that special music paper had to be printed for him). Richard Strauss was impressed with Schoenberg's work and helped him obtain a teaching position at the Stern Conservatory in Berlin. Schoenberg taught theory and composition there from 1902 to 1903. In 1903 Schoenberg moved back to Vienna, where he gathered disciples like composers Alban Berg and Anton von Webern and pianists Edward Steuermann and Rudolf Serkin. Their support was invaluable as each new Schoenberg work brought storms of criticism. That same year, he finished *Pelleas und Melisande,* a tone poem.

Inspired by the artists Wassily Kandinsky, Oskar Kokoschka, and Paul Klee, Schoenberg began to paint. An exhibition of his work in 1910 documented his considerable artistic talent and represented the Expressionist style, a style that focused on inner experience as the supreme reality and often rejected what had once been considered beautiful. Expressionist painters were active in Germany, many involved with the Blaue Reiter (Blue Rider) group, and interested in pursuing new artistic directions, particularly in regard to technical innovations. The linkage between the arts of painting, composition, and writing was important to the innovations that developed in each field.

Schoenberg himself moved toward rejection of conventional tonality and created his own brand of musical expressionism. "There is only one greatest goal," he wrote, "towards which the artist strives: to express himself." *Five Orchestral Pieces* (1909) illustrates this philosophy. Descriptive titles like "Vorgefühle" (Premonitions) suggest what is to come. The composition bears no key signature and is built on intricate, many-voiced textures, fluctuating rhythms, quicksilver melodies, and the tensions of unresolved dissonances. By 1911 he was in Berlin again, composing and conducting. *Gurrelieder* had its first performance in Berlin in 1913 and was well received.

In the years just before World War I, Schoenberg's music had already become fully chromatic—that is, each of the twelve tones of the chromatic scale had an equal role rather than having some notes heard as members of the diatonic scale of the going key, while others were heard as raised or lowered versions of diatonic members. Indeed, the sense of key or tonal center was kept in constant flux, so as to be fleeting at best. Having abandoned the traditional harmonic formulas of eighteenth- and nineteenth-century music, Schoenberg increasingly relied on motivic procedures. By using the same or similar configurations of intervals in many guises—to form chords, or melodies, or to govern the relationship between a chord and a melody—he created a sense of coherence and connectedness. Although tonal composers had used such techniques (and Schoenberg was always quick to show how it was the greatest of them—Bach, Mozart, Beethoven, and Brahms—who did so most cunningly), in Schoenberg's hands they came to have a governing force that took the place of tonality.

In 1915 Schoenberg returned to Austria; though he was past forty, he was called up for military service. In the years immediately following the war, Schoenberg appears to have completed no new pieces, but instead concentrated his efforts on rationalizing his compositional procedures into a kind of general method. In this "method for composing with twelve tones which are related only to one another," as Schoenberg referred to it, each tone of the chromatic scale is thought of in terms of the relationships it can form with any of the other eleven rather than in terms of its relation to a single privileged tone, the tonic or central tone. Basic to the method is the idea of the "tone row," which is simply a particular ordering of all twelve tones. This row may be transformed without losing its inherent intervallic shape by transposing it, by turning it backward, by turning it upside down, or by turning it upside down and backward. The resulting forty-eight transformations function as a common source for all the motivic configurations—the melodies, the chords, and their combinations—in the piece. Each piece has its own row, and the intervallic structure of that row takes the syntactic place of the intervallic structure of triads and scales

in tonal music. Although other composers of the time had been working along similar lines, it was, in the words of Joseph Machlis, Schoenberg "who set the seal of his personality upon this development, and who played the crucial role in creating a new grammar and syntax of musical speech."

By 1923 Schoenberg had composed the first work to use the new method, the Five Piano Pieces, and by 1924 his first piece to use it throughout, the Suite for Piano, op. 25. A host of other compositions followed as he explored the new method.

In 1926 Schoenberg traveled to Berlin again to take over the composition master class at the Prussian Academy of Arts, but he was dismissed from his post by order of the Nazi government in 1933.

He went first to France, where he returned to the Jewish faith (he had become a Roman Catholic in 1921), and then, when he was offered a position at the new Malkin Conservatory in Boston, Massachusetts, to America. Daunted by his first New England winter, he moved to Los Angeles in the fall of 1934. By 1936 he was a full-time professor at the University of California, Los Angeles, and in 1941 he became a naturalized American citizen.

By 1944 Schoenberg's health began to fail, but he continued to teach until his retirement at the mandatory age of seventy. Because his pension was so small, he continued to give private lessons and in 1946 lectured at the University of Chicago. That year, after a violent asthma attack, his heart stopped. He was revived but never fully recovered. In 1947 he was elected a member of the American Academy of Arts and Letters but could not attend the ceremony. He was still composing, however, and completed a textbook, *Structural Functions of Harmony,* in 1948. He taught one summer at the University of California, Santa Barbara (1948), but essentially he remained an invalid until he died in Los Angeles on July 13, 1951.

Schoenberg's works during his years in the United States have a kind of repose and sense of retrospection that is a far cry from his early expressionism. Some even return to traditional tonality. The String Quartet no. 4, op. 37 (1936) and the Piano Concerto, op. 42 (1942) belong to this period, along with the powerful *Survivor from Warsaw*, op. 46 (1947), the String Trio, op. 45 (1946), and the Fantasia for Violin and Piano, op. 47 (1949).

Schoenberg had a profound effect on his American students from Marc Blitzstein to JOHN CAGE and Oscar Levant. Two nonstudents, MILTON BABBITT and Robert Craft, have furthered Schoenberg's work: Babbitt as teacher and theorist, Craft as conductor and advocate. The Arnold Schoenberg Institute, established in 1974, houses the composer's manuscripts and memorabilia and publishes a journal.

Schoenberg's music is usually described as atonal. He rejected the term saying, "I regard the expression atonal as meaningless," and suggested the word "pantonal," noting that his work was aimed at the "synthesis of all tonalities," the interrelationship of all tones. However, "atonal" is the term that prevailed.

BIBLIOGRAPHY

Boretz, B., and E. Cone, *Perspectives on Schoenberg and Stravinsky*, 1968, rev., 1972; Macdonald, M., *Schoenberg*, 1976; Rosen, C., *Arnold Schoenberg*, 1975; Schoenberg, A., *Style and Idea*, 1950.

Schwartz, Delmore David

(December 8, 1913–July 11, 1966)
Dramatist, Poet, Short-Story Writer

With his first book, *In Dreams Begin Responsibilities*, Delmore Schwartz achieved precocious success as both a short-story writer and a poet whose work was rooted in the experience of his Jewish immigrant family. His subsequent failure led to tragedy and the making of a literary legend.

Schwartz was born in Brooklyn, New York, the son of immigrants from Romania. His troubled family life became the subject of much of his later poetry, especially the vicious arguments that led to his parents' divorce when he was fourteen. Schwartz knew early that he wanted to become a poet, and he kept voluminous journals.

Schwartz attended the University of Wisconsin for a year before enrolling at New York University, where he earned a bachelor's degree in philosophy in 1935. While an undergraduate, he helped edit a Marxist literary magazine, *Mosaic*. He enrolled in graduate study in philosophy at Harvard University in 1935 but left after two years without completing a degree.

In 1937 Schwartz's work began to appear in *Poetry* and *Partisan Review*. He received high praise, even comparison with the poet W. H. AUDEN. When his first book appeared the following year, it was recognized immediately for its precocious brilliance.

In Dreams Begin Responsibilities (1938) includes a short story, a play, and several poems. The title story evokes a Coney Island film house, where the narrator observes the couple who will marry and become his parents; seeing signs of the alienation that would eventually ruin their marriage, he tries to prevent their engagement. "The Heavy Bear Who Goes with Me," one of Schwartz's most anthologized poems, concerns the poet's alienation, which extends even to his own body. "Prothalamion" helped break ground for such confessional poets as JOHN BERRYMAN and ROBERT LOWELL. "The Ballad of the Children of the Czar" remembers Schwartz's family's roots in Eastern Europe.

Schwartz struggled to live up to his early reputation. However, subsequent work received consistently negative reviews, including a 1939 translation of Arthur Rimbaud's *A Season in Hell;* a verse play, *Shenandoah* (1941); an epic poem, *Genesis: Book One* (1943); and a collection of poems, *Vaudeville for a Princess* (1950). Only *Summer Knowledge: New and Selected Poems, 1938–1958* (1959), which contained a number of poems from *In Dreams Begin Responsibilities,* as well as the often-praised "Seurat's Sunday Afternoon Along the Seine," fared better: it won Schwartz the Bollingen Prize in 1960. He was the youngest person to have received the prize.

Schwartz worked as an editor at *Partisan Review* from 1943 to 1955 and as poetry editor at the *New Republic* from 1953 to 1957. He taught at Harvard, New York, and Princeton universities before becoming a professor of English at Syracuse University from 1962 to 1966.

Schwartz was driven to distraction by an overwhelming sense of failure. His body became ravaged by years of dependence on alcohol, plus barbiturates to sleep and amphetamines to wake up. His life ended tragically in a rundown hotel in New York City, where he suffered a heart attack on July 11, 1966. The poet was memorialized in John Berryman's *His Toy, His Dream, His Rest* (1968) and as the model for writer Von Humboldt Fleischer in SAUL BELLOW's novel *Humboldt's Gift* (1975).

BIBLIOGRAPHY

Atlas, James, *Delmore Schwartz: The Life of an American Poet,* 1977; McDougall, Richard, *Delmore Schwartz,* 1974; Pallett, Elizabeth (ed.), *Portrait of Delmore,* 1986.

Scorsese, Martin

(November 17, 1942–   )
Film Director

Martin Scorsese, like Francis Ford Coppola, George Lucas, and Steven Spielberg, belongs to the "film school" generation of directors, whose passion for and knowledge of film history inspired them to become filmmakers. His best films—including *Mean Streets* and *Raging Bull*—trace the torturous journey of a protagonist through violence to redemption.

He was born in Flushing, New York, into an Italian Catholic family. Scorsese's parents, Charles and Catherine, both worked in the garment industry. The family moved back to Little Italy in Manhattan, where Martin attended Old St. Patrick's School. Prevented from playing sports because of asthma, he spent countless hours at the movies. In 1956 he attended Cathedral College, intending to study for the priesthood, but transferred to Cardinal Hayes High School, from which he graduated with honors.

Scorsese majored in film at both undergraduate and graduate levels at New

The Museum of Modern Art/Film Stills Archive

York University, where he also taught briefly. After several short films, his first feature, *Who's That Knocking at My Door?* premiered at the Chicago Film Festival in 1967. In 1971 he moved to Hollywood, where he directed *Boxcar Bertha* (1972) for producer Roger Corman.

His first major work, *Mean Streets,* premiered at the New York Film Festival in 1973, receiving excellent reviews and placing Scorsese in the forefront of new American directors. His next, *Alice Doesn't Live Here Anymore* (1974), won Ellen Burstyn an Oscar for Best Actress. *Taxi Driver* (1976), for which he won a Golden Palm Award at the Cannes Film Festival, brought international fame for him and actor Robert De Niro, whose chilling performance as the psychotic Travis Bickle brought him instant stardom.

Scorsese's work is deeply personal. The moral and psychological conflicts of his characters are reflections of his own need to "exorcise the demons of my psyche." His style is an amalgam of the Hollywood studio films he so loved, the neorealism of Italian cinema, and the urban realism and improvisational look of American independents like John Cassavetes. When he successfully translates his personal obsessions into these cinematic terms, the results are powerful.

Often his moving camera and expressionist style reflect the state of mind of disturbed characters. In *Taxi Driver,* New York is awash in lurid colors and lights and slow tracking shots through seedy nighttime streets, the whole atmosphere a projection of Travis Bickle's distorted perspective. In what many believe his best film, *Raging Bull* (1980), the story of boxer Jake LaMotta, the moral myopia of the character is mirrored in the black-and-white photography, and the hyperrealism and

slow motion of the brutal fight scenes are commensurate with the outsized ego of the protagonist. In both films De Niro's intense performances complement the heightened uses of mise-en-scène.

Performance is of central importance in Scorsese's films. Actors often improvise behavior and dialogue that become part of the film. *The King of Comedy* (1983) is as much about De Niro's performative qualities as it is about the exhibitionism of its eccentric protagonist. Scorsese himself appears briefly in a number of his films, most memorably as a passenger in *Taxi Driver.*

Some of Scorsese's commercial successes are his least impressive works. Neither *The Color of Money* (1986), which won Paul Newman the Best Actor Oscar, nor *Cape Fear* (1991), a box-office hit, are considered among his best films. Conversely, two of his most personal works—*New York, New York* (1977), a loving evocation of the Hollywood musical, and *The Last Temptation of Christ* (1988), his adaptation of Nikos Kazantzakis's controversial novel—were disappointingly received. The latter drew intense criticism from religious groups for its all too human portrayal of Christ.

Other critically acclaimed films include *The Last Waltz* (1978), a lyrical documentary on the rock group The Band, and *Goodfellas* (1990), a violent adaptation of a memoir about the Mafia.

BIBLIOGRAPHY

Kelly, Mary Pat, *Martin Scorsese: The First Decade,* 1980, and *Martin Scorsese: A Journey,* 1991; Keyser, Les, *Martin Scorsese,* 1992; Kolker, Robert Philip, *A Cinema of Loneliness,* 1980; Thompson, David (ed.), *Scorsese on Scorsese,* 1989.

Segal, George

(November 26, 1924–   )
Sculptor

George Segal gained international fame for his life-sized cast-plaster figures frozen in everyday moments and often set in commonplace, assembled environments like a diner or phone booth. The dominance of abstract idioms in modern American sculpture of the 1960s and 1970s put Segal's reality-based works, with links to Pop art and Environmental art, in a unique position.

Segal was born in New York City, but moved with his family to South Brunswick, New Jersey, in 1940. After studying at Cooper Union, Rutgers University, and Pratt Institute (1941–1947), he received an art education degree from New York University (1949) and an M.F.A. degree from Rutgers (1963). In 1950 he bought a chicken farm near the family spread, pursued painting, and taught art in various New Jersey high schools (1957–1964). Exhibits of his paintings at New York's Hansa Gallery (1956, 1957) revealed Segal's conflict between the prevailing Abstract Expressionist style (see BARNETT NEWMAN), which emphasized an artist's subjective feelings, and his own impulse toward representational figures. He stated that he was drawn to sensual things, "things I could touch."

During the late 1950s, Segal shifted his interest to sculpture, influenced by sculptor Allan Kaprow and his staged "Happenings." These plotless, collaborative events, which achieved prominence in the 1950s and 1960s in the New York area, sought to synthesize theater and the visual arts, inviting public involvement. Happenings actively combined real people and real objects in living environments, thus creating a "total art environment," which intrigued Segal. He began experimenting in plaster on wire mesh and burlap to produce primitive sculptures, then created his seminal work, *Man Sitting at a Table* (1961), composed of a figure reconstructed from a plaster cast of his own body.

Segal gained widespread acclaim when his plaster figures in real-life situations were shown as part of the New Realists (Pop art) exhibit at New York's Sidney Janis Gallery in 1962. He has been linked to the Pop art movement (see ROY LICHTENSTEIN), the creation of art based on mass-produced images and everyday objects, through his use of real objects and real settings. However, his desire to penetrate into real space and populate it with his own creations distinguishes him from Pop art style. Segal also worked on a psychological plane, seeking to explore the "mystery" of how people relate to shapes and objects in "the intimacy of daily life." A hallmark of his style is the expressiveness of his white "phantomlike" figures: he captures characteristic body stances as in *Woman Shaving Her Leg* (1963) and revelatory psychological gestures like the sagging bodies in the *Depression Bread Line* series.

Using a direct casting method, Segal makes plaster casts of the head, torso, and legs of a real person, then assembles the sections, altering the surfaces. After 1960 he often incorporated fragments from the real environment of the model in order to explore the tension between the real and the created, and the spatial relationship of figures to their surroundings. *The Butcher Shop* (1965), inspired by his father's Bronx store, combines a real butcher's block with plaster-cast chickens and a plaster-cast, knife-wielding figure modeled by his mother. One of his famous works, *Cinema* (1963), shows an early use of electrical illumination. Inspired by an actual city scene, the sculpture shows a plaster figure removing the last letter from a back-lit Plexiglas theater marquee.

Segal was also noted for his compositions containing two or more figures in minimally defined real environments, such as *The Diner* (1964–1966). In this tableau the white plaster figures of a waitress and a male customer are isolated in the context of a Formica counter, coffee urn, fluorescent light, and other props. The scene's ambiguous yet powerful presence envelopes the spectator, eliciting feelings of identification and distancing. Segal's tableaux are linked to Environmental art through his attempt to obliterate barriers between art and life.

Segal's sculptures became more lifelike during the 1970s. He achieved greater physical detail by making casts of the insides of his plaster molds, instead of casts of the rough-textured, "bandaged" outer shells of his earlier works. More detailed figures and suggested movement add to the impact of *Times Square at Night* (1970) with its white plaster figures striding in front of illuminated movie and restaurant signs. In *Resting Dancer* (1984) Segal used color to integrate the figure in a more painterly way with the props and setting. The blue-painted figure reclines on a red-painted stool against a deeper blue, textured wall.

Many of his later works (from 1980 onward) are designed for site-specific installations, such as *The Commuters* in New York's Port Authority Bus Terminal and *The Holocaust* (1983) in San Francisco's Lincoln Park. He also works with fragments of figures, as in *Nude in Doorway* (1984), which is a wall piece composed of half a painted plaster nude seen through a doorway. He also continues to paint and exhibit large, figurative canvases done in pastels.

Segal's figures in their environmental sets have been variously described as "human museums," "petrified happenings," "pseudo-living," and "gestures frozen in time." His figures often evoke feelings of sadness, the spiritual isolation and alienation of modern humanity.

BIBLIOGRAPHY

Glueck, Grace, "George Segal's Plaster People," *New York Times*, April 27, 1984; Henri, A., *Environments and Happenings*, 1974; Seitz, William C., *George Segal*, 1972; Zeiffer, Ellen, "George Segal: Sculptural Environments," *American Artist*, January 1975.

Sendak, Maurice

(June 10, 1928–   )
Author, Illustrator, Opera Designer

Maurice Sendak is the author of the children's book *Where the Wild Things Are* and the first American illustrator to win the international Hans Christian Andersen Award.

Sendak was the third child of Sarah and Philip Sendak, both immigrants who had come to New York from Warsaw. He was frail and sickly and a bit of a loner, but he found escape in adventure books, the imaginative bedtime tales told him by his father, and the image of Mickey Mouse on the neighborhood movie screens. Many of his later books, like *Kenny's Window* and *Very Far Away*, would reflect his childhood loneliness.

By the age of ten he was writing and illustrating his own stories. After desultory high school years (he was only interested in drawing), he went to work in 1945 for All-American Comics, where he filled in the backgrounds for the *Mutt and Jeff* strip. A year later, he designed window displays for several stores in New York City, including F. A. O. Schwartz, in whose children's book department he would make many influential contacts. Through an editor at Harper and Brothers, he got the commission to illustrate his first book, *The Wonderful Farm* (1951), by Marcel Ayme. Among the books for Harper that followed, *A Hole Is to Dig* (1952), written by Ruth Krauss, was one of the most important. It was thoroughly Sendakian—organized around children's definitions of the details of their world, printed on brown paper, and executed in the cross-hatch pen-and-ink style reminiscent of nineteenth-century wood engravings that was to become one of his stylistic trademarks.

Now working as a full-time free-lance illustrator, Sendak took on many projects by other writers, such as a series of books by Meindert DeJong (*Shadrach*, 1953, *The Wheel on the School*, 1954, *The Singing Hill*, 1962, etc.), Ruth Krauss's *Charlotte and the White Horse* (1955), Else Holmelund Minarik's *Little Bear* books, Doris Orgel's *Sarah's Room* (1963), and stories by Hans Christian Andersen and Clemens Brentano. His first book as both writer and illustrator was the classic *Kenny's Window* (1956). It established the prototypical Sendakian hero, a child entangled in worlds of dream and reality. Other solo efforts followed: *The Sign on Rosie's Door (1960)*, the *Nutshell Library* series, and his greatest success to date, *Where the Wild Things Are* (1963).

In this tale, Max, a small boy banished to his room for misbehaving, sails away on an imaginary trip to a fantastic land where he conquers larger-than-human, wild, outlandish creatures, drawn in pen and ink with horns, beaks, claws, pointed teeth, and rolling yellow eyes, then returns to the comfort of his room, "where someone loved him best of all."

Since then, the indefatigable Sendak has produced more of his own stories, such as the autobiographical *Higglety Pigglety Pop!* (1967) and *In the Night Kitchen* (1970), as well as collaborations (he calls them "participations") with classic tales by George MacDonald and the Brothers Grimm. He has written screenplays and drawn storyboards of his works for animated films, designed the ballet of *The Nutcracker* (filmed by Carroll Ballard), and several operas, including his own *Where the Wild Things Are*, Mozart's *The Goose from Cairo* and *The Magic Flute*, and Prokofiev's *Love for Three Oranges*.

BIBLIOGRAPHY

Lanes, Selma G., *The Art of Maurice Sendak*, 1980.

Sennett, Mack

(January 17, 1880–November 5, 1960)
Film Director, Producer

Mack Sennett, creator of the Keystone Kops and purveyor of the pie-in-the-face brand of slapstick, was the first important comic figure in film history. Legendary stars CHARLIE CHAPLIN, Mabel Normand, Ben Turpin, Roscoe ("Fatty") Arbuckle, and Marie Dressler all appeared in Sennett's films.

He was born Michael Sinnott in Quebec to Irish Catholic parents. Sennett had little formal education and dreamed of being a singer. When he was seventeen, the family moved to Con-

necticut, where his father worked as a contractor, his mother ran a boarding house, and he worked in an iron works. When the family moved again to Massachusetts, he was determined on a stage career. Actress Marie Dressler, in local theater at the time, referred him to playwright/impresario DAVID BELASCO, who advised him to try burlesque.

Sennett made his stage debut at the Bowery Theater Burlesque in New York as the hind end of a horse. He learned that mocking authority was a sure way to get laughs, an idea he later developed in his Keystone comedies.

As Mack Sennett, he worked at the Biograph studios in New York as actor and writer for director D. W. GRIFFITH, an experience he described as "my day school, my adult education program, my university." After some leading parts, he directed his first one-reel comedy, *One Round O'Brien*, in 1911 and was given his own comedy unit.

Unsatisfied, he welcomed an offer from Adam Kessel and Charles Bauman, who wanted to start a film company strictly for comedies. The Keystone Film Company was established in 1912, and Sennett arrived in Los Angeles as managing director with total authority over talent, scripts, and footage.

His first stars were Fred Mace, Ford Sterling, and Mabel Normand, all of whom had worked at Biograph. Normand, the most talented female comic of the time, was romantically involved with Sennett, but they never married.

Distributed through the Mutual Film Corporation, Keystone comedies were immediately successful with audiences and exhibitors. In the days before Chaplin, BUSTER KEATON, and Harold Lloyd, they became the standard of film comedy. While many of their slapstick routines were indebted to French farces—like those of Georges Méliès—Keystone added time-tested burlesque formulas, such as perilous situations, coincidence, and disguise, to satirize authority figures and social pretensions.

A favorite target were the police. At first, one or two policemen were the butt of a gag, but soon there were seven Keystone Kops. This exemplified one of Sennett's guiding principles:

"If one of a kind is funny, more than one is funnier." Undoubtedly, the Kops were Sennett's major contribution to Americana; not only do they symbolize the era of silent comedy, but their name is still evoked to describe nonsensical action in films like *It's a Mad, Mad, Mad, Mad World* (1963).

Oblivious to official orders and rarely acting as a unit, the Kops created perennial chaos, further enhanced by the acceleration of action through camera speed and editing. In addition to the cross-cutting methods he learned from Griffith, Sennett removed every third or fourth frame from the filmstrip, causing that jerky motion so characteristic of Keystone chase sequences.

The actors who played the Kops performed dangerous stunts without doubles. Snub Pollard said, "I've been bathed in ten tons of very wet cement. . . . I'd caught about fourteen thousand pies in my puss and had been hit by six hundred automobiles and two trains. Once I was even kicked by a giraffe."

By 1915 Sennett had virtually every important comic in the business, but he often overlooked or underappreciated genuine talent. He missed out on Harold Lloyd and at first did not appreciate Arbuckle's talents, although he and Normand became Keystone's most popular couple. He completely underestimated Chaplin, who spent his year at Keystone complaining that he was being misdirected.

Chaplin appeared in a dozen Keystones and directed himself in more than twenty others. His last Keystone appearance was in *Tillie's Punctured Romance* (1914), directed by Sennett and starring Marie Dressler, although it is revived as an early Chaplin film. At six reels this was Sennett's first attempt at feature-length comedy, which he saw the advantages of long before it became the norm.

In late 1915 Triangle Pictures became Keystone's distributor and expanded the company's facilities, making it the biggest comedy studio in the industry. In 1916, his last year at Keystone, Sennett introduced his Bathing Beauties, a lineup of attractive women in daring (for the time) swimsuits. Admittedly a publicity gimmick, a few stars, including Gloria Swanson, emerged from this. In the same year Ben Turpin became Keystone's biggest star, but left to work with Sennett in the following decade.

By mid-1917, as a result of further power struggles, the Keystone Comedy was effectively dead. Sennett signed a contract with ADOLPH ZUKOR at Paramount and continued to make two-reelers, but with less success.

Lacking adequate copyright protection, Keystone comedies were duped, reduped, and rereleased long after the demise of the company. Sennett lost millions in the stock market crash of 1929 and went bankrupt. A picture made in England in 1935 was never released; in 1949 he assembled several of his shorts into the feature *Down Memory Lane*. He remained unmarried and died penniless.

BIBLIOGRAPHY

Fowler, Gene, *Father Goose*, 1934; Lahue, Kalton C., and Terry Brewer, *Kops and Custards*, 1968; Sennett, Mack, *King of Comedy*, 1954.

Sessions, Roger Huntington

(December 28, 1896–March 16, 1985)
Composer

Roger Sessions is remembered for his dense, demanding music and for fifty years of teaching. He reached beyond American interest in a strictly national style to lead an international approach to composition. He encouraged students, among them MILTON BABBITT, to master their craft and to pursue the highest ideals.

Roger Huntington Sessions was born in Brooklyn, New York. At eleven young Sessions intended to become a composer. At fourteen he entered Harvard and earned a B.A. in 1914. Sessions next studied with CHARLES IVES's teacher at Yale, Horatio Parker, and in 1917 earned a B.Mus. degree and the Steinert Prize for his Symphonic Prelude. While teaching theory at Smith College (1917–1921), he studied with composer Ernest Bloch in New York and in 1921 became Bloch's assistant at the Cleveland (Ohio) Institute of Music. In 1923 Sessions composed incidental music for *The Black Maskers*, a symbolist play of Leonid Andreyev that was to be performed at Smith College. The score, dedicated to Bloch, is thought by most to be Sessions's first real masterpiece.

Sessions resigned his Cleveland position in 1925 after Ernest Bloch was dismissed from the institute. Sessions traveled abroad and spent several years in Florence, Rome, and Berlin. He produced his First Symphony (1926–1927) while abroad, a piece that reflects Sessions's neoclassicism and the influence of IGOR STRAVINSKY. This early symphony, the first of nine, is Stravinskian in that it is less dense and less chromatic than Sessions's later symphonies. In the Piano Sonata no. 1 of 1930, Sessions began to move away from the neoclassic idiom to create a work that composer AARON COPLAND called "a cornerstone upon which to build an American music."

By 1935, when Sessions joined the faculty at Princeton University, he had completed a violin concerto. The work reveals his individualism and Copland notes "an almost tactile sensibility" in the music.

Sessions expended most of his energy on teaching and was composing very little. To remedy the dearth of new works, he forced himself to write at least one short piece every day or so. Under pressure from his publisher to provide something for publication, he agreed to submit four of these pieces, which together were published as *Pages from a Diary* (1940). The work shows Sessions's music becoming more and more chromatic.

The Second Symphony (1944–1946) is dedicated to the memory of Franklin Delano Roosevelt, and exhibits a new emotional strength and drama. Some sense of key remains in this and in other works of the period, such as the Piano Sonata no. 2 and the one-act opera *The Trial of Lucullus* (1947).

In 1947 Sessions began to work on his opera *Montezuma*, finished in 1963, and within a few years had incorporated the twelve-tone system into his work. He noted later that he "came to [the system] by degrees and used it for my own purposes. I never tried to force myself into a style ... because I wanted to find my own style." *Montezuma*, an ambitious work, was scored to a libretto by Antonio Borgese. The libretto was based on Bernal Díaz del Castillo's chronicle of the Spanish conquest of the Aztecs in the sixteenth century. Peter Maxwell Davies said in his *New York Times* review, April 21, 1964, "There is little doubt that this is Sessions' masterpiece; it is also his most problematic and difficult work ... [and] marks ... a huge step in the history of American music."

The Idyll of Theocritus (1954), for soprano and orchestra, was commissioned by the Louisville, Kentucky, Symphony. Scholar Joseph Machlis calls the striking music "both subtle and strong" and notes its emotional intensity, difficult vocal leaps, chromatic-atonal idiom, and full orchestral texture. The Third Symphony (1957), composed for the Boston Symphony Orchestra's seventy-fifth anniversary, is more lyric and accessible. Sessions had flowered as a teacher, writer, and composer at Berkeley (1944–1953), then at Princeton again, as Conant Professor of Music. At sixty-seven, the composer was beginning his most productive decade.

After Sessions retired from Princeton University in 1965, he became Bloch Professor at Berkeley (1966–1967) and Norton Professor at Harvard (1968–1969), and a faculty member of the Juilliard School. He completed four more symphonies, the very successful cantata *When Lilacs Last in the Dooryard Bloomed* (1970), after WALT WHITMAN, and in 1981, at eighty-four, composed the Concerto for Orchestra to mark the Boston Symphony Orchestra's 100th anniversary.

BIBLIOGRAPHY

Cone, E. T. (ed.), *Roger Sessions on Music: Collected Essays*, 1979; Olmstead, A., *Conversations with Roger Sessions*, 1987.

Shapiro, Karl Jay

(November 10, 1913–   )
Critic, Editor, Poet

Over a sixty-year career, the poet Karl Shapiro has demonstrated versatility and skill with forms both traditional and open. He has a reputation as a wide-ranging social critic and a poetic iconoclast. He also is regarded as having written some of the finest poetry to emerge from World War II.

Shapiro was born in Baltimore, Maryland. He matriculated at the University of Virginia in 1932 but did not finish out the year. Self-conscious about his Russian Jewish heritage, he felt excluded by the non-Jewish students. After he privately published a volume called *Poems* in 1935, he won a scholarship to the Johns Hopkins University, which he attended for two years without earning a degree. In 1941 he was drafted into the army and sent to the South Pacific.

At the end of four years' war service, Shapiro had published four more volumes of poetry and made his poetic reputation. While *The Place of Love* (1942) was considered unremarkable, the poems in *Person, Place, and Thing* (1942) won wide praise for their vivid imagery and qualities of clarity and directness. *V-Letter and Other Poems* (1944) offered wider range to Shapiro's social commentary; such poems as "V-Letter," "Elegy for a Dead Soldier," and "Christmas Eve: Australia" are considered among the finest written about World War II. The volume won Shapiro the Pulitzer Prize in 1945. With *Essay on Rime* (1945), a long poem in blank verse, Shapiro took aim at what he regarded as the stultifying effect of too much modern literary criticism, arguing that poetry ought to spring more from experience than from abstract ideas.

Shapiro joined the faculty of Johns Hopkins in 1948 and from 1950 to 1956 served as editor of *Poetry*. Subsequently, he taught at the University of Nebraska and became editor of the *Prairie Schooner*, positions he held from 1956 until 1966.

In *Poems of a Jew* (1958), Shapiro explores his religious heritage with pride and humor, as in "The Alphabet" and "Messias." In *The Bourgeois Poet* (1964), he turns exclusively to the prose poem; the manner of these works, which suggest free association, has drawn comparison to the poem "Song of Myself" by WALT WHITMAN.

Shapiro taught for two years at the University of Chicago before joining the faculty of the University of California at Davis in 1968. He remained at Davis until his retirement in 1984.

With *White-Haired Lover* (1968), Shapiro returned to more traditional verse forms, particularly the sonnet. This volume, together with his *Selected Poems* (1968), earned him the Bollingen Prize in 1969.

The poems in *Adult Bookstore* (1976) retain this formal polish but range widely in subject matter, as suggested by the titles "The Humanities Building," "My Father's Funeral," "Garage Sale," and "Girls Working in Banks."

Other volumes of Shapiro's poetry include *Trial of a Poet and Other Poems* (1947), *Poems 1940–1953* (1953), and *Love and War, Art and God* (1984). Shapiro also published several volumes of criticism, the most noteworthy of which are *In Defense of Ignorance* (1960) and *The Poetry Wreck* (1975), in which he attacked the poets EZRA POUND and T. S. ELIOT for their intellectualism and lionized Whitman and WILLIAM CARLOS WILLIAMS.

Shapiro lives in New York City.

BIBLIOGRAPHY

Raino, Joseph, *Karl Shapiro*, 1981; Shapiro, Karl, *An Autobiography in Three Parts*, 2 vols., 1988, 1990.

Sheeler, Charles, Jr.

(July 16, 1883–May 7, 1965)
Painter, Photographer

Charles Sheeler, American painter and photographer in the 1920s through the 1950s, expressed the idealization and optimism of a confidently expanding, industrial America. His style and vision, rooted in Cubism, and his closely observed architectural and mechanical factualism placed him in the forefront of the movement known as Precisionism.

Sheeler's early art training began in his native Philadelphia in 1900 in applied design at the School of Industrial Art. Three years later, he was accepted into the Pennsylvania Academy of Fine Arts, where he studied with William Merritt Chase. After a tour of England and Holland with Chase's class, during which he absorbed the works of classical and modern masters like Velázquez, Goya, and JOHN SINGER SARGENT, Sheeler had his first one-man show in 1908 at the McClees Gallery in Philadelphia.

For the next decade Sheeler, having studied more European trends, notably Cubism, Fauvism, and Synchromism (particularly the paintings of Cézanne, Matisse, and Stanfield Macdonald-Wright), struggled to apply Modernism as he understood it to the American scene, both rural and industrial. He combined the fractured forms of Cubism with the bright, prismatic colors of Synchromism, and applied this analysis to the industrial forms of turbines, factories, and bridges—revealing their elementary structures and absolute orders. In 1916 Sheeler said he felt the artist should establish contact with "the profound scheme, system or order underlying the universe." From his Bucks County home in Doylestown, Pennsylvania, he studied the American craft tradition and the interiors and architecture of the farmhouses, barns, and silos. The appeal of the spare economy of these forms was to become an essential part of his vision.

Meanwhile, he began to study photography as a means to support his painting. He photographed houses and commercial buildings for Philadelphia architect clients. Soon, however, he realized that photography had great direct value in his painting—it not only sharpened his vision but could furnish material for his paintings. Gradually, the mannerisms and fragmentations of Cubism—a movement whose imprint never left Sheeler's work—were replaced by a more sharply observed realism and a more severe geometry. As early as *Barn Abstraction* (1917) can be seen a foreshadowing of his most typical works to come.

After his move to New York in 1919, he became associated with several influential salons and galleries, notably the salon of Walter Arensberg. Here he met ISADORA DUNCAN, Amy Lowell, WILLIAM CARLOS WILLIAMS, and Charles Demuth, as well as MARCEL DUCHAMP and Francis Picabia. Through the ALFRED STIEGLITZ group, at the same time, his reputation as a photographer grew. But in his paintings he went his own way, and the decade of the 1920s brought Sheeler his first celebrity as a mature painter. *Church Street El* (1920) and *Offices* (1922), for example, were dubbed skyscraper Cubism, reducing urban architecture to generalized forms that were both planar and three-dimensional. The images were rendered fastidiously, even clinically, their grimy, urban reality replaced by confectionary colors and smooth surfaces. One particular painting, *Upper Deck* (1929), was a pivotal work in his career. While a wholly realistic depiction of an ocean liner's machinery, it was also an inherently abstract work.

Inspired by several photographic assignments of the late 1920s and 1930s, like documenting the Ford plant in River Rouge and the reconstruction of Williamsburg, Virginia, Sheeler moved into a new phase of his career where he began to execute extremely detailed and photographically realistic interiors and industrial exteriors. *Classic Landscape* (1931), *American Interior* (1934), *City Interior* (1936), and *Rolling Power* (1939) all presented forms of idealized utility, efficiency, and energy.

After being appointed the photographer-in-residence at the New York Metropolitan Museum of Art in 1942, Sheeler advanced into still another phase of his career during the next two decades. A new formalism, essentially a throwback to Cubist tendencies, was shaping the work of younger artists. By contrast, Sheeler's responses were paintings that were direct and object-centered, reductions of architecture and machines into a greater abstraction than he had hitherto attempted. *Fugue* (1945) and *Incantation* (1946) were Mondrian-like patterns that were flat and formal. However, with the advent of Abstract Expressionism (see BARNETT NEWMAN) near the end of the 1940s and its emphasis on the improvised, gestural nature of the artist, Sheeler's work was eclipsed. Despite the increasing formalism of his work at this time, he never was able to take the step into total abstraction. He remained essentially a factual artist with a consummate sense of composition.

BIBLIOGRAPHY

Friedman, Martin, *Charles Sheeler*, 1975; Rose, Barbara (ed.), *Readings in American Art Since 1900*, 1968.

Shepard, Sam

(November 5, 1943–)
Actor, Playwright

Sam Shepard, a Pulitzer Prize– and Obie Award–winning playwright and screen actor who emerged in the middle 1960s from the Off-Broadway theater movement in New York, has written plays noted for their quirky, back-road vernacular. "He explored the American landscape like a pathfinder," wrote critic John Lahr.

He was born Samuel Shepard Rogers in 1943 in Fort Sheridan, Illinois. His father was a career army officer, and the family moved frequently from post to post. Unhappy with home life, the boy at age eighteen joined a repertory group called the Bishop's Company and got his first experience

The Museum of Modern Art/Film Stills Archive

as an actor touring across the country. A year later he settled down in New York and, for the next several years, worked as an apprentice playwright in the Bowery for the Off-Broadway Theatre Genesis at Saint Mark's Church-in-the-Bowery. His first works were one-act plays like *The Rock Garden* (1964), which, although some critics dismissed them as minor-league Samuel Beckett, already revealed his distinctive stamp—open acting spaces, poetically charged monologues, and discontinuous story lines.

During the next ten years he wrote more than two dozen plays, staged them in several Off-Broadway houses, and collected his first Obies. Their dialogues and monologues flared and flickered against the dark emptiness of the stage; and their nightmarish metaphors were startling and new—picnickers describe a jet plane's vapor trail as a premonition of apocalypse in *Icarus' Mother* (1965); a man's flesh is disintegrating as he talks in *Red Cross* (1966); a military computer is transformed into a 6-foot rattlesnake in *Operation Sidewinder* (1970). When the latter play moved "uptown" to Lincoln Center, it repelled audiences and, from avant-garde playwright Jack Gelber, earned the remark: "It was the best play ever done at Lincoln Center."

In London from 1971 to 1974 he and his wife, the former O-Lan Johnson, raised their son, Jesse, while he wrote some of his finest plays, including *The Tooth of Crime* (1972), a tour de force of rock and roll imagery and vernacular whose invented language Shepard's biographer, Don Shewey, describes as a "rock-talk corollary to Lewis Carroll's 'Jabberwocky'"; and *Little Ocean* (1973), a play whose title is a metaphor for child birth. Upon his return he wrote a cycle of dramas dealing with the disintegration of families—*Curse of the Starving Class* (1977), the Pulitzer Prize–winning *Buried Child* (1978), and *True West* (1980). The latter dismantled fantasy conceptions of the American West as an earthly paradise and a frontier experience. Indeed, Shepard's position toward the need for myth and dream has always been ambivalent. As a character says in his Hollywood drama, *Angel City* (1976): "I look at the movie and I am the star. I hate my life not being a movie. I hate my life not being a star. . . . I hate . . . having to live in this body which isn't a star's body and all the time knowing that stars exist."

A tall, lanky man of a few mumbled words, Shepard currently divides his time between California and New Mexico. He continues to write about cowboys, celebrities, rock and rollers, drifters, and dreamers. Shepard's own resemblance to the GARY COOPER style of character has helped him in movies like *The Right Stuff* (1983), where he earned an Oscar nomination for his portrayal of test pilot Chuck Yeager, and *Country* (1984), where he played a beleaguered farmer in danger of losing his land. Indeed, for critics like John Lahr there is something quintessentially American about him: "He dredged the detritus of the society for the pure gold of its diction and its daydreams. Out of his distinctive and audacious work came a very special sense of America's deliriums."

Shepard's most recent plays include *Fool for Love* (1983), *A Lie of the Mind* (1985), which won the 1986 New York Drama Critics' Circle Award, and *States of Shock* (1991).

BIBLIOGRAPHY

DeRose, David, *Sam Shepard,* 1992; Shewey, Don, *Sam Shepard,* 1985.

Sherwood, Robert Emmet

(April 4, 1896–November 14, 1955)
Editor, Playwright

Robert Sherwood, a film critic, Pulitzer Prize–winning playwright, and Academy Award–winning screenwriter, was best known for his socially conscious plays of the 1930s, including *Idiot's Delight* and *Abe Lincoln in Illinois.*

He was born in 1896 into a family of artists. His mother was an artist, and his father was the founder and first editor of the *Harvard Lampoon.* Amidst the idyllic setting of the Skene Wood estate in Westport, New York, Sherwood's childhood was spent entertaining family and friends with his own amateur theatricals. His prep school years at the Milton Academy and his college days at Harvard University were marked by a lackluster interest in academics and a passionate devotion to theater and journalism. In 1918, after being expelled three times from Harvard, Sherwood left to join the war effort. Too tall for the army and navy (he was 6 feet, 6 inches in height), he enlisted in the Canadian Expeditionary Force and was assigned to the Forty-second Battalion of the Fifth Royal Highlanders (the Canadian Black Watch). He was gassed twice and wounded on active duty in France.

Back in the United States after his discharge, he moved to New York City and spent most of the 1920s as a journalist, including stints as film critic for *Vanity Fair* and *Life* magazines (for which he also served as editor). With his friends Dorothy Parker and Robert Benchley, he became an active member of the fabled Round Table at the Algonquin Hotel. ("Sherwood stood out like a grandfather's clock," biographer John Mason Brown aptly noted. "The tick of his talk was measured, his words seeming to be spaced by minutes, but when he chimed he struck gaily.") His first professional play, *The Road to Rome* (1927), a tongue-in-cheek fable told in contemporary vernacular about Hannibal's threatened invasion of Rome, was one of his greatest successes. It was a strong beginning for a new playwright, although there would be four failed plays (*The Love Nest*, 1927; *The Queen's Husband*, 1928; *Waterloo Bridge*, 1930; *This Is New York*, 1930) before his next big hit, *Reunion in Vienna* (1931). Reunion was a Theatre Guild production starring ALFRED LUNT and LYNN FONTANNE. The play was a frothy tale of love and deception in contemporary Vienna, although, as Sherwood stated in the play's preface, it was really a comic mask worn over the growing desperation and disruption of postwar Europe.

The decade of the 1930s was Sherwood's most fruitful. With MAXWELL ANDERSON, Elmer Rice, and others he formed the Playwrights' Company, a producing aggregate formed as a protest against the policies of the Theatre Guild. It was a decade that also marked a radical shift in his pacifist sensibilities, which he had formulated as a result of his ordeal in World War I. His gradual shift toward a decisively interventionist posture by the end of the decade can be seen in four plays, three of which won him Pulitzer Prizes—*The Petrified Forest* (1935), an allegorical confrontation in Arizona between a disillusioned idealist and a brutal gangster (played by Humphrey Bogart in both stage and film versions); *Idiot's Delight* (1936), a pacifist drama set amidst events portending a second world war; *Abe Lincoln in Illinois* (1938), whose portrait of Lincoln's shift away from noncommittal attitudes toward war and slavery paralleled America's situation during the outbreak of war in Europe; and *There Shall Be No Night* (1940), set during the Russian attack on Finland and firmly denouncing American isolationism.

Except for some screenplays—*Rebecca* (1940), *The Best Years of Our Lives* (1946; for which he won an Academy Award), *The Bishop's Wife* (1947)—and a couple of failed plays, Sherwood forsook theater and film during the 1940s for the greater drama of politics. He joined the Committee to Defend America by Aiding the Allies in 1940, worked as a speech writer for President Franklin Roosevelt, and headed the Overseas Branch of the Office of War Information. After the war he won another Pulitzer Prize for his book *Roosevelt and Hopkins* (1948), an "intimate biography."

Sherwood was both a skilled craftsman and a social dramatist, one of the most successful of the depression era playwrights. At their best, his dramas were witty and eloquent commentaries on the changing political consciousness of the day. However, for audiences of the Vietnam era, the political underpinnings of the later plays proved unpopular. "Few of our contemporaries have lived so many lives with such abundance as Sherwood," says John Mason Brown. "Few have so reflected the changing decades with their changing issues, interest, and climates as this skyscraper of a man, mournful of face, gay at heart, slow in talk, fluent with pen, and serious of purpose, who could seem solitary even in company."

BIBLIOGRAPHY

Brown, John Mason, *The Worlds of Robert E. Sherwood*, 1965, and *The Ordeal of a Playwright*, 1970.

Shubert, Levi

(1875–December 25, 1953)

Shubert, Samuel S.

(1876–May 12, 1905)

Shubert, Jacob J.

(1880–December 26, 1963)
Theater Managers, Producers

The Shubert brothers, Lee, Sam, and J. J., were the most powerful force in American theater production and exhibition during most of the first half of the twentieth century.

The brothers were born in Neustadt, East Prussia. Because of the anti-Jewish pogroms, their father, David, a peddler, emigrated to America in 1882; the rest of his family joined him by 1892. The boys grew up in Syracuse, New York, and, because their father was a chronically unemployed alcoholic, Lee and Sam were forced to go to work at an early age, selling papers and running errands in front of the local theater houses. For the next twelve years, the brothers pulled themselves up from poverty to a living wage and soon were managing the very theaters before which they had formerly scrambled for nickels and dimes.

After Sam purchased the touring rights to Charles Hoyt's play *A Texas Steer* in 1894, the brothers launched a campaign that soon saw them competing with the powerful New York–based theater syndicate of Marc Klaw and Abraham Erlanger. This syndicate, whose avowed aim had been to bring order into chaotic booking practices along the touring routes, actually was a monopoly and had put a stran-glehold on competition. Beginning with the Herald Square Theater in New York, where the three Shuberts booked Augustus Thomas's spectacularly successful play *Arizona* (1900), a prototype of the modern western drama, they successfully competed with the syndicate and eventually would become the largest theater owners and most active producers in America.

In the next few years the brothers wrestled with the syndicate and doggedly began to produce their own shows. Many of them were musicals, beginning with the tuneful, if forgettable *Chinese Honeymoon* (1902) and including a few prestigious operettas, like Sir Arthur Sullivan's *Emerald Isle* (1902). Among the dramas, *Old Heidelberg* (1902) would eventually become, after several revivals, one of their most successful hits. They also began building their own theater houses in New York, Chicago, and other cities.

In 1905 Sam was killed in a train wreck. He had been the driving force behind the Shubert interests; now J. J. and Lee took over. J. J. attended to importing and staging operettas, and Lee presided over the remainder of the operations, which now included thirteen theaters. More theaters were acquired, including the fabulous New York Hippodrome and the Winter Garden, site of their biggest extravaganzas.

The Shuberts represented talent like Richard Mansfield, Sarah Bernhardt, Eddie Foy, Lillian Russell, FRED ASTAIRE, and Al Jolson, who became their biggest moneymaker. Their series of "Passing Show" revues rivaled the Ziegfeld Follies in popularity. Other hit shows included *Sinbad* (1918), *The Chocolate Soldier* (1921), *Blossom Time* (1921), *Sally, Irene and Mary* (1922), *The Student Prince* (1924), and *Cynara* (1931), among many others. Quick to capitalize on the growing motion picture business, they went into partnership with the short-lived World Film Corporation in 1914 and made many of their productions available to the cameras. They instituted a policy of fireproof brick walls for their theaters, employed for the first time female ushers, installed coin-operated beverage machines, and developed the best ticket tally system in the business.

In all they became a syndicate in themselves, every bit as ruthless as the Klaw-Erlanger group, and produced 520 plays on Broadway, controlling fully one-quarter of all the shows presented during that time. At their height, in the early 1940s, more than 75 percent of Broadway's attractions were, to varying degrees, Shubert investments; and among those not connected to Shubert money, 90 percent were compelled to play in Shubert theaters. They had carved out theater districts in a dozen cities. And at the center of it all, between 44th and 45th streets, just west of Broadway in the space between the back of the Astor Hotel and the Shubert and Booth theaters, was the famed Shubert Alley.

When they were not at war with the Klaw-Erlanger syndicate and with each other, they were at war with the vaudeville interests controlled by B. F. Keith. And they fought the unions. They battled Actors Equity, founded in 1912 to protect actors from unscrupulous managers, and ASCAP (the American Society of Composers, Authors and Publishers), which had been formed in 1914 to protect the interests of composers and lyricists. At the end, while J. J. languished near death, his son, John, ran the business, still the largest theatrical empire in the world. When John died in 1962 (his father succumbed a year later), the Shubert estate was left wracked by private and public scandals. Today, the Shubert interests have been restructured as the Shubert Organization. It leases theaters and office space, and manages the real estate holdings. Resuming production in 1978, it has been responsible for some of the great Broadway successes of the last two decades, including *Ain't Misbehavin'* (1978), *Amadeus* (1980), and *Cats* (1982).

BIBLIOGRAPHY

McLaughlin, Robert, *Broadway and Hollywood: A History of Economic Interaction*, 1974; McNamara, Brooks, *The Shuberts of Broadway*, 1990; Stagg, Jerry, *The Brothers Shubert*, 1968; Tibbetts, John C., *The American Theatrical Film*, 1985.

Simon, Marvin Neil

(July 4, 1927–   )
Playwright

Pulitzer Prize–winning Neil Simon has consistently produced more Broadway hits than any other American playwright. His plays are an adroit mix of autobiographical elements with comic dialogue and memorable character studies.

Simon was born in the Bronx, New York, in 1927, the second of two sons of Irving Simon, a garment salesman, and Mamie Simon. He attended Woodside High School where the anti-Semitism he suffered was soon ended when he became the star hitter of the baseball team. During his high school years he and his older brother, Danny, imitated radio comedians, read the humorous sketches of Robert Benchley and Ring Lardner, and sold material to standup comics and radio shows.

During World War II, Simon was stationed at Lowry Field, Colorado, where he covered sports for the *Rev-Meter,* the base newspaper. After his discharge, he joined Danny at Warner Brothers in New York City and got a job in the mailroom. For the next decade the Simons wrote comedy material for many popular radio shows, including *The Phil Silvers Arrow Show, The Tallulah Bankhead Show,* and *The Jackie Gleason Show.* After Danny left writing for directing, Neil switched over to television, writing for *The Sid Caesar Show* (1956–1957), Phil Silvers's *Sergeant Bilko* (1958–1959), and *The Garry Moore Show* (1959–1960). Eventually, Simon grew restless at the routine. "Television meant doing the same thing for the rest of my life, writing what other people wanted me to write," he said in a 1985 interview. "I wanted freedom of expression and you're never going to get it in television. . . . Writing for the theatre you have no one but the public and the critics to answer to."

His first plays were light comedies. *Come Blow Your Horn* (1961) took its inspiration from the bachelor life of his brother, Danny. A much greater success was his next play, *Barefoot in the Park* (1963), directed by Mike Nichols, an autobiographical comedy about the marital difficulties of a newlywed couple in New York. Its four-year run (with Robert Redford and Elizabeth Ashley) established Simon's reputation. A string of hits followed—*The Odd Couple* (1965), with Art Carney and Walter Matthau, which won Simon his first Tony; *The Star-Spangled Girl* (1966), a satire about two radicals who vie for the attentions of a conservative southern belle; and *Plaza Suite* (1968), a trilogy of one-act sketches set in the same hotel suite. A more serious note was evident in Simon's next plays—*The Last of the Red Hot Lovers* (1969), about a man's midlife crisis; *The Prisoner of Second Avenue* (1971), about a recently fired advertising executive's nervous breakdown; and *The Sunshine Boys* (1972), about the reunion of two estranged vaudeville partners. Simon regards the latter as among his best works.

After his wife's death from cancer in 1973, Simon moved to California and promptly wrote *California Suite* (1976), a spin-off from *Plaza Suite; Chapter Two* (1977), based on Simon's own experience with actress Marsha Mason; *I Ought to Be in Pictures* (1980), which portrays a screenwriter's rapprochement with the daughter he has not seen in many years; and the offbeat *Fools* (1981), about the efforts of a teacher to educate the inhabitants of a Ukrainian village who are cursed with stupidity.

Simon reached a new phase of work with his trilogy, *Brighton Beach Memoirs* (1983), *Biloxi Blues* (1985), which won Simon a Tony Award for Best Play, and *Broadway Bound* (1986). They are an autobiographical account of Eugene Morris Jerome, from his youth in Brooklyn, to his army days, to his first work as an aspiring comedy writer. Simon's most recent plays are *Lost in Yonkers* (1991), which won a Pulitzer Prize, and *Jake's Women*

(1992). Among his original screenplays are the excruciating, underrated *The Heartbreak Kid* (1972), the broadly vulgar *The Cheap Detective* (1978), the elegiac *Max Dugan Returns* (1983), and a baseball comedy, *The Slugger's Wife* (1984).

Simon has been married three times and has two grown daughters and a stepdaughter. He divides his time between an apartment in Man- hattan and a house in Bel Air, California. He writes tirelessly, claiming to put aside ten or more plays for each one he finishes.

BIBLIOGRAPHY

Johnson, Robert K., *Neil Simon*, 1983; McGovern, Edythe M., *Neil Simon: A Critical Study*, 1979.

Sinatra, Francis Albert

(December 12, 1915–)
Actor, Singer

Known in the 1940s as the Voice, Frank Sinatra projected such intimacy as he sang that he had youngsters swooning at his feet. The mass hysteria he inspired in his early fans and his later personal notoriety have not overshadowed his gifts as a dramatic actor and the warmth and effortless style of his singing.

The child of an Italian immigrant family, Francis Albert Sinatra was born in Hoboken, New Jersey. Unable to read music and with no vocal training, he nonetheless dropped out of school when he was sixteen to sing.

From 1937 to 1939 Sinatra was singing at the Rustic Cabin, a roadhouse near Englewood, New Jersey, where he was also headwaiter. Trumpeter Harry James, having heard Sinatra on radio, hired him as a vocalist in mid-1939. James had just left BENNY GOODMAN's orchestra to found his own big band. A *Metronome* re-

Scoop Marketing

view, Sinatra's first notice, noted the singer's "easy phrasing."

A CBS executive advised bandleader Tommy Dorsey to "go listen to the skinny kid who's singing with Harry's band." Dorsey did and in 1940 hired Sinatra. Sinatra became a celebrity. By mid-1941 a *Billboard* survey of colleges rated him outstanding male band vocalist. Later that year a *Down Beat* poll had Sinatra outranking Bing Crosby. Songs like "I'll Never Smile Again" and "There Are Such Things" were hit recordings in the 1940s.

When Sinatra left Dorsey in 1942, he was in constant demand as a soloist and his voice, now overworked, began to falter. By 1947 his popularity was waning, though he continued to record with Columbia, backed by Alex Stordahl's rich arrangements that complemented the pleasant intimacy of the baritone voice so thrilling to young bobbysoxers. However, by 1952 he was without contracts for records or films and without a manager.

In 1953 Sinatra's career turned around. He won an Academy Award for his dramatic role in the film of the James Jones novel, *From Here to Eternity*, and signed a contract with Capitol Records, then known as an innovative organization. Capitol issued a number of best-selling Sinatra tunes, many of them backed by Nelson Riddle arrangements, including HAROLD ARLEN's "I've Got the World on a String." Sinatra regained his position and at last was recognized for the excellence of his performance rather than for his ability to draw a frenzied audience response. He continued to make films like *Guys and Dolls* and *The Man with the Golden Arm*, both in 1955. After retiring in 1971, the irrepressible Sinatra returned to television, touring and recording in 1973, and received the Presidential Medal of Freedom in 1985.

Frank Sinatra became the epitome of the American popular ballad singer. He developed his own personal and much copied style, having learned about phrasing and breathing from Tommy Dorsey, and having picked up pointers about jazz singing from BILLIE HOLIDAY and story telling from singer Mabel Mercer. Like crooner Bing Crosby, Sinatra turned the microphone into an ally to help him articulate the nuances of shading and volume that made his performances so winning.

BIBLIOGRAPHY

Kahn, E. J., *The Voice,* 1947; Rockwell, J., *Sinatra: An American Classic,* 1984.

Skidmore, Louis

(April 8, 1897–September 27, 1962)
Architect

Owings, Nathaniel Alexander

(February 5, 1903–June 13, 1984)
Architect, Planner

Merrill, John Ogden

(August 10, 1896–June 10, 1975)
Engineer

Bunshaft, Gordon

(May 9, 1909–August 6, 1990)
Architect

Founded in Chicago in 1939, Skidmore, Owings & Merrill (or SOM) became famous for its large-scale, "glass-box" commercial buildings based on the International style, its team approach to design, and its meticulous planning and attention to detail.

Louis Skidmore was born in Lawrenceburg, Indiana, and received an architectural degree from the Massachusetts Institute of Technology (MIT; 1924). He then worked for the Boston firm of Maginnis & Walsh (1924–1926), traveled in Europe and the Near East on a fellowship (1926–1929), and was chief of design (1929–1935) for the Chicago World's Fair (1933). In 1936 he opened a firm in Chicago with his brother-in-law, Nathaniel Owings.

Nathaniel Owings was born in Indianapolis, Indiana, and earned an architectural and engineering degree from Cornell University (1927). He worked briefly in the New York office of York & Sawyer before joining Skidmore on the Chicago Fair project. Owings championed environmental planning and became involved in civic programs outside the firm, such as the U.S. Secretary of the Interior's Advisory Board on National Parks, Historic Sites, Buildings and Monuments (1966–1972).

John Ogden Merrill was born in St. Paul, Minnesota, graduated from MIT (1921), worked in various architectural offices and for the Federal Housing Administration, and then joined with Skidmore and Owings to form SOM in 1939. In addition to his work with the firm, Merrill directed a major revision of Chicago's building code (1947–1949).

SOM's founding fathers set the guiding tenets for the firm: expand the architect's role and responsibilities in the design process, design only in the modern idiom, and maintain consistency and integrity of design. Focusing attention on large-scale commissions, SOM developed a multidisciplinary approach to architectural design based on the medieval guild system ideals of cooperation and anonymity. Because of the organizational skills of Owings, the design sensitivity of Skidmore, and the practical engineering savvy of Merrill, the firm flourished. Additional offices were opened in New York City (directed by Skidmore), San Francisco (directed by Owings), Portland, Oregon, Washington, D.C., Los Angeles, Houston, Boston, and Denver.

Merrill produced a complex (1942–1946) for the government's Manhattan Project (atom bomb development), including an entire town in Oak Ridge, Tennessee. He also encouraged SOM's emphasis on the relationship between structure and architecture, and promoted the prominence of such engineers as Fazlur Khan and Myron Goldsmith.

SOM's early work included plants for H. J. Heinz Company in Tracy, California (1946), and Pittsburgh, Pennsylvania (1950–1952), and New York's Sloan Kettering Institute for Cancer Research (1948). The firm also enlivened the Chicago tradition of urban organization through skillful redevelopment projects, such as the Lake Meadows Housing complex (1950–1960). The partners' streamlined designs of big buildings and clear, careful planning of exteriors and interiors brought national prominence. During the 1950s worldwide recognition was stimulated by the emergence of its foremost architect, Gordon Bunshaft, who designed many of SOM's outstanding buildings. This reinforced the founders' claim that they could "produce the people who produce the architecture."

Gordon Bunshaft was born in Buffalo, New York, earned bachelor's and master's degrees from MIT (1929–1935), then worked for Edward Durrell Stone and industrial designer RAYMOND LOEWY before joining SOM in 1937. After World War II service in the Army Corps of Engineers (1942–1946), he returned to SOM, becoming a partner and core member of the New York office in 1949. In 1952 his first major building, Lever House (headquarters for Lever Brothers Corporation) in New York, ushered in a new era of skyscraper design. This 24-story structure is composed of a glazed vertical slab on piers above an elevated 1-story "square donut." Its skin of heat-resistant green glass articulated with aluminum was the first commercial building in the city featuring a glass-curtain facade. Bunshaft's use of only 25 percent of available airspace for the building's tower redefined the relationship between a skyscraper and its urban setting. The building also served as an advertisement for the Lever firm's products, as the curtain wall was cleaned with a Lever household product.

The business community embraced the image of sophistication and efficiency created by Bunshaft's elegant shiny tower surrounded by open space. A hallmark of SOM's design became the firm's ability to establish a strong identity for its clients through architecture, as seen in the string of corporate headquarters that the firm built using Lever House as a model. SOM exerted a pioneering influence on American corporate architecture with its prefabricated glass-and-curtain walls, and Bunshaft became a major interpreter of the post–World War II International style (see LUDWIG MIES VAN DER ROHE), stressing clear geometric form, minimal surface detail, and the machine aesthetic. He stated: "I believe in disciplined architecture, in logical, rational building that makes sense." His skyscrapers are famous for their monumental yet light and airy presence, sleek glass-curtained towers lined with steel, and emphasis on volume over mass.

Bunshaft's Manufacturers Hanover Trust Bank Branch Headquarters, New York (1953–1954) revolutionized bank design by enclosing the structure in glass and placing the vault on full public display, giving the subliminal message that banks are open trading centers and that glass banks are as secure as masonry temples. Just as SOM was reaching its height in productivity and influence, Skidmore and Merrill retired, leaving Owings to maintain the firm's founding ideals until his retirement in the 1970s.

By the mid-1960s Bunshaft was shifting his aesthetic from glass and steel to more heavy, sculptural forms, as seen in the Lyndon Baines Johnson Library (University of Texas at Austin, 1971). The library is composed of two large, travertine-faced walls placed around a central "podium" with a massive staircase connecting five floors of glass-enclosed bookstacks and a top administrative floor. Another such work is the Hirshhorn Museum and Sculpture Garden in Washington, D.C. (1974), a huge windowless, fortresslike, donut-shaped building with a masterfully arranged sculpture garden. Other famous Bunshaft designs are the Beinecke Rare Book and Manuscript Library at Yale University (1963), with its boxlike structure in translucent marble; the W. R. Grace building (New York, 1973), with its innovative sloping facade; and the 27-story National Commercial Bank in Jeddah, Saudi Arabia (1983), with its deep window loggias to protect offices from direct sunlight.

Additional major works of SOM include the campus plan and buildings for the U.S. Air Force Academy in Colorado Springs, Colorado (1962), the New World Center, a multiuse complex in Hong Kong (1978), and the landmark Sears Tower in Chicago (1974). This 110-story tower is an excellent example of the firm's use of engineering principles to influence architectural design. It is composed of a cluster of nine framed shafts of varying heights—each with its own structural integrity—that work together to support and stabilize the building, which remains the world's tallest.

BIBLIOGRAPHY

Danz, Ernst, and Henry-Russell Hitchcock, *SOM: Architecture of Skidmore, Owings & Merrill, 1950–1962,* 1963; Drexler, Arthur, and A. Menges, *SOM: Architecture of Skidmore, Owings & Merrill, 1963–1973,* 1974; Krinsky, C. H., *Gordon Bunshaft,* 1988; Owings, Nathaniel Alexander, *The Spaces in Between—An Architect's Journey,* 1973; Woodward, Christopher, *Skidmore, Owings & Merrill,* 1970.

Smith, Bessie

(April 15, 1894–September 26, 1937)
Singer

An important early jazz singer, Bessie Smith, the "Empress of the Blues," was probably the greatest of the classic blueswomen. As she sang, her rich voice and personal intensity spoke directly and emotionally of common folks' troubles, and she would move listeners deeply with both her message and her passionate delivery.

Tennessee-born, some say as late as 1900, Bessie Smith was one of five children of William and Laura Smith. Her father, a Baptist preacher, died soon after her birth, and within a few years her mother and two brothers died. She went to work early on street corners singing for tips. The black entertainment circuit was to be her escape from the Chattanooga slums.

Through her brother Clarence, a comedian with Moses Stokes's minstrel troupe, Smith auditioned for that show in 1912, was hired as a dancer, and met Gertrude ("Ma") Rainey, the "mother" of the blues, who became a lifelong friend, though Rainey seems less influential as Smith's mentor than has been thought. In 1913 Smith moved to Atlanta, sang at Charles Bailey's 81 Theater, and began to tour, "strikingly beautiful and very black, with a belling blues cry [that] was stopping shows all around the South," according to jazz writer Ian Carr.

In the early 1920s she moved to Philadelphia, where she performed at theaters as well as at Paradise Gardens, a well-known nightclub in Atlantic City, New Jersey. After some unsuccessful record auditions, she was approached by Frank Walker, chief of Columbia Records' race catalog. Race records were aimed specifically to blacks. Though Walker later claimed he heard her first in Selma, Alabama, in 1917, it was probably pianist/composer Clarence Williams who was responsible for the contact. In the early 1920s Williams became her manager and led her to record his own material. Because of Williams's financial scheming, the business relationship was short. Walker took over and directed Smith's recording career from 1923 to 1931.

Her first release, "Down Hearted Blues," made in February 1923, with Clarence Williams on piano, was a success. FLETCHER HENDERSON appears on subsequent 1923 blues recordings, and in 1924 and 1925 Bessie began to call on the remarkably talented members of his band to accompany her, among them LOUIS ARMSTRONG, saxophonists COLEMAN HAWKINS and Don Redman, and clarinetist Buster Bailey.

Smith's early records brought her stardom. She played to overflow city crowds in the South, Midwest, and along the Atlantic seaboard. One of the few black artists to perform for white audiences, she was the first black woman to be broadcast live on local radio stations in Memphis and Atlanta. Poet LANGSTON HUGHES spoke of her "sadness . . . not softened with tears, but hardened with laughter, the absurd, incongruous laughter of a sadness without even a god to appeal to."

In 1929 Smith appeared in the film *St. Louis Blues*, but by then her excessive drinking and the depressed economy had damaged her prospects. Her last recording in 1933, intended for the European jazz market, was arranged by producer/critic JOHN HAMMOND and featured Jack Teagarden and BENNY GOODMAN.

Bessie Smith's personal life was shot through with the tragedies she described in song. Her first husband died shortly after their marriage, and she separated from her second husband after seven difficult years. Her misfortunes were matched by her love of food and drink and nightlife, extremes of living that SIDNEY BECHET ascribed to "this trouble in her, this thing that wouldn't let her rest."

According to jazz writer Richard Hadlock, Smith was the "one woman [who contributed] significantly to the development of jazz in the twenties." She sang the blues until she died in 1937, the victim of an automobile accident in Mississippi. Her death was the subject of an EDWARD ALBEE play, *The Death of Bessie Smith* (1959).

BIBLIOGRAPHY

Albertson, C., *Bessie*, 1972; Barlow, W., *Looking Up at Down: The Emergence of Blues Cultures*, 1989; Feinstein, E., *Bessie Smith*, 1985; Hadlock, R., *Jazz Masters of the Twenties*, 1965, rep., 1986; Lyons, L., and D. Perlo, *Jazz Portraits: The Lives and Music of Jazz Masters*, 1989; Schuller, G., *Early Jazz: Its Roots and Musical Development*, 1968.

Smith, David Roland

(March 9, 1906–May 23, 1965)
Sculptor

David Smith, the most original American sculptor of his generation, was a pioneer of welded metal pieces. He was a strong individualist who created during a prolific career metal calligraphic "drawings in space," totemic sculptures incorporating "found objects," and monumental, geometrically abstract pieces in the Cubist mode, all with moral undertones.

Smith was born in Decatur, Indiana, and studied art at Ohio University (1924), Notre Dame (1925), and George Washington University (1926). During the summers he worked as a riveter at the Studebaker automobile plant in South Bend, Indiana, acquiring the metalworking skills that would become central to his later career. In 1926 he moved to New York City and studied painting at the Art Students League (1926–1932). Through such teachers as Jan Matulka and such friends as abstract painter STUART DAVIS, Smith was introduced to the concepts of Surrealism (in which imagery is based on fantasy or the subconscious), Constructivism (a movement advocating innovative, nonobjective art based on experimentation with geometric forms in space, light, and motion), and Cubism (a movement concerned with the "image of the visible" achieved through geometric abstraction, often combined with strong color and expressive distortions). Smith assimilated aspects of these artistic movements and examined them in new, imaginative ways.

A painter until the early 1930s, Smith moved into sculpture, as he said, when his "painting developed into raised levels from the canvas. Gradually, the canvas became the base and the painting was a sculpture." He added "found" and shaped wooden objects to the paintings' surfaces, and created his first free-standing painted wooden piece in 1931. Partially inspired by published reproductions of Pablo Picasso's and Julio Gonzalez's iron constructions, Smith's first metal sculpture, *Head* (1933), was made of cut and shaped scrap iron and boiler plates welded together. He had found his artistic medium in iron and steel, and began to create revolutionary works that united artistic concepts, personal themes and imagery, and the methods of modern technology.

Smith established a studio at Brooklyn's Terminal Iron Works (1934–1940), where he created such early abstract works as *Aerial Construction* (1936), an open-space calligraphic piece of welded thin metal strips. He wrote:

The equipment I use, my supply of material come from what I learned in the factory, and duplicate as nearly as possible the production equipment used in making a locomotive. . . . What associations the metal possesses are those of this century. It is structure, movement, progress, suspension, cantilever and at times destruction and brutality.

After a trip through Europe, Russia, and the Middle East (1935–1936), Smith produced *Medals for Dishonor* (1937–1940), a series of fifteen bronze bas-reliefs. His most overt work of social commentary, the medallions attack war and social injustice using Surrealist imagery. Humanity's potential for violence and brutality, and the need to neutralize it, are recurring themes underlying much of his work. In embracing the techniques and materials of the machine age, he said, "Possibly steel is so beautiful because of all the movement associated with it, its strength and functions. . . . Yet it is also brutal; the rapist, the murderer and death-dealing giants are also its offspring."

In 1940 he moved to a farm in Bolton Landing, New York, near Lake George, and set up a machine shop/factory-style studio for making sculpture, calling it Terminal Iron Works. He worked as a welder in a Schenectady, New York, defense plant (1942–1944), producing little sculpture during the war years. After 1945 his creativity burst forth in many directions as he explored industrial steel shapes and developed a personal, more linear visual language using surrealist and expressionist imagery. He redefined the traditional approach to sculpture as to volume, mass, material, and color, by producing open, welded-steel constructions that were often painted and appended with found objects (pieces originally made for other purposes) and frequently resembled a two-dimensional painting or linear drawing. Smith's best known open-space metal "drawings" of this period were *Hudson River Landscape* and *Australia* (both 1951). Designed for frontal viewing against a wall or sky, these hieroglyphiclike pieces have self-contained suspensions within tangled frameworks of slender metal strips, which echo the twists of the river, and a kangaroo silhouette. One of his most powerful metal designs is *Blackburn: Song of an Irish Blacksmith* (1950), which creates a visual disjunction between frontal and profile views. From the front this emblematic figure appears symmetrically

aligned with detail along the periphery of the open metal frame, while the side view creates tension with displaced alignment of the head and jumbled overlay of metal shapes inside the frame.

During the late 1940s and 1950s, Smith's work became increasingly larger in scale and more spontaneous, and he began exploring ideas in related series of sculptures. Such series as *Agricola* and *Tanktotem* had anthropomorphic connotations expressed in a powerful verticality which often incorporated found or "recycled" elements like farm tools and machine parts. His lifelong interest in the subconscious manifested itself in his use of the totem image to express the underlying dark feelings and desires within modern society. Wedding sculptural form to totemic idea, he achieved a profound physical separation or distancing between viewer and art object in his aim to create "contemporary symbols." The emblematic figure of *Tanktotem V* (1955–1956), with its disclike projections assembled from boiler plates and tank tops, welded on a vertical metal trunk is extremely planar and immobile, yet aggressive in the way it activates the immediate space.

From the late 1950s until his untimely death in an auto accident in 1965, Smith created several series of massive sculptures for which he is most famous. These increasingly abstract pieces composed of strong geometric shapes, often appearing haphazardly arranged, and of painted metal or polished stainless steel were designed to be placed in a landscape. In 1962 he created twenty-seven sculptures, the *Voltri* series, in thirty days for the Spoleto Festival in Italy. These were his last pieces based on the human figure, although later works still retained human references. Paralleling the development of hard-edged painting, the assemblages of flat, cut-out geometric forms of the *Zig* series were painted in bright colors and had clearly defined edges.

Smith's most abstract sculptures, the *Cubi* series, are regarded as forerunners of the "primary structures" of Minimal art. He returns to three-dimensional volume with these assemblages of welded cubes, cylinders, and squares of polished and abraded stainless steel, which balance precariously one on top of another. *Cubi I* (1963) has a square base supporting a square balanced on one corner from which four cubes reach vertically culminating in a smaller square, and a gleaming buffed surface that reflects shifting patterns.

Smith viewed himself as a painter who "paints with steel." Indeed, his sculptural development paralleled changes occurring in American painting at the time. He moved from a personal, expressionistic, and surrealistic art to a more objective, Cubist-influenced monumentality. Smith and JACKSON POLLOCK are often considered the two most significant post–World War II artists in America.

BIBLIOGRAPHY

Gray, Cleve (ed.), *David Smith by David Smith*, 1968; Hess, T. B., *David Smith*, 1964; Krauss, Rosalind E., *Terminal Iron Works: The Sculpture of David Smith*, 1971.

Smithson, Robert

(January 2, 1938–July 20, 1973)
Painter, Sculptor

Robert Smithson, an experimental artist who took art out of the museum and gallery and created it in situ (exterior place or environment), was a pioneer of Earthworks or Land art. He is also known for his many incisive articles on art.

Smithson was born in Passaic, New Jersey, and began to develop his lifelong love of nature and prehistory after a childhood visit to the Museum of Natural History in New York City. Other early influences were a family cross-country trip, which introduced him to the wonders of America, and the poetry of WILLIAM CARLOS WILLIAMS, the family's physician.

While attending high school, Smithson studied at the Art Students League in New York on scholarship. He also served in the Army Special Services branch (1956–1957), painting watercolors for the Fort Knox mess hall, then hitchhiked throughout the United States and Mexico. His first solo exhibit of abstract paintings in 1959 was followed by a successful exhibit in Rome (1961). While abroad he became fascinated with Byzantine culture and the works of Freud and Jung, which influenced his later artistic focus on mythology, archetypes, and past ages.

After a 1962 exhibit, Smithson withdrew temporarily from the art world, partly in confusion over his artistic direction. In 1963 he married sculptor Nancy Holt. He reappeared on the art scene in 1965 with an exhibit of plastic sculptures. Some major innovative ideas and techniques were introduced in a series of solo shows at New York's Dwan Gallery (1966–1970). With the sculpture *E Chambers* (1965) he experimented with reflection and mirror image, while in *Alogon #2* and *Plunge* (both 1966) he focused on mathematical progression, perspective, and repetition.

Smithson is often identified with the Conceptual artists, who believe that concepts or ideas that lead to the physical realization of an art object are the true work of art, because they focus on the process of creating art, rather than art itself. Such geological refuse as rock fragments and gravel was collected by Smithson during visits to abandoned industrial sites and decaying urban areas, then arranged in containers or into heaps. Mirrors, along with photographs and maps of the sites where the materials were found, were next used to create his famous *Nonsites.* He wrote that this use of natural debris for artistic purposes would bring "a wholly new premise for contemporary sculpture."

By pushing his ideas one step further, Smithson created some of the first Earthworks or Land art in which the land itself is sculpted into an artwork. In deserted places, such as old quarries, he created mounds or trenches of earth and natural rubble that would continually be transformed by the elements. Since these works could not be exhibited in museums, he kept a photographic record of their transformation and decomposition. The development of Land art in the 1970s paralleled society's increasing awareness of the finiteness of natural resources.

Earthwork sculptures first found acceptance in Europe with such works as *Asphalt Rundown* (1969) in a quarry near Rome and *Broken Circle/Spiral Hill* (1971) in an abandoned sand quarry in Emmen, Netherlands.

Smithson's best-known earthwork structure was *Spiral Jetty* (1970), a tail-shaped structure of rocks, debris, and salt crystals that curved into Utah's Great Salt Lake. Its shape echoed the tail of the Great Serpent Mound in Ohio and reflected Smithson's typical method of evoking myths and the past in his work. The sculpture is no longer visible since the lake has risen and covered it.

Smithson died in a plane crash while trying to photograph the staked-out site at a desert lake near Amarillo, Texas, for his last earthwork, *Amarillo Ramp.* The earthwork was completed by friends of the artist.

BIBLIOGRAPHY

Hobbs, Robert, *Robert Smithson—Sculpture*, 1981; Holt, Nancy (ed.), *The Writings of Robert Smithson: Essays with Illustrations*, 1979; Tsai, Eugenie, *Robert Smithson Unearthed: Drawings, Collages, Writings*, 1991.

Sondheim, Stephen Joshua

(March 22, 1930–   )
Composer, Lyricist

Stephen Sondheim has been challenging conventional musical theater since 1970 with the dramatic range, serious intent, command of language, and compositional innovation that make him a force on Broadway. A consummate craftsman, Sondheim creates beautiful, haunting songs from dramatic roots and tailors them to character and situation.

As a ten-year-old the precocious Sondheim moved with his mother from New York City to a Pennsylvania farm after his parents' divorce. Lyricist Oscar Hammerstein II (see RICHARD RODGERS), a neighbor, encouraged the youngster's theatrical interests and guided him through four early scores and librettos.

Sondheim attended the George School in Pennsylvania and Williams College in Massachusetts. At Williams he was awarded the Hutchinson Prize, a two-year fellowship, which he used to study composition with avant-garde composer MILTON BABBITT.

After writing scripts for television and the score for a never-produced musical in the early 1950s, Sondheim had two major successes as a lyricist: *West Side Story*, with LEONARD BERNSTEIN in 1957, and *Gypsy* with composer Jule Styne in 1959. A reluctant wordsmith, Sondheim wanted to establish himself as a composer. He did so with *A Funny Thing Happened on the Way to the Forum* in 1962.

The 1970 production of *Company* began Sondheim's long association with producer/director Harold (Hal) Prince. In their six collaborations they probed serious themes and experimented with new formats. In *Company* and *Follies* (1971), both plotless, the themes take the place of plots. *A Little Night Music* (1973), based on Ingmar Bergman's film comedy *Smiles of a Summer Night,* includes the song "Send in the Clowns," which became a popular hit. In the ambitious *Sweeney Todd, the Demon Barber of Fleet Street* (1979), the score stretches the conventional materials of musical comedy even further.

After the failure of *Merrily We Roll Along* (1981), Sondheim had a hit with *Sunday in the Park with George* (1984), which won a Pulitzer Prize and the New York Drama Critics' Circle Award. Based on the life of artist Georges Seurat, the musical poses questions about creativity and probes the ties between the artist and his world. Here music reflects the painter's techniques. Sondheim notes, "Seurat experimented with the color wheel the way one experiments with a scale." More recently, Sondheim found success with *Into the Woods* (1987).

BIBLIOGRAPHY

Green, S., *The World of Musical Comedy,* 4th ed., 1980; Swain, J., *The Broadway Musical, a Critical and Musical Survey,* 1990; Zadan, C., *Sondheim & Co.,* 2d ed., 1986.

Sousa, John Philip

(November 6, 1854–March 6, 1932)
Bandmaster, Composer, Writer

Of the nearly 140 marches composed by the "March King," many, such as "The Stars and Stripes Forever" (1896), remain popular. The most famous American composer and bandmaster of his day, Sousa and his ensemble were public darlings for years while the energetic composer wrote operettas, songs, and band suites.

Born in Washington, D.C., Sousa attended local schools and studied violin and orchestration with John Esputa, Jr., in a small nearby music school. He also learned trombone, baritone and E-flat alto horns, and cornet. In 1868 Sousa's father, Antonio, a trombonist with the U.S. Marine Corps Band, foiled the youngster's plan to join the circus as a musician by enrolling Sousa in the Marine Band as an apprentice.

During his seven years with the band Sousa studied violin and harmony with George Felix Benkert, and played violin in Benkert's Washington Orchestral Union and with other groups.

Sousa was composing, too: dances for piano, like "Moonlight on the Potomac," and his first march, "The Review."

Discharged from the Marine Corps in 1875, Sousa played in theater orchestras and turned down an opportunity to study in Europe. The following year he was in Philadelphia playing violin in a theater orchestra directed by French composer Jacques Offenbach at the Centennial Exposition. Offenbach's successful operettas and bandmaster Patrick Gilmore's popular style became touchstones for Sousa. He stayed in Philadelphia four years, playing violin in orchestras, teaching, arranging, and composing.

In 1879 Sousa conducted Gilbert and Sullivan's *H.M.S. Pinafore* and in 1880 put together and conducted the music for *Our Flirtations,* a variety show. The production opened in Philadelphia and toured. The group had reached St. Louis when Sousa received a telegram inviting him to become leader of the U.S. Marine Band. He accepted the position, joined the group October 1, 1880, and stayed until 1892. Under his leadership the band was reorganized and reshaped (forty-nine musicians in 1891) into a fine performing ensemble.

Sousa continued to compose, including the operettas *The Queen of Hearts* (1885) and *The Wolf* (1888), as well as a group of marches. "The Gladiator" and "The Rifle Regiment," written in 1886, Sousa's first successes, were followed by "Semper Fidelis" (1888), "The Washington Post" (1889), and "The High School Cadets" (1890). Now known everywhere, Sousa had piano arrangements of his works ordered by dealers in lots of 20,000. "The Washington Post" coincided with a new dance rage, the two-step. In Europe, in fact, the two-step was often called the "Washington post."

The businessman in Sousa surfaced in the early 1890s. He obtained royalty contracts from publishers, thus avoiding flat fees, resigned from the Marines to establish his own band, took on David Blakely as manager, and developed the sousaphone, a reshaped tuba that could be carried while marching. The Sousa Band opened in Plainfield, New Jersey, September 26, 1892, and carried on almost until Sousa died in 1932. It became the best-known band America had ever known. During the 1920s Sousa increased the size of the group from the original forty-six to about seventy players.

The Sousa Band toured the United States and Europe and made a world tour in 1910–1911. During World War I, Sousa served in the U.S. Navy, where he organized a group of over 300 sailors, the Jackie Band (named after their navy blue jackets), and toured to support the war effort. After the armistice, Sousa went back touring with his own group. The Sousa Band broke up in 1931 because of the bandmaster's failing health. Sousa died in Reading, Pennsylvania, as he prepared for a guest appearance with the city's Ringgold Band.

Sousa, active along with VICTOR HERBERT in promoting copyright reform, was a founding member of ASCAP (American Society of Composers, Authors and Publishers). He was awarded many honors both during his life and posthumously, including being remembered through the Sousa Stage in the John F. Kennedy Center for the Performing Arts in Washington, D.C.

BIBLIOGRAPHY

Newsom, J. (ed.), *Perspectives on John Philip Sousa,* 1983; Sousa, J. P., *Marching Along: Recollections of Men, Women, and Music,* 1928.

Stegner, Wallace Earle

(February 18, 1909–April 13, 1993)
Biographer, Novelist, Short-Story Writer

The twentieth-century writer Wallace Stegner published a large number of realistic novels, as well as biographies and other nonfiction historical studies. His novels often explored the lives of characters who seek to make homes for themselves amid the rootlessness of the rural West.

Stegner was born in Lake Mills, Iowa. The family moved frequently about the West, Midwest, and Canada, as his father sought to make his fortune through a variety of enterprises. Stegner began writing at the University of Utah, from which he graduated in 1930, and pursued this work more seriously as a graduate student at the University of Iowa, where he received his doctorate in 1935. He took teaching jobs successively at the University of Utah, the University of Wisconsin, and Harvard University; from 1945 until 1971, he directed the writing program at Stanford University.

Stegner's first novel, *Remembering Laughter* (1937), about a rivalry between two sisters, made him an immediate success, winning a prize from its publisher and earning him the beginnings of a national reputation.

On a Darkling Plain (1940), a more ambitious novel, concerns an embittered veteran of World War I who goes to Saskatchewan hoping to find seclusion. An influenza epidemic forces him into contact with the villagers, and, ironically, his spirit heals, though his body weakens and dies.

Stegner spent years writing *The Big Rock Candy Mountain* (1943), a novel of broad scope about a family's wanderings throughout the West in an effort to find their fortune. The book recounts Stegner's own family history, though critics have observed that the story is rendered as fully realized fiction.

Stegner wrote only three novels over the next twenty years, though he also produced a substantial amount of nonfiction and many short stories. The three novels—*Second Growth* (1947), *The Preacher and the Slave* (1950), and *A Shooting Star* (1961)—were narrower in scope than *The Big Rock Candy Mountain* and considered subjects and themes further from his own experience. Stegner's nonfiction had begun with a study of Mormon culture, called *Mormon Country* (1942), and included a biography of the ex-

Copyright Leo Holub; Courtesy Random House

plorer and conservationist John Wesley Powell, *Beyond the Hundredth Meridian* (1954). Such short stories as "The Women on the Wall" (1946) and "The Blue-Winged Teal" (1950) received the highest critical praise. With "Field Guide to Western Birds" (1956), Stegner introduced the character of Joe Allston, a rough-edged, retired literary agent, who returns to narrate two novels.

The first of these novels, *All the Little Live Things* (1967), takes place as Allston is coming to grips with his adult son's apparent suicide and the death by cancer of another young family friend. The second Allston novel, *The Spectator Bird* (1976), features the story, told in retrospect, of an infatuation he had experienced twenty years earlier while traveling with his wife in Denmark. *The Spectator Bird* won the National Book Award in 1977.

Angle of Repose (1971) concerns an aging history professor, Lyman Ward, who is suffering through a degenerative illness and his wife's abandonment. Ward absorbs himself with the project of ordering the papers of his grandmother, a writer and illustrator. The process triggers in him a host of reflections on his own life, particularly as he confronts his grandmother's decision many years earlier to leave her husband, his grandfather, a gifted man with a failed career as a mining geologist. Stegner drew the characters of the grandparents from the papers of the American writer and illustrator Mary Hallock Foote, which he had collected for Stanford's library many years earlier. *Angle of Repose* won the Pulitzer Prize for Fiction in 1972.

Among his nonfiction works are *The Uneasy Chair* (1974), a biography of Bernard

DeVoto, and *One Way to Spell Man* (1982), collected essays.

Stegner died in Santa Fe, New Mexico, in 1993.

BIBLIOGRAPHY

Robinson, Forrest G., and Margaret C. Robinson, *Wallace Stegner*, 1977.

Steichen, Edward

(March 27, 1879–March 25, 1973)
Painter, Photographer

E dward Steichen, one of America's greatest photographers, embraced in his seventy-seven-year career the worlds of pictorial and straight photography—ranging from the commercial work of fashion and photojournalism to the documentation of combat during wartime.

Eduard J. Steichen (he later dropped the middle initial and changed the spelling of his first name) was born in Luxembourg in 1879. The family moved to America in 1881, residing in Hancock, Michigan, and, later, Milwaukee, Wisconsin. At age sixteen he was apprenticed as a designer at the American Fine Art Company, a commercial lithographic company in Milwaukee. He also studied painting and organized the Milwaukee Art Students' League. Meanwhile, he was experimenting in photography. He grew dissatisfied with his first camera, a Kodak box, because he could not control the exposure and development of single plates. With his new Primo Folding View Camera, a 4-by-5-inch camera that used glass plates, he was able to develop and print his own work. His first images were used as models for designs in his work at the lithographic company. "So my first real effort in photography was to make photographs that were useful," he wrote in his autobiography, *A Life in Photography* (1963), defining what was to become his artistic credo. "And, as I look back over the many intervening years, I find that usefulness has always been attractive in the art of photography."

In 1899 he sent some photographs to the Philadelphia Salon. A year later, he joined other progressive photographers, including F. Holland Day, Frank Eugene, Clarence H. White, and Gertrude Kasebier, in the "New School of American Photography" exhibition in Paris. Steichen's early photographs—*A Frost-Covered Pool* (1901), for example—were dubbed Impressionistic because of their soft focus, lack of definition, and extremes of lights and darks. He worked extensively in techniques that manipulated the plate, producing platinum, palladium, gum-bichromate, and pigment prints.

Establishing a studio in Paris, Steichen had his first one-man show in 1901. His series of portraits of leaders in the art world (including Rodin, Matisse, and Maeterlinck) and a number of nudes (*The Little Round Mirror*, 1901, *La Cigale*, 1901, *Figure with Iris*, 1902) elicited the scorn of critic George Bernard Shaw and the admiration of Ernst Juhl, editor of the German magazine *Die Photographische Rundschau*. Back in New York a year later, he established a portrait studio at 291 Fifth Avenue and renewed his friendship with ALFRED STIEGLITZ. They founded a society dedicated to promote pictorial photography, the Photo-Secession (a name borrowed from the German avant-garde). The Photo-Secession's first show in 1902 presented the kind of Impressionistic images that divided the critics. In the words of Beaumont Newhall, "Art critics were positive about it: some found it a revealing demonstration of hitherto unsuspected aesthetic possibilities of the camera, others condemned it as a pretentious display of imitation paintings and wondered if the aim of the photographers was 'to hold as 'twere a smoked glass up to nature.'" Utilizing the gum-bichromate print process—a nonsilver process that allowed manual control in developing with a brush (resulting in images often confused with drawings and watercolors)—much of Steichen's early landscape work revealed a predilection for the misty, hazy light of twilight and dawn. "Under those conditions the woods had moods," he wrote, regarding images like *The Pool—Evening* (1899) and *Edge of the Woods* (1899)—"and the moods aroused emotional reactions that I tried to render in photographs." Similarly, his city scenes, like *Brooklyn Bridge* (1903) and *The Flatiron Building* (1905) are studies in moody, diffused light. Memorable portraits from these years include striking chiaroscuro studies of J. P. Morgan (1903) and Richard Strauss (1906).

Steichen turned his studio over to the members of the Photo-Secession in 1905. On November 24 of that year "The Little Galleries of the Photo-Secession," as it was now called (later dubbed simply 291), opened to the public. Subsequent exhibitions introduced the most avant-garde paintings, sculptures, and photographs that the American art world had ever seen—drawings by Rodin, watercolors by Cézanne, Cubist paintings by Picasso and Braque, and so on. "[291] was a laboratory, an experimental station," proclaimed the journal *Camera Work*, "and must not be looked upon as an Art Gallery, in the ordinary sense of the term."

During World War I, Steichen commanded the American Air Service's Division of Aerial Photography. Faced with the challenge of securing high-definition photographs from a vibrating, speeding airplane at altitudes of 20,000 feet aroused in him a fascination for the aesthetic and the utility of straight photography (see also EDWARD WESTON). It was at this time that he decided to abandon painting and devote himself exclusively to photography. By 1920 he had rejected the manipulations of his earlier gum-print processes and began working primarily with silver prints. Three years later he joined the staff of the Condé Nast Publications as chief photographer and provided a great quantity of fashion photographs and celebrity portraits for magazines like *Vogue* and *Vanity Fair*. His theatrical portraits were especially noteworthy, capturing such luminaries as JOHN BARRYMORE, CHARLIE CHAPLIN, MARTHA GRAHAM, Lillian Gish, GRETA GARBO, and Paul Robeson in striking, dramatic poses. The solid design, dramatic use of artificial light, and an uncanny flair for those moments when a face reveals character transcended the commercial origins of the images.

Steichen again became involved in wartime activities when he was commissioned a lieutenant commander in the U.S. Navy in 1942. As director of the U.S. Naval Photographic Institute, he was in charge of all navy combat photography. He mounted two important wartime exhibitions—"Road to Victory" and "Power in the Pacific." Retiring with the rank of captain, Steichen served as director of the Department of Photography at the Museum of Modern Art from 1947 to 1962. The most famous of his projects during these years was the famed "Family of Man" exhibition, which opened in January 1955. Winner of many awards, including a Front Page Award from the Newspaper Guild, it brought together 503 images by 273 photographers from 68 countries. The U.S. Information Agency circulated it among 38 countries. In attempting to explain its unprecedented success, Steichen wrote: "The people in the audience looked at the pictures, and the people in the pictures looked back at them. They recognized each other." In 1961, in honor of his eighty-second birthday, the exhibition "Steichen the Photographer" opened at the Museum of Modern Art.

"Photography is a medium of formidable contradictions," wrote Steichen. "It is both ridiculously easy and impossibly difficult. . . .

[T]he photographer is the only imagemaker who begins with the picture completed. His emotions, his knowledge, and his native talent are brought into focus and fixed beyond recall the moment the shutter of his camera has closed."

BIBLIOGRAPHY

Juhl, Ernst, "Edward Steichen," in Beaumont Newhall (ed.), *Photography: Essays and Images*, 1980; Longwell, Dannis, *Steichen: The Master Prints, 1895–1914, The Symbolist Period*, 1978; Steichen, Edward, *A Life in Photography*, 1963.

Stein, Gertrude

(February 3, 1874–July 27, 1946)
Novelist, Poet

Gertrude Stein wrote novels, essays, and poetry in which she sought to change not only the ways in which language is used in literature but also our understanding of the nature of meaning. She spent forty years of her life in France and, like her contemporary James Joyce, she used her own past all the while she was a staunch expatriate.

Stein was born in Allegheny, Pennsylvania, on February 3, 1874, the daughter of a wealthy family. After studying psychology with William James at Radcliffe, she spent four years at medical school at the Johns Hopkins School of Medicine, but she left without taking her degree due to boredom.

In 1903 Stein moved to Paris with her brother Leo, and they began their influential collection of paintings by such modern artists as Cézanne, Matisse, Picasso, and Juan Gris. *Three Lives,* unconventional stories written in 1906 and published at Stein's own expense in 1909, presented vivid character studies of two white servant girls and one unhappy black girl named Melanctha. Their inspiration included a Cézanne portrait, Stein's own friendship with Picasso, and her memories of life in Baltimore at Johns Hopkins.

From 1906 to 1908 Stein wrote *The Making of Americans,* a novel based on her own family's cultural history over three generations. She devised a complex narrative style that abandoned formal plotting and adopted a free prose with odd syntax and punctuation. She concentrated on psychological portraiture rather than suspenseful storytelling. The book remained unpublished until 1925.

In 1909 Stein invited Alice B. Toklas, a Californian visiting in Paris, to join her household. Four years later Leo Stein moved out and Toklas became her secretary, cook, confidante, and lifelong companion. Their apartment was a salon for the elite of the art and literary world, especially the young American novelists whom she dubbed "the lost generation."

Stein's writing was heavily influenced by Picasso's Cubist paintings, which reduced natural forms to geometric shapes in order to call attention to the plastic nature of art itself. She meant to isolate words from their ordinary meanings and relations, to "let come what would happen to come," as she said later.

In 1914 she published *Tender Buttons,* which jettisons conventional syntax and semantics, even in its subtitle: *Objects Food Rooms.* The first piece in the collection, "A Carafe, That Is a Blind Glass," typifies Stein's difficult style: "A kind in glass and a cousin, a spectacle and nothing strange a single hurt color and an arrangement in a system to pointing. All this and not ordinary, not unordered in not resembling. The difference is spreading."

Stein's third book, *Geography and Plays,* published in 1922, contained her early experiments with dramatic form. Plays were reduced to speeches by characters often unnamed, devoid of action but aware of scenic background or landscape. "Sacred Emily," one of the portraits in this volume, contains the first appearance of Stein's famous sentence, "Rose is a rose is a rose is a rose." She was referring to a woman, not a flower.

Stein, not surprisingly, had difficulty getting her work published. Even when published, it did not sell, despite its influence on other writers, such as ERNEST HEMINGWAY, MARIANNE MOORE, THORNTON WILDER, and WILLIAM CARLOS WILLIAMS. Between 1930 and 1933, Toklas edited five volumes of Stein's work under her own private Plain Edition imprint, including *Lucy Church Amiably* and *Before the Flowers of Friendship Faded Friendship Faded.*

In 1926 Stein began at last to produce accessible explanations of her work. She lectured at Oxford and Cambridge on "Composition as Explanation," about her attempts to use writing to effect a new awareness of time, "a prolonged present," and to reflect on postwar consciousness. In 1933 she published *The Autobiography of Alice B. Toklas,* in which she assumes Toklas's persona in order to write her own autobiography, from 1907 to 1932, in clear and simple prose. The book takes on the problem of Stein's identity versus her perception by her audience, and it offers literary self-justification. Perhaps because it contained so much gossip about members of Stein's bohemian artistic circle, the book became an instant bestseller in the United States.

Stein made a triumphant lecture tour of the United States in 1934–1935; her book *Lectures in America* appeared soon after. Capitalizing on her new popularity, Random House reissued *Three Lives* and brought out *Portraits and Prayers* in 1934 and *The Geographical History of America* in 1936. Stein further explored her interests in problems of identity and audience in *Everybody's Autobiography* (1937) and *Ida: A Novel* (1941).

During World War II, Stein and Toklas fled Paris for southeastern France. In early 1943 she started keeping a journal describing the details of daily life in the village of Culoz during the Nazi occupation and after liberation in August 1944. It was published as *Wars I Have Seen* in 1945. By that time Stein and Toklas had returned to their Paris apartment, where they welcomed swarms of American soldiers whom she called her "military god-sons." After touring U.S. Army bases in Germany, she began a second book on the GIs in Europe. *Brewsie and Willie* (1946) mimicked their speech patterns in dialogues that she had stored in her keen memory. "The voices," as one critic wrote, "dominate the book. These are the new Americans talking about the faults they see in the world."

Her last book was a collaboration with Virgil Thomson on an opera about Susan B. Anthony, the nineteenth-century suffragist. *The Mother of Us All* was published posthumously in 1947. Stein died from cancer in 1946 in Paris.

BIBLIOGRAPHY

Hoffman, Michael J., *Gertrude Stein,* 1976; Mellow, James R., *Charmed Circle: Gertrude Stein & Company,* 1974.

Steinbeck, John Ernst

(February 27, 1902–December 20, 1968)
Journalist, Novelist, Short-Story Writer

John Steinbeck, best known for his novel *The Grapes of Wrath,* explored the lives of common people and their ties to their environment. As they struggle against adversity or the dehumanizing aspects of modern society, his characters often must come to grips with the meaning of shared experience.

Steinbeck was born in Salinas, California. He attended Stanford University intermittently between 1919 and 1925 but finally dropped out to go to New York City. There he held a job as a reporter for the New York *American.* Returning to California, he worked as an apprentice painter, chemist, surveyor, and fruit picker while writing his first novel, *Cup of Gold* (1929), a fictionalized life of the pirate Sir Henry Morgan.

Steinbeck's next book, *Pastures of Heaven* (1932), was an episodic account of the lives of farm workers in a California valley. The book explores their ties to the land, emphasizing their seclusion from the corrupting pressures of society. *To a God Unknown* (1933), an allegorical tale about four brothers attempting to farm a parched valley, concludes with a strong statement about the individual's relationship to the land, as one brother sacrifices himself to bring rain.

Tortilla Flat (1935) established Steinbeck's reputation. It concerns Mexican American *paisanos* in Monterey, California, and compares their simple camaraderie to that of the knights of the Round Table of Arthurian legend. *In*

The Nobel Foundation

Dubious Battle (1936) earned praise for its realistic depiction of a failed strike by fruit pickers and the efforts of radical leaders to organize migrant farm workers.

Of Mice and Men (1937) is a short novel, written in the manner of a play, which dramatizes the lives and friendship of two field laborers who dream of buying a farm of their own. Lennie, a giant of a man, has the mental capacities of a child. He loves to handle soft creatures, but he lacks control of his immense strength and kills them. His own death dashes the hopes of his friend and protector, George. The book sold well, and the story was also produced as a play (it won the New York Drama Critics' Circle Award for 1938) and as a movie released in 1939.

A collection of stories, *The Long Valley* (1938), included a popular four-story cycle called *The Red Pony* (1937), about a boy's maturing experiences on his father's ranch.

Steinbeck's career reached its zenith with *The Grapes of Wrath* (1939), a book that captured the economic despair of the 1930s and spawned popular outrage against conditions faced by migrant farm workers. The Joad family has moved from Oklahoma to California to escape the droughts that ruined farmers in the Midwest. They encounter strike violence and police harassment even as they face starvation and death. Unlike Steinbeck's earlier novels, in which characters often fail to fully understand their own circumstances, the Joads come to realize how their plight mirrors those of people around them and so begin to transcend their suffering for the good of others. The book won a Pulitzer Prize in 1940 and was made into an unforgettable film starring HENRY FONDA the following year.

Steinbeck traveled to Mexico in 1940 to work with the marine biologist Edward F. Ricketts, with whom he published a book about marine life, *Sea of Cortez* (1941). Ricketts apparently became the model for the character Doc in two subsequent Steinbeck novels, *Cannery Row* (1945) and its sequel, *Sweet Thursday* (1954). *Cannery Row* returns to Monterey, where Doc joins in the simple, happy lives Steinbeck first depicted in *Tortilla Flat.*

Critics agree that most of Steinbeck's subsequent novels lacked the scope and intensity of *The Grapes of Wrath.* With *The Moon Is Down* (1942), he turned his attention to World War II, writing about resistance to Nazi oppression in an occupied country. *The Wayward Bus* (1947) depicts travelers stranded overnight at a roadside station in California. In *The Pearl* (1947), a Mexican fisherman's greatest find brings him tragedy, and he throws it back into the sea. *Burning Bright* (1950), another short novel written in the manner of a play, addresses a woman's determination to seek out a man other than her sterile husband to father a child.

With *East of Eden* (1952), Steinbeck again set out to frame a novel of broad scope, mingling the story of a family living in Salinas Valley, California, with the biblical tale of Cain and Abel. Adam Trask is abandoned by his wife, Cathy, and is left to raise their two sons, Cal and Aaron. Jealous of Adam's affection for Aaron, Cal tells his brother their mother has become a prostitute; this knowledge drives Aaron to his death.

The Short Reign of Pippin IV (1957) satirizes French politics and culture in the era of the premier Charles De Gaulle, post–World War II. *The Winter of Our Discontent* (1961) frames a meditation by the central character on betrayal, his own and others'.

Steinbeck was awarded the Nobel Prize for Literature in 1962. Two years later, he received both the Presidential Medal of Freedom and the U.S. Medal of Freedom.

Steinbeck's nonfiction includes *Their Blood Is Strong* (1938), a collection of newspaper articles he wrote while traveling with migrant farm workers; *A Russian Journal* (with Robert Capa) (1948); *Once There Was a War* (1958), derived from his work as a war correspondent; and *Travels with Charley in Search of America* (1962), about a cross-country trip with his dog. He also wrote or cowrote screenplays for *The Forgotten Village* (1941), *Lifeboat* (1944), *A Medal for Benny* (1945), *The Pearl* (1946), *The Red Pony* (1949), and *Viva Zapata!* (1952).

Steinbeck died in New York City on December 20, 1968.

BIBLIOGRAPHY

Benson, Jackson J., *The True Adventures of John Steinbeck, Novelist,* 1984; Kiernan, Thomas, *The Intricate Music: A Biography of John Steinbeck,* 1979; McCarthy, Paul, *John Steinbeck,* 1980.

Steinway & Sons

(1853–   )
Firm of Piano Makers

A leader in the industry, Steinway & Sons set lasting standards for piano making in the United States and Europe. The firm's success springs from innovative technology, quality craftsmanship, and superior marketing skills. The instruments constructed in the 1880s by the Steinways are the prototypes of all modern pianos.

Born in Wolfshagen, Germany, in 1797, Heinrich Engelhard Steinweg fought at Waterloo in 1815 and turned to cabinetmaking after his discharge. His first piano, still held by the family, was completed in 1836. Fourteen years later he moved his family to New York City, anglicized his name to Henry Steinway, and founded Steinway & Sons in 1853.

In 1855 a Steinway square overstrung instrument won a prize at the American Institute Exhibition in New York. Overstringing, a method that fanned bass strings over the others, allowed greater string tension, alleviated overcrowding, simplified construction, and improved tone. The firm built the first overstrung upright in 1863.

The eldest son of Henry Steinway, Theodore (1825–1889), had remained in Germany to manage his own piano business. After the deaths of Henry's younger sons, Charles (1829–1865) and Henry, Jr. (1830–1865), Theodore sold his firm in Germany and emigrated. Theodore consolidated technical innovations to change the design of pianos: cross-stringing and improved iron frames that bore the tension of longer strings; and machine-produced felt-covered hammers. The changes increased the volume of the pianos and enriched their tone. Thanks to the work of Theodore and another brother, Albert (1840–1877), instruments manufactured by the late 1880s were "a generation before their competitors," and, continues writer Cyril Ehrlich, "essentially modern pianos."

William (1835–1896), Henry's fourth son, oversaw production and turned his agile brain and musical interests to promoting and marketing Steinways. Associating excellence with the Steinway product, William recruited artists to tour by rail with Steinway pianos. The first Steinway Hall, built at 14th Street in New York City in 1866, promoted pianists and instruments. The second Steinway Hall, with domed ceiling and Italian marble pillars, went up on 57th Street in 1925.

Steinways won prizes in competitions and endorsements from leading pianists. Demand for instruments prompted the replacement of the Fourth Avenue piano works with a factory and company village in Astoria, Queens, in the 1870s. The firm promoted itself abroad, too, building Steinway Hall in London in 1876 and a factory in Hamburg in 1880.

In 1903 Steinway's 100,000th piano was presented to the White House. In 1938 the 300,000th replaced it. Edward Rothstein observes in *The Smithsonian* that "by the time Henry Z. Steinway, of the fourth generation, took over in 1955, there were conflicts within the expanding family, a smaller skilled-labor market, an aging plant, an uncertain future."

In 1972 the company was sold to CBS, then in 1985 to a small group of investors. Three years later, a Carnegie Hall gala celebrated 135 years of Steinway & Sons and introduced piano number 500,000. Scholar Craig H. Roell notes that "Steinway was the first to promote itself successfully as art in the age of mechanical reproduction. It is the Steinway legacy."

BIBLIOGRAPHY

Ehrlich, C., *The Piano: A History,* 1976; Loesser, A., *Men, Women, and Pianos: A Social History,* 1954; Steinway, T., *People and Pianos,* 1953.

Stella, Frank Philip

(May 12, 1936–   )
Painter

Frank Stella, a leader in the Post-Painterly Abstraction movement that began in the 1950s, is known for the flat linear images of his early work, the later shaped, geometrical canvases, and his more recent three-dimensional constructions.

Stella was born in 1936 in Malden, Massachusetts, the son of a doctor. He attended Phillips Academy in Andover, where he first began to study painting. In his book *Working Space* (1986), he recalled that, at the time, smearing cadmium red pigment onto shellacked cardboard was a pleasurable alternative to the chemistry lab. It was while painting a still life of a pot of sickly ivy that he first decided to abandon mere representation and proceed in an abstract direction. "I knew that my hand was not going to make any more renditions," he said. "In that small moment of confrontation when I felt I had to do it or forget it, I formed my basic feeling about abstract painting." He entered Princeton University in 1954, where he continued to paint in an extracurricular studio. Eventually Stella chose not to imitate the gestural abstraction of Abstract Expressionism (see BARNETT NEWMAN), which was then at its peak; rather, he began working in the mode that would first gain him attention, the formulation of linear patterns.

The years 1958 and 1959 were a crucial time in his career. Living in New York City, he decided to pursue easel painting as a career (supporting himself by jobs as a house painter). He began with austere, black paintings in which stripes repeated a central motif (*Delta* in 1958 and *Jill* in 1959). His work was exhibited at the Museum of Modern Art in the winter of 1959–1960, where he attracted the attention of influential critics and museum curators. That institution acquired its first painting by him, *The Marriage of Reason and Squalor* (1959). His stripes of aluminum and copper paint on shaped canvases established him as a standard-bearer for the movement that would dominate the 1960s, subsequently referred to by a variety of labels: Abstract Imagism, Post-Painterly Abstraction (see MORRIS LOUIS), Color Field painting (see BARNETT NEWMAN), and Systemic painting (to name but a few).

All the while, as Stella recalls, he was absorbing the images of others: "Exciting abstract expressionist painting seemed to be everywhere. I went from gallery to gallery, museum to museum, opening to opening, and then back to my studio to look at my own painting." As opposed to the presumed tyranny of the individual gestural and/or brush stroke, Stella's interest resided in isolating simplified formal elements in large, flatly painted color areas. "I saw in front of me a system that would guarantee the exclusion of painterly gestures which in seemingly abstract painting always brought the ghost of figuration with them." As he explored more intricate patterns, he began working with bright colors, as in *Jasper's Dilemma* (1962–1963) and *BAM* (1965). In the late 1960s came the *Protractor* series, huge canvases of sometimes fluorescent colors in combinations of circular and semicircular shapes.

Increasingly, Stella insisted that an abstract painting existed as an object as much as a metaphor for an emotional state. After his first retrospective at the Museum of Modern Art in 1969, he entered a second career, as art historian William Rubin has described it, in the 1970s. His work began displaying an almost extravagant energy and materiality. He introduced three-dimensional geometrics and a more complex arsenal of materials into his works, thereby infusing them with sculptural implications. Complicated arrangements in aluminum and other media like *Montenegro I* (1974–1975) evaded the traditional distinctions dividing sculpture and easel painting;

rather, as William Rubin insists, they were at once pictorial and sculptural. Stella was retrieving the spatial considerations that had been lost in the essential flatness of his earlier works. The *Indian Bird* (1977–1979) and *Exotic Bird* (1976–1980) series were assemblies of metal alloy sheets, curved wooden cutouts, wire mesh, and splashes of paint, crayon, and glitter markings (*Jungli kowwa*, 1978). These ambitious constructions continued, with many variations, through the 1980s.

In his Charles Eliot Norton Lectures at Harvard University (published as *Working Space*, 1986), Stella admitted that his zeal in the 1960s to abandon "ordinary" representational painting in favor of a more "special" abstraction had been wrongheaded. Over the years he had come to believe in the reverse—that there was much in the former that was special and much in the latter that was ordinary. He said that too much of the abstract painting of his contemporaries, in this "difficult present," was facing a crisis of ordinariness. By 1970 it had lost contact with what had always made representational painting special—it had "lost its ability to create space" that was open to feeling, either emotional or literal. This achievement of a self-contained space had been declining into a series of "excruciatingly dull" shallow surfaces and misguided quests for the primacy of color. "What we are left with is illustrated space which we read; what we have lost is created space which we could feel." Stella concluded that if abstract painting were to be rejuvenated, it needed to reestablish contact with the important precedents established in the late sixteenth and early seventeenth centuries—the Rome of Caravaggio, Rubens, and the Carracci—the creation of pictorial space, a space independent of architecture, a space with a special, self-contained character. This should remain the "heart of modern painting," insisted Stella. "The aim of art is to create space—space that is not compromised by decoration or illustration, space in which the subjects of painting can live."

BIBLIOGRAPHY

Inboden, Gudrun, et al., *Frank Stella: Black Paintings, 1958–1960: Cones and Pillars, 1984–1987,* 1988; Rubin, Lawrence, *Frank Stella: Paintings, 1958 to 1965,* 1986; Rubin, William, *Frank Stella, 1970–1987,* 1987; Stella, Frank, *Working Space,* 1986.

Sternberg, Josef von

(May 29, 1894–December 22, 1969)
Film Director

Among the directors of Hollywood's Golden Age, Sternberg was the most in love with the image for the image's sake. He conceived of the screen as a canvas on which the filmmaker "paints with light and shadow." For many, he is best known for discovering MARLENE DIETRICH.

Born Jonas Sternberg in Vienna to a poor Orthodox Jewish family, Sternberg came to the United States, for the second time, at age fourteen. As a teenager, he worked in a millinery shop and at the World Film Corporation in Fort Lee, New Jersey, where he cleaned and repaired damaged films.

During World War I he made training films for the U.S. Army Signal Corps. In Hollywood he was assistant director on *The Mystery of the Yellow Room* (1921) and *By Divine Right*

(1923), during which director Roy William Neill added the "von" to his name.

Sternberg's penchant for exploring the symbolic value of light and shadow, rather than rely on editing to tell a story, was strikingly evident in his first feature, *The Salvation Hunters* (1924). While the general audience and critical reaction to this story of social derelicts was not favorable, the film drew the attention and admiration of CHARLIE CHAPLIN and MARY PICKFORD, two of the most powerful forces in the industry.

Throughout the decade he directed nine more features, including *A Woman of the Sea* (1926), produced by Chaplin, but for mysterious reasons suppressed and unseen to this day. *Underworld* (1927) is considered the first gangster movie, and along with *The Docks of New York, The Dragnet,* and *The Last Command* (all 1928), confirmed Sternberg's mastery of visual style and atmospheric mise-en-scène.

Because he was equally creative with sound (his first sound feature was *Thunderbolt,* 1929), he was invited by producer Erich Pommer to direct Germany's first talking film, *The Blue Angel* (1930). The story of this production, of Sternberg's problems with the temperamental German actor Emil Jannings, and of his insistence that the relatively unknown Dietrich play the cabaret singer Lola-Lola, is related in Sternberg's autobiography.

His instincts about Dietrich's star quality proved correct, and he convinced her to come to Hollywood, where their second film, *Morocco* (1930), introduced her to American audiences. In quick succession came *Dishonored* (1931), *Shanghai Express,* and *Blonde Venus* (both 1932).

Sternberg's talent for creating stunning compositions was never more apparent than in *The Scarlet Empress* (1934) and *The Devil Is a Woman* (1935), his last and most deliriously stylized films with Dietrich. Sternberg photographed as well as directed the latter, as if to acknowledge that a certain end had been reached.

Other films of the 1930s included two flawed versions of literary classics, THEODORE DREISER's *An American Tragedy* (1931) and Fyodor Dostoyevski's *Crime and Punishment* (1935).

Sternberg's pictorialism received mixed critical reaction. Andrew Sarris aptly appraised his art when he remarked that unlike a realist like ERICH VON STROHEIM, Sternberg understood that "the appearances of things were more impressive than the things themselves." On the other hand, John Grierson, an important critic of the 1930s, disappointed after the promise of Sternberg's first film, labeled him the "sophisticated purveyor of the meretricious Dietrich" and concluded that "his aesthetic conscience [was] devoted to making hokum as good looking as possible."

Sternberg was less than deferential to actors, whom he describes in his autobiography as raw material: "The actor . . . is little more than a tube of color which must be used to cover my canvas." While Dietrich seemed content with this role, most male actors vehemently protested. William Powell and GARY COOPER described him as a tyrant, and Edward Arnold declared him a "raper of egos." His most exasperating experience with an actor was with Charles Laughton, whose endless difficulties playing the Roman emperor Claudius resulted in the killing of the project, *I, Claudius* (1937).

After the critically unappreciated *Shanghai Gesture* (1941), he was inactive until millionaire producer Howard Hughes invited him to direct *Jet Pilot* (1950, but unreleased until 1957) with John Wayne and Janet Leigh, and *Macao* (1952) with Robert Mitchum and Jane Russell, neither of which boosted his reputation.

His last film, *The Saga of Anatahan* (1953), while his least successful financially, was his "favorite," made "under almost ideal conditions." While he went to Japan to film it, he made the entire film in a studio, where once more he could create an illusion with sets, lights, and shadows, thus reviving the very strengths that made him unique.

Sternberg spent his last years in Los Angeles, where he painted and studied his collection of twentieth-century art. He was married and had two children, but considered his personal life so private that he made no mention of it even in his autobiography.

BIBLIOGRAPHY

Baxter, John, *The Cinema of Josef von Sternberg*, 1971; Baxter, Peter (ed.), *Sternberg*, 1980; Sarris, Andrew, *The Films of Josef von Sternberg*, 1966; Sternberg, Josef von, *Fun in a Chinese Laundry*, 1965.

Stevens, Wallace

(October 2, 1879–August 2, 1955)
Essayist, Poet

Wallace Stevens's complex lyrical poetry has probably spawned more criticism than any other modern American poet. His work, always open to many varied interpretations, uses sensuous and innovative language to pose psychological and philosophical questions.

Stevens was born in 1879 in Reading, Pennsylvania, the son of a prominent lawyer. Although his family were members of the Dutch Reformed Church, Stevens himself became an agnostic. As a special student at Harvard University from 1897 to 1900, Stevens contributed poems and short stories to the campus literary magazine, *The Harvard Advocate*. He then worked for a year as a reporter for the New York *Tribune* before entering New York Law School.

Stevens worked for four different law firms before joining, in 1908, the New York office of the American Bonding Company of Baltimore as a member of their legal staff. This last job gave him the financial security he needed to marry Elsie Viola Moll, a young woman from his hometown, in 1909. In March 1916 he was invited to join the New York office of the Hartford Accident and Indemnity Company, of which he eventually became a vice president. He and his wife moved permanently to Hartford, Connecticut, in May 1916. Their only child, Holly Bright Stevens, was born there in 1924.

Though Stevens nearly stopped writing poetry when he entered law school, and the hiatus stretched for a decade, he kept up with a circle of writers in Greenwich Village in New York City, including WILLIAM CARLOS WILLIAMS, MARIANNE MOORE, and E. E. CUMMINGS.

Stevens developed interests in the French Symbolists, in Oriental art, and especially in the work of the Imagist poets, who stressed absolute precision in presenting the image itself rather than oblique description. He returned to his own poetry with a vengeance. In 1915 he published in little magazines two of his best-known poems, "Peter Quince at the Clavier" in *Others* and "Sunday Morning" in *Poetry*. By the time these and many more were collected in his first book, *Harmonium*, in 1923, he had published over 100 poems in such magazines.

"Sunday Morning" begins to express Stevens's conviction that the loss of a belief in God—for Stevens, the social and cultural milestone that defines modernity—is no different than the loss of the gods of Greek mythology. Written in the tradition of religious verse, the poem takes an elegiac tone, observing the meditations of a woman over her own loss of faith. The voice of the poet suggests that the woman might find the same divinity within herself and in the natural world around her. "Death is the mother of beauty," the poet asserts, because it is part of the cycle of renewal.

Inspired by avant-garde theater he had seen in New York, Stevens wrote three plays in verse. *Three Travelers Watch a Sunrise* won the Players' Producing Company prize in 1916 for the best one-act play in verse, but he soon lost interest in theater.

"The Comedian as the Letter C," written in 1922 and published in *Harmonium*, tells the story of Stevens's own poetic development. A mock epic, it follows the travels of the hero Crispin—Stevens's invention and mask—from Bordeaux to the Yucatan and finally to Carolina. Much of Crispin's voyage is interior: he seeks a new mythology to replace the romantic vision of the late nineteenth century. He finds his new poetry in the majestic sea and the brilliant colors of the Yucatan. As the poem progresses, Stevens describes his fears for the poet: that his new realistic bent will lead him either to overgeneralize his experience or to subsume his art in the details of daily life. The title of the poem refers in part to Stevens's comic playing on the sounds of the letter *C*.

Discouraged by the reception of *Harmonium* and absorbed by his business and family responsibilities, Stevens gave up writing for almost a decade. When he resumed, around 1933, his work had found a new assurance. *Ideas of Order* (1935) reflects his new thinking on the role of the poet in a world without God. He finds a salvation by combining the poetic imagination and the realities of the moment. Stevens's poetic style had become at once sparer and more abstract.

In "The Idea of Order at Key West," Stevens describes a girl walking along a beach, singing of the sea. By her song, the girl makes meaningful "the meaningless plungings of water and the wind." She inspires in the poet the "blessed rage for order" that Stevens sees at the center of the artistic impulse.

His poems now earned the attention of critics, some of whom found fault with their dense aestheticism at a time of economic depression and threatened war. Stevens justified his work by saying that poetry helps people live their lives by renewing their spiritual resources. He later wrote: "Poetry is a purging of the world's poverty and change and evil and death. It is a present perfecting, a satisfaction in the irremediable poverty of life."

Stevens's theory of poetry served as a theme uniting much of his work for the remainder of his life. In *Parts of a World* (1942), he evolved the ideas most fully presented in his long poem, *Notes Toward a Supreme Fiction*, first published in the same year. It embraces both objective reality and the individual imagination in its attempt to elaborate a huge subject: the nature of poetry. Stevens wrote: "The final belief is to believe a fiction, which you know to be a fiction, there being nothing else. The exquisite truth is to know that it is a fiction and that you believe in it willingly." Poetry and religion were mingled.

Transport to Summer (1947) and *The Auroras of Autumn* (1950) reflect the poet's embrace of the seasons and of his own aging. His poetry became ever simpler and more abstract as he sought a unity between ordinary realities and the sublimity of poetry.

Many of Stevens's finest essays were collected as *The Necessary Angel* in 1951. His final work (poems, essays, plays, and adages) appeared in *Opus Posthumous* in 1957. His work was honored with a Bollingen Prize in 1949, National Book Awards in 1951 and 1955, and a Pulitzer Prize for *The Collected Poems* in 1955.

Stevens died of cancer in 1955. It was reported that he had converted to Roman Catholicism on his deathbed. In 1966 Holly, his daughter, published *Letters of Wallace Stevens*, a major source of biographical details.

BIBLIOGRAPHY

Bates, Milton J., *Wallace Stevens: A Mythology of Self*, 1985; Richardson, Joan, *Wallace Stevens: The Early Years, 1879–1923*, 1986, and *Wallace Stevens: The Later Years, 1923–1955*, 1988.

Stewart, James Maitland

(May 20, 1908–)
Actor

For nearly fifty years and in over seventy-five films Jimmy Stewart played the often awkward, but honest and decent hero, whose face and voice inspired trust. Like GARY COOPER, he was one of the great "naturals" of film history, an actor whose charisma and personality were mythologized on the big screen.

Stewart was born in Indiana, Pennsylvania, to Alexander Maitland and Elizabeth Ruth Jackson Stewart. The family ran a hardware business. Stewart graduated from Mercersburg Academy in 1928. He was an accomplished accordion player when he entered Princeton University, where he performed in productions of the Triangle Club and earned a B.S. in architecture in 1932. In later life he became an adviser to Princeton's Theatre in Residence.

He made his stage debut with the University Players in *Goodbye Again* and his New York debut in *Carrie Nation* in 1932. His first important Broadway role was in *Yellow Jack* in 1934, but in 1935 he left the stage for Hollywood, returning only once in 1947 in *Harvey*, a role he repeated in the 1950 film version.

A screen test at MGM won him a contract in 1935, and his first role was a news reporter in *Murder Man.* In *Next Time We Love* (1936) and *Shopworn Angel* (1938) he played opposite Margaret Sullavan, and in 1938 made his first film with director FRANK CAPRA, *You Can't Take It With You,* which won the Academy Award for Best Picture. *Destry Rides Again*

The Museum of Modern Art/Film Stills Archive

(1939), a lively western with MARLENE DIETRICH, followed, and in 1940 two fine films, again with Sullavan, *The Mortal Storm* and ERNST LUBITSCH's *The Shop Around the Corner.*

Splendid as he was in these, it was his performance as the idealistic senator fighting corruption in Capra's *Mr. Smith Goes to Washington* (1939) that set his quintessential style—a cracking voice suggesting vulnerability, overcome by an honest, open-faced obstinacy. It was for his performance as the reporter in *The Philadelphia Story* (1940), however, that he won an Oscar.

The first star to enlist during the Second World War, Stewart flew twenty-five bomber missions over enemy territory in Europe, and returned in 1945 highly decorated with the rank of full colonel. His record enhanced his popularity and was invoked in the film *Strategic Air Command* (1955). A member of the Air Force Reserve, he attained the rank of brigadier general in 1959.

His first film after the war, Capra's *It's A Wonderful Life* (1946), was for many his most memorable. As George Bailey, an average citizen of a small town who learns on the brink of suicide that his life is worthwhile, Stewart was genuinely inspiring. The film is a perennial favorite on television during the Christmas season.

In the next decade, his homey persona was tapped in the film bios *The Glenn Miller Story* (1954) and *The Spirit of St. Louis* (1957), but a more brittle, neurotic personality was seen in ALFRED HITCHCOCK's *Rear Window* (1954) and *Vertigo* (1958); and a tough frontiersman emerged in the westerns directed by Anthony Mann—especially *The Naked Spur* (1953) and *The Man from Laramie* (1955)—and JOHN FORD—notably *Two Rode Together* (1961) and *The Man Who Shot Liberty Valance* (1962).

Stewart remained active until 1983, making comedies, westerns, and several television movies. His private life has been so free of

scandal that gossip columnist Louella Parsons called him "the most nearly normal of all Hollywood stars."

BIBLIOGRAPHY

Eyles, Allen, *James Stewart*, 1985; Hunter, Allan, *James Stewart*, 1985; Jones, Ken D., Arthur F. McClure, and Alfred Twomey, *The Films of James Stewart*, 1970; Robbins, Jhan, *Everybody's Man*, 1985.

Stickley, Gustav

(March 9, 1858–April 21, 1942)
Designer, Furniture Maker

Gustav Stickley was the leading designer and manufacturer among the American Arts and Crafts furniture producers, and became famous for his Mission style of furniture, which featured simple, durable, hand-finished pieces, primarily made of oak. He also published an influential magazine, *The Craftsman* (1901–1916).

Born in Osceola, Wisconsin, Stickley first became a stonemason before settling on a career in furniture design and production. He worked in his uncle's workshop in Pennsylvania, where he developed his skills for making chairs. In an 1898 visit to Europe, he embraced the ideas of the English Arts and Crafts movement, which advocated a return to simplicity and improved standards of design, by emphasizing craftsmanship. This movement, led by art critic and social theorist John Ruskin and poet and designer William Morris, became the seminal influence on Stickley's design concepts and social ideas. During this visit, he also met many designers whose works contributed to his evolving stylistic development. Most important of these was English architect and designer C. F. A. Voysey, who effectively translated the concepts of the Arts and Crafts movement into practical reality.

When he returned to the United States, Stickley founded his own furniture company, the Gustav Stickley Company, in Eastwood, New York (near Syracuse), to produce designs inspired by the Arts and Crafts movement (1899). Rejecting the mass-produced, overly ornamental, cluttered look of Victorian design with its marble tabletops and plush upholstery, he created sturdy pieces with rectilinear lines, plain leather or canvas upholstery, and exposed joints, such as dovetails (wedge-shaped joints) or dowel pins (cylindrical peg joints). According to Stickley, each piece was to be "simple, durable, comfortable, and fitted for the place it was to occupy and the work it had to do." The style of his furniture became popularly known as Mission because of its utilitarian function or "mission" and its association with the unadorned architecture and benches of the early Franciscan missions in California. His earliest pieces were solid and attractive, but rather plain with a hint of Art Nouveau ornamentation (a decorative style popular from the 1890s to 1915 that stressed curving lines, asymmetry, and motifs of flowers, leaves, and tendrils; see LOUIS COMFORT TIFFANY).

Stickley first displayed his new work at the furniture exhibition in Grand Rapids, Michigan, in 1900, and it quickly became popular. This public acceptance produced many imitators, including his brothers, L. and J. G. Stickley, who formed a company in Fayetteville, New York, to make similar furniture by capitalizing on the Stickley name. To distinguish his furniture from that of his brothers, Gustav Stickley adopted the trade name Craftsman in 1901, and reorganized his firm as a profit-sharing cooperative of craftsmen called United Crafts (based on the socialist ideas of William Morris).

In 1901 he began publishing *The Craftsman* magazine through which he promoted the need of giving careful attention to the design and proportion of objects and the design and furniture of houses. The magazine presented the craftsman's aim as "to substitute the luxury of taste for the luxury of costliness; to teach that beauty does not imply elaboration or ornament; to employ only those forms and materials which make for simplicity, individuality and dignity of effort." In addition, Stickley used the magazine as a forum for his progressive social ideas, based primarily on the ideas of Morris.

Stickley's furniture became so popular that he expanded his activities beyond the Crafts-man Workshops in Eastwood. Between 1905 and 1913 he established the Craftsman Farms in New Jersey and the Craftsman Building in New York City, which contained a library, showrooms, offices, a lecture hall, and home builder's exhibits. He also issued mail-order catalogs that reached a wide market. Among the best-selling items were his adjustable back or reclining armchair known as the Morris chair and his Mission dining room furniture and long, narrow library tables, which were inspired by medieval stretcher tables.

By 1915 demand for his products was declining, and his company declared bankruptcy. Stickley spent the rest of his life in relative anonymity, still tinkering with his unpretentious ideas. His best designs, however, exerted strong influence on other designers and architects, including FRANK LLOYD WRIGHT.

BIBLIOGRAPHY

Freeman, J. C., *The Forgotten Rebel*, 1966; Smith, Mary Ann, *Gustav Stickley: The Craftsman*, 1983.

Stieglitz, Alfred

(January 1, 1864–July 13, 1946)
Photographer

Alfred Stieglitz, photographer, editor, and gallery owner, was, in the early decades of the twentieth century, an influential force in the development of modern art and photography in America.

He was born in Hoboken, New Jersey, and grew up in a cultured upper-middle-class immigrant Jewish family. When his father retired and moved to Germany in 1881, young Alfred went to Karlsruhe and Berlin to study mechanical engineering and photochemistry. He became fascinated with the technical and artistic aspects of photography, "first as a toy, then as a passion, then an obsession." Upon his return to New York in 1890, he worked in the photoengraving business until 1895. Two years later he founded *Camera Notes*, the journal of the Camera Club of New York, and in 1903 expanded it into *Camera Work*, the leading organ of the photography movement known as the Photo-Secession. *Camera Work* was the first American magazine to publish the writings of GERTRUDE STEIN, Benjamin de Casseres, Sadakichi Hartmann, and Charles Caffin. But it relentlessly criticized the lack of true culture in the United States and objected to the prevailing elitist attitudes toward art that removed it from contact with ordinary citizens.

The Photo-Secession movement, founded in 1902 by Stieglitz and his associate of many years, EDWARD STEICHEN, consisted of a loosely knit group of photographers, including Gertrude Käsebier, Clarence H. White, Joseph T. Keiley, Frank Eugene, and Alvin Langdon Coburn. The name was a reference to Stieglitz's early years abroad when a number of artists in Germany and Austria, who called their group the Secession, were breaking away from academic establishments; thus, Photo-Secession was intended to represent the Americans' own break from doctrinaire standards of photography.

Stieglitz's own views of the medium were essentially inherited from Peter Henry Emerson, a prominent late–nineteenth-century photographer who believed that the camera should not be used to imitate the effects of paintings; rather, it was essentially an optical instrument that could reveal nature truthfully to the viewer. This view became the basis for modernist, or as it was named in the twentieth century, "straight" photography (see also EDWARD WESTON). Stieglitz took his hand-held camera to the streets and, in all kinds of weather and light, shot his most important images: *The Flat-Iron Building, The Terminal, The Rag Picker, Winter—5th Avenue,* and *The Steerage* (all dating from 1892 to 1907). These photographs became part of a new spirit of realism that was emerging in the 1890s, a movement that also saw the appearance of plays by James A. Herne, the sketches and novels of STEPHEN CRANE, and the newspaper illustrations and street paintings of ROBERT HENRI's group of young New York artists.

However, there was no unified vision in the Photo-Secession, and Stieglitz quarreled with some of the members. He objected when a few of them, like Käsebier and Eugene, rejected photography in favor of negative manipulation and darkroom alterations to imitate the pictorial effects and hazy imagery of the Impressionist painters. Some of the photographers, on the other hand, decried Stieglitz's increasing

use of his 291 Gallery to display the work not just of photographers, but of painters. He withdrew from the group in 1910.

The 291 Gallery (so named after its Fifth Avenue street address) had been established in 1905 to promote modernist American and European artists. With the invaluable assistance of Edward Steichen, Stieglitz gave major one-man shows for the first time in this country to figures like Picasso (1911), Picabia (1913), and Brancusi (1914). Other artists frequently represented in the exhibitions included Matisse, Rodin, and Rousseau. In the years after World War I, Stieglitz established other galleries, like the Intimate Gallery and An American Place, where he continued to exhibit the works of such new young artists as Marsden Hartley, JOHN MARIN, and GEORGIA O'KEEFFE, whom he married in 1924.

Stieglitz received many honors. He was the first American to be elected to the British photographic society, The Linked Ring. He received the Progress Medal of the Royal Photography Society of Great Britain in 1924, the Townsend Harris Medal in 1927, and an Honorary Fellowship of the Photographic Society of America in 1940. Yet he was a difficult and temperamental man, reclusive and contentious, quick to imagine slights against him. Unlike the more expansive Steichen, who insisted that artistry can exist even in commercial and fashion photography, Stieglitz worked increasingly in his last years for a more intensely felt personal vision. Even his cloudscapes of the late 1920s, the *Equivalents* series, were, he insisted, primarily private, artistic expressions. It is representative, perhaps, of his growing detachment from everyday life that some of his later photographs of New York were from elevated positions, removing him from the immediate, closely observed style of the city scenes of his youth.

To varying degrees he remained a steadfast advocate of straight photography all his life. "Personally, I like my photography straight, unmanipulated, devoid of all tricks," he explained in 1924, with "a print not looking like anything but a photograph, living through its own inherent qualities and revealing its own spirit." However, he was not opposed to making certain alterations in his images, enlarging them, cropping (or "editing") them to improve their composition. Never a very prolific photographer, his importance today is best measured by his long fight to win a place for photography among the fine arts—not to mention inclusion of it in the art museums. There should be no differentiations between the so-called major and minor media, he said: "I have refused so to differentiate in all the exhibitions that I have ever

held. . . . It is the spirit of the thing that is important. If the spirit is alive, that is enough for me."

Stieglitz died in New York City in 1946.

BIBLIOGRAPHY

Homer, William Innes, *Alfred Stieglitz and the Photo-Secession*, 1983; Norman, Dorothy, *Alfred Stieglitz: An American Seer*, 1973.

Stokowski, Leopold Anthony

(April 18, 1882–September 13, 1977)
Conductor

A perfectionist in the sound of the orchestras he led, Leopold Stokowski was a pioneer in bringing contemporary music into American concert halls and a daring innovator in his use of recording, radio, and film technologies to bring classical music to a larger public.

Born in London, England, Leopold Anthony Stokowski began musical studies early and learned to play violin, piano, and organ. He entered the Royal College of Music at thirteen, the youngest student to have been admitted there, and studied composition with Hubert Parry and C. V. Stanford. He received a degree in organ in 1900. Two years later he was organist and choirmaster at St. James, Piccadilly, and in 1903 earned a B.Mus. at Queen's College, Oxford.

In 1905 Stokowski was appointed organist of St. Bartholomew's in New York City and during summers studied in Berlin, Munich, and Paris. In 1908 he substituted for an ill conductor in Paris and went on to make his London debut in 1909. Recommended by the music critic of the *Cincinnati Enquirer,* the inexperienced conductor was hired by the Cincinnati Symphony Orchestra in 1909. *New York Times* critic Harold Schonberg writes in his

1967 book *The Great Conductors* that during the three years in Ohio Stokowski "brought a new concept of conducting, a new kind of glamour, a new set of instrumental standards."

Stokowski's success in Cincinnati resulted in a position with the Philadelphia Orchestra in 1912. In 1915 he became an American citizen and in his twenty-five years in Philadelphia gained worldwide fame for himself and for the orchestra, and, suggests critic Noël Goodwin, "revolutionized the American musical scene."

A strong, elegant, and idiosyncratic conductor, Stokowski continually tinkered with orchestral seating, lighting effects, and dress. He improved the standards of performance, creating what became known as the "Philadelphia sound." In 1929 he began conducting without a baton, but what was most controversial was his penchant for altering scores. "You must realize that Beethoven and Brahms did not understand instruments," he said, and many considered his Bach transcriptions "monstrosities," notes Schonberg.

However, Schonberg goes on to say that "Stokowski, in his years with the Philadelphia Orchestra (1912–1936) created one of the most brilliant groups that had ever existed, a marvel for its color, precision, power and virtuosity. . . . More than any other conductor in the history of music, Stokowski was governed by sound, pure sound." Always searching out improved tonal quality, he investigated acoustics and electronics, and his discoveries were used to better recording and radio transmission techniques.

Stokowski is noted, too, for the music he introduced. In 1971 it was estimated that he had conducted over 2,000 first performances in some 7,000 concerts. SERGE KOUSSEVITZKY, when he arrived in Boston in 1924, was another advocate and performer of contemporary works, but until then, says Schonberg, "nowhere else in America . . . could one hear so much important new music as in Philadelphia."

The premieres included works by Rachmaninoff, EDGARD VARÈSE, CHARLES IVES, and AARON COPLAND, as well as American premieres of IGOR STRAVINSKY's *The Rite of Spring,* Gustav Mahler's Eighth Symphony, and the orchestral music of ARNOLD SCHOENBERG. Most of Stokowski's efforts, however, supported works by American composers.

Stokowski used the radio and phonograph extensively. He made his first recording with the Philadelphia Orchestra in 1917 and left an extraordinary body of music. He participated, too, in several films, including *100 Men and a Girl* in 1937 and, with WALT DISNEY, the experimental *Fantasia* in 1941.

Leopold Stokowski shared leadership of the Philadelphia Orchestra (1936–1938) with Eugene Ormandy, his successor, before launching an independent career. He established other orchestras: the All-American Youth Orchestra (1940), the New York Symphony Orchestra (1944), the Hollywood Bowl Symphony Orchestra (1945), and the American Symphony Orchestra (1962). He conducted the Houston Symphony Orchestra for several seasons (1955–1960), and continued to conduct in Europe until July 1975 and recorded until 1977. His only book, *Music for All of Us,* was published in 1943.

Schonberg recalls that "even in the twilight of his career the octogenarian Stokowski . . . remained a sight to behold: stiffly erect, his head framed by . . . snow-white hair, his behavior still unpredictable, his interpretations . . . still full of fire, sonority, and personality . . . that made [the] public idolize him."

Stokowski died in England at age ninety-five.

BIBLIOGRAPHY

Chasins, A., *Leopold Stokowski: A Profile,* 1979; Daniel, O., *Stokowski: A Counterpoint of View,* 1982; Schonberg, H. C., *The Great Conductors,* 1967.

Stravinsky, Igor Fedorovich

(June 17, 1882–April 6, 1971)
Composer

S travinsky's supple and energetic sense of rhythm, his extraordinary ear for instrumental timbre and texture, and his restlessly searching mind combined to produce over a career that spanned six decades a dazzling series of masterpieces that make him, together with ARNOLD SCHOENBERG, one of the titans of twentieth-century music.

Igor Fedorovich Stravinsky was born in Oranienbaum, Russia, a summer resort near St. Petersburg. His father, a leading bass at the St. Petersburg Imperial Opera, sent him to the University of St. Petersburg to study law. Stravinsky pursued his musical studies as an avocation (he had studied the piano early on) until Nicolai Rimsky-Korsakov encouraged his work in 1902. Stravinsky studied with the composer until 1907.

Sergei Diaghilev, the Russian ballet impresario, impressed by an early work, commissioned the young composer to provide music for a ballet, *The Firebird,* staged in Paris in 1910. The Ballets Russes next performed his *Petrushka* in 1911. While these successful early ballets draw on Russian folklore and in their shimmering orchestral textures owe a debt to Rimsky-Korsakov and the Russian tradition, they also contain hints of what was to follow. In 1913

Library of Congress

Diaghilev premiered a third ballet, *The Rite of Spring,* in Paris. The upheaval during the performance (some believe it was partly staged) was so severe the police were called and, according to conductor Pierre Monteux, Stravinsky "disappeared through a window backstage." What provoked the audience was the ballet's primitive subject matter and the score's reflection of it through raging rhythms, dissonant polychords, and melodic fragmentation.

Stravinsky lived in Switzerland between 1914 and 1920. Despite World War I, he continued to compose, although not for the huge orchestras and lavish production standards of the prewar years. These works include the ballet cantata *Les Noces* (The Wedding), a Russian text that evokes peasant weddings, for soloists, chorus, four pianos, and seventeen percussion instruments; and *The Soldier's Tale* (*L'Histoire du soldat,* 1918), with a French text by the Swiss poet C. F. Ramuz in the style of a village morality play, for seven instrumentalists, a narrator, and two or three dancers or actors. They also show an increasing appropriation of preexisting musical ma-

terials and styles other than those of the folk tradition of his native land, as, for example, in his Etude for Pianola (player piano) (1917), Ragtime for Eleven Instruments (1918), and Piano Rag-Music (1919).

With the Russian Revolution, Stravinsky became a permanent exile. He lived in France between 1920 and 1939, becoming a French citizen in 1934. In these years he continued his practice of borrowing elements from other kinds of music and began to consolidate what was later to be called his neoclassical style. *Pulcinella* (1920), a ballet with commedia dell'arte characters, presents almost verbatim music written by or attributed to Pergolesi in sparkling—though by prewar standards, chaste—instrumentations. The one-act opera *Mavra* (1922), with a text by Pushkin, returns to the kind of accompaniment figures Glinka would have used. The Concerto for Piano and Wind Instruments (1923–1924) harks back to the Baroque style with its rhythmic formulas and sharply contrasting blocks of tone color. Writing in 1920, Stravinsky said of this new music that "the structure underneath is that of classicism, in the sense of construction and form." Later, he expanded on this idea: "The phenomenon of music is given us with the sole purpose of establishing an order in things...its indispensable and single requirement is construction."

Although the structure underneath may always have been that of classicism, the musical materials on the surface were to come from many periods—accompaniment figures from the late eighteenth century, tunes from Tchaikovsky (*The Fairy's Kiss,* 1928), textures and rhythms from American big bands (the *Ebony Concerto,* written for Woody

Herman in 1945). But the construction was always Stravinsky's, and the rhythms were always fascinating.

The composer toured the United States in 1925 and in 1935. The visits resulted in important commissions that produced some of the masterpieces of the 1930s: *Symphony of Psalms* (1930), written for the fiftieth anniversary of the Boston Symphony Orchestra; *The Card Party* (1936), a ballet, one of many fruitful collaborations with GEORGE BALANCHINE; and the *Dumbarton Oaks Concerto* (1937–1938), for Mr. and Mrs. Robert Bliss, named for their house. In 1939–1940 Stravinsky delivered the Charles Eliot Norton Lectures at Harvard University. He was in Cambridge, Massachusetts, when war broke out in Europe.

Stravinsky settled in Hollywood, California, where he completed Symphony in C (1940) to mark the fiftieth anniversary of the Chicago Symphony Orchestra. During World War II (he became an American citizen in 1945), he accepted several commissions, the most important from the New York Philharmonic Orchestra for Symphony in Three Movements. He conducted it himself January 24, 1946.

In his mid-sixties Stravinsky began to revise works to correct errors in earlier editions and to protect copyrights and his financial interests. He was composing, too, works like the ballet *Orpheus* (1947) for Balanchine, an austere Mass (1944–1948) for ten winds and chorus, and an opera, *The Rake's Progress* (1948–1951), based on Hogarth's eighteenth-century engravings. The libretto was written by poets W. H. AUDEN and Chester Kallman. *Rake* premiered in Venice, Italy, Stravinsky conducting, September 11, 1951. Its format and instrumentation are like those of Mozart's Italian operas (arias and ensembles are linked by secco recitatives accompanied by harpsichord), and the work is considered by many to be the apotheosis of Stravinsky's neoclassical style.

In any case it was to be the last work in that style, for at the age of seventy, the ever unpredictable Stravinsky made the most startling move of his career: he began to explore the tone row techniques invented by his archrival, Arnold Schoenberg.

Stravinsky and Schoenberg had met in 1913. Stravinsky mentioned the occasion later, remarking that in Schoenberg's *Pierrot Lunaire,* "the merits of instrumentation are beyond dispute," though he disliked the work. According to critic Peter Yates, Stravinsky's "disdain for—and . . . misunderstanding of—Schoenberg's aesthetic attitude, and Schoenberg's reciprocal disdain, did not end during Schoenberg's lifetime."

However, in the early 1950s Robert Craft (the conductor who became his collaborator, chronicler, and amanuensis) convinced Stravinsky of the importance of the methods developed by Schoenberg and his illustrious students, Anton Webern and Alban Berg. The ways in which Stravinsky was to use these methods were entirely his own. At first, as in works like *Three Songs from William Shakespeare* (1953), *In Memoriam Dylan Thomas* (1954), or the 1957 ballet for Balanchine, *Agon,* he used rows of less than twelve tones. But with *Threni,* a 1958 work for chorus and orchestra, *Movements* (1958–1959) for piano and orchestra, and his final major work, the *Requiem Canticles* (1965–1966), he was using rows to control intervals both within and between lines in a totally chromatic context.

During these last years Stravinsky and Craft collaborated on both an ambitious series of recordings and a considerable literary output. A flood of literary essays in the form of conversations created an enduring record of the last years of one of the century's liveliest minds. His health began to fail in 1967, and he died in New York City in 1971.

Stravinsky's impact on the language of twentieth-century music has been enormous. There is scarcely a composer in the United States—or for that matter in the entire Western world—whose music has been untouched by his.

BIBLIOGRAPHY

Boretz, B., and E. Cone, *Perspectives on Schoenberg and Stravinsky*, 1968, rev., 1972; Craft, R., and I. Stravinsky, *Memories and Commentaries*, 1960; Stravinsky, V., and R. Craft, *Stravinsky in Pictures and Documents*, 1978.

Stroheim, Erich von

(September 22, 1885–May 12, 1957)
Actor, Film Director, Screenwriter

Erich von Stroheim was the supreme realist of the silent film. In an effort to make the narrative cinema the equal of the novel in descriptive and psychological detail, he exceeded all production and budgetary constraints. His film *Greed* is the most celebrated example of a masterpiece destroyed by the studio system.

Erich Oswald Stroheim was born in Vienna. Little is known about his early life, other than a brief military career and his debts as a result of philandering. This absence of data allowed Stroheim to create his own biography upon his arrival in America, including his claim that he sprang from aristocracy, thus the "von." This image, publicized extensively in the 1920s, was fueled by the repeated preoccupation with European aristocracy in many of his films.

Arriving in the United States around 1906, he held various jobs, including working as a singing waiter in New York's German community. After a short stint in the National Guard, he worked as a traveling sales representative for a garment business and eventually landed in San Francisco. Stroheim was an extra in many films, including D. W. GRIFFITH's *Birth of a Nation* (1915), *Intolerance* (1916), and *Hearts of the World* (1918). On the latter two, as well as on *Old Heidelberg* (1915), he was also technical adviser and assistant.

In 1917 Stroheim played a cruel Prussian officer in *For France,* a role with which he became identified and for which he was called "the man you love to hate." Through CARL LAEMMLE, head of Universal, he directed his first film in 1919—*Blind Husbands*—and, not surprisingly, wrote and designed it, and played the lead.

This film, as well as his next two, *The Devil's Pass Key* (1920)—unfortunately lost—and *Foolish Wives* (1922), concerns a love triangle, involving sophisticated sex, seduction, and intrigue in a Continental setting, themes that weave through much of Stroheim's work. Originally intended as a two-part film, *Foolish Wives* is rich in characterization, subplots, and social satire, much of which remains despite the studio's cutting it by a third.

Stroheim suffered a second defeat when he was replaced by director Rupert Julian on *Merry-Go-Round* (1923) after a contest of wills with Universal's production supervisor, IRVING THALBERG. While many directors before and after him had to bow to studio dictates, Stroheim was the first—and remains the most famous casualty.

This was never more dramatically demonstrated than with his production of *Greed* (1924), a labor of love based on FRANK NORRIS's novel *McTeague*. The only really American subject he ever tackled, Stroheim filmed virtually every page of the novel down to the last detail, many scenes a visual duplication of phrases and sentences. The result was a film of forty-five reels running nearly ten hours.

As fate would have it, the film's producer, the Goldwyn Company, was taken over by the newly formed Metro-Goldwyn-Mayer, with Thalberg, Stroheim's nemesis, as production supervisor. Declaring that Stroheim had a "footage fetish," Thalberg demanded substantial cuts. A series of feuds and negotiations ensued until *Greed* was reduced to one-fourth its length, a shadow of the film Stroheim had conceived, painstakingly designed, and shot.

Even in its two-hour form, however, the film has undeniable power. It depicts the destruction of a friendship and a marriage through the corrosive effect of greed. Consistent with his passion for authenticity, Stroheim did not use one studio set, shooting in the actual locations described in the novel, from the rooming houses in San Francisco to Death Valley, where the concluding fight between the two male protagonists is set. This scene, filmed in 132 degree heat, caused actor Jean Hersholt to become ill.

Stroheim's commitment to cinematic and novelistic realism went beyond any of his contemporaries. He believed that only through establishing a credible milieu with contextual detail would the depiction of character psychology and class conflict convince an audience.

Despite the debacle of *Greed*, MGM hired Stroheim to direct *The Merry Widow* (1925), based on the operetta by Franz Lehár. Typically, Stroheim's approach cut deeper than the original into the fabric and class divisions of a mythical European society, amassing detail to expose perversity and the underlying decadence of the aristocracy. His intentions were somewhat muted by the studio's insistence that he use stars John Gilbert and Mae Murray, who Stroheim felt ill-suited to his purposes.

The Wedding March (1928), another love story with a Continental setting, was also planned in two parts. The first was released fairly intact, but Paramount removed him in the middle of the second part and the film was edited by JOSEF VON STERNBERG. Similar fates met *Queen Kelly* (1929), produced in partnership with Gloria Swanson and Joseph Kennedy (father of John F. Kennedy), but released incomplete; and *Walking Down Broadway* (1933), reshot by the studio and released as *Hello, Sister.*

Stroheim continued to write screenplays and act as technical adviser, but never directed another film. Over the next two decades he acted in many films: with GRETA GARBO in *As You Desire Me* (1932), as German general Erwin Rommel in BILLY WILDER's *Five Graves to Cairo* (1943), and most memorably in Jean Renoir's *Grand Illusion* (1937) and Wilder's *Sunset Boulevard* (1950).

BIBLIOGRAPHY

Curtiss, Thomas Quinn, *Von Stroheim,* 1971; Finler, Joel, *Stroheim,* 1967; Koszarski, Richard, *The Man You Loved to Hate: Erich von Stroheim and Hollywood,* 1983.

Stuart, Gilbert Charles

(December 3, 1755–July 9, 1828)
Portrait Painter

Gilbert Stuart was the most important painter of portraits in the years after the American Revolution, and his many paintings of the new country's president, George Washington, were in great demand. The luminosity and transparency of his facial skin tones are the most memorable characteristics of his style.

Stuart was born in Narragansett, Rhode Island. When his father's snuff factory failed, the family moved to Newport. He attended a school founded "to teach ten poor boys their grammar and mathematics" without charge. He was copying pictures when he was thirteen and trying to draw portraits with black lead. In 1769, when a Scottish artist, Cosmo Alexander, came to Newport and painted portraits of some of the town's citizens, Stuart took lessons from him. Alexander took him back to Scotland with him, but died three years later.

Alone in a foreign country, the teenage Stuart tried, but failed, to support himself by his art. He worked his way back to Newport on a coal cargo ship and earned money painting portraits while he also studied music. Just before the revolution, the American colonies did not offer much opportunity for the portrait painter. In 1775, with very little money and only one letter of recommendation, Stuart sailed for London, determined to be a painter.

While he painted a few portraits, he had to find work as a church organist to help pay his modest living expenses. Finally, he asked for help from BENJAMIN WEST, an American painter who had been in London since 1763. When West responded immediately, Stuart became his apprentice and moved his studio into the West household, where he worked for five years. Stuart learned a great deal from the sober, successful West and began to make his way, showing portraits at the Royal Academy of the Arts. *The Skater* (1782) was a full-length portrait of William Grant, dignified, with arms folded, wearing a broad-brimmed black hat, black frock coat, and knee breeches, ice skating in St. James Park. The piece won him many commissions for portraits.

Stuart moved to his own studio in 1782, but continued to help West with the backgrounds of his history paintings when he had time from his own work. He used bright, clear colors applied with great skill to capture the character as well as the appearance of his subjects, but was sometimes careless in the drawing of accessories. As Stuart became a leading London portrait painter, West admired his former pupil's accomplishments and said, "He *nails* the likeness to the canvas." An engraver made prints of a series of fifteen portraits of artists, including West, and sold them. By the time he left London in 1787, Stuart and his wife, Charlotte Coates of Reading, England, were living lavishly in a house in New Burlington Street, with a French chef and professional

musicians for parties. The Stuarts had twelve children (of whom two, Jane and Charles Gilbert, became artists) and were soon living beyond their means.

To avoid debtors' prison, Stuart left London for Dublin, where he painted many portraits. Once again, he maintained an extravagant way of life and incurred debts. He decided to return to the United States so he could, as he said, make enough money by painting portraits of George Washington to pay his debts in London and Dublin. He sailed for New York early in 1793, painting the portrait of the ship's owner to pay for his passage. He set up a portrait studio in New York, but in 1794 he moved to Philadelphia, then the federal capital. There he painted his initial two portraits of Washington. The first, in 1795, was a head and shoulders version showing the right side of Washington's face. (This portrait is known as the Vaughan type because it was owned by Samuel Vaughan, a friend of Washington's.) In 1796 he painted a life-size standing portrait that showed the left side of Washington's face, right hand stretched out. (This was given by Senator William Bingham to the marquis of Lansdowne and is known as the Lansdowne type.) So many people visited his studio that he had trouble finishing the portraits and moved to a stone barn in Germantown. Here in the early fall of 1796 the president sat for a third life portrait. Commissioned by Martha Washington, it was never finished. Yet it became the most popular image of Washington, and it appears on the U.S. one dollar bill. Stuart never delivered the portrait to Mrs. Washington but kept it, so he could make copies for sale. (It is known as the Athenaeum type because it was sold to the Boston Athenaeum after Stuart's death.)

Following the national government to Washington, Stuart painted THOMAS JEFFERSON, James Madison, and James Monroe. In the summer of 1805 he moved to Boston, where he lived the rest of his life. There he had more commissions than he could fill, but he was such a bad businessman that he often did not know if a finished portrait had been paid for or not.

He was extremely careless about correspondence and did not even answer a letter from the Pennsylvania Academy of the Fine Arts, which wanted to buy a replica of his Washington portrait of the Lansdowne type. Nor did he answer a letter from a museum in Florence, Italy, which wanted his own portrait to hang among those of other eminent painters.

In July 1828 he died at his home on Essex Street and was buried in the Central Burying Grounds on Boston Common.

BIBLIOGRAPHY

Flexner, James Thomas, *America's Old Masters,* 1980; McLanathan, Richard, *Gilbert Stuart,* 1986.

Sullivan, Louis Henry

(September 3, 1856–April 14, 1924)
Architect

L ouis Sullivan is, next to FRANK LLOYD WRIGHT, America's most important modern architect. His contributions were the development of high-rise commercial buildings at the end of the nineteenth century and the invention of a rich, abstract ornamentation.

He was born in Boston in 1856 to immigrant parents. His father, Patrick, was a dancing master from Ireland, and his mother, Andrienne, had family roots in Switzerland. During Louis's first ten years the family moved in and out of various homes and hotels in the Boston environs. When the family moved to Chicago in 1868, twelve-year-old Louis, already determined to become an architect, remained near Boston with relatives. Four years later, he entered the Massachusetts Institute of Technology, where, under the direction of William R. Ware, his architectural studies included calculus, languages, drawing skills, mechanics, and military drill.

In the first of what would be many rebellions against established order, Sullivan, dissatisfied by what he found to be a dull routine at MIT, left for Philadelphia for a stint as apprentice to architect Frank Furness. He learned a lot from this celebrated, idiosyncratic figure who had a penchant for semiabstract floral ornamentation and whose distinctive, bold buildings included the Pennsylvania Academy of Fine Arts and the Guarantee Trust and Safe Deposit Company, both in Philadelphia. Sullivan's tenure with Furness was cut short by the Panic of 1873. Out of work, he headed back to Chicago, which was then a place of great opportunity for architects. It had been devastated two years before by fire and was in the midst of a rebuilding program. Sullivan came under the tutelage of William Le Baron Jenney. Despite their aesthetic limitations, Jenney's buildings were major contributions to the development of skeletal, metal-framed, high-rise buildings (his 10-story Home Insurance Company Building would be constructed in 1885). Aware that American architecture at the time was predominantly French-inspired, and knowing that the center of advanced architectural thinking lay in Paris, Sullivan went in 1874 to Paris to study at the Ecole des Beaux-Arts. Within a year, however, despite liberating contacts with the architectural monuments of Paris, London, and Rome, Sullivan again grew dissatisfied with that education, which he decided was too confined by moribund formulas and attitudes. Soon he was back in Chicago.

In 1883 he entered his first important phase when he became a partner with one of the most prominent architects in Chicago, Dankmar

Adler. (It was for this firm that the young Frank Lloyd Wright came to work in 1887 as an assistant.) For the next twelve years or so Sullivan worked on many commercial buildings, warehouses, theaters, and music halls. Perhaps the best known project of the 1880s was Chicago's Auditorium Building (1886–1890), a massive complex of 136 offices and stores, 400 hotel rooms, and a theater and recital hall. Especially noteworthy were Adler's engineering and acoustics and Sullivan's ornamental virtuosity, his use of color, and his innovations with artificial light. For the World's Columbian Exposition in Chicago of 1893, he designed the Transportation Building, an exhibition space whose nonclassical aspects, as distinguished from most of the exposition's Franco-Roman architecture, aroused some controversy.

It was with the development of the highrise building that Sullivan would make his most important contribution to modern American architecture. "Understanding the highrise to be the characteristic edifice of the era," wrote Robert Twombly, "Sullivan felt that by working out its aesthetics, he could make a real contribution toward an American style." He was determined, in other words, to unite the priorities of commercial endeavor with aesthetic imperatives. "[The high rise] must be tall," Sullivan wrote in 1896. "It must be every inch a proud and soaring thing, rising in sheer exultation . . . from bottom to top . . . without a single dissenting line." The Auditorium Building's facade, with its 17-story tower, was influenced by the aesthetic simplifications and powerful massing of HENRY HOBSON RICHARDSON's nearby Marshall Field Building, which had been completed just before the premature death of Richardson in 1886. In the Wainwright Building in St. Louis (1890–1891), designed when Sullivan was thirty-four years old, he emphasized verticality with startling clarity. He extended the piers separating the windows in an uninterrupted vertical flow through the main body of the building. Horizontals were deemphasized by recessing the richly ornamented spandrils that covered the intervening floors. A floriated frieze and projecting cornice crowned the building. "[The Wainwright Building] was a sudden and volcanic design (made literally in three minutes)," noted Sullivan in 1903, "and marks the beginning of a logical and poetic expression of the metallic frame construction. . . . All my commercial buildings since the Wainwright are conceived in the same general spirit." Frank Lloyd Wright agreed on the Wainwright's significance: "This was Louis Sullivan's greatest moment—his greatest effort. The 'skyscraper' as a new thing under the sun, an entity with . . . beauty all its own, was born."

These ideas were perfected in the Guaranty Trust Building in Buffalo (1894–1895), and the more horizontal implications of steel construction were beautifully expressed in the Schlesinger & Mayer Department Store in Chicago (1898–1903).

After 1895 Sullivan's career took a tragic downturn. Hit hard by the depression that had struck in 1893, the firm of Adler and Sullivan eventually broke up. Sullivan's growing cantankerousness toward personal friends and professional colleagues alienated them and resulted in fewer commissions after 1900, although he created a number of exquisite small-town banks throughout the Midwest. Unlike his protégé, Wright, Sullivan cared little about residential architecture. His obsession with integral ornament was against the new trend toward more simplified decoration. He began to drink heavily and became severely depressed. After auctioning off all his effects, his wife, Margaret, left him. "With the future blank I am surely living in hell," he wrote Frank Lloyd Wright in 1918. His *Autobiography of an Idea*, which he began in 1922, was not just an account of his life, but an attempt to describe both his philosophy and his current situation. He died in 1924 of kidney disease.

Sullivan always rejected attempts to constrain art by label, category, and style. For him, art was something that solved problems. "Predigested solutions from the library, that is, historical styles, might be acceptable for critics who praised tradition," assesses biographer Twombly. "But for him style was not so much chosen as arrived at spontaneously, by instinct. . . . [His] principal interest was to encourage architects to abandon historic styles, rethink design problems without relying on precedent, and develop a poetic sensitivity toward life itself."

BIBLIOGRAPHY

Bush-Brown, Albert, *Louis Sullivan,* 1960; Sullivan, Louis, "The Tall Office Building Artistically Considered," *Lippincott's,* March 1896; Twombly, Robert, *Louis Sullivan: His Life and Work,* 1986.

Tarkington, Newton Booth

(July 29, 1869–May 19, 1946)
Novelist, Playwright, Short-Story Writer

Booth Tarkington is best known for realistic novels, such as *The Magnificent Ambersons* and *Alice Adams,* which render middle-class life in the Midwest during an era of industrial expansion in the early twentieth century. His comic novels about adolescents—Penrod and his friends—were also very popular.

Newton Booth Tarkington was born in Indianapolis, Indiana, and was named in honor of an uncle who had served as governor of California and as a U.S. senator. Tarkington attended Phillips Exeter Academy and then Purdue University for a year before enrolling at Princeton University in 1891. There he became president of the new Triangle Club and wrote the book for the group's first musical comedy, *The Honorable Julius Caesar.* He left Princeton without a degree and became a full-time writer in 1893.

Tarkington's first novel, *The Gentleman from Indiana* (1899), describes the efforts of a young newspaper editor to root out corruption in a small town. John Harkless's eventual

Library of Congress

triumph over his political enemies leads him to run for Congress. (Tarkington himself served in the Indiana House of Representatives in 1902 and 1903, then drew on the experience for a novel, *In the Arena,* published in 1905.) *Monsieur Beaucaire* (1900) is a romantic adventure, featuring a French duke who travels to England in search of a bride. Others of Tarkington's early novels are *Cherry* (1903) and *The Conquest of Canaan* (1905).

Tarkington's most successful period began in 1914 with the publication of his novel *Penrod.* The misadventures of the twelve-year-old central character, Penrod Schofield, are depicted in a manner that is nostalgic without being idealized. The comic rendering of Penrod's first experience of romantic infatuation, for example, or even his daydreaming in school, endeared him to the reading public, both adult and juvenile. Tarkington followed *Penrod* with two more novels about the same character, *Penrod and Sam* (1916) and *Penrod Jashber* (1929).

Seventeen (1916), a novel about the first love of its teenage protagonist, Willie Baxter, is written in the same vein as the Penrod stories. The absurdity of Willie's longings for Lola Pratt, a woman who speaks in baby talk, made the book popular in its day, though the joke seems to have been lost on the more sophisticated teenagers of later generations.

Most critics agree that Tarkington's most serious literary contribution comprised the trilogy he called *Growth*, published as a set in 1927, written in about the same time period as his stories of adolescence. The three novels constitute a social satire of America's industrial expansion. *The Turmoil* (1915) describes the ascent to prominence of a family, the Sheridans, who have made their wealth in industry; the book both renders in caricature their nouveau riche sensibilities and offers a critique of the simple ugliness and the environmental neglect that seemed to characterize the new industry. *The Magnificent Ambersons* (1918) concerns an established family whose fortunes decline in the new era. The proud, mean-spirited George Amberson Minafer gets his due at the end of the story, though he is forgiven by many he has wronged. The story won Tarkington the Pulitzer Prize in 1919. ORSON WELLES filmed it in 1941. *The Midlander* (1924) recounts the story of Dan Oliphant, a prosperous developer and a generous man whose fortunes reverse tragically before he is able to see his greatest dream—the construction of a truly beautiful American city—come to fruition.

Alice Adams (1921), originally conceived for the *Growth* trilogy but supplanted in Tarkington's plan by *The Midlander*, is often counted his finest novel. Lacking the broad intention of social criticism that informs *Growth*, *Alice Adams* nonetheless offers an acute rendering of middle-class ambition and pretension. The protagonist hopes desperately to lure a prominent husband in order to rescue herself from a future of menial employment; her efforts fail poignantly because she cannot put on the tastes and manners of the wealthy. *Alice Adams* won Tarkington his second Pulitzer, in 1922. A film version starring KATHARINE HEPBURN was made in 1935. He also wrote more than two dozen plays, some of them with Harry Leon Wilson. Two of the most successful were *The Man from Home* (1908) and *Clarence* (1921).

BIBLIOGRAPHY

Fennimore, Keith J., *Booth Tarkington*, 1974; Tarkington, Booth, *The World Does Move*, 1928; Woodress, James, *Booth Tarkington: Gentleman from Indiana*, 1955.

Tate, John Orley Allen

(November 19, 1899–February 9, 1979)
Critic, Poet

In his poetry and criticism, Allen Tate sought to revive the moral and aesthetic values of the preindustrial era, especially those of the agrarian South, and to stress the formal aspects of modern poetry.

Born in Winchester, Kentucky, John Orley Allen Tate faced a choice of allegiance to the South or to the dominant Yankee culture. Believing materialism was poisoning human character and society, Tate sought to understand the South's literary heritage.

Entering Vanderbilt University in 1918, Tate studied under JOHN CROWE RANSOM and joined the so-called Fugitives, a group of writers opposed to what they saw as the social decadence reflected in contemporary poetry and to the influence of Victorian sentimentalism. Another student member was ROBERT PENN WARREN, with whom Tate briefly shared a dormitory room. Tate helped found the magazine *The Fugitive* (1922–1925) and contributed poetry to it.

Tate finished his undergraduate course work in 1923 and the next year married Caroline Gordon, whom he had met through Warren. They spent the next few years in New York City, Patterson, New York, and France, while Tate wrote two biographies, *Stonewall Jackson: The Good Soldier* (1928) and *Jefferson Davis: His Rise and Fall* (1929).

During the winter of 1925–1926, while living with Caroline, their newborn daughter, Nancy, and a penniless HART CRANE in a rented farmhouse in Patterson, Tate crafted "Ode to the Confederate Dead." Perhaps his best-known poem, it was revised again and again over the course of a decade. It depicts a man at the gate of a Confederate cemetery, struggling to understand the buried heroes and to define a modern form of heroism. Hindered by self-absorption and the loss of objective values, modern humanity must turn to history to find meaningful direction in life, the poem suggests. An early form of the poem was published in *Mr. Pope and Other Poems* in 1928.

After visiting London, Oxford, and Paris on a Guggenheim Fellowship in 1928 and 1929, the Tates moved in 1930 to a large old house and farmland his brother had bought them near Clarksville, Tennessee. They returned to Europe for a year in southern France when Caroline won a Guggenheim in 1932.

In 1930 he helped edit *I'll Take My Stand: The South and the Agrarian Tradition,* a collection of essays affirming the agrarian way of life, some of them written by former Fugitives. Tate wrote that he sought to restore "the moral and religious outlook of Western Man," as well as the civility and humanism he believed typified southern life in the pre-industrial era.

Tate's first full-length volume of poetry, *Poems: 1928–1931,* was published in 1932, followed by *The Mediterranean and Other Poems* (1936) and *Selected Poems* (1937). In two of his most important poems, "The Mediterranean" and "Aeneas at Washington,"

Tate melds classical characters and events with the present in order to contrast ancient and modern values. In "The Mediterranean," for example, a picnic at Cassis serves to frame a reverie about the boldness and bravery of Roman soldiers who arrived by boat to conquer the coastal lands; their disciplined valor is contrasted with the wastefulness of the settlers of North America, seen as careless plunderers of the natural bounty of the land.

In 1938 Tate published his only novel, *The Fathers,* a pre–Civil War story set in Virginia.

Tate's first volume of criticism, *Reactionary Essays on Poetry and Ideas,* appeared in 1936. It was followed by *Reason in Madness: Critical Essays* (1941), *On the Limits of Poetry: Selected Essays: 1928–1948* (1948), and *The Man of Letters in the Modern World* (1955). In his criticism, Tate sought not only to justify the direction he had taken as a poet, but to refocus attention on the form of the poem itself. He defined poetry as "the art of apprehending and concentrating our experiences in the mysterious limitations of form." He advocated close textual analysis. These ideas were integral to the so-called New Criticism, which dominated literary theory through the 1950s.

Between 1938 and 1946 Tate taught at the Woman's College (now the University of North Carolina at Greensboro) and Princeton University, served as Consultant in Poetry at the Library of Congress, and edited the *Sewanee Review.* He and Caroline were divorced in January 1946 but remarried in April, settling in New York City, where Tate worked as a literary editor for Henry Holt and Company.

Tate's poem "Seasons of the Soul," published in *The Winter Sea: A Book of Poems* (1944), uses the classical figures of Venus and Sisyphus to suggest humanity's heroic capacity, despite its flawed nature. Critics noted that the poem seemed to mark a shift in Tate's poetry toward the religious. Tate converted to Catholicism in 1950.

In 1948 Tate left Holt to teach at New York University. In 1951 he accepted an offer, with tenure, as professor of English at the University of Minnesota, from which he retired in

1968. After 1951 he wrote few new poems, though he wrote many prose pieces for periodicals and edited several books, notably *The Complete Poems and Selected Criticism of Edgar Allan Poe* (1968). Tate was given the Bollingen Prize in 1956.

He and Caroline were separated again in 1955 and divorced finally in 1959. He then married Isabella Gardner. After divorcing again in 1966, Tate married Helen Heinz, a student at the University of Minnesota. The couple had three sons. They left Minneapolis after Tate's retirement and settled in Sewanee, Tennessee, where he died in 1979.

BIBLIOGRAPHY

Bishop, Ferman, *Allen Tate*, 1967; Hemphill, George, *Allen Tate*, 1964; Squires, Radcliffe, *Allen Tate: A Literary Biography*, 1971.

Tatum, Arthur, Jr.

(October 13, 1910–November 5, 1956)
Jazz Musician

The remarkable Art Tatum is one of the greatest pianists jazz has produced. His reputation rests on an amazing technique and outstanding powers of invention. A major influence on alto sax great CHARLIE PARKER, Tatum's free improvisations and technical acrobatics were forerunners of modern jazz.

Tatum was born in Toledo, Ohio. Nearly blind from birth, he had no sight in one eye and only partial vision in the other. His parents were sympathetic to and supportive of his musical bent. From the age of three he played by ear. Later he studied piano and managed to master braille so that he could read music.

Tatum did not pursue a career as a classical pianist despite being encouraged to do so by his teacher, Overton G. Rainey. Extraordinary talent notwithstanding, career opportunities in classical music were, for black musicians, non-existent at the time. Tatum turned instead to what he heard on piano rolls, recordings, radio broadcasts, and from musicians who played in the area. Stride pianist Fats Waller was an early important influence.

By 1926 Tatum was playing locally. In 1929 and 1930 his performances were broadcast over WSPD in Toledo, once as a partner of Teddy Wilson. He went to New York in 1932 as accompanist for jazz singer Adelaide Hall, and in 1933 he recorded his first solo. New York City was the scene of Tatum's first "cutting" contest, a performance competition among musicians. He won with a formidable rendering of "Tiger Rag," having faced down James P. Johnson, Willie ("The Lion") Smith, and Fats Waller.

After-hours solos at New York's Onyx Club did not bring in enough money, and Tatum returned to the Midwest. He was in Cleveland from 1934 to 1935 and in Chicago the following year. By 1937, thanks to New York club dates and radio jobs, his reputation was established. He toured England in 1938, conquered London, and appeared in New York and Los Angeles in the late 1930s and early 1940s. In 1943 he founded his own trio with Tiny Grimes, electric guitar, and Slam Stewart, double bass. Until his death in Los Angeles, California, in 1956, he played solo or in ensemble, in clubs or in concert.

Tatum, a complex person, was a favorite of jazz fans but never became generally popular. Recordings produced by Norman Granz in the

1950s brought together some fine small ensembles and yielded an extraordinary series of solo performances. Tatum, however, was a subject of controversy, especially during the years preceding and following his death.

According to critic/scholar Gunther Schuller, conflicting opinions about the pianist's importance stem from "the uniqueness and solitary nature of his art." Not of the mainstream, Tatum was essentially a loner: most often he performed alone and did not follow musical fashion. The disagreements spring from differing assessments of his creativity and of his influence on the course of jazz. As *New Yorker* writer Whitney Balliett says, "No one ever knew exactly what he was or what to do with him."

Schuller suggests Tatum was neither composer nor arranger, but rather was at his best as a "reharmonizer" of others' songs. "In that role he was brilliant," says Schuller, "for he frequently improved even fine composers like [GEORGE] GERSHWIN or [RICHARD] RODGERS or [IRVING] BERLIN. . . . The melodies were always already there, waiting for Tatum to ornament them, reconstruct them, dissect them, elaborate them."

All critics concede that his technical mastery was matchless. Balliett writes that Tatum's astonishing style was distinguished by "its speed and accuracy, and its harmonic and rhythmic imagination." Tatum continued to grow musically until the end of his life. By abandoning the restrictions imposed by the stride style, he was able to play with greater rhythmic freedom. Tatum's recordings of 1953 to 1955 for Norman Granz, 121 titles, sum up his work. They include "Too Marvelous for Words" (according to Schuller, "almost what one would have to say of this performance"), "Somebody Loves Me," "If I Had You," and a stirring rendition of "Embraceable You."

BIBLIOGRAPHY

Balliett, W., "One Man Band," *New Yorker*, Sept. 9, 1968, and *Ecstacy at the Onion*, 1971; Distler, J., *Art Tatum*, 1981; Schuller, G., *The Swing Era: The Development of Jazz, 1930–1945*, 1989.

Taylor, Paul Belville, Jr.

(July 20, 1930–)
Choreographer, Dancer

An artistic descendant of RUTH ST. DENIS, TED SHAWN, and MERCE CUNNINGHAM, the unpretentious Paul Taylor heads what many consider the last great dance company of the Post-Modern era. Rich in imagination, Taylor has choreographed brilliantly for individual dancers and brought physical lightness, dazzling humor, ironic sensibility, and sometimes anger to considerations of American life.

Born in Edgewood, Pennsylvania, near Pittsburgh, Paul Taylor was the youngest of four and the only child of his widowed mother's second marriage. The marriage broke up in the 1930s and Taylor, brought up in Washington, D.C., completed his secondary education at Virginia Episcopal School in Lynchburg, Virginia. He won a partial art scholarship at Syracuse (New York) University to study painting, then a full swimming scholarship.

When Taylor decided to pursue dance, he transferred to the Juilliard School in New York City, but spent the prior summer, 1952, studying dance at the American Dance Festival at Connecticut College in New London. Taylor was twenty-two when he began his dance career. That summer MARTHA GRAHAM invited him to join her company. As a scholarship student at Juilliard, he studied with Doris Humphrey but took evening classes at the Graham school, and, after seeing a Merce Cunningham performance, took classes with Cunningham as well.

Following a summer at Black Mountain, North Carolina, with Cunningham, Taylor struggled to hone his technique and to support himself in New York. He studied, choreographed, and even performed as an acrobat in *Peter Pan,* choreographed by JEROME ROBBINS. In 1955 he joined Graham's five-month tour of the Orient. His own first concert, *Epic,* was performed in New York in 1957. The sets and costumes were designed by Taylor's friend, painter ROBERT RAUSCHENBERG. Set to recorded telephone time signals, *Epic* contained no dance steps, only occasional gestures. He continued to dance leads with Graham in works like *Clytemnestra* and *Alcestis* until 1962, appearing in the GEORGE BALANCHINE/Graham collaboration, *Episodes,* in 1959.

By 1962, when the sunny *Aureole* was completed, Taylor had been choreographing since the mid-1950s and had established his own small company. Following its premiere at Connecticut College, *Aureole* was performed many times around the world and became a repertory piece. "*Aureole* is a brilliant, intelligent neoclassic dance to music by Handel," says critic Moira Hodgson. She goes on to note, "As Balanchine's classic choreography reveals STRAVINSKY to us, so Taylor's choreography reveals Handel."

Critic Edwin Denby wrote in 1964 that "Taylor's first choreography [*Epic*] was anti-dance." Denby goes on to note that Taylor's "gift defined itself as one not for anti-dance but for prodance. What he has been doing since 1960 is new in the sense that such dance momentum had not existed before in the modern dance (i.e., in nonclassic technique). The technical as well as the creative discovery is his." Technique aside, Taylor reveled in the unexpected and the witty and often commented on American hypocrisy in his works. His energetic, fluid dance style embraced both neoclassical and expressionist movement.

Taylor toured with his small company through the 1960s, all the while performing his own works, dances like the sardonic *From Sea to Shining Sea,* the large-scale *Orbs,* set to music from late Beethoven string quartets (hailed by some critics as a masterpiece of choreography), and *Private Domain.* He continued to tour and choreograph, devising the satirical *Agathe's Tale* and *American Genesis* in the early 1970s. Like so many American artists, he was better received abroad than at home.

By 1974, exhausted by a brutal touring schedule and plagued by injuries, Taylor gave up dancing, though he continued to choreograph. *Esplanade* (1975), the first work created after his retirement, relied on natural motion like walking, running, and jumping, rather than on danced movements, a challenge to create, according to Taylor.

Paul Taylor created dances through the 1970s and 1980s, works like *Images* (1977) and *Sacre du Printemps* (1980). *Company B,* subtitled *Songs Sung by the Andrews Sisters,* premiered in June 1991 in Houston, Texas. Anna Kisselgoff of the *New York Times* wrote, "The mix of catchy harmonies by the famous trio and Mr. Taylor's fleeting jitterbug references, coupled with a stream of wartime images, would suggest that "Company B" is about the 1940s. Actually it is about us—humans at large and Americans in particular. . . . It is the jewel in Mr. Taylor's crown of dances about hypocrisy in America."

Arlene Croce said of Taylor in a *New Yorker* magazine review, "[Some] speak of Paul Taylor's company as the last of the great modern dance companies. . . . But Taylor was also a prophet of post-modernism. His first works predicted (and his *Esplanade* summed up) the era of the deconstructed dancer. Taylor [is] a major establishment figure with a style as individual as a thumbprint."

BIBLIOGRAPHY

Hodgson, M., *Quintet: Five American Dance Companies,* 1976; Taylor, P., *Private Domain,* 1987.

Thalberg, Irving Grant

(May 30, 1899–September 14, 1936)
Producer

Irving G. Thalberg was the most prestigious motion picture producer in Hollywood until his brilliant meteoric career was terminated by his death at age thirty-seven. It was largely owing to his talent and taste, often dictatorially imposed, that Metro-Goldwyn-Mayer— between 1924 and 1936— became the most powerful studio in the industry.

Born in Brooklyn, Irving was the son of William and Henrietta Thalberg. His father ran an import business; his mother dreamed

The Museum of Modern Art/Film Stills Archive

of wealth, success, and social status, pinning her hopes on her son. She remained an important influence throughout his life.

Doctors predicted that Irving would die before age thirty. Frail at birth, beset by childhood illnesses and a heart condition, he was unable to participate in physical exercise, but became an avid reader and was considered superior academically. Thanks to his mother's nursing, he completed grammar school and attended Bushwick High School.

At age eighteen Thalberg worked as a secretary at CARL LAEMMLE's Universal Film Manufacturing Company, handling correspondence and correcting "Uncle Carl's" broken English. Laemmle often asked his opinion of new productions. Thalberg's instincts for moviemaking were already evident; later he claimed he could find cinematic material in everything, even a cookbook.

Laemmle made him general manager in charge of production at Universal, where his authority was tested in a clash with director ERICH VON STROHEIM on *Foolish Wives* (1922).

Stroheim was notorious for exceeding budgets and shooting schedules. Thalberg ordered him to "stick to the script . . . no added scenes, no excess photography." Stroheim retorted, "Since when does a child supervise a genius?" On the production of *Merry-Go-Round* (1922), Thalberg replaced Stroheim with another director. The film suffered, but Thalberg emerged a respected figure.

Thalberg's tie with Laemmle ended when he did not agree to be Laemmle's son-in-law. In 1923 he became production assistant to LOUIS B. MAYER. Initially compatible—because Thalberg did not drink, smoke, or swear, which impressed the puritan Mayer—they had their differences during the last few years before Thalberg's death.

When Metro-Goldwyn-Mayer was formed in 1924, Thalberg became supervisor of production. The studio was established at Culver City, Los Angeles, and Mayer and Thalberg became "commanders in chief of an army of filmmakers," producing twenty-six films in their first year.

One of Thalberg's first challenges was— again—a Stroheim film, *Greed* (1924), which he eventually took out of the director's hands and cut to one-fifth its length. While his decision seemed in the best interests of the studio, film scholars have criticized Thalberg for destroying a masterpiece of the silent cinema.

Among his productions in the 1920s were *The Big Parade* (1925), Stroheim's *The Merry Widow* (1925), and the epic *Ben-Hur* (1926). All three were very successful and made stars of John Gilbert, a Thalberg "discovery," and Ramon Novarro. Thereafter, Mayer believed in the value of promoting stars, and MGM became known as the studio with "more stars than there are in Heaven."

Other prominent stars of Thalberg's era included GRETA GARBO, Norma Shearer, Lon Chaney, and Joan Crawford. Thalberg produced *Flesh and the Devil* (1927), the film that echoed the real-life Garbo/Gilbert romance. Thalberg himself courted Shearer and married her in 1927.

Thalberg's ability to concentrate on many films simultaneously without neglecting other duties was legendary. However, his artistic control was often resented by creative directors, who were considered mere "contributors" and were expected to assist fellow directors.

Nevertheless, Thalberg's genius led MGM to fame and success into the sound era. The studio's first musical, *The Broadway Melody*, won the Academy Award for Best Picture of 1929. Thalberg produced Garbo's first talkie, *Anna Christie* (1930), and *Camille* (1936), one of her finest films, as well as the MARX BROTHERS' *A Night at the Opera* (1935). His production of *Mutiny on the Bounty* won the Best Picture Oscar of 1935.

His last films were *Romeo and Juliet* (1936) starring Shearer and Leslie Howard, which he considered his monument, and *The Good Earth* (1937), based on PEARL BUCK's novel about China.

While on a trip, Thalberg was stricken with a bad cold, from which he never recovered, finally dying of pneumonia. In his honor, the Academy of Motion Picture Arts and Sciences created the Irving G. Thalberg Memorial Award, a special Oscar given to creative producers in the industry. It was first awarded in 1937 to Darryl F. Zanuck; in 1992 *Star Wars* creator George Lucas was its recipient.

Thalberg was the model for the Monroe Starr character in F. SCOTT FITZGERALD's uncompleted novel, *The Last Tycoon*, written after Fitzgerald's unsuccessful sojourn as a Hollywood screenwriter.

BIBLIOGRAPHY

Crowther, Bosley, *Hollywood Rajah: The Life and Times of Louis B. Mayer*, 1960; Gabler, Neal, *An Empire of Their Own: How the Jews Invented Hollywood*, 1988; Marx, Samuel, *Mayer and Thalberg: The Make-Believe Saints*, 1975.

Thoreau, Henry David

(July 12, 1817–May 6, 1862)
Essayist, Natural History Writer, Social Critic

The essayist Henry David Thoreau is best known for his account of two years spent in seclusion in a cabin in the Massachusetts woods. In *Walden* and elsewhere, he gave memorable expression to a social theory that stressed self-reliance and close communion with nature as a route to meaning in life.

Thoreau was born in Concord, Massachusetts, and lived most of his life in that town, which became the center of the Transcendentalist movement in the 1840s. His family were shopkeepers who also ran a small business manufacturing pencils. Thoreau helped in the business from time to time but decided early that any such efforts would detract from the work he wished to pursue as a writer.

Thoreau attended Harvard University from 1833 to 1837 and there read RALPH WALDO EMERSON's essay *Nature* (1836), the first important Transcendentalist treatise. Thoreau was intrigued by the notion that the primary route to truth was through intuition and that the individual could, by meditating on his own reading and experience, divine universal truths. Thoreau also heard Emerson's address to Harvard's Phi Beta Kappa Society in 1837. Titled *The American Scholar*, it argued for an intellectual self-reliance informed by the study of nature as a step toward achieving cultural emancipation from Europe.

After his graduation from Harvard, Thoreau taught, first at the public school in Concord and then, from 1838 until 1841 with his older brother, John, as a master of the private Concord Academy. Thoreau stayed at Emerson's house in Concord from 1841 until 1843, contributing to the household by doing odd repairs. Thoreau then made a brief attempt to break into New York literary circles while working as a tutor to Emerson's nephews on Staten Island, but he had little luck with the New York magazines and shortly returned to Concord.

In 1842 Emerson, then editor of the Transcendentalists' magazine, *The Dial*, commissioned Thoreau to write the first of what became a series of essays drawing on his knowledge of natural phenomena, "Natural History of Massachusetts." Two more essays followed, in which Thoreau began to use the journey through natural settings as a metaphor for spiritual exploration: "A Walk to Wachusett" (1842) and "A Winter Walk" (1843).

The death of Thoreau's brother in 1842 led him to consider his first book, which was to commemorate a boating trip they had taken together in 1839. He wrote *A Week on the Concord and Merrimack Rivers* (1849) while living in seclusion in the small cabin he had built on Walden Pond.

Thoreau is best remembered for *Walden* (1854), his account of the experiment in living on Walden Pond. Thoreau had set out to discover whether he could sustain himself in a natural setting by living very simply and exerting himself minimally toward his own subsistence, preserving his energies for the tasks of observation and artistic creation.

Having built his own cabin, Thoreau moved in on July 4, 1845—a date deliberately chosen to celebrate his own "independence"—and stayed for a little over two years, returning to Concord in the fall of 1847. He did finishing work on the cabin, planted a crop of beans, and rambled about the woods. At the same time he was preparing the manuscript for *A Week on the Concord and Merrimack Rivers*, he made notes in his journal toward the memoir of his experience at Walden.

One experience during Thoreau's second summer at Walden is particularly noteworthy. As a protest against the war with Mexico, which he and many others considered merely a pretext for extending slavery into Texas, he had refused to pay a poll tax owed to the federal government. This act of resistance caused his arrest, and he spent a night in the Concord jail. The experience led Thoreau to write an essay, "Resistance to Civil Government" (1849), which held that individuals were obliged under certain circumstances to offer nonviolent resistance to unjust laws. Later republished as "Civil Disobedience," the essay became influential in the twentieth century among such political leaders as Martin Luther King, Jr., and Mohandas Ghandi.

By the time Thoreau left his cabin in 1847, he had completed a draft of *Walden*, but the difficulty he experienced finding a publisher for *A Week* and then the book's poor sales (an edition of 1,000 sold only 300 copies) led him to postpone any effort to get *Walden* into print. He supported himself as a lecturer and explored the wilderness in Maine and on Cape Cod while heavily revising the *Walden* manuscript during the early 1850s.

Published finally in 1854, *Walden* criticizes American culture for overvaluing commerce and material success at the expense of the inner life of the individual. Thoreau, in a taut, epigrammatic style of writing, recounts his own activities at Walden to demonstrate the possibility of a life spent in exploration of the self and nature.

In the mid-1850s, Thoreau succeeded in selling a few travel articles based on his trips to the Maine woods and Cape Cod to such publications as the *Atlantic Monthly* and *Putnam's Monthly*. His involvement in the anti-slavery movement led to a vital speech in Framingham, "Slavery in Massachusetts" (1854), followed by three on John Brown's actions at Harpers Ferry (1859–1860). He also developed a number of lectures about humanity's relation to nature, which he edited into essay form shortly before his death. The bulk of his creative energies, however, was spent on his journals, which he had begun in 1837 and in which he sought to make his natural observations ever more detailed and cohesive.

At the time of his death from tuberculosis in 1862, Thoreau had earned a reputation as a naturalist, though the vast majority of his writings remained unpublished. In the years following, many of his published works were collected, and an effort began to cull publications out of the journals, which themselves extended to 2 million words. Among the fruits of these efforts were *Excursions* (1863), edited by Emerson, as well as *The Maine Woods* (1864) and *Cape Cod* (1865), both edited by Sophia Thoreau and William Ellery Channing. In 1906 Houghton Mifflin published fourteen volumes of selections from Thoreau's journal; Princeton University Press began a more comprehensive edition in 1971.

BIBLIOGRAPHY

Harding, Walter, *The Days of Henry Thoreau*, rev., 1992; Howarth, William, *The Book of Concord: Thoreau's Life as a Writer*, 1982; Richardson, Robert D., Jr., *Henry Thoreau: A Life of the Mind*, 1986.

Thurber, James Grover

(December 8, 1894–November 2, 1961)
Artist, Essayist, Playwright, Short-Story Writer

The twentieth-century humorist James Thurber brought humane intelligence and biting wit to stories and sketches that describe human foibles. Thurber's hapless heroes, such as the protagonist of his best-known tale, "The Secret Life of Walter Mitty," go unredeemed except in the hilarity of the moment.

Thurber was born in Columbus, Ohio. Childhood experiences would become the source of many of his humorous sketches, as well as of his tongue-in-cheek memoir, *My Life and Hard Times* (1933). A childhood accident that impaired his vision precluded active duty during World War I, but he left Ohio State University in 1918 to serve as a code clerk at the American embassy in Paris.

After the war, Thurber began work as a reporter, first for the Columbus *Dispatch*, then for the Paris edition of the Chicago *Tribune*, and finally for the New York *Evening Post*. He later wrote that falling back on journalism as a career was "very much like falling back full-length on a kit of carpenter's tools." In 1927 Thurber met the writer E. B. White, who in turn introduced him to Harold Ross, the editor of a newly established magazine, *The New Yorker*. Ross hired Thurber, who became a staff writer and later a free-lance contributor.

Over the course of Thurber's long association with *The New Yorker*, which lasted until his death in 1961, he both found his own voice and helped define that of the magazine. His first sketch, "An American Romance," published in 1927, concerns a Walter Mitty–like little man who defies the fates by barricading himself in a revolving door. Most of Thurber's twenty-two books began as pieces for the magazine.

Thurber's first book, a collaboration with White, was a parody, *Is Sex Necessary?* (1929). White also discovered and encouraged Thurber's talent for cartooning. Soon Thurber's drawings became almost integral to his written pieces, and his cartoon figures graced not only the pages of *The New Yorker* but also its office walls. "Humor," Thurber believed, "is a kind of emotional chaos told about calmly and quietly in retrospect." His cartoons often featured the conflicts between men and women ("I love the idea of there being two sexes, don't you?" read one caption) and frequently used dogs and seals to lend an aura of absurdity to the proceedings. Thurber drew until the late 1940s, when his eyesight deteriorated so severely he could no longer continue.

Thurber's collections of humorous sketches, many of them featuring his own illustrations, include *The Owl in the Attic* (1931), *The Middle-Aged Man on the Flying Trapeze* (1935), *Let Your Mind Alone!* (1937), *Fables for Our Time* (1940), *My World—and Welcome to It* (containing "The Secret Life of Walter Mitty," 1942), *The Beast in Me, and Other Animals* (1948), *The Thurber Album* (1952), *Thurber's Dogs* (1955), and *Lanterns and Lances* (1961), his last book of essays.

Thurber also tried his hand at children's stories, most notably with *The 13 Clocks* (1950) and *The Wonderful O* (1957). He wrote two plays, *The Male Animal* (with Elliott Nugent, 1940) and *A Thurber Carnival* (1960). *The Years with Ross* (1959) is a memoir of Thurber's work with Harold Ross at *The New Yorker.*

Thurber died in New York City in 1961.

BIBLIOGRAPHY

Bernstein, Burton, *James Thurber: A Biography*, 1975; Long, Robert Emmett, *James Thurber*, 1988; Morsberger, Robert E., *James Thurber*. 1964.

Tiffany, Louis Comfort

(February 18, 1848–January 17, 1933)
Craftsman, Decorator, Designer, Painter

L ouis Comfort Tiffany, internationally recognized as a major talent of the Aesthetic and Art Nouveau movements, was an innovator in the art of glassmaking. He was also famous as a painter, an interior decorator, and a designer of jewelry and small art objects.

Tiffany was born in New York City, the son of the jeweler Charles L. Tiffany, who founded Tiffany and Company, one of the world's great jewelry stores. Rebelling against his father's conservatism and commercialism, Tiffany became a nonconformist and independent thinker, choosing to study painting rather than to learn the family business. He first studied with the American painter GEORGE INNESS, then with Leon Bailly in Paris (1868). He was fascinated by French Medieval stained glass windows, especially those at Chartres Cathedral, and was influenced by the English artist William Morris's revival of interest in the crafts generally and in stained glass particularly. Later travels through Spain and North Africa and a growing interest in Islamic and Japanese art exerted major influences on his subsequent design and craft work.

After his return to the United States, Tiffany gained prominence as an oil painter and watercolorist, and in 1871 became a member of the National Academy of Design in New York City. In 1877 he, along with such renowned artists as AUGUSTUS SAINT-GAUDENS, split from the academy because of that organization's conservative bent and formed the Society of American Artists. During the 1870s, Tiffany shifted his attention to the decorative arts, experimenting with stained glass as early as 1872 and establishing his first glassmaking plant in Cirona, New York, in 1878. He also formed Louis C. Tiffany and Associated Artists (1879–1885), which involved the collaboration of furniture makers, glassworks, textile and tile manufacturers in the coordinated creation of unified interior designs. His renown for highly decorated but original interiors earned a commission from President Chester A. Arthur to redecorate the reception rooms at the White House (1882–1883). Renamed the Tiffany Glass Company (1885–1892), then the Tiffany Glass & Decorating Company (1892–1900), the firm was reorganized as the Tiffany Studios in 1900.

Tiffany developed a new process for making an iridescent, freely shaped glass in which layers of colored glass flowed transparently or opaquely over one another,. creating abstract patterns. The delicate, jewel-like opalescence of this Favrile glass (popularly known as Tiffany glass) was the sensation of the 1893 World's Columbian Exhibition in Chicago and established his international reputation as a leading glassmaker. The trade name Favrile was patented in 1894 to apply to everything Tiffany created (except jewelry) in acknowledgment that each article was handmade. Calling himself the first industrial artist, Tiffany tried to fuse art and everyday life by creating beautiful objects that could "nourish the human spirit." He strove to implement his philosophy that "handicraft which possesses beauty and originality is independent of passing fashion." A versatile, determined perfectionist with a myriad of creative ideas, Tiffany designed and supervised the production of glass bowls, vases, lampshades, and ornamental windows, textiles, rugs, frescoes, metalwork, furniture, jewelry, small art objects, even tombstones.

Tiffany's emphasis on quality of craftsmanship, his motifs of flowers, stems, vines, and feathers, and the sinuous lines of his vases and lamps put him at the forefront of the blossoming Art Nouveau movement (1890–1915). An aesthetic, romantic movement concentrated primarily in the decorative arts, Art Nouveau stressed sensual, interlacing lines based on natural forms like flowers, tendrils, and waves. Tiffany's lamps had metal bases sculpted in naturalistic forms, like vines or branches, and leaded-glass shades in floral or insect patterns. The Wisteria lamp and the Lily Cluster lamp, which won the grand prize at the Turin Exhibition (1902), were two of his most popular patterns. He often used gold to achieve swirling rings and the metallic luster of blue-green peacock feathers.

Major large-scale achievements were the high altar in the Cathedral of St. John the Divine in New York City (never installed) and the huge glass curtain-screen for the National Theater in the Palacio de Belias Artes, Mexico City.

But perhaps Tiffany's grandest achievement was the design and construction of his estate, Laurelton Hall, at Oyster Bay, Long Island (1903–1904), the only major Art Nouveau residence built in America. The exotic mansion, with its marble floors, glass walls, colored lights, exotic plants, and artworks, was surrounded by landscaped terraces and fountains, also designed by Tiffany. Today, the loggia, as well as the famous Tiffany window, *View of Oyster Bay* (1905), form the centerpiece of New York's Metropolitan Museum of Art's American Wing.

When his father died in 1902, Tiffany became more involved in the family business, designing jewelry and enamels. That same year he reorganized his glass factory in Cirona, calling it the Tiffany Furnaces, and expanded production to include pottery, metal works, and enamels. Eventually he became vice president and director of Tiffany & Company, Jewelers, and Tiffany & Company Safe Deposit Company, as well as directing his own design and manufacturing companies. At the height of his popularity and influence, Tiffany's Favrile glass created a new fashion, especially in the United States and in Central Europe, and he revolutionized interior design in late–nineteenth-century America. His influence on decorative taste was so great that even train station waiting rooms sported Tiffany-style windows.

In 1918 Tiffany established and endowed the Louis Comfort Tiffany Foundation to help art students. At his estate, he built studios and living quarters as a summer retreat for working artists, and every summer until his death he invited artists from around the country to work there. Unfortunately, after his death, the estate was sold, and the foundation only provided funds to artists.

Tiffany's work became unfashionable by World War II, but it enjoyed a resurgence of popularity from the 1950s onward and is now highly collectible. Although he had no formal training in glassmaking or interior design, Tiffany left an indelible mark on the decorative arts.

BIBLIOGRAPHY

Koch, Robert, *Louis Comfort Tiffany, Rebel in Glass*, 1964, and *Louis C. Tiffany's Glass-Bronzes—Lamps*, 1971; McKean, Hugh F., *The "Lost" Treasures of Louis Comfort Tiffany*, 1980.

Toscanini, Arturo

(March 25, 1867–January 16, 1957)
Conductor

Toscanini's high standards remain models for orchestral performance. His belief that the performer had a moral obligation to realize the composer's intentions as faithfully as possible led to an almost fanatical attention to detail. His often stormy rehearsals resulted in a precision of rhythm, intonation, articulation, and dynamics that created the characteristically intense Toscanini sound.

Born to a nonmusical family in Parma, Italy, Toscanini's musical promise led to a scholarship at Parma's Royal School of Music. He was nine years old and remained at the conservatory until he graduated in 1885 with highest honors in cello, piano, and composition. Employed by Claudio Rossi's newly formed opera company and touring South America as first cellist and assistant chorus master, he was asked on June 30, 1886, to substitute for the orchestra conductor for *Aida* in Rio de Janeiro. At nineteen Toscanini had never before led a professional performance. He astonished everybody by conducting from memory and with no rehearsal. The performance was such a success that Toscanini was named principal conductor of the touring company and always conducted from memory.

The following decade saw the young conductor at work in various Italian theaters, where he led the premieres of Leoncavallo's *I Pagliacci* and Puccini's *La Bohème* and the first Italian performances of Wagner's *Götterdämmerung, Tristan und Isolde*, and *Siegfried*. His reputation as a conductor grew. In 1895 he became music director of the Teatro Regio in Turin, Italy, and in 1898 was appointed conductor of the Teatro La Scala in Milan, where he remained until 1908, though he was absent for three years because of a dispute over standards.

In 1908 Toscanini went to the Metropolitan Opera in New York as conductor. He made his New York debut conducting *Aida*, November 16, 1908, and in the ensuing years managed to exert his remarkable discipline over a stunning array of operatic talent. Among his American premieres were Mussorgsky's *Boris Godunov*, Puccini's *La fanciulla del West*, and Gluck's *Armide*. A dispute over standards and finance, aided by a tempestuous affair with leading soprano Geraldine Farrar and Italy's participation in World War I, led to Toscanini's resignation from the Met in 1915 and his subsequent return to his homeland.

In 1920 Toscanini was appointed artistic director of La Scala. Granted extraordinary powers, he formed a new orchestra of 100 players, toured Italy, the United States, and Canada (1920–1921), before returning to Milan, where he remained until 1929. In 1926 and 1927 he appeared as guest conductor with the New York Philharmonic Orchestra. After a brilliant company tour of Vienna and Berlin, Toscanini resigned his post at La Scala in 1929 to become principal conductor of the New York Philharmonic Orchestra, which had recently merged with the Symphony Society Orchestra. With this group he toured Europe in 1930 and remained with the orchestra until 1936. Many believe this period represents the peak of Toscanini's musical achievement.

New York was home base to Toscanini for the last twenty-five years of his career. During the 1930s, after conducting at Bayreuth in 1930 and 1931, he refused to conduct at the Wagner Festival again or at the Salzburg (Austria) Festival because of Hitler's ban on Jewish artists. His political sympathies led to his leadership of the inaugural performance of the Palestine Symphony Orchestra in 1936 and to other concerts in the Mideast.

In 1937 Toscanini returned to New York to lead the NBC Symphony Orchestra, which had been established especially for him by David Sarnoff and Samuel Chotzinoff. He conducted the group for seventeen years, toured South America in 1940 and the United States in 1950, and made many recordings. His final concert with the NBC Symphony Orchestra was April 4, 1954. He died two months short of his ninetieth birthday in New York and was buried in Milan, Italy.

Though he did not often perform works by twentieth-century composers, Toscanini's repertory was broad—Puccini to Richard Strauss, Brahms to Berlioz, and Tchaikovsky to Debussy. The music of Beethoven, Wagner, and Verdi were particular favorites. The way he combined prodigious musical gifts and respect for musical texts with energy, discipline, and demand for perfection made him a nearly legendary figure. Biographer Harvey Sachs concludes, "The most amazing thing about Toscanini . . . was that his struggle to achieve a beautiful performance was absolutely a matter of life and death—the struggle itself even more than the achievement. . . . This passion . . . possessed him so entirely that his work *became* communication at a level undreamed of by most performers."

BIBLIOGRAPHY

Antek, S., and R. Hupka, *This Was Toscanini,* 1963; Horowitz, J., *Understanding Toscanini: How He Became an American Culture God and Helped Create a New Audience for Old Music,* 1987; Sachs, H., *Toscanini,* 1978.

Twain, Mark

(November 30, 1835–April 21, 1910)
Novelist, Short-Story Writer, Travel Writer

Mark Twain, best known for his tales of boyhood along the Mississippi River, is remembered as America's greatest humorist and one of its finest novelists. In *The Adventures of Huckleberry Finn,* he has been credited with having written the first truly American novel.

Mark Twain was the pseudonym adopted by Samuel Langhorne Clemens at the age of twenty-seven; the name derives from a phrase called out on Mississippi riverboats to denote that a channel was 2 fathoms deep and thus safe for travel.

Clemens was born in Florida, Missouri, and, after the age of four, grew up in the small town of Hannibal, on the west bank of the Mississippi River. His father, a dreamer with notions of finding his fortune on the frontier, had wandered west from Virginia, stopping to marry in Kentucky. John Marshall Clemens died when his son was twelve, and young Clemens was apprenticed to a local printer. At eighteen he began selling humorous sketches to newspapers, and at twenty-one he began to pursue his childhood dream of becoming a riverboat pilot.

The Civil War shut down riverboat service on the Mississippi, and Clemens enlisted briefly as a Confederate soldier. He deserted after three weeks and traveled West with his brother Orion, an abolitionist who had been appointed by President Lincoln to serve as secretary to the governor of the Nevada Territory.

Library of Congress

Clemens worked briefly for his brother and even tried his hand at mining for gold before taking up a succession of reporting jobs, first at the Virginia City, Nevada, *Territorial Enterprise*—where, in 1863, he first used the name Mark Twain on a story—and later at the San Francisco *Morning Call.*

Twain's first real success came with the publication of "The Celebrated Jumping Frog of Calaveras County" in the New York *Saturday Press* in 1865. A folktale current among the miners he knew, the story concerned a bet by Jim Smiley that his frog, Dan'l Webster, could outjump a frog picked by a stranger—a bet the stranger wins by loading Dan'l Webster with buckshot while Smiley's back is turned. Twain made the tale the title story for his first book, published in 1867.

In 1866 Twain made his debut as a humorous travel writer with a trip to Hawaii for the Sacramento, California, *Union.* The following year, he signed on for the voyage of the steamship *Quaker City* to Europe and the Holy Land; his dispatches for the San Francisco *Alta California* were later rewritten as *The Innocents Abroad* (1869), the book that won him an international reputation and made his fortune. Twain's lengthy, energetic parody of the life of the traveler and his irreverence toward the hallowed landmarks of European culture endeared him to American readers, who wished both to be traveling and to feel a sense of their own worth and identity on the international scene.

In 1870 Twain married Olivia Langdon of Elmira, New York, the sister of a man he met on the steamship *Quaker City* and the daughter of a millionaire who had made his fortune in the coal industry. Twain began sharing the drafts of his work with his wife; her role as a censor attuned to the sensibilities of the book-buying classes has been questioned by some critics, though others insist it has been overstated. The couple settled first in Buffalo, New York, where Twain set himself up as the editor of a local paper, and then in Hartford, Connecticut, where Twain built an elaborate house that drew comparison to a riverboat.

Twain wrote a series of books in quick succession, including *Roughing It* (1872), an account of his adventures in California and Hawaii; *The Gilded Age* (1873), a satiric novel of the hectic post–Civil War development boom and a collaboration with Charles Dudley Warner; *A Tramp Abroad* (1880), a travel book featuring Germany, Switzerland, and Italy; and *The Prince and the Pauper* (1882), a novel set in Tudor England about two boys who change places in the days before one of them is to be crowned King Edward VI.

During this period, Twain also wrote the three books for which he is most remembered, all of which hearken back to his boyhood in Hannibal. *The Adventures of Tom Sawyer* (1876) concerns a mischievous boy and his experiences growing up in St. Petersburg, Missouri, a little town based on Hannibal. The novel recounts Tom's clever pranks on his schoolmates, his wearying effect on his proper Aunt Polly, his infatuation with his first sweetheart, Becky Thatcher, and his misadventures with Huck Finn, with whom he both witnesses a murder and eventually finds hidden treasure.

Life on the Mississippi (1883) is an autobiographical reminiscence of Twain's years training to become a riverboat pilot, mingled with an account of his monthlong travels along the river as he researched the book.

Twain's acknowledged masterpiece is *The Adventures of Huckleberry Finn* (1884). Huck escapes his father, a violent drunkard who has kidnapped him to gain control of Huck's share of the treasure found at the conclusion of *The Adventures of Tom Sawyer.* Huck teams up with Jim, an escaped slave, and the two head downriver on a raft. Their adventures reach a climax when one of a pair of wandering frauds sells Jim into slavery behind Huck's back. Tom Sawyer concocts an elaborate plot to rescue Jim, which fails; he then reveals that Jim had been freed under the terms of the will of his first owner. At the end of the novel, Huck announces his intention to depart civilization, despite his now secure claim to the treasure.

While the novel's apparent moral ambiguity has stirred debate, critics agree that the story remains true to Huck as a character and that Twain's achievement in narrating the tale in Huck's voice was to fully define for the first time an American literary vernacular.

When *The Adventures of Huckleberry Finn* was published, Twain was at the peak of his career, but his fortunes reversed soon thereafter. He had invested heavily in the prototype of a new typesetting machine, whose inventor, James Paige, never completed it. Twain wrote furiously in an attempt to stave off bankruptcy, but the project soaked up all the profits from such books as *A Connecticut Yankee in King Arthur's Court* (1889), *Tom Sawyer Abroad* (1894), and *The Tragedy of Pudd'nhead Wilson* (1894). Twain was forced into bankruptcy, though, fortunately, he managed to transfer his copyrights to his wife, and so protected his most valuable property.

Determined to pay off his debts, Twain began a lecture tour around the world. The death of a daughter, Susy, of meningitis during his absence depressed him terribly. He continued writing, but mostly in fragments. *Following the Equator* (1897) is a record of his tour. This emotional turmoil lasted until after the death of his wife in 1904.

The chief creative work of Twain's waning years were his short stories and his autobiography, dictated to his secretary, Albert Bigelow Paine, and published posthumously in 1924.

Twain died in Redding, Connecticut, in 1910.

BIBLIOGRAPHY

Emerson, Everett H., *The Authentic Twain: A Biography of Samuel Langhorne Clemens*, 1983; Gerber, John C., *Mark Twain*, 1988; Kaplan, Justin, *Mr. Clemens and Mark Twain: A Biography*, 1966; Leary, Lewis, *Mark Twain*, 1960; Paine, Albert B., *Mark Twain*, 3 vols., 1912, rep., 1980.

Updike, John Hoyer

(March 18, 1932–   )
Essayist, Novelist, Poet, Short-Story Writer

Best known for such novels as *Rabbit, Run* and *Rabbit Is Rich*, John Updike is concerned with the search for moral certainty in a world lacking religious signposts. Even as his characters explore their own sexual desires, they yearn for truths that might endow their lives with meaning.

Updike was born in Shillington, Pennsylvania, the son of a high school mathematics teacher. He attended Harvard University, where he majored in English and edited the *Harvard Lampoon*. After graduating in 1954, he spent a year in Oxford, England, studying at the Ruskin School of Drawing and Fine Art.

In October 1954 *The New Yorker* magazine published his story, "Friends from Philadelphia." In 1955 Updike joined the magazine as a staff writer. Two years later, he left the magazine and New York City and moved with his family to Ipswich, Massachusetts, to devote his full energies to writing. Updike has maintained his association with *The New Yorker*, as a frequent contributor of fiction, poetry, and reviews, for almost forty years.

Updike's first book, *The Carpentered Hen and Other Tame Creatures* (1958), is a collection of light verse culled largely from contributions to *The New Yorker;* similarly, *The Same Door* (1959) collects short stories from the magazine.

Updike's first novel, *The Poorhouse Fair* (1959), contrasts the traditional religion of one ancient inhabitant of a public home for the aged with the secular creed of the younger man who administers the home; the younger man seems able to address his clients' every need except their fears of death. Subsequent novels continued to reflect Updike's concern with the moral hollowness of secular society.

Rabbit, Run (1960), the first of a series of novels based on the misfortunes of Harry ("Rabbit") Angstrom, finds Rabbit trying to find moral footing in a life whose most important features include an aimless job in a five-and-ten-cent store, a bored wife in a seedy apartment, and too much television. Wanting desperately to stop feeling empty, Rabbit resorts to flights from home and adulterous sex. In later novels, *Rabbit Redux* (1971), *Rabbit Is Rich* (1981), and *Rabbit at Rest* (1990), Rabbit tries on a succession of lovers and lifestyles in the same ill-fated quest for meaning. *Rabbit Run* established Updike's reputation; *Rabbit Is Rich* won him the Pulitzer Prize, the American Book Award, and the National Book Critics Circle Award.

Updike's third novel, *The Centaur* (1963), frames a teenager's gradual awareness of the meaning of faith. Peter Caldwell believes his father, a high school science teacher, to be a good man living a good life, and he is deeply pained to see him mocked and misunderstood by his students—like the centaur in the myth of Chiron who must impart the wisdom of the gods to unwilling pupils. Peter comes to see his father's grace as sustaining. *The Centaur* won the National Book Award.

Updike explores the modern preoccupation with sex in such novels as *Couples* (1968) and *Marry Me* (1976). The first of these examines sexual exchanges among couples in a small Massachusetts suburb; the latter observes an adulterous liaison that is about to break up a marriage. In both cases Updike celebrates the human impulse that fuels these romantic entanglements at the same time he questions whether his characters have gained anything that can compensate for their faithlessness.

Again exploring adultery as a theme, Updike published a trilogy of novels that were meant to update the lives of central characters from NATHANIEL HAWTHORNE's *Scarlet Letter. A Month of Sundays* (1975) concerns a disgraced minister, after Arthur Dimmesdale; *Roger's Version* (1986) reworks the story of Roger Chillingworth; *S.* (1988) evokes Hester Prynne.

The Coup (1978) broadens Updike's familiar concerns and transplants them to a distant African state. The novel's protagonist is a dictator who faces marital woes on top of his country's political and economic morass. The novel exposes interference by the United States in the affairs of a sovereign nation.

The Witches of Eastwick (1984) concerns modern-day witchcraft and presents a comic satire on feminism. A circle of witches in New England—angry women living in isolation—ply their spells on others but do little to change themselves.

Updike's short stories are collected in many volumes, including *The Music School* (1966), *Bech: A Book* (1970), *Museums and Women* (1972), and *Bech Is Back* (1982). Among his volumes of poetry are *Tossing and Turning* (1977) and *Facing Nature* (1985). A collection of essays, *Hugging the Shore* (1983), won the 1984 National Book Critics Circle Award, and a volume of essays and criticism, *Odd Jobs*, appeared in 1991.

Updike now lives and works in Beverly Farms, Massachusetts.

BIBLIOGRAPHY

Detweiler, Robert, *John Updike*, 1984; Updike, John, *Self-Consciousness: Memoirs*, 1989; Uphaus, Suzanne H., *John Updike*, 1980.

Upjohn, Richard

(January 22, 1802–August 17, 1878)
Architect

Richard Upjohn is renowned for his church architecture, particularly in the Gothic Revival style, in which forms and details are derived from the medieval Gothic style. His masterpiece, Trinity Church in New York City, became a landmark of American ecclesiastical design. He also influenced his profession substantially as first president of the American Institute of Architects.

Upjohn was born in Shaftesbury, England, and trained as a cabinetmaker (1819–1824). He established his own cabinetry business (1824), but financial reverses motivated him to emigrate to the United States in 1829. He worked as a draftsman in New Bedford, Massachusetts, then settled in Boston (1834), where he worked in Alexander Parris's office and developed an independent practice. His earliest independent designs were for Maine residences, including one in Gardiner (1835) done in Gothic Revival (see RALPH ADAMS CRAM).

The first of his Gothic Revival churches, St. John's in Bangor (1835–1836), possessed rich decoration and accurate Gothic detail, reflecting Upjohn's careful study of architectural books and craftsmanlike use of ornament as a decorative aspect of construction rather than as superficial embellishment. A devout Episcopalian, Upjohn believed that the Gothic Revival style, with its characteristic pointed arches, steep roofs, and soaring spires, best represented the church, and could ignite religious fervor through the mystical and emotional connotations of its medieval allusions. Upjohn gained powerful patrons within the Protestant Episcopal clergy and by 1846 emerged as the leading ecclesiastical architect of his day.

He opened an office in New York City in 1839 and gained prominence with his design for Trinity Church (1841–1846), the first major building of national importance in the Gothic Revival style. Noted for its majestic spire and interior ornament, Trinity established a new standard for Gothic Revival in size and in wealth of accurate detail. Although Upjohn had no previous experience with such a monumental project, his structure proved so successful that it became a model for church design for decades.

As the Episcopal community prospered and expanded, Upjohn was in constant demand to build churches. Among his other Gothic Revival churches are Christ Church, Brooklyn (1841–1842), with its sparse ornament and centered tower fronting a building that externally expresses its massive internal space, and the Church of the Holy Communion, New York (1844–1846). The interiors of his Gothic churches are noted for the complex carpentry of their roofs. Upjohn seldom copied whole features; he adapted a style's characteristics to the materials, client's needs, and the workmanship and money available. "Reality" and "truth" dominated his design philosophy; he believed that "the purpose of every structure we build should be marked so as to need no other inscription than what it truly presents. Its exterior and interior expression ought to make plain the uses for which it was erected."

As smaller parishes sprung up in rural settings, Upjohn created church designs to meet their needs, stressing simplicity of form, ornament, and materials, as in the striking wooden Church of Saint John Chrysostom in Delafield, Wisconsin (1851–1853). His influential 1852 book *Upjohn's Rural Architecture*, which contained drawings of a prototype church and other buildings, estimates of materials needed and cost, and construction directions, brought affordable architectural design to outlying areas.

Upjohn also designed buildings in other styles to fit the purpose of each. For the Church of the Pilgrims, Brooklyn (1844–1846), and Bowdoin College chapel and library, Brunswick, Maine (1845–1855), he employed the Romanesque Revival style (see HENRY HOBSON RICHARDSON) based on the pre-Gothic masonry tradition of stone walls and round arches.

In 1853 Upjohn's son, Richard Michell Upjohn, joined his office and also became a well-known architect. In 1857 the father became a founder and first president (until 1876) of the American Institute of Architects. His ideas and policies shaped the organization's development and set the standards of professional ethics. Upjohn retired in 1872 and pursued his hobby of painting.

BIBLIOGRAPHY

Stanton, Phoebe B., *The Gothic Revival and American Church*, 1968; Upjohn, Everard Miller, *Richard Upjohn: Architect and Churchman*, rep., 1968; Upjohn, Richard, *Upjohn's Rural Architecture*, rep., 1975.

Valentino, Rudolph

(May 6, 1895–August 23, 1926)
Film Actor

Rudolph Valentino was the first male superstar of film history and, according to historian Richard Griffith, "the most maniacally adored man of the twentieth century." In films such as *The Four Horsemen of the Apocalypse* and *The Sheik* he defined male screen sensuality in the silent era and spawned dozens of imitators.

Born and baptized Rodolfo Alfonzo Rafaelo Pierre Filibert Guglielmi di Valentina d'Antonguolla at Castellaneta, Italy, he was the son of a veterinarian. After his father's death, he was educated at boarding schools until 1911 and emigrated to the United States in 1913.

Library of Congress

He worked as a gardener on the estate of Cornelius Bliss on Long Island, and later as a dancer at Maxim's, a New York cabaret. There he met Bonnie Glass, a professional dancer whom he partnered at the Winter Garden, the Palace, and other New York houses until she married in 1916. In 1917 he worked in musicals, as a dance instructor and chorus boy, then joined Al Jolson's *Passing Show*, which brought him to Los Angeles where he broke into movies.

Between 1917 and 1920 he appeared in at least sixteen films, first as an extra and then in supporting roles. In 1919 he married starlet Jean Acker, but they separated a month later and were divorced in 1922.

His big chance finally came in 1920 when screenwriter June Mathis proposed that he play Julio in Metro's *Four Horsemen of the*

Apocalypse, based on a novel by Vicente Blasco Ibañez. It was the year's biggest hit (1921) and made Valentino a star. During its production, Valentino met Natasha Rambova, set and costume designer for Alla Nazimova's films. She became his second wife in 1922. Valentino appeared in four other Metro films in 1921, including Nazimova's offbeat production of *Camille* and *The Conquering Power,* an adaptation of Balzac's *Eugénie Grandet.*

Before Metro assessed Valentino's impact, Paramount had signed him for *The Sheik* (1921), a costume melodrama in which the actor played an Arabian sheik who abducts and seduces a proper English lady, played by Agnes Ayres. Considered hammy by some, the film crystallized the Valentino appeal—combining an aggressive sexuality with a pained sensitivity—and was an even bigger hit than *The Four Horsemen,* earning over a million dollars for the studio and creating the most sensational phenomenon the industry had yet witnessed.

While it may be difficult for contemporary viewers to comprehend the effect Valentino had on his mostly female audience, it was verifiably fanatical and immense. Recent scholars have theorized that he was the first male sex object of the movies offered exclusively to women, thus tapping a previously unacknowledged and powerful segment of the audience.

But he fascinated men as well. Director D. W. GRIFFITH found him "an exciting discovery," struck not only by "his perfect features" but by his "charm and gracious manner." The ever cynical social critic H. L. Mencken described him as "a curiously naive and boyish fellow. There was an obvious fineness in him.... His words were simple and yet very eloquent. [He was] for want of a better name, a gentleman."

Certainly, his effect on the screen had little to do with acting, which his Paramount boss, ADOLPH ZUKOR, unflatteringly described as "largely confined to protruding his large, almost occult, eyes until the vast areas of white were visible, drawing back the lips of his wide, sensuous mouth to bare his gleaming teeth, and flaring his nostrils."

Yet Valentino did sometimes give affecting performances, particularly in *Blood and Sand* (1922), based on another Ibáñez novel about a matador led into dissipation by a temptress played by Nita Naldi. The film was another box-office smash. Equally interesting was *Monsieur Beaucaire* (1924), a film version of the novel by BOOTH TARKINGTON, although a bewigged Valentino, dressed in silks and satins and sporting beauty spots on his cheek, proved less appealing to his fans.

This "new" Valentino image, in striking contrast to that of the aggressive seducer, was largely the work of Rambova, who, after their marriage, fought with studio heads and demanded creative control over his films, until a separate production unit was established. As a result, such films as *A Sainted Devil* (1924) and *Cobra* (1925) were less enthusiastically received. Eventually, Rambova was excluded from creative participation.

Valentino's last two films, produced by United Artists, were *The Eagle* (1925) and *Son of the Sheik* (1926), both costarring Vilma Banky. After Rambova divorced him in 1926, he suffered from depression and had a number of serious automobile accidents. On August 15, he was rushed to a hospital and operated on for a ruptured appendix and an acute gastric ulcer. Pleurisy set in days later, leading to his death.

In New York City thousands of women blocked the streets outside the funeral parlor waiting their turn to pass by his bier. And for many years a mysterious woman dressed in black placed flowers on his grave. Whether a genuine act or a publicity stunt, the gesture became part of the Valentino legend.

Ten years after his death, *The Sheik* and *Son of the Sheik* were reissued with musical soundtracks and Agnes Ayres came out of obscurity to accompany showings on a publicity tour, billing herself, misleadingly, as "Rudy's girl," an indication that his legend lived on.

BIBLIOGRAPHY

Arnold, Alan, *Valentino*, 1952; Mackenzie, Norman A., *The Magic of Rudolph Valentino*, 1974; Shulman, Irving, *Valentino*, 1967.

Vallee, Rudy

(July 28, 1901–July 3, 1986)
Actor, Bandleader, Publisher, Saxophonist, Singer

Rudy Vallee, an early crooner and sex symbol, kept his audiences swooning with songs like "Good Night, Sweetheart," "Marie," and "I'm Just a Vagabond Lover." The Ivy League Vallee seemed the very embodiment of the 1920s, yet he continued to perform in clubs until shortly before his death in 1986.

Born Hubert Prior Vallée in Island Pond, Vermont, Vallee grew up in Westbrook, Maine, where his father was a pharmacist. At sixteen Vallee could play piano, clarinet, and drums. He taught himself to play saxophone, then a rather rare instrument, using clarinet skills and by listening to recordings and copying the style of

Rudy Wiedoeft. Vallee soon adopted Wiedoeft's first name. In 1920 Vallee began his professional career playing sax in a Portland, Maine, theater orchestra.

After a year at the University of Maine (1921), Vallee transferred to Yale University in New Haven, Connecticut, graduating in 1927. At Yale he established a band, the Yale Collegians (later the Connecticut Yankees), and played with the group at parties and in nightclubs to help defer college costs. In 1924 he took a year off from Yale to perform in London.

Vallee opened with the Connecticut Yankees at the Heigh-Ho Club in New York. The group, two violins, two saxophones, and a rhythm section, played arrangements of college and popular songs. Vallee was known for his saxophone vibrato, which created a singing tone, and for his crooning vocal style.

Vallee was an early pop idol, though he said, "I never had much of a voice . . . one reason for the success was that I was the first articulate singer—people could understand the words." Radio helped make him popular. He appeared on several shows, but with *The Fleischmann Hour* (1929–1939) he was broadcast on four stations. His trademark introduction ("Heigh-ho, everybody") and theme song ("My Time Is Your Time") were heard everywhere as the variety show, radio's first, promoted entertainers like Eddie Cantor, George Burns and Gracie Allen, and singer Alice Faye.

In 1929 Vallee began his film career with *The Vagabond Lover* and sang the title song, for which he was coauthor. He was to appear in over thirty-two films, his image gradually changing from romantic lover to the comic, pompous rich man who never wins the girl.

On Broadway, Vallee starred in *George White's Scandals* in 1931 and in 1936. Thirty years later, in 1961, he returned to Broadway in the Burrows-Loesser musical *How to Succeed in Business without Really Trying.* One reviewer applauded, saying, "Rudy Vallee is very funny in a tough-minded, high-handed, majestically incompetent way." The film version was released in 1967, and Vallee took part in a 1975 San Francisco production.

Vallee served in the U.S. Coast Guard during World War II and became bandmaster of the Eleventh Naval District Coast Guard Band. After the war his popularity declined, though he continued as a comic in nightclubs. In the 1930s Vallee founded a talent agency and in the 1940s, two publishing companies. He died in Hollywood, California, of a heart attack in 1986.

BIBLIOGRAPHY

Smith, W., *The Vaudevillians,* 1976; Vallee, R., and G. McKean, *My Time Is Your Time: The Story of Rudy Vallee,* 1962.

Varèse, Edgard

(December 22, 1883–November 6, 1965)
Composer

Long ignored, the pioneering Varèse reorganized music's structural components to emphasize masses of sound rather than linear elements. His influential experiments of the 1920s broke with traditional concepts and forms. He later manipulated technological advances in post–World War II electronics to construct major works from sounds on tape.

Edgard Varèse was born in Paris, France, but moved with his family to Turin, Italy, in 1893. Intending a career in engineering for his son, Henri Varèse steered Edgard toward a science and mathematics curriculum. However, young Varèse managed, despite opposition, to study music.

At the turn of the century Varèse returned to Paris to enter the Schola Cantorum. In 1905 he began to study composition with organist Charles-Marie Widor, and in 1907 traveled to Berlin. There he met and became friendly with Ferruccio Busoni, whose ambitious musical ideas were to help shape his own.

Varèse served in the French army in 1914 and was discharged a year later because of a serious illness. He sailed for the United States on December 18, 1915, and arrived in New York aswirl with the ideas and works of artists bent on changing the ways painting and other arts were perceived. Varèse quickly involved himself in musical circles. After his December 1917 American debut conducting the Berlioz Requiem, he went on to lead the Cincinnati Symphony Orchestra and his own New Symphony Orchestra in concerts of new music.

In 1921, to promote work of contemporary composers, he founded, with harpist-composer Carlos Salzedo, the International Composers' Guild. For six years the guild organized concerts of chamber works by ARNOLD SCHOENBERG, IGOR STRAVINSKY, Henry Cowell, and others. Works by Varèse included *Hyperprism* in 1923 and *Intégrales* in 1925.

Varèse's music, revolutionary in its day, replaced melody and harmony with sound and rhythm as unifying elements. What distressed audiences were the jagged, percussive rhythms and the lack of tonal harmony of Varèse's consciously emotionless style. However, the composer's dissonances, presented as sound masses, reflect twentieth-century city tensions, and the titles of his works refer to the sciences that so intrigued him.

Ionisation (1931), one of Varèse's most celebrated scores, is, writes British scholar Michael Nyman, "the first musical piece to be organized solely on the basis of *noise.*" It calls on thirteen performers to use thirty-five instruments (largely percussion), including sirens, cymbals, and bongos. Scholar Joseph Machlis notes that here Varèse frees percussion and bell sounds "from their traditional subservience to melody and harmony, . . . project masses of tensile sound that generate a sense of space," and causes the siren wail to emerge "as a vast shadowy image of our Age of Anxiety."

In the early 1930s Varèse made an unsuccessful attempt to raise funds for an electric-instrument research center. Depressed over that failure and over a lack of support for his music, he ceased composing after he completed *Density 21.5* in 1936, a solo work intended for the inauguration of Georges Barrère's platinum flute. (The specific gravity of platinum is 21.5.) By 1950, when Varèse resumed composing and began to work on *Déserts,* completed in 1954, the public was more receptive to experimental music. A recording of four of his works was released, and the U.S. State Department invited him to conduct master classes in composition in Darmstadt, Germany, in 1950. The young European composers in attendance recognized Varèse as an early and neglected forerunner of their own experiments with sound, and he, at last, received acclaim for his pioneering work.

Déserts, for twenty instruments and two-track tape, includes electronic interludes of factory sounds and percussion instruments. When it was played in Paris, it was broadcast live in stereo, a first for French radio. In 1957, at seventy-four, the composer was back in Europe to work on *Poéme électronique,* for three-track tape, commissioned for the Le Corbusier pavilion at the 1958 Brussels Exposition. There, says Peter Yates, in "a building resembling a circus tent with three poles somewhat inaccurately pitched, . . . four hundred loudspeakers projected the sound-composition from every point inside the continually curving structure; the music consists of natural sound, electronically altered, and electronically generated sound."

Varèse died in New York a few years later, in 1965, having completed only a few self-sustaining works, leaving a number of unfinished compositions and a remarkable legacy of musical experiments.

BIBLIOGRAPHY

Machlis, J., *Introduction to Contemporary Music,* 1961; Ouellette, F., *Edgard Varèse,* 1964, trans., 1981; Salzman, E., *Twentieth Century Music: An Introduction,* 3d ed., 1988.

Venturi, Robert

(June 25, 1925–   )
Architect

Scott Brown, Denise

(October 3, 1931–   )
Architect, Urban Planner

Robert Venturi and his wife, Denise Scott Brown, partners in their Philadelphia firm, are influential Post-Modern architects. Their books have provided a major theoretical basis for the movement away from the strict tenets of Modernism. Their buildings reveal a commitment to context and tradition, while exhibiting the realities of late–twentieth-century urban and suburban culture.

Venturi was born and raised in Philadelphia and studied at Princeton University, where Jean Labatut of the School of Architecture and art historian Donald Drew Egbert strongly influenced him. He then worked two and a half years for the Finnish-American architect EERO SAARINEN. Having won the Rome Prize Fellowship in 1954, he spent two years in Rome at the American Academy. After his return to this country, he worked for LOUIS I. KAHN, a Philadelphia architect, and taught a course on architectural theory in the School of Architecture at the University of Pennsylvania.

Venturi opened his own architectural office in Philadelphia in 1958 and formed a partnership with John Rauch in 1964. From 1957 to 1965 he taught at the University of Pennsylvania, where he met Denise Scott Brown, who was born in Nakana, Zambia, grew up in South Africa, graduated from the Architectural Association in London, and was studying architecture and city planning at Penn. They immediately became "a coterie of two," as Venturi has put it, since they were the "only two non-Harvard, non-Bauhaus, people at

Penn." In 1966 Venturi became a professor of architecture at Yale University, where he stayed four years. In 1966 he also lectured in classes taught by Scott Brown, who was by then teaching at the School of Architecture and Urban Planning at the University of California at Los Angeles. They married in 1967, when Scott Brown joined the firm of Venturi & Rauch. She became a partner in 1969. After Rauch retired in 1987, the firm became Venturi, Scott Brown and Associates.

Venturi has designed a number of houses, including one for his mother, Vanna Venturi, in Chestnut Hill, a suburb of Philadelphia (1962). Although a small house, it is an almost monumental gesture with its gabled facade and large central chimney. The windows and doors, however, are taken from the American postindustrial, suburban vernacular.

His early public buildings include the Guild House, a home for the elderly in Philadelphia (1960–1963); the Humanities Building at the State University of New York at Purchase (1968), which demonstrates Venturi's ideas for using the "ordinary" and the "boring," or responding to the vernacular architecture, in Post-Modern architecture (see MICHAEL GRAVES); and the Dixwell Fire Station (1970–1974) in New Haven. Venturi and Scott Brown have designed several buildings at Princeton University, including Gordon Wu Hall (1983), a residential college with flamboyant decorative motifs and one of the most critically acclaimed buildings of the 1980s, and the exterior of the Lewis Thomas Molecular Biology Building (1986), for which they used many-colored bricks, cast stone, and stucco to weave a fabriclike and checkerboard effect.

The Venturis collaborated on the new Sainsbury Wing addition to the National Gallery on Trafalgar Square in London (1986–1991), for which they borrowed some of the classical vocabulary of the existing building, designed by William Wilkins in 1838, but used it in unexpected ways and in juxtaposition with brick and glass walls.

They also designed the new building for the Seattle Art Museum (1992). "Mr. Venturi and Ms. Scott Brown have rejected a simplistic, self-indulgent replication of the past in favor of designs that make highly studied comments on other styles—more stimulating intellectually, but less likely to provoke a comfortable visceral response," wrote Paul Goldberger in the *New York Times*. Yet Goldberger found that the new Seattle Art Museum "possesses comfort, is easy and exciting to look at, and . . . is energizing and even fun."

Scott Brown has been more devoted to urban planning than Venturi, and their planning work includes the South Street Rehabilitation Plan for Philadelphia (1970), the "City Edges Study" for Philadelphia (1973), the Galveston Development Project (1975), and the Pennsylvania Avenue Project for Washington, D.C. (1978–1979).

Their work has been controversial. In 1991 a poll of readers of *Architecture*, the magazine of the American Institute of Architects, placed Venturi fifth among the most admired architects and in the same place on the list of the most despised architects. He was the only architect to appear on both lists.

Venturi's book, *Complexity and Contradiction in Architecture*, published in 1966, called for a more varied architecture than the bare, square boxes of Modernism and argued for a "messy vitality" and for ambiguity and paradox. He lampooned LUDWIG MIES VAN DER ROHE's pronouncement, "Less is more," with his own statement, "Less is a bore." When he won the prestigious Pritzker Architecture Prize in 1991, the jury said the book was "generally acknowledged to have diverted the mainstream of architecture away from modernism."

In *Learning from Las Vegas* (1972), which he coauthored with Scott Brown and Steven Izenour, he argued that architects should pay attention to "ordinary" buildings and even to strip malls and billboards and think about accommodating public taste, not reforming it. Venturi values his classical training, however, and once said, "We could not have written about Las Vegas if we had not studied in Italy." Scott Brown published a collection of her writings on planning, *Urban Concepts*, in 1990.

BIBLIOGRAPHY

Goldberger, Paul, "An Art Museum Lifts Seattle's Cultural Profile," *New York Times*, February 16, 1992; Leigh, Catesby, "Visions of Venturi," *Princeton Alumni Weekly*, November 6, 1991; Muschamp, Herbert, "American Gothic," *New Republic*, August 12, 1991; Scully, Vincent, *The Architecture of Robert Venturi*, 1989.

Vidal, Gore

(October 3, 1925–)
Essayist, Novelist, Playwright, Short-Story Writer

The contemporary writer Gore Vidal is best known for novels about historical figures, such as *Burr* and *Lincoln*, and for satiric treatments of modern themes, such as *Myra Breckinridge*. Pointed social criticism underlies many of his novels and essays.

Eugene Luther Vidal, Jr., was born in West Point, New York, the son of an army instructor of aeronautics. He later adopted the name Gore in honor of his maternal grandfather, Thomas P. Gore, Oklahoma's first U.S. senator, with whom he spent a great deal of time after his parents' divorce in 1935.

Educated at Phillips Exeter Academy, he enlisted in the army in 1943 and was trained as an engineer. He served as a maritime warrant officer during World War II.

Vidal wrote his first novel, *Williwaw* (1946), while serving on a ship for the U.S. Army Transport Corps near the Aleutian Islands. The story concerns a storm, or williwaw, which tests the mettle of a naval commander as his ship makes a run near the Aleutian Islands. Vidal's second novel, *In a Yellow Wood* (1947), takes place after the war, as a veteran decides whether to pursue a wartime love affair or accept a more secure, but lonelier, life as a company man.

The City and the Pillar (1948) was controversial for its sympathetic depiction of homosexuality. Two subsequent novels were more favorably received: *The Judgment of Paris* (1952), about an American's European love affair, and *Messiah* (1954), the story of the establishment of a new religion.

After a period spent writing extensively for television, Vidal began to publish a long succession of novels centered on historical figures. *Julian* (1964) depicts the fourth-century Roman emperor renowned for his liberality toward non-Christian religions. Most of Vidal's historical novels concern America's own past: *Washington, D.C.* (1967), on the New Deal; *Burr* (1973), about the renegade politician Aaron Burr; *1876* (1976), on the election of Rutherford B. Hayes as president; *Lincoln* (1984), about the most-admired president;

Copyright Jane Brown; Courtesy Random House

Empire (1987), on the post–Civil War period; and *Hollywood* (1990), about Tinsel Town in the 1920s.

Myra Breckinridge (1968) caused controversy for its focus on transsexuality, as well as its satiric depiction of American culture and mores. Other novels by Vidal include *Myron* (1974), *Kalki* (1978), *Creation* (1981), and *Live from Golgotha* (1992).

Though he has often expressed disillusionment with the United States and its system of government, Vidal twice ran for seats in Congress, in 1960 and 1982. His essays on political and literary themes are collected in several volumes including *The Second American Revolution* (1982) and *At Home* (1988).

His most popular plays were *Visit to a Small Planet* (1957), *The Best Man* (1960), and *An Evening with Richard Nixon and . . .* (1972).

Vidal lives and works in Ravello, Italy.

BIBLIOGRAPHY

Kiernan, Robert F., *Gore Vidal*, 1982; White, Ray Lewis, *Gore Vidal*, 1968.

Vonnegut, Kurt, Jr.

(November 11, 1922–   )
Essayist, Novelist, Playwright, Short-Story Writer

Kurt Vonnegut, Jr., is best known for his novels *Slaughterhouse-Five; or, The Children's Crusade* and *Breakfast of Champions; or, Goodbye Blue Monday!* Vonnegut's stories are fantastic and often funny, but they also express a fatalistic sense that the violence of modern life precludes true moral action.

Vonnegut was born in Indianapolis, Indiana. He studied biochemistry at Cornell University, where he wrote for the student newspaper, the *Cornell Sun.* In 1943 Vonnegut left school to enlist in the army. Captured by Germans during the Battle of the Bulge, he was taken to Dresden, where he survived the Allied air raid that destroyed the city. He was freed when Soviet troops occupied the city in April 1945. Vonnegut returned briefly to Cornell, then enrolled at the University of Chicago to pursue a master's degree in anthropology.

In 1947 Vonnegut went to work as a public relations writer for the General Electric Research Laboratory in Schenectady, New York. He succeeded in placing his first short story, "Report on the Barnhouse Effect," in *Collier's* magazine in 1950. The following year, he quit his job and moved to Provincetown, Massachusetts, in order to write full time.

Vonnegut's first two novels, *Player Piano* (1952) and *The Sirens of Titan* (1959), were classified by many as science fiction, though Vonnegut preferred to describe them as realistic novels concerned with the impact of technology on the lives of ordinary people. *Player Piano* extrapolates from Vonnegut's experience in Schenectady, spinning the tale of an engineer who rebels against the overwhelming power of the company he works for. *The Sirens of Titan* is more purely fantasy, as it centers on an earthly millionaire taken against his will to live among Martians.

Mother Night (1962) concerns an American playwright who goes undercover as a Nazi propagandist during World War II. In *Cat's Cradle* (1963), a scientist invents a form of ice that remains solid at room temperature, leading to the end of the world. *God Bless You, Mr. Rosewater* (1965) tells the story of a millionaire determined to do good with his money; the stresses of life in contemporary society drive him to madness.

Vonnegut's best-known novel, *Slaughterhouse-Five* (1969), re-creates his experience at Dresden. Billy Pilgrim survives the city's conflagration in an underground meat-storage locker and then is forced to dig corpses from the ashes of the city. Much of the novel is fantasy, as Billy "time trips" into the future and visits the planet Tralfamadore. Vonnegut introduces himself into the narrative to allude to moments that are autobiographical.

In *Breakfast of Champions; or, Goodbye, Blue Monday* (1973), Vonnegut appears as Philboyd Studge, the author of the novel, which concerns a Pontiac salesman who goes mad after reading a novel by Kilgore Trout, the science-fiction writer who created Tralfamadore. *Breakfast of Champions* is perhaps Vonnegut's most popular novel.

Slapstick; or, Lonesome No More! (1976) describes an effort to create a truly human community by renaming people to establish elaborate familial interconnections.

More recent Vonnegut novels are *Bluebeard* (1987) and *Hocus Pocus* (1990). His plays include *Happy Birthday, Wanda June* (1971) and *Between Time and Timbuktu* (1972). His essays are collected in *Wampeters, Foma, and Granfalloons* (1974) and in *Palm Sunday* (1981).

Vonnegut now lives and works in New York City.

BIBLIOGRAPHY

Allen, William Rodney, *Understanding Kurt Vonnegut*, 1991; Klinkowitz, Jerome, *Kurt Vonnegut*, 1982; Lundquist, James, *Kurt Vonnegut*, 1977; Schatt, Stanley, *Kurt Vonnegut, Jr.*, 1976; Vonnegut, Kurt, Jr., *Fates Worse than Death*, 1991.

Warhol, Andy

(August 6, 1928–February 22, 1987)
Filmmaker, Graphic Designer, Painter

Andy Warhol was the foremost prophet and practitioner of the American Pop art movement of the late 1950s and 1960s.

Warhol was born in Pittsburgh in 1928 of Czech immigrant parents named Warhola. His father's early death meant he had to take occasional jobs while still in high school. After graduating in 1945, he studied technical drawing and design with Richard Lepper for several years at the Carnegie Institute of Technology (now Carnegie-Mellon University). With his friend, the painter Philip Pearlstein, he moved to New York in 1949 and worked as a commercial artist for *Vogue* and *Harper's Bazaar*, designed window displays for Bonwit Teller, and did advertisements for the I. Miller shoe company. In 1953, after his first one-man exhibition at the Hugo Gallery, he moved into a house on Lexington Avenue with his mother and several cats.

Encouraged by filmmaker Emile de Antonio, and stimulated by paintings by JASPER JOHNS and ROY LICHTENSTEIN he saw in the Leo Castelli Gallery, Warhol rejected the still-prevalent style of Abstract Expressionism (see BARNETT NEWMAN) and moved his commercial art to center stage. He made his debut as a Pop art (see ROY LICHTENSTEIN) painter in 1962 when he exhibited stenciled pictures of multiple dollar bills (*200 One Dollar Bills*), Marilyn Monroe (*Marilyn Monroe*), Campbell's soup cans (*Big Torn Campbell's Soup Can [Vegetable Beef]*), and Coca-Cola bottles (*Green Coca-Cola Bottles*). These were "all the great modern things that Abstract Expressionists tried so hard not to notice at all," he said. He plunged into the "Happenings" (see GEORGE SEGAL) and the avant-garde scene below 14th Street. He cultivated galleries and managed a show at New York's ultra-fashionable Stable Gallery in 1963. He established his celebrated Factory at 231 East 47th Street in midtown Manhattan. It was a loft measuring 50 by 100 feet and was furnished with trash recovered from the streets. "Knowing how to use what somebody else didn't was a knack you could really be proud of," he recalled. The walls and pipes were covered in silver foil. "Silver was the future, it was spacy," said Warhol. "And silver was

Copyright *Washington Post;* Reprinted by permission of the D.C. Public Library

also the past—the Silver Screen.... And maybe more than anything, silver was narcissism— mirrors were backed with silver." His art was intentionally devoid of emotional and social comment. He produced more than 2,000 images, including a silk-screen series of star portraits and a series of sculptures that duplicated product wrappings. News events and disaster pictures, many of them silk-screen transfers, included *129 DIE (Plane Crash)* (1962), the *Most Wanted Men* series (1963), *Orange Car Crash 10 Times* (1963), and *Lavender Disaster,* which depicts an electric chair (1963). The head-on, deadpan style recalled Dada and anticipated Conceptual art (see ROBERT SMITHSON).

In 1966 Warhol announced his retirement as an artist in order to devote himself to producing films. He frequently had said that as an artist he felt passive; now, with cinema, he could pursue his favorite activity of observing. Three years earlier, with cameraman Paul Morrissey, he had already begun making experimental movies, including *Sleep* and *Empire,* six and eight hours long, respectively (continuous,

views of the subjects from a single perspective). By 1967 the team had made more than fifty-five films, many of them silent, ranging in length from four minutes (*Mario Banana,* 1964) to twenty-four hours (****, also known as *Four Stars,* 1967). They recorded the antics of Warhol's coterie of friends—artists, junkies, transvestites, rock singers, and hustlers—and were all informed by a passive, mechanical aesthetic. With such "breakthrough" features as *The Chelsea Girls* (1966), *Bike Boy* (1967), and *Lonesome Cowboys* (1968), the team moved from an austere style to a more classical, even commercial cinema— story films with sound, split-screen, and color. While Warhol recovered from gunshot wounds inflicted by Factory regular Valerie Solanas, Morrissey took over principal directing responsibilities for *Flesh* (1968) and, with Warhol as producer, made some mainstream pictures like the 3-D *Andy Warhol's Frankenstein* (1973).

Warhol's literary activities included a magazine, *Interview,* which began in 1969; an autobiography, *The Philosophy of Andy Warhol,* in 1975; and his own history of Pop art, *POPism, the Warhol '60s* in 1980.

From the very beginning, notes critic Philip Core, Warhol was clearly preoccupied with techniques that removed, in effect, the artist's "handwriting." Warhol's famous dictum, "I like boring things," acknowledged the lack of authorial presence in fashion images as well as in much great art—the smoothness and polish that was especially attractive to Americans. Thus, he used repetition and duplication (*210 Coke Bottles* and *Twenty-Five Colored Marilyns*) to alter our concepts of meaning in art. "Apparently most people love watching the same basic thing, as long as the details are different," he wrote in *POPism, the Warhol '60s.*

> But I'm just the opposite: if I'm going to sit and watch the same thing I saw the night before, I don't want it to be essentially the same—I want it to be *exactly* the same. Because the more you look at the same exact thing, the more the meaning goes away, and the better and emptier you feel.

At the same time, he was fascinated with glamour, particularly the star images and careers of Marilyn Monroe and TRUMAN CAPOTE (Warhol wrote him a letter every day in 1949), and with surface and packaging. Historian Patrick S. Smith has called it an "idolization of Hollywood's idealization." In *POPism, the Warhol '60s,* Warhol documents with exhaustive detail his cultivation of the famous and the idiosyncratic in the art circles of New York and Los Angeles. As Tilman Osterwold writes:

> His art is informed by the knowledge that it is the appearance given to a thing or an event, the manner in which it is mediated or presented, which gives it its meaning. . . . Warhol not only wanted to turn the trivial and commonplace into art, but also to make art itself trivial and commonplace.

"Contrary to what many people may think," writes Philip Core, "Warhol did not force himself on the world; the world altered, and was ready for someone with his taste, his stance, his outsider's point-of-view." Indeed, his international fame proved to be much more durable than the fifteen minutes he allotted to "everybody." His appearance—the oversize sunglasses, the white pallor, the platinum white wig, the half-open smile—became as much of a public cliché as the nature of his work. Exhibitions included major shows at the Moderna Museet, Stockholm, in 1968, the

Kunstmuseum in Basel in 1972, the Wurttembergischer Kunstverein in 1976, the Whitney Museum of American Art in 1979, the Kestner-Gesellschaft in Hanover in 1981, and the American Museum of Natural History in New York in 1983.

In his last book, *America* (1985), Warhol had described death as "the most embarrassing thing that can ever happen to you." He died under rather mysterious circumstances following a routine gallbladder operation in 1987. When the appraisers entered his townhouse at 57 East 66th Street, they found a veritable Xanadu, an amazing clutter of objets d'art and junk. "It wasn't the room of a collector who liked to gaze on his treasures with the eye of a connoisseur," wrote biographer Victor Bockris. "It was, instead, the room of a shopper, an accumulator, a pack rat with all the money in the world." Two years later the Museum of Modern Art in New York fulfilled Warhol's prediction—"It will take my death for the Museum of Modern Art to recognize my work"—and organized the largest retrospective of an artist since the Picasso blockbuster of 1980.

BIBLIOGRAPHY

Bockris, Victor, *The Life and Death of Andy Warhol,* 1989; Core, Philip, "Drella's Idols," *Times Literary Supplement,* May 1, 1987; Osterwold, Tilman, *Pop Art,* 1991; Smith, Patrick S., *Andy Warhol's Art and Films,* 1988; Stitch, Sidra, *Made in U.S.A.: An Americanization in Modern Art, the '50s and '60s,* 1987; Warhol, Andy, *POPism, the Warhol '60s,* 1980.

Warren, Harry

(December 24, 1893–September 22, 1981)
Songwriter

Harry Warren's delightful songs were popularized by radio and film, and many climbed to the charts' top ten between 1932 and 1957. A versatile and influential songwriter, Warren wrote hits like "Lullaby of Broadway" and "On the Atchison, Topeka and the Santa Fe," songs that continue to be standard fare.

Born Salvatore Guaragna in Brooklyn, New York, Warren was the eleventh of twelve children to Italian immigrant parents. As a youngster he sang in a church choir and taught himself to play musical instruments from the piano to the accordion to drums. He worked as a drummer in his godfather's carnival band before he began singing with a vocal quartet and playing piano in movie theaters and in New York saloons. In 1920 he joined Stark and Cowan as a song plugger.

Four years later Warren joined Shapiro, Bernstein & Co., a music publishing firm, and by 1926 he had success with his own song, "I Love My Baby, My Baby Loves Me." Warren moved to the Remick Music Corporation, another music publisher, in 1928, as staff composer. After Remick was purchased by Warner Brothers, he went to Hollywood to write for early musical films.

At Warner Brothers, Warren, along with choreographer Busby Berkeley and lyricist Al Dubin, designed the extravagant musical films of the Great Depression. His first task for Warner was to compose six songs for the film version of RICHARD RODGERS's *Spring Is Here* (1930).

Warren continued to write for Broadway revues, including several produced by Billy Rose, but eventually he settled in Hollywood where he turned out music that was sung by Dick Powell, Carmen Miranda, Judy Garland, Gene Kelly, FRED ASTAIRE, and Bing Crosby. Forty-two Warren songs reached the top ten on the popular music charts. Three received Academy Awards: "Lullaby of Broadway," "You'll Never Know," and "On the Atchison, Topeka and the Santa Fe."

With "I Found a Million Dollar Baby" from the 1931 Broadway revue *Crazy Quilt,* Warren went on to a string of Hollywood successes in the 1930s: "You're Getting to Be a Habit with Me," "I Only Have Eyes for You," and "Jeepers Creepers"; and in the 1940s: "Chattanooga Choo Choo," "There Will Never Be Another You," "At Last," and "I've Got a Gal in Kalamazoo." The films are forgotten now, but the songs live on.

Almost all of Warren's nearly 250 songs were published and performed. Four Jays Music, Warren's publishing company, controlled the rights to songs published by Harry Warren Music and other companies. The Harry Warren Collection of musical comedy material is in the Archive of Popular American Music at the University of California, Los Angeles, and recorded interviews with Warren are in the libraries of ASCAP (American Society of Composers, Authors and Publishers) and Southern Methodist University. Warren, considered by song historian Alec Wilder to be "among the foremost pop song writers," died in Los Angeles, California, in September 1981.

BIBLIOGRAPHY

Thomas, T., *Harry Warren and the Hollywood Musical,* 1975; Wilder, A., *American Popular Song: The Great Innovators, 1900–1950,* 1972.

Warren, Robert Penn

(April 24, 1905–September 15, 1989)
Critic, Novelist, Poet

Robert Penn Warren, best known for his novel *All the King's Men,* wrote prolifically in three genres: fiction, poetry, and criticism. Drawn from southern history and experience, his writings often concern human failure in the face of moral dilemmas posed by changing social circumstances.

Warren was born in Guthrie, Kentucky. While in attendance at Vanderbilt University, from which he graduated in 1925, he developed an interest in poetry through his association with a professor of English, the poet JOHN CROWE RANSOM. With a roommate, ALLEN TATE, another fledgling poet, Warren was introduced to an informal literary discussion group led by Ransom. Known as the Fugitives, the writers in the group were generally opposed to what they saw as the social decadence reflected in contemporary poetry and to Victorian sentimentalism. Warren contributed to the group's journal, *The Fugitive.*

Warren earned a master's degree in literature at the University of California at Berkeley in 1927 and then continued his graduate work at Yale University before moving on to Oxford as a Rhodes scholar from 1928 to 1930. Upon his return to the United States, he accepted the first of a succession of teaching appointments that over time included Vanderbilt and Louisiana State universities, the University of Minnesota at Minneapolis, and, finally, Yale, from which he retired in 1973.

In 1930 Warren and eleven other writers contributed their voices to *I'll Take My Stand,* a collection of essays attacking northern industrialism and affirming the more traditional social and religious values associated with southern agrarianism. Warren later renounced his essay, "The Briar Patch," which had suggested that African Americans were better off in the South than at the mercy of northern factory owners. His subsequent thinking on the issues of race and changing southern society is contained in his books *Segregation: The Inner Conflict in the South* (1956) and *Who Speaks for the Negro?* (1965).

Warren's most pervasive influence as a critic was through his association with the movement known as the New Criticism, which held that poetry could best be understood through a close analysis of its structure and language rather than through historical scholarship. While at Louisiana State, Warren and the poet and critic Cleanth Brooks wrote a series of textbooks, beginning with *An Approach to Literature* (1936) and including *Understanding Poetry* (1938) and *Understanding Fiction* (1943), which described techniques·for close reading of literary texts that transformed the teaching of literature. During the same period, Warren, Brooks, and Charles Pipkin founded *The Southern Review,* a distinguished literary journal that continues to publish.

Warren's first three volumes of poetry, *Thirty-Six Poems* (1935), *Eleven Poems on the Same Theme* (1942), and *Selected Poems 1923–1943* (1944), feature taut, formal lyric poems written in a tone that is distant and ironic. Then, after a decade-long poetic silence during which he concentrated on fiction, he published *Brother to Dragons* (1953), a long narrative poem about the brutal murder of a slave by nephews of THOMAS JEFFERSON. Warren's subsequent work became more intensely personal and even occasionally autobiographical. *Promises* (1957) marks a lasting change in form, as Warren began to utilize a looser poetic structure and frequent shifts in rhythm and in diction. It won him a Pulitzer Prize. Among his important later volumes of poetry are *Being Here* (1980) and *New and Selected Poems 1923–1985* (1985).

Warren's fiction drew on southern history, making universal the experiences of its people. His first published novel, *Night Rider* (1939), concerns a dispute among Kentucky tobacco farmers, which turns violent when some farmers slightly undersell the association formed to stabilize prices. The protagonist, Percy Munn, is an attorney and a vigilante whose failure to come to terms with the meaning of his own actions destroys him. Warren's second novel, *At Heaven's Gate* (1943) is based on a political murder that occurred in Nashville while Warren was attending Vanderbilt.

Warren's best-known novel, *All the King's Men* (1946), is drawn from the story of the Louisiana politician Huey Long. Long's fictional counterpart, Willie Stark, rises to governor on a populist platform but corrupts himself in the process. The novel focuses on Stark's assistant, Jack Burden, who must confront the moral significance of his own actions on Stark's behalf.

The novel *World Enough and Time* (1950) reprises a murder that took place in Kentucky in 1825. *Band of Angels* (1955) and *Wilderness* (1961) are Civil War novels. *The Cave* (1959) fictionalizes the true story of a man trapped in a cave and examines particularly the men who try to rescue him.

Over the course of his career, Warren was honored with Pulitzer Prizes in 1947, 1958, and 1978; National Book Awards in 1958 and 1978; and a Bollingen Prize in 1967. He was named America's first Poet Laureate in 1986.

Warren died of cancer at his summer home in Stratton, Vermont, in 1989.

BIBLIOGRAPHY

Bohner, Charles H., *Robert Penn Warren*, 1964, rev., 1981; Snipes, Katherine, *Robert Penn Warren*, 1983; Watkins, Floyd C., et al. (eds.), *Talking with Robert Penn Warren*, 1990.

Weill, Kurt Julian

(March 2, 1900–April 3, 1950)
Composer

Kurt Weill and playwright Bertolt Brecht were known abroad for theatrical innovations designed to shock audiences into recognizing social realities. The composer drew heavily on jazz idioms and later brought his talents to Broadway, where he joined uncommon dramatic material to complex musical ideas with simple melodies and subtle harmonies.

Born in Dessau, Germany, Weill was the son of a cantor. He left for Berlin when he was eighteen to study with composer Engelbert Humperdinck, and in 1920 entered the master class of pianist/composer Ferruccio Busoni for three years of training. Along with PAUL HINDEMITH, Weill came to be considered one of Germany's most gifted post–World War I composers.

Weill's theater music made his name. He collaborated with Bertolt Brecht to produce the darkly satiric *Die Dreigroschenoper* (*The Threepenny Opera*, based on John Gay's *The Beggar's Opera*, 1727) in 1928 and the despairing *Aufstieg und Fall der Stadt Mahagonny* (The Rise and Fall of the City of Mahagonny) in 1930. Both works express Brecht's criticism of capitalist society, a hostility leavened by the playwright's compassion for humanity. Both seek to communicate directly with audiences, to shock with reality stripped of illusion. Weill enhanced and supported the message and the stripped down presentations with music that brilliantly fused jazz with other popular music.

In 1933, after the Nazis came to power in Germany, Weill went to Paris with his wife, actress Lotte Lenya, and worked again with Brecht before leaving for New York in 1935. Weill's first work for the American commercial theater was the antiwar *Johnny Johnson*. It pleased critics but not the public. *Knickerbocker Holiday* (1938), a comic/satiric operetta written with playwright MAXWELL ANDERSON, fared better. The bittersweet "September Song," sung by Walter Huston, produced, according to Weill biographer Ronald Sanders, "one of the great moments in the history of the American musical theatre."

During the 1940s Weill collaborated successfully with MOSS HART (see GEORGE S. KAUFMAN) and IRA GERSHWIN (*Lady in the Dark*, 1941) and S. J. Perelman and Ogden Nash (*One Touch of Venus*, 1943). *Venus* starred Mary Martin and included ballet sequences by AGNES DE MILLE. A more somber Weill is revealed in a dramatization of tenement life (*Street Scene*, 1947) written with Elmer Rice

and LANGSTON HUGHES and in the tragic view of South Africa found in *Lost in the Stars* (1949; from Alan Paton's *Cry the Beloved Country*).

Weill's greatest triumph came posthumously with the English language version of *The Threepenny Opera*, which had over 2,500 performances in New York between 1954 and 1961. A revival of *Street Scene* in 1978 led Andrew Porter to comment in the *New Yorker*: "In much the same way that Handel can be claimed as Britain's greatest opera composer, Kurt Weill might be claimed as America's: a master musician, master musical dramatist, and large soul who found song for people of his adopted country, learned its idioms, joined them to his own, and composed music of international importance."

BIBLIOGRAPHY

Jarmen, D., *Kurt Weill: An Illustrated Biography*, 1982; Sanders, R., *The Days Grow Short: The Life and Music of Kurt Weill*, 1980.

Welles, George Orson

(May 6, 1915–October 10, 1985)
Actor, Radio Broadcaster, Director

Although he made one of the greatest of all films, *Citizen Kane*, at the age of twenty-five, this wunderkind of broadcasting, theater, and cinema never was able thereafter to realize the enormous potential of his youth. Nonetheless, for all his imperfections and shortcomings, Welles is ranked among this century's creative geniuses.

He was born in Kenosha, Wisconsin, in 1915 and grew up in a well-to-do and cultured family. His father was an inventor and his mother a concert pianist. A precocious child, he staged Shakespearean plays in his playroom. He left school at the age of sixteen and spent the next

four years traveling extensively and working in a variety of theatrical pursuits, acting in Dublin's Gate Theater, coediting and illustrating three Shakespearean plays and a commercial textbook, *Everybody's Shakespeare*, and appearing on Broadway as Mercutio in KATHARINE CORNELL's production of *Romeo and Juliet*. In the mid-1930s he met John Houseman and collaborated with him on productions for the Federal Theater Project. In 1937 they founded the Mercury Theater, a New York City repertory company intended to offer "classical plays excitingly produced." The Comedy Theater on 41st Street was leased and renamed, an ensemble formed (including actors Joseph Cotten, Martin Gabel, and Agnes Moorehead; composers Virgil Thomson and Bernard Herrmann; and writer Howard Koch), and productions mounted of *Julius Caesar* (a modern-dress version reflecting Fascist conditions in Italy), *The Cradle Will Rock* (a modern opera by Marc Blitzstein), *The Shoemaker's Holiday* (a madcap Elizabethan comedy), and *Five Kings* (a collage of Shakespeare's history plays).

The notoriety of the Mercury Theater's radio projects, especially the October 30, 1938, broadcast of *The War of the Worlds* (a series of simulated news reports that recounted the Martian invasion of New Jersey), brought Welles an invitation to come to Hollywood. He became fascinated with the possibilities of the camera. RKO studios gave him a relatively free hand, and for the first and only time in his career he exercised total control over a project—the extraordinary *Citizen Kane* (1941). Few films in the history of the medium have created more of a stir and exerted greater influence on subsequent generations of filmmakers. Particularly noteworthy were Welles's performance as newspaper publisher Charles Foster Kane, photographer Gregg Toland's hallucinatory imagery, Herman Mankiewicz's complex script, and the movie's canny dissection of public celebrity and private failure. However, problems attendant upon the production and exhibition of the film—particularly the pressures brought against it by the Hearst newspapers for its alleged travesty of William Randolph Hearst's personal life—wrecked its chances for success and recognition. Out of its nine Oscar nominations, it received only a Best Original Screenplay Award.

Welles's next project, a film version of Booth Tarkington's *Magnificent Ambersons* (1942), might have been his masterpiece, but studio infighting and Welles's involvement with location shooting in South America on another project disrupted the project, and it was finished by other hands. Welles would never again enjoy financial independence or have total control over his work. Moreover, without the re-sources of the Mercury Theater ensemble to draw on, he lost artistic stability. Just ten years after the release of *Citizen Kane* Welles was being described by critic Walter Kerr as "an international joke, and possibly the youngest living has-been."

For the rest of his life he restlessly roamed the world, from Spain to Hollywood to Las Vegas, from project to project, acting on the stage, doing television commercials, touring the lecture circuit, and appearing in secondary movie roles—most memorably as Harry Lime in Carol Reed's *The Third Man* (1949), Father Mapple in John Huston's *Moby Dick* (1955), and Cardinal Wolsey in Fred Zinnemann's *A Man for All Seasons* (1966). His personal life was erratic. There were many sensational affairs, including a notorious liaison with Rita Hayworth, who became his second wife.

Meanwhile, Welles managed to piece together a small number of distinguished, if idiosyncratic movies. *The Stranger* (1946), *The Lady from Shanghai* (1948), and *Touch of Evil* (1958) were thrillers about corruption and deceit; *Mr. Arkadin* (1955) and *The Trial* (1963) were labyrinthine social satires; and *Macbeth* (1948), *Othello* (1955), and *Chimes at Midnight* (1966) featured Welles in Shakespearean roles. In later years Welles declined into a caricature of himself. His vast bulk ballooned out to almost 400 pounds. The protean genius had turned into a talk-show magician and raconteur, wittily discoursing in that rich, rumbling voice on topics like politics, literature, and broiled fish.

Welles's last projects, some of which remained unfinished and unreleased at his death in 1985, constitute a fascinating, if peculiar catalog of might-have-beens. *Don Quixote* (loosely adapted from Cervantes) and *The Other Side of the Wind* (a parable about modern-day Hollywood) consumed decades of shooting in locations all around the world. All that remains are tantalizing collections of vivid fragments. *The Big Brass Ring,* a satire on New Deal politics, exists only in screenplay form and was published in 1987. *F Is for Fake* was released in 1973. It was a witty commentary on fraud and forgery in the art world, intercutting scenes of Welles as an onscreen narrator with documentary footage about the art forger Elmyr de Hory.

In 1975 Orson Welles was presented a "Life Achievement Award" by the American Film Institute. It was ironic that America's greatest living filmmaker had not been able to make a movie in this country for almost twenty years. "We are a vanishing breed," said Welles. "This honor I can only accept in the name of all the mavericks."

BIBLIOGRAPHY

Brady, Frank, *Citizen Welles*, 1989; Kael, Pauline, *The Citizen Kane Book*, 1971; Leaming, Barbara, *Orson Welles: A Biography*, 1985; Naramore, James, *The Magic World of Orson Welles*, 1978.

Welty, Eudora Alice

(April 13, 1909–   )
Novelist, Short-Story Writer

The twentieth-century writer Eudora Welty is best known for her short stories and for novels such as *Delta Wedding* and *The Optimist's Daughter*. Her fiction, most often set in her native Mississippi, explores with sympathy the hearts of humble characters challenged by circumstance, whether by poverty, loneliness, or grief.

Welty was born in Jackson, Mississippi. She attended the Mississippi State College for Women for two years, then transferred to the University of Wisconsin at Madison, from which she graduated in 1929. The following year, she studied advertising at the Columbia University School of Business.

Returning to Mississippi at the height of the Great Depression, Welty found part-time work in radio and newspapers. In 1933 she went to work as a publicity agent for the

© 1991 Nancy Crampton; Courtesy Harcourt Brace Jovanovich

Works Progress Administration. For three years, she traveled throughout Mississippi, writing feature stories about WPA projects and taking photographs of the people she met. The impressions she formed of these people, in this time and place, fed her fiction for many years.

Welty's first published short story, "Death of a Traveling Salesman," appeared in *Manuscript* in 1936. Soon after, she began to publish in *The Southern Review* and later, the *Atlantic*. Her reputation was established with her first two volumes of short stories, *A Curtain of Green* (1941) and *The Wide Net* (1943). Three early stories won O. Henry Awards: "A Worn Path" (1941), "The Wide Net" (1942), and "Livvie" (1943).

Most of Welty's stories are set in Mississippi towns or countryside. As she wrote in an essay, *Place in Fiction* (1957), she uses physical settings to frame affect, as well as action. While her attention to place and her uncanny ear for dialect earned her a reputation as a local colorist, Welty's profound interest in universal human nature eventually won her a wide audience.

Welty's first long fiction was published as *The Robber Bridegroom* (1942), a novella set along the Natchez Trace, originally a wilderness trail traveled by traders and settlers between Natchez and Nashville. *Delta Wedding* (1946), a full-length novel, frames a complex interplay among individuals in an extended family. The central event of the novel is George Fairchild's rescue of a retarded cousin from injury by a passing train. The reactions of family members gathered for the wedding of George's niece reflect both on themselves as individuals and on the family dynamic.

The Golden Apples (1949) is a collection of short stories that have been recast slightly and linked into a story cycle that suggests a novel. The stories concern families in the Delta town of Morgana, and characters in search of some form of satisfaction, amorous or aesthetic.

In another novella, *The Ponder Heart* (1954), Edna Earle Ponder recounts the tale of her uncle's trial in the death of his wife. The comic aspects of the story—Daniel Ponder has tickled his wife to death—helped make it popular; in 1956 it was made into a play and enjoyed a successful run on Broadway. Welty's novel *Losing Battles* (1970) describes a clan reunion celebrating the ninetieth birthday of Granny Vaughn and the release from prison of the protagonist, Jack Renfro. The novel mingles a farcical tangle of talk and action with serious insights into the hearts of individuals. The book was a best-seller.

In *The Optimist's Daughter* (1972), the loss of her parents' home to her father's surviving spouse provides Laurel McKelva Hand with an occasion for soul-searching and remembrance. Recollections of her parents' marriage and of her own to a young man killed in World War II finally enable Laurel to set aside her resentment of her father's remarriage, as well as her anger at his widow. *The Optimist's Daughter* became a best-seller and earned Welty a Pulitzer Prize.

A new collection of short stories, *Moon Lake*, was published in 1980, the same year Welty's *Collected Stories* saw publication. She was awarded the National Medal for Literature in the same year.

Welty lives in Jackson, Mississippi.

BIBLIOGRAPHY

Ruth Vande Kieft, *Eudora Welty*, 1987; Welty, Eudora, *One Writer's Beginnings*, 1984; Westling, Louise, *Eudora Welty*, 1989.

West, Benjamin

(October 10, 1738–March 11, 1820)
Painter

Benjamin West, who painted historical, mythological, and religious subjects, left his native America at the age of twenty-two and lived the rest of his life in England, where he had a profound influence on three generations of American artists who came abroad to study.

Born in Springfield, Pennsylvania, near Philadelphia, the son of a Quaker innkeeper, West was interested in drawing as a child. The work of the adventurous English portraitist, William Williams, who came to town when West was about nine years old, fascinated the child. After Williams lent him books and encouraged him, West decided to be a painter.

In his teens, West was painting portraits in Lancaster, Pennsylvania, and completed his first history painting, *The Death of Socrates*

(1756). A Philadelphia merchant named William Allen and some of his colleagues raised the money to send West to Europe to study. West went first to Rome, where European artists and social leaders were surprised he was not a savage from the American wilderness, but a talented, civilized young man. He studied for three years in Rome, then traveled through France to England.

Arriving in London in 1763, he was immediately acclaimed for the biblical and classical scenes he had painted in Italy. At first, to earn a living, West resumed the painting of portraits. He broadened his style, however, and became a charter member (and, later, a long-time president) of the Royal Academy of Arts when it was founded in 1768 to improve the status of artists and to promote the grand style of history painting, which was regarded as the highest form of art.

West's large history painting *Agrippina with the Ashes of Germanicus* (1766–1768), is the best example of his neoclassical paintings, both in subject and style. It impressed George III so much that he became a friend and patron. West made no secret of the fact that he was loyal to the cause of American independence, but he never lost favor with the king, even during the revolutionary war. The king paid West a salary that assured him financial independence so he would do history paintings without having to do portraits.

West also treated historical subjects in a new, realistic manner. *The Death of General Wolfe* (1771), for example, showed the death of British general James Wolfe, fatally wounded in the successful battle for the capture of Quebec during the French and Indian War. West painted the figures in contemporary dress instead of Greek robes or Roman togas, a revolutionary concept at the time. The English were delighted to have in their midst such a splendid, innovative practitioner of history painting.

Finally, West painted in an emotional and literary style. He exhibited a study for his painting *Death on the Pale Horse* in Paris in 1802, where it caused a sensation. The finished painting, done in 1817, demonstrated that West could still be an innovator at the age of eighty. The picture, with the pale horse plunging through thunderbolts and lightning, conveys an emotion that predated French romantic painting and was in stark contrast to his neoclassical works.

Remarkably, West worked in all three styles—neoclassical, realistic, and preromantic—at various times during his life, and there are important landmarks in his oeuvre of the changing styles and approaches to art in the eighteenth century.

As an American who was painting in London, West was accepted as a British painter as well and became Painter to the King. Unfailingly helpful and generous to other American painters who came to London to study, he was on hand for JOHN SINGLETON COPLEY, GILBERT STUART, John Trumbull, CHARLES WILLSON PEALE, Rembrandt Peale, Thomas Sully, Samuel F. B. Morse, and Washington Allston.

After his death West was buried in St. Paul's Cathedral near the great English painter Sir Joshua Reynolds and architect Christopher Wren.

BIBLIOGRAPHY

Abrams, Ann Uhry, *Benjamin West and Grand Style History Painting*, 1988; Flexner, James Thomas, *American Old Masters*, 1980; Von Erffa, Helmut, *Benjamin West*, 1986.

West, Mae

(August 17, 1892–November 22, 1980)
Actress, Playwright

Mae West, the buxom, flamboyant, wise-cracking comedienne, made a sensation burlesquing sex on stage and screen. In slinky, tight-fitting gowns, she was both seductive and ironic. Unlike other sex symbols, she wrote her own material and never descended to the stereotype of the "dumb blonde."

Born Mary Jane West in Brooklyn, her parents were John Patrick West, a livery stable owner and prizefighter, and Matilda Delker-Dolger, a fashion model before marriage. As a child, Mae took dancing lessons and worked in Hal Clarendon's stock company from ages eight to eleven. She had little schooling, entering vaudeville at thirteen determined to be a big star. She secretly married song-and-dance man Frank Wallace in 1911, but they separated soon after; their divorce was finalized in 1943. She never remarried and had no children.

A sensation in her first major theatrical revue, *A La Broadway and Hello Paris* (1911), she later appeared with Al Jolson in *Vera Violetta.* Returning to vaudeville a star, she created havoc with what one reporter described as "a swaying, sin-promising strut, a nonchalant and lazy line delivery, and a simultaneous caress of her undulating hip with one hand and her chiseled blonde hair with the other." In 1918 she introduced the "shimmy" to the Broadway stage, a continuous movement of shoulders, torso, and pelvis, which she had seen in black cafés in Chicago.

West developed a nightclub act after World War I, then wrote and produced her own plays. The first, *Sex,* created such a scandal in New York in 1926 that she was arrested, found guilty of corrupting morals, fined $500, and sentenced to ten days in jail. Two other plays—*The Pleasure Man* in 1928 and *The Constant Sinner* in 1931—encountered similar fates.

Her most durable creation was *Diamond Lil,* about an 1890s saloon girl with a good heart who sings "Frankie and Johnny." It opened in Brooklyn in 1928 and had a successful run before it went on tour.

In 1932 she made her first movie, *Night After Night,* for which she rewrote her own role. Her most famous addition was the line she delivered to a hat check girl when the latter exclaims, "Goodness, what beautiful diamonds"—to which West replied, "Goodness had nothing to do with it, dearie." The phrase became the title of her autobiography.

While West was less risqué than she was on stage, her film dialogue sparkled with enough insinuations to have helped bring about enforcement of the Motion Picture Production Code in 1934. Her famous come-on to CARY GRANT in *She Done Him Wrong* (the film version of her 1933 play *Diamond Lil*)—"Come up and see me sometime"—is tamer than most. In the same year she made *I'm No Angel,* also with Grant.

Her Hollywood career spanned a mere decade and ten films, none of them memorable in themselves, but leaving behind "a patchwork of bits and lines and scenes," as critic Andrew Sarris phrased it. Even her teaming with the irrepressible W. C. Fields in *My Little Chickadee* (1940) disappointed audiences, perhaps because these two strong personalities could not complement each other.

West entered the dictionary during World War II when the British Royal Air Force named an inflatable life jacket after her. Like BETTE DAVIS, she became a standard subject for female impersonators.

One of her last Broadway appearances was in 1944 as the empress of Russia in *Catherine Was Great,* and her last film appearance was in an adaptation of her play *Sextette* (1978), which is about a Hollywood glamour queen with numerous ex-husbands. Even with a supporting cast including Tony Curtis, Ringo Starr, Dom DeLuise, Timothy Dalton, George

Hamilton, and George Raft, the film was a critical and box-office disaster, although it has not dimmed the brightness and wit of West in her prime.

West herself accurately summed up her style and impact: "It isn't what I do, but how I do it. It isn't what I say, but how I say it and how I look when I do it and say it."

BIBLIOGRAPHY

Eells, George, *Mae West: A Biography,* 1982; Tuskan, Jon, *The Films of Mae West,* 1973; Weintraub, Joseph (ed.), *The Wit and Wisdom of Mae West,* 1967; West, Mae, *Goodness Had Nothing to Do with It,* 1959, rep., 1981.

Weston, Edward Henry

(March 24, 1886–January 1, 1958)
Photographer

Edward Weston was an important advocate in the first half of the twentieth century of straight, or unaltered, photography. No matter whether the subject matter was treated in an abstract or realistic way, he demanded clarity of form and precise sharpness of focus.

Weston was born in Highland Park, Illinois, in 1886, the son of a physician. He was sixteen years old when his father gave him his first camera, a Bulls-Eye no. 2. He grew so preoccupied with the medium that he quit school to attend Illinois College of Photography from 1908 to 1911, during which time he married. Then, after working as an errand boy at the Marshall Field department store in Chicago, he worked at odd jobs in California—surveying for the railroads and selling photographs from door to door. Deciding to become a professional portrait photographer, he opened his first studio in Tropico (later Glendale) in 1911, photographing family reunions, babies, and pets.

At first, he was distressed by the "irrelevant" details that cluttered up his portraits. "I couldn't think what to do with all that wonderful detail," he recalled, "so I used a soft-focus lens and dissolved it away in a romantic haze." However, he soon grew impatient with the tricks of the trade employed to flatter the subjects—soft lenses, soft papers, vignetting, and other discreet retouchings. (Later, his second wife, Charis Wilson, noted that Weston did

not stop flattering his subjects—he just stopped doing it with artificial means.) By 1920 he was starting all over again, making sharply realistic studies of cypress roots, rocks, and vegetables. "I just wanted to make it the most cabbagy cabbage a man ever looked at," he said, defining his credo. It was at this time that he began what biographer Nancy Newhall referred to as "years of ruthless self-scrutiny and growth," working in New York with ALFRED STIEGLITZ and living three years in Mexico. His images in the bright open air of landscapes, Mayan pyramids, maguey plants, people, and culture brought him praise from leaders of the Mexican Renaissance, like Diego Rivera and José Orozco. Back in California in 1926, he began to isolate the details of his subjects, including his famous nudes, in extreme closeups. In 1928 he moved to Carmel, which became his permanent home. His son Brett, already a fine photographer, worked with him.

His first one-man show was held in New York in 1930. He was awarded Guggenheim Fellowships in 1937 and 1938, and he spent time in California, capturing the details and immensity of Death Valley. He spent the early part of the war years working on an assignment from the Limited Editions Club to produce images (he called them a "counterpoint") for an edition of WALT WHITMAN's *Leaves of Grass.* By the time he had his important one-man retrospective at the Museum of Modern Art in 1946, he had already had more than seventy other exhibitions. He was the subject of Willard Van Dyke's 1948 documentary, *The Photographer*.

He generally used a large, 8 by 10 viewfinder camera on a tripod for his landscapes and a 4 by 5 Graflex for his portraits. His lens was specially built for him so that he could stop it down to f/256 (actually, another system's designation of f/64). "You must remember I work with long-focus lenses," he said, "and the nature of my work requires that everything from a few feet in front of the camera to infinity be in sharp focus." This required inordinately long exposure times for his preferred panchromatic sheet film, which was capable of registering all visible wavelengths. He used no enlarger and preferred chloride paper and tray developing for his contact prints. He never trimmed these sheets. "Trimming is an admission of poor seeing," he said, "or seeing nothing, in the first place." The old-fashioned developing solution left lifelong brown stains on his fingernails.

Weston's legacy is a respect for the untampered photographic image. In 1932 he and ANSEL ADAMS and Willard Van Dyke organized the Group f/64 (a reference to a shutter stop associated with sharp focus) in the avowed service of what they called "pure photography." Although the Group lasted only a year, Nancy Newhall noted that "as the violent peak of a great contemporary movement, its influence still persists." So fiercely did he cleave to the idea that his images should not be altered or adjusted in any way that he hung a sign in his Carmel studio in 1934—"Unretouched Portraits." He eschewed pictorial photography, photojournalism, and scientific-technical photography. He gave only generic titles, or numbers, to his images. As Adams assessed: "Edward was not a preacher, aggressive teacher, promulgator, or verbal prophet. He was, simply, there—and his work is almost everywhere."

He died in 1958 after a ten-year struggle with Parkinson's disease.

BIBLIOGRAPHY

Maddow, Ben, *Edward Weston*, 1978; Newhall, Beaumont, and Amy Conger, *Edward Weston Omnibus*, 1984.

Wharton, Edith

(January 24, 1862–August 11, 1937)
Novelist, Short-Story Writer

Best remembered for her tragic novel *Ethan Frome* and for her lighter satires of life amid the American upperclass, Edith Wharton probed the personal conflicts faced by individuals who understand the limitations of social and moral conventions.

Born Edith Newbold Jones to a well-to-do family in New York City, she was raised in a house near Washington Square, educated at home by governesses, and taken often on trips to Europe. Her early efforts at poetry were published anonymously in the *Atlantic Monthly* in 1880. Five years later, she married Edward Wharton, a Boston banker. Subsequently, she spent her time at home in Newport, Rhode Island, or traveling in Europe.

In 1897 Wharton and the architect Ogden Codman wrote a book based on their experience redecorating the interior of the Whartons' Newport house. *The Decoration of Houses* presented the notion—novel at the time—that interior design could reflect homeowners' personalities. The book sold widely.

Wharton turned to writing in earnest, in part to find an outlet, given increasingly apparent mental instability on the part of her husband.

During the 1890s, she began to publish short stories in *Scribner's Magazine.* She moved to Lenox, Massachusetts, and cultivated a set of literary acquaintances. In quick succession, she published several volumes of short stories and two novels.

Wharton's first major novel, *The House of Mirth* (1905), concerns Lily Bart, a young woman from a socially prominent family that has fallen on financial hard times. Lily must choose between marrying the man she loves and living in relative discomfort, or marrying to preserve her status and achieve security. The novel's rendering of the manners of New York society made it extremely popular.

In 1907 Wharton moved to France. She published two more novels, *Madame de Treymes* and *The Fruit of the Tree,* in the same year. Her next novel, *Ethan Frome* (1911), carries a theme similar to *The House of Mirth.* The protagonist, a poor farmer, must choose between happiness and preserving a social standard—in this case represented by his marriage to a drab, complaining woman. Ethan Frome falls in love with his wife's young cousin, Mattie Silver. Feeling they cannot elope, the lovers attempt suicide, but they succeed only in crippling themselves and landing in the permanent care of the woman they had sought to escape. *Ethan Frome* remains one of Wharton's briefest but best-known novels.

Wharton divorced her husband in 1913 and chose to remain in Europe even during the world war. Her efforts on behalf of the Allied relief effort won her the cross of the French Legion of Honor. Two novels, *The Marne* (1918) and *A Son at the Front* (1923), drew on her war experiences.

The Age of Innocence (1920) won Wharton the Pulitzer Prize. The novel is an ironic treatment of the quandary facing a man from a prominent family: marry the conventional woman who is his fiancée or pursue her more attractive and interesting cousin. Newland Archer chooses propriety; Ellen Olenska returns to Europe. Years later, after his wife's death, Archer visits Europe, and, though he contemplates visiting Ellen, he prefers instead to cling to the remembered satisfactions of his life with May Welland.

In 1924 Wharton published *Old New York,* comprising four short novels set in the mid-nineteenth century. One of the novels, *The Old Maid,* won a Pulitzer Prize and was made into a play and a movie starring BETTE DAVIS.

Subsequent novels by Wharton include *The Children* (1928), *Hudson River Bracketed* (1929), and its sequel, *The Gods Arrive* (1932). Among her collections of short stories are *Certain People* (1930), *The World Over* (1936), and *Ghosts* (1937).

Wharton also wrote several travel books and a book of criticism, *The Writing of Fiction* (1925). In the latter volume, she acknowledges the influence of her friend and mentor, the novelist HENRY JAMES, who, like her, wrote fiction around complex moral issues.

Wharton died at her home in St.-Brice-sous-Forêt, France, in 1937.

BIBLIOGRAPHY

Auchincloss, Louis, *Edith Wharton: A Woman in Her Time,* 1971; Lewis, R. W. B., *Edith Wharton,* 1975; Wharton, Edith, *A Backward Glance,* 1934.

Whistler, James Abbott McNeill

(July 10, 1834–July 17, 1903)
Painter

James A. M. Whistler was an important painter of landscapes and portraits and a highly esteemed printmaker. His misty, poetic style, in which tonality—the subtle arrangement of tones in a painting—was of first importance, anticipated the way for the emergence of completely abstract painting in the next several generations.

Whistler was born in Lowell, Massachusetts, where his father, a former army officer, was an engineer for the locks and canals. In 1843 the family followed the father to Russia, where he had been hired to manage the building of the railroad line from Moscow to St. Petersburg. "Jimmy" Whistler began his art training at the Imperial Academy of the Fine Arts in St. Petersburg.

After the elder Whistler died in Russia in 1849, Whistler's mother brought her sons back to the United states, to Pomfret, Connecticut, and Whistler, against his will, in 1851 entered the U.S. Military Academy at West Point. Always at the head of the drawing class, but at the bottom in chemistry, he was expelled in 1854. He found a job drafting coastal maps at the U.S. Coast and Geodetic Survey in Washington, D.C., where he also learned how to do etchings. In 1855, with a yearly allowance of $350, he sailed for Paris, never to return to America. He studied with Charles Gleyre, who also taught Claude Monet and Pierre Auguste Renoir. Whistler was a colorful figure in the art world of Paris and an exponent of the idea of "art for art's sake," as opposed to the belief that art must be morally uplifting. His belief that art and the pursuit of the beautiful were more important than anything else helped to inspire the Aesthetic movement.

Many people and movements influenced Whistler in Paris: the realist painter Gustave Courbet, who urged him to paint what he saw; Edouard Manet, a younger, more revolutionary French painter later associated with the Impressionists; the work of Japanese artists, who could indicate whole scenes with a few spare elements.

In 1859 Whistler moved to London and became well known as an eccentric man about town, whom some called a poseur, a snob, a dandy. Still, Whistler was a hard worker and by the early 1860s had refined his own style. *The White Girl* (1862) was one of Whistler's first paintings with a monochromatic palette (tones of one color). In the picture, his Irish mistress, Joanna Heffernan, dressed in white, stands on a bearskin rug, with flowers at her feet. *The White Girl* was refused admission to the 1863 Salon, the big annual exhibition that the French government sponsored in Paris each year, but along with Manet's *Déjeuner sur l'Herbe*, it made a sensation at the Salon des Refusés, where the pictures that had been refused were hung. Whistler renamed the picture *Symphony in White, No. 1: The White Girl* after a critic compared his painting to music, pointing out that color, like music, could suggest moods. Although there is surely some message of lost virtue in this image, the title removes it somewhat from the obvious subject and hidden meaning and emphasizes the more abstract quality of form and color.

Whistler's mother came to live in London in 1863 and his best-known portrait, *Arrangement in Grey and Black, No. 1: Portrait of the Painter's Mother* (1871), in which a straight-backed older woman sits in profile, is more commonly known as *Whistler's Mother*. The government of France bought the painting. Very similar in composition is *Arrangement in Grey and Black, No. 2: Portrait of Thomas Carlyle* (1872), which depicts the English writer sitting in profile.

Whistler's first landscapes were realistic; examples are *The Thames in Ice* (1860), *Coast of Brittany: Alone with the Tide* (1861), and *The Blue Wave, Biarritz* (1862).

Like figure paintings, they became more ethereal and more involved with pure tones. He liked to paint scenes at twilight when the light was quite dim. As his work became more abstract, critics disliked it. In 1875 he painted an abstract nighttime impression of fireworks bursting in the sky, *Nocturne in Black and Gold: The Falling Rocket.* John Ruskin, a famous English critic, venomously attacked the picture when it was exhibited in London and accused Whistler of "flinging a pot of paint in the public's face." Whistler sued for libel and, after a famous trial, won, although he collected damages of only a farthing, one-fourth of an English penny. Whistler always wore the famous farthing on his watch chain as a sign of triumph, but he had to pay half the court costs, an expense that bankrupted him.

After he was forced to sell many of his paintings for absurdly low prices, a commission in 1879 for a series of etchings of Venice saved him financially. A master of the techniques of printmaking, Whistler made over 400 etchings in his life, including a set inspired by a trip through northern France in 1858 and a set of the Thames River. He also made many lithographs.

Whistler tried to explain his theories of painting in a book, *The Gentle Art of Making*

Enemies (1890). "Take the picture of my mother, 'Arrangement in Grey and Black,'" he wrote. "Now that is what it is. To me it is interesting as a picture of my mother; but what can or ought the public to care about the identity of the portrait?" In another passage, he discussed *Harmony in Grey and Gold,* saying that it was "an illustration of my meaning—a snow scene with a single black figure and a lighted tavern. I cared nothing for the past, present, or future of the black figure, placed there because the black was wanted at that spot."

Whistler, who had many mistresses and two illegitimate children, married late in life to Beatrix Godwin, whom he adored. Grief stricken when she died, Whistler returned to live briefly in Paris, traveled in North Africa, but was living in London when he died in 1903. He is buried in Chiswick.

BIBLIOGRAPHY

Fleming, G., *James Abbott McNeill Whistler: A Life,* 1991; Spalding, Frances, *Whistler,* 1979; Walker, John, *James McNeill Whistler,* 1987.

Whiteman, Paul Samuel

(March 28, 1890–December 29, 1967)
Bandleader

Showman Paul Whiteman, an enormously successful bandleader in the 1920s and 1930s, pioneered a symphonic approach to dance music and created the "band show" format still in use today. He hired and encouraged many fine instrumentalists and vocalists and through his efforts helped jazz gain popular attention and acceptance.

Born in Denver, Colorado, where his father taught music at a public school, Paul Whiteman

was a violist with the Denver Symphony Orchestra from 1912 to 1915 and with the San Francisco Symphony Orchestra from 1915 to 1916. He led a navy band during World War I. In 1918 he established a dance band in San Francisco, moved to Los Angeles and then to Atlantic City, New Jersey, before going to New York in 1920. His popularity on the rise, the 1920 recording of "Whispering" and "Japanese Sandman" sold over a million copies. By the time he toured abroad—Britain in 1923, Europe in 1926—his rich orchestral style was a model for many musicians.

Whiteman commissioned GEORGE GERSHWIN to write *Rhapsody in Blue* for use on an extended tour of the United States. Gershwin performed the piece in New York in 1924, part of a Whiteman concert held in Aeolian Hall called "An Experiment in Modern Music." Whiteman, gaining a reputation for fast-paced presentations, put on seven such stage performances between 1925 and 1938. These spectaculars popularized American composers, among them DUKE ELLINGTON, VICTOR HERBERT, William Grant Still, and, of course, George Gershwin.

A major figure in American music, Whiteman was nonetheless controversial. Some jazz musicians of the day resented the bandleader for his success, pointing out that what he did was not jazz. Others admired his versatility and high standard of performance and noted the quality of his instrumentalists from Bix Beiderbecke (cornet) to Bunny Berigan (trumpet), Jack Teagarden (trombone), and Joe Venuti (violin), and singers from Bing Crosby to Mildred Bailey. Critic Gunther Schuller points out that Whiteman and his arrangers were not innovators and that "what evolved on average was a skillful dance and show band" overly dependent on instrumentation and often overarranged, pretentious scores that lacked focus.

However, Whiteman was dubbed, some say undeservedly, the "King of Jazz" after a 1930 movie of that name. He appeared in films, provided music for six Broadway shows, and produced over 600 recordings. Perhaps one of this consummate showman's most significant contributions is the publicizing of jazz and his success in making it acceptable. He developed the "band show" format and was noted for his kindness to and support of his musicians. After World War II, when his popularity was in decline, he gave up his band and became a director at ABC.

After his 1967 death in Doylestown, Pennsylvania, his memorabilia, including over 3,000 arrangements, went to Williams College in Williamstown, Massachusetts, to establish the Whiteman Collection.

BIBLIOGRAPHY

DeLong, T. A., *Pops: Paul Whiteman, the King of Jazz*, 1983; Johnson, C., *Paul Whiteman: A Chronology*, 1977; Whiteman, P., and M. McBride, *Jazz*, 1926.

Whitman, Walt

(May 31, 1819–March 26, 1892)
Essayist, Journalist, Poet

The poet Walt Whitman addressed themes that were uniquely American, celebrating in particular the life of common people in a democracy. His free verse changed forever the form of American poetry. His important volume *Leaves of Grass*, first published in 1855, expanded as his work evolved over a lifetime.

Walter Whitman was born in the rural community of West Hills, Long Island, New York, the second son among nine children of Walter Whitman and Louisa Van Velson. His father, a carpenter, moved the family to Brooklyn, New York, in 1823, and there he built houses, though supporting his family remained difficult. Young Walt, as he was called, attended public schools in Brooklyn, then apprenticed as a law clerk and as a printer, working in Brooklyn and Manhattan.

Whitman moved to Huntington on Long Island in 1836 and taught for several years in country schools. He founded and edited for a year the Huntington *Long Islander,* and then worked as a compositor at the *Long Island Democrat.* He returned to New York City in 1840, working as a printer and briefly as an editor at a string of newspapers publishing poems and stories in popular magazines.

In 1845 Whitman returned to Brooklyn as a reporter for the *Star,* and a year later assumed the editorship of the *Daily Eagle.* He lost the latter position in 1848 over his editorial support of the Free Soil movement, which sought to prevent the legal extension of slavery into new U.S. territories. Traveling south to New Orleans, he worked briefly at the *Crescent* before quitting over disagreements with the editors; the trip did leave a lasting impression on Whitman, however, as he observed much about the lives of American people that would surface later in his poetry.

Returning to Brooklyn, Whitman founded a Free Soil newspaper, the *Freeman,* which lasted for a year (1848–1849). He then spent several years working with his father and writing poetry in his spare time. In 1855 he published at his own expense twelve untitled poems in a slim volume called *Leaves of Grass.*

This publication, unnoticed except by a few intellectuals, became an American literary milestone. As Whitman's hero, the poet and essayist RALPH WALDO EMERSON, wrote to him, "I find it the most extraordinary piece of wit & wisdom that America has yet contributed. . . . I greet you at the beginning of a great career." The poems lacked both rhyme and meter; they featured repetitive lines. The central poem, later called "Song of Myself," seemed audaciously personal:

Library of Congress

I celebrate myself,
And what I assume you shall assume,
For every atom belonging to me as good belongs to you.

Whitman worked from 1857 to 1859 as editor of the Brooklyn *Daily Times.* He continued writing poetry. In 1860 a Boston publishing house brought out a third edition of *Leaves of Grass,* including many new poems. Three groups of poems were particularly noteworthy: "Chants Democratic," "Enfans d'Adam," and "Calamus." The "Calamus" poems, which celebrated the love of men for each other, became controversial, because some readers felt the poems celebrated homosexuality.

During the Civil War, Whitman volunteered to help nurse wounded soldiers at army hospitals in Washington, D.C. He occasionally assisted the doctors, but spent most of his time distributing reading material, talking to patients, and helping them write letters. He subsequently published a volume of poems called *Drum-Taps* (1865), which gathered impressions from his service. *Sequel to Drum-Taps,* published the following year, included "When Lilacs Last in the Dooryard Bloom'd," a now famous elegy to Abraham Lincoln, as well as the popular rhymed poem, "O Captain! My Captain!"

Whitman's war service earned him a clerk's job at the Bureau of Indian Affairs, but he was fired when the new interior secretary, James Harlan, discovered that Whitman had authored *Leaves of Grass.* Whitman's friends promptly helped him find a similar slot in the attorney general's office, where he worked from 1865 until he suffered a paralyzing stroke in 1873.

In 1871 Whitman published a new edition of *Leaves of Grass,* containing his poem "Passage to India," a celebration of engineering advances such as the Suez Canal, which Whitman hoped would open the way to intercultural understanding and eventually a utopian world community.

After his stroke, Whitman recuperated at the home of his brother George in Camden, New Jersey. Subsequently, he remained in Camden, earning a living by lecturing and through the sales of his books, particularly in England, where he had developed a significant reputation.

In 1881 a new edition of *Leaves of Grass* was published in Boston, but distribution halted after a suit was threatened over poems with sexual content that Whitman refused to remove. The suppression of the book in Boston actually boosted sales elsewhere, and in 1884 Whitman used the proceeds to buy a house in Camden.

Whitman lived in Camden for the rest of his days, enjoying an intellectual circle of friends, as well as entertaining prominent visitors from the United States and abroad. With some help, he assembled a final edition of *Leaves of Grass* (1891–1892), which became known as the deathbed edition, because Whitman prepared it during his final illness. He died in 1892 and was buried in Camden's Harleigh Cemetery.

BIBLIOGRAPHY

Allen, Gay Wilson, *The Solitary Singer: Walt Whitman,* 1955, rev., 1967; Arvin, Newton, *Whitman,* 1938, rep., 1969; Kaplan, Justin, *Walt Whitman: A Life,* 1980; Miller, James Edwin, *Walt Whitman,* 1990.

Whittier, John Greenleaf

(December 17, 1807–September 7, 1892)
Poet

The poet John Greenleaf Whittier is best remembered for his "schoolroom" poems celebrating the life and values of rural New England, though his efforts toward the abolition of slavery took most of his energy and yielded much of his poetry during the first half of his career.

Whittier was born on a farm near Haverhill, Massachusetts, that had been established by his great-great-grandfather in 1648. His family were devout Quakers, and Whittier learned an abiding emphasis on family, hard work, and broad social concern.

Whittier apprenticed as a cobbler, saving enough to pay for two terms at Haverhill Academy (1827–1828). In 1829 a friend who had taken an interest in his writing, the abolitionist newspaperman William Lloyd Garrison, helped Whittier get a job as editor of the *American Manufacturer,* a weekly political magazine with headquarters in Boston. He published his first book, *Legends of New-England,* a collection of poetry and folktales, in 1831.

A committed abolitionist, Whittier turned his energies to the fight against slavery. In 1833 he printed a pamphlet called *Justice and Expediency,* which attacked the Colonization Society, a group that proposed to address the injustice of slavery by sending all the slaves back to Africa. Later in the same year, Whittier became a delegate to the convention that founded the American Anti-Slavery Society. He was elected to the state legislature in 1835, and there organized efforts to lobby Congress on the slavery question. His work encountered opposition. He and a colleague, George Thompson, were mobbed in Concord, New Hampshire, before an antislavery lecture in 1835.

Whittier sold the family farm in 1836 and moved to Amesbury, Massachusetts, with his mother and sister. He then traveled to New

York City to work in the office of the American Anti-Slavery Society and to Philadelphia to assume the editorship of an abolitionist newspaper, the *Pennsylvania Freeman*. In 1837 a group of his friends published without his knowledge a collection of his abolitionist verse, *Poems Written During the Progress of the Abolition Question in the United States, Between 1830 and 1838*. The following year, Whittier participated in the publication of an expanded volume, *Poems*.

In 1840 Whittier returned permanently to Amesbury and worked on behalf of candidates from the newly founded Liberty party. He published another volume of abolitionist poetry, *Voices of Freedom* (1846) and became a contributing editor to the antislavery journal *National Era*. One of Whittier's best-known abolitionist poems, "Ichabod," was written to protest Daniel Webster's advocacy of a compromise with the South. Whittier continued his efforts against slavery until the question was settled finally during the Civil War. An ardent pacifist, he had hoped to see abolition without violence, a position that made him seem overly hesitant to many in the movement.

After 1843, with the publication of his collection *Lays of My Home*, Whittier resumed his interest in poetry that celebrated rural life in New England. These poems were featured in such volumes as *Ballads* (1844), *The Chapel of the Hermits* (1853), *The Panorama* (1856), containing "Maud Muller" and "The Barefoot Boy," and *Home Ballads* (1860). The founding of the *Atlantic Monthly* in 1857 gave Whittier an important outlet for his verse, and such long-remembered poems as "Skipper Ireson's Ride" and "Telling the Bees" were first published there.

Snow-Bound (1866) is the volume that firmly established Whittier's literary reputation. The title poem, which recalls the experience of being snowbound at his father's farm as a child, is his acknowledged masterpiece:

> We looked upon a world unknown,
> On nothing we could call our own,
> Around the glistening wonder bent
> The blue walls of the firmament,
> No cloud above, no earth below,—
> A universe of sky and snow!

The poem describes the family encircled about the fireplace while the winter elements beat against the door, metaphorically suggesting the power of the heart to withstand physical and spiritual challenges.

Snow-Bound brought Whittier his first commercial success, which continued the following year with the publication of *The Tent on the Beach*. Thereafter, he lived more comfortably, moving in 1876 to a more spacious home in Danvers, Massachusetts. He continued to write poetry, publishing several volumes, including *Among the Hills* (1869), *The Pennsylvania Pilgrim* (1872), and *At Sundown* (1890).

Whittier died at his summer retreat in Hampton Falls, New Hampshire, in 1892.

BIBLIOGRAPHY

Leary, Lewis, *John Greenleaf Whittier*, 1961;
Wagenknecht, Edward, *John Greenleaf Whittier: A Portrait in Paradox*, 1967.

Wilder, Billy

(June 22, 1906–)
Film Director, Producer, Writer

The enfant terrible of the American cinema, Billy Wilder is probably the most successful writer/director in Hollywood, applying European sophistication to "naive" American subjects. Few films display the wit and cynicism of Wilder's best, which includes *Double Indemnity, Sunset Boulevard,* and *Some Like It Hot.*

He was born Samuel Wilder to Jewish parents in Sucha, Austria (now part of Poland) during the waning years of the Hapsburg Empire. His father was a hotel owner who dabbled in other businesses. After high school, Wilder attended the University of Vienna for a few months, then worked as a reporter for the newspaper *Die Stunde.*

During the 1920s in Berlin, Wilder wrote for several newspapers while writing scripts to break into the movies and worked as a dancer/gigolo. Hired as a ghostwriter for UFA, the biggest film studio in Germany, he wrote over 200 scripts, uncredited, in 1928 and 1929.

His first credited screenplay was *People on Sunday* (1929), followed by the delightful *Emil and the Detectives* (1931). When Hitler came to power in 1933, Wilder left for Paris, where he codirected his first film, *Mauvaise Graine* (1934). Remaining behind in Austria, his mother and other members of his family were lost to the Holocaust.

With help from respected German director and fellow expatriate Joe May, Wilder emigrated to Hollywood, where, after a few years of occasional employment, he was hired as a writer for Paramount and soon teamed with screenwriter Charles Brackett.

Wilder and Brackett wrote some of their best screenplays over the next decade, including *Bluebeard's Eighth Wife* (1938) and *Ninotchka* (1939), both directed by ERNST LUBITSCH; *Ball of Fire* (1941), directed by HOWARD HAWKS; and six of the first seven films directed by Wilder, notably *The Major and the Minor* (1942); *The Lost Weekend* (1945)—which won Oscars for Best Picture, Director, Actor (Ray Milland), and Original Screenplay; *A Foreign Affair* (1948); and *Sunset Boulevard* (1950).

Double Indemnity (1944), cowritten with novelist Raymond Chandler, and based on James M. Cain's novel, is the first great *film noir,* a darkly atmospheric and cynical style of crime melodrama that emerged in the 1940s but had not yet been named as such at the time. In addition to superb performances by Fred MacMurray and Edward G. Robinson, Barbara Stanwyck created what became the prototype of the femme fatale of Hollywood cinema—a beautiful, worldly, and dangerously neurotic woman who lures a man toward his and her destruction. A bitter fable of desire and greed, the film was a natural for Wilder's perversely ironic point of view and made his directorial reputation overnight.

Equally memorable is *Sunset Boulevard,* a macabre critique of Hollywood values, viewed through an affair between a young, ambitious writer, played by William Holden, who sells himself to an older has-been silent film star. The latter is played by real-life silent film actress Gloria Swanson, one of many unnerving convergences between the film's narrative and Hollywood history. The presences of directors ERICH VON STROHEIM, BUSTER KEATON, and CECIL B. DEMILLE add to the film's irony.

Ace in the Hole (1951), a savage attack on the American press and mob mentality, did not fare well at the box office, leading Wilder to leaven his bite with more wit and even belly laughs in *Stalag 17* (1953), an engaging war comedy that won William Holden an Oscar for Best Actor; *Sabrina* (1954), in which playboy Holden loses Audrey Hepburn to older brother Humphrey Bogart; and two films in which Marilyn Monroe gives memorable comic performances—*The Seven Year Itch* (1955) and the hilarious parody of the 1920s *Some Like It Hot* (1959), also starring Tony Curtis and Jack Lemmon. On the latter and on his subsequent films, Wilder enjoyed his second successful writing collaboration, with I. A. L. Diamond.

Lemmon embodied the archetypal Wilder character of the 1960s: the naive "shnook" confronted with a callous world, especially in *The Apartment*—which won the Oscar for Best Picture of 1960 and gave Wilder three more Oscars—and *The Fortune Cookie* (1966), the first of three films in which Lemmon costarred with Walter Matthau. The other two are *The Front Page* (1974), a second remake of the popular play, and *Buddy, Buddy* (1981), Wilder's last film. In all of these, however, Wilder's treatment is ambiguous: Lemmon's "innocents" are often as unlikable as the cads who corrupt them.

Other films of interest include *Love in the Afternoon* (1957), Wilder's tribute to fellow German expatriate filmmaker Ernst Lubitsch, in which Audrey Hepburn falls for older man GARY COOPER; *Witness for the Prosecution* (1958), a melodramatic adaptation of Agatha Christie's stage success, starring MARLENE DIETRICH; *The Private Life of Sherlock Holmes* (1970), a surprisingly affectionate portrait of the detective; and *Fedora* (1979), a haunting exposé of the lies on which film legends are based.

Wilder received the American Film Institute's Life Achievement Award in 1986 at a ceremony at which he was enthusiastically praised by many of his collaborators.

BIBLIOGRAPHY

Madsen, Axel, *Billy Wilder*, 1969; Schickel, Richard, *Double Indemnity*, 1992; Zolotow, Maurice, *Billy Wilder in Hollywood*, 1977.

Wilder, Thornton Niven

(April 17, 1897–December 7, 1975)
Novelist, Playwright, Teacher

Thornton Wilder is best known for *The Bridge of San Luis Rey* and the play *Our Town*. As his work seeks to uncover universal aspects of human experience, it relies on formal experimentation to make each piece unique.

Wilder was born in Madison, Wisconsin, the son of a newspaperman. He lived briefly in Hong Kong, after his father, Amos Parker Wilder, became U.S. consul general there. Subsequently, he settled with his mother and sisters in Berkeley, California, and there attended public schools. He graduated from Yale University in 1920 and studied for a year at the American Academy in Rome.

In 1921 Wilder began four years' service as a teacher of French at the Lawrenceville School in New Jersey. He earned a master's degree at Princeton University in 1926. In the same year, he published his first novel, *The Cabala*, a fictionalization of his experiences in Rome.

Wilder's second novel, *The Bridge of San Luis Rey* (1927), became a surprise bestseller. The story concerns the collapse of an ancient rope bridge in Peru in the early eighteenth century. Brother Juniper, who has witnessed the tragedy, sets out to study the lives of its five victims, hoping to understand whether the incident was truly accidental or rather showed the hand of God. The book won a Pulitzer Prize.

The success of *The Bridge of San Luis Rey* enabled Wilder to travel to Europe, where he met and befriended such literary notables as ERNEST HEMINGWAY and GERTRUDE STEIN, and it earned him a part-time teaching position at the University of Chicago, which he held from 1930 until 1936.

Wilder's next two novels received ambivalent reviews, though the first of these, *The Woman of Andros* (1930), was another popular success. The novel, drawn from the comedy *Andria* by the classical Roman author Terence, presents a story of love and loss cast against the death of classical Greek society and the advent of Christianity. *Heaven's My Destination* (1935) is a novel about a traveling salesman, George Brush, whose earnest attempts to uplift the people he meets fail comically.

Wilder next turned his full attention to theater. He had already published two volumes of one-act plays, *The Angel That Troubled the Waters* (1928) and *The Long Christmas Dinner* (1931), as well as *Lucrèce* (1933), an adaptation of a play by André Obey. He next produced an adaptation of *A Doll's House* by Henrik Ibsen, performed in New York in 1937.

Wilder's play *Our Town* (1938) opened in New York to rave reviews, despite poor reception in prior engagements. The play won Wilder his second Pulitzer. Set on a stage with no props and relying on a narrator to unify its loose, episodic structure, the play focuses on the simplest aspects of life in a small town, most poignantly rendering the love of a young couple and the tragedy of the woman's early death.

Later that same year, Wilder's *Merchant of Yonkers* opened in New York. Though the play was unsuccessful in its first run, Wilder revised it years later as *The Matchmaker* (pro-

duced in 1955). In 1964 Michael Stewart and Jerry Herman rewrote the play yet again, and it opened as the smash-hit musical *Hello, Dolly!*

The Skin of Our Teeth (1942) became Wilder's second real Broadway success and earned his third Pulitzer. The play traces the struggles of humanity since the Ice Age through the experiences of a contemporary family from New Jersey. Like *Our Town*, it relies on unconventional staging and dramatic devices—such as having the characters comment on the action of the play in frequent asides to the audience.

After service as an intelligence officer in the U.S. Army Air Force during World War II, Wilder wrote a new novel, *The Ides of March* (1948), which treats the last months in the life of Julius Caesar. Though the novel sold well, it received poor reviews from critics, and it was not until 1967 that Wilder wrote a new novel, *The Eighth Day*, which recounts the impact of a tragic shooting on two families in Illinois. The book won the National Book Award. Wilder's final novel, the partly autobiographical *Theophilus North*, was published in 1973.

Wilder was honored with the first National Medal for Literature in 1965. He died in 1975 at his home in Hamden, Connecticut.

BIBLIOGRAPHY

Castronovo, David, *Thornton Wilder*, 1986; Harrison, Gilbert A., *The Enthusiast: A Life of Thornton Wilder*, 1983; Simon, Linda, *Thornton Wilder: His World*, 1979.

Williams, Hiram Hank

(September 17, 1923–January 1, 1953)
Country Music Singer, Guitarist, Songwriter

The country music star Hank Williams, steeped in southern gospel and black music, delivered his lyrics so poignantly that listeners knew he sang just for them. His songs, successfully recorded by others, crossed over to pop, among them "Cold, Cold Heart" (Tony Bennett), "Half as Much" (Rosemary Clooney), and "Jambalaya" (Jo Stafford).

Born in Mount Olive, Alabama, Hiram Hank Williams moved with his family to Georgiana, near Montgomery, five years later. His father, Lonnie, a part-time farmer and log-train engineer for the W. T. Smith Lumber Company, soon fell ill and retired to a veteran's hospital. Hank never knew him well. Lilly, his domineering mother, raised him, and it was she who introduced Williams to the hymns and gospel tunes of fundamentalist Baptist churches.

At twelve Hank was trailing after a black street singer, Rufus Payne, nicknamed Tee-Tot, in Greenville and Georgiana. Tee-Tot allowed Williams to sing with him, and some believe he taught Williams basic guitar chords. Young Williams won an amateur night contest at the Empire Theatre in Montgomery singing "The WPA Blues," a song he had written.

In 1937 Williams formed his own hillbilly band, the Drifting Cowboys. The group appeared on WSFA radio in Montgomery and wherever else they could. One honky-tonk (dance hall) that hired the group, Thigpen's Log Cabin, located north of Georgiana in dry Butler County, encouraged patrons to bring their own moonshine. It was here that Hank began the drinking that shadowed his life.

As a youngster Hank had absorbed the popular music of the day as performed by commercial singers like Roy Acuff and Ernest Tubb. His style became a mix of country gospel and honky-tonk—the loud, rhythmic country music popular during the 1930s and 1940s that expressed rural folk's pain in facing urban realities.

Williams's early singing career was hard, in fact, so difficult that he gave it up during World War II when he went to work in the shipyards of Mobile in 1942. That year he married Audrey Sheppard. Four years later Williams and Audrey auditioned for Fred Rose in Nashville, Tennessee. Williams was hired as a songwriter for Acuff-Rose Publications. Fred Rose managed Williams's career ever after: produced his recordings for Sterling and for MGM, edited his songs, even collaborated on some. Williams's first recordings for MGM were "Move It on Over" and "I Heard You Crying in Your Sleep."

Hank Williams was to guarantee the fame of Acuff-Rose and MGM as he bolstered the reputation of "Louisiana Hayride," a Shreveport, Louisiana, radio show. His audience expanded even more when he became guest host for the daily "Johnny Fair Syrup Hour," another KWKH Shreveport show. Williams was on his way to becoming the best known and most copied country entertainer in America.

Some early recordings did well, but the breakthrough came with "Lovesick Blues," an old song recycled by Williams with a kind of yodeling style. This was the song that established his reputation and landed him a job at Grand Ole Opry despite misgivings about his drinking.

From 1949 Williams was secure financially: earnings from recordings and personal appearances continued to be strong until his death on New Year's Day 1953. In October 1951 he signed a five-year movie contract with MGM, but no film was ever made.

The hits "Lovesick Blues" (1949), "Cold, Cold Heart" (1951), "Your Cheatin' Heart" (1952) reflect his unsettled life: pain from a back ailment, divorce and rapid remarriage to model/singer Billie Jean Jones, and dismissal by the Grand Ole Opry for drunkenness. He died of a heart attack in West Virginia. His funeral, called "the greatest emotional orgy" in Montgomery's history by writer Eli Waldron, drew some 20,000 people to the city auditorium, where gospel songs were sung by Ernest Tubb, Carl Smith, Roy Acuff, and Red Foley.

Hank Williams took country music to new peaks of popularity and was one of the first honored by the Country Music Hall of Fame in

1961. His son, Hank Williams, Jr., also became a country music performer.

BIBLIOGRAPHY

Flippo, C., *Your Cheating Heart*, 1980; Malone, B. C., *Country Music, U.S.A.: A Fifty-Year History*, 1968; Williams, R. M., *Sing a Sad Song: The Life of Hank Williams*, 1970, rev., 1981.

Williams, Thomas Lanier ("Tennessee")

(March 26, 1911–February 25, 1983)
Playwright, Short-Story Writer

Tennessee Williams was a Pulitzer Prize–winning playwright whose themes of isolation, breaches in communication, breakdowns between illusion and reality, and the survival of values in a chaotic world link him to the southern literary tradition of WILLIAM FAULKNER and CARSON MCCULLERS.

While growing up in Columbus, Mississippi, and St. Louis, Missouri, Williams had only to observe his own family to find the models for many characters in his plays—his father was a sales representative who was on the road a lot, his mother was the puritanical daughter of a minister, and his elder sister was emotionally disturbed. Himself a solitary character due to a near-fatal bout with diphtheria as a child, he turned to alcohol and the writing of short stories as an escape from an unhappy

Library of Congress

adolescence. He entered the University of Missouri in 1929, but was forced to withdraw two years later for financial reasons. After a nervous breakdown in 1935, he began writing plays while resuming studies at Washington University and, later, the University of Iowa.

Restless wandering, odd jobs, and numerous stories and one-act plays marked the next four years. It was not until 1940 that Williams (by now irrevocably known as Tennessee, a name he appended to a short story in 1939) first achieved a major production of a play, *Battle of Angels* (1940), which the Theatre Guild opened in Boston. Unfortunately, the play—which would gain the dubious distinction of becoming perhaps his most reworked play—was closed due to bad notices and a theater house fire. Yet it introduced many of Williams's themes and styles—the setting of a small southern town, a mix of sex and religion, lyrical dialogue, and characters who tend to be metaphors rather than real people.

A short time in Hollywood with Metro-Goldwyn-Mayer studios (1943–1944) resulted in only a few aborted scenarios. However, one of them, tentatively titled *The Gentleman Caller,* was reworked as a play, *The Glass Menagerie,* which premiered in New York with Laurette Taylor in the role of Amanda Wingfield in 1945. It would become his most critically acclaimed play, winning the New York Drama Critics' Circle Award and a Broadway run of over two years. The influence of Williams's family background was obvious, with the character of Tom, a poet trapped in a mundane existence, patterned after Tennessee ("I seem dreamy, but inside—well, I'm boiling"), and the mother and invalid sister, Laura, drawn from his real mother and sister. The father, significantly, is portrayed as a family deserter, "the telephone man who fell in love with long distances."

Although the next two decades saw a measure of failures, notably the surreal fantasy *Camino Real* (1953) and the sexual violence of *Orpheus Descending* (1958), Williams won great acclaim and a Pulitzer Prize for *A Streetcar Named Desire* (1947), the story of the downfall of a woman living with delusions of grandeur; *Summer and Smoke* (1947–1948), which portrayed the sexual tensions between a minister's daughter and a young doctor; *The Rose Tattoo* (1951), about a widow who finds rekindled romance with a younger man; *Cat on a Hot Tin Roof* (1955), a portrait of yet another dysfunctional southern family, which won Williams his second Pulitzer Prize; *Suddenly Last Summer* (1958), a violent tale of extremes; *Sweet Bird of Youth* (1959), the story of the relationship between a gigolo and a fading actress; and *The Night of the Iguana* (1961), Williams's last major success, about a group of mismatched characters in an isolated Mexican resort hotel.

Williams continued to write until his death in 1983. Indeed, few playwrights can match his prolific output. His career, however, had been in eclipse since the early 1960s. Only *Small Craft Warnings* (1972), about a group of derelicts in a sleazy bar on the California coast, had achieved any degree of popularity. More and more involved with drugs, alcohol, and psychoanalysis, preoccupied with the degeneracy of social structures, and caught up in a homosexual lifestyle that had been an increasingly important element of his plays' thematic material, he had spent his last decades in relative obscurity and continual depression over failed plays.

Even more than EUGENE O'NEILL, writes Harold Clurman, Williams is "the dramatist of lost souls"; his work "describes a long laceration." His fascination with sin and his affinity with sinners opens our eyes to the company of the "somehow unfit," of "the fragile, the frightened, the different, the odd and the lonely, whose presence in our world we have so long sought to avoid thinking about and recognizing as our kind."

A substantial collection of Williams's manuscripts and letters is held by the Humanities Research Center, the University of Texas at Austin.

BIBLIOGRAPHY

Hughes, Catharine R., *Tennessee Williams: A Biography,* 1978; Smith, Bruce, *Costly Performances,* 1990; Windham, Donald, *Lost Friendships,* 1987.

Williams, William Carlos

(September 17, 1883–March 4, 1963)
Essayist, Novelist, Poet

A poet and novelist who made his living as a physician, William Carlos Williams struggled in his writing to define a distinctively American idiom. He chose simple themes, reflected, he felt, in the hearts of common people, and wrote in the language of everyday speech.

Writing in his *Autobiography* (1951) about the marriage of his two professions, Williams said that medicine gave him access to the "secret gardens of the self" he described in his poetry. Furthermore, listening to his patients helped him find the right language.

Born in 1883 in Rutherford, New Jersey, Williams studied medicine at the University of Pennsylvania (1902–1906) and later the University of Leipzig. While at Penn, Williams met the poet EZRA POUND, an undergraduate there, and the two became lifelong friends. After 1910 Williams practiced medicine in Rutherford and nearby Paterson.

Williams's first volume, *Poems*, was published at his own expense in 1909. Pound unceremoniously informed him that the poems' flowery style was at least twenty years out of date. Williams's second volume, *The Tempers*, published in 1913, showed Pound's heavy influence. By 1917 in *Al Que Quiere!* Williams seems to have found his own poetic voice.

Kora in Hell, a series of prose improvisations, was printed in 1920. In its influential prologue, Williams outlined the direction he hoped American poetry would follow. *Spring and All*, published in 1923, contained poems interspersed with prose describing what Williams meant by modern poetry.

In the American Grain, published in 1925, was Williams's first important prose work. An idiosyncratic collection of essays on American history, it was widely read. He later wrote that "the plan was to try to get inside the heads of some of the American founders or 'heroes,' if you will, by examining their original records."

Williams's first novel, *A Voyage to Pagany*, published in 1928, followed the complete itinerary of Williams and his wife, Flossie, during six months spent traveling in France, Italy, and Austria in celebration of their twelfth anniversary.

His poetry came to reflect the influence of the Imagists in that it rejected sentiment and concentrated on concrete images presented in spare language. Williams helped define a new movement known as Objectivism, which held that the poem was itself an object that had to be shaped syllable by syllable. "No ideas but in things" became a maxim identified with Williams. His volume, *Collected Poems, 1921–1931*, was published in 1934 by the Objectivist Press.

Williams wrote a series of three novels about a family of European immigrants—based on his in-laws, the Hermanns—as they came to terms with life in the United States. *White Mule* appeared in 1937, *In the Money* in 1940, and *The Build-Up* in 1952.

In the late 1930s, he began an extended poem describing the American scene during the depression years of the 1930s. Called *Paterson*, it was published in five volumes over the period 1946 to 1958. An autobiographical epic, it was Williams's answer to WALT WHITMAN's *Song of Myself*, Pound's *The Cantos*, and T. S. ELIOT's *The Waste Land*.

Williams published three more volumes of poetry in the 1940s: *The Wedge* in 1944, *The Clouds* in 1948, and *Selected Poems* in 1949. While the first two were printed in runs of only a few hundred apiece, the third was reprinted in batches of up to 10,000 and Williams began to reach a wider audience, due largely to the success of *Paterson*. In 1950 he was awarded the first National Book Award for poetry given by the American Book Publishers Council.

Later in the 1950s, Williams began to search again for a "new poetry." *The Desert Music* and

Journey to Love, printed in 1954 and 1955, respectively, reflect his experimentation with new line forms. "He was willing to be reckless," as his old friend MARIANNE MOORE said. "If you can't be that, what's the point of the whole thing?"

Williams's last volume, *Pictures from Brueghel and Other Poems,* published in 1962, won him a posthumous Pulitzer Prize.

Williams died in 1963 in Rutherford.

BIBLIOGRAPHY

Breslin, James, *William Carlos Williams: An American Artist,* 1970; Mariani, Paul, *William Carlos Williams: A New World Naked,* 1981; Whittemore, Reed, *William Carlos Williams: Poet from Jersey,* 1975.

Wilson, Edmund

(May 8, 1895–June 12, 1972)
Critic, Novelist

The writer Edmund Wilson explored many genres, including poetry and fiction, but his greatest contribution was as a critic depicting cultural figures and analyzing their social contributions within a historic context. A learned popularizer, he combined the skills of the journalist, the biographer, and the scholar to fashion broad social critique.

Wilson was born in Red Bank, New Jersey, the son of a prominent lawyer. He attended Princeton University, where he edited the *Nassau Literary Magazine.* After graduating in 1916, he worked as a reporter for the New York *Evening Sun.* The following year, he entered an army hospital unit; he served in France for two years during World War I.

Wilson became managing editor of *Vanity Fair* in 1920 and an associate editor at the *New Republic* in 1921. As a magazine writer, he was a jack-of-all-trades, reviewing films, books, and other products of popular culture, as well as reporting on crimes, protests, and social events. He developed a style that was at once literate and direct; he advocated experimentation, precision, and coherence and freely admonished writers who failed by his standards.

Wilson's first book, *The Undertaker's Garland* (1922), was a collection of poetry on which he collaborated with his college friend John Peale Bishop. In 1929 he published a novel, *I Thought of Daisy,* about a disillusioned Jazz Age intellectual who finds solace with a Broadway chorus girl.

In *Axel's Castle* (1931), Wilson surveyed modern poets who had been influenced by the French Symbolists. The Symbolists had sought to suggest a state of mind using only sensory images. Included in Wilson's survey were T. S. ELIOT, James Joyce, William Butler Yeats, and GERTRUDE STEIN. *Axel's Castle* features both concise biography and thoughtful analysis of difficult texts, yet it is written for a general audience.

The American Jitters (1932) reports on Wilson's travels around depression-scarred America before the advent of the New Deal. It vividly evokes the sufferings of workers and the unemployed, and brilliantly articulates Wilson's own rage against the economic system he held accountable.

The Triple Thinkers (1938) is a loose collection of essays on such writers as Gustave Flaubert, A. E. Housman, HENRY JAMES, and George Bernard Shaw. The piece "Marxism and Literature" analyzes the uses of Marxist methodology in criticism of art and literature;

it also suggests the depth of Wilson's own interest in grounding criticism in a broad social awareness.

To the Finland Station (1940) traces the evolution of socialist thought and particularly the roots of the Russian Revolution of 1917. The book is a social history, though it also frames criticism of important socialist texts. Wilson drew on techniques from fiction—particularly careful plotting and character development—to bring the historic action to life.

In *The Wound and the Bow* (1941), Wilson described the link between childhood suffering and the artist's expressive impulse. Using the metaphor of Philoctetes, the mythic warrior who compensates for an enduring injury by honing his skill as an archer, Wilson observes traumas in the early lives of such writers as Charles Dickens, ERNEST HEMINGWAY, Rudyard Kipling, and EDITH WHARTON and finds their reflections in the art produced by each.

The 1940s were a period of change for Wilson. He parted company with the intellectual circle surrounding the *New Republic* and became a book reviewer for *The New Yorker* in 1943. He divorced his third wife, the novelist MARY MCCARTHY, in 1946 and married Elena Thornton Mumm, settling, at last, for domestic stability. He also diversified his literary pursuits, returning to fiction and play writing and producing his first travel essays.

Wilson's collection of loosely connected short stories, *Memoirs of Hecate County* (1946), constituted his critique of life in the suburbs. The book was removed from shelves in New York bookstores because one story, "The Princess with the Golden Hair," frankly treated the narrator's sexual liaisons with two women. Wilson's play *The Little Blue Light* (1950) offers an apocalyptic vision of America's future.

Wilson spent almost a decade at work on *Patriotic Gore* (1962), which considers the impact of the Civil War on the lives of creative individuals. The book offers profiles of political and literary heroes such as Abraham Lincoln, OLIVER WENDELL HOLMES, and Harriet Beecher Stowe, vividly rendering them as characters in part by analyzing their prose.

Other books by Wilson include *Classics and Commercials* (1950), *A Piece of My Mind* (1956), *The American Earthquake* (1958), *Apologies to the Iroquois* (1960), *The Cold War and the Income Tax* (1963), and *The Bit Between My Teeth* (1965). *Upstate* (1971) is a memoir written from Wilson's family retreat in Talcottville, New York.

Wilson died in 1972 in Talcottville.

BIBLIOGRAPHY

Castronovo, David, *Edmund Wilson,* 1984; Costa, Richard Hauer, *Edmund Wilson: Our Neighbor from Talcottville,* 1980; Kriegel, Leonard, *Edmund Wilson,* 1971.

Wolfe, Thomas Clayton

(October 3, 1900–September 15, 1938)
Novelist, Playwright, Short-Story Writer

Thomas Wolfe, best known for his first novel, *Look Homeward, Angel*, wrote fiction that sought to forge autobiographical fact into an American mythology concerned broadly with the tempering of youthful aspirations through time and against imposing social realities.

Wolfe was born in Asheville, North Carolina, the son of a stonecutter and the proprietor of a guest house. He attended the University of North Carolina at Chapel Hill, where he edited the *Tar Heel* magazine. He graduated in 1920 and enrolled in a graduate play writing program at Harvard University, from which he received a master's degree in 1922.

In 1924 Wolfe accepted a part-time teaching post at New York University. He continued writing plays, though he had no luck selling them. Later that year he made the first of several voyages to Europe; on the return boat, he met Aline Bernstein, a set designer who was married and nineteen years older than he. They began an intense relationship that was to last five years.

During a second trip abroad with Bernstein, in 1926, Wolfe began writing a novel. Returning to New York, the couple shared an apartment, which Bernstein kept as an office, and Wolfe completed the draft, influenced importantly by Bernstein. When the novel was accepted by Scribner's for publication, Wolfe began a close collaboration with the editor Maxwell Perkins, who helped him cut his prodigious manuscript. *Look Homeward, Angel* was published just days before the great stock market crash of October 1929.

The novel tells a story of youth and coming of age in Altamont, a small Carolina town. The protagonist, Eugene Gant, is Wolfe's fictional counterpart, and the novel recounts his conflicts with both members of his immediate family and individuals in the larger community. Wolfe demonstrated penchants for copious de-

scription and intense lyricism, as well as a burlesqued form of characterization that lent the novel a comic aura. However, despite the book's success, residents of Asheville failed to get the joke, and Wolfe became unwelcome in his own hometown.

Fortified with a Guggenheim Fellowship, Wolfe quit his teaching post at New York University, split with Aline Bernstein, and sailed again for Europe in 1930. He returned almost a year later, moving to an apartment in Brooklyn, New York, where he began work on a sequel to *Look Homeward, Angel*. His manuscript stretched to the thousands of pages; again, Maxwell Perkins's editorial advice was vital in shaping the final novel.

Of Time and the River (1935) takes Eugene Gant to Harvard as a student of play writing, settles him as a teacher in New York, then sends him voyaging to Europe. Thematically, the novel is concerned with the swift passage of time, with the individual's essential loneliness, and with one man's intense need to locate the greatness of America. Much of the story is told in terms of Gant's fascination with the city. As he faces the harsh realities before him, Gant learns the discipline he needs as a writer. *Of Time and the River* received mixed critical reviews, but it became a best-seller.

Later in 1935, Wolfe published a collection of short stories, *From Death to Morning*. In 1936 he described his approach to writing fiction, using *Of Time and the River* as the primary instance, in the controversial lecture *The Story of a Novel*.

Wolfe continued traveling, to Germany to witness the 1936 Olympic Games; to Asheville, where his welcome was warmer than he might have imagined; and, finally, on a trip to the national parks. It was during this last trip, in 1938, that Wolfe fell suddenly ill and was hospitalized, first in Seattle, then at the Johns Hopkins University Hospital in Baltimore. He had developed pneumonia and tuberculosis of the brain. He died on September 15, 1938, in Baltimore, just weeks short of turning thirty-eight.

Wolfe had been working on a voluminous manuscript, which he had delivered to his new editor, Edward Aswell at Harper's, in a packing crate shortly before his final illness. Over the next three years, Aswell carved three books out of the manuscript. Two are novels: *The Web and the Rock* (1939) and *You Can't Go Home Again* (1940). *The Hills Beyond* (1941) is a collection of short stories.

Sensitive to criticism that his style was excessively lyrical and that he lacked the discipline to structure his fiction, Wolfe had sought to write more "objectively." *The Web and the Rock* continues in the autobiographical vein, but Wolfe shows greater stylistic restraint. The protagonist, now called George Webber, settles in New York and begins a turbulent love affair with Mrs. Esther Jack, a set designer. As Web-

ber matures, he faces disillusionment with the city and with the relationship, and he turns to travel.

In *You Can't Go Home Again*, Webber finally breaks with Jack and moves to Brooklyn. Webber's trips to Germany and home to Carolina offer Wolfe opportunities to convey detailed impressions of Nazi bigotry and Great Depression–era social devastation. Even his critics acknowledged that, by the end of his final novel, Wolfe's fiction had matured and broadened into an effective social realism.

BIBLIOGRAPHY

Austin, Neal F., *A Biography of Thomas Wolfe*, 1968; Donald, David Herbert, *Look Homeward: A Life of Thomas Wolfe*, 1987; Evans, Elizabeth, *Thomas Wolfe*, 1984; Payne, Ladell, *Thomas Wolfe*, 1969.

Wright, Frank Lloyd

(June 8, 1867–April 9, 1959)
Architect

Frank Lloyd Wright was one of America's most important and influential modern architects. He was a proponent of "organic architecture," a phrase he coined to describe buildings that harmonized with their environments and complemented (but often challenged) the lives and work of their inhabitants.

He was born Frank Lincoln Wright (he would later change his middle name to Lloyd) in 1867, the son of a schoolteacher, Anna Lloyd Jones, and preacher and musician, William C. Wright. The family moved frequently during his youth, and he grew up in Iowa, Rhode Island, Massachusetts, and Wisconsin. He enrolled at the University of Wisconsin in Madison, but, disappointed that there were no courses in architecture, he left in 1887 for Chicago, where

until 1893 he worked as a chief assistant to the architects Dankmar Adler and LOUIS SULLIVAN. Rejecting an opportunity to study in Europe at the expense of DANIEL BURNHAM, another influential Chicago architect, Wright determined to remain in America and create an architectural style appropriate to the Midwest.

In 1889 Wright married Catherine Tobin, with whom he would have six children, and, with the financial help of Sullivan, built his own home in Oak Park, Illinois. It was at first a modest, gabled house, built on a platform and around a chimney core. In its often extended form, it was the working place for many of the ideas in Wright's future houses.

Wright's philosophy of architecture, drawn mainly from the medievalistic visions of John Ruskin and William Morris, was expressed primarily in houses and furniture, which are major monuments of the Arts and Crafts movement in America (see GUSTAV STICKLEY). After 1900 Wright became the magnetic leader of the so-called Prairie school of architecture, whose radical domestic style featured low-spreading roofs with wide eaves, boldly detailed elevations, and open, free-flowing plans that defied the conventional boxlike layout of traditional American houses. From 1900 to 1910 he designed an estimated fifty prairie houses. Many of these dwellings, like his early masterwork, the home of Ward W. Willitts (1902–1903) in Highland Park, Illinois, and the later Frederick G. Robie House (1908–1910) in Chicago, had strong axes, large fireplaces with adjacent built-in seating, and sanctuary-like dining rooms. The main spaces were ornamented with finely milled woodwork and leaded glass in the spirit of the Arts and Crafts movement.

His early works had some remarkable innovations. For example, the Larkin Company Administration Building (1903–1904) for a mail-order soap firm in Buffalo, New York (demolished in 1950), featured mechanical ventilation, a balance of natural and artificial light, and metal furniture. Its central nave, with biblical inscriptions in the frieze, was almost a church of the ethics of work. Unity Temple (1905–1908), in Oak Park, was a small Protestant fortress of concrete, which, like the Larkin building, used natural light to great effect.

Wright's personal life was complicated in 1904 when he became involved in a relationship with Mamah Borthwick Cheney, with whom he "eloped" to Europe in 1909. There Wright and several draftsmen prepared the stunning presentations of his architecture, published by the Berlin firm of Ernst Wasmuth (portfolio of drawings, 1910; photographs, 1911). They were to be some of the most influential architectural publications of the early twentieth century.

Back in the United States, Wright's unconventional tie with Mamah Cheney brought notoriety and kept many clients away. He was able to build himself a handsome new house, Taliesin (1911), in Spring Green, Wisconsin,

where he moved with Mrs. Cheney. In 1913 and 1914, he created the lively Midway Gardens on the South Side of Chicago, a complex of restaurant clubrooms and bandshell around an open court, with abstract murals and sculpture designed by the architect or in collaboration with him. As the project neared completion in August 1914, Wright learned that Mrs. Cheney, her children, and several employees had been murdered at Taliesin by a mad servant, who also nearly destroyed the house by setting it on fire. It took Wright many years to recover from this ghastly tragedy.

In 1916 he went to Tokyo to design the Imperial Hotel (1916–1922). Because of its revolutionary, floating cantilever construction, it was one of the few large buildings to survive the Tokyo earthquake of 1923 (only to be razed in 1968). He also received many commissions in southern California, including the houses for Aline Barnsdall in Los Angeles (1916–1920) and for Mrs. George Madison Millard in Pasadena (1923). The latter house was of vertical composition, built of precast concrete blocks with cruciform patterns. This idea became the "textile-block" system of other Wright houses of the Los Angeles area in the 1920s.

The stock market crash in 1929 worsened Wright's already erratic fortunes, which had been further complicated by a liaison with the unstable Miriam Noel, whom he met in late 1914 and married in 1923, when his first wife finally agreed to a divorce. This marriage plagued the architect in many ways and brought him to the brink of financial disaster. Salvation was his third wife, Olgivanna Lazovich, with whom he had a daughter and spent the rest of his life. It was she who urged him to begin writing his autobiography, which was published in 1932 (in a longer version in 1943).

In 1930 Wright was invited to lecture at Princeton University. These lectures, which summed up much of his career and propagandized his ideas of the future, were published in 1931 as *Modern Architecture*. In 1932 he founded the Taliesin Fellowship, a program at his twice-rebuilt home and farm in Spring Green, which provided residential apprenticeships for paying students. This helped the architect survive the Great Depression.

Wright's most universally admired work from these often lean years was a retreat in the Alleghenies, the Edgar Kaufmann House (1935–1937), which was cantilevered over a waterfall and thus called Fallingwater. It is an unforgettable gesture, combining the horizontal forms of the International style (which Wright disliked but had helped to inspire; see LUDWIG MIES VAN DER ROHE) and his romantic response to the dramatic site. The stones of the main vertical core were quarried nearby.

At about this time, Wright started to plan his winter home, Taliesin West, near Scottsdale, Arizona (1937–1938), that fit the horizontal expanse of the landscape and revealed his renewed interest in geometry. The Goetsch-Winckler House (1939) in Okemos, Michigan, represents his so-called Usonian house, a single floor on a heated concrete foundation slab with planes of bricks and wood for the walls and roof. Wright hoped that this type would be a model for low-cost dwellings suitable for a wide range of people across America.

Among the many commissions that came his way in the 1940s and 1950s were designs for the campus of Florida Southern College at Lakeland (1938–1954), the Marin County Civic Center, San Raphael, California (1957–1966), and the Solomon R. Guggenheim Museum in New York City (1943–1946; 1956–1959). The original commission for the Guggenheim called for a structure to house a permanent collection of nonobjective art. Construction was not begun until 1956 and was completed shortly after Wright's death. Financial constraints and building codes had altered the donor's intentions and the architect's vision. Critics said it was more of a sculpture than a functioning building, and that it had far too little conventional wall space to display adequately the works of art. But after a restoration and expansion by the firm Gwathmey Siegel and Associates, completed in 1992, the Guggenheim more comfortably accommodates exhibitions in Wright's ideal of continuous space, defined by the winding ramp and circular skylight. It is a place as awe-inspiring as a domed cathedral. Art historian John Richardson has said: "The ascent up that empty spiral ramp which heads for the sky verges on the spiritual, just as Wright intended."

Frank Lloyd Wright designed approximately 1,000 buildings, of which 400 were actually built and about 280 are still standing. His books and lectures have been as influential as his buildings. A product of the Arts and Crafts movement a century ago, he had several careers, reinvented himself often, and attempted almost everything—even a mile-high skyscraper (project, 1956). When he died in 1959, he was compared with WALTER GROPIUS, Ludwig Mies van der Rohe, and Le Corbusier, who were a generation younger.

BIBLIOGRAPHY

Richardson, John, "Go Go Guggenheim," *The New York Review of Books,* July 16, 1992; Secrest, Meryle, *Frank Lloyd Wright,* 1992; Twombly, Robert C., *Frank Lloyd Wright: His Life and His Architecture,* 1979.

Wright, Richard Nathaniel

(September 4, 1908–November 28, 1960)
Essayist, Novelist, Short-Story Writer

Richard Wright, best known for his first published novel, *Native Son*, introduced a new realism to literary treatments of America's racial problems, rendering sympathetically the always fearful, sometimes violent psychology of the oppressed.

Wright was born on a plantation near Natchez, Mississippi, the son of a sharecropper and a teacher. Abandoned by their father in 1911, Wright and his younger brother lived with their mother in the homes of relatives in Tennessee, Arkansas, and Mississippi. The children were often hungry and had little opportunity for formal schooling. After his mother suffered a stroke in 1919, Wright lived with an aunt and uncle, then with his grandmother. He attended a public junior high school in Jackson, Mississippi, and graduated first in his ninth-grade class in 1925.

At fifteen he left home, moved to Memphis, and took a succession of menial jobs in order to support himself. Four years later, he moved to Chicago and found a job as a postal clerk, which he held until it was eliminated during the Great Depression in 1931. He joined the Communist party in 1933.

Wright moved to New York City in 1937 to become Harlem editor of the *Daily Worker*. In the same year, he completed a manuscript for a first novel, "Cesspool," but was unable to find a publisher. This heavily autobiographical work remained unpublished until three years

Library of Congress

after Wright's death, when it was printed as *Lawd Today* (1963).

Wright's first published volume was a collection of short stories, *Uncle Tom's Children* (1938). Included is "Big Boy Leaves Home," a tale of truant black youths caught swimming in a whites-only stream. Their discovery leads to violence and the killing of a white man; Big Boy escapes, but his friend Bobo is lynched. *Uncle Tom's Children* caused a sensation for its honest rendering of the victimization of blacks in a society marked by Jim Crow laws and mob justice. The novel won first prize in a contest sponsored by *Story* magazine for writers supported by the Federal Writers Project.

The novel *Native Son* (1940) proved even more shocking to prevailing literary sensibilities, and it became a best-seller. Acting out of fear, the protagonist, Bigger Thomas, accidentally smothers a wealthy young white woman when he holds a pillow over her head to avoid having his innocent presence in her bedroom detected by her mother. His act is discovered, and he flees with his mistress, Bessie. Desperate for his own survival, he murders Bessie and goes into hiding. He is finally caught and executed, but he comes to see his own violence as a necessary rebellion against his fate as a black man. Until *Native Son*, most American fiction had treated men like Bigger stereotypically as either subhuman thugs or helpless victims; the novel lent a new complexity to literary discourse on the subject of race and opened a new channel for black fiction.

Wright became a national spokesman on issues relating to black experience, a role he pursued in his next two books, *Twelve Million Black Voices* (1941) and *Black Boy* (1945). The first, a social history, recounts African Americans' struggles from slavery, their oppression in the contemporary South, the migration of many blacks to the North, and their sufferings in urban, industrial society. *Black Boy* is an autobiographical account of Wright's life from ages four to nineteen. It compellingly places Wright's own experience of extreme poverty and racism into a broad social context. Portions of the original manuscript that dealt with his life after his move to Chicago were published separately as *American Hunger* in 1977.

Alienated by the continuing experience of racism in America, Wright moved permanently with his wife and daughter to Paris in 1947. There, he wrote *The Outsider* (1953), a novel about a man who escapes the pressures of marriage and family by taking advantage of a mistaken report of his death to create a new identity for himself. *Savage Holiday* (1954), remarkable because it features white characters and ignores the subject of race, concerns a white man's suppressed love for his own mother and the violent rage that leads him to murder the woman he marries as a substitute for her. *The Long Dream* (1958) recounts a young black man's coming of age in Mississippi and his coming to terms with the white man's political and economic power.

During the Paris years, Wright began to use the American experience of slavery as a framework for the interpretation of world events. *Black Power* (1954) offers his impressions as a black American of a trip to the Gold Coast shortly before it became the independent nation of Ghana. *The Color Curtain* (1956), a report on the Bandung Conference of nonaligned nations of the Third World, argues that race is the key factor determining the development of emerging nations in Asia and Africa. *Pagan Spain* (1956) indicts the mores of Catholic Spain during the regime of Francisco Franco, comparing religious intolerance to racism. *White Man, Listen!* (1957) collects lectures made throughout Europe warning Western society of the perils of continuing to deny freedom to large portions of the world's population.

At the time of his sudden death, in Paris, of a heart attack in 1960, Wright was at work on a new collection of short stories. *Eight Men* was published in 1960.

BIBLIOGRAPHY

Fabre, Michel, *The Unfinished Quest of Richard Wright*, 1973; Gayle, Addison, *Richard Wright: Ordeal of a Native Son*, 1980; Walker, Margaret, *Richard Wright, Daemonic Genius*, 1988.

Wyeth, Andrew Newell

(July 12, 1917–   )
Painter

Andrew Wyeth has been one of this century's most popular painters of the rural regions of Pennsylvania and the coastal areas of Maine. Unlike his father, the illustrator N. C. Wyeth, Andrew was not tied to commercial art and was able to pursue a lifelong interest in landscape and portraits.

Andrew was the last of five children born to N. C. and Carolyn Wyeth. It was a close-knit family, and there were many group outings, readings, and pageants celebrated around their home in Chadds Ford, Pennsylvania. Andrew, particularly, shared with his father, a world-renowned painter and illustrator, an innate artistic ability, along with a love of the romance and legends of the countryside. His only drawing lessons came from the elder Wyeth; because of ill health, the boy was frequently at home and was able to take advantage of the opportunity to learn from his father first hand. "I had no intent except to put down what I felt and saw in front of me," recalled Andrew. "[My father] helped me *simplify* things. He rarely talked about technique." There were other shared staples in life between the two, particularly a love for cinema, the music of Bach, and the writings of HENRY DAVID THOREAU and ROBERT FROST.

In 1936 Wyeth exhibited thirty watercolors at the Art Alliance in Philadelphia. In the next few years there were one-man shows at the Macbeth Gallery in New York and the Currier Gallery of Art in Manchester, New Hampshire. A major turning point in his life came with the tragic death of his father in 1945. As art historian James Duff has noted, Wyeth's very personal loss was expressed in works dating from this time, like *Winter 1946.* His palette, which had always been less colorful and more muted than his father's, grew even darker. Virtually all illustrative/narrative implications in the scenes disappeared. "A very personal iconography began to develop from this time," says Duff, "an

iconography of hills, paths, windows, doorways—the details and shapes with which Andrew Wyeth has built his pictures and endowed them with meaning." His father had taught him that an artist can paint only what he knows and where he has lived; Andrew documented the areas around Chadds Ford and the coast of the peninsulas of Port Clyde and Thomaston, Maine, with the scrupulousness of the historian and the sensitivity of a poet— creating in their catalogs of the ordinary, says Duff, not the history of these regions, but their "remnants," those "vestiges that affect the present." The Kuerner Farm in Chadds Ford, particularly the home of a German immigrant family, was the inspiration for many works throughout his life, including *Evening at Kuerners* (1970), *Wolf Moon 1975,* and *Spring* (1978). In Maine he got to know the Olson family and their farm, which he also painted for many years. There he produced one of his finest works, *Weather Side* (1965), and his most famous painting, *Christina's World* (1948).

Perhaps because of a prolonged, life-threatening illness sustained after the death of his father, Wyeth was sympathetic to other survivors, tough people who had endured a harsh and lonely life. There is a melancholy strength to *Christina's World, The Kuerners* (1971), and *The Drifter* (1964). On the other hand, in his famous series of nude studies of a woman named Helga Testorf, executed in Chadds Ford between 1972 and 1986, he captured a sturdy, sensuous vitality. Art historian Thomas Hoving calls this series a "rebirth of creativity" for the artist.

Prior to 1940 he worked mostly in watercolor, for he disliked oils. Thereafter he turned increasingly to the medium of egg tempera. With the former he achieved a combination of freely applied washes and precisely controlled dry-brush line that is unsurpassed. The latter medium, by contrast, was more opaque and substantial. As he put it, "I wanted something I could chew on for months at a time and pour myself into." One of the images of Kuerner Farm, *Spring Fed* (1967), is a particularly effective example with its layered surfaces and meanings. "I'm very conscious of the ephemeral nature of the world," Wyeth said. "I feel things are just hanging on the surface and that it's all going to blow away."

BIBLIOGRAPHY

Duff, James H., et al., *An American Vision: Three Generations of Wyeth Art*, 1987; Brandywine River Museum, *The Brandywine Heritage*, 1971; Hoving, Thomas, "The Prussian: Andrew Wyeth's Secret Paintings (1972–1985)," *Connoisseur*, September 1986; Wilmerding, John, *The Helga Pictures*, 1987.

Zappa, Francis Vincent

(December 21, 1940–)
Composer, Guitarist

The versatile Frank Zappa foreshadowed punk, with his anticonformist attitudes and derisive lyrics, while his technically demanding, unconventional compositions influenced the fusing of jazz and rock. Many well-known musicians started their careers playing Zappa's complex and demanding music with the Mothers of Invention.

Born in Baltimore, Maryland, Zappa moved to Lancaster, California, in the Mojave Desert near San Diego with his family in 1956, graduating from Antelope Valley High School in June 1958. He began drumming at twelve but soon switched to guitar, sang blues and rock with the Blackouts when he was in high school, and, for one semester after graduation, studied music theory at Chaffey College in Alta Loma, California.

"The rest of my musical training," Zappa said, "comes from listening to records and play-

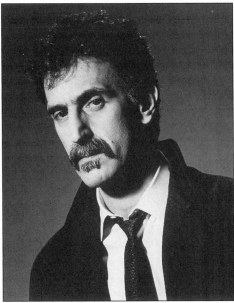

Rykodisc USA

ing in assorted little bands in beer joints and cocktail lounges, mostly in small towns." He had been learning from recordings of rhythm and blues, doo-wop, and blues guitarists like Clarence ("Gatemouth") Brown, as well as absorbing the work of avant-garde composers like EDGARD VARÈSE. "It didn't make any difference to me if I was listening to Lightnin' Slim, or a vocal group called the Jewels, or Webern or Varèse, or [IGOR] STRAVINSKY. To me it was all good music."

In the early 1960s Zappa bought a small recording studio, renamed it Studio Z, and began relentlessly experimenting. In 1964 he joined the Soul Giants, eventually renamed the Mothers on Mother's Day 1964, and finally, the Mothers of Invention. The group provided a forum for Zappa to explore concepts of total audience involvement—called enforced recreation by Zappa—wherein music shared equal time with social satire, bad theater, and performance art.

The group's first album for MGM's Verve label, *Freak Out!* was rock's first two-record set. The 1966 set included parodies, social protest, even rock-opera themes. As the decade wore on, Zappa continued to break new ground with his compositions as well as explore new techniques in the art of sound recording, particularly in the use of multitracking.

When Zappa left MGM for Warner Brothers, he gained greater artistic control over albums he produced, among them recordings by Captain Beefheart, Los Angeles street entertainer Wild Man Fischer, Alice Cooper, and some made under his own name. His first solo album, *Hot Rats* (1969), brought Zappa's guitar improvisations to the fore.

After Mothers of Invention broke up in late 1969, Zappa directed and produced *200 Motels*, a surrealistic film. In 1971, when Zappa's film score was performed by the Los Angeles Philharmonic Orchestra conducted by Zubin Mehta, the attempt to merge rock with classical music received mixed reviews.

Mothers of Invention reconvened that year. The group toured and recorded (*Live at the Fillmore East*, 1971; *Just Another Band from L.A.*, 1972) and set a new style that featured the vocal talents of Howard Kaylan and Mark Volman, formerly of the soft rock group the Turtles. More Zappa material was recorded on *Overnite Sensation* in 1973. The album contained his first hit single, "Don't Eat the Yellow Snow."

Zappa toured and recorded through the 1970s. Three albums, the contents drawn from tape archives, were issued: *Studio Tan* (1978), and *Sleep Dirt* and *Orchestral Favorites* (both 1979). Zappa established the Zappa label, which was distributed by Mercury Records.

Zappa's controversial lyrics continued to skewer the hypocritical and shallow side of American life, wherever he saw it. "Jewish Princess" prompted a B'nai Brith Anti-Defamation League complaint to the FCC. He responded with "Catholic Girls." In 1980 Mercury refused to issue "I Don't Wanna Get Drafted," and Zappa departed to establish Barking Pumpkin, a label distributed by CBS. During the early 1980s Zappa showcased his guitar skills with *Shut Up 'n' Play Yer Guitar*, directed the film *Baby Snakes*, organized an Edgard Varèse concert with the composer's widow, and recorded the 1982 single "Valley Girl," with his teenage daughter, Moon Unit.

Zappa's classical forays, inspired in part by avant-garde composer Varèse, hark back to the instrumental flights of his rock compositions. As symphony orchestras took up his work, Zappa appeared as conductor and in 1984 was keynote speaker for the American Society of University Composers. Zappa could not resist controversy, always pushing musical boundaries. His compositions include tape-collages and require daunting instrumental technique. Often tasteless, he forecast punk but affected jazz-rock composers with his instrumental concepts.

In 1990 Zappa appeared before the Senate against the Parents' Music Resource Center, led by Tipper Gore, to challenge proposed legislation to label albums in a manner similar to film ratings in order to warn parents of possible offensive content. Zappa believed this to be in violation of the First Amendment and soundly renounced it.

BIBLIOGRAPHY

Denyer, R., *The Guitar Handbook*, 1980; Stambler, I., *Encyclopedia of Rock and Roll*, 1974.

Ziegfeld, Florenz, Jr.

(March 21, 1869–July 22, 1932)
Theatrical Impresario

Florenz Ziegfeld was a theater producer whose name became synonymous with extravagant shows and revues in the first quarter of the twentieth century. The term "Ziegfeld Girl," derived from his famous series of Follies revues, still connotes a particular image of idealized (if exotic) American womanhood.

Ziegfeld was born into a musical family in 1868 in Chicago. His father, who was director of musical events for the Columbian Exposition of 1893, dispatched his son to Europe to secure talent for the exposition. Characteristically, rather than bringing back distinguished artists, the young man signed up a motley company of circus acts and vaudeville performers.

Most of Flo Ziegfeld's first Broadway productions were vehicles for his wife, the popular singer Anna Held, including an 1896 revival of *The Parlor Match, Papa's Wife* (1899), *Mam'selle Napoleon* (1903), and *A Parisian Model* (1906). The Follies series, which began with the *Follies of 1907,* inaugurated the form of revue that would make him an American institution. In addition to featuring headline performers like comedian/monologist Will Rogers, comedienne Fanny Brice, juggler W. C. Fields, and knockabout singer Eddie Cantor, these shows emphasized elaborate *tableaux vivants,* or living pictures of extravagantly clad females in sculptural poses arranged against spectacular backdrops. By 1911 each edition of the Follies bore Ziegfeld's name, and they continued annually until 1925. After 1922, through

Library of Congress

1931, the revues were advertised as "Glorifying the American Girl." After 1915 each production was designed by the inimitable Joseph Urban, whose art deco stylings and vivid colors made them among the finest stage conceptions in the history of the American musical stage. Song hits that came from the Follies series included "Shine on, Harvest Moon" (1908), "By the Light of the Silv'ry Moon" (1909), "A Pretty Girl Is Like a Melody" (1919), and "My Man" (1921).

While most of the Follies productions were staged in the sumptuous New Amsterdam Theater, some of Ziegfeld's greatest non-Follies productions were premiered in his showcase, the Ziegfeld Theater, which opened in 1927 with *Rio Rita.* In quick succession, from 1927 to 1929 other landmarks in American musical stagecraft followed, like *Show Boat, Rosalie, The Three Musketeers, Whoopee,* and *Bitter Sweet.*

In the late 1920s Ziegfeld was at the zenith of his career, with a beautiful second wife, actress Billie Burke, and a penchant for high living and gambling. The 1929 stock market crash wiped him out, however, and in 1930 he sought new pastures in Hollywood. He personally supervised the production of *Glorifying the American Girl* (1929), whose second half is a virtual re-creation of the Follies style of revue (starring Eddie Cantor, Helen Morgan, and Mary Eaton in duplications of their stage roles); and *Whoopee* (1930), a Technicolor film for which he collaborated with film producer

SAMUEL GOLDWYN and dance choreographer Busby Berkeley.

Mounting debts and personal extravagance, always a part of Ziegfeld's lifestyle, became a real problem at the dawn of the 1930s. Hounded by creditors, Ziegfeld turned to radio, hosting a weekly show for Chrysler. Nonetheless, when he died of pleurisy in 1932, he left his wife burdened with enormous debts. Ziegfeld has been the subject of several motion pictures—*The Great Ziegfeld* (1936), which starred William Powell as the showman;

Ziegfeld Follies (1945), in which Powell reappeared briefly; and *Funny Girl* (1968), with Walter Pidgeon in the role. Needless to say, all these films were based more on the spirit, rather than the fact, of the Ziegfeld legend.

BIBLIOGRAPHY

Carter, Randolph, *The World of Flo Ziegfeld*, 1974; Tibbetts, John C., *The American Theatrical Film*, 1985; Toll, Robert C., *On with the Show*, 1976.

Zukor, Adolph

(January 7, 1873–June 10, 1976)
Film Producer

Adolph Zukor, cofounder of Paramount Pictures, was a self-made man who helped shape the course of the film industry. He was also a founder of the Academy of Motion Picture Arts and Sciences, which honored him with a special Oscar in 1949 as "the father of the feature film in America."

He was born in Hungary to Jewish parents. His father, a farmer, died before Adolph was a year old. His mother remarried but died seven years later, leaving Adolph and his brother, Arthur, in the care of an uncle. A Judaic scholar, the uncle adopted Arthur, who later became a rabbi, leaving Adolph feeling "unchosen," as a result of which his identification with his faith remained tenuous.

Zukor emigrated to the United States at age sixteen, leaving behind a culture from which he felt disconnected. "No sooner did I put my foot on American soil than I was a newborn person," he said. He worked himself up in the fur trade in New York from floor sweeper to designer, later forming Zukor's Novelty Fur Company in Chicago. Facing bankruptcy in 1896, he began a new partnership with furrier Morris Kohn, which lasted

nearly a decade and made Zukor wealthy. He married Kohn's niece, Lottie Kaufman, in 1897.

While his life seemed settled, Zukor was restless, and having been "drawn irresistibly by that fascinating marvel [the movies]" as early as 1897, he teamed up with Mitchell Mark, an operator of penny arcades, and opened the Automatic Vaudeville Company on 14th Street in 1903, with his friend Marcus Loew as fellow investor.

By 1905 Zukor and Loew were full-time proprietors of nickelodeons (early movie theaters), eventually combining the one-reelers with variety shows and presenting the whole program in real theaters. In 1910 they established Loew's Consolidated Enterprises, with Loew as president and Zukor as treasurer, and controlled a circuit of theaters.

Convinced that the future of movies depended on attracting the middle class, Zukor believed that only longer and better films would accomplish this. In 1910 he bought the exhibition rights to a ninety-minute Passion play filmed in Oberammergau, Germany. The film's success in New York demonstrated that audiences would sit through movies just as they did through stage plays.

In 1912 Zukor distributed a French four-reel film version of Sarah Bernhardt's performance in *Queen Elizabeth*. Premiering at Broadway producer Daniel Frohman's Lyceum Theater, the film helped to make movies, regarded as a pastime for the masses, "socially respectable." Inspired by his success, Zukor opened a studio in New York and established his Famous Players in Famous Plays Film Company, and with Frohman's influence drew well-known stage stars to play their roles on film.

Without the sanction of the Motion Picture Patents Company, which set limits on film length and denied licenses arbitrarily, Zukor suffered financially, but—like CARL LAEMMLE and other independents—he persevered, believing he was making films that would "elevate" the industry. The year 1913 brought *The Count of Monte Cristo*, starring James O'Neill, EUGENE O'NEILL's father, and *The Prisoner of Zenda*, one of Frohman's stage successes.

Zukor eventually shifted to younger performers—like MARY PICKFORD—dropped "Famous Plays" from the company's name, and increased production to thirty films a year. In 1916 he merged with Jesse L. Lasky's Feature Players–Lasky Corporation, which took over W. W. Hodkinson's Paramount Pictures, a distribution outfit. Zukor became president of the entire operation, and the Paramount trademark still used today—a mountain encircled by stars—became the symbol of the production/distribution company. To control exhibition, Zukor acquired and built theaters, establishing the industry's largest film theatrical chain—the Publix.

In 1921 the industry was rocked by scandal: comic Roscoe ("Fatty") Arbuckle was accused of the rape and death of a young girl during a riotous party. Zukor absorbed a huge financial loss by withdrawing Arbuckle's films from theaters. In response to public outcry over Hollywood's "immorality," Zukor and industry leaders brought in Will Hays to head the Motion Picture Producers and Distributors of America (later the Motion Picture Association of America) to monitor moral issues on and off screen. In 1930 the MPAA issued the Production Code, compelling the industry to censor itself.

Despite setbacks, Paramount was the most successful studio in Hollywood until the mid-1920s, when MGM was formed by Marcus Loew. In 1933 Paramount went into bankruptcy, largely as a result of theater buying, and when it was officially reorganized in 1935, Zukor was made board chairman, a post he held until 1964.

While Zukor was reputed to be dogmatic and puritanical, the stars and directors who worked under him were among the biggest in silent and early sound films: RUDOLPH VALENTINO, Gloria Swanson, Clara Bow, GARY COOPER, W. C. Fields, MAE WEST, and Bing Crosby, among the stars; CECIL B. DEMILLE, D. W. GRIFFITH, JOSEF VON STERNBERG, and ERNST LUBITSCH, among directors.

BIBLIOGRAPHY

Eames, John Douglas, *The Paramount Story*, 1985; Gabler, Neal, *An Empire of Their Own: How the Jews Invented Hollywood*, 1988; Zukor, Adolph, with Dale Kramer, *The Public Is Never Wrong: The Autobiography of Adolph Zukor*, 1953.